Charles de Gaulle

In this new biography, Andrew Knapp concisely dissects each of the major controversies surrounding General Charles de Gaulle, leader of the Free French during the Second World War and President of France from 1959 to 1969.

From the beginning of de Gaulle's military career in 1909 to an analysis of legacies and myths after his death in 1970, this study examines the path by which the French came to honour him as the greatest Frenchman of all time, and as the twentieth century's pre-eminent world statesman. In each chapter, Knapp analyses de Gaulle's participation in key events such as the development of France's resistance against Nazi Germany, the decolonisation of Algeria, the birth of the French Fifth Republic, and the gigantic upheaval of May 1968. Simultaneously, this study questions de Gaulle's actions and motives throughout his life. By exploring the justification of the contemporary 'de Gaulle myth', Knapp concludes by shedding new light on the influence of de Gaulle in the political culture of twenty-first-century France.

Through careful analysis of primary sources as well as recent scholarship, this biography is an invaluable source for scholars and students of modern history, the history of France, political institutions, and international relations.

Andrew Knapp is Emeritus Professor of French Politics and Contemporary History at the University of Reading. He is author of *Gaullism since de Gaulle* (1994) and *Parties and the Party System in France* (2004), joint author of *The Government and Politics of France* (2006) and *Forgotten Blitzes: France and Italy under Allied Air Attack* (2012), and editor of *The Uncertain Foundation: France at the Liberation, 1944–47* (2007).

ROUTLEDGE HISTORICAL BIOGRAPHIES
Series Editor: Robert Pearce

Routledge Historical Biographies provide engaging, readable and academically credible biographies written from an explicitly historical perspective. These concise and accessible accounts will bring important historical figures to life for students and general readers alike.

In the same series:
Bismarck by Edgar Feuchtwanger (second edition)
Calvin by Michael A. Mullett
Charles I by Mark Parry
Charles de Gaulle by Andrew Knapp
Edward IV by Hannes Kleineke
Elizabeth I by Judith M. Richards
Emmeline Pankhurst by Paula Bartley
Franco by Antonio Cazorla-Sanchez
Gladstone by Michael Partridge
Henry V by John Matusiak
Henry VI by David Grummitt
Henry VII by Sean Cunningham
Henry VIII by Lucy Wooding (second edition 2015)
Hitler by Michael Lynch
Ho Chi Minh by Peter Neville
Isabella d'Este by Christine Shaw
John F. Kennedy by Peter J. Ling
John Maynard Keynes by Vincent Barnett
Lenin by Christopher Read
Louis XIV by Richard Wilkinson (second edition 2017)
Martin Luther by Michael A. Mullet (second edition 2014)
Martin Luther King Jr. by Peter J. Ling (second edition 2015)
Mao by Michael Lynch (second edition 2017)
Marx by Vincent Barnett
Mary Queen of Scots by Retha M. Warnicke
Mary Tudor by Judith M. Richards
Mussolini by Peter Neville (second edition 2014)
Nehru by Benjamin Zachariah
Neville Chamberlain by Nick Smart
Oliver Cromwell by Martyn Bennett
Queen Victoria by Paula Bartley
Richard III by David Hipshon
Stalin by Christopher Read
Thatcher by Graham Goodlad
Thomas Cranmer by Susan Wabuda
Trotsky by Ian Thatcher
Wolsey by Glenn J. Richardson

Charles de Gaulle

Andrew Knapp

Routledge
Taylor & Francis Group
LONDON AND NEW YORK

First published 2021
by Routledge
2 Park Square, Milton Park, Abingdon, Oxon OX14 4RN

and by Routledge
52 Vanderbilt Avenue, New York, NY 10017

Routledge is an imprint of the Taylor & Francis Group, an informa business

© 2021 Andrew Knapp

The right of Andrew Knapp to be identified as author of this
work has been asserted by them in accordance with sections 77
and 78 of the Copyright, Designs and Patents Act 1988.

All rights reserved. No part of this book may be reprinted or reproduced
or utilised in any form or by any electronic, mechanical, or other means,
now known or hereafter invented, including photocopying and recording,
or in any information storage or retrieval system, without permission in
writing from the publishers.

Trademark notice: Product or corporate names may be
trademarks or registered trademarks, and are used only for
identification and explanation without intent to infringe.

British Library Cataloguing in Publication Data
A catalogue record for this book is available from the British Library

Library of Congress Cataloging-in-Publication Data
Names: Knapp, Andrew, author.
Title: Charles de Gaulle / Andrew Knapp.
Description: London ; New York, NY : Routledge/Taylor & Francis Group,
2021. | Series: Routledge historical biographies | Includes
bibliographical references and index. | Contents: De Gaulle before
Gaullism, 1890-1940 – Allies and Rivals: De Gaulle, the Free French and
their Partners – Free France: Foundations, 1940-42 – Towards a
provisional government, 1942-44 – Liberation and Recognition,
June-October 1944 – The Liberation Government, October 1944-January
1946 – A Study in Failure, 1946-58 – The Return, 1958 – Setting an
example? De Gaulle, decolonisation and the Third World – De Gaulle's
constitution and the politics of presidential primacy – Superpowers and
bombs – De Gaulle's Europe – May 1968: Economy, Society, and the
Limits of Presidential Power – Departure, Death, Afterlives, 1968-2020.
Identifiers: LCCN 2020023828 | ISBN 9781138839182 (hardback) | ISBN
9781138839199 (paperback) | ISBN 9781003098751 (ebook)
Subjects: LCSH: Gaulle, Charles de, 1890-1970. |
Presidents–France–Biography. | Generals–France–Biography. |
Statesmen–France–Biography. | France–Politics and government–20th century.
Classification: LCC DC420 .K628 2021 | DDC 944.083/6092 [B]–dc23
LC record available at https://lccn.loc.gov/2020023828

ISBN: 978-1-138-83918-2 (hbk)
ISBN: 978-1-138-83919-9 (pbk)
ISBN: 978-1-003-09875-1 (ebk)

Typeset in Sabon
by Taylor & Francis Books

For Sara and Viveca

Contents

List of tables xii
List of abbreviations xiii
Preface xv

1 De Gaulle before Gaullism, 1890–1940   1

   Decline and the Third Republic 2
   De Gaulle and the de Gaulles 8
   An army career, 1909–1940 12
   Soldier, intellectual, nonconformist 15
   An element of balance? Charles de Gaulle at home 24
   Conclusion 25

2 Allies and rivals: De Gaulle, the Free French, and their partners   33

   Breaking-point: the Appel du 18 juin 33
   De Gaulle: the personal equation 37
   The Free French 41
   The British 44
   The Empire 48
   The internal Resistance 51
   Franklin D. Roosevelt and the United States 53
   The old alliance: Free France and the USSR 56
   Conclusion 57

3 Free France: foundations, 1940–1942 — 65

   London, 1940–1942 65
   Imperial imbroglios, 1940–1942 68
   De Gaulle and the Resistance, 1940–1942 77
   Organisation and politics, 1940–1942: Free France turns Left 82
   De Gaulle, the Americans, and Torch 85
   Conclusion 89

4 Towards a provisional government, 1942–1944 — 96

   Darlan in Algiers: the 'temporary expedient' 97
   Resisting the Allies: Anfa, January 1943 99
   Rallying the Resistance, 1942–1943 101
   De Gaulle vs. Giraud (1): duel at a distance, January–May 1943 103
   De Gaulle vs. Giraud (2): duel in Algiers, June–November 1943 106
   Building a state-in-waiting 108
   Competing legitimacies: de Gaulle and the Resistance, 1943–1944 115
   De Gaulle and the Allies, 1943–1944 118

5 Liberation and recognition, June–October 1944 — 128

   D-Day and after 128
   Rome, Washington, Algiers 131
   Paris, August 1944 132
   'A monopoly of the legitimate use of physical force': de Gaulle versus the Resistance, autumn 1944 137
   Reluctant recognition, October 1944 142
   Conclusion 143

6 The Liberation Government,
  October 1944–January 1946   149

  Parties, elections, and the Constitution 150
  Reform without radicalism? 151
  The impossible épuration 153
  'Worse than under the Germans': hard times 155
  A diminished world power 156
  Cracks in the Empire 160
  Departure, January 1946 166
  Conclusion 169

7 A study in failure, 1946–1958   175

  Constitution-making, 1946 176
  The RPF surge, 1947 178
  Reflux, 1948–1953 181
  Restless retirement, 1953–1958 186
  Conclusion 191

8 The return, 1958   197

  Algeria: the jewel in the crown? 198
  A dirty war, 1954–1958 199
  A crisis of ungovernability 202
  Sakhiet and after, February–May 1958 204
  Insurrection, 13–19 May 206
  Resurrection, 20–29 May 208
  Endgame, 29 May 1958 – 8 January 1959 211
  Conclusion: coup d'état or democratic transition? 214

x   Contents

9   Setting an example? De Gaulle, decolonisation, and the Third World   220

   Algeria: a five-stranded narrative 221
   An Algerian balance-sheet 233
   The French Community and its failure 240
   'Co-operation' and Françafrique 242
   France and the wider Third World 246
   Conclusion 251

10 De Gaulle's Constitution and the politics of presidential primacy   259

   The sources of presidential power 260
   The practice of presidential primacy 269
   Presidential primacy under de Gaulle: functional or flawed? 279
   Conclusion 281

11 Superpowers and bombs   286

   Hoisting the colours, 1958–1962 291
   Developing independence, 1962–1966 298
   The zenith, 1966–1968 307
   Returning to the fold? 1968–1969 316
   Conclusion 319

12 De Gaulle's Europe   331

   De Gaulle and European integration, 1950–1958 332
   A strong Europe with weak institutions: the Fouchet Plan, 1960–1962 335
   France–Germany: the troubled partnership 339
   The CAP wars and the Empty Chair 346
   The United Kingdom: two vetoes and Soames 350
   Conclusion 358

13 May 1968: economy, society, and the limits of
presidential power 368

*Economic growth and social inequality 369
Education: expansion and its discontents 378
The 'Events' of May 1968 383
The triumph of the Right, 1 June – 10 July 1968 395
Conclusion 398*

14 Departure, death, afterlives, 1968–2020 411

*Reform and reaction, 1968–1969 412
Pompidou and the succession 415
Towards the referendum, February–April 1969 416
Defeat and departure, April 1969 419
A brief retirement, 1969–1970 421
Afterlives 422*

Index 440

Tables

1.1 De Gaulle's military career, 1909–1940   13
2.1 Free France and the French Empire   49
9.1 The Algerian War, 1958–1962   222

Abbreviations

2DB	Deuxième Division Blindée (2nd Armoured Division)
AEF	Afrique Équatoriale Française
ALN	Armée de Libération Nationale (Algeria)
AMGOT	Allied Military Government in Occupied Territory
AML	Amis du Manifeste et de la Liberté
AOF	Afrique Occidentale Française
BBC	British Broadcasting Corporation
BCRA	Bureau Central de Renseignements et d'Action
CDE	Conseil de Défense de l'Empire
CDLs	Comités de Libération
CDRs	Comités de Défense de la République (May 1968)
CFDT	Confédération Française Démocratique du Travail
CFLN	Comité Français de (la) Libération Nationale
CGT	Confédération Générale du Travail
CIA	Central Intelligence Agency (United States)
CNF	Comité National Français
CNR	Conseil National de la Résistance
CODER	Comité de Développement Économique Régional
COMAC	Comité d'Action Militaire (of CNR)
CPL	Comité Parisien de Libération
DM	Discours et Messages (De Gaulle)
ECSC	European Coal and Steel Community
EEC	European Economic Community
ÉNA	École Nationale d'Administration
FFI	Forces Françaises de l'Intérieur
FLN	Front de Libération Nationale (Algeria)
FO	Force Ouvrière

FTP	Francs-Tireurs et Partisans
GATT	General Agreement on Tariffs and Trade
GDP	Gross Domestic Product
GNP	Gross National Product
GPRA	Gouvernement Provisoire de la République Algérienne
GPRF	Gouvernement Provisoire de la République Française
IFOP	Institut Français de l'Opinion Publique
LNC	Lettres, Notes et Carnets (De Gaulle)
MH	Memoirs of Hope (De Gaulle)
MNA	Mouvement National Algérien
MRP	Mouvement Républicain Populaire
MUR	Mouvements Unis de la Résistance
NATO	North Atlantic Treaty Organisation
OAS	Organisation de l'Armée Secrète
OCM	Organisation Civile et Militaire
ORA	Organisation de Résistance de l'Armée
PCF	Parti Communiste Français
PRC	People's Republic of China
PTBT	Partial Test Ban Treaty
RAF	Royal Air Force
RPF	Rassemblement du Peuple Français
SAC	Service d'Action Civique
SAS	Sections Administratives Spéciales
SHAEF	Supreme Headquarters Allied Expeditionary Force
SNESup	Syndicat National de l'Enseignement Supérieur
SOE	Special Operations Executive
UDMA	Union Démocratique du Manifeste Algérien
UDR	Union pour la Défense de la République
UDSR	Union Démocratique et Sociale de la Résistance
UK	United Kingdom
UN	United Nations
UNEF	Union Nationale des Étudiants Français
UNR	Union pour la Nouvelle République
US	United States
USSR	Union of Soviet Socialist Republics
WM	War Memoirs (De Gaulle)

Preface

Why another de Gaulle book? I wondered when Routledge suggested I write this one. Other biographers have been here before. And there is no great unexploited archive to transform our view of the man (Julian Jackson, who started on the same road a bit earlier than me, confirmed that). So mine would be based on published works: de Gaulle's own, of course – his memoirs, speeches, and notebooks, all in print – plus a selection from the mass of secondary material that has accumulated over three-quarters of a century.

So why this book? First, it is a medium-length biography. It is meant for readers who lack either the time or the inclination to wade into the weighty (and excellent) tomes of Julian Jackson, or Éric Roussel, or Jean Lacouture – but who seek a deeper level of understanding available from the mini-biographies on offer. Second, it is organised, as far as possible, thematically, and is designed to be dipped into. This cannot be an absolute choice. An element of chronology is inevitable, especially in the (closely interrelated) chapters on the war. But the aim is to allow the reader interested in a particular theme to find the relevant material easily without the chronology bogging her, or him, down. Third, within each theme I have tried to confront head-on the major controversies, such as de Gaulle's wartime relations with the Allies, or Algeria, or the Constitution, or his policies on Europe or East-West relations, or his handling of the May 1968 crisis, and give the reader the tools to do his, or her, own interpreting. If the book does these things it will have fulfilled its purpose.

Much of my academic career has been spent in de Gaulle's company, close or distant. I am grateful to Christopher Andrew for first pointing me towards the Gaullist party (1951 vintage) in 1975; to David Goldey for getting me to teach on Gaullism; to Bill Johnson for suggesting I return to the party (1990 vintage) for my first book; to the University of Reading for keeping me in employment for 25 years and for giving me emeritus status when I left; to the Universities Superannuation Scheme for the pension which sustains me as I write; to PriceMinister for selling me almost all the secondhand de Gaulle books I needed; to Julian Jackson, Cyril Buffet, Beatrice Heuser, Claire Andrieu and two anonymous readers for going over some or all of the manuscript; to James Hoggan for finding the house in the Cantal where I have done so much of the work. But most of all I thank Sara and Viveca, who have never known me not to be writing a book, who have borne patiently all the demands that that entails, and to whom I dedicate this volume. It's about time.

AK, La Roquebrou, May 2020

1 De Gaulle before Gaullism, 1890–1940

Colonel Charles de Gaulle gave his first radio broadcast on 21 May 1940. In command of France's Fourth Tank Division, he had just fought a fierce battle against General Heinz Guderian's XIX Panzer Corps at Montcornet, north of Reims. 'One day', he assured listeners, 'we will win right along the line.'[1]

That day was long in coming. At Montcornet, then at Crécy-sur-Serre and at Abbeville, de Gaulle valiantly attempted to halt Guderian's Panzers. His offensive spirit helped secure his promotion to brigadier-general on 1 June.[2] But he never came near halting a German advance that defeated the French army in just six weeks. The debacle led Marshal Philippe Pétain, an octogenarian World War I hero newly appointed as Prime Minister, to request an armistice on 17 June. That would lead to four years of German occupation. Next day, in a better-known broadcast, from London, de Gaulle called on the French people to carry on the fight.

In doing so he stepped out of the soldier's role he had inhabited since entering the Saint-Cyr officer training school in 1909, and onto the stage of world history. That, given the danger de Gaulle had courted on the battlefield, might never have happened. Dead, he would have been just one of the 100,000 French losses of the 1940 campaign: a tank colonel, known to a narrow circle of army officers and politicians as an advocate of mechanised warfare. Alive, de Gaulle changed history. He rallied the French to the cause of a Free France, not only free of Germans but also speaking to its allies as an equal. As leader of the post-war Provisional Government (1944–1946), he oversaw a vast programme of economic and social reform. Returning to power as Prime Minister then President (1958–1969), he ended the world's bloodiest colonial war, conceding Algeria's independence in 1962; he replaced France's constitution, dramatically shifting power from the legislature to the executive; he transformed France's foreign policy; and he presided over a decade of internal prosperity, only shaken by the unrest of May 1968. Taken together, these achievements ensure his position as one of the twentieth century's pre-eminent world statesmen, and, for the French, as their outstanding national figure.

Why de Gaulle? What was it about the first half-century in a life spanning eight decades that led him to the BBC studios on that Tuesday 18 June? What qualities enabled him to transform this founding, defiant gesture into a powerful political movement? The answers lie in his upbringing, in his development as a soldier, and in the determination with which he forged his own persona. In addition, and however much de Gaulle liked to present himself as a force beyond time,[3] he developed in a specific context. That context was France's relative decline as a major power, which de Gaulle would set out to reverse.

Decline and the Third Republic

Late seventeenth- and eighteenth-century France had been Europe's demographic, strategic, and economic giant. In 1800 France had the largest population in Europe, at over 29 million. In 1900, at 39 million, it was barely greater than Italy's, no higher than the UK's, and well below those of Germany (67 million), Austria-Hungary, Russia, or the United States. That damaged military capacity. For over 150 years before 1815, it had taken a coalition of other European nations to defeat France. In the 1870–1871 war against Prussia, however, France had succumbed to a single adversary, and lost the eastern provinces of Alsace and Lorraine. Worse, in 1871 the Prussian Chancellor, Otto von Bismarck, had declared the unification of a new German Empire around Prussia. For the next 33 years France's politicians and strategists dreamt of *revanche*, a war to regain the lost provinces from Germany. World War I (1914–1918), fought in alliance with Britain, Russia (till 1917), and the United States (after 1917), delivered the hoped-for victory, but at the price of 1.3 million dead. These losses drove the birth rate down. In 1939, France faced a third war against Germany in a single human lifetime; only 600,000 troops were available, against 1.2 million in 1914.[4]

Demographic and military, France's relative decline was also economic. Despite some spurts of industrialisation, France's overall growth rate through the century from 1840 was among Europe's slowest. France had too little coal or high-quality iron ore, key materials for industrialisation – and too many peasants. Nearly half of France's active population in 1900, over a third in 1939, still worked on the land; in the UK, the figure was under 10% by 1900. France's millions of small peasant proprietors, protected against foreign competition by high tariffs, saw no reason to stop working their little farms as their parents had done. But they were so inefficient that in 1914 France was still importing grain from Russia.

Slow development did not ensure political stability. Since revolution had ended France's absolute monarchy in 1789, no lasting consensus had existed about the nation's political institutions. In less than a century after 1789, France lived under eight regimes: three limited monarchies (1789–1792, 1814–1830, 1830–1848); two empires (1804–1814, 1852–1870) headed by Napoleon I and his nephew Napoleon III;[5] and three republics (1792–1804, 1848–1852, 1870–1940).[6] A closely linked and divisive issue was that of Church–State relations. The ideological and material power of the Catholic Church had underpinned the pre-1789 *ancien régime* and conservative monarchists wanted to revive that close relationship, and therefore a monarchy. For many republicans, the Church was a purveyor of pernicious superstitions, to be excluded from politics and if possible from its historic role in education too.

The Third Republic, under which de Gaulle grew up, was proclaimed on 4 September 1870, after France's catastrophic defeat by Prussia at Sedan and Napoleon III's abdication. Assailed from Right and Left, it suffered unpromising beginnings: a (divided) monarchist majority in the first National Assembly, and the Paris Commune, a full-scale left-wing rebellion of France's capital city against the new regime, ferociously repressed by the government of Adolphe Thiers in May 1871. The republicans only prevailed against their monarchist opponents, President MacMahon and his parliamentary supporters, in 1879.

The Third Republic nevertheless lasted nearly 70 years. Supported by most of the people most of the time, it achieved much.

It oversaw a rapid recovery from the humiliation of 1870–1871. It furthered France's industrialisation in advanced sectors – chemicals, automobiles, and aviation. It spread primary education – universal, secular, compulsory, and free – into every town and village in France, and from the 1920s began to extend secondary education as well. It enshrined most democratic freedoms: universal (male) adult suffrage, freedom of the press, of assembly, of political organisation. It modernised France's armed forces after the defeat of 1870–1871 and instituted a truly universal system of military service. That, and universal education (in one language, French), created a stronger sense of nationhood out of culturally and linguistically disparate provinces.

Yet the Third Republic's weaknesses were equally striking. The social base of its support was always thin. France's industrial working class, smaller than its German or British counterparts and more weakly represented by trade unions and parties, was left without workplace rights, without welfare, and exposed to repression by troops if it went on strike. The political Left suffered from its divisions: in 1920 a large left-wing contingent split away from the Socialist Party to form the French Communist Party, loyal to Moscow. A second 'out-group' were devout Catholics, who had to swallow the advent of secular education and, in 1905 the separation of Church and State. To be a good republican and a good Catholic was widely seen, by both sides, as incompatible. A third group had no political rights: women would have to wait till 1945 to vote.

The Third Republic also suffered from a political culture hostile to strong individual leadership – not least because both of the Napoleons had held high office in a republic before overthrowing it.[7] Neither president nor prime minister wielded overarching authority under the constitution. Instability resulted: Third Republic governments lasted, on average, less than nine months. Political parties were weak and divided, more clubs of like-minded independent parliamentarians than nationwide organisations.[8] The near-permanent governing party of the later Third Republic, the Radical Party, owed its position to a place at the centre of France's political spectrum: it formed majorities with parties of the moderate Right, or with the Socialists to its Left. Radical only in its anti-clericalism, it enacted its core programme with the separation of Church and State. Thereafter it settled to a safe conservatism while paying lip service to left-wing republican traditions. Unstable government was matched by stability in (some) policies, especially the protection of agricultural interests behind high tariffs. That was guaranteed by the conservative upper house of Parliament, the Senate, where rural interests were over-represented; in turn, protectionism ensured that inefficient rural producers remained numerous and industrialisation slow.

On three occasions between the Commune and 1940, a crisis borne of France's deep-seated social and political tensions threatened to overwhelm the Republic.[9] From 1885, the War Minister, General Georges Boulanger, became the focus of (mostly) right-wing plots to replace the Republic with an authoritarian regime: lacking the stomach for a coup, he fled France in 1889. Altogether more serious, from 1898, was the 'Dreyfus Affair', the political fallout arising from a gross miscarriage of justice in which a Jewish army officer, Captain Alfred Dreyfus, had been convicted of spying on what proved to be forged evidence. 'Dreyfusards' like the novelist Émile Zola sought to overturn the unsound conviction; for the anti-Dreyfusards, the honour and prestige of the army mattered more than one man's guilt or innocence. Their hatred of Dreyfus and his supporters extended to Jews in general and to the secular Republic. The Affair crystallised a new Catholic, anti-Semitic, anti-republican, and nationalist French Right, exemplified by the brilliant young polemicist Charles Maurras and the *Action Française* newspaper he edited. Against them, progressive republicans not only championed the rights of the accused but also grew increasingly anti-clerical and anti-militarist.

The Republic prevailed, but the Affair split France. Dreyfus was fully rehabilitated in 1906. By then, Radical-dominated governments, using the opportunity of the Church's strongly anti-Dreyfusard stance, had dissolved religious orders engaged in teaching, closed some 2,500 Catholic schools, and separated the Church from the State. Inventories were made of Church goods, provoking near-riots. War Minister General André started to block the careers of Mass-going army officers and promote only 'good republicans'. Both episodes deepened the divisions left by the Affair. Only war in 1914 brought together nationalists, republicans, and even (most) Socialists in a (temporary) 'sacred union' against Germany.

The third crisis was again provoked by the anti-republican Right. On 6 February 1934, riots on the Place de la Concorde, opposite the

Chamber of Deputies, left 31 people, mostly rioters, dead. They were protesting against the sacking of a prefect of the Paris police, Jean Chiappe, who had favoured them, and at a cover-up surrounding the death of Alexandre Stavisky, a crooked financier who happened to be Jewish. Stavisky's supposed links with senior politicians turned the protests into an attack on the government and the Republic itself.

In a charged international context (Hitler had become German Chancellor a year earlier), the Left's anti-fascist reaction was vigorous. Socialists and Communists co-operated for the first time since 1920. A 'Popular Front' alliance, incorporating Socialists, Communists, and (with reluctance) Radicals as well, won the 1936 elections and gave France its most left-wing government since 1871. Its reforms, which gave French workers their first paid holidays and a 40-hour working week, and dissolved the anti-republican leagues, were inevitably hateful to the far Right. The anti-republican Right never forgave the Popular Front for this, or for bringing Communists into the parliamentary majority, or, worst of all, for putting Léon Blum, not only a Socialist but a Jew, into the office of prime minister. Its militants physically assaulted Blum; a smear campaign in the right-wing press drove his Interior Minister to suicide. Economic difficulties, and the Senate, forced Blum's resignation in June 1937. The governing coalition, now under Radical prime ministers, shed the support first of the Communists, then of the Socialists, before turning back to the moderate Right for allies. The Radical Édouard Daladier, Prime Minister from 12 April 1938, reversed or watered down key Popular Front legislation, notably the 40-hour week, and accepted, at the Munich conference on 29–30 September 1938, Hitler's annexation of strategic areas of Czechoslovakia.

Daladier's premiership of nearly two years lent France a little stability. At the same time, as the crisis of the 1930s bled into the approach to war, political alignments became more complex. The formerly pacifist-leaning Left split as some sought peace at any price while anti-fascists prepared for a war against Hitler. Within the formerly nationalist, militarist, anti-German Right, some favoured Nazi Germany as a bulwark against Communist Russia, now the Union of Soviet Socialist Republics (USSR); for others, the rise of Nazism only intensified their hostility to Germany.

Daladier sought peace but prepared for war. When, with his British counterpart Neville Chamberlain, he signed the Munich Agreement in September 1938, he believed that war with Germany then would be suicidal. But he also passed a long-delayed law preparing France's economic and institutional mobilisation. The defence budget tripled in 1939. That April, after Hitler had swallowed up the rest of Czechoslovakia, Daladier and Chamberlain guaranteed Poland's independence and integrity. On 3 September 1939, with Poland now invaded, they declared war on Germany.

Daladier passed for a resolute figure. But he remained committed to France's defensive military posture, which excluded offensive action to support France's eastern allies. So the 94 divisions that France mobilised sat out an eight-month 'phoney war' marked by excruciating boredom, sagging discipline, and steady drinking through the half-litre daily wine ration.[10] Nor was the 'Sacred Union' of 1914 replicated. The Nazi–Soviet pact of August 1939 led the Communist Party, at Moscow's behest, to oppose the war. The government banned the party in September, dismissed its parliamentarians four months later, and persecuted ordinary Communist workers. When the USSR invaded Finland in November 1939, French right-wingers suggested that France had picked the wrong fight, and both French and British governments prepared to send troops to assist Finland. Too late: the Finns were forced into a humiliating peace treaty on 12 March 1940. Daladier, criticised as too slow to help them, resigned eight days later. His conservative Finance Minister, Paul Reynaud, replaced him – but Reynaud's wafer-thin parliamentary majority testified to continuing divisions, not just over the conduct of the war with Germany but over whether it was worth fighting a war at all.

It was Reynaud who presided over the Third Republic's terminal failure, the six-week collapse of French forces after Germany's invasion on 10 May 1940. As the debacle unfolded, Reynaud used military appointments to shore up his government. Pétain, France's most prestigious soldier, became vice-premier on 18 May at age 84; de Gaulle became Under-Secretary of State for War on 5 June. Neither, of course, could stave off defeat, and when Reynaud resigned on 16 June he knew that the armistice with Germany would follow. But the two soldiers became Reynaud's successors. Pétain signed the armistice on 22 June and became France's head of state during the four years of German occupation that followed; de Gaulle headed the Free French, and, from 1944, what would become France's first post-war government.

De Gaulle and the de Gaulles

Placing the de Gaulle family, into which Charles was born on 22 November 1890, on the spectrum of Third Republic politics might appear straightforward. They were strongly Catholic, 'bourgeois' at least in a loose sense, keenly sensitive to France's humiliation in 1871. Charles himself became an army officer in the wake of the Dreyfus Affair. Yet the family's individuality meant that his background was not simply that of right-wing anti-republicanism.

Catholicism was the most marked of the de Gaulle family traits. Bible readings were an evening fixture at home. De Gaulle's mother, Jeanne (1860–1940), attended Mass daily at 7am. His father, Henri (1848–1932), had resigned from the civil service in 1884 to avoid serving what he saw as an anti-clerical government. Thereafter, his career was spent teaching in Catholic institutions: first at the Jesuit College of the Immaculate Conception, where the first three of his four sons (Xavier, Charles, Jacques, and Pierre) studied; then, when the post-Dreyfus ban on religious teaching orders closed the college in 1907, at the Cours Fontanes, the school Henri de Gaulle founded himself, which included religious teaching in its syllabus. With the de Gaulles' Catholicism went a hostility towards both Protestants (Henri called both the Protestant Reformation and the French Revolution 'essentially Satanic') and Jews, regarded as deicides – though Henri privately conceded their 'superior intelligence'.[11]

Despatched for his final year's schooling to a college in Antoing, Belgium, and sent for his summer holiday in 1908 to stay with a Catholic priest at Baden, in Germany, de Gaulle entered another Catholic establishment, the Collège Stanislas in Paris, to prepare the entrance examination to Saint-Cyr.[12] Antoing inspired a phase of adolescent piety, which proved temporary.[13] But de Gaulle remained a Catholic by conviction as well as by upbringing. He attended Mass as an officer without display and without courting the army chaplains. His quiet Christianity was a resource to confront human tragedies, or to face decisions of life and death.[14]

De Gaulle was not a political Catholic. The 'religious strife' of the post-Dreyfus years distressed him, but chiefly for the damage it did France.[15] He had little time for the literature of France's eighteenth-century Enlightenment, but nor was there any nostalgia for a mythologised past of religious devotion, nor yet, as we shall see, any rejection of Jews or Protestants.[16] He saw France as a Catholic country, but never supported a return to an established Church. In 1938 he joined an association of friends of *Temps présent*, a Christian Democratic, and strongly anti-fascist, review.[17] Christian Democrats, Catholics who accepted the Republic and sought to promote a progressive Catholic social doctrine, would grow in importance after 1945. De Gaulle's association with them showed a certain distance from the Catholicism of his upbringing. But he was never a Christian Democrat. For de Gaulle, nation came before faith, at least in politics.

It is harder to call the de Gaulles 'bourgeois'. They certainly respected the bourgeois virtues of hard work, thrift, and outward respectability. But the family fortune had been lost at the Revolution. What money there was came from Jeanne's family, the Maillots, Lille merchants and also distant cousins of the de Gaulles. It was they who rented a house at Wimereux, near Boulogne-sur-Mer, for the de Gaulles to spend seaside holidays. Henri de Gaulle did buy a holiday home in the Lot, which he could not keep up, and sold. Charles de Gaulle never became wealthy. Officers' pay was far from princely during his army years; he refused most of his pension entitlements; and the (significant) royalties from his memoirs went into a charitable trust, the Fondation Anne de Gaulle. Like his father, he married into a northern business family: Yvonne Vendroux, whom he wedded on 6 April 1921, was the daughter of a Calais biscuit manufacturer.[18] There would be occasional holidays in the Vendroux château in the Ardennes, and (rare) loans from Yvonne's brother Jacques, but the Vendroux money went no further than that.

There was also a touch of eccentricity about this 'family of intellectuals with strange specialities'.[19] De Gaulle's paternal grandfather Julien-Philippe wrote a five-volume history of Paris; his grandmother Joséphine, some 80 books – travelogues, pious and improving novels, and biographies. One uncle, Jules, catalogued over 5,000 species of wasps and bees; another, Charles, though crippled by polio, became a sort of Breton bard, whom de Gaulle quoted in one of his last speeches.[20] Charles de Gaulle grew up in an atmosphere that might be described as curious in both senses of the word. Academic excellence was expected; 'Grace at meals was followed by short extempore speeches in Latin'; intense discussion of contemporary political events was encouraged.[21] At 14, de Gaulle wrote a drama in verse, which won a prize and was published.[22] As a young man he wrote two stories of doomed love, of a young colonial army officer for a 'native' woman. The second was also published.[23] This was hardly yet the magisterial author of the *War Memoirs*; but de Gaulle at 20 knew how to handle a pen.

At the very least, the de Gaulles were ardent patriots. Henri, described by his son as 'imbued with the dignity of France', would take the family to visit the symbols of France's glory – the Arc de Triomphe, or Napoleon's tomb – or the spot near Paris where he had been wounded as a volunteer during the war of 1870–1871. Jeanne's childhood memories of the defeats of 1870 marked her for life.[24] Did that make them right-wing anti-republican nationalists? Certainly Henri subscribed to *Action Française* – until the Pope disowned the movement in 1927. He would describe himself as a 'monarchiste de regret' – a monarchist who reluctantly accepted that the Republic was there to stay. As for Jeanne, she worried that her sons had turned into republicans.[25] But reading *Action Française* does not mean sharing the movement's views. Henri appears to have been too inquiring, and probably too decent, to share the convictions of the anti-Dreyfusards. According to Charles de Gaulle, as recollected by his son Philippe, Henri had 'fought for Dreyfus with the same passion with which he fought for the Church and for religious teaching in schools'.[26]

Jeanne de Gaulle's concerns about her sons' republicanism were half-founded in Charles's case. He was no ardent republican. His anger at the ineffectiveness of France's parliamentary system boils over in wartime letters to his parents.[27] But he never associated with *Action Française* or any of the anti-parliamentary leagues that led the Stavisky riots.[28] When he had a political agenda, as in the 1930s, he used established – republican – political channels to promote it, and ultimately accepted ministerial office in the Republic's twilight days. His condemnation of the politics of those years was largely retrospective. Recalling a meeting with Blum, on 16 October 1936,

De Gaulle before Gaullism, 1890–1940 11

he describes a Prime Minister interrupted by ceaseless telephone calls over minor political issues.[29] Of Albert Lebrun, President during the disaster of 1940, he later observed that 'as the leader of the state, he had lacked two essential things: he was not a leader, and there was no state'.[30]

Less of a Catholic fundamentalist, more of a republican than his parents, de Gaulle was just as much a nationalist. He belonged to a generation of young educated Frenchmen who, according to a 1913 study, had abandoned the anti-militarism of their immediate post-Dreyfus elders, and become 'traditionalist, nationalist, Catholic and sporting'.[31] They read the philosopher Henri Bergson, theorist of the balance between reason and intuition, but also fervent nationalists like Maurice Barrès, or Ernest Psichari, a young soldier-novelist whose 1913 novel *L'Appel aux armes* (*The Call to Arms*) was a programme in itself; or poet and essayist Charles Péguy, a former Socialist who by 1911 was calling for the Socialist leader Jean Jaurès to be shot when war broke out. They went to war with enthusiasm: a far-Right nationalist duly assassinated Jaurès on 31 July 1914; Psichari and Péguy were both killed in action weeks later.

These authors marked de Gaulle. He quotes Bergson on the first page of his second book, *Le Fil de l'épée*; he borrowed Barrès's expression, 'a certain idea of France', for the first sentence of his *War Memoirs*; he sent for a copy of Psichari from the front in 1940; as for Péguy, he would say in 1964 that no writer had marked him as much.[32] By contrast, de Gaulle barely mentioned Maurras in his writings, and shared none of his (and Barrès's) exclusionary, anti-Semitic nationalism.[33] We find one censorious mention of Jewish profiteers in a letter sent to his mother from Poland, written in 1919 during a phase which he himself described as one of 'generalised xenophobia' at the end of World War I.[34] But in the inter-war years he was friendly with a Jewish former colonel, Émile Meyer, and sought and obtained an interview with Blum. After 1940, he readily accepted Jews at the top of the Free French movement.[35]

De Gaulle's nationalism, in the end, was very much his own. The opening of his *War Memoirs* is a deeply personal statement of his 'certain idea of France'.

> This is inspired by sentiment as much as by reason. The emotional side of me tends to imagine France, like the princess in

fairy stories or the Madonna in frescoes, as dedicated to an exalted and exceptional destiny. Instinctively I have the feeling that Providence has created her either for complete successes or for exemplary misfortunes. If, in spite of this, mediocrity shows in her acts and deeds, it strikes me as an absurd anomaly, to be imputed to the faults of Frenchmen, not to the genius of the land. But the positive side of my mind also assures me that France is not really herself unless she is in the front rank; that only vast enterprises are capable of counter-balancing the ferments of disintegration inherent in her people; that our country, as it is, surrounded by the others, as they are, must aim high and hold itself straight, on pain of mortal danger. In short, to my mind, France cannot be France without greatness.[36]

For a man who thought this, the idea of an armistice with Germany in 1940 would clearly be anathema. France's peculiar place in the world, her capacity for grandeur, and her vulnerability to misfortunes, whether internally or externally generated, would be constant themes of de Gaulle's statesmanship. So would the restoration and safeguarding of France's place at the 'front rank'.

An army career, 1909–1940

De Gaulle's strictly military career lasted just under 31 years from his arrival in September 1909 at Saint-Cyr, France's Sandhurst or West Point. Unlike many candidates, de Gaulle won admission at his first attempt. For his mandatory year in the ranks, de Gaulle joined the 33rd Infantry Regiment, stationed at Arras, close to the Belgian frontier, before becoming a full officer cadet in October 1910. He passed out of Saint-Cyr 13th out of 211, and was commissioned as a second lieutenant in September 1912. Fashionable postings in the cavalry or the colonies beckoned. De Gaulle preferred the 33rd Infantry. His commanding officer was Pétain, who believed that 'firepower kills' – an unconventional view, which had stalled his career in the offensive-minded pre-1914 French army. It was probably not Pétain's heterodoxy that attracted de Gaulle to the 33rd. Rather, Arras was close to his mother's family; it was a stone's throw from the likely future battlefront; it was home to some of France's finest troops.[37]

Table 1.1 De Gaulle's military career, 1909–1940

1909 (Sept.)	Enters Saint-Cyr military academy.
1909–1910	Compulsory year in the ranks with 33rd Infantry Regiment, Arras: corporal (April 1910); sergeant (September 1910).
1910–1912	Cadet at Saint-Cyr. Passes out 13th out of 211, commissioned 2nd lieutenant.
1913 (1 Oct.)	Promoted lieutenant.
1914–1916	Service on Western Front. Wounded at Dinant (15 August 1914) and Mesnil-lès-Hurlus (15 March 1915).
1915	Promoted temporary captain (10 February), full captain (3 September).
1916 (2 March)	Wounded and taken prisoner at Verdun.
1916 (April)–1918 (Nov.)	Prisoner of war, mostly in the fortress of Ingolstadt. Five documented escape attempts.
1919 (Jan.–March)	Training period, Saint-Maixent officer school.
1919 (April) – 1921 (Jan.)	On secondment as military adviser to the Polish army. Takes part in operations against Soviet Russia.
1921 (Feb.) – 1922 (June)	Assistant professor at Saint-Cyr.
1922 (Nov.) – 1924 (Oct.)	Student at the Higher War School.
1924 (Nov.) – 1925 (June)	Posted to staff of French Rhine Army, Mainz.
1925 (July) – 1927 (Oct.)	Posted to staff of Marshal Pétain.
1927 (April)	Gives three lectures at the Higher War College.
1927 (25 Sept.)	Promoted major.
1927 (Oct.) – 1929 (Oct.)	Commands 19th Light Infantry Battalion at Trier.
1929 (Oct.) – 1931 (Oct.)	On staff of high command of French forces in the Levant.
1931 (Nov.) – 1937 (June)	Posted to Secretariat-General of the Higher Council for National Defence.
1933 (Dec.)	Promoted lieutenant-colonel.
1937 (July) – 1939 (Sept.)	Commands 507th Tank Regiment, Metz.

(*continued*)

Table 1.1 (continued)

1937 (Dec.)	Promoted full colonel.
1939 (Sept.) – 1940 April	Commander of tanks of 5th Army.
1940 (April–June)	Commander of 4th Tank Division.
1940 (1 June)	Promoted acting brigadier-general.
1940 (5 June)	Appointed Under-Secretary of State for War.

A lieutenant from September 1913, Gaulle was wounded, three times, in the first 18 months of World War I. He took a bullet in the knee on his first day of combat, on 15 August 1914, and was out of action for two months. His hand became infected after receiving a shell splinter on 10 March 1915, shortly after his promotion to captain. Finally, on 2 March 1916 at Verdun, at the start of what became, for France, the symbolic, terrifying, meat-grinding battle of the war, de Gaulle was bayoneted in the left thigh, knocked out by a grenade, and recorded missing presumed dead. He awoke a prisoner, and remained in German captivity for the rest of the war. Prisoners are not promoted, even if, like de Gaulle, they try to escape. So he ended the war a captain, returning to France in early December 1918.

After a few weeks' refresher training at the Saint-Maixent officer school, de Gaulle began 21 months' secondment to France's military mission in Poland. Partitioned between Prussia, Austria, and Russia from 1795, Poland had only regained statehood with the German defeat in 1918. It was soon attacked by Soviet Russia. De Gaulle's posting renewed his experience of active service, and offered pay nearly three times higher than a captain's in France.[38] He ran training courses for middle-ranking officers, took an occasional part in operations, and won the respect of both French and Polish senior officers.

Thereafter de Gaulle's inter-war years saw a fairly conventional succession of study, staff jobs, and field postings. Combat opportunities were limited to colonial rebellions, and de Gaulle's only colonial posting, in the Levant (Syria and Lebanon, 1929–1931), came just after a rising there had been crushed. The most original feature of de Gaulle's record was his connection with Pétain. Now known as the victor of Verdun, Pétain was a Marshal of France, vice-president of the Higher War Council and probably France's most influential soldier. It was Pétain who wrote the citation that secured de Gaulle the Légion d'Honneur for his bravery at Verdun.[39] It was probably Pétain who intervened to shore up de Gaulle's mediocre marks at the Higher War School, whence he passed out 52nd out of 129 in 1924. It was certainly Pétain, later that year, who picked the man he called 'the most intelligent officer of the French Army' to serve two years on his personal staff, rescuing de Gaulle from a dull post handling supplies in Mainz. And it was probably Pétain who ensured that the Higher War School invited him to give three lectures in 1927.[40] Promoted major that September, de Gaulle concluded his staff job with Pétain and served in Trier (Germany) for two years, before sailing to Beirut in 1929. His longest posting – nearly six years – was at the secretariat-general of France's Higher War Council, where he helped draft the law on France's wartime organisation. His final inter-war postings, from 1937, were in command of tank units, in the last of which he fought at Montcornet and Abbeville.

No-one rose fast in France's inter-war army,[41] and de Gaulle's career was held back by two handicaps: his 32 months of captivity, and a growing reputation as a difficult, opinionated officer.[42] These, however, were offset by powerful supporters. Pétain first: their closeness can be overstated, and was waning by 1928 – but he still, probably, recommended de Gaulle for posts beyond then.[43] The second backer was the conservative politician Paul Reynaud, who helped secure de Gaulle's promotion to colonel in 1937 and his command of a tank division in 1940 – and who brought him into government.[44]

Soldier, intellectual, nonconformist

What kind of soldier was de Gaulle? He was, in the first place, a true believer in the military virtues, in France's military genius, and in his own military destiny. War, he told his fellow-officers in 1913, is a necessary ill that awakens 'manly virtues and noble enthusiasms'; a long peace endangers a people's 'moral value'.[45] As for the pre-1914 French army, battered by the Dreyfus Affair, with applications to Saint-Cyr down from 2,000 in 1900 to 900 in 1909, de Gaulle still recalled it as 'one of the greatest things in the world'.[46] And as his choice of the 33rd Infantry showed, he wanted to be at the centre of the only war that mattered – against Germany.

Secondly, he was a soldier bound, in his own mind, by an extraordinarily *personal* relationship to his country. He aimed for Saint-Cyr from age 14, despite a civilian background; at 15, he wrote an account of himself leading an army of 200,000 men to victory against Germany; at 17, a poem about dying for France.[47] 'I did not question', he wrote 47 years later, 'that France would have to go through gigantic trials, that the interest of life consisted in one day rendering her some signal service, and that I would have the occasion to do so.'[48] As his aide Olivier Guichard recalled, 'De Gaulle's love affair was with France ... He could never stand someone else getting close to his mistress; and he could stand even less having a relationship with her that was mediocre or uncertain – he preferred to leave her'.[49] His relationship with France was thus more than personal; it was exclusive; in his own mind it set him apart. This was clear to others from his youth onwards. He quickly earned the nickname *le Connétable* – the Constable of France, the first officer of state and commander-in-chief of the medieval French army.[50]

Passion for profession and country was reflected in action. Pétain described him, when presumed dead, as 'a peerless officer in every respect'.[51] De Gaulle chafed at inaction, especially at the informal understandings between Allied and German troops on quiet sections of the front not to exchange fire.[52] In prison, inactivity was 'the cruellest thing imaginable', he wrote to his parents in December 1917.[53] Hence his persistent escape attempts, recognised by an Escapee's Medal in 1927.[54] Nor, as his physical bravery in 1940 showed, was this merely a young man's passion.

Courageous as a fighting soldier, de Gaulle was less than ideal as a leader of men. Certainly, his physique (he was 6 feet 4 inches tall, a foot higher than the average Frenchman of the time)[55] and his behaviour could inspire. He learnt before 1914 to give clear and forceful lectures to other officers, and to rank-and-file troops, in language they understood.[56] A prodigious memory enabled him to learn and remember the names and personal details of his men.[57] He sometimes quietly helped men under his command with minor financial problems.[58] On the other hand, both at Trier and at Metz he drove his men (and, at Metz, his tanks) extremely hard.[59] Above all, in battle at Mortcornet and Abbeville, he remained a solitary, peremptory commander, incapable of galvanising his junior officers; not one joined de Gaulle in London.[60] This combination of distance and cold authority with rare, and self-effacing, human warmth was to reappear throughout de Gaulle's life.

If de Gaulle was indisputably a man of action, he was also an 'intellectual in uniform'.[61] His lectures to fellow-officers, wide-ranging and detailed, continued in the fort of Ingolstadt where he was held prisoner.[62] His pedagogical capacity was noted as he completed his teaching at Saint-Cyr in 1922; when Pétain invited him to speak at the Higher Military College in 1927, he was calling not just on a protégé but on an exceptionally talented lecturer.[63] In addition, de Gaulle's publication record between 1920 and 1936 would be respectable for a full-time academic: 4 books and 21 articles in both specialised reviews and more general periodicals.[64]

The intellectual development that underpinned the books began during his captivity, from March 1916 till November 1918. In between frequent (and unsuccessful) escape attempts, and lectures to his fellow-prisoners, he would read, think – and take notes. The prison notebooks offer a unique insight into de Gaulle aged 25–7. We find him reflecting on Bergson, and applying Bergson's ideas on reason and intuition to the sculptures of Rodin.[65] His curiosity covers ancient Greece, Japanese and American influences on the Chinese governing classes, the government of Iran, the constitution of the United States, Indian religions, or the strength of monarchist sentiments in Britain. This was not mere dilettantism. A commander, he would later write, must be equipped with a solid general as well as military culture in order to think deeply and judge wisely.[66] Hence the later assessment of American President Richard Nixon that 'No leader I met could surpass his remarkable ability to discuss any subject or any part of the world with such competence, intelligence, and at times profound insight.'[67]

The core of his prison reflections, however, concerns 'the philosophy of action', the 'principles and methods of command', the nature of leadership, and the need – clearly applied to himself – to become a 'man of character'. To achieve this, a 'perpetual domination of oneself' is required, to be gained through a 'constant gymnastic of the will' in all things – thought, clothing, working habits, conversation. The 'man of character' should speak rarely, but then, with authority: *still waters run deep*, he notes in English. 'Analyser le prestige' is another self-exhortation. These ideas led directly into his three 1927 lectures at the Higher War School, and thence into his second book, *Le Fil de l'épée*.[68] De Gaulle not only saw himself as destined for exceptional things; he also consciously developed himself as an exceptional, and literally commanding, being.

Each of the four inter-war books develops themes that were to be crucial in de Gaulle's later life. *La Discorde chez l'ennemi*, which appeared in March 1924 (before he had left the Higher War College), is a study of the German defeat of 1918 which drew both on reading (of the German press) and thinking in captivity, and on post-war German memoirs.[69] Two themes dominate. One is a sense of measure and balance; the German leaders, he claims, courted disaster by losing both.[70] The other is political control of the military. Government, de Gaulle argued, must control the general conduct of the war, but leave the military operational freedom. Neither should impinge on the other. The successful partnership between Chancellor Bismarck and Commander-in-Chief Moltke had secured Prussia's victory against France in 1870. By contrast, Admiral Tirpitz and Generals Ludendorff and Hindenburg badly overstretched the military's proper role: they imposed the policy of unrestricted submarine warfare which brought America into the war, forced the resignation of Chancellor Theobald von Bethmann-Hollweg, and took effective political control for themselves.[71] Defeat followed within 18 months. De Gaulle's insistence on political control of the military would be a constant in his thinking, especially important during the Algerian War of 1954–1962.

It reappeared in *Le Fil de l'épée* (*The Edge of the Sword*), based on his Higher War School lectures and published in 1932.[72] In this second, most obviously intellectual, and most clearly personal of his inter-war books, two new themes also stand out. One of them, inspired by Bergson, launches the first sentence: warfare depends on contingency, which may upset the best-laid plans; success in war requires not only well-informed and logical planning but also instinct and intuition, to apprehend and act upon a reality in constant flux.[73] But the book's core theme is leadership. Here de Gaulle returns to his prisoner's reflections on the 'man of character': superior in the strength of his will, in his powers of decision, in his ability, in a crisis, to break free of established hierarchies and take charge. These chapters are a self-portrait, at least of the man de Gaulle aspired to be. He appears to know the role from the inside, and evokes a constant internal struggle to rise to the occasion which 'imposes pain at every moment'. And it offers fascinating clues as to his own future behaviour. 'Nothing', he states, 'raises authority better than silence'; and 'the man of action is scarcely imaginable without a strong dose of egoism, pride, toughness, and cunning'.[74]

If *Le Fil* is the most personal of the inter-war books, the third, *Vers l'armée de métier*, published in April 1934, is probably the best known.[75] Here he confronts head-on the reality of a resurgent Germany. Germany held a lifelong and ambiguous fascination for de Gaulle. In captivity he read the German press – a habit he continued into his presidency – but also books like Friedrich von Bernhardi's *Germany and the Next War* (1911), which appeared to prove Germany's aggressive war aims.[76] At the same time he had opened *La Discorde chez l'ennemi* with a tribute to the German people's warlike virtues – a will to conquer and endurance in hardship, which 'will certainly win the admiration of History'.[77] In *Vers l'armée de metier*, written a year after Hitler had come to power, the ambiguity is pushed further. He likens Germany to a cathedral, in which the multicoloured nave 'becomes a symphony for the senses, for the mind, the soul, the emotions, the light and the religion of the world, but whose gloomy transept, echoing a barbaric din, offends the eyes, the spirit, and the heart'.[78]

France, he noted, with its north-eastern frontier opening out onto the north European plain, was extraordinarily vulnerable to this overbearing neighbour: 'the Franco-German border is the lip of a wound'.[79] Nor did the signature of the Treaty of Versailles in 1919 lessen the danger. Germany, he wrote to his mother, would not execute the treaty 'unless constrained ... by the last degree of brutality'.[80] In December 1928 he clearly foresaw Germany's plans for the 1930s: union with Austria, and recovery, by diplomacy or force, of eastern territories from Poland and Alsace from France.[81] In this de Gaulle followed the *Action Française* journalist and historian Jacques Bainville.[82] But he diverged from the conservative Right by supporting a close alliance with the USSR – whatever horror the Soviet regime might inspire – to fight the (inevitable) war against Germany.[83] The Munich Agreement of 1938, for de Gaulle, was a 'surrender without fighting' dressed up to look like peace by a French 'national' press replete with German subsidies.[84] The line that would separate de Gaulle from the pro-German Right in 1940 was already drawn.

Vers l'armée is chiefly remembered for its call for *offensive* capacity, whether to deter German aggression or to attack in support of eastern allies like Poland. De Gaulle wanted an army corps of six tank divisions, plus one light armoured division. Manned by an elite cadre of 100,000 professional soldiers, the corps would seize strongpoints, disrupt the enemy's mobilisation, and win territory in the first days of war. In making his case, de Gaulle, a convert to massed armour only since 1932, was giving a decade-old debate much wider visibility.[85] *Vers l'armée* remains a flawed book. De Gaulle was not (yet) a tank expert and said little about keeping thirsty, fast-moving armoured divisions supplied. In the first edition, he neglected the uses of air power in co-ordination with tanks. His call for a *professional* army, couched in militarist language, ran against France's republican, citizen-army tradition, and was thus an inexpedient addition to the plea for massed armour. Only 800 of the initial print run of 1,500 sold. However, German and Russian translations followed within a year. *Vers l'armée* was read by Hitler, and by Heinz Guderian, the Panzer commander who spearheaded the attack on France in 1940. The French High Command took less notice.

Vers l'armée, finally, is notable for what it leaves out. De Gaulle envisages the coming conflict as primarily a Franco-German affair from which the 'Anglo-Saxons', as de Gaulle would come to call them, are largely absent. For the USA, this was justified by continuing American isolationism. De Gaulle's inter-war writing about the United States is limited to a 1934 article on 'Economic Mobilisation Abroad': he noted America's enormous economic potential, but disapproved of the dominance of business in policy-making.[86] In his view, the state should act more forcefully in a future war than in 1914–1918 to requisition adequate labour and war supplies at reasonable prices.[87]

De Gaulle's treatment of Britain, which he never visited before 1940, is universally chilly and lacks any confidence in Britain's value as an ally. He identified Britain as a potential enemy in 1912.[88] Letters to his parents in 1914–1915 are scathing about the British contribution to the war effort. In 1936 he observes that the British 'have their navy, but no army and an out-of-date air force'.[89] His Levant posting convinced him that the British in the Middle East were at best rivals, at worst enemies.[90] Established French strategy envisaged a defensive war on the Western Front, leaving the British fleet to strangle the German economy by blockade, as in 1918. De Gaulle dissented; and his lack of trust in the British would inevitably generate tension once he became dependent on them from 1940.

Each of de Gaulle's first three books caused offence. *La Discorde* gave lessons to France's high command while its author was still studying at the Higher War School. *Le Fil*'s plea for pragmatism in strategy was an implicit critique of France's rigid post-1918 defensive-mindedness; its portrait of the 'man of character' challenged a military establishment deeply attached to its own hierarchies. *Vers l'armée*, finally, displeased both the military establishment, which still conceived armour chiefly as an infantry support weapon, and republican politicians for whom de Gaulle's advocacy of a professional army as the repository of national values, and his apparent obsession with leadership, all resembled fascism.

The fourth book, *La France et son armée*, published in 1938, was far more consensual in content.[91] A dramatic opening ('France was built by strokes of the sword') begins a historical survey of France's army that celebrates the military glories of every regime, republics and empires as well as the pre-1789 monarchy. In doing so, de Gaulle establishes a clear distance with the sectarian, anti-republican Right. He applauds adequacy of military means to political projects (as in the 'grand siècle' of Louis XIV), and great moments of national unity (as in the Revolutionary victories of 1793), while deploring periods of national division (including much of the Middle Ages, and the Dreyfus Affair). As for Napoleon, de Gaulle's 'judgement remains suspended between condemnation and admiration': admiration for the military genius and for the national energies he called into being; condemnation of the fact that, like Hindenburg and Ludendorff, Napoleon lacked a sense of measure, and left France diminished, confined within indefensible frontiers, and diplomatically isolated.[92]

But the most dramatic impact of *La France et son armée* concerned de Gaulle's relations with Pétain. 'The Marshal' had recruited de Gaulle to his staff in 1925 primarily as a ghost-writer, to help him win election to the Académie Française by preparing a book to be called *Le Soldat*. The project, unfinished when de Gaulle left for Trier in 1927, was soon suspended: in 1929 Pétain had won election to the Académie without the help of a book. Then, in 1938, de Gaulle informed Pétain that he planned to publish his material, complemented by new chapters, under his own name. Pétain objected; de Gaulle responded by inviting him to write a preface; Pétain suggested a dedication, which de Gaulle did not adopt, preferring to write 'to Marshal Pétain, who wished this book to be written' (which he had not). The two men never spoke again after publication. De Gaulle became one of the very rare Frenchmen who did not revere Pétain.[93]

De Gaulle's nonconformity, and cultivated apartness, easily passed for arrogance, and not only through his literary production. A succession of senior officers took exception to what they saw as his inflated view of himself.[94] General Henri Giraud, Gaulle's superior when he commanded the 507th Tank Regiment in 1937, considered that 'His ideas may be brilliant but they are of a type which could lose us the next war'.[95] Many superiors – including, by 1938, Pétain – thought de Gaulle had an attitude problem. This did not assist his career progression.

His circle of friends, too, was unorthodox. One of his fellow-captives in Germany, Étienne Répessé, became his editor with the publisher Berger-Levrault and introduced him to an octogenarian former colonel, Émile Meyer, whose opposition to received army doctrine had stalled his career in 1898. The Meyer circle included journalists, civil servants, and lawyers (de Gaulle was the only serving officer) and met regularly in a Montparnasse café.[96] These acquaintances gave him the political contacts to pursue his crusade for massed armour. They included Blum, who as Prime Minister had dropped his earlier Socialist pacifism and converted to rearmament – but on the defensive lines consistent with General Staff orthodoxies. Their meeting was friendly but inconclusive.[97] De Gaulle had more luck with a conservative, Paul Reynaud. The two men had been introduced in December 1934; by 15 March 1935, Reynaud was speaking up for armoured divisions in the Chamber. Over the next four years, de Gaulle wrote him over 60 letters.[98]

In public, de Gaulle could still act as a spokesman for government policy: he presented the national wartime organisation plan to the Higher Defence College in October 1936.[99] But he attracted more attention as a dissenter, publishing at least three articles on the need for armoured divisions between 1934 and 1936 and encouraging journalist friends like Jean Auburtin or Rémy Roure, another former fellow-prisoner, to do the same. In private, his view of France's defence posture was close to contempt. On 2 April 1936, after Hitler's first major coup against the Versailles peace settlement, the remilitarisation of the Rhineland, he castigated the defeatism and sloppiness of established army doctrines in a letter to Reynaud.[100] In January 1940, after a dinner with Blum and Reynaud, de Gaulle took the extraordinary step of expressing his concerns in writing to Prime Minister Daladier, Reynaud, the supreme commander Gamelin, and some 80 other senior generals and politicians. Germany, he argued, was rapidly acquiring the weapons to defeat France; France's army, committed to a sedentary and defensive war, was prey to boredom and demoralisation. Only new doctrines and vastly more advanced weapons would save France.[101]

De Gaulle apparently thought there was still time: he did not expect major operations on the western front in 1940.[102] In fact the German invasion came less than four months after his memo. The balance of forces that April illustrated the limited success of de Gaulle's campaign for armour. Three-quarters of France's tanks were scattered in penny packets among infantry or light cavalry regiments. Few had radios; most needed refuelling after travelling 20 kilometres. There were just three French armoured divisions proper (plus de Gaulle's 4th, still being cobbled together as he took command); each had only half the number of tanks of a Panzer division, of which ten attacked France in May, piercing the front within days.[103]

It is easy to see why de Gaulle's campaign for armour achieved so little. No army, and certainly not the extremely hierarchical French army of 1940, readily tolerates a colonel who dissents publicly from official military doctrine, and proposes a radical strategic overhaul to generals and ministers in time of war. The crusade for armour nevertheless had two important consequences. First, it brought de Gaulle into politics – to the point of writing Reynaud's speech to the Chamber as France's incoming Prime Minister, on 21 March 1940. De Gaulle's own appointment as a junior minister in the reshuffle of 5 June secured him that vital place in government that would be crucial for later events.[104] The second consequence concerned de Gaulle's relationship with the army. His record in May 1940 shows de Gaulle as a brave and disciplined soldier. His writings show the importance that he attached to the subordination of military to civilian authority. Yet legitimate disobedience, when the fate of France was at stake, was part of the de Gaulle code before the defeat of June 1940.[105] Without that, there could have been no De Gaulle, leader of Free France.

An element of balance? Charles de Gaulle at home

After 1940, de Gaulle's belief in France's exceptional destiny, and in his own exceptional relationship with France, led to his being viewed as a 'prima donna', if not a fascist or an aspiring dictator.[106] Overbearing, cold, and distant he could certainly be; a dictator he never sought to become. One element of balance in his developing character was his own family life.

We know little of de Gaulle's private life before he married. Yvonne Vendroux was not his first love. He told his mother of a brief (pre-war) attraction to a distant German cousin, Theresa Kolb; another letter tells of a young woman, 'almost my fiancée', who was killed by a stray British shell in northern France in 1917.[107] More speculative are the recollection by his former wartime Chief of Staff that de Gaulle had spoken of 'satisfying the same women' as his then commanding officer, none other than Philippe Pétain, and the claim by Éric Roussel that he had had at least two affairs while in Poland in 1919–1921: both strenuously denied by de Gaulle's son.[108]

No affairs were alleged, even by his fiercest enemies, over the nearly five decades of de Gaulle's marriage to Yvonne. Mocked in the press for her bourgeois conventionality and supposed Catholic prudery, shunning the news media, practically absent from de Gaulle's own memoirs, Yvonne was nevertheless more than a devoted and self-effacing wife. She was an immensely resilient companion who lent much-needed balance to de Gaulle's life; she travelled almost everywhere with him; when she could not, he became irritable and out of sorts.[109] There were three children: Philippe (born 28 December 1921), Élisabeth (15 May 1924), and Anne (1 January 1928).

In July 1934 he bought a 14-room house, La Boisserie, in the village of Colombey-les-Deux-Églises. A cheap location compared with fashionable regions like Normandy, Colombey is roughly halfway between Paris and the German frontier. He purchased it *en viager*: that is, he paid the vendor a lump sum plus lifetime annuities, taking possession only on her death. As she died within two years of the sale, the de Gaulles got a bargain. This was the family home in which de Gaulle would die in 1970. But before the outbreak of war, they could only use it in summer: it lacked heating and, initially, running water as well.[110]

La Boisserie provided a big, safe, and sheltered space, with grounds, for the de Gaulles' younger daughter Anne, who was born with Down Syndrome. Other parents of their generation would have placed such a handicapped child in a home. The de Gaulles kept her with them, and paid a carer who became part of the household. There is a photograph of de Gaulle on a beach in Brittany in 1934, sitting in a deck chair, wearing a civilian suit and hat, with Anne on his knee. A gaze of extreme tenderness passes between them. No image of this much-photographed man is more eloquent. Even in the turmoil of the war years, de Gaulle managed to spend an hour with her at the day's end. De Gaulle's relationship with Anne and his Catholic faith reinforced one another. As he told the chaplain of his tank division in 1940, 'Anne is my joy and my strength. She is a grace of God in my life.'[111]

Conclusion

The answers to *why de Gaulle?* are both political and highly personal. First, de Gaulle's transition into politics secured him access, during his 12 days as a junior minister, to Churchill, and thence, on 18 June 1940, to the BBC. A minister of the Republic, however ephemeral, carries more of the authority of the state than a brigadier-general. Second, de Gaulle's break with Pétain allowed him to denounce the armistice of 22 June with a (necessary) ferocity that would have been impossible to anyone with even a residual regard for the Marshal. Third, despite his sense of military discipline and his belief that soldiers should obey the political authorities, de Gaulle was clear in 1940 that the strategy fixed by France's high command and by its politicians was doomed. And he had theorised the necessary breaking of established hierarchies in his writings about the 'man of character'. Both would be necessary for the leap into rebellion that his denunciation of the armistice represented.

Fourth, de Gaulle in June 1940 was independent in the French political context. The narrow reason for this is that while he had received favours – notably from Pétain and Reynaud – he owed no-one any favours back. The broader reason is that de Gaulle did not fit into any group defined by the controversies of the late Third Republic. He kept his dislike of the Third Republic in the private sphere and showed, as a military historian, that he was no doctrinaire anti-republican. A practising Catholic, he still accepted the separation of Church and State and gave only guarded support to France's social Catholic movement. A passionate nationalist, intransigent against Germany – essential for the task he assigned himself – he refused not only the inward-looking, exclusive nationalism of Maurras and his followers but also what had become the flabby, complacent nationalism of the mainstream Republic, now identified with paralysis and defeat. In none of these areas of controversy was de Gaulle anyone's man but his own. That allowed him, in time, to gather support from the full range of French patriots, from the far Right to the Communists, from Catholics to the most secular-minded – and from Jews.

None of these attributes would have sufficed without de Gaulle's personal equation. A sense of measure and a salutary private humility, often well hidden but exemplified by his tenderness towards his daughter Anne, always prevented de Gaulle from becoming the dictatorial figure of his detractors' imagination. But he did believe, with almost mystical intensity, in the values of leadership, in his *own* exceptional destiny, and in his unique relationship with France. And he had devoted considerable effort into becoming De Gaulle, into forging himself as the 'man of character' he had theorised. That was necessary not only to his act of rebellion against established France on 18 June 1940 but also to sustaining a divided and quarrelsome Free French movement against his overbearing allies.

Notes

1 Alain Peyrefitte, *C'était de Gaulle*, vol. I (Paris: Éditions de Fallois/Fayard, 1994), p. 28.

De Gaulle before Gaullism, 1890–1940   27

2 De Gaulle was a *général de brigade*, technically a brigadier-general in English. But from June 1940 he was always General de Gaulle.
3 Maurice Druon, 'De Gaulle avant de Gaulle', in Institut Charles de Gaulle, *De Gaulle en son siècle*, vol. I: *Dans la mémoire des hommes et des peuples* (Paris: Plon, 1991), pp. 115–21: p. 115.
4 Alistair Horne, *To Lose a Battle: France 1940* (London: Macmillan, 1969), p. 156n.
5 Napoleon I's only legitimate son, Napoleon II (1811–1832), never reigned.
6 Dividing the First Republic into its three distinct phases (Convention, Directory, Consulate) brings the total to ten.
7 Sudhir Hazareesingh, *Political Traditions in Modern France* (Oxford: Oxford University Press, 1993), p. 83.
8 Raymond Huard, *La Naissance du parti politique en France* (Paris: Presses de Sciences Po, 1996).
9 Michel Winock, *La Fièvre hexagonale: les grandes crises politiques depuis 1870*, 2nd edn (Paris: Le Seuil, 1995).
10 Eugen Weber, *The Hollow Years: France in the 1930s* (New York: W. W. Norton, 1994), p. 271; Horne, *To Lose a Battle*, pp. 91–2, 156.
11 Jean Lacouture, *De Gaulle*, vol. I: *Le Rebelle, 1890–1944* (Paris: Le Seuil, 1984), p. 15; Philippe de Gaulle, *De Gaulle mon père. Entretiens avec Michel Tauriac*, vol. II (Paris: Plon, 2003), p. 335; Ilan Greilsammer, 'De Gaulle et le judaïsme', in Fondation Charles de Gaulle, *Charles de Gaulle, chrétien, homme d'État* (Paris: Plon, 2005), pp. 371–9: pp. 371–2.
12 Alain Larcan, *Éducation religieuse et références spirituelles*, in Fondation Charles de Gaulle, *Charles de Gaulle, chrétien*, pp. 17–37: pp. 17, 21; Éric Roussel, *Charles de Gaulle* (Paris: Gallimard, 2002), p. 12.
13 Julian Jackson, *A Certain Idea of France: The Life of Charles de Gaulle* (London: Allen Lane, 2018), pp. 23–4.
14 Jacques Prévotat, 'De Gaulle croyant et pratiquant', in Fondation Charles de Gaulle, *Charles de Gaulle, chrétien*, pp. 39–66: pp. 47, 40; Xavier Boniface, 'L'Officier catholique', in *ibid.*, pp. 121–32.
15 Charles de Gaulle, *War Memoirs*, vol. I: *The Call to Honour, 1940–1942*, tr. Jonathan Griffin (London: Collins, 1955: hereafter WMI), p. 10.
16 Philippe de Gaulle, *De Gaulle mon père*, II, p. 325.
17 See the chapters by Xavier Boniface, Philippe Portier, Jérôme Grondeux, and Jean-Pierre Rioux in Fondation Charles de Gaulle, *Charles de Gaulle, chrétien, homme d'État* (Paris: Plon, 2005).
18 Lacouture, *De Gaulle* I, p. 109.
19 Jean Touchard, *Le Gaullisme 1940–1969* (Paris: Le Seuil, 1978); Lacouture, *De Gaulle* I, p. 13.
20 Olivier Guichard, *Mon Général* (Paris: Grasset, 1980), pp. 15–17.
21 Peter Mangold, *The Almost Impossible Ally: Harold Macmillan and Charles de Gaulle* (London: I.B.Tauris, 2006), p. 9.

De Gaulle before Gaullism, 1890–1940

22 Lacouture, *De Gaulle* I, p. 29.
23 Charles de Gaulle, *Zalaïna*, and *Le Secret du Spahi*, in *Lettres, Notes et Carnets*, vol. I (Paris: Robert Laffont, 2010 [Plon, 1980–1997]: hereafter *LNC*I), pp. 47–51, 57–61.
24 *WM*I, pp. 9–10; Roussel, *De Gaulle*, p. 12.
25 Lacouture, *De Gaulle*I, pp. 15–16.
26 De Gaulle, *De Gaulle mon père*II, p. 317.
27 De Gaulle to Jeanne de Gaulle, 23 December 1915, and to Henri de Gaulle, 31 December 1915, *LNC*I, pp. 231–2, 236–7.
28 Roussel, *De Gaulle*, p. 57.
29 *WM*I, p. 31.
30 Charles De Gaulle, *War Memoirs*, vol. III: *Salvation, 1944–1946*, tr. Richard Howard (London: Weidenfeld & Nicolson, 1960: hereafter *WM*III), p. 28.
31 Touchard, *Le Gaullisme*, p. 20.
32 Alain Peyrefitte, *C'était de Gaulle*, vol. II (Paris: Éditions de Fallois/Fayard, 1997), pp. 188–9.
33 Jacques Julliard, 'Bernanos, Claudel, Mauriac, Péguy et de Gaulle', in Fondation Charles de Gaulle, *Charles de Gaulle, chrétien*, pp. 87–114; pp. 90, 111.
34 De Gaulle to Jeanne de Gaulle, 23 May 1919, and to Henri de Gaulle, 7 June 1919, *LNC*I, pp. 458–61. The word 'Jews' is replaced by dots in the published edition.
35 René Cassin, *Les Hommes partis de rien: le réveil de la France abattue (1940–1941)* (Paris: Plon, 1975), p. 138.
36 *WM*I, p. 9.
37 Jackson, *A Certain Idea*, p. 29; Philippe de Gaulle, *De Gaulle mon père* I, p. 376.
38 De Gaulle to Jeanne de Gaulle, 24 February 1920, *LNC*I, pp. 493–4.
39 De Gaulle to Henri de Gaulle, 26 August 1919, *LNC*I, p. 468.
40 Lacouture, *De Gaulle*I, p. 139; Jackson, *A Certain Idea*, pp. 56–9.
41 General Maurice Gamelin was 67 when, as France's Commander-in-Chief, he faced the German onslaught of May 1940; he was succeeded on 17 May by the 73-year-old Maxime Weygand.
42 François Cochet, 'La Société militaire en France: réalité et perception par Charles de Gaulle (1919–1940)', in Fondation Charles de Gaulle, *Charles de Gaulle, 1920–1940: Du militaire au politique* (Paris: Plon, 2004), pp. 17–32: pp. 26–7.
43 Roussel, *De Gaulle*, pp. 43, 50.
44 De Gaulle to Reynaud, 14 December 1936, *LNC*I, pp. 826–7; Paul-Marie de La Gorce, 'De Gaulle: la presse et le monde politique', in Fondation Charles de Gaulle, *Charles de Gaulle, 1920–1940*, pp. 354, 360–1.
45 Charles de Gaulle, 'Du patriotisme', *LNC*I, pp. 70–7: p. 76.
46 Jackson, *A Certain Idea*, pp. 30–1; *WM*I, p. 10.
47 'Campagne d'Allemagne', *LNC*I, pp. 1–14; 'Je voudrais', *LNC*I, pp. 50–1.

48 *WM*I, p. 10.
49 Guichard, *Mon Général*, p. 9.
50 Lacouture, *De Gaulle* I, p. 38.
51 Touchard, *Le Gaullisme*, p. 21.
52 Lacouture, *De Gaulle* I, p. 65.
53 Letter to parents, 19 December 1917, *LNC*I, pp. 337–8.
54 'Récits d'évasions', 31 January 1927, *LNC*I, pp. 673–85.
55 Jackson, *A Certain Idea*, p. 29.
56 'Aux nouvelles recrues', *LNC*I, pp. 64–9.
57 Charles Williams, *The Last Great Frenchman* (New York: John Wiley, 1993), p. 39.
58 Pierre Debray, 'Le Colonel de Gaulle vu par un jeune officier, le futur colonel Pierre Debray', in Fondation Charles de Gaulle, *Charles de Gaulle, 1920–1940*, pp. 442–6.
59 Williams, *Last Great Frenchman*, pp. 67–8; Jackson, *A Certain Idea*, p. 61; Debray, 'Le Colonel de Gaulle'; Roussel, *De Gaulle*, p. 44.
60 Jackson, *A Certain Idea*, p. 107; Lacouture, *De Gaulle*I, p. 318.
61 Cochet, 'La Société militaire en France', p. 30.
62 'De la guerre' and 'De la direction supérieure de la guerre', both 1917, *LNC*I, pp. 338–74, 375–404.
63 Claude Carré, 'Charles de Gaulle, professeur et conférencier', in Fondation Charles de Gaulle, *Charles de Gaulle, 1920–1940*, pp. 204–16; Lacouture, *De Gaulle* I, p. 113.
64 Fondation Charles de Gaulle, *Charles de Gaulle, 1920–1940*, p. 425.
65 *LNC*I, pp. 301–2.
66 Charles de Gaulle, *Vers l'armée de métier* (Paris, Berger-Levrault, 1934), in Charles de Gaulle, *Le Fil de l'épée et autres écrits* (Paris: Plon, 1994), pp. 227–325: p. 321.
67 Richard Nixon, *Leaders: Profiles and Reminiscences of Men Who Have Shaped the Modern World* (New York, Warner Books, 1982), p. 76.
68 *LNC*I, pp. 276–9, 304, 318, 642.
69 Charles de Gaulle, *La Discorde chez l'ennemi* (Paris, Berger-Levrault, 1924), in Charles De Gaulle, *Le Fil de l'épée et autres écrits* (Paris: Plon, collection Omnibus, 1994), pp. 7–140. German was de Gaulle's first foreign language at school; he perfected his knowledge while a prisoner of war.
70 De Gaulle, *Discorde*, pp. 12–13.
71 De Gaulle, *Discorde*, pp. 50, 112; Alain Larcan, 'Pouvoir politique et pouvoir militaire', in Fondation Charles de Gaulle, *Charles de Gaulle, 1920–1940*, pp. 295–320: p. 305.
72 Charles de Gaulle, *Le Fil de l'épée*, in Charles De Gaulle, *Le Fil de l'épée et autres écrits* (Paris: Plon, collection Omnibus, 1994), pp. 141–225.
73 De Gaulle, *Le Fil*, pp. 145–60.
74 De Gaulle, *Le Fil*, pp. 178, 182–3.

75 Charles de Gaulle, *Vers l'armée de métier*, in Charles de Gaulle, *Le Fil de l'épée et autres écrits* (Paris: Plon, 1994), pp. 227–325. A literal translation is *Towards a Professional Army*; the English version of 1940 was called *The Army of the Future*.

76 *LNC*I, pp. 292–316; Pierre Maillard, *De Gaulle et l'Allemagne. Le rêve inachevé* (Paris: Plon, 1990), p. 60.

77 De Gaulle, *La Discorde*, p. 12.

78 De Gaulle, *Vers l'armée*, p. 238.

79 De Gaulle, *Vers l'armée*, p. 237.

80 De Gaulle to Jeanne de Gaulle, 25 June 1919, *LNC*I, pp. 462–3.

81 De Gaulle to Mayer, 21 December 1928, *LNC*I, p. 706.

82 Guichard, *Mon Général*, p. 70.

83 De Gaulle to Jeanne de Gaulle, 20 December 1936, *LNC*I, pp. 828–9.

84 De Gaulle to Yvonne de Gaulle, n.d. (1938), *LNC*I, p. 864; Maurice Vaïsse, 'De Gaulle face aux crises internationales des années trente', in Fondation Charles de Gaulle, *Charles de Gaulle, 1920–1940*, pp. 328–35.

85 General Bruno Chaix, 'Charles de Gaulle et le débat doctrinal du début des années trente', in Fondation Charles de Gaulle, *Charles de Gaulle, 1920–1940*, pp. 91–101; Touchard, *Le Gaullisme*, p. 34; Roussel, *De Gaulle*, p. 61; Jackson, *A Certain Idea*, pp. 73–6.

86 Christopher S. Thompson, 'Prologue to Conflict: de Gaulle and the United States, from First Impressions through 1940', in Robert O. Paxton and Nicholas Wahl (eds.), *De Gaulle and the United States: A Centennial Reappraisal* (Oxford: Berg, 1994), pp. 13–32: pp. 14–18.

87 De Gaulle, 'Projet de loi sur l'organisation de la nation au temps de guerre, conférence au Collège de Hautes Études de la Défense Nationale', 22 October 1936, *LNC*I, pp. 806–24: p. 809.

88 *LNC*I, p. 65.

89 De Gaulle to Henri de Gaulle, 14 September 1914, *LNC*I, pp. 90–1; to Jeanne de Gaulle, 2 May 1915, *LNC*I, pp. 157–8, and 20 December 1936, *LNC*I, pp. 828–9.

90 Bernard Ledwidge, *De Gaulle* (London: Weidenfeld & Nicolson, 1982), p. 36.

91 Charles De Gaulle, *La France et son armée* (Paris: Plon, 1938), in Charles de Gaulle, *Le Fil de l'épée et autres écrits*, pp. 327–500.

92 De Gaulle, *Armée*, pp. 421–2; Touchard, *Le Gaullisme*, pp. 41–4.

93 Jackson, *A Certain Idea*, pp. 91–2; de Gaulle, letters to Pétain, 23 January 1928, 18 August and 7 October 1938, *LNC*I, pp. 704–6, 858–60, 867–8.

94 Roussel, *De Gaulle*, p. 17; Touchard, *Le Gaullisme*, p. 21.

95 Jean-Luc Barré, *Devenir de Gaulle, 1939–1943* (Paris: Perrin, 2003), p. 28.

96 Henri Lerner, 'Le Cercle des amis', in Fondation Charles de Gaulle, *Charles de Gaulle, 1920–1940*, pp. 244–51.

97 *WM*I, p. 31.

98 Roussel, *De Gaulle*, pp. 64–7; Raymond Krakovitch, 'Charles de Gaulle et Paul Reynaud', in Fondation Charles de Gaulle, *Charles de Gaulle, 1920–1940*, pp. 371–80; *LNC*I, pp. 766–916.
 99 *LNC*I, pp. 806–24.
100 De Gaulle to Reynaud, 2 April 1936, *LNC*I, p. 792.
101 Charles de Gaulle, 'Mémorandum adressé par le colonel Charles de Gaulle aux généraux Gamelin, Weygand et Georges et à MM. Daladier et Reynaud le 26 janvier 1940', in *Le Fil de l'épée et autres écrits*, pp. 797–810; De La Gorce, 'De Gaulle: la presse et le monde politique', pp. 358–61.
102 De Gaulle to Répessé, 11 February 1940, *LNC*I, p. 918.
103 Horne, *To Lose a Battle*, pp. 155–6; Jackson, *A Certain Idea*, p. 104.
104 De La Gorce, 'De Gaulle: la presse et le monde politique', pp. 360–1.
105 Cochet, 'La Société militaire', p. 29.
106 Views held strongly though far from exclusively by President Franklin D. Roosevelt.
107 De Gaulle's great-great-grandfather was a Bavarian, Louis-Philippe Kolb. Cf. Pierre Maillard, *De Gaulle et l'Allemagne. Le Rêve inachevé* (Paris: Plon, 1990), pp. 17–18; letters to Jeanne de Gaulle, 17 July 1919, *LNC*I, pp. 464–5, and to J.-C. Pagès, 9 March 1942, *LNC*II, pp. 42–3.
108 Claude Bouchinet-Serreulles, *Nous étions nés pour être libres. La Résistance avec de Gaulle et Jean Moulin* (Paris: Grasset, 2000), p. 187; Roussel, *de Gaulle*, pp. 34–5; Philippe de Gaulle, *De Gaulle mon père*I, pp. 79, 376–7.
109 Pierre-Louis Blanc, *De Gaulle au soir de sa vie* (Paris: Fayard, 1990), p. 83.
110 Lacouture, *De Gaulle* I, p. 188.
111 Prévotat, 'De Gaulle croyant et pratiquant', p. 53.

Further reading

Julian Jackson, *A Certain Idea of France: The Life of Charles de Gaulle* (London: Allen Lane, 2018) has become the standard big one-volume work in English. Other good one-volume biographies are Charles Williams, *The Last Great Frenchman* (London: Little, Brown, 1993) and Bernard Ledwidge, *De Gaulle* (London: Weidenfeld & Nicolson, 1982).

The leading French biography remains Jean Lacouture's monumental three-volume *De Gaulle* (Paris: Éditions du Seuil, 1985–1986), translated in an abridged two-volume version (New York: Norton, 1990 and 1993).

The day-by-day chronology of de Gaulle's life is admirably charted in Olivier Germain-Thomas and Philippe Barthelet, *Charles de Gaulle jour après jour* (Paris: Nathan, 1990).

The Institut (now Fondation) Charles de Gaulle organised a gigantic conference in the de Gaulle centenary year, from which emerged six volumes of proceedings: Institut Charles de Gaulle, *De Gaulle en son siècle* (Paris: Plon, 1991–1992). Some of the contributions, from eyewitnesses as well as academics, tend towards the hagiographic – but by no means all.

No book in English is specifically devoted to de Gaulle's pre-1940 career, but all the main biographies cover it.

De Gaulle's own four pre-war books are grouped in French, with other writings, as *Le Fil de l'épée et autres écrits* (Paris: Plon, Collection Omnibus, 1994). The English versions are *The Enemy's House Divided* (*La Discorde chez l'ennemi*), tr. Robert Eden (Chapel Hill: University of North Carolina Press, 2002); *The Edge of the Sword* (*Le Fil de l'Épée*), tr. Gerard Hopkins (London: Faber, 1960); *The Army of the Future* (London: Hutchinson, 1940); *France and Her Army* (*La France et son Armée*), tr. F.L. Dash (London: Hutchinson, 1945).

De Gaulle's memoirs, of the war and of the presidency, present his own case with eloquence and at times tendentiousness. In the three-volume *War Memoirs*, the opening chapter of *The Call to Honour, 1940–1942*, tr. Jonathan Griffin (London: Collins, 1955) is crucial for his early life and outlook on France. The first volume of his miscellaneous letters and papers *Lettres, Notes et Carnets* (3 volumes: Paris: Robert Laffont, 2010) includes, for example, his prison notebooks.

The best general survey of French history since 1870 is Charles Sowerwine, *France since 1870: Culture, Politics and Society*, 3rd edn (Basingstoke: Palgrave Macmillan, 2018). Good analyses of the pre-war years are found in Wilfrid Knapp, *France: Partial Eclipse* (London: Macdonald, 1972) and Eugen Weber, *The Hollow Years: France in the 1930s* (New York: W.W. Norton, 1994).

2 Allies and rivals
De Gaulle, the Free French, and their partners

How did de Gaulle, brigadier-general of a collapsing French army in June 1940, become the undisputed leader of France's Provisional Government, recognised by every Allied power, in the liberated Paris of October 1944? Much of the answer lies in the twists and turns of the intervening 53 months, without doubt the densest of his career. But that narrative, which occupies Chapters 3–5, has a structural framework: the intricate set of relationships between de Gaulle, the Free French organisation that he created, and five other players – the British, the French Empire, the internal Resistance, the Americans, and the Russians. They are the subject of this chapter.

Breaking-point: the *Appel du 18 juin*

De Gaulle's brief, as Under-Secretary of State for War from 5 June 1940, was to look after zones behind the front line and to liaise with the British.[1] But the front was now irreparably broken and the assumptions of the start of the battle useless. The British had rescued 224,320 British and 141,842 French servicemen off the coast at Dunkirk in the week to 4 June.[2] But the balance of forces in France was now tilted massively in the Germans' favour. Meanwhile Weygand, France's Commander-in-Chief since 16 May, was actively promoting an armistice.[3] Pétain, vice-premier since 17 May, led the defeatists in Paul Reynaud's government. Another defeatist, Hélène de Portes, shared Reynaud's bed. His government left Paris for Tours on 10 June, and thence reached Bordeaux on 14 June, just as German forces entered an undefended capital.

All de Gaulle's efforts to halt the dash to armistice failed. His requests to Churchill (at Reynaud's behest) for more British fighter aircraft, during visits to London on 9 and 16 June, were twice refused: Britain would need them for her own defences, as de Gaulle (according to Churchill) well understood.[4] No more successful were his proposals made at the Supreme Allied War Council near Briare on 11 June, and at an inter-Allied meeting at Tours on 13 June: to amalgamate French and British armoured forces still in France, or to organise an orderly retreat, first to Brittany, and then, eventually, to North Africa.[5] But the grandest project to stave off France's defeat was sprung upon de Gaulle, during his London visit of 16 June, by Jean Monnet, the planning expert co-ordinating British and French war supplies, and France's ambassador Charles Corbin: a union of the British and French states. Personally sceptical, de Gaulle nevertheless persuaded Churchill, then the British War Cabinet, and finally, by telephone in the afternoon, Reynaud to back the plan. That evening he flew back to Bordeaux in a Dragon Rapide lent him by Churchill, only to find that the French government had rejected the union. Reynaud had resigned, knowing that Pétain would succeed him and request an armistice.

Signed on 22 June, the armistice provided for Germany's indefinite military occupation of the northern half of France and the whole Atlantic coast; the effective annexation of Alsace and Lorraine to the Reich; the limitation of France's army to 100,000 men; and the payment of huge so-called occupation costs, again for an indefinite period. The government was not permitted to return to Paris; it settled at the spa town of Vichy, in the so-called 'free' zone in the South. Here, on 10 July, the combined houses of the French Parliament abolished the Third Republic (and themselves) by voting Pétain full constituent powers. Not that Pétain ever enacted a constitution: the 'French State' (not Republic) founded at Vichy was simply an authoritarian regime, with neither parliament nor elections nor free press nor civil liberties. It collaborated willingly with the German occupiers.

In retrospect, only two things were important about de Gaulle's 12 days as Under-Secretary of State. First, as a minister of France's last republican government he would be vastly more qualified to speak for France than as a mere brigadier-general. Second, he had established a close relationship with Churchill over their four meetings, two face-to-face in London and two at the Allied conferences in France. 'If de Gaulle had not found Churchill', he would tell his son later, 'then de Gaulle would not have existed and France would have been finished.'[6] Churchill, for his part, identified de Gaulle as 'the man of destiny' (at the Tours meeting on 13 June), and even, in London three days later, as 'the Constable of France' – a striking echo of de Gaulle's Saint-Cyr comrades.[7]

So it was Churchill who lent de Gaulle the Dragon Rapide, in which he returned to London on 17 June, carrying 100,000 francs from the Prime Minister's funds – a parting gesture from Reynaud – and accompanied by Major-General Sir Edward Spears, a friend of Churchill's and Britain's chief military liaison officer with the French. It was Spears who found de Gaulle offices – shabby, cramped, fortunately temporary – at St Stephen's House on the Victoria Embankment. It was Churchill who sent a Sunderland flying-boat to search for de Gaulle's family (the Sunderland was lost with its crew; Yvonne, Philippe, Élisabeth, and Anne reached Plymouth on 20 June on the last ferry out of Brest).[8] And it was, crucially, Churchill and Spears who – overruling a sceptical War Cabinet – supplied the instrument with which de Gaulle entered history: a microphone at the BBC. For de Gaulle, having failed to prevent the armistice, had resolved to take another road.

The *Appel du 18 juin* was a five-minute, 355-word, call to continue the fight, broadcast on the BBC's French service at 10pm on 18 June 1940 and repeated four times.[9] It was also edited down to a 133-word poster.[10] In the confusion of defeated France, few heard it live. Yet it ranks with Abraham Lincoln's (270-word) Gettysburg Address for its historic importance.

The first reason for this was the *Appel*'s content. Against all apparent evidence, it gave the French reasons to believe the war was not lost. France's Empire; undefeated Britain, and the Commonwealth; the huge potential of Allied, especially American, industry to turn mechanised warfare, spearhead of the German victory, against the Nazis; the inevitably global nature of the war: all this meant that Britain, France, and their (future) Allies were sure of victory.[11] In its grasp of an as yet unrealised global balance of forces, this was the polar opposite of Pétain's broadcast of the previous day, focused entirely on France's weakness and Germany's strength. De Gaulle concluded with a call to action, inviting any

French citizen in Britain, especially military personnel, but also key officials such as colonial governors, wherever they were, to join him. In declaring that 'the flame of the French Resistance must not and will not go out', de Gaulle, in effect, coined the term Resistance, the most resonant of France's war.

Secondly, the *Appel* marked the defining break in de Gaulle's personal trajectory, an act of flagrant insubordination from a man hitherto devoted to the military virtues of discipline and obedience.

> As the irrevocable words flew out upon their way, I felt within myself a life coming to an end – the life I had lived within the framework of a solid France and an indivisible army. At the age of forty-nine I was entering upon adventure, like a man thrown by fate outside all terms of reference.

Within six weeks a Vichy military tribunal condemned him to death *in absentia* for 'damaging State security and desertion abroad in wartime'. The sentence was signed by Weygand, whom de Gaulle had actually invited to lead the Resistance in his own place. The verdict gave a violent new twist to de Gaulle's (never simple) relations with the French army.[12]

Third, the *Appel* had an impact even in the short term. De Gaulle was not the only Frenchman to reject the armistice, but he was the only former minister with radio access. Certainly the immediate response was disappointing. Weygand was an instant enemy. So was Charles Noguès, Resident-General (effectively, governor) in the French protectorate of Morocco, and, crucially, commander of French forces across North Africa. When a group of politicians, including former Interior Minister Georges Mandel, arrived in Casablanca hoping to continue the fight, Noguès had them arrested or repatriated. Among Frenchmen in London, many, including Corbin and Monnet, chose to cross the Atlantic; de Gaulle devotes a bitter page of his memoirs to their mealy-mouthed excuses.[13] Indeed, when Churchill's government recognised de Gaulle on 28 June as 'leader of all the Free French wherever they might be' it was not only an endorsement but also a recognition that no more eminent figure had stepped up.[14] But across France, the news of the *Appel* spread, whether by word of mouth or through the regional newspapers, still largely uncensored in France's 'free' southern zone.[15] De Gaulle as a symbol of resistance began, slowly, to take shape.

The final importance of the *Appel* was best expressed in the poster version. That Germany would be crushed, it claimed, was inevitable. 'On that day', it added, 'France must be present at the victory. Thus she will regain her freedom and grandeur. That is my aim, my only aim!' De Gaulle's purpose was thus not just to liberate France, which would happen anyway, but to retrieve her status as a first-rank power. That could only be done by the French themselves, if necessary against 'the tendency of the great Powers to take advantage of our weakness in order to push their interests at the expense of those of France'.[16] He was thus embarking on a conflict, not only with Vichy and the German occupiers, but also with the allies on whom he depended for his very existence.

De Gaulle: the personal equation

We have already seen how de Gaulle's personal characteristics, developed before 1940, fitted him for the role he was to play: an absolute belief in France and a complete self-identification with his country; an intellectual non-conformity and modernism; an ability to think and act ahead of events; a belief in the power of leadership and a painstaking construction of himself as a 'man of character'.[17] It remained to apply these traits to the task in hand.

Most obviously, through the spoken word.

> General de Gaulle was always, above all, a voice, the voice I heard through the four years of the Occupation, in penury, arbitrary rule, fear and horror. To hear that voice of hope, of courage, of honour, of rectitude, of liberation was something absolutely extraordinary.[18]

Thus Stanley Hoffmann, a Viennese Jewish boy, who survived the Occupation in France and became a Harvard professor in 1955, described the effect of his 67 wartime broadcasts, mostly on the BBC, which Vichy believed reached an audience of 300,000 in 1941 and 3 million in 1942.[19] Added to the broadcasts were the great public speeches, for example at London's Albert Hall on 15 November 1941, 18 June and 11 November 1942, or Oxford on

25 November 1941, Algiers on 14 July 1943 or Tunis on 7 May 1944: each calculated, with careful consideration of time and place, to move, to provoke thought, and above all, however resounding the tributes paid to the Allies, to assert the strength and independence of Free France.

De Gaulle's second technique, more complex than the first, lay in his self-construction as a symbol of France's resistance. This emerges most vividly from his account of arriving at Douala, the main port of Cameroon, on 8 October 1940, and being surrounded, for the first time, by a cheering crowd:

> The fact of embodying for my comrades the fate of our cause, for the French multitude the symbol of its hope, and for foreigners the image of a France indomitable in the midst of her trials, was to dictate my bearing and to impose upon my personality an attitude I could never again change. For me this meant, without respite, a stubborn self-supervision as well as an extremely heavy yoke.[20]

As if, observed Olivier Guichard, the flesh-and-blood human de Gaulle henceforth had a permanent larger-than-life double. And it was this symbolic de Gaulle, difficult and unbending, both illuminated and weighed down by his symbiotic relationship with France, who presented himself to the internal Resistance and to the British.[21]

The third aspect of de Gaulle's personal equation was his intransigence towards his allies: certain of his value to them, he regularly threatened to withdraw co-operation. To his Free French associates, he insisted that 'Our grandeur and our strength consist entirely in our intransigence concerning French interests. We will need this intransigence up to and including the Rhine.'[22] Churchill wrote that de Gaulle 'had to be rude to the British to prove to French eyes that he was not a British puppet'.[23] Or, as he put it to his physician Lord Moran, 'Look at him! ... He might be Stalin, with 200 divisions behind his words!'[24] To be unbending, to behave as if heading a great and undefeated power, were deliberate, strategic attitudes; both also sprang readily from de Gaulle's own character.

De Gaulle could, finally, bind (some) men to him. When he tried, he could be charming. The novelist André Gide, who met him in

Algiers in June 1943, remembered politeness, simplicity, and attentiveness.[25] Harold Macmillan, British Minister Resident in Algiers in 1943, recalled with pleasure their wide-ranging conversation as they visited the Roman ruins at Tipasa together that same month.[26] Other men's allegiance, by contrast, was won precisely through his granite-like inflexibility. François Jacob, an early Free French recruit, recalled seeing de Gaulle 'looking like a Gothic cathedral' in a camp at Aldershot in 1940, thinking 'Never seen a man like that' – and concluding that 'this was the man of the situation'.[27] Pierre Lefranc, who led a Gaullist demonstration in Paris in November 1940, wrote of the loyalty he inspired, and of a desire to be worthy of the task de Gaulle set.[28] Jacques Chaban-Delmas, de Gaulle's military delegate in France in 1944, 'loved him like a father'.[29] Loyalty and even love towards de Gaulle, though far from universal, remain essential to understanding the Free French phenomenon.

Yet de Gaulle was also, as Sir Anthony Eden, Churchill's Foreign Minister from 1940, put it, 'the victim of his qualities'.[30] His intransigence could spill into pig-headedness, his passion for France into xenophobia, his rigorous conception of leadership into coldness and ingratitude.

Intransigence could accrue short-term benefits but lasting resentments. Spears wrote that his technique with the British was to embarrass them by being intolerably rude, and at the next meeting to be easy and polite, whereupon the British would be so relieved they would concede all of the substantive points at issue.[31] But repetition of the technique bred mistrust and bitterness. Intransigence, moreover, became a reflex for de Gaulle as much as a calculated gambit. He often behaved as if compromise meant surrender and firmness required brutality. And so, to the despair of others in the Free French movement, he alienated his friends – and appeared not to care.[32]

Was de Gaulle also an Anglophobe, as the Free French economist (and later ambassador to the United States) Hervé Alphand claimed?[33] Certainly, de Gaulle found much to admire among the British: stable institutions, steadfastness among soldiers (who did not mutiny in World War I, unlike the French), and among civilians under the Blitz, a determination not just to survive but to destroy their tormentors. But he was contemptuous of the British record in the 1930s – the appeasement of Hitler, and the slowness to mobilise in 1939–1940, which left just 10½ British divisions in France in May 1940, of the 60 he claimed were promised.[34] He resented British offhandedness after 1940; and he constantly suspected the British of wanting to take over the French Empire. This mistrust, strengthened by 'a persecution complex, common to exiles',[35] and by incomprehension of the English language (at least at first), of English habits of thought, of the 'Anglo-Saxon world' generally,[36] blossomed into a generalised suspicion in which he was 'unable to come across a muddle without seeing a conspiracy behind it'.[37] André Dewavrin, alias Colonel Passy, was told 'don't trust the British' as he started to put together the Free French secret services from scratch (and, inevitably, with British help), in London.[38] Where de Gaulle led, many subordinates followed – and damaged their own cause by annoying all manner of British officials.[39] Pierre Brossolette, an outstanding *résistant* and Free French operative, observed that 'The General must be constantly reminded that our enemy number one is Germany. For if he followed his natural inclination it would rather be Britain.'[40]

Equally damaging was de Gaulle's lack of human warmth even to the Free French. He offered no congratulations to new Free French recruits, who he considered were doing no more than their duty.[41] He memorised no personal details of troops he reviewed, as he had as an army officer.[42] François Jacob might appreciate his gruffness; many others did not. Things were no better at Free French headquarters. Legal expert René Cassin wrote of his unnecessary severity towards his entourage; André Philip, a Socialist economist who came to London in 1942, of his pride, lack of charity and pointless harshness.[43] Brossolette wrote de Gaulle a four-page letter about the damage his gratuitous brutality was doing to the movement: with so many people afraid of him, de Gaulle was surrounded by yes-men and no proposal could be effectively tested in discussion.[44]

A final reproach levelled against de Gaulle was that he was bored by administration and inept in his choice of men. Jacques Bingen, a leading *résistant* who, like Brossolette, did not survive the war, observed a combination of authoritarianism with an inability to keep order in his own house.[45] The questionable choice of men applied especially to Émile Bollaert, designated as de Gaulle's delegate in occupied France, and General Charles Delestraint, chosen to head the 'secret army' of the Resistance in the northern zone. Eminently qualified in late Third Republic terms, neither was suited, or trained, for clandestine activity; both would be captured, in Delestraint's case with devastating results.[46]

De Gaulle, then, was in some ways a dysfunctional leader. This was partly due to stress; not only bearing almost the whole weight of the Free French movement (and therefore, for de Gaulle, of France) on his shoulders, but also suffering intensely from his country's humiliation and its state of near-total dependence on Allies. Churchill discerned in de Gaulle 'a remarkable capacity for feeling pain'.[47] Lady Spears, who had created an ambulance unit for French soldiers, observed a man 'skinned alive' who could barely tolerate contact with 'friendly wellmeaning people'.[48] Small wonder, perhaps, that he should so rarely remember to be nice to his friends. And yet, however damaging de Gaulle's shortcomings as a leader, the big picture is one of success. Lacking direct political experience, he proved a very able political operator.[49] Jean Monnet's assistant René Pleven, who became a leading Free French figure from June 1940, wrote in 1942 that 'I have seen him operate in the most difficult circumstances and each time he comes out of it bigger in my eyes.'[50]

The Free French

De Gaulle would have achieved nothing without the men and women of Free France. That group was, initially, exceedingly small. A huge haul of potential recruits, French servicemen arriving from Norway and Dunkirk, returned to France almost immediately. By 15 August, de Gaulle's 'first brigade of the French legion' counted just 2,721 men and 123 officers. At 4 Carlton Gardens, the much smarter premises which replaced dingy St Stephen's House in July, there were 129 staff: 75 military and 54 civilians including secretaries and cooks.[51] By late 1940 Free France had recruited a mere five senior officers; one senior civil servant, Pierre Tissier; no diplomats; no senior politician except Pierre Cot, who as Aviation Minister under the Popular Front had so incensed Air Force chiefs that de Gaulle refused his services – even to sweep the stairs – for fear of losing his handful of Free French airmen. De Gaulle had not expected to be so shunned by France's elites.[52] 'From those first two years of Free France', he would tell his aide-de-camp Claude Guy, 'I have kept the memory of an incredible solitude'.[53] That memory permeates his memoirs – and contrasts with wartime speeches written as if the whole of France was behind him.[54]

Why were they so few? De Gaulle, a quarter-century later, put it down to property. People with nothing to lose, or Jews certain of their impending dispossession, joined him; but 'people who had to choose between their material goods and the spirit of France – the material goods chose for them'.[55] This was over-simple. French servicemen often got little opportunity to join de Gaulle. The British military saw them as defeatists and wanted them repatriated. When Spears did manage to get Free French recruiters into camps where French soldiers were held, the obstruction came from the overwhelmingly Pétainist French officers. Inept Free French propaganda took no account of such constraints. For the ordinary French soldier, money and family worries, the hardship of British camps, the belief that the war was lost, and mistrust of the British did the rest.[56]

Nor was de Gaulle himself, largely unknown, dependent on the British, unable to offer decent pay to supporters or protection for families at home against Vichy or the Germans, a very attractive material proposition. If you needed to survive in London in June 1940, Lord Bessborough's French Welfare organisation was a better bet. Influential among French exiles, it remained extremely suspicious of de Gaulle.[57]

Few though they were, the early Free French numbered a handful of outstanding men. Among the military recruits were Lieutenant Claude Hettier de Boislambert, the first Free French officer; Émile Muselier, an opium-smoking admiral who built up the Free French fleet before falling out with de Gaulle in 1941–1942; André Dewavrin, alias Colonel Passy, a lecturer in fortifications at Saint-Cyr who conjured a Free French intelligence organisation into being; the airman and future minister Christian Fouchet; Pierre Messmer, lieutenant and future Prime Minister, who hi-jacked a ship to Gibraltar; Colonel Edgard de Larminat, Chief of Staff of French forces in the Levant, and General Paul Legentilhomme, previously Allied commander in Somalia; two of France's outstanding officers of World War II, Captains Philippe de Hautecloque (Leclerc became his *nom de guerre*), and Marie-Pierre Koenig; and Georges Catroux, a five-star general and governor of French Indochina, sacked by

Vichy in July 1940, who placed himself under de Gaulle's orders in September notwithstanding his own higher rank.[58] Civilians included Reynaud's and Blum's former chiefs of staff, Gaston Palewski and Georges Boris, and a single Free French Deputy, the Socialist Pierre-Olivier Lapie; and two assistants of Jean Monnet – Pierre Denis, who would manage the Free French finances (from an initial treasury of 14 shillings),[59] and René Pleven, who undertook countless delicate missions abroad and would become Prime Minister in 1950. The journalist Maurice Schumann would become Free France's (second) best-known broadcaster, and Foreign Minister in 1969. René Cassin, Free France's jurist, later helped draft the Universal Declaration of Human Rights, and received the Nobel Peace Prize for it. From overseas came Georges Gorse, lecturer at Cairo University and future minister, and from Mexico Jacques Soustelle, a brilliant ethnologist and future governor of Algeria; François Coulet left his post at the French embassy in Helsinki for London.[60] These were not the ministers, generals, and ambassadors whom de Gaulle had expected; but many would mark post-war France.

Free France attracted more awkward, even quarrelsome people than quiet pragmatists. Passy saw it as an extreme example of a French propensity to turn any organisation into bedlam, adding that he himself probably resigned 48 times.[61] This was the normal state of things when de Gaulle himself was present and his rudimentary people-management skills functioning; during his long absences in Africa or the Middle East, they got worse.[62] To the usual turf quarrels inherent in any organisation were added difficult individual temperaments; the over-promotion of some people beyond their competence, inevitable given the small pool of volunteers; and the political gap between the often very right-wing, even anti-Semitic, military men, and the centrist or left-wing civilians, among them Jews like Cassin or Boris (de Gaulle defended the Jews against the officers).[63] Free France's problems did not disappear as men and women from the internal Resistance began to arrive from 1942, or with its partial uprooting to Algiers in June 1943. The dispersal of Free France by then, beyond London and across the world, led Crémieux-Brilhac to describe it as a 'collection of micro-societies' as much as a movement with a common purpose.[64]

Yet the common purpose was there. The Free French were courageous men and women, often young, galvanised by de Gaulle's passion and charisma to give of their best.[65] The 1,038 individuals awarded the Cross of the Liberation – the Order having been created in November 1940, and initially mocked among the Free French,[66] were called companions. The term has stuck to Gaullism ever since and the ties of Free France lasted long after the war, supplying the top leaders of the Gaullist party into the late 1960s.[67]

Without the Free French military, however tiny at first, de Gaulle had no claim to be continuing the war for France; without Passy's intelligence services, a far weaker bargaining position with the British; without the political figures, no embryo government to suggest the revival of a French state. They also influenced de Gaulle's decisions. De Gaulle did listen to advice, though he often rebuked those who offered it. Some, hyper-Gaullists like Soustelle or Palewski, might encourage his intransigence. More important were the moderates – Catroux, Pleven, or René Massigli, the former ambassador to Turkey who joined the Free French early in 1943.[68] More than once, they pulled de Gaulle back from the brink when he was tempted to break with his difficult but necessary allies.

The British

The British were the first to recognise de Gaulle and the Free French, on 28 June 1940, and to supply them with the resources they needed. They provided a headquarters – St Stephen's House, then, quickly, 4 Carlton Gardens, and later 10 Duke Street for the intelligence services. Confidential Free French telegrams went through the Foreign Office network. The British Special Operations Executive (SOE) helped organise radio contact with France, and undertook training and transport of agents (by boat, then, from 1942, on the reliable short take-off Lysander aircraft). Free French soldiers fought with British equipment (until 1943, when they were increasingly American-supplied). The Royal Navy protected Free French colonies in Africa. And, crucially, under an agreement of 7 August 1940, the British financed Free France. By mid-1943, Free French debt to the British had reached £35 million, and monthly subventions were running at £1.5m: comparatively small sums but absolutely indispensable.[69]

British support for Free France was always self-interested. First, the British needed a symbol to show, in 1940–1941, that they did not face Nazi Germany alone, that the main ally of 1939–1940 was still in the fight – and de Gaulle was the only one who offered. Secondly, they needed intelligence from German-occupied France, initially as the territory from which air raids were launched against Britain and an invasion might be, later as the obligatory starting-point for the Allied liberation of Europe. In early 1942 they estimated that 40% of their intelligence on France was of Free French origin; Passy claimed 75% by 1943.[70] Third, as the Allied landings in France approached, the need grew for intelligence but also for active disruption of the German war effort; this required the services of the French internal Resistance. Fourth and finally, British policymakers like Eden believed that in post-war Europe, a strong France allied to Britain was the best bulwark against a potentially hostile Soviet Union. As long as de Gaulle controlled intelligence traffic out of France, held the allegiance of the internal Resistance, and looked like France's future post-war leader, he was indispensable to the British. He knew this and behaved accordingly.

But British support was never unconditional; other interests always weighed in the balance. The first of these was Vichy. Under the armistice of 22 June 1940, France's fleet was simply kept in port and Vichy remained in charge, not only of southern France but also of the French Empire. Britain's nightmare was the prospect of Germany controlling Vichy's navy (hence the devastating British attack on a French naval squadron at Mers-el-Kébir on 3 July 1940), or its Empire, especially North-West Africa; Britain's dream was winning the same assets for the Allies.[71] Late in 1942 the Allies did gain control of North Africa, Vichy's fleet was scuttled in Toulon harbour, and the Vichy danger receded. Until then, however, the British tended to prefer a quiet *modus vivendi* with Vichy to confrontation which risked pushing it into more active co-operation with Germany.

A second complication arose from security concerns. These developed after an Anglo-Free French operation against the African port of Dakar in September 1940. The (unjust) perception that French security lapses were solely to blame became ingrained in the British military: Sir Alan Brooke, Chief of the Imperial General Staff from 1941, was convinced that no serious military planning could be done with the Free French for this reason.[72]

A third British concern arose in the Middle East, the main theatre of Britain's land war between mid-1940 and 1943. After 1919 the

British and French had carved up this strategic region, with the British dominant in Egypt, Palestine, Transjordan, and Iraq and the French in the Levant – Syria and Lebanon. The Levant was a running sore in Anglo-Free French relations from its transfer from Vichy to Free France in 1941. The British worried that heavy-handed Free French rule there would damage British relations with the (increasingly nationalist) Arabs, just as they were fighting the German–Italian Axis in Egypt and Libya.[73]

Fourth, British perspectives were altered by the (forced) entry of the Soviet Union (with the German invasion of 22 June 1941) and the United States (with the Japanese attack on Pearl Harbor on 7 December 1941) into what was now truly a world war. Free France became a less prominent ally compared with the two future superpowers. Britain's 'special relationship' with the United States, crucial since 1940, now took on an overwhelming importance. De Gaulle understood from Pearl Harbor that while an Allied victory was now certain, the British would henceforth do nothing without American permission.[74] More generally, in a complex, many-fronted war, the temptation, too often, was to view the Free French not as an asset, but as a complication, their leader not as a partner but as an obstacle to be circumvented. Accordingly, while the British continued to support the Free French, they often treated them shabbily.

The Free French charge sheet against the British was a long one. They talked secretly to Vichy, without keeping the Free French informed; they behaved with duplicity in the Levant; they excluded the Free French from three major landings on French territory – in Madagascar in May 1942, in North Africa in November 1942, and in Normandy in June 1944. They periodically restricted de Gaulle's movements (he needed British transport to leave the UK), blocked or censored his broadcasts, withheld intelligence, or briefed against him in Parliament and to the press. They tried to use rivals in the Free French movement to undermine him. More than once Churchill tried to break with de Gaulle altogether. While they exchanged intelligence with the Free French, the British also poached their agents, ran non-Gaullist agents in France behind their backs, and even created fake 'Gaullist' cells in their own services.[75] They followed, with little demur, the prolonged American refusal to accept the Free French as representing the French people.[76] They invented technical or administrative excuses when they did not wish to co-operate; and when they did help, it was too often with pettiness and ill grace.[77]

While there was another side to many of these stories, British behaviour regularly enraged de Gaulle, and generated the gigantic de Gaulle–Churchill rows that were a hallmark of Anglo-Free French relations. Though he tried to avoid evening meetings because of Churchill's drinking,[78] de Gaulle was more than capable of holding his own during these clashes. And if the British knew that part of de Gaulle's anger on such occasions was staged, de Gaulle believed that Churchill was also playing a role for President Roosevelt. But the British were more than Churchill. The pattern of British support for de Gaulle was complex and shifting.

At the outset, Churchill, Spears, and Churchill's assistant Desmond Morton, faced almost universal opposition to their support for de Gaulle. The Foreign Secretary, Lord Halifax, the Foreign Office, and its Permanent Secretary Sir Alexander Cadogan feared it would upset the vital relationship with Vichy.[79] The Chief of the Imperial General Staff, Sir John Dill, disliked the French military from the defeat of 1940; his successor Brooke had no time for de Gaulle.[80] They long set the tone for the whole British military, who in the words of Eden's private secretary 'cannot get out of their stupid heads the idea that de Gaulle is a "rebel", whereas Vichyites are "loyalists"'.[81] Britain's Arabists in the Middle East, whether soldiers or diplomats, disliked any French presence there.[82] The Labour Party thought de Gaulle too right-wing and authoritarian.

But Churchill insisted on co-operation with de Gaulle from all government departments and required maximum media (especially newsreel) coverage for the Gaullists' celebration in London of France's national day on 14 July 1940. In doing so he helped secure de Gaulle the lasting support of British public opinion; de Gaulle would recall how he would be cheered by Londoners as he walked to work in Carlton Gardens, and how he received jewels from anonymous donors. Most MPs became consistent supporters;[83] so did King George VI and the royal family.[84]

By mid-1942 the position had changed dramatically. Churchill, much affected by his own quarrels with de Gaulle and influenced by the Americans, swung between lukewarm support and outright opposition. Churchill's unpredictability matched de Gaulle's; both served to complicate the relationship further. But as de Gaulle's detractor, Churchill was now almost as isolated within the British establishment in 1942–1944 as he had been as his backer in summer 1940.[85] His negative messages about de Gaulle to the Cabinet, to Parliament, and via the press to the public, had far less impact than the earlier positive ones. Eden, Halifax's successor, had moved in spring 1942 from an early scepticism to warm endorsement of de Gaulle as France's most likely post-war leader, and had carried the Foreign Office with him.[86] Macmillan would note after a meeting in October 1943 that 'Once again I ended the day feeling that de Gaulle stood head and shoulders above all his colleagues in the breadth of his conceptions for the long term.'[87] His successor in Algiers, Alfred Duff Cooper, was if anything more favourable. The Labour Party was won over as de Gaulle's politics moved leftwards. Even some British officers grew to appreciate Free French troops in combat: 'Well played' Montgomery radioed to Leclerc late in February 1943 after a Free French success in southern Tunisia.[88] Public opinion, moreover, remained solid: 59% of respondents to a British Gallup poll in June 1942 considered that de Gaulle's movement represented true French opinion. This bedrock of British support would be crucial for de Gaulle whenever Churchill contemplated dropping him.[89] His certainty that he was indispensable to the British could only be reinforced by the growing Free French hold on France's Empire.[90]

The Empire

'"Give me some land", the General kept saying, "some land that is France. Anywhere. A French base. Somewhere to start from".' De Gaulle was already craving his own base in July 1940.[91] He had failed to win over any of France's major imperial 'proconsuls': not Noguès in North Africa, not Pierre Boisson in French West Africa (Afrique Occidentale Française, or AOF), nor Gabriel Puaux, High Commissioner in the Levant. In Indochina, Catroux leant towards de Gaulle and was sacked for it. The Dakar expedition of September 1940, aimed at securing the whole of AOF, failed disastrously. Those who did rally to Free France governed smaller, more far-flung outposts: New Caledonia, Polynesia, the New Hebrides, or the French enclaves in India, economically dependent on the British Raj (Table 2.1). The exception to this pattern was French Equatorial Africa (Afrique Équatoriale Française, or AEF), comprising

Table 2.1 Free France and the French Empire

Colony	Free French rule from ...	Other details
Chandernagor (India)	20 June 1940	Governor rallied
New Hebrides	22 July 1940	Governor rallied
Most of French Equatorial Africa (AEF): Chad, Oubangui-Chari, French Congo, plus Cameroon	26–28 August 1940	Governor rallied (Félix Éboué, Chad) plus Free French military takeover with British logistical support
Other French enclaves in India (Mahé, Karikal, Pondicherry, Yanaon)	9 September 1940	Governor rallied
New Caledonia, French Polynesia	September 1940	Governors rallied
Gabon	8–9 November 1940	Free French military takeover with British logistical support
Levant (Syria, Lebanon)	July 1941	Anglo-Free French military operation
St-Pierre-et-Miquelon	24 December 1941	Free French naval operation
Madagascar	May–November 1942	British military operation: Free French invited in in November
La Réunion	28 November 1942	Free French military operation with British support
North Africa (Morocco, Algeria, Tunisia)	November 1942 / July 1943	Anglo-American invasion, November 1942; Free French effectively in control, June/July 1943
French West Africa (AOF)	June 1943	Vichy Governor resigns after peaceful insurrection
French West Indies, French Guyana	June 1943	Vichy governors resign after peaceful insurrections
Indochina	August 1945	Free French enter after Japanese defeat

Chad, the French Congo, Oubangui-Chari, and Gabon. The first three of these, plus the mandated territory of Cameroon, were brought over to Free France during the 'three glorious days' of 26–8 August 1940, thanks to local initiatives (Félix Éboué, governor of Chad, declared for de Gaulle), British logistics (with Nigeria as a jumping-off point), Free French diplomacy (notably Pleven) and a modest but decisive use of armed force (under Leclerc, and Hettier de Boislambert). Gabon followed in November. For the rest of the war, AEF, four times the size of France but with six times fewer inhabitants (about 6.5 million) was Free French territory. Its economy received a monthly British subsidy of £200,000 to compensate for the severing of economic ties with colonies loyal to Vichy.[92]

For de Gaulle, taking, and fighting from, AEF

> was to bring back, as it were, a fragment of France into the war. It was to defend her possessions directly against the enemy. It was, as far as possible, to deflect England – and perhaps one day America – from the temptation to make sure of them on their own account, for their fighting needs and for their advantage. It was, lastly, to wrench Free France free from exile and install her in full sovereignty on national territory.[93]

Brazzaville, capital of French Congo, was the official Free French capital from 1940 to 1943, and de Gaulle was sometimes tempted to move there from London.[94]

These colonies offered more tangible assets too. First, AEF plus Cameroon supplied some 27,000 troops to the Free French forces; two-thirds of the 50,000 Free French troops in July 1943 were colonial soldiers.[95] Second, the colonies represented a base from which to fight the Axis and contribute to the Allied victory. Third, the colonies' strategic importance to the Allies enhanced Free French bargaining power. The 'Takoradi air route' allowed British aircraft to travel securely over Free French AEF, and to refuel, between Nigeria and Cairo, thus avoiding a long journey around the Cape to supply the Egypt-based Desert Air Force.[96] For the United States, bases in New Caledonia and Polynesia were important assets in the Pacific War.[97] Finally, the colonies were sources of war materials. New Caledonia holds over one-fifth of world reserves of nickel: AEF helped supply British and American requirements of other minerals, foodstuffs, and lumber. And the Free French saw AEF gold supplies as a means to financial autonomy. Like the British in their colonies, the Free French increased production of colonial goods by intensifying the exploitation of local workers: as Jennings writes, 'forced labour redoubled under Gaullist rule, coerced military recruitment as well'.[98]

For all that, the jewels in the French imperial crown remained in Vichy hands in 1940–1942. The major colonial development came in 1943, after the Allied conquest of North Africa, with the Free French capture of French institutions there. Now de Gaulle had a proper base, in Algiers, for what was virtually a provisional government, as well as, for the first time, enough troops (formerly loyal to Vichy, and stationed in North Africa) to make a substantial contribution to the Allied war effort.

Free France was not, of course, very free for colonial subjects. On 30 January 1944 de Gaulle opened a conference of colonial governors at Brazzaville with a speech suggesting that native populations be 'raised' to a level where they might take part in running their own affairs.[99] In Gaullist mythology, the speech began de Gaulle's long and glorious record as a decoloniser. But Brazzaville closed with a firm rejection of anything resembling colonial self-government.[100] Whatever de Gaulle's personal views about liberalising the French Empire, they were trumped both by the immediate usefulness of colonial possessions to the Free French cause and by the risk of Vichy claiming that he was 'giving away' colonies for which, as Spears said, 'he regarded himself as the trustee'.[101]

The internal Resistance

From 1941 onwards, the Vichy authorities paid de Gaulle a backhanded tribute by calling most resistance movements they encountered 'Gaullist', whatever their political leanings. Many of them did indeed express a general support for de Gaulle. But few came into being at de Gaulle's behest, and their support was never unconditional. Like the Allies, 'the Resistance' (rarely united) was another partner, half-ally, half-rival, in de Gaulle's complex game.

Militarily, clandestine Resistance networks could do much of use to the Allies – and therefore to de Gaulle if he could be the intermediary between the two. They supplied intelligence to Passy's secret services, the Central Bureau for Intelligence and Action (BCRA); they sabotaged German installations; they helped well over 2,000 Allied prisoners of war, many of them valuable, highly trained airmen, to get home and fight another day.[102] With the Normandy landings in 1944, the armed Resistance slowed German reinforcements moving to the beachheads and guarded prisoners as the Allied armies drove east.

But the Resistance's effectiveness depended on money, radio equipment, arms, and training, all from outside France. The Free French, with better Resistance contacts than the Allies, were well placed to channel these things where they were needed. There were thus the makings of a bargain. De Gaulle would supply the Resistance with vital resources; the Resistance would give de Gaulle the intelligence that would make him indispensable to the Allies. Plus, in principle, recognition: the alternative, a leader from the internal Resistance ranks, would be more divisive within the fiercely competitive Resistance groups and less well known to the French public.[103]

Even such an exclusively military bargain had its weaknesses; de Gaulle could offer less money and fewer weapons than the Resistance wanted. Moreover, few Resistance groups were exclusively military. Especially in the unoccupied south, where clandestine presses were more easily operated, they had political aims: to convince the population that the fight was not over, but also to play a role in the construction and government of liberated France. For this purpose, they might be happy to adopt de Gaulle as a symbol, without endorsing his political views or accepting his orders.[104]

There were many reasons for this. Resistance groups were often fiercely independent, divided by competing ambitions. They disagreed about strategy and, because they ranged from Pétainists to Communists, about politics. Meanwhile most Resistance groups suspected de Gaulle of anti-republican sympathies well into 1942. Some also mistrusted a man who claimed to lead France from the comparative safety of London, while they were risking arrest, deportation, or death every day. Then there was a cultural gulf between de Gaulle's belief in military hierarchy and discipline, and Resistance groups, free associations of men and women who, given the events of 1940, held the military in no high regard. Relations were further complicated by de Gaulle's attempt, from 1943, to reinforce his credentials with the Allies by bringing Third Republic politicians into a National Resistance Council alongside Resistance leaders. The politicians might command better name-recognition with the Allies; but for many Resistance chiefs and many Free French, they represented a discredited political elite.[105] For all of these reasons de Gaulle might be a figurehead for the Resistance forces but could never be their undisputed commanding officer.

One party posed a specific problem. The Communists had fully joined the Resistance fight only after Germany's invasion of the USSR in June 1941. But when they did so, they outclassed other parties (and many Resistance organisations) by their capacity to operate under cover, a historic requirement for all Communist parties. They also managed both to place their own men in umbrella organisations of the Resistance, and to create powerful Communist-led front organisations that drew in many non-Communists. To outsiders, it might look as if they were preparing to seize power at the Liberation. At all events, the Communists insisted that the internal Resistance had its own legitimacy, independent from that of the Free French. France's Liberation, therefore, was played out not only between de Gaulle and his allies but also between de Gaulle and an internal Resistance over which he never established full control.

Franklin D. Roosevelt and the United States

De Gaulle's wartime relations with the Americans were so bad that it is worth underlining what the Americans did for Free France. The United States extended Lend-Lease, its wartime aid programme, from Britain to the Free French in 1941.[106] American troops did most of the fighting that liberated France from German occupation. The French armies that joined the Allies to defeat Italy, then Germany, in 1943–1945, were American-equipped. The cost to the United States was $2.3 billion of military plus $548 million of civilian aid.[107] De Gaulle had been right to predict, on 18 June 1940, that American industry would benefit France as well as Britain.

Yet for long periods the Roosevelt Administration simply did not see the Free French as partners. De Gaulle was viewed at various stages as a creature of the British, or as a fascist, or later, when his relations with the Soviets developed, as a crypto-Communist.[108]

Formal recognition of his Provisional Government was delayed, at American insistence, until 23 October 1944, long after the Soviets and (most of) the British were ready to offer it. The President himself was chiefly responsible. Roosevelt never got the measure of de Gaulle, and probably never tried. In letters to Churchill, Roosevelt not only called de Gaulle 'unreliable, unco-operative, and disloyal' (in July 1943) but chose epithets like 'jackanape' and 'prima donna' to describe him. Part of the problem in US-Free French relations, therefore, was simply presidential antipathy.[109]

It was underpinned by strongly held (mis-)perceptions. First among these was that since June 1940, 'France was finished' as a great power.[110] This view, shared by many Americans, clashed with Free France's very *raison d'être* — to re-establish France's great-power status. In Britain, by contrast, shock at the defeat of 1940 was mitigated both by de Gaulle's willingness to stand with Britain at the 'finest hour', and by the view that the future balance of power in Europe depended on France's full recovery. Second, Roosevelt believed that colonial empires were finished. Britain's might be temporarily tolerated, but he saw no reason why France, unable to defend its own territory, should still aspire to rule Indochina or North Africa. Third, Roosevelt shared both Churchill's worries about the fate of the French fleet and the North African empire, and the British military's contempt for Free French security.[111] Fourth, Roosevelt believed the assurances of his close friend Admiral William Leahy, whom he appointed ambassador to Vichy, that the French overwhelmingly supported Pétain.[112] Fifth, he was correspondingly convinced, by Leahy and by many in the French exile community in the United States, that de Gaulle had negligible support in France. It followed that de Gaulle was merely 'a general among others', that the Free French enterprise was not democratic, and that promoting it would constrain the French people's freedom to choose their government when the time came.[113]

Nor did de Gaulle do enough to reassure the Americans. The possible reactions of the White House or the State Department rarely weighed in his decision-making. And he failed to build a stable, effective US representation in Washington or New York capable of developing contacts in the Administration.

Two consequences followed. One was that complications arose even over mutually beneficial arrangements, as after the offer of bases to the United States in Africa or New Caledonia.[114] Second, Roosevelt enjoyed musing aloud about carving up the French Empire and even France itself, and his comments got back to de Gaulle. This merely confirmed both his suspicions of the 'Anglo-Saxons' generally, and a particular dislike of what he saw as Roosevelt's hypocrisy in wrapping great-power politics in the cloak of 'spreading democracy'. As for his personal relations with Roosevelt, there were no epic rows, as with Churchill; but the two men still quietly loathed one another.[115]

Roosevelt was not the United States, but he had no monopoly on anti-Gaullist prejudices. Left-wingers in the Administration disliked de Gaulle's authoritarianism; conservatives thought him too left-wing. The State Department (the American foreign ministry), including Cordell Hull, the Secretary of State, Under-Secretary Sumner Welles, and Assistant Secretary for France Ronald Matthews (who referred to de Gaulle as 'the French Adolf') all shared the President's view. So did Secretary for War Henry Stimson.[116]

American public opinion, fortunately for de Gaulle, did not follow. In August 1941, 58% of respondents to an American poll said that Vichy was 'helping Hitler'; a month later, 74% favoured supplying war materials to the Free French. In May 1942, 75% of Americans thought de Gaulle represented French opinion best, compared with just 13% for Pétain.[117] Hollywood helped this perception by romanticising the Free French in films like *Casablanca* (1942).

De Gaulle also had better luck with the Administration's representatives in Europe than with Washington. John Winant, US ambassador to London from 1941–1946, Edwin Wilson and Harold Stark, respectively Washington's diplomatic and military representatives to the Free French, and Allen Dulles, who headed the Berne-based US secret services in Europe, were all more sympathetic than their chiefs to Free France. In addition, the US military was more open than the British to de Gaulle. Both Dwight D. Eisenhower, Supreme Commander of Allied Forces in the Mediterranean (1942–1943) and North-West Europe (1944–1945) and his Chief of Staff Walter Bedell Smith, formed a good, though not always cloudless, working relationship with de Gaulle. By late 1943, Eisenhower's views had filtered upwards to John McCloy, Stimson's assistant in the War Department; that autumn, too, Hull met de Gaulle for the first time in Algiers, and for once de Gaulle turned on the charm, to good effect. So by the year's end Free France was no longer quite frozen out of Washington.[118]

With the approach of the Normandy landings, scheduled for June 1944, pressure built on Roosevelt from within the Administration to soften his hostility. Eisenhower, in particular, wanted to ensure the active co-operation of the Resistance before, during and after the landings, and the maintenance of order in liberated areas. And by spring 1944 it was clear that only the Free French could deliver these. The President relaxed his opposition with painful slowness; but he was quickly overtaken in France by the developing co-operation on the ground between his generals and de Gaulle's men.

The old alliance: Free France and the USSR

'Nothing in foreign policy opposes us to Russia', de Gaulle remarked in September 1942.[119] Free French relations with the USSR were correspondingly smooth – in general. De Gaulle had grown up in a world where the Russian alliance was seen as vital to France's security. He had supported a full Soviet alliance in the 1930s. Certainly, the Nazi–Soviet non-aggression pact signed in August 1939 was an obstacle to good relations in 1940, but even then Soviet official views were more favourable than the Soviet press. De Gaulle established discreet contacts in London even before the Soviets entered the war on 22 June 1941.[120] The Soviets recognised Free France in similar terms to the British the following 26 September; relations became noticeably warmer after a meeting between de Gaulle and Soviet Foreign Minister Vyacheslav Molotov, in London on 24 May 1942. And on 28 September 1942, in the midst of an Anglo-Free French crisis, the Soviets recognised the Free French, in much fuller terms than Britain or the USA, as having the *sole* right to organise the participation of French citizens and territories in the war.[121]

Like the British, de Gaulle contemplated sending troops directly to assist the hard-pressed Soviets on the Eastern Front. The plan fell through when the British refused to supply transport. Easier to send were airmen. On 1 December 1942, some 60 Free French aviators arrived to crew what would become the 'Normandie-Niemen' squadron on the Eastern Front. By the war's end, 'Normandie-Niemen' claimed 273 German aircraft downed. This was a tiny detail on the vast canvas of the war in the East – but of great symbolic significance because France, alone among the Western Allies, actually supplied fighting men to the USSR.[122] From 1943, de Gaulle's speeches included flattering references to 'our dear and powerful Russia', cited as a 'natural ally' in Ajaccio (Corsica) on 8 October 1943, a 'permanent ally' in Tunis on 7 May 1944.[123] On 10 December 1944, he signed an alliance treaty in Moscow: the only such treaty signed by France before the war's end.

There was no ideological convergence: de Gaulle had no more affinity than Churchill with the Soviet system. But he valued the Soviets as 'a balancing element over against the Anglo-Saxons, of which I was determined to make use'.[124] He even, at a low point in relations with the British and Americans, sounded out the Soviets about moving Free French headquarters to Moscow: the Soviets advised caution, and de Gaulle may have been bluffing for the benefit of the Western Allies.[125] De Gaulle's second reason for cultivating the Soviets arose from the expected challenge from the French Communists, who, though more hostile than the Soviets to de Gaulle, took their orders in the last analysis from Stalin.[126] Good relations with Moscow would contain the Communist challenge at home.

Stalin, for his part, never worried about the level of de Gaulle's support in France. Dismissive of French military power, he was interested by France's diplomatic and strategic position. In 1942, the Soviets hoped that de Gaulle might put pressure on the British and Americans to open a second front in Western Europe quickly (though willing, the French were largely powerless). Stalin was also attracted by de Gaulle's independence; too realistic to seek a Communist Western Europe, he saw the next best thing as promoting a French post-war leader who would not be subservient to the Anglo-American camp.[127]

In the end, however, no critical interests were at stake on either side. The Soviet Union was neither a resource base for the Free French nor a threat to France's Empire; while the Free French could offer the Soviets very little practical help. The limited importance of the Free French-Soviet link meant there was little to quarrel about.

Conclusion

The Free French, the British, the colonies, the internal Resistance, the Americans, the Russians: these were the partners in the complex game de Gaulle began on 18 June 1940 and which ended, at least provisionally, with the recognition of his government on 23 October 1944. Each player had powerful reasons to co-operate with the others, but also reasons to mistrust and compete with them. It was de Gaulle's colossal achievement to wield his own exiguous resources to act on his partners, and his leverage with his partners to gain additional resources, gradually engaging Free France in a virtuous, upward, circle. Most obviously, he drew on his position with the British, and the resources it made available, to win the allegiance of the Resistance movements within France, and he used his support from the internal Resistance to reinforce his legitimacy with the Allies. De Gaulle showed exceptional flair in making each partner a lever to enhance his position with the others; but genuinely opposed interests, misperceptions, and even personal animosity were so many obstacles on the long road to full recognition.

Notes

1 Jean-Luc Barré, *Devenir de Gaulle, 1939–1943* (Paris: Perrin, 2003), pp. 38, 42, 59; Charles Williams, *The Last Great Frenchman* (New York: John Wiley, 1993), pp. 95–6.
2 Nicholas Atkin, *The Forgotten French: Exiles in the British Isles, 1940–1944* (Manchester: Manchester University Press, 2003), p. 94.
3 Julian Jackson, *A Certain Idea of France: The Life of Charles de Gaulle* (London: Allen Lane, 2018), p. 108.
4 Winston S. Churchill, *The Second World War*, vol. II: *Their Finest Hour* (London: Cassell, 1949), p. 189.
5 Julian Jackson, *The Fall of France: The Nazi Invasion of 1940* (Oxford: Oxford University Press, 2003), p. 134; Éric Roussel, *Charles de Gaulle* (Paris: Gallimard, 2002), pp. 98–105.
6 Philippe de Gaulle, *De Gaulle mon père. Entretiens avec Michel Tauriac*, vol. I (Paris: Plon, 2003), p. 160. Cf. also WMi, p. 63.
7 Churchill, *Finest Hour*, pp. 62, 189. Cf. also above, p. 16.
8 Roussel, *de Gaulle*, pp. 134–6; Philippe de Gaulle, *De Gaulle mon père*i, pp. 110, 184–5. De Gaulle's wider family suffered badly in the German occupation. By late 1943, his sister Marie-Agnès had been arrested, her husband deported to Buchenwald; brother Xavier was on the run, his daughter Geneviève deported to Ravensbrück; brother Pierre had been deported to Eisenberg, and paralysed Jacques smuggled into Switzerland by a priest, the Abbé Pierre. Williams, *Last Great*, pp. 237–8, 262.
9 Jackson, *A Certain Idea*, p. 127.

10 Literally, the 'call' or the 'appeal' of 18 June. But 'call' is too non-specific and 'appeal' too resonant of law-courts or fundraising. There are two texts of the *Appel*. The published version, in Charles de Gaulle, *Discours et Messages*, vol. I (Paris: Plon, 1970: henceforth *DM*I), pp. 3–4, is what de Gaulle wrote. An English translation is at https://www.ordredelaliberation.fr/en/order-of-the-liberation/le-grand-maitre/the-appeal-of-june-18th-1940, accessed 1 February 2019. However, when he spoke, de Gaulle toned down the first two sentences, as required by the British government. This version is on www.charles-de-gaulle.org/?s=appel+du+18+juin. For the poster, cf. www.charles-de-gaulle.org/espace-pedagogie/dossiers-thematiques/refus-de-larmistice-lappel-18-juin/affiche-a-francais-placardee-murs-de-londres-3-aout-1940/, accessed 31 January 2019.

11 De Gaulle was already convinced in July 1940 that Germany would attack the Soviet Union, that the United States would enter the war, and that victory was therefore certain. Cf. Olivier Guichard, *Mon Général* (Paris: Grasset, 1980), p. 122.

12 *WM*I, pp. 89–90; Barré, *Devenir de Gaulle*, pp. 79–80.

13 *WM*I, p. 103.

14 Williams, *Last Great*, p. 115.

15 Jean-Louis Crémieux-Brilhac, *La France Libre, de l'appel du 18 juin à la Libération* (Paris: Gallimard, 1996), p. 44.

16 *WM*I, p. 88; Roussel, *de Gaulle*, p. 148.

17 René Cassin, *Les Hommes partis de rien: le réveil de la France abattue (1940–1941)* (Paris: Plon, 1975), pp. 124–6; Crémieux-Brilhac, *France Libre*, pp. 916–17.

18 Stanley Hoffmann, intervention in Institut Charles de Gaulle, *De Gaulle en son siècle*, vol. I: *Dans la mémoire des hommes et des peuples* (Paris: Plon, 1991), p. 291.

19 Peter Mangold, *Britain and the Defeated French: From Occupation to Liberation, 1940–1944* (London: I.B.Tauris, 2012), p. 113; Williams, *Last Great*, pp. 188–9.

20 *WM*I, p. 136.

21 Guichard, *Mon Général*, p. 83; Crémieux-Brilhac, *France Libre*, p. 124. The Resistance leader Emmanuel d'Astier de la Vigerie, who in his book *Sept fois sept jours* (Paris: Union Générale d'Éditions, 1963 [1961]), perversely invents a pseudonym for each character in the Free French and the Resistance, refers to de Gaulle simply as 'le symbole'.

22 Jackson, *A Certain Idea*, p. 180 (quoting an unpublished de Gaulle letter of 13 August 1941).

23 Churchill, *Finest Hour*, p. 451.

24 Lord Moran, *Winston Churchill: The Struggle for Survival, 1940–1965* (London: Constable, 1966), p. 81.

25 Quoted in Simonne Servais (ed.), *Regards sur de Gaulle* (Paris: Plon, 1990), p. 179.

26 Harold Macmillan, *The Blast of War, 1939–1945* (London: Macmillan, 1967), p. 345.
27 Servais, *Regards*, pp. 209–10.
28 Pierre Lefranc, *Avec de Gaulle* (Paris: Plon, 1989 [1979]), pp. 53, 56–7.
29 Jacques Chaban-Delmas, *Mémoires pour demain* (Paris: Flammarion, 1997), p. 89.
30 Sir Anthony Eden (Earl of Avon), *The Reckoning* (Memoirs, vol. II) (London: Cassell, 1965), p. 250.
31 Sir Edward Spears, *Fulfilment of a Mission: Syria and Lebanon, 1941–1944* (London: Seeley, Service and Cooper 1977), p. 138.
32 Mangold, *Defeated French*, p. 243.
33 Hervé Alphand, *L'Étonnement d'être* (Paris: Fayard 1977), p. 125.
34 Philippe de Gaulle, *De Gaulle mon père* I, pp. 161–5.
35 Crémieux-Brilhac, *France Libre*, p. 293.
36 Cassin, *Les Hommes*, p. 132; Roussel, *de Gaulle*, p. 146.
37 Mangold, *Defeated French*, p. 11.
38 Passy in Georges-Marc Benamou, *C'était un temps déraisonnable. Les premiers résistants racontent* (Paris: Robert Laffont, 1999), p. 137.
39 Atkin, *Forgotten French*, pp. 256–7.
40 François Kersaudy, *Churchill and de Gaulle* (New York: Atheneum, 1981), p. 184.
41 Pierre Messmer, Pierre Lefranc, Daniel Cordier in Benamou, *Déraisonnable*, pp. 47, 267, 311.
42 Colonel Passy (pseudonym of André Dewavrin), *Mémoires du chef des services secrets de la France libre*, ed. Jean-Louis-Crémieux-Brilhac (Paris: Odile Jacob, 2000), p. 131.
43 Cassin, *Les Hommes*, p. 124; Rémi Fabre, 'De Gaulle et les protestants', in Fondation Charles de Gaulle, *Charles de Gaulle, chrétien, homme d'État* (Paris: Plon, 2005), pp. 351–69: p. 361.
44 Pierre Brossolette, 'Lettre au général de Gaulle' (2 novembre 1942), in Pierre Brossolette, *Résistance (1927–1943): Textes rassemblés et présentés par Guillaume Piketty* (Paris: Odile Jacob, 2015), pp. 144–7.
45 Cassin, *Les Hommes*, p. 124; Claude Bouchinet-Serreulles, *Nous étions nés pour être libres. La Résistance avec de Gaulle et Jean Moulin* (Paris: Grasset, 2000), p. 165; Jackson, *A Certain Idea*, p. 163.
46 Benamou, *Déraisonnable*, pp. 28, 146.
47 Churchill, *Finest Hour*, p. 189.
48 Quoted in Jackson, *The Fall of France*, p. 241.
49 Crémieux-Brilhac, *France Libre*, p. 37.
50 Quoted in Jackson, *A Certain Idea*, p. 223.
51 Crémieux-Brilhac, *France Libre*, pp. 88, 117, 182–3. The Carlton Gardens numbers had tripled to 446 by 1941.
52 Philippe de Gaulle, *De Gaulle mon père* I, p. 143; WMI, p. 103.
53 Claude Guy, *En écoutant de Gaulle. Journal 1946–1949* (Paris: Grasset, 1996), p. 48.
54 Jean Touchard, *Le Gaullisme, 1940–1969* (Paris: Le Seuil, 1978), p. 62.

55 Alain Peyrefitte, *C'était de Gaulle*, vol. I (Paris: Éditions de Fallois/Fayard, 1994), p. 148.
56 Atkin, *Forgotten French*, pp. 117–19, 124–9.
57 Atkin, *Forgotten French*, pp. 127, 256.
58 Crémieux-Brilhac, *France Libre*, p. 89.
59 Crémieux-Brilhac, *France Libre*, p. 80.
60 Crémieux-Brilhac, *France Libre*, p. 84.
61 Passy in Benamou, *Déraisonnable*, pp. 135–6.
62 Alphand, *L'Étonnement*, p. 88; Passy, *Mémoires*, pp. 69–75; Roussel, *de Gaulle*, pp. 206–7.
63 Passy, *Mémoires*, pp. 113; Cassin, *Les Hommes*, pp. 136–8.
64 Crémieux-Brilhac, *France Libre*, pp. 34–5.
65 Crémieux-Brilhac, *France Libre*, pp. 96, 97, 100, 917.
66 Bouchinet-Serreulles, *Nous étions nés*, p. 134. Only 6 of the 1,038 were women; 238 of the awards were posthumous.
67 Jean Charlot, *L'UNR. Étude du pouvoir au sein d'un parti politique* (Paris: Armand Colin, 1967), p. 26.
68 Crémieux-Brilhac, *France Libre*, pp. 37, 475–9; Jackson, *A Certain Idea*, pp. 257–8; Roussel, *de Gaulle*, p. 424.
69 Mangold, *Defeated French*, pp. 124–5.
70 Passy in Benamou, *Déraisonnable*, p. 133; Crémieux-Brilhac, *France Libre*, pp. 233–7, 738; Mangold, *Defeated French*, p. 90.
71 Crémieux-Brilhac, *France Libre*, pp. 309–10.
72 Field Marshal Lord Alanbrooke, *War Diaries 1939–1945* (London: Weidenfeld & Nicolson, 2001), p. 101. Poor security was one reason why Passy (confirming Brooke) moved his intelligence operations to 10, Duke Street in March 1942. He also remarked that if you wanted something known around London, the best course was to tell M. Schumann and swear him to secrecy. Passy in Benamou, *Déraisonnable*, p. 136; Passy, *Mémoires*, pp. 115.
73 Cf. Churchill to Lyttleton, 7 July 1942, in Mangold, *Defeated French*, pp. 129–30.
74 Crémieux-Brilhac, *France Libre*, p. 277.
75 Crémieux-Brilhac, *France Libre*, pp. 407–9, Passy in Benamou, *Déraisonnable*, pp. 137–8; Passy, *Mémoires*, p. 298.
76 Mangold, *Defeated French*, pp. 250–1.
77 Passy, *Mémoires*, p. 223; Bouchinet-Serreulles, *Nous étions nés*, pp. 206–7 (21 May 1942).
78 Philippe de Gaulle, *De Gaulle mon père* I, p. 178.
79 Mangold, *Defeated French*, p. 123.
80 Williams, *Last Great*, p. 123; Alanbrooke, *War Diaries*, p. 101.
81 Mangold, *Defeated French*, p. 146.
82 A.B. Gaunson, *The Anglo-French Clash in Lebanon and Syria, 1940–1945* (Basingstoke: Macmillan, 1987), pp. 5–6.
83 Cassin, *Les Hommes*, pp. 161–2.
84 Kersaudy, *Churchill and de Gaulle*, pp. 87–9; WMI, pp. 106–7.

85 Crémieux-Brilhac, *France Libre*, p. 826; Macmillan, *Blast*, p. 441; David Reynolds, 'De Gaulle face à Churchill', in Fondation Charles de Gaulle, *De Gaulle chef de guerre. De l'Appel de Londres à la libération de Paris, 1940–1944* (Paris: Plon, 2008), pp. 442–59: p. 445.

86 Crémieux-Brilhac, *France Libre*, pp. 410–11, 828; Eden, *Reckoning*, p. 398; Jackson, *A Certain Idea*, pp. 180, 233.

87 Macmillan, *Blast*, p. 420.

88 Crémieux-Brilhac, *France Libre*, p. 497.

89 Philip Bell, 'L'Opinion publique britannique solidaire du général de Gaulle', in Fondation Charles de Gaulle, *De Gaulle chef de guerre*, pp. 564–71. Crémieux-Brilhac, *France Libre*, pp. 75, 828.

90 Crémieux-Brilhac, *France Libre*, pp. 38–9.

91 Eric T. Jennings, *Free French Africa in World War II: The African Resistance* (New York: Cambridge University Press, 2015), p. 15.

92 Jennings, *Free French Africa*, p. 21.

93 *WM*I, p. 111.

94 Jennings, *Free French Africa*, p. 7.

95 Jennings, *Free French Africa*, pp. 4, 143–65; André Martel, 'De Gaulle et le réarmement des forces françaises, un outil militaire et diplomatique, 1940–1944', in Fondation Charles de Gaulle, *De Gaulle chef de guerre*, pp. 319–36: p. 324.

96 Mangold, *Defeated French*, p. 123.

97 Memorandum of 5 June 1941, *LNC*III, pp. 350–3 (*LNC*I, pp. 1223–6).

98 Martin Shipway, *Decolonization and its Impact: A Comparative Approach to the End of the Colonial Empires* (Oxford: Blackwell, 2008), pp. 68–9; Jennings, *Free French Africa*, pp. 5, 175–85, 204–15.

99 *DM*I, pp. 370–3.

100 Martin Shipway, 'Whose Liberation? Confronting the Problem of the French Empire, 1944–47', in Andrew Knapp (ed.), *The Uncertain Foundation: France at the Liberation, 1944–1947* (Basingstoke: Palgrave, 2007), pp. 139–59.

101 Spears, *Fulfilment of a Mission*, p. 97.

102 J.M. Langley, *Fight Another Day* (London: Collins, 1974), p. 251.

103 Henri Frenay, *La Nuit finira: mémoires de la Résistance, 1940–1945* (Paris: Robert Laffont, 1973), pp. 109–10.

104 Barré, *Devenir de Gaulle*, p. 193.

105 Cf. the contributions to Benamou, *Déraisonnable*, of Bouchinet-Serreulles (p. 32), Serge Ravanel (pp. 120–1), Passy (p. 147), Stéphane Hessel (pp. 284–6) and Daniel Cordier (p. 324).

106 Crémieux-Brilhac, *France Libre*, pp. 267–8.

107 Frank Costigliola, *France and the United States: The Cold Alliance since World War II* (New York: Twayne, 1992), p. 34.

108 Kim Mulholland, 'The United States and the Free French', in Robert O. Paxton and Nicholas Wahl (eds), *De Gaulle and the United States: A Centennial Reappraisal* (Oxford: Berg, 1994), pp. 61–94: pp. 76–9, 88–9.

109 Robert Dallek, 'Roosevelt and De Gaulle', in Paxton and Wahl, *De Gaulle and the United States*, pp. 49–60: p. 57; Costigliola, *France and the United States*, p. 24.
110 Costigliola, *France and the United States*, pp. 8–9, 13.
111 Cassin, *Les Hommes*, p. 191; Crémieux-Brilhac, *France Libre*, pp. 820–4.
112 Costigliola, *France and the United States*, p. 15.
113 François Kersaudy, 'De Gaulle face à Roosevelt', in Fondation Charles de Gaulle, *De Gaulle chef de guerre*, pp. 460–3; Servais, *Regards*, p. 355.
114 Crémieux-Brilhac, *France Libre*, pp. 294–305; Jackson, *A Certain Idea*, p. 212, 238.
115 Bouchinet-Serreulles, *Nous étions nés*, p. 248; David Reynolds, 'De Gaulle face à Churchill', p. 458.
116 Crémieux-Brilhac, *France Libre*, pp. 820–4; Alphand, *L'Étonnement*, p. 141.
117 Costigliola, *France and the United States*, p. 17; François Kersaudy, *De Gaulle et Roosevelt: Le Duel au Sommet* (Paris: Perrin, 2004), p. 130n.
118 Crémieux-Brilhac, *France Libre*, pp. 419, 567–9, 832; Dwight D. Eisenhower, *Crusade in Europe* (London: Heinemann, 1948), p. 452; Robert Belot, 'Le Général de Gaulle et le gaullisme vus par les services spéciaux américains', in Fondation Charles de Gaulle, *De Gaulle chef de guerre*, pp. 586–608; Alphand, *L'Étonnement*, p. 84; Kersaudy, 'De Gaulle face à Roosevelt', p. 462.
119 Bouchinet-Serreulles, *Nous étions nés*, p. 230.
120 Marina Arzakanian, 'De Gaulle pendant la Seconde guerre mondiale à travers les archives soviétiques', in Maurice Vaïsse (ed.), *De Gaulle et la Russie* (Paris: CNRS Éditions, coll. 'Biblis', 2012 [2006]), pp. 61–73; Henri-Christian Giraud, 'Les Relations de Gaulle-Staline pendant la guerre', in Stéphane Courtois and Marc Lazar (eds), *Cinquante ans d'une passion française. De Gaulle et les communistes* (Paris: Balland, 1991), pp. 57–74: pp. 57–8.
121 Crémieux-Brilhac, *France Libre*, pp. 330–1.
122 Patrick Facon, 'Le "Normandie-Niemen", vecteur de la politique soviétique du général de Gaulle', in Vaïsse, *De Gaulle et la Russie*, pp. 45–59.
123 *DM*I, pp. 328–30, 401–5.
124 *WM*I, p. 228.
125 Crémieux-Brilhac, pp. 311–12.
126 Arzakanian, 'Archives soviétiques', pp. 67–8.
127 Entretien avec M. Gaston Palewski sur les relations entre le général de Gaulle et l'URSS, in Vaïsse, *De Gaulle et la Russie*, pp. 127–32; François Lévêque, 'Les Relations entre l'Union soviétique et la France Libre (juin 1941-septembre 1942)', in Vaïsse, *De Gaulle et la Russie*, pp. 19–44.

Further reading

The best accounts of the fall of France in 1940 are Alistair Horne, *To Lose a Battle: France 1940* (London: Macmillan, 1969), and Julian Jackson, *The Fall of France: The Nazi Invasion of 1940* (Oxford: Oxford University Press, 2003).

Julian Jackson's *France: The Dark Years, 1940–1944* (Oxford: Oxford University Press, 2001) is an excellent survey covering Vichy, Free France, and the internal Resistance.

For the colonies of sub-Saharan Africa, see Eric T. Jennings, *Free French Africa in World War II: The African Resistance* (New York: Cambridge University Press, 2015).

For Anglo-French relations, see François Kersaudy, *Churchill and de Gaulle* (New York: Atheneum, 1981), and Peter Mangold, *Britain and the Defeated French: From Occupation to Liberation, 1940–1944* (London: I. B.Tauris, 2012).

For the (chiefly internal) Resistance, see Robert Gildea's *Fighters in the Shadows: A New History of the French Resistance* (London: Faber, 2015). The definitive history of Free France is in French: Jean-Louis Crémieux-Brilhac, *La France Libre, de l'appel du 18 juin à la Libération* (Paris: Gallimard, 1996).

For Franco-American relations, see the relevant chapters in Charles Cogan, *Oldest Allies, Guarded Friends: The United States and France since 1940* (Westport, CT: Praeger, 1994); Robert O. Paxton and Nicholas Wahl (eds), *De Gaulle and the United States: A Centennial Reappraisal* (Oxford and Providence RI: Berg, 1994); and Frank Costigliola, *France and the United States: The Cold Alliance since World War II* (New York: Twayne, 1992). François Kersaudy's excellent *De Gaulle et Roosevelt: Duel au Sommet* (Paris: Perrin, 2004) has not been translated.

For Franco-Soviet relations, see Hélène Carrère d'Encausse, *Le Général de Gaulle et la Russie* (Paris: Fayard, 2017) and Maurice Vaïsse (ed.), *De Gaulle et la Russie* (Paris: CNRS Éditions, coll. 'Biblis', 2012 [2006]). Neither has been translated.

De Gaulle's own account of the early war years is in his *The Call to Honour, 1940–1942*, tr. Jonathan Griffin (London: Collins, 1955). His wartime speeches (in French) are in Charles de Gaulle, *Discours et Messages*, vol. I (Paris: Plon, 1970).

3 Free France: foundations, 1940–1942

The Allied victories of late 1942, at Stalingrad and in North Africa, neatly divide the war against Germany into two halves: almost unbroken German victories before, an almost continuous German retreat after. For the Free French, the earlier period was one of slow and painful establishment. They organised themselves in London, secured several footholds in the Empire, won the partial and conditional support of the internal Resistance, and created a political organisation firmly within France's republican tradition. These were considerable but fragile achievements. As the war moved into its second, victorious phase, the Free French still risked being sidelined. It would take them another six months to become indispensable.

London, 1940–1942

The summer of 1940 saw a brief honeymoon between de Gaulle and the British. Londoners offered him encouragement as he walked to Carlton Gardens; the Royal Family approved; Churchill was warm, even enthusiastic, promoted a successful 14 July commemoration, and regularly invited de Gaulle to Chequers, the Prime Minister's country residence.[1]

Paradoxically, a ferocious British attack on France's navy facilitated this harmonious moment. Pétain had undertaken not to let the French fleet fall into German hands, but he had a record of broken promises; the British did not believe him.[2] So when, on 3 July 1940, Admiral James Somerville confronted a French naval squadron anchored at Mers-el-Kébir in French Algeria, and his French counterpart Admiral Gensoul refused three possible courses of action to put his ships out of German reach, Somerville's Force H opened fire, killing 1,295 French sailors, sinking one battleship and badly damaging two others. The British also seized 130 French naval and merchant vessels in British ports and negotiated the neutrality of a French squadron in Alexandria.[3]

Furious at first, de Gaulle broadcast on 7 July in terms which, without minimising the 'odious tragedy' of Mers-el-Kébir, justified the attack in the light of the risk of the vessels being used by Germany.[4] Into this coldly realistic broadcast Churchill read a warmth of sentiments towards Britain that was not there, gratefully telling the House of Commons that 'Our old comradeship with France is not dead. In General de Gaulle and his gallant band, that comradeship takes an effective form.'[5]

Later, Churchill would say many less flattering things about de Gaulle. And Mers-el-Kébir badly damaged recruitment to Free French forces. But that summer Britain and the Free French established structural links that held good through many crises. The first was the Anglo-Free French agreement of 7 August, setting out financial, military, and political relations. The Free French would be financed by British loans, reimbursable at the war's end. They would have their own army (by 15 August, a 'first brigade of the French legion' counted 123 officers and 2,721 men) and navy (a dozen vessels at the end of 1940, 60 by June 1943, mostly British-supplied), with their own ranks, regulations, pay structure, officer training school, and (a first) a women's section.[6] Free French forces would accept orders from the British High Command, and help defend British territory when required; air force units (four squadrons by 1941) would serve with the RAF.[7] But this was to be more than just a French legion fighting for Britain. Crucially, the agreement allowed the creation of Free French civilian departments which later became the embryo of a state.[8] And when René Cassin, the jurist who negotiated the agreement, asked de Gaulle what was Free France's legal basis, de Gaulle's reply, from which he never varied, defined his movement to the world: 'We are France.'[9] The British, without going that far, undertook to defend the grandeur and freedom of France, if not the territorial integrity of its Empire.[10]

Military links extended to intelligence co-operation. This faced many difficulties. The French team, from its chief André Dewavrin (alias colonel Passy) down, lacked experience and depended on the British for everything, including, in effect, Passy's own training. And de Gaulle harboured intense suspicions of the British. But the British needed intelligence, and quickly undertook to train and parachute a handful of Free French agents into France.[11] Passy's organisation grew slowly. Only by late 1941 had it developed services for intelligence, archives, action, escapes, codes, and counter-intelligence. Despite these modest beginnings, Free French agents still managed, for example, to alert the British to the arrival of German battle-cruisers in Brest early in 1941, and their departure a year later, and to supply intelligence leading to a successful British operation against a Würzburg radar at Bruneval on the Channel coast in February 1942.[12] Intelligence co-operation survived most crises in Anglo-Free French relations and demonstrated the two sides' interdependence.[13]

A third component of Free France's relationship with Britain was the BBC. France was 'the most important British propaganda target in Europe'.[14] The BBC's French broadcasts ran for 2½ hours daily in September 1940, five hours from September 1942. Only five minutes of this was explicitly Free French; and of de Gaulle's 67 broadcasts, 40 went out in 1940–1941, when audiences were still under half a million.[15] But the chief Free French broadcaster Maurice Schumann spoke for Free France over 1,000 times; and for most French listeners, the Free French slot proper and the BBC French Service's longer programmes were indistinguishable.[16]

Promoted by the BBC in France, de Gaulle also enjoyed favourable publicity in Britain, thanks to a public relations consultant hired by Churchill's assistant Desmond Morton. A promotional brochure appeared in British, American, and French editions in September 1940.[17] And the publicity machine survived every vicissitude in Anglo-Free French relations: *Picture Post* published a noticeably sympathetic feature on de Gaulle and the Free French in May 1942, when relations with Churchill were especially frosty.[18] The support of British public opinion, sustained in part by these efforts, carried de Gaulle through more than one crisis.

All four structural elements – the 7 August agreement, intelligence co-operation, the BBC broadcasts, and publicity – help explain the resilience of the Anglo-Free French relationship. But the crises were many. Three concerned Admiral Émile Muselier, the only one of France's 60 admirals to join the Free French. By May 1941 Muselier had 2,500 men and 6 vessels on active service, and the genuine respect of the British Admiralty. He was also an intriguer who wanted to replace de Gaulle as leader of the Free French.[19]

In the first of the three 'Muselier affairs', in January 1941, two agents working for Passy conspired unsuccessfully to discredit the admiral. In the second (September 1941) Muselier himself attempted, with the support of 'his' fleet and of several leading Free French and British figures including Morton, to refashion Free France and confine de Gaulle to an honorary position. De Gaulle countered, at a press conference on 23 September, by unveiling a new French National Committee (Comité National Français, or CNF) ostensibly less autocratic than previous structures – but with himself still firmly in the chair. The third affair opened in March 1942 after Muselier's successful mission to seize the islands of Saint-Pierre-et-Miquelon, off the Newfoundland coast, from Vichy. Returning in triumph, the admiral entered into open rebellion and tried to remove 'his' fleet from Free French control.[20] The British, initially supportive, withdrew their backing as Muselier's behaviour grew more extreme, and Muselier eventually quit the Free French altogether. De Gaulle, outraged by the initial British attitude, suspended contact with his allies and withdrew to his house at Berkhamsted. He even contemplated abandoning the Free French enterprise, and wrote to his inner circle in terms suggesting his possible removal by the British. That spring he remained at Berkhamsted, depressed and suffering from malaria.[21]

The three Muselier affairs, especially the second and third, exhibit common features. One was the tension between an overbearing leader and strong-willed personalities under him. Second, the British showed poor judgement in lending their support, however cautious, to Muselier's efforts to destabilise de Gaulle. Third, de Gaulle's suspicions of British perfidy were reinforced. This view was certainly compounded by his experiences in the colonies, especially Syria.

Imperial imbroglios, 1940–1942

Three times in the year after the *Appel du 18 juin*, the Free French used British backing in bids to seize Vichy-held territory. The first, in French Equatorial Africa (AEF), was successful; the second, in Dakar, was a total failure; the third, in the Levant, was a Pyrrhic victory that did lasting damage to Anglo-Free French relations.

The seizure of AEF, plus Cameroon, in late August 1940, was a largely Free French operation, though the small forces involved had started out from British Nigeria, which they had reached on British transport. AEF was not France's wealthiest or most populous territory. But it was large (at 2.5 million square kilometres, or four times larger than France, for 6.5 million people), and offered Free France several assets: a political base at Brazzaville independent of London; a geopolitical resource – the Nigeria-Cairo air route – to bargain with the British; raw materials for war production; colonial troops; and a base from which to attack Italian Libya.[22]

For their first three years, the Free French did most of their ground fighting in Africa. They fought alongside the British in Sudan, Egypt, Ethiopia, and Eritrea. In March 1941 Colonel Philippe Leclerc, starting from Chad with 400 mostly colonial troops, took the Libyan oasis of Koufra, plus 300 Italian prisoners.[23] Meanwhile Marie-Pierre Koenig's First Free French Brigade, consisting of troops from AEF and other colonies, halted the advance of Rommel's Afrika Korps at Bir Hakeim in June 1942, covering the British Eighth Army's left flank, facilitating the later British recovery in North Africa – and showing the Allies that the Free French had military value. Though small, these engagements were vital to de Gaulle's aim of earning France a place among the war's victors. Hence his intense emotion on hearing of Bir Hakeim, recorded in an uncharacteristic passage of his Memoirs: 'O heart throbbing with emotion, sobs of pride, tears of joy!'[24]

But the big African goal was missed. Dakar is the westernmost point of Africa, with a magnificent sheltered anchorage. Its value to the British as a base for Atlantic naval operations was inestimable. For the Free French, Dakar was also a huge prize: as capital of Senegal and of French West Africa (AOF), with a population of over 12 million, it could be used to destabilise Vichy's North African colonies of Morocco, Algeria, and Tunisia.

Churchill believed, with de Gaulle's sceptical backing, that the arrival, one day at dawn, of a large Royal Navy squadron would overawe Vichy's governor there, Pierre Boisson, into speedy surrender. A big Anglo-Free French squadron duly left Liverpool on

31 August 1940. De Gaulle was on board the troop-carrying liner *Westernland*. After halting at Freetown (Sierre Leone), it appeared off Dakar on 23 September, beginning Operation Menace. But after three days' fighting, the squadron turned back for Freetown. Operation Menace ended, not in a bloodless victory, but in a fiasco.

Bad luck played a part: shrouded in unseasonable fog, the Anglo-Free French force was hardly visible, let alone awe-inspiring, to Governor Boisson. But the failure also resulted from epic incompetence. Security was non-existent on the British and (perhaps especially) the Free French sides, but this was not the chief failing.[25] Far worse was a failure of military and political intelligence. The British Admiralty grossly underestimated the strength of French naval forces in Dakar.[26] Boisson, believed susceptible of being nudged into support for Free France, was in fact a Vichy proconsul determined to use military force against any attack. His resolution, moreover, was stiffened by the arrival in Dakar of reinforcements: one heavy and three light cruisers, part of a 'Force Y', despatched from Toulon, which had sailed under the noses of the British fleet stationed at Gibraltar. The Admiralty, though informed twice of their course and intentions, had given no orders to intercept Force Y in the Straits. The British Cabinet, learning that part of it had reached Dakar, gave the Anglo-French force, then at Freetown, the option of aborting Operation Menace. Both de Gaulle and the Allied commanders opted to continue.

Thus reinforced, Boisson rejected both de Gaulle's polite request of 23 September for permission to land his Free French forces, and a sterner British ultimatum. When Commander Thierry d'Argenlieu tried to sail into Dakar under a flag of parley, he was fired on and wounded; Major Hettier de Boislambert was captured after attempting to infiltrate the town from the land. The 15-inch rounds fired from the British battleships on 24 and 25 September made little impression; but Vichy fire damaged two battleships, prompting the Anglo-Free French withdrawal.[27]

Operation Menace had just one positive consequence: Force Y never reached AEF, its initial target. Indeed, the Free French added Gabon to their bag in November. De Gaulle was reassured by a rapturous reception, on 8 October in Douala (Cameroon), where he had travelled from Freetown. And Churchill strongly defended de Gaulle in the Commons. Nevertheless the negative fall-out was enormous. De Gaulle, though outwardly stoical, was inwardly tempted to throw in the towel.[28] Free French recruitment fell away, as after Mers-el-Kébir. Boisson's fierce resistance led the British government to reassess Vichy, as a force to be conciliated where necessary. The British press blamed de Gaulle for the setback. Poor Free French security was widely pilloried – unjustly, given the shared security and intelligence failures. The British military lost faith in the Free French as partners. Roosevelt found another reason to write France off. The Free French lost their chance to win control of AOF and thence possibly of French North Africa too.[29] But taking Dakar against Boisson's opposition would have required forces that the Free French did not have and the British could not spare.

In the Levant, a joint Anglo-Free French operation did, in June 1941, wrest territory from Vichy rule. It also poisoned relations between the two allies, and between de Gaulle and Churchill personally: four of the biggest Anglo-Free French wartime quarrels concerned this region.

British and French had been rivals in the Middle East for 150 years. France accepted British pre-eminence in Egypt only in 1904. After the collapse of the Ottoman Empire in 1918, the British gained control of modern-day Iraq, Jordan, and Palestine/Israel while the French took over the Levant, or Syria and Lebanon. Officially the League of Nations 'mandated' the two powers to administer the territories in preparation for self-rule; effectively, however, they became colonies. The British tried to apply a light-touch rule just sufficient to safeguard their own interests. Iraq even became formally independent in 1932, but with a strong British military presence guaranteed by treaty; France's Senate, by contrast, blocked the Popular Front government's attempt to grant Syria independence in 1936. The Arab populations, promised freedom when they rebelled against the Ottomans in 1916 with British help, bitterly resented the mandates: Iraq, Syria, and Palestine all saw Arab nationalist insurrections. These inspired no solidarity between the imperial powers. The British believed France's intrusive style of rule, underpinned by a belief in an imperial 'civilising mission', fanned the flames of Arab nationalism. The French (including de Gaulle during his 1929–1931 posting) thought the British were stirring up the Arabs against them.[30]

The defeat of 1940 temporarily smoothed out Anglo-French relations in the region. General Wavell, the British commander in the Middle East, hard pressed on fronts stretching from Eritrea to Libya to Greece, had no wish to disturb the Vichy-held Levant, and reached a *modus vivendi* with General Henri Dentz, France's High Commissioner there from December 1940.[31] Georges Catroux, the five-star general whom de Gaulle had appointed his representative in Cairo, shared Wavell's approach.[32] De Gaulle disagreed. Visiting Cairo in April 1941, he sought Wavell's backing for an operation against Syria. He got nowhere and left for Brazzaville.

Then events obliged the British, and Catroux, to act. A *coup d'état* in Baghdad brought to power a pro-German Arab nationalist, Rachid Ali al-Gaylani, who besieged the RAF's Habbaniyah base on 2 May. The Germans moved to assist Rachid Ali, and Vichy to assist the Germans: from 12 May German supply trains and aircraft were reaching Baghdad, via Syria. Hitler and Admiral François Darlan, Pétain's vice-premier from February 1941, then agreed formally the German use of Syrian bases.

A proxy German takeover of Iraq would threaten Britain's whole Middle East position. Churchill therefore determined to cut the Syrian link, and on 12 May wired de Gaulle to return to Cairo and ordered Wavell to prepare an Anglo-Free French expedition. But Dentz had 35,000 well-equipped men; the Free French could muster barely 6,000, with 8 guns, 10 tanks, and 24 aircraft. Wavell added an Australian division, a cavalry and two infantry brigades, and 60 aircraft. But that still left a numerical advantage to the defence.[33]

To overcome their handicap, the British and Free French, under the overall command of General Sir Henry Maitland Wilson, bid for Arab support with a promise of independence. This was a commitment fraught with political sensitivities. De Gaulle felt insulted by a British offer to guarantee the promise: the word of the Free French, he considered, should suffice.[34] More important was what independence meant. For Cassin, and for de Gaulle, real independence would have to wait till after the war; until then, the Free French were still mandated to govern Syria and Lebanon.[35] Churchill and Eden, however, 'were insistent that the Arab population should not be made to feel that they had exchanged one set of French masters for another'.[36] This difference dogged Anglo-French relations in the Levant for over four years. Catroux's declaration, however, was clear. Dropped by air over Syria and Lebanon, as Anglo-Free French troops crossed the border from Palestine at 2AM on 8 June 1941, it read: 'I am abolishing the mandate, and proclaim you free and independent.'[37]

The fighting took a month. French and Australian troops entered Damascus on 21 June. De Gaulle followed two days later, and appointed Catroux his 'plenipotentiary and delegate-general' – a title which still looked (to the British) too much like Dentz's. Rachid Ali's overthrow in Baghdad allowed the Allies' reinforcement, and Dentz, whose men had suffered 6,500 casualties (to 3,000 British and Commonwealth and 783 Free French) requested an armistice on 8 July.[38]

De Gaulle, expecting Free French participation in negotiations with Dentz, and in the longer term the transformation of the Levant into a Free French stronghold, had told Wilson on 19 June what he wanted: Vichy personnel to hand over all weapons and equipment to the Allies, and to be given the opportunity to remain in Syria and join the Free French. On 8 July de Gaulle departed for Khartoum and Brazzaville, leaving Catroux to represent French interests.[39] This was a mistake. When Dentz refused to negotiate with the Free French, Wilson simply relegated Catroux to observer status. Wilson's agreement, reached with Dentz's representative General de Verdhilhac at Acre on 14 July, banned any attempts to recruit Vichy troops to the Free French side and allowed those returning to France to keep their weapons.[40] For Wilson, the Free French were a complication: he aimed simply to speed Vichy troops out of the Middle East, and British and Commonwealth troops back to Egypt, where Rommel's Afrika Korps threatened.[41]

An incandescent de Gaulle returned to Cairo on 20 July and immediately confronted first Spears, still British liaison officer to the Free French, and then Sir Oliver Lyttleton, the British Minister to the Middle East. His anger and threats shocked the two Englishmen, especially when he told them that he was only interested in France's victory in the war, which he regarded as wholly distinct from Britain's, and when he announced that Free French forces would be withdrawn from British command by 24 July – a move bound to destroy the Anglo-Free French partnership.[42] Only on the night of 24 July did de Gaulle and Lyttleton agree to an 'interpretation' of the Acre armistice: the Free French could seek to recruit Vichy troops, weapons would be left behind, and Arab forces under Dentz's command transferred to the Free French.

On the ground, however, British officers proved obstructive. Barely one in seven Vichy soldiers joined the Free French. Those returning to France sabotaged the equipment they surrendered.[43] Returning to Brazzaville after a frustrating Levant summer, de Gaulle vented his spleen to the *Chicago Evening News* correspondent: England, he claimed, was co-operating with Nazi Germany at France's expense, with Vichy as go-between.[44] He could hardly have done more to provoke his Allies.[45] Back in London from 1 September, de Gaulle was denied access to the BBC and to ministers; intelligence-sharing was suspended. Only a conversation with Churchill on 12 September, in which he (unusually) expressed regret at the Brazzaville interview, cleared the air – for the moment.[46] At his 23 September press conference, de Gaulle even called reports of differences over Syria 'enemy propaganda'.[47]

He still believed, however, that the British aimed to replace France in the Levant.[48] True of some British officials and soldiers on the ground, this was not government policy. But the British were guilty of poor co-ordination (between Churchill and the Foreign Office, between London and Cairo, between diplomats and soldiers in Cairo), mixed messages, and high-handedness towards the Free French. Above all, the attempt to conquer Vichy territory on the cheap, as at Dakar (and later in Madagascar and North Africa) led the British into unsustainable, contradictory promises: to Arab leaders, independence; to the Free French, a continued presence in strength in the Levant.[49] Britain's double-dealing resulted in part from muddle; but de Gaulle was bound to see it as calculated.

De Gaulle's errors, strategic and tactical, were if anything worse. He quite failed to understand that insofar as the Arabs welcomed the Free French, it was not as harbingers of more French rule. Tactically, to leave the Levant at the start of armistice negotiations, only to return and denounce the Acre agreement, was barely rational – unless the purpose was to demonstrate British duplicity.[50] Reports of de Gaulle's rages in Cairo, moreover, seriously damaged relations with Churchill and other ministers, while Spears turned overnight from a staunch supporter into a dangerous enemy – who became, in December 1941, British Minister to Syria and Lebanon as well as liaison officer to the Free French.

Syria could, in fact, have been left alone with impunity.[51] The Anglo-Free French invasion was ordered to counter an emergency, in Iraq, which ended before it was launched. The shabby *modus vivendi* with Dentz might have survived indefinitely. The risk, however, was always that Vichy Syria might offer facilities to the Germans again. So Churchill and de Gaulle began a military occupation which did more than anything to sour their wartime relations.

It was Spears who set the scene for a second Syrian crisis in summer 1942. He began by presenting his credentials as minister to the (appointed) presidents of the new republics of Syria and Lebanon, not to the French, on the ground that the League of Nations mandate no longer existed.[52] He then took control of a new Wheat Office designed to prevent grain hoarding, profiteering, and thus civil unrest. The French viewed his (rather successful) efforts as meddling in their affairs.[53] Spears's local activities were complemented by the British government's pressure on the Free French to implement Syrian and Lebanese independence: to hold elections and, once governments were constituted, to sign treaties with them on the Anglo-Iraqi model.

De Gaulle arrived for his second wartime visit to the Middle East on 7 August 1942, resolved to eject Spears and to reaffirm Free French power in the Levant. To Richard Casey, the Australian who had replaced Lyttleton as British Minister in Cairo, he vigorously opposed any elections for 1942, observing that none were planned in Egypt or Iraq or Transjordan, and accusing the British of using Arab nationalism to remove France from the Levant.[54] De Gaulle also claimed, in a flurry of telegrams to Churchill, that Britain's behaviour in the Levant had breached the de Gaulle–Lyttleton agreements. Now that French Levant forces outnumbered the British, he added, the command should pass to a Frenchman. Churchill replied that his representatives were only protecting essential wartime interests, and invited de Gaulle back to London to talk.[55] But de Gaulle stayed in the Levant till mid-September and returned to London slowly via AEF. On 28 August he used a speech in Beirut to tell Syria and Lebanon that independence, though now accorded by the French, had to be 'organised'. Events of 1941, he said had sealed the Levantines' 'tacit' alliance with France; elections would wait till the war's end; for the moment, the French would continue their 'civilising mission'.[56]

In principle, British and French differences were limited. De Gaulle was ultimately prepared to contemplate elections in spring 1943, military conditions permitting; Churchill accepted the 'technical' need to maintain the French mandate temporarily.[57] But the tone of de Gaulle's progress through the Levant infuriated Churchill. All honey to Arab leaders, de Gaulle was all haughtiness to British officials, or else played them off against one another.[58] His complaints to the US consul in Beirut, William Gwynn, included a threat to go to war against Britain. This was immediately relayed to Washington and thence to the Foreign Office.[59]

De Gaulle's interview with Churchill on 30 September 1942 was a more hostile re-run of their conversation of a year earlier. Churchill told de Gaulle that he did not represent France; cipher telegrams to Africa, Levant, and the Pacific, co-operation with British intelligence, and subsidies to the French in the Levant were all suspended.[60] De Gaulle's main consolation was that the whole CNF supported him; the British no longer had a Muselier to back.[61] But relations came close to a break before Desmond Morton undertook a rapprochement late that October.[62]

Madagascar was a final bone of colonial contention. From late 1941, de Gaulle pressed on an unreceptive British government proposals for an Anglo-Free French operation to take the island from Vichy and prevent a possible Japanese attack.[63] Instead, the British launched their own amphibious assault (Operation Ironclad) on 5 May 1942. What was unprecedented was that, whether because of American pressure or fall-out from Syria, they had not consulted the Free French about an attack against a French colony.

Ironclad went painfully slowly. Again, the British tried to seize territory with threadbare forces. Again, Vichy's resistance surprised them: 20% of the British force that took the port of Diego Suarez became casualties in three days.[64] The British then sought Free French support, promising 'participation' in the island's future administration,[65] while simultaneously seeking an agreement with the Vichy authorities that would close Madagascar to Axis vessels. This attempt failed. British forces then fought slowly through the island, receiving the Vichy surrender only on 8 November.

His exclusion from the operation incensed de Gaulle, who in May 1942 considered breaking with the British and departing to AEF, or even Moscow. A cordial interview with Churchill after the Bir

Hakeim success on 10 June patched matters up; but clashes over Syria in August and September ruled out any Free French role in the island's final conquest. Only after Morton's visit to de Gaulle on 30 October 1942 were relations reset: the agreement that followed, on 6 November, established Free French General Paul Legentilhomme as High Commissioner in Madagascar. De Gaulle's declaration of 14 December accepted that the agreement 'wipes clean the consequences of recent painful events', and added a reference to 'the complete loyalty of our good old ally, England'.[66]

Thanks to British support, the Free French by late 1942 controlled AEF, the Levant, and Madagascar. These were useful, but not game-changing acquisitions, and the British had become steadily more overbearing, provoking exaggerated suspicions on de Gaulle's part and damaging Anglo-Free French relations. The Allied landings in North Africa in November 1942 would renew the same conflicts, on an altogether larger canvas.

De Gaulle and the Resistance, 1940–1942

Resistance within France faced colossal logistical and security challenges and was therefore slow to take root. It was even slower to bind itself to de Gaulle. A student demonstration at the Arc de Triomphe on 11 November 1940 used de Gaulle as a symbol but created no lasting structure. A network set up at the Musée de l'Homme in Paris in June 1940 fell victim to the Gestapo within a year. Most major Resistance movements existed, just, by spring 1941: the Organisation Civile et Militaire (OCM), Libération-Nord, and Défense de la France in the occupied northern zone; Combat, Franc-Tireur, and Libération in the 'free' south. Much of their early activity, however, consisted of distributing clandestine newsletters – essential for recruitment, of no direct use to London. The PCF, meanwhile, was paralysed by the Nazi–Soviet pact, whatever the efforts of some individual Communists.

The Free French were more interested in groups or individuals with intelligence to offer. Chief among these was Gilbert Renault, alias Colonel Rémy, a film-maker who appeared in Passy's office in July 1940. Rémy was a talented organiser with a range of contacts in both France (in all political camps, despite his own *Action Française* leanings) and Spain (key for exfiltrating Resistance figures to

London). His value was all the greater as Passy aimed to send agents into France who would organise intelligence networks of individuals able to observe from their homes and daily occupations.[67] Rémy got a first report on German deployments on the Atlantic Coast to London in December 1940; his Confrérie Notre-Dame became the major Gaullist intelligence network operating in France till 1943.

But the circuitous route for Rémy's first dispatch, via a friend in Vichy's Madrid embassy, illustrated the difficulty of communications with France. Sailing small boats out of a closely guarded coast was dangerous, crossing the Pyrenees safer but slower. Radio transmitters were heavy (nearly 30 kilograms), rare (Passy had two in France in mid-1941), and courted detection.[68] Until late 1941, therefore, Free France and the internal Resistance could only undertake small intelligence operations together.

De Gaulle initially thought of the Resistance as an intelligence, not a political, asset.[69] His own early attempts to lead or mobilise the French were amateurish. An invitation to the French to stay home for an hour on 1 January 1941 was well followed; a repeat performance that 11 May was not.[70] On 23 October 1941, after Communists had provoked the execution of 97 hostages by assassinating the German commandant at Nantes, de Gaulle ordered the Resistance to cease attacks on German soldiers – unaware that he was in no position to give *orders* to anyone within France.[71]

Three things changed from mid-1941. First, the PCF joined the fight wholeheartedly after Germany invaded the USSR on 22 June. With a ready-made clandestine organisation, arms saved from June 1940, and no scruples about violent action, the Communists instantly became major players and inspired emulation from other Resistance groups. Second, in creating the CNF in September 1941, de Gaulle acquired for the first time an *organisation* (rather than a group of individuals around himself) claiming to represent France. Its credibility, he realised, depended on its attractiveness to individuals within France who had their own following.[72] Third and finally, in Jean Moulin, who reached London in September and first met de Gaulle on 24 October, de Gaulle found the man who, more than any other, would draw together the internal Resistance and tie it to Free France.

Moulin had been Prefect of Eure-et-Loir, the most senior state official of the *département*, until Vichy sacked him as politically unsound in November 1940. His resulting enforced leisure ensured that by the time he reached London, Moulin was able to brief de Gaulle exhaustively on all major Resistance movements, until then barely known to the Free French. The Resistance, he claimed, could be 'an army of parachutists already in place, knowing the terrain' and ready to liberate France.[73] Within ten days of meeting Moulin, de Gaulle had made him the CNF's delegate in the southern zone and given him a mission. He was, firstly, to unify the three main Resistance groups in the south – Henri Frenay's Combat, Emmanuel d'Astier de la Vigerie's Libération, and Jean-Pierre Lévy's Franc-Tireur – and, secondly, to create, from existing and disparate armed groups, the nucleus of a unified Resistance army under Free French orders. To secure co-operation from Resistance groups, Moulin was given money and authorised to promise arms drops. After repeated delays, he was parachuted into France late on 1 January 1942. He would only return to London on 14 February 1943, making his final journey back to France five weeks later.[74]

Moulin did not initially target political parties. But the PCF's growing role in the Resistance changed his mind. He could not leave the Communists out of the big Resistance grouping that he envisaged without the risk of dangerous internecine competition. Brought inside, however, they risked dominating the organisation – unless other parties were also incorporated. Whatever de Gaulle's misgivings about the parties of the Third Republic, therefore, their revival appeared essential to the balance of the overarching Resistance body he and Moulin wanted.[75]

Three other developments early in 1942 helped transform Free French–Resistance co-operation. First, late in February Rémy brought to London 50 kilograms of maps, identity papers, and ration cards: false papers and real maps could now be readily supplied to the internal Resistance. Second, RAF Lysanders, short take-off and landing aircraft, began air links to clandestine airstrips in occupied France. After a slow start, between 1942 and 1944, the RAF landed 443 passengers in France and brought 635 out, mostly by Lysander and later in the larger Hudsons too.[76] Third, radio traffic increased: 30 transmitting radios were supplied for France in 1942, while messages into France were transmitted, in code, by normal broadcast channels.[77] Better radio traffic meant speedier intelligence for London, improved bargaining power for the Free

French for scarce British assets (such as space on Lysanders), and more internal and external Resistance operations.

Things became possible in 1942 that were hardly imaginable in 1941. Mass events could be undertaken. De Gaulle's call for silent demonstrations in French towns on May Day 1942, for example, was successful thanks in part to Moulin's organisation: 100,000 people came onto the streets of Marseille, for example, irritating the occupiers and showing goodwill towards the PCF.[78] Then, in spring 1942, contact was made with the Communists via Rémy and his associate François Faure. Rémy secured one parachute drop of weapons plus a monthly payment of 500,000 francs for the Francs-Tireurs et Partisans (FTP), the Communist-led paramilitary group.[79] The PCF was not thereby subordinated to the Free French. But as both parties were seeking to reinforce their legitimacy, recognition, even limited, was mutually beneficial.[80]

And now leaders reached London from France. Emmanuel d'Astier de la Vigerie, from Libération-Sud, visited Carlton Gardens in May 1942. De Gaulle sent him to plead the Resistance cause in the United States. Frenay, for Combat, reached London in September. Pierre Brossolette, the brightest journalist of the pre-war Socialist Party, sent a long report on the Resistance and political parties with Rémy, and appeared in person in April 1942. Christian Pineau, a leading trade unionist in the Confédération Générale du Travail (CGT), member of the clandestine Socialist Action Committee, and co-founder of Libération-Nord, arrived in March. Another Socialist, André Philip, economist, fluent English speaker, and former Deputy (1936–1940), was in London from July; de Gaulle immediately gave him the CNF's Interior portfolio.[81] Their conversations with de Gaulle were not always easy. Visitors found his opening line, 'Tell me about France', unnerving, though de Gaulle was an attentive listener.

Both Brossolette and Frenay opposed Moulin's plan to bring parties under the Resistance umbrella on the grounds that they were discredited, needed re-forming, and would tarnish the heroic image of the Resistance.[82] Many of the new arrivals, moreover, were men of the centre-Left who doubted de Gaulle's republicanism. Pineau confronted de Gaulle about this, demanding a declaration of principles to convince his and other Resistance movements. He had some leverage because de Gaulle wanted the Resistance to tell the

British that he, de Gaulle, was their recognised leader. But de Gaulle's draft declaration confirmed Pineau's misgivings, by attacking the Third Republic and Vichy in comparable terms. Only as Pineau was waiting at Tempsford aerodrome, on 28 April, for his Lysander to fly him to France, did a revised text arrive by despatch rider. This included the republican motto (Liberty, Equality, Fraternity) and promised the full restoration of pre-war freedoms and the free election by universal suffrage (including women) of a National Assembly to decide France's future at the Liberation. The text appeared in all main Resistance publications early in June and was distributed in leaflet form.[83]

De Gaulle's declaration underpinned the near-fulfilment of Jean Moulin's mission in October 1942. The three big southern movements, Combat, Libération, and Franc-Tireur, declared their attachment to Free France and agreed to the creation of a Co-ordinating Committee under Moulin.[84] Their military component would be united as the Secret Army and headed by a retired general, Charles Delestraint. On 17 November 1942, d'Astier and Frenay were sent to the southern zone with 20 million francs for Moulin to divide between the Resistance movements, which were also promised a shared monthly budget of 5 million.[85] A week earlier Moulin had sent a telegram congratulating the Allies for their speedy liberation of French North Africa, in the name of Combat, Franc-Tireur, Libération, the Socialist Action Committee, the two main trade unions (the CGT and the Confédération Française des Travailleurs Chrétiens), and 'different political parties'.[86]

This display of unity was greatly overdone. The Resistance movements' allegiance to de Gaulle was limited and conditional: Frenay, for example, had tried to sell intelligence to the Americans in Bern before the Gaullists intervened.[87] De Gaulle never liked the Resistance leaders personally and considered that whereas he served only France, they acted out of ideological allegiance or simple hunger for power.[88] For their part, the Resistance leaders needed the de Gaulle 'brand', and the arms and the money that recognition brought them, but expected to be treated as equals. They did not readily accept Moulin handing down an order to create a secret army under de Gaulle's command. Here were the roots of bitter future conflicts – though the Resistance groups' military wings were in any case still tiny, poorly trained, and ill-equipped. For all that, the internal Resistance and Free France were vastly closer than they had been at the CNF's creation in September 1941. Moreover, Free France itself had changed, developing a broader political appeal to France's people.

Organisation and politics, 1940–1942: Free France turns Left

How could de Gaulle and his tiny band turn their claim to represent the French nation into reality – and become the French state? It took four incarnations to transform Free France from a group of adventurers into something resembling a government: the Conseil de la Défense de l'Empire (Empire Defence Council, or CDE) in October 1940; the CNF in September 1941; the Comité Français de la Libération Nationale in June 1943; and finally the Gouvernement Provisoire de la République Française a year later.

The CDE was proclaimed in Brazzaville on 27 October 1940, during de Gaulle's post-Dakar African progress. But its nine members (de Gaulle, Cassin, plus colonial governors and service chiefs) held no ministerial portfolios, and were too geographically dispersed to meet. The Brazzaville Declaration irritated the Foreign Office by claiming Vichy's illegitimacy at a time when the British sought decent relations with Pétain's regime; so did the ensuing 'Organic Declaration' of 16 November 1940, with an opening proclamation ('We, Charles de Gaulle General de Gaulle, leader of the Free French, declare …') that the British viewed as 'typically fascist'.[89] But the British government still allowed a form of recognition of the CDE on 31 December.

And the Free French began to behave like the embryo of a state. A *Journal Officiel de la France Libre*, on the model of the pre-war *Journal Officiel*, appeared from January 1941, publishing Free French legislation (in the form of decrees, or *ordonnances*, as there was no parliament to debate laws) and major appointments. A Free French Administrative Conference met weekly from 29 January 1941 and included quasi-governmental members with portfolios such as Justice, Finance, and Foreign Affairs.[90] To underpin this, the Free French developed a constitutional doctrine. It proceeded in four steps: (a) Vichy was illegitimate both because the constitutional revision of 10 July 1940, giving Pétain full powers, was itself unconstitutional under the laws of the Third Republic, and because

Vichy had submitted to the dictates of an invading power; (b) the Third Republic therefore remained France's legal regime; but (c) because the occupation of France prevented the Third Republic from functioning, de Gaulle had taken power to continue France's war effort; and (d) he held this power in trust until the French people might choose their own representatives freely. This doctrine would be reiterated at the creation of the CNF on 24 September 1941 and of the CFLN on 3 June 1943.[91]

In principle, then, Free France was a republican enterprise. Its founding texts referred to the Rights of Man and the Citizen. Yet its early aspect was not very republican at all. It was presented as the endeavour of one man: the CDE's members were simply appointed to 'assist' de Gaulle. In de Gaulle's and Schumann's early broadcasts, the army motto – Honour and Fatherland – replaced the republican Liberty, Equality, Fraternity. Many of the first Free French figures, like Leclerc or Edgard de Larminat, whom de Gaulle had made governor of AEF, opposed Vichy's submission to Germany, not its internal policies. But de Gaulle's distance from republicanism also arose from a belief that the Third Republic was discredited for its role in France's defeat. A civilian republican like Cassin felt very much in the minority in the early Free France, and had to argue hard to persuade other republican figures to join.[92]

Free France was not, on the other hand, anti-Semitic, though it certainly included anti-Semites. De Gaulle accepted Jews like Cassin or Georges Boris into his entourage and did not tolerate anti-Semitic remarks in his presence. With his approval, Schumann specifically attacked Vichy's first Jewish Statute on the BBC in October 1940 and Cassin wrote a Free French protest against Vichy's treatment of Jews in March 1941. That was about as far as the anti-anti-Semitism of early Free France went. Vichy, for de Gaulle, was illegitimate for its treatment of France, not of Jews.[93]

Then, in September 1941, a leftward turn began. The Atlantic Charter, Churchill's and Roosevelt's joint statement of liberal democratic principles of 14 August, offered a propitious context. The CNF's creation on 23 September 1941 provided an occasion. Unlike the CDE, the CNF looked like a government, with quasi-ministers for Justice and Education (Cassin), Finance and Economic Affairs (Pleven), Foreign Affairs (Maurice Dejean), and Interior and Information (André Diethelm, a former senior official under the

Third Republic), as well as for each armed service.[94] The *ordonnance* of 24 September cited, as justification for the CNF's creation, Vichy's daily violation of 'the constitution and laws of the French Republic'.[95]

More was to come. If 1940 had been the year of the historic de Gaulle broadcasts, 1941–1942 was the period of the great wartime speeches, notably at Oxford (25 November 1941) and at London's Albert Hall (15 November 1941, 18 June and 11 November 1942). At Oxford he drew the very broad lines of a Gaullist, social Catholic-inspired, social policy.[96] Ten days earlier, at the Albert Hall, he had resoundingly reinstated Liberty, Equality, and Fraternity in the Gaullist lexicon, called for a future in which every French person should be able to live, to think, to work, to act, in dignity and security, and evoked France's revolutionary tradition ('if this war is a revolution, it is true of France more than for any other people').[97]

De Gaulle's revolutionary rhetoric peaked in April 1942, when he mentioned 'revolution' seven times.[98] On 1 April he proclaimed that France was on the threshold of 'the greatest revolution in her history'; 17 days later, that 'national liberation cannot be separated from national insurrection' – a clear nod to the Communists, who had hitherto monopolised talk of insurrection.[99] Just as frequent were the references to 'the laws of the Republic'.[100] Meanwhile the manifesto that Pineau took to France included a plea, along broadly social-democratic lines, for each person to 'enjoy equal chances to those of others, that each should be respected by all and assisted in case of need' in the name of 'the centuries-old French ideal of liberty, equality and fraternity'.[101] This war, de Gaulle declared at the Albert Hall on 18 June 1942, quoting US Vice-President Henry Wallace, was the 'war of the common man'.[102]

The aim of the republican, left-wing, even guardedly revolutionary turn was to win over republican forces within France, as well as international opinion. Resistance movements (Libération, Franc-Tireur, and Combat) first got a named mention in a press conference on 27 May, and again at the Albert Hall on 18 June. In the most moving passage in the sequence of speeches, at the Albert Hall on 11 November 1942, he glorified Resistance fighters shot in Paris, Nantes, Lille, Bordeaux, or Strasbourg alongside the dead of Free French armed forces: 'France will live', said de Gaulle, 'because you knew how to die for her.'[103]

By late 1942, Free France – or Fighting France, as de Gaulle had started calling it that spring, prematurely claiming unity with the internal Resistance – was a vastly more attractive organisation than its early incarnations. The clandestine manifesto published in June had won the support of politicians from Socialists (Léon Blum, André Le Troquer), Radicals (Édouard Daladier, Daniel Mayer, or Jules Jeanneney) and the Right (Louis Marin).[104] Moulin's success in winning over the southern Resistance movements in October depended on de Gaulle's democratic credentials as well as on money and arms. On 14 July, meanwhile, de Gaulle had so charmed 300 members of the British Parliament that they had spontaneously risen and sung the *Marseillaise*. Even the Roosevelt administration was finally accrediting representatives to him.[105]

This transformation showed two things about de Gaulle the politician. The first was his astonishing ability, remarkable given his lack of pre-war experience, as an orator on the big stage and on radio. The second was his pragmatism. More of a republican than the right-wing officers of the early Free France, de Gaulle was probably less so than the mid-1942 Fighting France. He never took Resistance leaders or Third Republic politicians to heart. But this supposedly unbending man was prepared to make the necessary gestures, even to the Communists, to win their support when he needed it – without losing sight of his main goal. Unfortunately, de Gaulle showed fewer political skills in his dealings with the Americans.

De Gaulle, the Americans, and Torch

The fundamental premise of the *Appel du 18 juin* was that France was engaged in a world war. And indeed, by mid-1942, there were 412 Free French Committees, undertaking propaganda, fundraising, and recruitment, in 42 countries, notably in the Middle East and Latin America.[106] Cassin targeted the British Commonwealth, and de Gaulle received warm support in Anglophone Canada – though not in largely Pétainist Francophone Quebec. Eighteen full-time delegates were sent across the world (though only six professional diplomats could be found), while consular offices represented Free French supporters deprived of citizenship rights by Vichy.[107]

But the most important focus of Free French international activities was the United States, where Gaulle sent René Pleven in May

1941. Pleven persuaded the State Department to authorise an official Free French organisation, but without any diplomatic status: its full accreditation, under Adrien Tixier, former director of the International Labour Organisation in Washington, was delayed until December. Free France's US profile was in any case chaotic: three separate offices in New York hosted the official Free French mission, de Gaulle's personal representative, and a grass-roots organisation, France Forever.[108]

Dispersal of effort was especially damaging given the poor state of Free France's wartime relations with the United States.[109] They started badly in December 1941 with the Free French seizure of Saint-Pierre-et-Miquelon, Vichy-held islands off Newfoundland. For de Gaulle, the operation had everything to recommend it. Islanders were clamouring to be liberated; Saint-Pierre had a radio transmitter broadcasting Vichy propaganda, and possibly messages to German submarines; Free French action would pre-empt any possible Canadian takeover; and it got Muselier, after two 'affairs', out of London. Muselier, having reached Newfoundland ostensibly on an inspection tour, landed men on the islands on 24 December 1941; no shots were fired; a Christmas Day plebiscite of some 800 islanders confirmed their Free French preference; and Muselier's aide-de-camp, Alain Savary, took the head of a Free French administration. The syndicated reports of an American journalist on the spot ensured the operation wide publicity.

It was a success won against the US administration's express opposition. On 13 December, after Pearl Harbor, Roosevelt had reaffirmed his commitment to the July 1940 Havana Convention, under which the United States, Vichy, and other states had agreed to oppose any change of sovereignty in the Western hemisphere. Secretary of State Hull therefore condemned the intervention by the 'so-called Free French'. This embarrassed Churchill, on his first wartime visit to Washington: he had just commended the action in the Canadian Parliament.[110] Hull, meanwhile, received hundreds of letters addressed to the 'so-called Secretary of State': public opinion in the US, Canada, and Britain, backed de Gaulle, who therefore felt secure enough on the moral high ground to refuse demands to withdraw. And no Allied power would use force against an administration enjoying the islanders' clear support. So de Gaulle won – but at great cost. Roosevelt's and Hull's belief in his untrustworthiness was reinforced.[111] Free France was left out of the list of the 27 United Nations issued on 1 January 1942, and sidelined from the planning of all future Allied operations – including Madagascar, North Africa, Italy, and mainland France itself.

Relations improved in the spring and early summer of 1942. America's generals, pressing for an Allied landing in mainland France in 1942, knew they would need help from the French Resistance. In London, Ambassador Winant approached de Gaulle, who responded eagerly with notes on French participation in the operation.[112] Meanwhile Emmanuel d'Astier de la Vigerie, despatched to Washington in May to sell the Resistance to the Americans, met Roosevelt's special advisor Harry Hopkins and senior military figures.[113] In July, a successful French Week in New York reinforced that city's good opinion of the Free French.[114]

The bright interval was brief. The creation (with Free French agreement) of an American base on the French Pacific island of New Caledonia created tensions between American military personnel and the suddenly outnumbered inhabitants; these were aggravated by the behaviour of the newly promoted Admiral Thierry d'Argenlieu, Free French High Commissioner of Pacific Territories; and de Gaulle began to refer privately to US imperialism.[115] Meanwhile Free France's American representation remained chaotic. Tixier complained publicly about de Gaulle's authoritarianism; his assistant Étienne Boegner resigned after de Gaulle had called him an American agent.[116] D'Astier cut a dashing figure in Washington, but the still-hostile State Department easily demolished his overblown claims of Resistance numbers.[117] Worse, the Americans' need for French help was short-lived, for the moment. When de Gaulle met General Marshall, the US Chief of Staff, along with Generals Eisenhower and Clark and Admirals King and Stark, at Claridge's Hotel in London on 23 July, the Americans heard de Gaulle's detailed plans in polite silence. They had just learnt of the decision to land in North Africa, not metropolitan France.[118] News later that summer of de Gaulle's behaviour in Syria put paid to any chance of Washington letting him back into planning.

The Allied decision to land in North Africa was largely a British one. Brooke, Chief of the Imperial General Staff, saw shipping as the fundamental constraint on all Allied operations. For the British, making the Mediterranean safe for Allied vessels by conquering its

North African and Italian coastlines therefore became an essential preliminary to invading France.[119] But to secure American consent to the plan, they conceded the implementation of what became Operation Torch to the Americans. It was Dwight D. Eisenhower who commanded the mostly American forces that landed in Morocco and Algeria on 8 November 1942. They did not land in Tunisia; the Germans did, by air, without Vichy's consent.

Vichy had 120,000 troops in North Africa, twice as many as the planned landing force.[120] As at Dakar, therefore, as in Syria and Madagascar, the military planners counted on local co-operation to palliate their insufficient numbers. But Governors-General Noguès in Morocco and Châtel in Algeria were solidly pro-Vichy. The North African Gaullists, meanwhile, consisted of a small group in Algiers University. So the Americans, and specifically Robert Murphy, Roosevelt's personal representative in North Africa, tried other expedients. Externally, they relied on Henri Giraud, a five-star general captured by German troops on 19 May 1940. Giraud had escaped from captivity on 17 April 1942, and now resided in the southern zone. Here American consular officials discussed Torch with him in October, believing he might have sufficient authority to secure a Vichy cease-fire in North Africa; Giraud was exfiltrated to Gibraltar by submarine in time for the landings. In Morocco, meanwhile, Murphy expected General Antoine Béthouart, commander of the Vichy army's Casablanca division, to neutralise Noguès. In Algiers he relied upon a bizarre alliance between the military commander of Algiers, a handful of extreme right-wing anti-Vichyites, and a larger group of young left-wing French Algerian Jews led by José Aboulker, son of a former Radical Deputy. The main link between them was Henri d'Astier de la Vigerie, brother of Emmanuel. These groups met Murphy plus the American General Mark Clark, who arrived by submarine, at a villa on the Algerian coast on 23 October 1942. The third piece in Murphy's game was Admiral Darlan, head of the French navy and, until his replacement, at the Germans' instigation, by Pierre Laval on 18 April 1942, no. 2 in the Vichy regime. From early November Darlan was in Algiers, ostensibly to visit his son in hospital but very much open to American offers.

Only the Aboulker team's operation went to plan that 8 November. It neutralised all leading Vichy figures in Algiers, including

Darlan, for one vital night: Clark's troops controlled the city 15 hours after arriving.[121] In Casablanca, by contrast, Noguès took Béthouart prisoner and gave orders to resist American forces. And Giraud's broadcast call, from Gibraltar, for a general cease-fire had absolutely no effect. It took an order from Darlan, issued under extreme pressure from Mark Clark, and endorsed, then cancelled (too late) by Pétain, to persuade Noguès to sign a cease-fire on 11 November. By then Allied casualties, overwhelmingly in Oran (Western Algeria) and Morocco, had reached 1,469, including 530 killed; Vichy's were over twice as high. A general cease-fire across North Africa required a new order from Darlan, on 13 November. By then Clark had made Darlan, freshly sacked by Pétain, High Commissioner and Commander-in-Chief of Naval Forces; Giraud was Commander-in-Chief of Ground and Air Forces; Juin, formerly Commander-in-Chief of French North African forces, became Commander of the Eastern Sector (Algeria); and Noguès and Châtel kept their posts as Resident in Morocco and Governor in Algeria.[122] The government of liberated North Africa, in short, seemed barely distinguishable from that of Vichy North Africa.

Woken with news of Torch by his Chief of Staff, de Gaulle expressed the hope that 'the Vichy people throw them into the sea'.[123] But he accepted Churchill's embarrassed lunch invitation, and, as after Mers-el-Kébir, played the British game with exemplary loyalty. On the evening of 8 November he broadcast a message to North Africa's leaders to 'join up with the Allies without reservations'. His Albert Hall speech three days later included warm tributes to the Allies.[124] His proposal to send a mission to Algiers with a view to uniting the Free French to Giraud's supporters received guarded support from both President and Prime Minister.[125] But these optimistic perspectives were dashed within days, and de Gaulle soon faced his most gruelling confrontation as Free French leader.

Conclusion

What was de Gaulle's achievement in these first 29 months? In terms of territory, while AEF, and New Caledonia, and the Levant, and Madagascar, and even Saint-Pierre-et-Miquelon, were useful assets, they were not the French Empire. North-West Africa was still governed by Vichyites, and in Allied not Free French hands. In terms of troops, the tally was modest: Leclerc and Larminat mustered barely more than 10,000 Free French soldiers when they joined forces with Juin's established North African army in June 1943.[126] As to recognition, the British had recognised the Fighting French as representing all French citizens, wherever they might be, who sought to fight the Axis. The Soviets had been a little more generous, the Americans a good deal less so. None came close to recognising Free France as a government in exile. The southern Resistance leaders and a clutch of Third Republic politicians had given de Gaulle their backing; but de Gaulle could not claim to be the undisputed 'leader of the Resistance'. Moreover, he had squandered a part of his credit with the British Prime Minister, not through being inflexible, which Churchill usually respected, but through rudeness, anger, and suspicion. And his failure to establish good working relations with the Americans, while owing much to the Roosevelt administration's hostility, was also due to his own inability to unify Free France's US operation.

Given the lowly beginnings of Free France, however – a handful of officers, a few rooms in St Stephen's House – de Gaulle's accomplishment was enormous. He had engaged the virtuous circle, winning colonies with British backing, using the colonies as Free French bases, winning growing support among the French from his broadcasts, using his symbolic stature and British-sourced funds to secure recognition, albeit partial, from the internal Resistance. This in turn reinforced his position with the Allies – as was demonstrated, for example, by the American interest in him in spring 1942. And de Gaulle's refusal to compromise, added to his renewed commitment to democratic values from late 1941, had secured him a moral stature which French, British and American public opinion understood and welcomed. This was to prove de Gaulle's most precious asset in the two difficult years ahead.

Notes

1 François Kersaudy, *Churchill and de Gaulle* (New York: Atheneum, 1981), pp. 88, 91.
2 Kersaudy, *Churchill and de Gaulle*, p. 83.
3 Charles Williams, *The Last Great Frenchman* (New York: John Wiley, 1993), pp. 117–18.

4 *DM*I, pp. 13–15.
5 Hansard, House of Commons debates, 20 August 1940, pp. 1168–9.
6 Jean-Louis Crémieux-Brilhac, *La France Libre, de l'appel du 18 juin à la Libération* (Paris: Gallimard, 1996), pp. 84, 87–8, 91; Claude d'Abzac-Epezy, 'Le Rôle de l'armée dans le processus de légitimation du général de Gaulle, 1940–1944', in Fondation Charles de Gaulle, *De Gaulle chef de guerre. De l'Appel de Londres à la libération de Paris, 1940–1944* (Paris: Plon, 2008), pp. 324–6.
7 René Cassin, *Les Hommes partis de rien: le réveil de la France abattue (1940–1941)* (Paris: Plon, 1975), p. 86.
8 Éric Roussel, *Charles de Gaulle* (Paris: Gallimard, 2002), pp. 161–3.
9 Cassin, *Les Hommes*, p. 77; Jean-Luc Barré, *Devenir de Gaulle, 1939–1943* (Paris: Perrin, 2003), pp. 81–4, 110.
10 Cassin, *Les Hommes*, pp. 105–6, 112, 117–19; Crémieux-Brilhac, *France Libre*, pp. 65–71; Kersaudy, *Churchill and de Gaulle*, pp. 89–90.
11 Douglas Porch, *The French Secret Services from the Dreyfus Affair to the Gulf War* (Oxford: Oxford University Press, 1995), p. 179; Colonel Passy (pseudonym of André Dewavrin), *Mémoires du chef des services secrets de la France libre*, ed. Jean-Louis-Crémieux-Brilhac (Paris: Odile Jacob, 2000), p. 207; Passy in Georges-Marc Benamou, *C'était un temps déraisonnable. Les premiers Résistants racontent* (Paris: Robert Laffont, 1999), p. 137.
12 Passy, *Mémoires*, p. 147; Crémieux-Brilhac, *France Libre*, p. 237; Porch, *Secret Services*, pp. 245–6.
13 Cassin, *Les Hommes*, p. 311.
14 Tim Brooks, *British Propaganda to France, 1940–1944: Machinery, Method and Message* (Edinburgh: Edinburgh University Press, 2007), p. xvii.
15 Peter Mangold, *Britain and the Defeated French: From Occupation to Liberation, 1940–1944* (London: I.B.Tauris, 2012), p. 113; Williams, *Last Great*, pp. 188–9.
16 Crémieux-Brilhac, *France Libre*, pp. 212–14; Philippe de Gaulle, *De Gaulle mon père. Entretiens avec Michel Tauriac*, vol. I (Paris: Plon, 2003), p. 157.
17 Williams, *Last Great*, p. 123; Crémieux-Brilhac, *France Libre*, pp. 71–3; Kersaudy, *Churchill and de Gaulle*, pp. 86–7.
18 Philippe de Gaulle, *De Gaulle mon père* I, p. 195; *Picture Post* 15.05, 2 May 1942.
19 Crémieux-Brilhac, *France Libre*, pp. 93–4; Passy, *Mémoires*, p. 96.
20 Roussel, *de Gaulle*, pp. 243–6; Kersaudy, *Churchill and de Gaulle*, pp. 162–7; Crémieux-Brilhac, *France Libre*, pp. 200–10.
21 Williams, *Last Great*, p. 171; Jackson, *A Certain Idea*, pp. 208–9; Kersaudy, *Churchill and de Gaulle*, pp. 179–82; Roussel, *de Gaulle*, pp. 271–9; *LNC*II, pp. 50–1, 55; broadcast interview with Michel Droit, 7 June 1968, *DM*V, p. 295.
22 See above, p. 50.

23 Williams, *Last Great*, p. 143.
24 *WM*I, p. 302.
25 Roussel, *de Gaulle*, pp. 171–3; Porch, *Secret Services*, p. 181; Cassin, *Les Hommes*, pp. 189–90.
26 Claude Bouchinet-Serreulles, *Nous étions nés pour être libres. La Résistance avec de Gaulle et Jean Moulin* (Paris: Grasset, 2000), p. 100.
27 Roussel, *de Gaulle*, pp. 178–81; Williams, *Last Great*, pp. 128–33.
28 Interview with Michel Droit, 7 June 1968, *DM*v, p. 295.
29 Cassin, *Les Hommes*, pp. 189–92; Kersaudy, *Churchill and de Gaulle*, p. 103.
30 A.B. Gaunson, *The Anglo-French Clash in Lebanon and Syria, 1940–1945* (Basingstoke: Macmillan, 1987), pp. 4–8.
31 Williams, *Last Great*, p. 144.
32 Barré, *Devenir de Gaulle*, pp. 139–41.
33 Kersaudy, *Churchill and de Gaulle*, p. 136.
34 Barré, *Devenir de Gaulle*, p. 149; Gaunson, *Clash*, pp. 41–2.
35 Cassin, *Les Hommes*, p. 353.
36 Sir Anthony Eden (Earl of Avon), *The Reckoning* (Memoirs, vol. II) (London: Cassell, 1965), p. 249.
37 Quoted in Sir Edward Spears, *Fulfilment of a Mission: Syria and Lebanon, 1941–1944* (London: Seeley, Service and Cooper, 1977), p. 98.
38 Crémieux-Brilhac, *France Libre*, p. 153.
39 Kersaudy, *Churchill and de Gaulle*, p. 137.
40 Crémieux-Brilhac, *France Libre*, pp. 156–7.
41 Colin Smith, *England's Last War against France: Fighting Vichy, 1940–1942* (London: Weidenfeld & Nicolson, 2009), pp. 270–3.
42 Spears, *Mission*, pp. 121, 133–6.
43 Smith, *Britain's Last War*, p. 273; Gaunson, *Lebanon and Syria*, pp. 44–61; Kersaudy, *Churchill and de Gaulle*, pp. 139–49.
44 Mangold, *Defeated French*, pp. 134–5.
45 Hervé Alphand, *L'Étonnement d'être* (Paris: Fayard 1977), p. 89.
46 Kersaudy, *Churchill and de Gaulle*, pp. 155–60.
47 *LNC*I, pp. 1300–1307: p. 1301.
48 Jackson, *A Certain Idea*, p. 178.
49 Gaunson, *Clash*, p. 78.
50 Barré, *Devenir de Gaulle*, p. 162.
51 Guichard, *Mon Général*, pp. 105–6.
52 Gaunson, *Clash*, pp. 86–7.
53 Gaunson, *Clash*, pp. 89–91; *WM*I, p. 238.
54 *WM*II, pp. 21–2.
55 Charles de Gaulle, *War Memoirs*, vol. II: *Unity, 1942–1944: Documents*, tr. Joyce Murchie and Hamish Erskine (London: Weidenfeld & Nicolson, 1959: hereafter *WM*IIDocs), pp. 37–46.
56 *DM*I, pp. 215–21.

57 Churchill to de Gaulle, 23 August 1942, WMiiDocs, pp. 41–2; de Gaulle to Pleven and Dejean, 4 September 1942, WMiiDocs, pp. 48–9.
58 Gaunson, *Clash*, p. 97.
59 Kersaudy, *Churchill and de Gaulle*, p. 200.
60 Kersaudy, *Churchill and de Gaulle*, pp. 202–10; Mangold, *Defeated French*, p. 152.
61 Passy, *Mémoires*, p. 364.
62 Williams, *Last Great*, p. 190.
63 Kersaudy, *Churchill and de Gaulle*, p. 185; Barré, *Devenir de Gaulle*, pp. 219–21; Notes of 11 February 1942 in Charles de Gaulle, *War Memoirs*, vol. i: *The Call to Honour, 1940–1942: Documents*, tr. Jonathan Griffin (London: Collins, 1955) pp. 330–1.
64 Mangold, *Defeated French*, pp. 85–6.
65 WMi, p. 243.
66 *DM*i, pp. 248–9.
67 Passy, *Mémoires*, pp. 80–1.
68 Crémieux-Brilhac, *France Libre*, p. 235.
69 Crémieux-Brilhac, *France Libre*, pp. 241–3.
70 Cassin, *Les Hommes*, p. 325.
71 Broadcast of 23 October 1941, *DM*i, pp. 122–3.
72 Bouchinet-Serreulles, *Nous étions nés*, pp. 163–4.
73 Jackson, *A Certain Idea*, p. 196.
74 Crémieux-Brilhac, *France Libre*, pp. 346–9.
75 Jean Moulin par Laure Moulin, in Simonne Servais, *Regards sur de Gaulle* (Paris: Plon, 1990), pp. 302–3; Daniel Cordier, 'La France libre, Jean Moulin et les communistes', in Stéphane Courtois and Marc Lazar (eds), *Cinquante ans d'une passion française. De Gaulle et les communistes* (Paris: Balland, 1991), pp. 25–37; WMi, p. 273.
76 Passy, *Mémoires*, pp. 220–5; Crémieux-Brilhac, *France Libre*, p. 744.
77 Passy, *Mémoires*, pp. 320–1.
78 Broadcast, 30 April 1942, *DM*i, pp. 183–4; Mangold, *Defeated French*, p. 115; M.R.D. Foot, *SOE in France: An Account of the Work of the British Special Operations Executive in France 1940–1944* (London: Frank Cass, 2004), p. 206.
79 Crémieux-Brilhac, *France Libre*, pp. 334–5.
80 Philippe Buton, 'Le Parti communiste français et le général de Gaulle, de la Résistance à la Libération', in Courtois and Lazar, *Cinquante ans*, pp. 39–55.
81 Roussel, *de Gaulle*, pp. 281–3; Foot, *SOE in France*, p. 213; Crémieux-Brilhac, *France Libre*, pp. 333–6, 340–5.
82 Passy, *Mémoires*, p. 360; Henri Frenay, *La Nuit finira: mémoires de la Résistance, 1940–1945* (Paris: Robert Laffont, 1973), p. 257.
83 Christian Pineau, 'Le Général de Gaulle et la Résistance intérieure française (1940–1943)', in Institut Charles de Gaulle, *De Gaulle en son siècle*, vol. i: *Dans la mémoire des hommes et des peuples* (Paris: Plon, 1991), pp. 537–49.

84　Jackson, *A Certain Idea*, p. 224.
85　Passy, *Mémoires*, p. 386.
86　Guichard, *Mon Général*, p. 151.
87　Frenay, *La Nuit finira*, pp. 119–22, 142–7, 320–31.
88　Barré, *Devenir de Gaulle*, p. 197. Charles de Gaulle, *Mémoires* (Paris: Gallimard (Collection Pléiade), 2000), p. 1325.
89　Crémieux-Brilhac, *France Libre*, p. 140.
90　Cassin, *Les Hommes*, pp. 241–5.
91　Emmanuel Cartier, 'The Liberation and the Institutional Question in France', in Andrew Knapp (ed.), *The Uncertain Foundation: France at the Liberation, 1944–1947* (Basingstoke: Palgrave, 2007), pp. 23–40; www.france-libre.net/manifeste-brazzaville/ and http://www.france-libre.net/declaration-organique-16-novembre-1940/, accessed 25 January 2019.
92　Cassin, *Les Hommes*, pp. 217–21; Passy, *Mémoires*, p. 114; Jackson, *A Certain Idea*, p. 190.
93　Cassin, *Les Hommes*, p. 138; Dominique Schnapper, 'De Gaulle vu par les juifs', in Institut Charles de Gaulle, *De Gaulle en son siècle* I, pp. 458–71; Roussel, *De Gaulle*, p. 200.
94　Crémieux-Brilhac, *France Libre*, p. 207.
95　Roussel, *de Gaulle*, p. 246; *LNC*I, pp. 1300–07; *DM*I, pp. 104–7.
96　*DM*I, pp. 138–46. De Gaulle also declared that France's liberation was synonymous with a British victory – the precise opposite of what he had said to Spears five months earlier.
97　*DM*I, pp. 132–8.
98　Yves Lavoinne, 'De Gaulle en révolution. Du militaire au politique: 18 juin 1940–1948 mai 1945', in Institut Charles de Gaulle, *De Gaulle en son siècle*, vol. II: *La République* (Paris: Plon, 1992), pp. 69–77.
99　*DM*I, pp. 176–81, 181–2.
100　Jean Touchard, *Le Gaullisme 1940–1969* (Paris: Le Seuil, 1978), p. 63.
101　*DM*I, pp. 205–7.
102　*DM*I, pp. 197–204.
103　*DM*I, pp. 233–40.
104　Pineau, 'Le Général de Gaulle et la Résistance intérieure', p. 546.
105　Jackson, *A Certain Idea*, pp. 234–5.
106　Williams, *Last Great*, pp. 163–4; Cassin, *Les Hommes*, pp. 286–90, 372, 387; Crémieux-Brilhac, *France Libre*, pp. 267–74.
107　Cassin, *Les Hommes*, pp. 257–8, 283.
108　Williams, *Last Great*, pp. 163–4; Roussel, *de Gaulle*, p. 252.
109　See above, pp. 53–5.
110　Williams, *Last Great*, pp. 167–70.
111　Crémieux-Brilhac, *France Libre*, pp. 278–88; Roussel, *de Gaulle*, pp. 261–3.
112　*LNC*II, pp. 119–20; François Kersaudy, *De Gaulle et Roosevelt: Le duel au Sommet* (Paris: Perrin, 2004), pp. 132–4.

113 Emmanuel d'Astier de la Vigerie, *Sept fois sept jours* (Paris: Union Générale d'Éditions, 1963 [1961]), pp. 65–6.
114 Williams, *Last Great*, pp. 183–4.
115 Crémieux, *France Libre*, pp. 297–305.
116 Roussel, *de Gaulle*, pp. 298–300.
117 Passy, *Mémoires*, pp. 249–51.
118 Jean Lacouture, *De Gaulle*, vol. I: *Le Rebelle* (Paris: Le Seuil, 1986), pp. 557–8; Mangold, *Defeated French*, p. 157.
119 Field Marshal Lord Alanbrooke, *War Diaries 1939–1945* (London: Weidenfeld & Nicolson, 2001), pp. 281–2.
120 Williams, *Last Great*, p. 197.
121 Benamou, *Déraisonnable*, p. 218.
122 Robert Gildea, *Fighters in the Shadows: A New History of the French Resistance* (London: Faber, 2015), p. 252; Lacouture, *De Gaulle* I, p. 613; George F. Howe, *United States Army in World War II: The Mediterranean Theatre of Operations, Northwest Africa, Seizing the Initiative in the West* (Washington DC: Office of the Chief of Military History, 1957), pp. 81, 92–5, 172–3, 188–9, 249–50, 262–6, https://history.army.mil/html/books/006/6-1-1/CMH_Pub_6-1-1.pdf, accessed 18 February 2019.
123 Kersaudy, *Churchill and de Gaulle*, p. 217.
124 *DM*I, pp. 231–2, 233–40.
125 Howe, *Mediterranean Theatre*, p. 267.
126 Crémieux-Brilhac, *France Libre*, p. 35.

Further reading

The following material is in addition to that listed for Chapter 2.

Julian Jackson, *A Certain Idea of France* (London: Allen Lane, 2018), chapters 6–10, covers de Gaulle 1940–1942.

René Cassin, *Les Hommes partis de rien: le réveil de la France abattue (1940–1941)* (Paris: Plon, 1975) is an excellent inside story of the beginnings of Free France.

A.B. Gaunson, *The Anglo-French Clash in Lebanon and Syria, 1940–1945* (London: Macmillan, 1987) is the key book on the Syrian crises. Colin Smith, *England's Last War against France: Fighting Vichy, 1940–1942* (London: Weidenfeld & Nicolson, 2009) is also useful, while Sir Edward Spears, *Fulfilment of a Mission: Syria and Lebanon, 1941–1944* (London: Seeley, Service and Cooper, 1977) is a revealing, though partisan, first-hand account.

Georges-Marc Benamou, *C'était un temps déraisonnable. Les premiers résistants racontent* (Paris: Robert Laffont, 1999) is an excellent book of interviews with surviving Resistance heroes.

4 Towards a provisional government, 1942–1944

In November 1942, as in June 1940, de Gaulle aimed both to rid France and its empire of the Germans and Vichy and to restore France's great-power status. He would do so by pursuing his virtuous circle, taking the leadership of the Resistance to reinforce his position with the Allies, thereby winning control of territory, and in turn reinforcing his primacy over the Resistance. But the two years between the Operation Torch landings and the Allies' recognition of de Gaulle's provisional government, on 23 October 1944, were strewn with obstacles; for his partners were also competitors, and not all wished him to succeed.

Two processes advanced de Gaulle's undertaking in 1942–1943. Moulin's work with the Resistance bore fruit in the creation of the National Resistance Council (Conseil National de la Résistance – CNR) in May 1943. In parallel went a year-long battle with Giraud and with the Allies for control of French North Africa. In June 1943, de Gaulle joined Giraud in the new Algiers-based French Committee of National Liberation; by mid-November he had eliminated Giraud from it. Controlling French North Africa brought the same benefits – territory, an independent base, and troops – as control of other colonies, but on a larger scale. It was also indispensable to any claim to lead the French forces opposed to the Axis.

From late 1943, the main focus shifted to the future of mainland France after its liberation. A symbol of this was the transfer in December of General Eisenhower from his post of Supreme Allied Commander in the Mediterranean to London, where he would head preparations for the Normandy landings at SHAEF, the Supreme Headquarters Allied Expeditionary Force. De Gaulle therefore needed to ensure his primacy in France itself. To do so, he built the apparatus of a state capable of taking power from the moment of liberation, forestalling possible bids by the Americans or by an internal Resistance in which Communists were increasingly influential.

Darlan in Algiers: the 'temporary expedient'

On 22 November 1942 the Americans recognised Admiral François Darlan as High Commissioner in North Africa. Darlan had, after all, neutralised Vichy troops there by ordering a cease-fire, saving American lives. But the appointment shocked public opinion in France, Britain, and the United States; just seven months earlier, as the Vichy regime's head of government, Darlan had been collaborating actively with Nazi Germany.[1]

Both Churchill and Roosevelt initially tried to conciliate a shocked de Gaulle. The President publicly referred to Darlan as a 'temporary expedient'.[2] But when de Gaulle issued a communiqué dissociating the CNF from negotiations underway in North Africa, the Allies' attitude hardened. His broadcast of 21 November, underlining the gap between the Allies' democratic ideals and the grubby arrangements concocted in Algiers, went out from Beirut and Brazzaville, but was banned from the BBC along with other Free French messages.[3] To André Philip, who visited the White House on 20 November with a message from de Gaulle intended to smooth out their differences, and who unwisely attempted to harangue the President for his actions, Roosevelt replied that 'The important thing is to get to Berlin, nothing else matters. If Darlan gives me Algiers, long live Darlan! If Laval gives me Paris, long live Laval!'[4] On 4 December, de Gaulle talked to the Soviet ambassador Ivan Maisky in London about moving his headquarters to Moscow. He drew a very guarded Soviet response, but antagonised Churchill, who attacked de Gaulle in a secret session of the Commons.[5] Rebuffed by all three Allies and close to despair, de Gaulle wondered, to his British liaison officer Charles Peake on 18 December, whether Free France had any purpose if Allied policy was to use collaborators with Nazi Germany to further its aims.[6]

Darlan, meanwhile, issued decrees in Pétain's name, maintained Vichy legislation, including anti-Semitic measures, created a council of Vichy colonial governors, made Giraud his Commander-in-Chief, and kept some 25,000 French and foreign anti-fascists in prisons and camps. His announcement, on 16 December, of his regime's imminent liberalisation reflected American pressure, but also an expectation of becoming a permanent, not a temporary, expedient.[7]

Darlan was also lax about his personal security. It was therefore easy for a 22-year-old French nationalist, Fernand Bonnier de La Chapelle, to walk into the Algiers Summer Palace and shoot him there on Christmas Eve. Bonnier had been in Aboulker's teams on 8 November. He had met François d'Astier de la Vigerie, the emissary de Gaulle had sent to Algiers with $40,000 to reinforce the Gaullist presence there; he was even carrying $2,000 of d'Astier's money when, after assassinating Darlan, he was arrested.[8] But while Gaullists were certainly part of Bonnier's conspiracy, de Gaulle's personal involvement is unlikely: alive, Darlan was repulsive enough to act as a recruiting agent for Gaullism.[9] Bonnier, in any case, got no chance to talk. Having expected a hero's treatment for his act, he was given the most summary of trials and shot at dawn on 26 December.[10] The full truth around the assassination has never been elucidated.

Its main beneficiaries, however, were the Americans, and General Giraud. Darlan had served his purpose; his death removed an embarrassment. And on the insistence of Roosevelt's envoy Robert Murphy – which no one in Algiers was powerful enough to resist – it was Giraud who replaced him.[11] De Gaulle knew Giraud, who had been military commander of Metz during his pre-war period as a tank colonel there. On Giraud's escape from Königstein in April 1942, de Gaulle considered making him supreme commander of Free French forces.[12] On the other hand Giraud, on his own admission, was 'perfectly incompetent in politics'[13] – a positive point for the Americans, who wanted a figurehead not a leader, but not for Free France.

Giraud was as anti-democratic, and as anti-Semitic, as Vichy. As a condition of residing as an escapee in France's southern zone in 1942, he had signed an undertaking to Pétain not to harm the Vichy regime or its relations with Germany.[14] In Algiers in the last days of 1942, he used an alleged plot against himself to arrest leading Gaullists; only René Capitant, a law professor at Algiers University, escaped. Officers who had opposed Torch, by contrast, were decorated.[15] Darlan's Vichyite policies were maintained. This lamentable record was de Gaulle's opening to get into the North African game, just in time for a Churchill–Roosevelt summit in January 1943.

Resisting the Allies: Anfa, January 1943

De Gaulle had been sidelined in North Africa because the Americans preferred Giraud and the Gaullists were weak on the ground. Sending the tactless Philip to Roosevelt, and courting the Soviets, had also damaged his case. But there had been no rages, no foolish press interviews, as in the Levant. On 14 December 1942, days after Churchill's hostile speech to the Commons, de Gaulle had praised 'the complete loyalty of our old English allies' in handing Madagascar to Free French rule.[16] He had written to Giraud suggesting a meeting; Giraud responded by arresting the Algiers Gaullists.

De Gaulle now appealed to public opinion in a declaration and two broadcasts, reasonable yet firm in their criticism of the situation in Algiers. France, he stated, needed a single authority to apply the laws of the Republic in North Africa, and united armies to wage war alongside the Allies. Giraud was a fine soldier, but no North African authority would have legitimacy without Fighting France. Meanwhile Leclerc's exploits, in crossing Libya and (on 13 January 1943) joining Montgomery's Eighth Army in Tripoli, contrasted with the 'crumbling hierarchies and sordid scheming' elsewhere. Listeners were left to infer that elsewhere meant Algiers, and to note that Giraud was *not* applying the laws of the Republic.[17]

These appeals embarrassed Roosevelt and Churchill into trying to settle de Gaulle's position once and for all. They had scheduled a wide-ranging strategic conference, at Anfa, a luxurious suburb of Casablanca, from 14 to 24 January. Roosevelt invited Giraud. Churchill summoned de Gaulle on 16 January.[18]

De Gaulle detested receiving an Anglo-American convocation to a meeting on French territory. But as moderates on the CNF argued, he could hardly refuse. Arriving in Casablanca early on 22 January, he was driven in an American staff car with mudded-out windows to a villa surrounded by barbed wire and American soldiers, treatment he viewed as 'a flagrant insult'.[19] Over the next 48 hours, de Gaulle had two inconclusive encounters with Giraud, two affable meetings with Roosevelt (the two men disliked one another but never rowed), two shouting-matches with Churchill, and two conversations with Murphy and with Harold Macmillan, appointed British Minister Resident in Algiers in December. The efforts of these two intermediaries narrowly achieved a minimal communiqué, reporting 'complete agreement as to the aim to be achieved – the liberation of France and the triumph of democratic principles through the total defeat of the enemy'. And on 24 January, the General and the President gathered with Churchill, Giraud and their staffs and de Gaulle shook hands with Giraud for Roosevelt and for the cameras.[20]

But Anfa left two key issues unresolved. The first was a possible Gaullist–Giraudist merger. Churchill, backed by Roosevelt, proposed that Giraud and de Gaulle should jointly head a North African governing committee including two Vichy governors (Noguès and Boisson), two former Vichy ministers, and General Alphonse Georges, a friend of Churchill recently arrived from mainland France. Giraud would command French forces in North Africa. But de Gaulle refused to join an administration stuffed with Vichyites. Giraud, he insisted, should disavow Vichy and the 1940 armistice, and serve only as Commander-in-Chief of France's armies; his undertakings to Pétain had disqualified him as a political leader. Neither Murphy nor Macmillan could bridge the gap. De Gaulle's refusal to budge left Roosevelt disappointed and Churchill enraged.[21]

The second unresolved issue was the representativeness of Fighting France. For Roosevelt, the Allies held France in 'trusteeship' and could not hand power to any contender for it until post-war elections had been held.[22] For de Gaulle 'the national will had already made its choice' – Fighting France.[23] Each case was overstated. Roosevelt *was* willing to hand power in North Africa to any group or individual acceptable to him. De Gaulle's claim that the French had chosen Fighting France was really work in progress; hence the missions given to Moulin, Passy, and Brossolette after his return to London.

Anfa was also important for the damage it did to trust between the major protagonists. Churchill felt betrayed by de Gaulle's refusal to accept the 'compromise' offered him.[24] De Gaulle, meanwhile, knew that Roosevelt had discussed Moroccan independence over dinner with the French Resident, Noguès, and the Sultan, Mohammed V; and Murphy had shown him a text committing Americans and British to backing Giraud as commander of *all* French forces fighting Germany, with the 'right and duty' to represent all French interests in North Africa.[25] He left Anfa convinced that the Americans sought to establish their own puppet governments throughout French territory, and that Roosevelt therefore threatened France's independence and great-power status.[26]

Finally, Anfa revealed much about the power relations between the protagonists. De Gaulle believed that Giraud had little *personal* political following and was stuck, even as a soldier, in 1939, but also knew that he could not break with Giraud without alienating the Allies. Hence his willingness to sign a minimal communiqué and to shake hands for the cameras.[27] Churchill, for his part, had the opportunity at Anfa to abandon Fighting France altogether in Giraud's favour, but did not take it: presented with the Roosevelt–Murphy text which Murphy had shown de Gaulle, he insisted that de Gaulle's name be included. Three reasons may be suggested: a lingering admiration for de Gaulle's intransigence; Foreign Office and parliamentary support for de Gaulle; and a refusal to be taken for granted, even by the Americans.[28] Roosevelt, finally, had behaved at Anfa as if on conquered territory, and was perfectly prepared to drop de Gaulle when he withheld co-operation – but would not take sole responsibility for doing so.

So the drama between the four men would roll on for months to come. De Gaulle had stayed in the game with neither rages nor concessions, relying on the force of his personality, his commitment to democracy (excluding, like the other protagonists, North Africa's Moslem majority) and its resonance with public opinion, and the fact that he, unlike Giraud, had actually raised an army, albeit a small one, that was fighting alongside the Allies.[29] But his position remained precarious: to reinforce it, he needed stronger backing from within France.

Rallying the Resistance, 1942–1943

In January 1942 Jean Moulin had set out to unify the southern Resistance movements; to bring recognised party leaders into a Resistance structure; and to forge an alliance with the Communists. He also hoped to extend the future unified Resistance structure to the northern zone. These missions were partially accomplished by October 1942. But the Resistance movements' jealousy of their own independence, and deep suspicion of political parties, remained significant obstacles. So was the effective abolition of the 'free' zone: on 11 November 1942, German and Italian troops occupied southern France in response to Operation Torch. But Torch, and the Allies' near-elimination of de Gaulle from their North African plans, also made consolidating Gaullist support in metropolitan France all the more urgent.

The merger of Combat, Franc-Tireur, and Libération into the Mouvements Unis de la Résistance (MUR), prefigured by the October 1942 co-ordinating committee, was finally agreed late in January 1943, after much haggling about money.[30] The movements would pool military resources into an *Armée Secrète*, while still publishing separate clandestine journals. Progress was also made with the PCF: Fernand Grenier, a PCF Central Committee member, was brought to London in January 1943. Having praised de Gaulle warmly on the BBC, Grenier became an adviser to the CNF's Interior Commissioner.[31]

Moulin himself reached London, after living 13 months undercover in France, on 15 February 1943, along with General Delestraint, newly appointed commander of the *Armée Secrète*. He now undertook with de Gaulle to create a nationwide Resistance Council including party representatives, starting with Socialists and Communists, and an executive to direct clandestine action. Appointed de Gaulle's sole representative for both northern and southern zones, Moulin returned for his last mission to France on 30 March.[32] De Gaulle's broadcast of 12 March, urging unity of the Resistance under Free French leadership, primed his efforts.[33]

Bringing the northern Resistance together was left to Brossolette and Passy. Over six weeks in France from 26 February 1943, they produced an inventory of Resistance networks, created two central organisations for intelligence, and set up a Co-Ordinating Committee for the northern zone, including Ceux de la Libération and Ceux de la Résistance, the Organisation Civile et Militaire, Libération-Nord, and the Communist-based Front National and Francs-Tireurs et Partisans (FTP). Brossolette secured these movements' support for de Gaulle and the CNF, but dragged his feet over the inclusion of parties in Resistance representation, which he opposed. This issue led to a fierce clash with Moulin, who reached Paris on

31 March. Moulin's seniority as de Gaulle's delegate prevailed, and on 12 April he and Delestraint chaired a first meeting of the Co-Ordinating Committee for the North.[34]

Increased cohesion enhanced the Resistance's attraction for the Allies. Senior Allied officers received Moulin and Delestraint to discuss sabotage operations prior to a future Allied landing in France. Both the nascent American secret services and Admiral Harold Stark, commander of US naval forces in Europe, now viewed Fighting France more favourably than did the Roosevelt administration. But little concrete help, aside from 3 million francs for the MUR from the US Office of Strategic Services, followed, and especially no big arms drops: Yugoslavia had priority for these.[35]

Moulin's greatest achievement, however, was the CNR's creation in May 1943. This crowned six weeks of negotiations by Moulin with Resistance movements still deeply suspicious of what they saw as his dictatorial methods. De Gaulle had had to make significant concessions, for example leaving operational control of the *Armée Secrète* with local leaders.[36] Moulin had to overcome Resistance misgivings about including political parties, and sometimes poisonous personal relations – for example, between himself and Brossolette and between Frenay and d'Astier de la Vigerie.[37] His assets were authority, both personal and as de Gaulle's delegate, and the power of the purse.[38] The CNR finally assembled on 27 May, at 48, rue du Four in Paris, for the first of only two plenary meetings in wartime. Present were Moulin and two assistants, plus representatives from eight Resistance organisations (three from the south, four from the north, plus the Communist-led Front National); from the two main trade union confederations; and from the six main Third Republic parties (Communists, Socialists, Radicals, Christian Democrats, and two conservative parties). All backed a resolution calling for a provisional government of France under de Gaulle.[39] De Gaulle concluded that the CNR was his to command – optimistically, as the ensuing months would show. But the meeting greatly strengthened his hand in relation to the Allies – and to his rival Giraud.

De Gaulle vs. Giraud (1): duel at a distance, January–May 1943

After Anfa, it took four months of negotiations before de Gaulle and Giraud formed a joint French authority for North Africa. With de Gaulle confined to London, this was a duel at a distance. Intermediaries, more conciliatory than the two principals, engineered the final compromise: on Giraud's side, Murphy but also Jean Monnet (officially in Algiers simply to organise the re-equipment of Giraud's North African army); on de Gaulle's, Catroux, head of the Fighting French mission to Algiers from February. Macmillan broadly backed de Gaulle, to whom, with Catroux, he counselled patience. In any confrontation, they warned, the Americans would back Giraud to the hilt. But Giraud's following in Algiers, they added, was draining away; de Gaulle need only wait, then accept a compromise merger, and finally manoeuvre himself into a dominant position. This was roughly what happened.[40]

On 23 February 1943, the CNF wrote to Giraud demanding that any merged authority in North Africa should reject both the armistice and Vichy ideology, personnel, and organisations. It should have 'all the attributes of a government', and be underpinned by a consultative assembly representing the Resistance, until full democracy could be restored in liberated France.[41] Macmillan and Monnet soon gave Giraud a nudge towards the CNF position, drafting a speech, which Giraud gave on 14 March, denouncing Vichy and praising the Resistance and the Republic.[42] Here, in principle, were the premises of an agreement.

But the practice of Giraud's administration in North Africa was far removed from his newly discovered democratic principles. Unrepentant Vichy figures – Boisson, Noguès, and former Interior Minister Marcel Peyrouton – remained on North Africa's governing council; Giraud refused to reverse Vichy legislation depriving Algerian Jews of French citizenship; and he planned to remain civil and military Commander-in-Chief in a merged North African administration.[43] De Gaulle made two devastating attacks on this record, at a press conference on 9 February and a speech on 4 May, highlighting the reality of 15,000 people imprisoned for anti-Vichy activities, anti-Semitic and anti-democratic legislation still in force, and ubiquitous portraits of Pétain. Giraud's administration had no legitimate base, he added, whereas Fighting France was committed to the 'laws and the spirit of the Republic' and United Nations principles.[44]

Right but brutal, de Gaulle was kept in London, by common agreement between the British, Catroux, and Eisenhower, for fear that his arrival in Algiers would derail Giraud's slow rapprochement with Free France.[45] In May, after Giraud had finally proposed a meeting at Biskra, a small, quiet town in eastern Algeria, it was de Gaulle who held back: counting on the support of local (white) public opinion, he would leave London for Algiers – but not for Biskra.[46]

Then, as de Gaulle was probably expecting, a trump card arrived from mainland France.[47] A telegram from Moulin, dated 15 May, stated the support of the nascent CNR for an Algiers-based provisional government under de Gaulle, with Giraud as military Commander-in-Chief; de Gaulle, Moulin added, would remain the chief of the Resistance whatever happened.[48] Within two days, Giraud sent de Gaulle proposals for a merged authority, drafted by Monnet, Murphy, and Macmillan. It would be governed by an executive committee, chaired by de Gaulle and Giraud in turns; each general would appoint two committee members; three other posts would be filled later; members would accept collective responsibility. The committee would relinquish power at the Liberation of France, when the Republic would be restored under procedures set out in a law of 1872.[49]

Was Giraud's proposal a response to the CNR's endorsement of de Gaulle, which the Fighting French hastened to publicise?[50] A more important factor was probably troops. Some 75,000 'Giraudist' North African soldiers, against 13,000 Free French, paraded through liberated Tunis on 20 May. But Giraud's men had joined the battle late, while Leclerc's and Larminat's had covered themselves with glory; their prestige, indeed, had led men from Giraudist units to defect to them.[51] To obtain the equipment to make his armed forces battle-ready, from the Americans via Monnet, Giraud was prepared to accept the (considerable) political concessions the Allies required in the name of a workable compromise.[52]

American behaviour in May 1943, however, was inconsistent. As Murphy helped plan the unified North African authority, his President, meeting Churchill in Washington, was seeking a complete break with de Gaulle.[53] Churchill wrote to Britain's War Cabinet to support this line on 21 May. Foreign Secretary Eden, however, opposed Roosevelt's views on France.[54] And in the light of Giraud's letter of four days earlier, the British War Cabinet turned Churchill down, considering a break 'extremely difficult'. Perhaps Churchill expected this outcome, and was going through the motions for the President.[55]

Unaware of these manoeuvres, de Gaulle flew to Algiers, where Giraud greeted him on 30 May with a guard of honour – a striking improvement on his earlier welcome at Casablanca.[56] But the de Gaulle–Giraud confrontation was about to enter its most brutal phase.

De Gaulle vs. Giraud (2): duel in Algiers, June–November 1943

Within five-and-a-half months of his arrival in Algiers, de Gaulle had stripped Giraud of all substantive responsibilities. Having started, with Giraud, as co-president of the merged authority, known from 3 June as the French National Liberation Committee (Comité Français de la Libération Nationale, CFLN), he had become its sole chief by mid-November.

In this tortuous process, de Gaulle's main advantage lay in Giraud's own multiple failings. Giraud's habit of signing papers without reading them helped.[57] More broadly, his political ineptness and vacillation exasperated Macmillan, and even Murphy. His inability to grasp the realities of equipping a modern, mechanised army irritated Eisenhower and Monnet. So the key Allied representatives in Algiers turned Gaullist by default, and cushioned de Gaulle against the hostility of President and Prime Minister (Churchill's last attempt to drop de Gaulle was rejected by the War Cabinet in June). Giraud also failed to keep a grip on his own French supporters. The three key Vichyite governors on his former governing council had all resigned their posts by the end of June: Marcel Peyrouton as Governor-General of Algeria, Charles Noguès as Resident-General in Morocco, and Pierre Boisson as Governor-General of AOF. All were replaced by Gaullists. Two key CFLN members who started in Giraud's camp left it: Maurice Couve de Murville (a former senior financial official in Vichy) in June, and General Georges by November.

Nor did Giraud's excursions outside Algiers promote his cause. He spent July 1943 in North America, where he failed to attend any 14 July celebrations, basked in Roosevelt's praise, even when the President stated that 'for the moment France no longer exists', and told an audience in Ottawa that there were 'good things' about

National Socialism in Germany.[58] De Gaulle, meanwhile, officiated at grand 14 July ceremonies in Algiers, and appointed his own supporters to key posts.[59] In mid-September, Giraud left for Corsica, where he had despatched troops in support of a rising against the occupying Italian and German forces (Italy had surrendered to the Allies on 3 September). The island was liberated by 4 October, but the military success brought a political backlash. Giraud had not sought CFLN approval for the operation, and had effectively handed Corsica to the Communists who dominated the local Resistance: Charles Luizet, installed by de Gaulle as prefect, took two months to settle his authority over them.[60]

De Gaulle's main aim was to confine Giraud to his military command, incompatible in his view with his functions as CFLN co-president, and to subordinate the military to the CFLN's political leadership – in effect, to himself. When he tried to do this frontally, however, he failed. In June he actually resigned from the CFLN when it rejected his proposal that Giraud should drop one of his two posts, as co-president or Commander-in-Chief; only the intervention of Macmillan and Murphy stopped Giraud and Georges from accepting the resignation, and de Gaulle was reinstated. Similarly, on 18 September de Gaulle proposed a single, elected presidency for the CFLN, which he was confident of winning. But the CFLN rejected major institutional change in the middle of the Corsican operation.

De Gaulle was far more effective when he deployed hitherto untapped skills of political manoeuvre to squeeze Giraud out by slow, incremental institutional changes. In an agreement sanctioned by Macmillan and Monnet in June, the supreme command of French forces was divided, with Giraud in charge of North Africa and de Gaulle of other forces. And, crucially, a CFLN military committee was created, including the Commander-in-Chief and three service heads – but chaired by de Gaulle.[61] After Giraud's return from America, de Gaulle ensured that his rival would only chair those CFLN meetings devoted to military questions. As Commander-in-Chief, moreover, Giraud now had three Gaullists as assistant Chiefs of Staff, and the army staff was explicitly subordinated to the CFLN, which would 'assure the general conduct of the war'; and this function was effectively delegated to the National Defence Committee – under de Gaulle.[62]

The final blow to Giraud came when the CFLN's new Consultative Assembly convened for its inaugural session on 3 November. Mooted in London in 1941, agreed in principle during the spring 1943 negotiations, its composition fixed in September, the Assembly included 20 Deputies who had refused to vote full powers to Pétain in 1940, 12 local councillors from liberated areas, and 12 delegates from the external and 40 from the internal Resistance – the latter flown in secretly from mainland France.[63] De Gaulle used the shake-up caused by the Consultative Assembly's creation to propose the CFLN's full renewal, and Giraud carelessly agreed. When the revamped body was announced, neither Giraud nor Georges was on it.[64] Giraud continued as a largely impotent Commander-in-Chief until 8 April 1944, when he was told that his post had been abolished.[65]

De Gaulle grounded his victory in the year-long struggle with Giraud on his certainty, often tested to breaking-point, that in the end the Allies would not abandon him. He already believed this at Anfa; the CNR's declared support strengthened his position. This enabled him to deploy, against a rival whom he outclassed at every turn, considerable personal qualities: inflexibility, clarity of goals, a clear identification with the ideals for which Resistance, Fighting France, and the Allies were fighting, and a newly revealed talent for base, opportunistic, political manoeuvre. By 9 November he had become the undisputed head of the CFLN. But this, as he was well aware, was not the same as a head of state.

Building a state-in-waiting

Max Weber famously defined, as the essential attribute of a state, the 'monopoly of the legitimate use of physical force within a given territory'.[66] The CFLN had no hope of meeting this criterion. Split between London and Algiers, it had no control over metropolitan France; in several colonial territories it shared the 'monopoly' of force with the Allies. But a strong state was essential to de Gaulle's aim of restoring France's great-power status. The Americans, he believed, favoured a weak French state under their influence; the Communists, he suspected, sought to take power from below as France was liberated. Against both dangers, he needed his own state-like apparatus to be ready. So he attempted five things: to build 'regalian' state-like attributes, especially armed forces; to reinforce the CFLN's political legitimacy; to absorb and neutralise the Communists; to develop cadres ready to govern future liberated territory; and to reinforce and renovate France's imperial role. Both developing policies and choosing people, however, demanded a difficult balance between ambitions for renewal and the realities of a war that inhibited swift reform and required the re-employment of competent former Vichyites. For de Gaulle himself, disappointment at the behaviour of France's elites in 1940 had not effaced a continuing respect for established institutions and hierarchies.

Thirty-seven governments recognised the CFLN by December 1943, all requiring diplomatic representation. The CFLN's diplomatic service was the achievement of René Massigli, from February 1943 Commissioner for Foreign Affairs, who built a proper ministry from Giraud's skeletal establishment and bridged the divided loyalties of France's diplomats across the globe.[67] Diplomacy was a necessary regalian attribute, but for de Gaulle France's great-power status required, above all, a contribution to the Allies' military victory. Hence the importance of merging, equipping, and augmenting the Fighting French and the North African armies. The merger was fraught with tensions. Men who left the 'Giraudist' North African units for the Fighting French were treated as deserters by their former officers; two separate army staffs cohabited in Algiers till August 1943; de Gaulle purged some 1,100 officers with strong Vichy links; regular North African officers resented their swiftly-promoted Free French counterparts.[68] The confusion led the Allies to exclude both armies from the invasion of Sicily in July 1943.[69] In addition, the French had difficulty training with the newly available American equipment, and configuring divisions to include the necessary support personnel, along the lines of modern American units. French divisions therefore took months to become operational – yet only after shared combat experience would the armed forces merger 'take' fully.

Meanwhile the numbers rose. France had 75,000 'Giraudist' and 13,000 Fighting French troops in Tunis in May 1943, but 300,000 troops in North Africa by 26 August, and 400,000 by mid-autumn. General Alphonse Juin, de Gaulle's former Saint-Cyr comrade, who had stayed with Vichy's North African army, led 110,000 men into Italy from September 1943. Their fighting record would reinforce the CFLN's legitimacy with the Allies.[70] By August 1944, General de Lattre de Tassigny could land 250,000 men in Provence. In the war's last winter, the French army in Europe, complemented by mainland French troops but still one-half African-recruited, numbered a million.

De Gaulle also aimed to reinforce the CFLN's civilian legitimacy. Since 1941 he had stressed the restoration of 'republican legality' in liberated territories. So in Algeria, elected local authorities reassembled; Jews regained their citizenship and goods, both confiscated under Vichy; sacked civil servants were reinstated, political prisoners released, and freedom of the press and of assembly revived. De Gaulle might tolerate rather than celebrate press freedom, but his regime was vastly more liberal than Giraud's.[71] Meanwhile the new Consultative Assembly gave the CFLN the best parliament available without elections. Party chiefs did, it is true, manoeuvre inexperienced Resistance leaders into subordinate positions; Félix Gouin, a Socialist politician, became the Assembly's President.[72] But while the CFLN was not formally responsible to it, the Assembly debated widely and affected policy, for example in outlining the transitional regime and social reforms to be undertaken at the Liberation. This had a positive impact on British opinion.[73] And de Gaulle took the Assembly seriously enough to address it 20 times.[74]

His discourse changed during the year in Algiers, partially undoing the left turn of 1941–1942. Out went revolution and insurrection, at a time when much of the internal Resistance aspired to both; in came 'renewal', but also order and the state.[75] Renewal was central, for example, in de Gaulle's speech opening the Consultative Assembly on 3 November 1943, and again at Constantine on 12 December.[76] It meant an ambition, beyond simple 'republican legality', for wide-ranging social reform, dignity, and decent living standards for all.[77] But along with renewal went an insistence on order and a strong state. On 18 March 1944 he warned, in highly Weberian terms, that 'Nothing can be done without order ... there must not be, let me state this with some force, any other public authority than that which proceeds from the responsible authorities at the centre' and that the future government would need 'the strength and the stability required to ensure the authority of the state and France's greatness in the world'.[78] Authority of the state, national grandeur, and national renewal: these themes were the heart of what would become known as Gaullism. But he was also, in March 1944, telling the Americans that he could prevent social unrest, while simultaneously warning off the PCF.

De Gaulle found the PCF a useful bogeyman: only he, he told the Americans, or Macmillan, or ex-Vichyites in Algiers, could face down the Red Peril in liberated France.[79] He deliberately exaggerated this threat, both then and in his *War Memoirs*: in fact, he believed that Stalin was counting on *him* to limit British and American influence in post-war Europe, and would therefore restrain the PCF.[80] Hence his pointed references, designed to reassure the Kremlin of his independence from the Western Allies, to 'our dear and powerful Russia', our 'natural ally' (Ajaccio, 8 October 1943) or a 'permanent ally' (Tunis, 7 May 1944).[81] He almost certainly exaggerated his, and France's, importance to the Soviets; but they still preferred him to Giraud.[82]

Whatever Stalin's attitude, within France de Gaulle still faced a palpable Communist challenge. The PCF aimed to accrue power through its front organisations, the (political) Front National and the (military) FTP, but also by dominating organisations of the unified Resistance like the CNR's Military Action Committee, by gaining footholds in the CFLN, and by controlling newly liberated localities: in Corsica, notably, Communists won control of newly revived local authorities by a show of hands at mass meetings. Meanwhile André Marty, the PCF delegate sent (from Moscow) to join the Consultative Assembly, was thoroughly hostile to de Gaulle.[83]

To meet the challenge, de Gaulle had agreed with Moulin to try and draw the PCF into a unified Resistance movement under his leadership. This now meant bringing Communists into the CFLN – but de Gaulle insisted on choosing which ones. The PCF's equal insistence on its own right of appointment produced a six-month stand-off.[84] Only in March 1944, under Moscow's orders, did the Party agree to de Gaulle's nominees, François Billoux and Fernand Grenier, joining the CFLN as Commissioners on 4 April.[85]

But the power struggle would continue for the rest of 1944. It centred on how the state would reappear in liberated France. The PCF's vision, based on its own grass-roots organisational strength, was bottom-up: 'patriotic delegations', elected in each locality (as in Corsica) by a show of hands, would send representatives to assemblies in France's 90 *départements*, which in turn would choose a national delegation. By contrast, de Gaulle's project, voted by the CFLN and the Assembly in April 1944, was top-down. The CFLN would govern from Paris, assisted by a reinforced Consultative Assembly; elections, with women voting for the first time, would be held within a year of the liberation of French territory. On the ground, CFLN-appointed *Commissaires de la République* would replace Vichy officials in each *département*: de Gaulle's former Chief of Staff Claude Bouchinet-Serreulles set to work secretly in Paris with the young civil servant Michel Debré to identify nominees for these key posts.[86] They would be assisted (a concession to the Resistance) by Liberation Committees, local versions of the CFLN representing the same groupings.[87] De Gaulle also instructed each member of the CFLN to list Vichy laws and decrees to be repealed, and to prepare substitute legislation where necessary.[88]

By May 1944, de Gaulle and the CFLN therefore had a clear plan for returning democracy to mainland France. Their imperial project, by contrast, was more equivocal. Fighting a war for freedom and democracy faced Britain and France with an awkward question: did these ideals apply to their millions of imperial subjects? The most optimistic answer was 'Not yet'. Everything was subordinate to the war effort: so exploitation was stepped up in British and French African colonies. De Gaulle himself understood both the anti-colonial impulses engendered by the war and his American allies' hostility to old-style imperialism. But as Vichy accused him of handing over France's Empire to the Allies, he was correspondingly determined to keep it in French hands for the duration.[89] Liberal rhetoric consequently coexisted with repressive policy – a combination which would outlast the conflict.

Days after Giraud's removal from the CFLN, a third Levant crisis arose. Elections had finally been held there in August 1943 – by which time the liberal Catroux, appointed Governor-General of Algeria, had been replaced by Jean Helleu. The elections returned strongly nationalist majorities (blamed by de Gaulle on Spears's meddling) in both Syria and Lebanon. The new Lebanese Prime Minister, Riad Solh, backed by his Parliament and by Spears, initiated a plan to abolish the French mandate, deleting references to it from Lebanon's Constitution.[90] Helleu responded, on the night of 10–11 November, by arresting Lebanon's President and Cabinet and

Towards a provisional government, 1942–1944

suspending the Constitution. De Gaulle telegraphed his support for Helleu two days later.[91] Civil unrest flared across Lebanon; French and colonial forces fired into the crowds, causing some 20 deaths and 60 injuries. A general strike followed.[92]

Old Anglo-French differences immediately resurfaced. The Foreign Office threatened a British military takeover unless the ministers were reinstated; de Gaulle threatened to resign if the British imposed a settlement.[93] In the short term, however, conciliation won. Macmillan showed the British ultimatum to Massigli, but only informally; Massigli successfully persuaded the CFLN to recall Helleu to Algiers and release the ministers; and Spears was told to allow the mandate to stand.[94] By the end of 1943, therefore, France's soldiers and officials were still in the Levant – but with their anti-British resentments intensified.[95] They would boil over again in 1945.

The record in North Africa was no better. In the protectorate of Morocco, a nationalist party, the Istiqlal, was founded on 11 January 1944 with the tacit support of Sultan Mohammed V. Demonstrations ensued; Leclerc's tanks were briefly called in; estimated casualties were 42 dead and 100 wounded. In Tunisia, the titular sovereign, Moncef Bey, also sympathised with a nationalist party, the Néo-Destour. General Juin deposed the Bey in May 1943; some 10,000 largely indiscriminate arrests and a handful of death sentences followed.[96]

But the major problem was Algeria, unlike Tunisia and Morocco considered a part of France, but where only white settlers, plus Jews under the Republic, enjoyed citizenship rights. An established nationalist movement, Ferhat Abbas's Parti du Peuple Algérien, had published an independence manifesto in February 1943. De Gaulle had recognised the need for greater social justice in Algeria at Constantine on 12 December 1943.[97] He encouraged Catroux, as Governor-General from June, to propose granting full French citizenship to 128,000 educated Moslems (out of a total Moslem population of 8 million). They would vote at national and local elections in an electoral college alongside some 200,000 white voters. A second college, electing the same number of parliamentarians, would represent the rest of the Moslem majority. The CFLN was more cautious: under the *ordonnance* (decree) of 7 March 1944, just 70,000 Moslems received citizenship. Modest in strictly political terms, the reform also did nothing to relieve the Moslem population's chronic economic distress, and Catroux's economic development plan launched in August 1944 fell victim to budgetary constraints.[98] Even this much liberalism, moreover, provoked a white settlers' backlash. Within a decade, Algeria's divisions would turn to war.

Yet in Gaullist mythology, de Gaulle's wartime record appears as the start of a benign process of decolonisation culminating in Algerian independence in 1962.[99] The symbol of this was the conference of colonial governors held in Brazzaville from 30 January to 8 February 1944, and especially the liberal passages in de Gaulle's opening speech. He did indeed declare that progress in colonies should benefit colonised peoples and raise them 'to the level where they will be capable of taking part in the management of their own affairs'.[100] But the first half of the speech was a celebration of France's 'civilising mission' in the colonies, and the potential of Brazzaville to deliver change was tightly limited. The 21 conference delegates were all appointed governors; the only black face was that of Félix Éboué, de Gaulle's Governor-General of AEF; and they 'represented' only the formal colonies of sub-Saharan Africa, Madagascar, and La Réunion. Algeria was excluded as 'French' territory, Tunisia and Morocco as protectorates, Indochina as still under Vichy rule, Syria and Lebanon as technically independent states. The conference's conclusion explicitly rejected any 'eventual establishment of *self governments* in the colonies, even in a distant future'.[101]

Brazzaville did also, it is true, make some modestly liberal recommendations. These included the abolition, at the war's end, of forced labour (but France had already signed a convention banning it, in 1930) and of the *indigénat*, the system of arbitrary colonial justice; and the inclusion of elected colonial representatives in the post-war constituent assembly, which would open a door to colonial activists like Léopold Senghor or Félix Houphouët-Boigny.[102] But Brazzaville was perhaps above all a propaganda event, designed to show Americans and others that the colonies were and would remain firmly in 'capable, and possibly liberal, French hands under de Gaulle's leadership'.[103]

In the light of post-war events, de Gaulle's imperial record appears excessively timid. But no one was undertaking major colonial reforms while the war persisted. The imperial question, indeed, highlights a wider problem: state-building in conditions of partial sovereignty and war was not easily combined with state transformation. No other government-in-exile, however, had what de Gaulle had by autumn 1943: a clear territorial base, an administration, an assembly resembling a parliament and significant if partial international recognition. From autumn 1943, indeed, de Gaulle began to speak of the CFLN as the Provisional Government and Macmillan to call it 'virtually a French Government'.[104] But not everyone was so sure.

Competing legitimacies: de Gaulle and the Resistance, 1943–1944

Never was the relationship between Fighting France and the internal Resistance closer than when the CNR pledged its support to de Gaulle on 27 May 1943. It loosened in the following months, for two reasons. First, vital intermediaries were captured. General Delestraint, head of the *Armée Secrète*, was taken on 9 June 1943; Moulin and six other Resistance leaders on 21 June.[105] Moulin died following torture on 8 July; Delestraint in Dachau in 1945. From 1 September, Moulin's role as de Gaulle's delegate passed to Émile Bollaert, a former prefect like Moulin but without his charisma.[106] In February 1944, however, both Bollaert and Pierre Brossolette, who had accompanied him to France as a mentor, were themselves captured: Brossolette committed suicide at the Gestapo's Paris headquarters on 22 March, and Bollaert ended the war in a German camp. Jacques Bingen, de Gaulle's delegate for the southern zone, swallowed a cyanide pill after being cornered by the Gestapo near Clermont-Ferrand in May 1944. These terrifying losses were compounded, at least over summer 1943, by an apparent loss of attention on de Gaulle's part. He delayed replacing Moulin, allowing the CNR, without consulting him, to elect as its new president Georges Bidault, a Christian Democratic journalist. Henceforth, therefore, Moulin's twin roles of de Gaulle's delegate-general in France and CNR president were separated. The internal and external Resistance maintained multiple and close links, but not as the fully integrated organisation de Gaulle and Moulin had sought. Douglas Porch, indeed, suggests that the Resistance was simply less important for de Gaulle once it had publicly stated its support for him.[107] The CFLN occupied most of his energies from June 1943;[108] and the Consultative Assembly, which included five times as many members, from parties and Resistance movements, as the CNR, and could debate freely in Algiers, was now a surer source of legitimacy.

The Resistance grew fast in 1943–1944, but largely independently of the CFLN and its emissaries. Resistance papers tripled their readership, and more, in 1943, several exceeding 100,000; *Armée Secrète* numbers ran to the tens of thousands;[109] acts of sabotage multiplied, as did assassinations of German soldiers and of their paramilitary accomplices in the Vichy *Milice*.[110] Meanwhile men avoiding compulsory labour in Germany took to the French countryside – the *maquis*, a (rapidly generalised) term for Corsican scrubland. There, many organised a rural Resistance. In February–March 1944, a pitched battle on the Glières plateau near Annecy pitted *maquis* forces against the *Milice* and Germans. The *maquisards*, inevitably, lost – but gave the internal Resistance an added heroic stature.[111]

The Resistance also developed specialised structures. The CNR met in plenary session only twice after May 1943, but its smaller *bureau* convened more regularly. It created a military action committee (Comité d'Action Militaire, or COMAC), a medical committee, a financial committee, and committees to subvert the Vichy administration and to fight deportations to Germany. Embryonic local Liberation Committees were set up, the biggest being the Paris Liberation Committee (CPL). In these groups Communists like Pierre Villon, the dominant figure on the COMAC, were increasingly influential. The USSR's prestige from 1943, the Communists' willingness to kill and die for the Resistance cause, and its own vigorous propaganda all earned the PCF wide recognition, even among non-Communists, as the vanguard of the Resistance, deserving a leading role in CNR bodies.[112] It was Villon, in close liaison with his party, who produced a 'Resistance Charter' which, after lengthy debates, consultations with Resistance movements, and modifications, would become the CNR's most influential single text, the Programme of 15 March 1944. This set out ambitious goals for post-war France – the restoration of civil and political liberties, the confiscation of war profits and punishment of collaborators, public ownership of major firms, economic planning, and a comprehensive social security system.[113]

But while the CFLN and the internal Resistance might develop along parallel lines, they still needed one another. To bargain with the Allies, de Gaulle still required Resistance intelligence and the promise of a secret army ready to assist the Allied landings. His vision of a revived post-war France, moreover, required that the French participate actively in their own liberation.[114] The Resistance still needed weapons (Churchill finally agreed in February 1944 to increase arms shipments to France), money, and technical assistance.

Intelligence operations relied heavily on close collaboration between the internal Resistance and Passy's Bureau Central de Renseignements et d'Action (BCRA). Intelligence networks had attained high levels of specialisation and complexity by 1943.[115] The 226 telegrams sent monthly from France to London in early 1943 had risen to 5,255 by July 1944, thanks to 200 radio operators spread across 50 centres in France.[116] In Passy's possibly exaggerated estimate, some 80% of British intelligence on France originated with Resistance and BCRA sources; even Porch acknowledges a major Resistance contribution.[117] Similarly, pre-D-Day plans for sabotage operations were co-ordinated between the BCRA and the internal Resistance, assisted by technicians sent from London.[118]

Political links also remained important despite the separation at the summit. It was Bingen who, in February 1944, brought together the armed Resistance groupings – the *Armée Secrète*, the Communist-led FTP and the army-based, and initially Giraudist, Organisation de Résistance de l'Armée (ORA) – into the Forces Françaises de l'Intérieur (FFI); Bingen, too, who created the Financial Committee, and ran the CNR *bureau* until his death. Equally, the CNR charter was not drafted in isolation: despite the Communists' role in the drafting, it was still a broadly social-democratic document, and its themes appeared in deliberations of the CFLN and the Consultative Assembly, and in de Gaulle's own speeches.

From early 1944 de Gaulle moved to reinforce the CFLN's positions within the internal Resistance. Alexandre Parodi replaced Bollaert as his delegate. He continued nominating future *Commissaires* to take over in France's regions and secretaries-general for key ministries.[119] The FFI Commander-in-Chief, in principle, was General Koenig, hero of Bir Hakeim. From April 1944, he was also CFLN delegate to Eisenhower's SHAEF. Under Koenig, within

France, was de Gaulle's national military delegate from May 1944, Jacques Chaban-Delmas, with regional delegates beneath him.[120]

In principle, therefore, a chain of command led from de Gaulle to Koenig to Chaban-Delmas to the FFI's most ragged *maquisard*. In practice, relations were looser. The CNR, the COMAC, and the FFI, Communists and non-Communists alike, might view de Gaulle as a necessary symbol of the Resistance. But they considered themselves, not the CFLN, as repositories of the 'provisional organisation of national sovereignty'.[121] Despite de Gaulle's best efforts, therefore, two legitimacies were now competing for control of post-Liberation France.

De Gaulle and the Allies, 1943–1944

Whatever his Resistance support, de Gaulle would need Allied backing to win control of liberated France – ideally by formal recognition of the CFLN as France's government-in-exile, otherwise through a 'civil affairs' agreement with Allied forces empowering the CFLN to govern liberated areas behind the front line, or, at the very least, through informal agreements with Allied military commanders.

Formal recognition was partial and insufficient, despite the efforts of Eden and others. From 26 August 1943 the United States accepted the CFLN as 'the body governing the overseas territories that recognise its authority' – leaving out metropolitan France. The (somewhat) more generous British called it 'the organisation qualified to carry forward the French war effort within the framework of Allied co-operation'. Only the Soviets treated the CFLN as 'guarantor of the interests of the French Republic' and 'sole representative of the patriots fighting Hitlerism'; but the Soviets would not be liberating France.[122] Similarly, the other 36 governments that recognised the CFLN by the year's end, though useful, counted for less than the reluctant 'Anglo-Saxons'.[123]

Nor did the Allies respond to the CFLN's proposal, dated 3 September 1943, of a civil affairs agreement. Most worrying for the French was the alternative model favoured by Roosevelt: an Allied Military Government in Occupied Territory (AMGOT), which would leave the Allied military in charge and free to work with any individuals or authorities it chose. An AMGOT would either sideline the CFLN altogether or leave its representatives dependent on Allied goodwill. One already existed in Italy, a defeated Axis power. That made the idea positively insulting to de Gaulle.

Roosevelt was, admittedly, increasingly isolated in his support for an AMGOT. Macmillan opposed it from the start; so, by late 1943, did the US State Department: 'We neither aim nor wish to govern France', wrote Cordell Hull on 9 April 1944. So did Eden, in 41 separate memos during spring 1944. Along with Canada's Prime Minister Mackenzie King, they considered an agreement with the CFLN vital to ensure Resistance support and a friendly public reception to Allied landings in France.[124] But Roosevelt still resisted, believing that 'de Gaulle is on the wane'. The most he would do was to order Eisenhower, on 15 March 1944, not to negotiate with Vichy authorities. For Roosevelt, this was a major concession; almost everyone else found it frustrating, as it still left Eisenhower to choose who should govern each locality, CFLN nominees or not; to de Gaulle the order was, again, insulting. Unable to impose an AMGOT, Roosevelt had still blocked any pre-D-Day civil affairs agreement. On 14 May he reiterated to Eisenhower that the French people should choose their future without the 'domination' of any external force, meaning the CFLN. Even a memo from Churchill recommending negotiation had no effect.[125]

De Gaulle's wider relations with the Allied political leaders over the year from June 1943 were stalemated. Neither Roosevelt nor Churchill could afford to drop him altogether. Even the third Syrian crisis produced no break. But with recognition minimal and civil affairs on ice, no progress was possible either. Each side, moreover, irritated the other, and not just over Syria. The CFLN arrested several senior ex-Vichy (and pro-American) figures in Algeria. Most were tried after the war. But Pierre Pucheu, Vichy's former Interior Minister, was convicted of treason after a show trial in Algiers in March 1944, and shot. De Gaulle had refused to commute the sentence. Gratifying to the Consultative Assembly, the Communists and the Resistance, intentionally alarming to leading Vichyites in France, Pucheu's execution infuriated Churchill and Roosevelt alike. From Algiers, Macmillan and his successor Alfred Duff Cooper, and Murphy's successor Edwin Wilson, were left to calm their ire.[126]

The Allies, for their part, signed the Italian armistice on 3 September without the CFLN.[127] More dramatically, they intensified a bombing campaign against French targets linked to Germany's war effort: 40,000 tons of bombs fell on France in 1943, killing 7,500 French civilians, and over 400,000 tons between March and September 1944, with over 35,000 civilian losses.[128] Massigli complained to Eden in 1943, and the CFLN to Duff Cooper in May 1944, to little avail. Even Churchill tried to get the spring 1944 raids on rail targets scaled down, before accepting Roosevelt's final decision in their favour.[129] Yet de Gaulle never took the issue up personally, viewing the civilian deaths, like those from First World War Allied shelling, as inevitable.[130] No slight to *France*, real or imagined, could pass; but thousands of French civilian deaths could. The bombing briefly reinforced Pétain, who was greeted by big crowds when he appeared in Paris on 26 April after a deadly run of raids on northern France – suggesting to Roosevelt that he still commanded mass support.[131]

Unsuccessful in securing either formal recognition or a civil affairs agreement from the Allied chiefs, de Gaulle had better luck with Eisenhower, appointed Supreme Commander for the Normandy landings in December 1943. Eisenhower knew as he prepared for D-Day that he would need Resistance help and that any 'open clash' with de Gaulle would be damaging, and costly in American lives.[132] For once, therefore, de Gaulle was delighted with the behaviour of an Allied leader when, at two meetings on 27 and 30 December 1943, the Americans actually consulted him about the future deployment of his country's troops. Most French forces, it was agreed, would remain in the Mediterranean and land in southern France. But a French armoured division, Eisenhower accepted, should fight in the north and help liberate Paris (de Gaulle stipulated that the division should be all-white, claiming that the British would object to coloured troops on British soil).[133] Eisenhower's co-operation triggered that of most of the US War Department.[134]

A more formal agreement with the Allies, however, still eluded de Gaulle. In April 1944 Churchill offered, via Duff Cooper, to arrange a meeting with Roosevelt if de Gaulle requested it. De Gaulle, reluctant to ask anything of the President with no guarantee of a positive answer, declined.[135] Then, on 17 April, the pre-D-Day security lockdown of the United Kingdom began. No communications could reach London except through secured British or American channels. For the CFLN, this was both inconvenient and proof of its exclusion from D-Day preparations. De Gaulle's view of his allies deteriorated accordingly.[136] There was a riposte of sorts. On 3 June 1944, on the Consultative Assembly's proposal with CNR support, the CFLN became the Provisional Government of the French Republic (Gouvernement Provisoire de la République Française – GPRF).[137] On the same day, Eisenhower pressed Roosevelt to concede political recognition – without success.[138]

By the eve of D-Day de Gaulle had advanced decisively along his virtuous circle. Marginalised from the government of French North Africa after Torch, he had won for himself and the Free French, first a coequal role, and then absolute dominance, on the newly constituted CFLN. Despite its limited official recognition, this body was viewed, at least, as a necessary partner by the Allied Commander-in-Chief; as the virtual government of France by Allied leaders like Macmillan; and as the 'legitimate government of France' by the Constituent Assembly and the CNR. But Roosevelt and Churchill still opposed full recognition, and the Resistance maintained its claim to a parallel legitimacy. It would take a summer's fighting and a turbulent liberation to break this double impasse.

Notes

1 Robert Gildea, *Fighters in the Shadows: A New History of the French Resistance* (London: Faber, 2015), pp. 252–4, 257; Jean-Louis Crémieux-Brilhac, *La France Libre, de l'appel du 18 juin à la Libération* (Paris: Gallimard, 1996), pp. 436, 443.

2 Éric Roussel, *Charles de Gaulle* (Paris: Gallimard, 2002), pp. 319–20; Peter Mangold, *Britain and the Defeated French: From Occupation to Liberation, 1940–1944* (London: I.B.Tauris, 2012), pp. 165–6, 170.

3 *DM*1, pp. 241–3; Jean-Luc Barré, *Devenir de Gaulle, 1939–1943* (Paris: Perrin, 2003), p. 255; Mangold, *Defeated French*, p. 171.

4 Philip, quoted in Crémieux-Brilhac, *France Libre*, p. 442; Colonel Passy (pseudonym of André Dewavrin), *Mémoires du chef des services secrets de la France libre*, ed. Jean-Louis-Crémieux-Brilhac (Paris: Odile Jacob, 2000), p. 441.

5 Crémieux-Brilhac, *France Libre*, pp. 444–5; Roussel, *de Gaulle*, pp. 324–6; François Kersaudy, *Churchill and de Gaulle* (New York: Atheneum, 1981), pp. 227–8.

6 Crémieux-Brilhac, *France Libre*, p. 445.

7 Crémieux-Brilhac, *France Libre*, pp. 431, 451; Kersaudy, *Churchill and de Gaulle*, p. 229.

8 Crémieux-Brilhac, *France Libre*, pp. 450–1.

9 Gildea, *Fighters*, p. 257.
10 Passy, *Mémoires*, pp. 446–7.
11 Crémieux-Brilhac, *France Libre*, p. 452.
12 René Cassin, *Les Hommes partis de rien: le réveil de la France abattue (1940–1941)* (Paris: Plon, 1975), p. 135.
13 Simonne Servais (ed.), *Regards sur de Gaulle* (Paris: Plon, 1990), p. 184.
14 Passy, *Mémoires*, p. 431.
15 Passy, *Mémoires*, p. 448.
16 *DM*I, pp. 246–7.
17 The broadcasts were on 28 December 1942 and 13 January 1943, the declaration on 2 January 1943 (respectively *DM*I, pp. 250–2, 256–7, and 255–6).
18 Roussel, *De Gaulle*, pp. 340–2; François Kersaudy, *De Gaulle et Roosevelt: Le duel au Sommet* (Paris: Perrin, 2004), p. 238; Peter Mangold, *The Almost Impossible Ally: Harold Macmillan and Charles de Gaulle* (London: I.B.Tauris, 2006), pp. 38–9.
19 Kersaudy, *Churchill and de Gaulle*, pp. 243, 249; Roussel, *de Gaulle*, p. 343; *WM*II, p. 81.
20 Barré, *Devenir de Gaulle*, p. 292.
21 Charles Williams, *The Last Great Frenchman* (New York: John Wiley, 1993), p. 201; Barré, *Devenir de Gaulle*, pp. 212, 289; *WM*II, pp. 85–6.
22 Kersaudy, *Churchill and de Gaulle*, pp. 249–51. Frank Costigliola, *France and the United States: The Cold Alliance since World War II* (New York: Twayne, 1992), p. 23.
23 *WM*II, p. 84.
24 Barré, *Devenir de Gaulle*, pp. 282–92.
25 Mangold, *Almost Impossible*, p. 41; Williams, *Last Great*, p. 214.
26 Au commandant Tochon, à Casablanca, 23 janvier 1943, *LNC*II, pp. 266–7.
27 *WM*II, p. 85; Philippe de Gaulle, *De Gaulle mon père. Entretiens avec Michel Tauriac*, vol. I (Paris: Plon, 2003), p. 285.
28 Julian Jackson, *A Certain Idea of France: The Life of Charles de Gaulle* (London: Allen Lane, 2018), pp. 254–6.
29 Crémieux-Brilhac, *France Libre*, p. 462.
30 Henri Frenay, *La Nuit finira: mémoires de la Résistance, 1940–1945* (Paris: Robert Laffont, 1973), pp. 290–3.
31 Barré, *Devenir de Gaulle*, pp. 278–9; Crémieux-Brilhac, *France Libre*, pp. 513–15; Jackson, *A Certain Idea*, p. 252.
32 Crémieux-Brilhac, *France Libre*, pp. 515–18.
33 *DM*I, pp. 272–3.
34 Passy, *Mémoires*, pp. 565–98; Passy in Georges-Marc Benamou, *C'était un temps déraisonnable. Les premiers Résistants racontent* (Paris: Robert Laffont, 1999), pp. 144–5; Crémieux-Brilhac, *France Libre*, pp. 523–7; M.R.D. Foot, *SOE in France: An Account of the*

Work of the British Special Operations Executive in France 1940–1944 (London: Frank Cass, 2004), p. 214.
35 Crémieux-Brilhac, *France Libre*, pp. 519–22; Robert Belot, 'Le Général de Gaulle et le gaullisme vus par les services spéciaux américains', in Fondation Charles de Gaulle, *De Gaulle chef de guerre. De l'Appel de Londres à la libération de Paris, 1940–1944* (Paris: Plon, 2008), pp. 586–608; Frenay, *La Nuit finira*, p. 307.
36 Crémieux-Brilhac, *France Libre*, pp. 527–34; Frenay, *La Nuit finira*, pp. 310–11.
37 Claude Bouchinet-Serreulles, *Nous étions nés pour être libres. La Résistance avec de Gaulle et Jean Moulin* (Paris: Grasset, 2000), p. 276.
38 Daniel Cordier in Benamou, *Déraisonnable*, p. 321.
39 Crémieux-Brilhac, *France Libre*, pp. 535–9.
40 Crémieux-Brilhac, *France Libre*, pp. 37, 468–74; Mangold, *Almost Impossible*, pp. 44–7; Catroux to de Gaulle, 18 February 1943, *WM*IIDocs, pp. 133–4.
41 CNF memorandum to Giraud, *WM*IIDocs, pp. 135–7.
42 Barré, *Devenir de Gaulle*, pp. 308–10.
43 Jackson, *A Certain Idea*, pp. 256–7; Mangold, *Defeated French*, p. 187; Barré, *Devenir de Gaulle*, p. 309.
44 *DM*I, pp. 260–9, 284–90.
45 Kersaudy, *Churchill and de Gaulle*, p. 266; Crémieux-Brilhac, *France Libre*, pp. 466–8.
46 Kersaudy, *Churchill and de Gaulle*, p. 271, and the exchanges in *WM*IIDocs, pp. 155–63.
47 Crémieux-Brilhac, *France Libre*, pp. 480–2.
48 *WM*IIDocs, pp. 165–6.
49 *WM*IIDocs, pp. 166–7; Mangold, *Defeated French*, pp. 191–2; Jackson, *A Certain Idea*, p. 269.
50 Julian Jackson, *France: The Dark Years* (Oxford: Oxford University Press, 2001), p. 456.
51 Jackson, *A Certain Idea*, p. 268.
52 Crémieux-Brilhac, *France Libre*, p. 544; André Martel, 'De Gaulle et le réarmement des forces françaises, un outil militaire et diplomatique, 1940–1944', in Fondation Charles de Gaulle, *De Gaulle chef de guerre*, pp. 319–36: pp. 332–4.
53 Kersaudy, *Churchill and de Gaulle*, pp. 272–3.
54 Sir Anthony Eden (Earl of Avon), *The Reckoning* (Memoirs, vol. II) (London: Cassell, 1965), pp. 370–1.
55 Jackson, *A Certain Idea*, pp. 269, 272.
56 Mangold, *Almost Impossible*, p. 51.
57 Costigliola, *France and the United States*, pp. 23–4.
58 Kersaudy, *De Gaulle et Roosevelt*, p. 325.
59 Crémieux-Brilhac, *France Libre*, pp. 569–71.
60 Barré, *Devenir de Gaulle*, p. 388n.

61 Harold Macmillan, *The Blast of War, 1939–1945* (London: Macmillan, 1967), pp. 346–51; Williams, *Last Great*, p. 230.
62 Crémieux-Brilhac, *France Libre*, p. 574.
63 René Cassin, *Les Hommes*, pp. 252–3; WMiiDocs, pp. 231–2; Barré, *Devenir de Gaulle*, p. 386.
64 Macmillan, *Blast*, pp. 418–20.
65 Crémieux-Brilhac, *France Libre*, pp. 579, 628. Ordonnance du 4 avril 1944, WMiiDocs, p. 263.
66 Max Weber, 'Politics as a Vocation' (1919 lecture), http://anthropos-lab.net/wp/wp-content/uploads/2011/12/Weber-Politics-as-a-Vocation.pdf, accessed 29 January 2019.
67 Jackson, *A Certain Idea*, p. 283; Maurice Vaïsse, 'Rebâtir une diplomatie', in Fondation Charles de Gaulle, *De Gaulle chef de guerre. De l'Appel de Londres à la libération de Paris, 1940–1944* (Paris: Plon, 2008), pp. 407–26.
68 Jackson, *A Certain Idea*, p. 268. The division also affected the French secret services until at least November 1943. Cf. Douglas Porch, *The French Secret Services from the Dreyfus Affair to the Gulf War* (Oxford: Oxford University Press, 1995), pp. 218–22.
69 Benamou, *Déraisonnable*, pp. 51–2; Crémieux-Brilhac, *France Libre*, pp. 573.
70 Claude d'Abzac-Epezy, 'Le Rôle de l'armée dans le processus de légitimation du général de Gaulle, 1940–1944', in Fondation Charles de Gaulle, *De Gaulle chef de guerre*, pp. 299–318; Crémieux-Brilhac, *France Libre*, pp. 629–40; Julie Le Gac, 'L'Armée, un outil de politique internationale? Le Corps expéditionnaire français en Italie', in Fondation Charles de Gaulle, *De Gaulle chef de guerre*, pp. 337–54. Williams, *Last Great*, p. 249; Crémieux-Brilhac, *France Libre*, pp. 629–40, 647–51. French troops in Italy were also guilty of widespread rape and looting: cf. Julie Le Gac, *Vaincre sans gloire: le Corps expéditionnaire français en Italie* (Paris: Les Belles Lettres/Ministère de la Défense, 2013).
71 Crémieux-Brilhac, *France Libre*, p. 614, 627.
72 Emmanuel d'Astier de la Vigerie, *Sept fois sept jours* (Paris: Union Générale d'Éditions, 1963 [1961]), pp. 103–5.
73 Crémieux-Brilhac, *France Libre*, pp. 585–605.
74 Jackson, *A Certain Idea*, pp. 288–9; Roussel, *de Gaulle*, p. 396.
75 Touchard, *Le Gaullisme*, pp. 66–7; Jackson, *A Certain Idea*, pp. 23, 290–1.
76 *DM*i, pp. 336–42: p. 341, and pp. 351–4: p. 353.
77 *DM*i, p. 341.
78 *DM*i, pp. 384, 390.
79 Crémieux-Brilhac, *France Libre*, pp. 621, 626; Macmillan, *Blast*, p. 417.
80 Crémieux-Brilhac, *France Libre*, p. 627.
81 *DM*i, pp. 330, 405.

82 Mikhail Narinski, 'De Gaulle face à Staline', in Fondation Charles de Gaulle, *De Gaulle chef de guerre*, pp. 464–82: p. 469.
83 Crémieux-Brilhac, *France Libre*, pp. 622–3.
84 Philippe Buton, 'Le Parti communiste français et le général de Gaulle, de la Résistance à la Libération', in Stéphane Courtois and Marc Lazar (eds), *Cinquante ans d'une passion française. De Gaulle et les communistes* (Paris: Balland, 1991), pp. 39–55: p. 41; Jackson, *A Certain Idea*, p. 300.
85 Crémieux-Brilhac, *France Libre*, pp. 625–6; Barré, *Devenir de Gaulle*, pp. 390–3.
86 Barré, *Devenir de Gaulle*, p. 375.
87 Crémieux-Brilhac, *France Libre*, pp. 616–18.
88 Letter to CFLN members, 22 December 1943, WMiiDocs, pp. 242–3.
89 Cf. Gaston Palewski, 'Allocation d'Ouverture', in Institut du Droit de la Paix et du Développement de l'Université de Nice and Institut Charles de Gaulle (eds), *De Gaulle et le Tiers Monde*, actes du colloque de Nice, 25–6 février 1983 (Paris: Pedone, 1984), pp. 9–13.
90 A.B. Gaunson, *The Anglo-French Clash in Lebanon and Syria, 1940–1945* (Basingstoke: Macmillan, 1987), p. 121.
91 Gaunson, *Clash*, p. 125: WMiiDocs, pp. 292–3.
92 Gaunson, *Clash*, p. 127; Sir Edward Spears, *Fulfilment of a Mission: Syria and Lebanon, 1941–1944* (London: Seeley, Service and Cooper 1977), pp. 230, 239.
93 De Gaulle to Catroux, 19 November 1943, *LNC*ii, pp. 424–5.
94 Macmillan, *Blast*, pp. 424–9.
95 Gaunson, *Clash*, pp. 142, 147.
96 Crémieux-Brilhac, *France Libre*, pp. 660–2.
97 *DM*i, pp. 351–4.
98 Crémieux-Brilhac, *France Libre*, pp. 670–2.
99 Martin Shipway, 'Whose Liberation? Confronting the Problem of the French Empire, 1944–47', in Andrew Knapp (ed.), *The Uncertain Foundation: France at the Liberation, 1944–1947* (Basingstoke: Palgrave, 2007), pp. 139–59: p. 140.
100 *DM*i, pp. 370–3: p. 373.
101 Quoted in Shipway, 'Whose Liberation?', pp. 146–7. '*Self governments*' was in English in the French text.
102 Paul Smith, '*Sénat ou pas Sénat*? The "First" Council of the Republic', in Knapp, *The Uncertain Foundation*, pp. 41–56: p. 46.
103 Roussel, *de Gaulle*, p. 408; Martin Shipway, *Decolonization and its Impact: A Comparative Approach to the End of the Colonial Empires* (Oxford: Blackwell, 2008), p. 127.
104 Crémieux-Brilhac, *France Libre*, p. 694; Macmillan, *Blast*, p. 409.
105 M.R.D. Foot, *SOE in France: An Account of the Work of the British Special Operations Executive in France 1940–1944* (London: Frank Cass, 2004), p. 213.
106 Roussel, *de Gaulle*, p. 374.

107 Porch, *French Secret Services*, pp. 225–6.
108 Jackson, *Dark Years*, p. 464.
109 Jackson, *Dark Years*, pp. 475–6.
110 Jackson, *Dark Years*, pp. 478–80. In addition, by spring 1944 over 70% of French households with a radio listened to London (Crémieux-Brilhac, *France Libre*, p. 717).
111 Jackson, *Dark Years*, pp. 483–91, 531–2.
112 Philippe Buton, *Les Lendemains qui déchantent: le Parti communiste français à la Libération* (Paris: Presses de Sciences Po, 1994), p. 72; Jackson, *Dark Years*, pp. 473–4; Gildea, *Fighters*, p. 336.
113 Buton, *Les Lendemains*, p. 53; Claire Andrieu, 'Le Programme du CNR dans la dynamique de la construction de la nation résistante', *Histoire@Politique. Politique, culture, société*, no. 24, September–December 2014, p. 6 (www.histoire-politique.fr, accessed 4 April 2020).
114 Porch, *French Secret Services*, p. 226.
115 Passy, *Mémoires*, pp. 389–420.
116 Crémieux-Brilhac, *France Libre*, pp. 739–41.
117 Passy, *Mémoires*, p. 382; Porch, *French Secret Services*, pp. 240–51 and 558 n.5.
118 Porch, *French Secret Services*, p. 256.
119 Guichard, *Mon Général*, pp. 165–6.
120 Crémieux-Brilhac, *France Libre*, pp. 628, 696–8, 769–71; Jackson, *A Certain Idea*, pp. 303–4; John Keegan, *Six Armies in Normandy* (London: Pimlico, 2004 [1982]), p. 289; Williams, *Last Great*, p. 247.
121 Crémieux-Brilhac, *France Libre*, pp. 754–60.
122 Kersaudy, *Churchill and de Gaulle*, pp. 296–7 and n.
123 Jackson, *A Certain Idea*, p. 283.
124 Mangold, *Defeated French*, pp. 217–18; Olivier Wieviorka, 'Négocier la Libération: l'Amgot en question, Imposer la reconnaissance', in Fondation Charles de Gaulle, *De Gaulle chef de guerre*, pp. 499–516: p. 507.
125 Mangold, *Defeated French*, pp. 218–19; Alfred Duff Cooper, ed. John Julius Norwich, *The Duff Cooper Diaries* (London: Weidenfeld & Nicolson, 2005), p. 299.
126 Kersaudy, *Churchill and de Gaulle*, pp. 303–5; Mangold, *Almost Impossible*, pp. 67–8; Duff Cooper diaries, pp. 298–9; Roussel, *de Gaulle*, pp. 409–10, 419.
127 Macmillan, *Blast*, p. 410.
128 Andrew Knapp, *La France sous les bombes alliées* (Paris: Tallandier, 2014), p. 55.
129 CFLN letter to British and US governments, 5 May 1944, WMiiDocs, pp. 387–8.
130 Letter to J.-C. Pagès, 9 March 1942, *LNC*ii, pp. 42–3.
131 Costigliola, *France and the United States*, p. 26.
132 Dwight D. Eisenhower, *Crusade in Europe* (London: Heinemann, 1948), p. 272.

133 Kersaudy, *De Gaulle et Roosevelt*, pp. 359–65; WMII, pp. 216–17; WMIIDocs, pp. 369–76.
134 Crémieux-Brilhac, *France Libre*, pp. 565, 609, 684.
135 Note for CFLN on conversations with Duff Cooper, 14 and 17 April 1944, WMIIDocs, pp. 320–2.
136 Crémieux-Brilhac, *France Libre*, p. 698.
137 Williams, *Last Great*, p. 248.
138 Jackson, *A Certain Idea*, p. 309.

Further reading

The following material is in addition to that listed for Chapters 2 and 3.

Julian Jackson, *A Certain Idea of France* (London: Allen Lane, 2018), chapters 11–12, covers the period from November 1942 to June 1944.

Peter Mangold, *The Almost Impossible Ally: Harold Macmillan and Charles de Gaulle* (London: I.B.Tauris, 2006) is excellent on the de Gaulle-Giraud power struggle.

Charles de Gaulle, War Memoirs, vol. II: *Unity, 1942–1944*, tr. Richard Howard (London: Weidenfeld & Nicolson, 1959) covers the period from November 1942 to August 1944.

5 Liberation and recognition, June–October 1944

The pace accelerated sharply with the Normandy landings on 6 June. Recognition of de Gaulle by the French reached a climax with the liberation of Paris on 25 August and de Gaulle's triumphal progress down the Champs-Élysées the following day. But the Allies were slow to accept even de Gaulle's right to control liberated areas of territory, let alone to govern France. Nor was the Resistance ready to fade into the background, its work done. The two months after the liberation of Paris therefore saw de Gaulle lead a fierce struggle to impose his authority both with the Allies and with the Resistance, in Paris and in the provinces.

D-Day and after

On 27 May 1944 de Gaulle received an invitation to England from Churchill. It was a tardy, ill-prepared summons. Against the wishes of practically every major Allied actor in London and Algiers, there had been no discussion with the CFLN on how liberated France should be governed, still less a proper civil affairs agreement.[1] Churchill had asked Roosevelt to send a senior official to discuss civil affairs, but the *New York Times* announced that none would be coming. So de Gaulle was being asked to London 'at the last moment as a spectator to events that vitally affected his country'.[2] He waited a week before agreeing – at the CFLN's urging – to go. When he did, he took advisers but no GPRF ministers, signalling that political discussions would be pointless without top-level US participation.[3]

On 4 June he lunched at the Prime Minister's 'forward headquarters' – a train near Portsmouth.[4] There Churchill outlined military plans for D-Day, which bad weather had postponed by 48 hours. De Gaulle accepted that initial French participation would be extremely limited: 10 Allied divisions, but only 177 French commandos, landed in Normandy on 6 June. The discussions became more heated when Churchill asked de Gaulle for a proclamation to the French, and proposed to prepare a civil affairs agreement for submission to Roosevelt. This triggered the last full-scale Churchill-de Gaulle row before the liberation of France. French civil affairs proposals, said de Gaulle, had been ignored since September; France's government existed, without needing the President's approval; relations between it and the Allied armies could not be discussed without a senior American present. This provoked Churchill's furious reply that 'each time we have to choose between Europe and the open sea, we shall always choose the open sea. Each time I have to choose between you and Roosevelt, I shall always choose Roosevelt'.[5] No two sentences have done more to shape French perceptions of British foreign policy. De Gaulle maintained his refusal of political talks even after Churchill had offered US Ambassador John Winant as a negotiating partner. The British were now *asking* for the co-operation that they had withheld from de Gaulle for nine months; de Gaulle's stalling was partly a demonstration of how dependent on *him* they had become.[6]

A visit to Eisenhower's nearby tent was no more fruitful. After outlining military plans, Eisenhower showed de Gaulle a text he planned to broadcast on D-Day morning. It invited the French population to obey *his* orders, mentioning neither CFLN nor GPRF. De Gaulle told Eisenhower the text was unacceptable; Eisenhower invited him to propose amendments; de Gaulle did so, only to discover on the morning of 5 June that Eisenhower's text had already been printed and recorded.[7]

By 5 June de Gaulle was inclined to dissociate himself entirely from the landings. He would certainly not appear to endorse Eisenhower's broadcast to the French by following it with one of his own. Nor, without a civil affairs agreement, would he send CFLN-trained liaison officers to Normandy. Nor, finally, would he recognise the currency that the Allies planned to issue without having consulted him: 'Go and make your war with your fake money!', he shouted during talks that night.[8] For the Allies to print 'French' money was to usurp French sovereignty. And indeed, without formally recognising the GPRF, the Allies could hardly ask it to back their 'francs'.[9]

Just hours before the Normandy landings, therefore, no agreement covered the Allies' relations with their principal French partner. De Gaulle and Churchill, moreover, were not speaking: Churchill wanted de Gaulle packed off to Algiers 'in chains if necessary'; even Eisenhower said that de Gaulle could 'go to the devil'. It was left to Eden and to Pierre Viénot, the GPRF ambassador to Britain, with Duff Cooper, Charles Peake, and Desmond Morton assisting, to bridge the gap. Under an agreement reached at 4am on 6 June, Eisenhower's broadcast was to go out at 9.30am, and de Gaulle's only at 6pm. Twenty CFLN liaison officers would accompany the Allied forces (in fact, 30 had already left). De Gaulle's message, recorded at 12.30, barely mentioned the Allies and told the French to obey orders from the French government and its military representatives. As the British had had to plead with de Gaulle to broadcast at all, Eden had judged it prudent not to censor his proclamation.[10]

This patched matters up temporarily, but Churchill was still telling Eden that 'de Gaulle must go' and de Gaulle was minded to refuse co-operation with the Allies without full recognition of the GPRF.[11] Churchill visited Normandy on 12 June without inviting de Gaulle. Under the pressure of British public and parliamentary opinion, however, de Gaulle was permitted a visit on 14 June. Landing at Courseulles, he briefly met General Montgomery before continuing to the liberated and largely intact town of Bayeux. Here small groups of onlookers swelled to a large, increasingly enthusiastic crowd.[12] This was visible public support in France, which the British and American press and newsreels amplified and British and US intelligence confirmed. Crucially, too, de Gaulle's representative, François Coulet, took over the administration of Bayeux from the Vichy-appointed authorities quickly and smoothly, the British military raising no objection.[13] The Allies might still be withholding a civil affairs agreement in principle, but events were moving as if one already existed.

Many formalities fell into place over the summer. An outline civil affairs agreement was signed on 19 June. By 20 June most of Europe's governments-in-exile had formally recognised the GPRF. Koenig and other FFI staff were included in the SHAEF command structure from 1 July.[14] Eden and Viénot reached a full civil affairs agreement covering administration and currency on 27 August. It excluded any Allied 'supervision' of French authorities, and provided for the steady absorption of the Allied currency issue by the Allied authorities themselves.[15] Meanwhile de Gaulle hosted a cordial visit from Eden to Carlton Gardens, before returning to Algiers on 16 June. His displays of anger at the Allies, though understandable, had been superfluous for practical purposes: Allied military commanders needed his co-operation, and Roosevelt disliked interfering with his generals on the ground. By 1 July, indeed, short of full recognition, de Gaulle had got most of what he wanted. Now he could go to Washington with a stronger hand to play – and turn his attention to the Resistance.[16]

Rome, Washington, Algiers

Late in June Gaulle travelled to Italy, to visit Allied commanders, French forces – and Pope Pius XII. The Church had so far given the Free French neither support nor recognition. While some Catholic activists and rank-and-file clergy had joined the Resistance, France's Catholic hierarchy were far closer to Vichy than they had been to the Republic.[17] De Gaulle now offered the Pope reassurance about a future republican France – while making clear that any difficulties were due to the recent behaviour of 'certain ecclesiastical circles'.[18]

He visited the United States for the first time from 6 to 11 July. After awkward exchanges about the trip's organisation and timing, Roosevelt provided de Gaulle with an aircraft, a 17-(not 21-) gun salute on his arrival in Washington, and three conversations in three days. The President expounded his vision of a four-power world directorate composed of the United States, the Soviet Union, China and Britain; de Gaulle tried to persuade Roosevelt that future world peace depended on the recovery of Western Europe.[19] There was no meeting of minds.

Four developments outweighed the summit talks in importance. First, de Gaulle consolidated his standing within Roosevelt's administration, even among old adversaries like Leahy and Hull.[20] Second, Alphand and Monnet undertook negotiations on US military and civilian aid for liberated France.[21] Third, de Gaulle scored a palpable hit with the American press and people, especially in

132 *Liberation and recognition, June–October 1944*

New York. Fascinated by American 'optimism, dynamism and creativity', he appeared for once almost happy, and made two speeches in English.[22] Fourth, on 11 July Roosevelt accepted the CFLN as 'the de facto authority for the civil administration of France'.[23] Public opinion, and impending elections, required at least that much.

Having partially mended relations during what would prove his last personal encounter with Roosevelt, de Gaulle might have done the same with Churchill. The Prime Minister did, after all, praise de Gaulle to the Commons on 2 August, and underlined Britain's interest in restoring France's great-power status.[24] Instead, de Gaulle indulged in gratuitous displays of ill temper. When Churchill, visiting Algiers, suggested a meeting for 11 August, de Gaulle refused. Four days later he flew into a rage because Churchill had visited Corsica without notifying the French authorities. This wounded Churchill and exasperated even natural supporters like Massigli or Duff Cooper, who wondered how long de Gaulle would last in Paris.[25]

Paris, August 1944

'The simple and sacred duty of the sons of France', de Gaulle had declared in his D-Day broadcast, 'wherever they are, is to fight with all available means.' But he added that 'our operations at the enemy rear should be co-ordinated as closely as possible with those undertaken at the front by the Allied and French armies'.[26] This was finely balanced. The call to arms was required to deny the Communists a monopoly of fighting talk; to demonstrate the FFI's usefulness, reinforcing the GPRF's legitimacy with the Allies; and to enable the French people to recover some of the self-respect lost in 1940.[27] The stress on co-ordination and orderly, militarised combat was part instinct, part politics (an insurrection could turn into a Communist revolution), and part prudence (an ill-prepared rising could become a bloodbath). Three weeks earlier, his directive to the FFI had been centred on disrupting German communication lines in *southern* France before the landings there, and on helping secure Breton ports – not on a general insurrection, and certainly not on Paris unless the Germans there were in full retreat or completely demoralised.[28]

The Communists, by contrast, wanted a mass rising inspired by the French revolutionary model. Did they also see it as a means to seize power? In principle, they did not. Rather, they aimed, as the Liberation progressed, to win control of territory, and of local institutions, and of key offices in the state such as that of Prefect of the Seine *département* around Paris, to be utilised as the opportunity arose.[29] To many non-Communist Resistance fighters, whatever the PCF's hidden strategy, its vision of a *people*'s struggle was much more attractive than the GPRF's, which saw the FFI as auxiliaries for Allied forces.

Naturally, these competing visions of the Liberation spilt over into the question of command. For the GPRF, the chain of command passed from Koenig to Chaban-Delmas, to the FFI chiefs of staff. But the COMAC, closer than Koenig to forces on the ground, claimed its own superior right to issue orders to the FFI. Again, this view, though pushed by the Communists (with two of the three full seats on the COMAC), appeared more realistic to many non-Communists than the GPRF's more distant command structure.[30]

As it turned out, neither the GPRF nor the COMAC fully controlled the Resistance forces unleashed at D-Day. The FFI grew from 50,000 in January 1944 to 100,000 in June and 500,000 in August. 'Resistance', as Foot observes, 'in fact called itself out over much of the country'.[31] The results, over summer 1944, were often disastrous. Ill-conceived *maquis* risings provoked barbaric German retaliation, in the Limousin, the Auvergne, the Ardennes. On the Vercors plateau above Grenoble, 639 *maquisards* and 200 civilians died in a pitched battle against some 10,000 German troops: the expected airlift of heavy weapons never arrived.[32]

But where the FFI worked closely with the military, it achieved significant results, especially after the Allied breakthrough in Normandy in late July and the landings in Provence on 15 August. Now de Gaulle could broadcast unambiguously from Algiers that 'Everyone can fight. Everyone must fight', and the BBC could call for a general rising in all major towns.[33] In Brittany, the FFI's 30,000 men covered the province and permitted Patton's Third Army to swing eastwards towards the Seine. In the south, Marseille was half-liberated before de Lattre's troops arrived, four weeks ahead of schedule; FFI operations enabled the Allies to reach Grenoble in a week, rather than the expected three months. Northern and southern Allied forces met at Dijon on 11 September, and 85% of French territory was liberated by the month's end. Henry Maitland Wilson, now Mediterranean Commander-in-Chief, stated that the FFI had reduced the German capability in southern France by 40%. Eisenhower put the FFI's value at 15 divisions.[34] Perhaps they exaggerated, but these results contrasted sharply with the disasters of uncoordinated risings.

Meanwhile COMAC and Koenig continued to dispute the command of the FFI. The Communists tried to consolidate their hold on the CNR and on local Liberation Committees, and Gaullists to thwart them by seizing key points such as railway and power stations and ration card offices.[35] This was the context for the liberation of Paris, which would bring the GPRF 'home' to France's capital by the end of August. The battle for Paris (15–25 August) left 901 FFI fighters, 71 soldiers of Leclerc's Second Armoured Division (Deuxième Division Blindée – 2DB), and 582 civilians dead and over 2,200 wounded: German casualties amounted to 3,000.[36]

It was preceded by a confused struggle between distinct actors with conflicting ideas of how to proceed. Eisenhower, having promised de Gaulle months earlier to give 2DB the honour of entering the capital, knew that it made better military sense simply to bypass it. De Gaulle wanted 2DB to sweep triumphantly into Paris, with the Parisians and FFI as largely symbolic auxiliaries, not actors in a spontaneous rising. The Communists, and the majority on the CNR and COMAC, sought an FFI-led popular insurrection, with 2DB back-up if necessary, from which the (Communist-dominated) CPL would emerge as the capital's chief political force. As for ordinary Parisians, their desire for liberation at (almost) any price was stimulated by growing hunger: thanks to Allied bombing, no trains were replenishing the capital's food supplies.[37]

De Gaulle's military and civilian delegates, respectively Chaban and Alexandre Parodi, were torn between three conflicting priorities: to apply de Gaulle's line, centred on 2DB; to prevent an urban Vercors tragedy; to avoid a break between de Gaulle and the internal Resistance, which might result if they tried to stop an insurrection. As messages from London or Algiers took days to reach Paris, they had to use their own initiative. Chaban even travelled to London to request aid from Koenig and Ismay, Churchill's chief military adviser. The Parisian FFI, he told them, though not heavily outnumbered by the Germans' 16,000 men, were massively outgunned. Ismay responded that Paris was expected to fall by siege within weeks and refused support for any insurrection. Hence Koenig's order to Chaban: no uprising without his orders.[38]

The uprising started anyway, rolling forward from a police strike beginning on 15 August to skirmishes between FFI and Germans, to the take-over of the Prefecture of Police by the GPRF's appointee Charles Luizet on 18 August, to a full-scale insurrection, ordered on 19 August by Rol-Tanguy, the (Communist) regional FFI chief, and backed by the CNR's *bureau*, and by Chaban and Parodi, who could hold the Koenig line no longer.[39] Almost immediately the Swedish consul, Raoul Nordling, brokered a truce between the insurgents and the German commandant, General von Choltitz, supposedly to allow an orderly German evacuation. Fiercely contested at three CNR meetings on 20 and 21 August, the truce lapsed at 4pm on 22 August.[40] By then German authority was breaking down: the FFI was taking over the town halls of Paris's 20 *arrondissements*, while Parodi was moving GPRF men into the ministries. But the Germans were still fighting hard in places, and Hitler's orders were to destroy the city. Even Rol-Tanguy was worried enough, on 21 August, to send an emissary, codenamed Gallois, westwards through German lines to appeal for Allied help.

De Gaulle, meanwhile, arrived in western Normandy on 20 August, officially on a military inspection tour. In his *Memoirs* he recalls aiming to head off two eventualities – a handover of power to the Americans by Laval, and a Communist bid to take control of Paris and then France.[41] The first of these had been blocked on 17 August when the Germans transported Pétain and Laval eastwards to Belfort and thence to Sigmaringen in southern Germany. The Communists, however critical of the GPRF, were less intent on seizing sole power than de Gaulle claimed to have believed.[42] But from the perspective of 20 August, anything appeared possible, including an even bloodier repetition of the 1871 Paris Commune.

That evening, therefore, de Gaulle asked Eisenhower to launch 2DB, then at Argentan, on a 125-mile dash to Paris. Eisenhower was non-committal.[43] Only two days later, after receiving a pressing letter from de Gaulle, plus Gallois's intelligence on the weakness of German defences west of Paris, did Eisenhower allow General Omar Bradley to order 2DB forward.[44] Leclerc's men moved on

23 August. The following evening an advance party of 130 men, 3 tanks and 15 half-tracks, under Captain Raymond Dronne entered Paris through side roads and parked in front of the FFI-controlled Town Hall. The main force began arriving from 7am on 25 August, destroyed the remaining pockets of German resistance, captured von Choltitz, and took his surrender.

The fighting had not ended when de Gaulle reached Leclerc's headquarters at the Gare Montparnasse shortly after 5pm, immediately expressing annoyance that Rol-Tanguy's signature appeared with Leclerc's on the surrender document. His movements that evening were loaded with political meaning. While the CNR and the CPL awaited him at the Town Hall, de Gaulle returned to his old office at the War Ministry, where Parodi and Luizet joined him, and took a ministerial car to the Prefecture of Police for a brief inspection with Luizet. Only then, at Parodi's urging, did he walk over to the Town Hall, arriving by 8pm.[45] The offices and officers of the state came first: the leaders of the national insurrection second.

There followed one of the historic de Gaulle speeches: 'Paris! Paris humiliated! Paris broken! Paris martyrised! But now Paris liberated! Liberated by herself, by her own people with the help of the armies of France, with the support and aid of France as a whole, of fighting France, of the only France, of the true France, of eternal France!'[46] Its interest lies partly in de Gaulle's visible emotion while delivering it, partly in its stern call to continue the fight and enter Germany as conquerors, but also in the gaps. Allies and FFI alike had made indispensable contributions to the liberation of Paris: each got only the briefest mention, in the second paragraph. The CNR did not get even that, despite Bidault's fulsome tribute paid to de Gaulle minutes earlier (and Georges Marrane's for the CPL). Nor would de Gaulle agree to proclaim the Republic from the balcony of the Town Hall, as in 1848 and 1870: according to Gaullist doctrine, embodied in an *ordonnance* of 7 August, 'In law, [the Republic] has never ceased to exist'.[47] The evening of Liberation thereby lost a symbol of the revolutionary republicanism with which the CNR identified. Bidault had to restrain its stunned members from publishing a formal protest.[48]

De Gaulle had been acclaimed by cheering crowds since reaching Paris, but the real celebration took place on the afternoon of

26 August. Having lit the flame at the tomb of the Unknown Soldier at the Arc de Triomphe, he led a great parade down the Champs-Élysées. For a brief moment, his dream of national unity seemed to come to life: 'In this community, with only a single thought, a single enthusiasm, a single cry, all differences vanished, all individualities disappeared'.[49] He knew that the summer's political and strategic tensions had not evaporated; but it is almost possible to believe it from the joyful, mildly chaotic, footage of the event. The footage also offers evidence of de Gaulle's coolness under fire. As he reaches Notre Dame, where a *Magnificat* is to be sung, shots ring out: the crowd dives for cover, but de Gaulle remains upright, smoking. To this day it remains unknown who fired; de Gaulle at first minimised the shots, then, in his *Memoirs*, ascribed them unconvincingly to Communist *agents provocateurs*.[50] What is certain, and not only in the *Memoirs*, is that as he returned to the task of state-building begun in exile, he saw the Communists, and the Resistance generally, less as partners than as elements of disorder.

'A monopoly of the legitimate use of physical force': de Gaulle versus the Resistance, autumn 1944

The GPRF decamped to Paris on 28 August. De Gaulle himself did not move to the Prime Minister's office, preferring the War Ministry. Here, in an atmosphere of optimistic improvisation, an administration took shape.[51] Here too, in those first days of the Liberation, the Head of the Provisional Government lunched with France's leading writers. The symbolism was eloquent. The War Ministry was about using hard power to secure France's place among the victorious nations; the literary luncheons were about revitalising France's soft, cultural power, by which de Gaulle set great store as the nation's lifeblood.[52]

But de Gaulle's most pressing task was restoring the French state, in its full Weberian sense. In his first Parisian broadcast, on 29 August, he called for 'republican order under the only valid authority, that of the State'; on 14 October he warned that 'The right to command any armed force whatsoever belongs solely to the chiefs appointed by the responsible ministers.'[53] The main competition he faced was from the PCF and the organisations it dominated. But the CNR also commanded wide support for its claim, based on the Resistance, to a role as an equal partner with the GPRF. De Gaulle was determined to overcome both challenges.

His first move, remarkably, was to enlist the help of Eisenhower, whose visit on 27 August amounted to a de facto recognition for the GPRF. De Gaulle 'asked for the temporary loan of two American divisions to use, as he said, as a show of force and to establish his position firmly'.[54] So two American divisions paraded through Paris on their way to the battlefront, a reminder of a massive Allied military presence and a warning against civil disorder. Not surprisingly, the episode features in Eisenhower's memoirs, not de Gaulle's.

De Gaulle then moved to decommission the FFI. The Resistance, in his view, had done its work; it was now for the army to fight the Germans, for the police to apprehend and for the courts to prosecute Vichyites. Accordingly, on 28 August, he summoned Villon and other Resistance chiefs, then the CNR, read them a decree merging the FFI into the army, and coldly advised FFI chiefs to return to civilian life. 'I have known human ingratitude, but I never imagined it reaching such a degree', recalled one of Villon's entourage.[55]

Brusqueness did not bring instant results. The COMAC issued its own orders to the FFI for two more weeks. General Billotte, de Gaulle's representative, had to visit Villon's headquarters, surrounded by barbed wire and sandbags, to persuade him to allow his Parisian FFI to become the Tenth Infantry Division.[56] A meeting with de Gaulle's new War Minister, André Diethelm, eventually produced a compromise – with the PCF's consent – on 12 September. Within the army, an FFI direction, responsible for the merging of forces, was created; the COMAC nominated its members, and in return gave up its independence. Decrees of 19 and 20 September integrated the FFI into the army at battalion level.[57] At a press conference on 25 October, de Gaulle was confident enough to call the FFI 'young people of extreme quality, almost all of them', of whom France would soon make an impressive army.[58] A little more slowly than hoped, he had secured the FFI's dissolution; that of the FFI direction in the army followed by January 1945.[59]

It remained to dissolve the Resistance leadership, and particularly the CNR, into de Gaulle's renascent state. This took place in three stages. First, the GPRF was enlarged on 9 September to include Resistance leaders, after tough negotiations during which de Gaulle had (already) threatened to resign.[60] The new arrivals included party politicians untainted by association with Vichy, and Free French figures like Parodi (as Labour Minister) and René Capitant (at Education). Bidault became Foreign Minister, resigning as president of the CNR. To the disappointment of the Resistance press, however, only one head of a Resistance movement joined the new government: Henri Frenay, minister for returning prisoners and deportees.[61] The second step, on 12 September, was a mass meeting at the Palais de Chaillot in Paris. Here, de Gaulle addressed the 'thanks of the Government and of the whole country' to the CNR and promised it a major role – within an enlarged Consultative Assembly. That was all. The main burden of his speech was an austere call to new efforts to conquer Germany and reconstruct France.[62] For the young Resistance fighters who were expecting the CNR to become a full partner in government, this was a cold shower – especially as representatives of the major civil service bodies that formed the backbone of the French state, and who had largely eschewed any form of Resistance, were also invited to Chaillot.[63]

As the third stage in the integration of the Resistance, a decree of 11 October enlarged the Consultative Assembly to 248 members, against 84 at its creation in Algiers. CNR members would sit *ex officio*, would vet new Assembly members appointed from political parties, and would sit on the committees formed to purge notorious collaborators from the civil service. But these roles were consolation prizes, not partnership. Through 1945, the CNR was steadily marginalised.[64] As Touchard remarks, 'while the Resistance generation dreamt, confusedly, of a generous revolution, of socialism on a human scale, General de Gaulle waged war, re-established order and undertook the restoration of the state. It is fairly fruitless to ask who was responsible for this profound divorce.'[65]

Paris, however, is not France. In liberated Limoges, Communist cadres including the prestigious *maquis* leader Georges Guingouin wondered how to replace 'de Gaulle-Kerensky' by 'Lenin-Thorez' (referring to the exiled PCF leader). True, few comrades supported them; the PCF, as Buton insists, was not openly revolutionary in 1944. But it did seek to create a parallel state from its positions on the ground.[66] This bid persisted longer in the provinces than in the capital, and provoked a fierce response.

The challenge in the provinces involved two types of organisation. One was the Liberation Committees. They had been grudgingly accepted by the CFLN as consultative bodies in *départements* and major localities. But in seven *départements* in the east and south-east, they actually prevented GPRF-appointed prefects from taking up their posts.[67] Foot describes much of south-western France as under the control of 'feudal lords'.[68] And 39 Committees from southern France held a congress in Avignon on 7–8 October – a rather clear attempt to build a parallel state-like authority, opposed at first by the CNR but approved by Maurice Thorez, the PCF's secretary-general, from Moscow. The Communist challenge also used the Patriotic Militias, plant-level and neighbourhood-level groups formed, supposedly, to complement the FFI as instruments of national insurrection – but which the GPRF never approved, and which went on recruiting *after* the Liberation.[69]

A show of military force to face down provincial challenges was hardly possible. The Allies would not send troops all across France – and de Gaulle had no wish to show weakness by asking them. He may have contemplated sending French troops, especially to the south-west, but he wanted them to fight the Germans alongside the Allies.[70]

Instead, he went himself, undertaking six provincial tours in two months: on 14–18 September to Lyon, Marseille, Toulouse and other southern towns; on 23–6 September to eastern France; in late September to the North; on 7–9 October to Normandy; on 21–3 October to eastern France again; and on 4–6 November to the south-east.[71] In each locality de Gaulle invariably visited the state's appointees – the regional military governor, the *Commissaire de la République*, the prefect – *before* meeting invited notables at the Town Hall. He would also inspect troops – and, crucially, would wade through crowds, with minimal police protection, not only seen but physically touched by his people, like a medieval sovereign.[72]

The local press celebrated the crowd scenes. But it did not report the brutality with which de Gaulle greeted Resistance fighters and (especially) leaders. This was particularly marked in Toulouse, where he had been infuriated by the appearance of Spanish republican fighters, and Spanish and even Soviet flags, in the Resistance parade.[73] For Serge Ravanel, head of the Toulouse FFI, de Gaulle's obsession with restoring the state blinded him to the fact that the local authorities in Toulouse were functioning effectively alongside the *Commissaire de la République*, and that the *résistants* who greeted him, whatever their political leanings, considered themselves Gaullists.[74] But de Gaulle was behaving as he had to Allied leaders: lacking, as yet, the overwhelming force of a state, he substituted extreme personal rudeness. In less turbulent Bordeaux, by contrast, de Gaulle readily supported the appointment, to assist the new *Commissaire de la République*, of Maurice Papon, who (as de Gaulle knew) had supervised the deportation of Jews, as secretary-general of the same prefecture under Vichy.[75] As Jackson remarks, 'De Gaulle, the rebel of 1940, felt more at home in this company of former Vichyites than with the ragged troupe of resisters encountered in Toulouse and Marseilles.'[76]

There remained the Patriotic Militias, whose dissolution provoked the clearest confrontation with the PCF – and the CNR. In the northern town of Maubeuge, the militias had challenged de Gaulle's authority openly by executing two collaborators whom he had just pardoned. On 28 October he announced their dissolution in the Council of Ministers. The PCF, the CPL, and the CNR all protested.[77] But the Communist *ministers* did not budge. Hence de Gaulle's confidence to Claude Mauriac on 30 October: 'As long as the Communists stay in the government and share responsibility, then we've won ... The Communists, you see, aren't dangerous ... You can't make a revolution without revolutionaries. And I'm the only revolutionary in France.'[78]

De Gaulle had two reasons for confidence. The first was public support. Opinion polls in the Paris region showed overwhelming backing for de Gaulle's stress on restoring public order; an equally general sense that the Resistance, however heroic, belonged to the past not the future; and a minimal demand, even among PCF supporters, for additional Communist ministers, let alone for revolution.[79] Second, de Gaulle was sure of Moscow's unspoken backing. On the day he dissolved the militias, he authorised Thorez, who had deserted from the army in 1939 and travelled to Moscow, to return to France with the guarantee of a pardon. The tacit bargain was that Thorez, once home, would play the game. De Gaulle would probably not have been surprised to hear Stalin's advice to the homeward-bound Thorez: the militias, said Stalin, 'needed to be transformed into a more political organisation; as for [their] weapons, they should be hidden'. The context, Stalin stressed, had changed, because 'there now existed in France a government recognised by the Allied powers'.[80] The GPRF's tardy recognition, on 23 October, by London, Washington, and Moscow, marked the closure of the long cycle opened by the *appel du 18 juin*.

Reluctant recognition, October 1944

Even after the liberation of Paris, Churchill and Roosevelt still refused to recognise the GPRF. Meeting at Quebec 12–16 September, they merely reinforced one another's prejudices – against their foreign ministers' urgings. Eden's 'Gaullism' was long-standing; Cordell Hull's was new. His long memo of 17 September cited, as reasons for recognition: clear public support for de Gaulle, the unlikelihood of a dictatorship, the risk of damage to America's standing in France, and the need to reinforce the GPRF's capacity to keep public order.[81] To no avail. On 19 September Roosevelt insisted that the GPRF 'has no direct authority from the people'; on 28 September, that elections, and the total liberation of French territory, should precede any recognition – although the Allies had, that same day, recognised the government of Italy, where no elections had been held and where the Germans still controlled the north.[82] Under pressure in the Commons, Churchill finally recommended recognition to Roosevelt on 18 October. He received yet another refusal, before learning on 21 October that the State Department had now instructed Jefferson Caffery, US envoy to Paris, to proceed after all. Recognition by Americans, British, and Soviets alike followed, in some confusion, in 48 hours.[83]

Perhaps unsurprisingly, de Gaulle remained intensely suspicious of the Western Allies. In early September, he had suspected the Americans of planning a separate peace with Germany: 'The Allies are betraying us and betraying Europe, the bastards', he told Claude Mauriac – 'but they'll pay for it!'[84] Over the next six weeks France was excluded from the Quebec conference, from the briefing on Churchill's and Eden's October visit to Moscow, from the European Advisory Commission, and from the Dumbarton Oaks conference on the future United Nations Organisation. American equipment for France's armies, meanwhile, arrived painfully slowly.[85] On 23 October, the day of recognition, de Gaulle exhorted the French to redouble their own efforts to overturn the 'sort of relegation in which the other powers currently hold France'.[86] A question about recognition at his press conference two days later received a laconic reply: 'The French government is pleased that it is to be called by its name.'[87]

Conclusion

The virtuous circle that de Gaulle had engaged with the British, the internal Resistance, and then the Americans and Soviets, was now, more or less, complete. Without the Allies, the Paris insurrection might have been crushed in blood; 2DB would never have existed, let alone dashed to Paris; de Gaulle could never have returned to his office at the War Ministry. Without his support from France's Resistance, and his ability to control the Communists, Allied recognition would have been withheld still longer. Throughout the process, de Gaulle deployed an impressive range of personal attributes: iron resolution (at all times), brutality (more often than necessary), a fine judgement of the balance of forces (enabling him to risk walking away from a negotiation), and an ability to articulate dreams of liberation and of honour in terms both lofty and accessible, and thereby to make them believable.

Did he make a difference? The Allies would certainly have liberated France without his assistance. And without a de Gaulle, the Communists would still not have taken France over; that was never Stalin's plan. In some areas, notably Syria, de Gaulle was more of a complication than a help. But without him there would have been no Bir Hakeim, no 2DB; no voice of 'hope, courage, honour, rectitude, and liberation' to sustain the French through the Occupation; no alternative to the quasi-Vichyite regime that the Americans considered good enough to govern Algeria; no sense among the French, whatever the exaggerations of the *Paris libérée* speech, that liberation was somehow *their own*, not merely delivered by the Allies. It is hard to imagine what sort of French government might have been concocted in August 1944; but it is reasonable to assume that it would have clashed with some Communists, locally, with arms: a rising in Antwerp was, after all, violently suppressed by police and British troops in November 1944.[88] For all these reasons, the verdict of Anthony Eden appears sound: 'Whatever de Gaulle's gifts or failings, he was a godsend to his country in this hour, when France must otherwise have been distracted by controversy or bathed in blood.'[89]

Notes

1 Jean-Louis Crémieux-Brilhac, *La France Libre, de l'appel du 18 juin à la Libération* (Paris: Gallimard, 1996), p. 832.
2 Peter Mangold, *Britain and the Defeated French: From Occupation to Liberation, 1940–1944* (London: I.B.Tauris, 2012), pp. 220–1.
3 Crémieux-Brilhac, *France Libre*, p. 817.
4 François Kersaudy, *Churchill and de Gaulle* (New York: Atheneum, 1981), pp. 326–9; Alfred Duff Cooper, *The Duff Cooper Diaries*, ed. John Julius Norwich (London: Weidenfeld & Nicolson, 2005), pp. 305–7.
5 *WM*II, pp. 226–7. Sir Anthony Eden (Lord Avon), *The Reckoning* (Memoirs, vol. II) (London: Cassell, 1965), p. 453, broadly confirms de Gaulle's account, though not the precise words.
6 Crémieux-Brilhac, *France Libre*, pp. 833–8; Mangold, *Defeated French*, pp. 220–1.
7 *WM*II, pp. 228–9.
8 Olivier Wieviorka, 'Négocier la Libération: l'Amgot en question, Imposer la reconnaissance', in Fondation Charles de Gaulle, *De Gaulle chef de guerre. De l'Appel de Londres à la libération de Paris, 1940–1944* (Paris: Plon, 2008), pp. 499–516: p. 506.
9 Kersaudy, *Churchill and de Gaulle*, pp. 342–5; Duff Cooper, *Diaries*, pp. 309–11.
10 Crémieux-Brilhac, *France Libre*, pp. 838–41. The strain of these meetings took its toll on Viénot's health: he died of a heart attack on 20 July at age 46.
11 Eden, *Reckoning*, pp. 454–6; Kersaudy, *Churchill and de Gaulle*, pp. 349, 352.
12 *WM*II, pp. 233–4; René Hostache, 'Bayeux, 14 juin 1944: étape décisive sur la voie d'Alger à Paris', in Fondation Charles de Gaulle, *De Gaulle et la Libération* (Brussels: Complexe, 2004), pp. 37–48. Cf. also newsreel footage at https://www.ina.fr/video/AFE99000037, accessed 11 March 2019.
13 Julian Jackson, *A Certain Idea of France: The Life of Charles de Gaulle* (London: Allen Lane, 2018), pp. 315–18; Kersaudy, *Churchill and de Gaulle*, pp. 354–6.
14 Crémieux-Brilhac, *France Libre*, p. 863.
15 François Kersaudy, *De Gaulle et Roosevelt. Le duel au Sommet* (Paris: Perrin, 2006), p. 411; Olivier Wieviorka, *Histoire du Débarquement en Normandie* (Paris: Le Seuil, 2007), p. 403; Crémieux-Brilhac, *France Libre*, pp. 851–2.

16 Crémieux-Brilhac, *France Libre*, p. 833; Mangold, *Defeated French*, p. 226; Kersaudy, *De Gaulle et Roosevelt*, pp. 407–9.
17 Étienne Fouilloux, 'Les Catholiques français et de Gaulle, 1940–1951', in Fondation Charles de Gaulle, *Charles de Gaulle, chrétien, homme d'État* (Paris: Plon, 2005), pp. 133–47: p. 133; Nicholas Atkin, 'Catholics and the Long Liberation: The Progressive Moment', in Andrew Knapp, *The Uncertain Foundation: France at the Liberation, 1944–1947* (Basingstoke: Palgrave Macmillan, 2007), pp. 121–38: pp. 125–9.
18 *WM*II, p. 236; Jean-Marie Mayeur, 'De Gaulle et l'Église catholique', in Institut Charles de Gaulle, *De Gaulle en son siècle*, vol. I: *Dans la mémoire des hommes et des peuples* (Paris: Plon, 1991), pp. 436–46.
19 *WM*II, p. 242.
20 Kersaudy, *De Gaulle et Roosevelt*, pp. 416–17.
21 Jean Lacouture, *De Gaulle*, vol. I: *Le Rebelle* (Paris: Le Seuil, 1985), pp. 789–90.
22 Lacouture, *De Gaulle* I, p. 796.
23 Charles Williams, *The Last Great Frenchman* (New York: John Wiley, 1993), pp. 262–5.
24 Hansard, 2 August 1944, https://api.parliament.uk/historic-hansard/commons/1944/aug/02/war-situation#S5CV0402P0_19440802_HOC_380, accessed 12 March 2019.
25 Duff Cooper, *Diaries*, pp. 317–18.
26 6 June 1944, *DM*I, pp. 407–8.
27 Crémieux-Brilhac, *France Libre*, pp. 779–87.
28 Directive to FFI, 16 May 1944, *WM*IIDocs, pp. 389–90.
29 Philippe Buton, *Les Lendemains qui déchantent: le Parti communiste français à la Libération* (Paris: Presses de Sciences Po, 1994), p. 99; Robert Gildea, *Fighters in the Shadows: A New History of the French Resistance* (London: Faber, 2015), p. 374.
30 M.R.D. Foot, *SOE in France: An Account of the Work of the British Special Operations Executive in France 1940–1944* (London: Frank Cass, 2004), p. 318; Julian Jackson, *France: The Dark Years, 1940–1944* (Oxford: Oxford University Press, 2001), p. 547.
31 Foot, *SOE in France*, p. 343.
32 Lacouture, *De Gaulle* I, pp. 812–13.
33 Broadcast from Algiers, 7 August, *DM*I, pp. 436–8; Mangold, *Defeated French*, p. 230.
34 Mangold, *Defeated French*, pp. 230, 233; Douglas Porch, *The French Secret Services from the Dreyfus Affair to the Gulf War* (Oxford: Oxford University Press, 1995), p. 260.
35 Crémieux-Brilhac, *France Libre*, pp. 857–63, 870–4; Patrick and Philippe Chastenet, *Chaban* (Paris: Le Seuil, 1991), pp. 63–7; Foot, *SOE in France*, p. 367; Olivier Guichard, *Mon Général* (Paris: Grasset, 1980), p. 169.
36 Jackson, *Dark Years*, p. 567; Wieviorka, *Histoire du Débarquement*, p. 408.

37 Matthew Cobb, *Eleven Days in August: The Liberation of Paris in 1944* (London: Simon & Schuster, 2013), p. 34.
38 Chastenet, *Chaban*, p. 70. The Allies had long limited arms drops to Paris, regarded as a nest of Communists. Cf. John Keegan, *Six Armies in Normandy* (London: Pimlico, 2004 [1982]), p. 288.
39 Keegan, *Six Armies*, pp. 291–2; Claire Andrieu, 'Le CNR et les logiques de l'insurrection résistante', in Fondation Charles de Gaulle, *De Gaulle et la Libération*, pp. 69–125: p. 88.
40 Andrieu, 'Le CNR', p. 89.
41 *WM*II, pp. 291–5.
42 Buton, *Les Lendemains*, pp. 82–3, 89–90, 99.
43 *WM*II, pp. 296–7.
44 Cobb, *Eleven Days*, p. 205; Crémieux-Brilhac, *France Libre*, pp. 894–6.
45 Serge Berstein, 'L'Arrivée du général de Gaulle à Paris', in Fondation Charles de Gaulle, *De Gaulle et la Libération*, pp. 127–42: p. 137; Cobb, *Eleven Days*, pp. 308–9.
46 *DM*I, pp. 439–40; translation Cobb, *Eleven Days*, p. 310: https://www.ina.fr/video/I12104905/charles-de-gaulle-paris-outrage-!-paris-brise-!-paris-martyrise-!-mais-paris-libere-!-video.html, accessed 5 January 2020.
47 Lacouture, *De Gaulle* I, p. 834; Andrieu, 'Le CNR', p. 92. He would add that the Town Hall, rebuilt after its predecessor had burnt down during the Commune in 1871, had no balcony (Jean Touchard, *Le Gaullisme, 1940–1969* (Paris: Le Seuil, 1978), p. 342).
48 Cobb, *Eleven Days*, p. 311.
49 *WM*II, p. 312.
50 Jean Lacouture, *De Gaulle*, vol. II: *Le Politique, 1944–1959* (Paris: Le Seuil, 1985), pp. 13–14; https://www.ina.fr/video/3959622001/mysteres-d-archives-1944-de-gaulle-dans-paris-libere-video.html, accessed 29 December 2019; *WM*II, p. 316.
51 Claude Mauriac, *Un autre de Gaulle: Journal 1944–1954* (Paris: Hachette, 1970), p. 43.
52 Éric Roussel, *Charles de Gaulle* (Paris: Gallimard, 2002), pp. 452–3; Nicole Racine, 'De Gaulle et la "République des lettres"', in Fondation Charles de Gaulle, *De Gaulle et la Libération*, pp. 173–93.
53 *DM*I, pp. 441–2, 454.
54 Dwight D. Eisenhower, *Crusade in Europe* (London: Heinemann, 1948), pp. 326–7; Crémieux-Brilhac, *France Libre*, p. 908.
55 Andrieu, 'Le CNR', p. 96; Lacouture, *De Gaulle* II, pp. 36–7.
56 Lacouture, *De Gaulle* II, p. 38.
57 Buton, *Les Lendemains*, pp. 133, 137.
58 *DM*I, p. 467.
59 Andrieu, 'Le CNR', pp. 97–8.
60 Mauriac, *Un autre de Gaulle*, pp. 21–2.
61 Roussel, *de Gaulle*, p. 456.
62 *DM*I, pp. 443–51.

63 Claude Bouchinet-Serreulles, *Nous étions nés pour être libres. La Résistance avec de Gaulle et Jean Moulin* (Paris: Grasset, 2000), p. 371.
64 Andrieu, 'Le CNR', pp. 99–103.
65 Touchard, *Le Gaullisme*, p. 81.
66 Buton, *Les Lendemains*, pp. 122–3, 163–4.
67 Buton, *Les Lendemains*, p. 142.
68 Foot, *SOE in France*, p. 369.
69 Gildea, *Fighters*, p. 376; Buton, *Les Lendemains*, pp. 89–90.
70 Mauriac, *Un autre de Gaulle*, pp. 44, 46–7.
71 Laurent Douzou and Dominique Veillon, 'Les Déplacements du général de Gaulle à travers la France', in Fondation Charles de Gaulle, *De Gaulle et la Libération*, pp. 143–63; Olivier Germain-Thomas and Philippe Barthelet, *Charles de Gaulle jour après jour*, pp. 86–8.
72 Mauriac, *Un autre de Gaulle*, pp. 44, 46–7; Douzou and Veillon, 'Les Déplacements', pp. 157–61.
73 Benamou, *Déraisonnable*, pp. 93–7.
74 Benamou, *Déraisonnable*, p. 128.
75 Roussel, *de Gaulle*, p. 458.
76 Jackson, *A Certain Idea*, p. 338.
77 Buton, *Les Lendemains*, pp. 158–9.
78 Mauriac, *Un autre de Gaulle*, p. 60.
79 Buton, *Les Lendemains*, pp. 175, 179.
80 Natalia Naoumova, 'Moscow, the Parti Communiste Français, and France's Political Recovery', in Knapp, *The Uncertain Foundation*, pp. 160–82: p. 167.
81 Chantal Morelle and Maurice Vaïsse, 'La Reconnaissance internationale: des enjeux contradictoires', in Fondation Charles de Gaulle, *De Gaulle et la Libération*, pp. 195–218; pp. 207–9.
82 Kersaudy, *Churchill and de Gaulle*, pp. 366–7; The National Archives of the United Kingdom, CAB120/524/T1834/4, Roosevelt to Churchill, 28 September 1944.
83 Kersaudy, *De Gaulle et Roosevelt*, p. 444; Duff Cooper, *Diaries*, pp. 327–8.
84 Servais, *Regards*, pp. 412–13; Mauriac, *Un autre de Gaulle*, pp. 22–5.
85 Kersaudy, *Churchill and de Gaulle*, p. 372.
86 Mauriac, *Autre de Gaulle*, pp. 55–6.
87 Charles de Gaulle, *War Memoirs*, vol. III: *Salvation*, tr. Richard Howard (London: Weidenfeld & Nicolson, 1960), p. 36.
88 Andrieu, 'Le CNR', p. 118.
89 Eden, *Reckoning*, p. 457.

Further reading

The following material is in addition to that listed for Chapters 2–4.

Julian Jackson, *A Certain Idea of France* (London: Allen Lane, 2018), chapters 13–14, covers the period from June 1944 to May 1945.

There are numerous books about D-Day and the ensuing military campaign, including John Keegan, *Six Armies in Normandy* (London: Pimlico, 2004 [1982]) and Antony Beevor, *D-Day* (London: Penguin Books, 2009). Matthew Cobb, *Eleven Days in August: The Liberation of Paris in 1944* (London: Simon & Schuster, 2013) is the pre-eminent narrative of the liberation of Paris.

Philippe Buton, *La Joie douloureuse. La Libération de la France* (Brussels: Complexe, 2004) is the best general history of the liberation of France. Fondation Charles de Gaulle, *De Gaulle et la Libération* (Brussels: Complexe, 2004) covers de Gaulle's role in it.

Charles de Gaulle, *War Memoirs*, vol. III: *Salvation, 1944–1946*, tr. Richard Howard (London: Weidenfeld and Nicolson, 1960) covers the period from August 1944 to January 1946.

6 The Liberation Government, October 1944–January 1946

In October 1944 de Gaulle appeared to have reached a political zenith. His stature as France's liberator was untarnished. His government, recognised by the Allies, could legislate by decree (or *ordonnance*) unencumbered by a constitution and unchecked by an Assembly that was still purely consultative. With Vichy and the Third Republic both discredited, there was scope for big reforms. And even after France's first post-war elections, on 21 October 1945, the new Assembly unanimously confirmed him in his post.

Yet he laboured under serious constraints. France's economy had all but collapsed. The Allies had recognised the GPRF, not France's great-power status. France's colonies were restless. And France's political parties, held in check during hostilities, intended to reassert themselves at de Gaulle's expense.

Extraordinarily effective as a war leader, de Gaulle was less equipped for these new conditions. Claude Mauriac, his loyal but critical private secretary from September 1944, described him as a 'block of pride', representing 'a demanding, incorruptible France wanting to ignore its current fragility in the name of its eternal grandeur'.[1] His primary goal, France's return to great-power status, was remote from ordinary people's (literally) bread-and-butter concerns. And he had no direct experience of ordinary democratic politics. The dramatic outcome was that de Gaulle resigned on 20 January 1946, just 17 months after the liberation of Paris.

What was his record over this period? How did he handle the enormous problems of a country emerging from the most destructive war in history? What does his behaviour under 'ordinary' political conditions tell us about de Gaulle the politician? And what made him leave?

Parties, elections, and the Constitution

Since August 1944 de Gaulle had made clear progress towards his primary aim of re-establishing the state. He found a new ally in the Communist Party leader Maurice Thorez, who returned from his wartime Soviet exile on 27 November, briefed by Stalin to get the PCF allies and government posts, not to make a revolution. In January 1945 Thorez told the PCF central committee that the Patriotic Militias should be dissolved. That July, he exhorted miners to produce more coal, as a 'class duty'.[2]

But de Gaulle remained wary of longer-term Communist ambitions. The spring 1945 municipal elections saw big gains for the PCF and its Socialist allies. Parliamentary elections would soon follow. De Gaulle had no wish to see the Communists dominate the new Assembly or shape France's future constitution. Hence the *ordonnance* of 17 August 1945, which linked elections to the new Assembly with a double referendum on its powers. Voters would be asked if they wanted the Assembly to have 'constituent' powers (to draft a new constitution – otherwise the Third Republic would return), and if so, whether they wanted to limit its other powers (the new draft constitution itself to go to referendum, and the Assembly to last seven months maximum). De Gaulle recommended Yes to both questions. The elections themselves would be held under proportional representation, which (unlike majority electoral systems) limits the advantage enjoyed by big parties (like the Communists in 1945).

De Gaulle got his Yes-Yes vote (by 96% to the first question and 66% to the second) on 21 October 1945. The elections saw the old dominant parties of the Third Republic trounced: conservatives and Radicals won under a quarter of the vote and just 92 out of 586 seats between them. The big winners were three parties whose alliance would become known as *tripartisme*. The Communists, now France's largest party, won 26.2% of the vote and 161 seats; the Socialists, 23.4% and 150 seats; and the new Christian Democratic Party, the Mouvement Républicain Populaire (MRP), 23.9% and 150 seats. No previous Assembly had leant so far Left.[3]

Confrontation with de Gaulle soon followed. Although the new Assembly unanimously confirmed him as head of government on 13 November, the three parties of *tripartisme*, now with a democratic mandate behind them, demanded an 'equitable share' of Cabinet places. That would mean one security-sensitive ministry – War, Foreign Affairs, or Interior – for the PCF. De Gaulle refused, in a radio broadcast which put his own post on the line.[4] The issue went even further than the right to choose the government. In France's republican tradition, de Gaulle's behaviour was a brazen challenge to the sacred rights of Parliament as the nation's representative.[5] De Gaulle's view of democracy, by contrast, centred on direct contact between leader and people, as when he waded into the crowd at public gatherings: 'Beneath the cheers and behind the stares, I saw the image of the people's soul. For the great majority, what mattered was the emotion provoked by this spectacle, exalted by this presence, and expressed with smiles and tears by *Vive de Gaulle!*'[6] The clash of November 1945, therefore, highlighted a profound and lasting difference of political culture between de Gaulle and the parties. Still, the Communists finally accepted five ministerial posts, all economic or industrial, and de Gaulle and the Assembly settled to an uneasy coexistence – for eight weeks.

Reform without radicalism?

On non-constitutional domestic issues, by contrast, there was considerable agreement between de Gaulle and the parties of *tripartisme*. All backed nationalisations and welfare provisions as envisaged in the CNR programme of 15 March 1944. For de Gaulle, such reforms corresponded to his social Catholic sensibility; to a sense that France's business elites had failed the country, and that while a big private sector should still exist, the state should hold the 'command levers' of the economy;[7] and to a belief that social cohesion must underpin France's *grandeur*.

Nationalisations of businesses began with the expropriation, by *ordonnances* in 1945, of two major contributors to Germany's war effort: Renault, and Gnome et Rhône aero-engines. In addition, in August 1944 the coal miners of the Nord took over the mines from their bosses, who had collaborated with the Germans: nationalisation would be formalised in December 1944. Another *ordonnance*, in February 1945, mandated the creation of works councils, including union representatives, in firms of over 100 employees. A second, non-punitive, wave of nationalisations began once France had an elected Assembly: a law of 2 December 1945 nationalised the Bank of France and the four biggest deposit banks. Gas and electricity, plus the 34 biggest insurance companies, followed after de Gaulle's resignation.

Meanwhile, *ordonnances* of 4 and 19 October 1945 created a wide-ranging social security system, including pensions, unemployment and sickness insurance, and family allowances. The new system, not at first fully comprehensive, overlaid rather than replaced pre-existing schemes, but did extend social protection to millions of workers for the first time. Family allowances, meanwhile, helped reverse France's long-term demographic decline – a perennial concern of de Gaulle's.

Two other measures completed the edifice. The first was the National School of Administration (École Nationale d'Administration, or ÉNA), created at de Gaulle's behest by an *ordonnance* of 9 October 1945. Recruited by hyper-competitive examination, ÉNA graduates, soon known as *énarques*, would spearhead France's economic modernisation. The second was the creation of a Planning Commissariat on 3 January 1946. Its founder, Jean Monnet, had convinced de Gaulle of the need for a national plan – and had also negotiated the American loans to finance it. Small, flexible, directly responsible to the head of government, the Commissariat would frame France's economic overhaul by selecting target sectors for new (and now state-led) investments, and by acting as 'a clearinghouse of [economic] ideas and objectives' so that 'the normal French aversion to expansive business practices could be overcome'.[8]

The settlement that emerged from this crucial post-war moment has parallels in the record of Britain's 1945–1951 Labour government. But it also had distinctive features: the Planning Commissariat's 'indicative' planning; state ownership of financial institutions, allowing planners to channel major investments; and the *énarques*' role as a new technocratic elite. The resulting model was widely credited with the French economy's 30 years of strong post-war growth.

Although the CNR had set the agenda, de Gaulle declared ownership of the result. *Dirigisme*, the idea of state intervention to promote economic development, goes back to Louis XIV's minister Jean-Baptiste Colbert (1619–1683). De Gaulle's unambiguous support ensured that it became a consensual, not just a left-wing, project.[9] This came at a price: for example, after the first, punitive nationalisations, he insisted on fair compensation for shareholders, and he kept merchant banks private. Works councils, confined to staff leisure activities, fell far short of the CNR vision of industrial democracy; for de Gaulle was more interested in modernisation and never questioned management's right to manage.[10] But the settlement still marked a radical departure from the past.[11]

The impossible *épuration*

The CNR programme also called for a purge – *épuration* – of those who had collaborated with Nazi Germany. De Gaulle broadly agreed, but retained his own, pragmatic, priorities. The first was to end the so-called *épuration sauvage* of summer 1944, in which FFI, *maquis* groups, and people's militias had killed some 10,000 real or suspected collaborators – relatively few compared to other West European countries – and publicly humiliated thousands of women accused of intimate relations with Germans, notably by shaving their heads.

Securing the state's monopoly of retribution and ensuring due process was difficult given the huge number of cases – and the judiciary's own record of loyalty to Vichy. Special courts were set up, their juries partly appointed by bodies close to the Resistance or Free France. Defendants were tried retroactively for acts which, under Vichy, had been perfectly legal. And the often-imposed penalty of 'national degradation' – permanent or temporary loss of civil rights – was not in the penal code before the Liberation. Imperfect, the courts were still vastly preferable to the *épuration sauvage*, and necessary, to punish crimes that were too many and too vile to be ignored.

According to Novick, they considered 163,077 cases and dismissed 73,501; 7,037 defendants were sentenced to death, 4,397 in their absence; 2,777 to life imprisonment, 10,434 to forced labour, and 26,649 to other prison terms. The (lower) Civic Chambers handed down 57,415 sentences of national degradation, 8,929 of them suspended for mitigating acts of resistance.[12] The High Court of Justice, meanwhile, tried just 100 very senior figures: 42 cases led to convictions, including 8 death sentences. In addition to the judicial condemnations, *ordonnances* of 1944 and 1945 banned former senior office-holders under Vichy from election to Parliament. Some 321 former Deputies and Senators were thus debarred; of the 581 members of the first Constituent Assembly, nearly four-fifths were new.[13]

As provisional head of state, de Gaulle had to decide whether or not to exercise his right of clemency, in respect of no fewer than 2,071 death sentences.[14] Of these he commuted 1,303, including all women, almost all minors, and most men who had acted on orders; 768 sentences were carried out.[15] Those executed included palpable villains – Laval, after perhaps the most obviously rushed trial, at which he had been eloquent in his own defence,[16] and Joseph Darnand, head of the notorious Vichy *Milice* – but also writers like Robert Brasillach and Paul Chack. De Gaulle, who considered writers particularly at fault for poisoning the national spirit, rejected pleas in their support from other intellectuals, even Gaullist ones.[17] Among the reprieved were General Dentz, commander of Vichy forces in Syria, and Pétain himself, whose sentence de Gaulle commuted on grounds of age: the Marshal would die in prison, aged 95, in 1951.

If de Gaulle had hoped for a fair *épuration* that would allow the French to move on together, he failed. For the Right, the *épuration* was victors' justice; from 1947 on, it engineered a round of early releases and amnesties, and just 62 persons were left in prison for collaboration by 1956.[18] For the Left, the *épuration* was far too lenient; the PCF even contested de Gaulle's right of clemency.[19] And indeed, relative to the population, the French courts imprisoned four times fewer collaborators than the Danish or Dutch, six times fewer than the Belgian or Norwegian.[20] Journalists, whose collaboration was open and public, were easily tried and convicted; the cases of civil servants and businessmen, who often claimed to have secretly helped the Resistance, were more difficult. They came to trial late if at all, when the courts had grown more lenient – and mindful that reconstruction required administrators and business leaders. This view chimed with de Gaulle's own. He might have a low opinion of French businessmen – 'I didn't see many of you in London', he is reported to have told a worried business delegation in October 1944[21] – but he had no wish to break the mainsprings of French capitalism. Among the civil servants, the most egregious case was that of Maurice Papon, secretary-general of the Gironde prefecture, who had organised the arrest and transport of Jews to the Drancy holding camp, en route for Auschwitz. De Gaulle knew this: but Papon kept his job and later served eight years under him as prefect of Paris police.

'Worse than under the Germans': hard times

'I had forgotten that such copious and refined meals existed', wrote Claude Mauriac after lunching for the first time in the War Ministry, the centre of de Gaulle's government.[22] 'Copious and refined' eating remained inaccessible to most French households, whose disappointment with the *épuration* was matched by dissatisfaction at grinding material hardship.

Penury resulted from France's loss of housing, industrial capacity, and food production. In 1944 alone, the Allies dropped over 450,000 tons of bombs on France, seriously damaging most major French towns and destroying 15% of the housing stock.[23] Industrial production, in December 1944, fell to 35% of 1938 levels; wheat output in 1945 to 52%. Only 2,800 railway locomotives out of 12,000 had survived, a third of France's lorries, a third of the merchant fleet. De Gaulle acknowledged on 2 March 1945 that 400,000 men were unemployed and a further 1.2 million on short-time.[24]

For households, that meant that daily food rations fell to 900–1,000 calories in spring 1945, well below even the meagre British levels; the franc lost roughly half its purchasing power between 1944 and 1946; and infant mortality exceeded one in ten live births for the first time since 1919. In Lille, following an enthusiastically received visit from de Gaulle, the *Commissaire de la République* saw life return to grim normality: belts tightened, ration tickets unredeemed, and dark grumblings about the government's failure to do better than under the German occupation.[25]

How to get a handle on this desperate economic situation? In spring 1945, de Gaulle's Economics Minister, Pierre Mendès-France, proposed a complete replacement of the currency, to curtail inflation and flush out hidden war profits. His Finance Minister, René Pleven, backed a more liberal approach, relying on American loans and domestic bond issues to expand the economy. De Gaulle, against type, backed Pleven's less rigorous policy, provoking Mendès's resignation. In an echo of the first lines of *Le Fil de l'épée*, he later wrote that 'In economy as in politics or strategy, I do not believe that there can be absolute truth, but only circumstances.' Circumstances, he claimed – the Mendès plan's practical difficulties, the austerity it would entail, the likely damage to business confidence – justified his choice.[26] But the economy failed to right itself in 1945 and the franc was massively devalued in December. And economic weakness hobbled de Gaulle's broader ambitions. 'The road to greatness lay open before us', he wrote, 'but France was in a pitiful condition to follow it!'[27]

A diminished world power

De Gaulle's central post-war foreign policy objective, he wrote in 1958, was to forge a West European bloc under French leadership. The bloc would prevent the rise of a new German Reich and become a third superpower, standing between the Soviet and 'Anglo-American' camps. He pursued this grand design with some consistency over 25 years. In 1944, he was well aware that 'the means were poor indeed!'[28] To compensate for economic weakness, de Gaulle employed the methods of Free France: assertiveness and intransigence.

To earn a place among the great powers, France had first to help defeat Germany. To maximise this contribution, de Gaulle wrote, it was even desirable 'from the viewpoint of France's higher interests' that the war should drag on.[29] So Leclerc's 2DB fought all the way to Hitler's lair at Berchtesgaden; French troops, American-equipped, made up nearly a quarter of the forces under Eisenhower's command.[30]

But politics disrupted military relations with France's allies more than once. This applied both to hardware (de Gaulle thought the Allies were equipping his armies far too slowly)[31] and to operations. In December 1944, faced with Hitler's Ardennes offensive, Eisenhower ordered the evacuation of Strasbourg, which 2DB had liberated weeks earlier. To return such a symbolic piece of French territory to Nazi rule without consulting the French government was unacceptable to de Gaulle. He threatened to withdraw French forces in the sector from the Allied command, until a meeting on 3 January 1945 with Churchill and Eisenhower got the order reversed.[32] Less justifiable were de Gaulle's attempts to grab territory for France at the war's end: Stuttgart, assigned to American troops in the overall military plan, in April 1945; and in Italy in May, the Val d'Aosta region and the towns of Tende and Brigue. For de Gaulle, France had not signed and was not bound by the 1943 armistice with Italy, and had legitimate territorial claims there. To the Americans, he was pursuing narrow national aims at the expense of the Allied cause. France kept Tende and Brigue, was forced to leave the Val d'Aosta, and lost part of the Allied goodwill earned by months of hard fighting.[33]

De Gaulle's design for post-war France certainly envisaged alliances – but under conditions. An obvious potential partner was Britain. When Churchill came to celebrate Armistice Day in Paris in November 1944, de Gaulle called the visit 'the practical manifestation of an alliance that cruel vicissitudes have made more necessary than ever'.[34] But no formal alliance would be signed until March 1947. Churchill was disinclined to choose the 'policy of frank solidarity' that de Gaulle sought if it meant committing to Western Europe at the expense of relations with the United States.[35] Other issues were involved too: the Levant, still a running sore, and Germany, where British and French priorities increasingly diverged. On 5 February 1945, de Gaulle reaffirmed his desire for an alliance if only these two questions could be satisfactorily resolved.[36] But as long as he was in power they never were.

De Gaulle did, by contrast, sign a treaty with the Soviet Union, after spending 2–10 December 1944 in Moscow. The visit was intended to signal France's return to the world stage; to win a voice in the shaping of Europe's future; to secure Soviet support for French plans for Germany; and, probably, to guarantee good behaviour from France's Communists. Stalin, for his part, wanted international backing for a new German–Polish frontier on the Oder-Neisse line, but above all recognition for the Communist-dominated Lublin Committee, which he supported as the government of Poland against the London-based government-in-exile. To secure this, he was willing to propose a treaty of alliance.[37]

According to his *Memoirs*, de Gaulle outmanoeuvred Stalin and got the alliance, without abandoning Poland to the Lublin

Committee.[38] This account is misleading in several ways. The Soviets' invitation was not spontaneous, as he states; he had fished for it.[39] De Gaulle recognised Oder-Neisse without any corresponding concession from Stalin. Withholding formal recognition of Lublin, he still sent a personal representative: Christian Fouchet, a trusted veteran of Free France, was received as a fully accredited diplomat – the first Western envoy to arrive. The alliance itself merely put into words what was happening anyway, a shared fight to the finish against Germany. The Soviets offered no concrete support, either over Germany's post-war status or for a seat at future summits. For Stalin, France, weak economically and militarily, was simply not worth it.[40] The first-ever issue of *Le Monde* might gush over the alliance;[41] *Pravda* contented itself with a routine announcement.

France was therefore excluded from the Allied conference hosted by Stalin at Yalta (4–11 February 1945). In Gaullist mythology, Yalta was the summit where the Allies carved up Europe between East and West: an outcome which France, if present, would have opposed, even prevented.[42] This view is incorrect. The Declaration on Liberated Europe, approved by Stalin, Churchill, and Roosevelt, was about free elections and did *not* mention any division of Europe. Stalin could and did ignore the Declaration; the Western Allies could only have stopped him by military force. But for de Gaulle, 'Yalta' became the symbol of a bipolar world system, dominated by the United States and the Soviet Union, which he utterly rejected.

In practice, de Gaulle conceded that Yalta offered France 'important satisfactions':[43] an occupation zone in Germany, carved out of the British and American zones, a seat on the Allied Control Council for Germany, and permanent membership of the future United Nations Security Council. It was the British – not de Gaulle's new Soviet allies – who had 'fought like tigers' to secure these marks of recognition for France, whose strength they saw as crucial to the security of Europe.[44]

This did not, however, lead to any convergence in British and French views on Europe's future. On the contrary: as the war ended, the Western Allies' views on Germany, in particular, changed rapidly while de Gaulle's remained fixed. The British and Americans moved from plans to dismember and deindustrialise

Germany (at the Quebec conference in September 1944) to a policy of reconstruction and consolidation, in order to avoid an economic and political void at Europe's heart. The Potsdam conference of summer 1945 (from which France was also excluded) was a landmark along this route. De Gaulle's very different priorities were threefold: to keep Germany divided and avoid the emergence of a 'new Reich'; to prevent the revival of a German military-industrial complex by detaching the Ruhr industrial area from any future German state, placing it under Allied control, and using its coal production to meet the needs of the victorious powers; and to secure France's vulnerable eastern frontier, by separating the left bank of the Rhine from Germany and stringing permanent French garrisons along it.[45]

This was not mere crude Germanophobia. Visiting France's occupation zone in October 1945, de Gaulle shook hands publicly with German officials and told them that 'we are all Europeans, we are all Westerners'.[46] In practice, however, the French zone, and especially the coal-rich Saar region, was vigorously exploited for France's benefit. And its commander, General Koenig, was ordered to veto any all-German structures (to handle questions such as transport) proposed in the Allied Control Council.[47] The creation of the German Federal Republic in 1949 testifies to the failure of de Gaulle's policy. And his confrontational strategy, as much as his political aims, damaged relations with the Anglo-Americans.[48]

This was all the more anomalous as in principle, US policy 'set out to make France a chief pillar of a revived post-war Europe', and to further economic recovery with loans.[49] The first political hitch after recognition in October 1944 came when de Gaulle declined an invitation from President Roosevelt to meet in Algiers, during his homeward trip from Yalta aboard USS *Quincy*. For de Gaulle, it was not for the President to invite *him* to a meeting in French waters.[50] The Americans, however, saw the refusal as a snub to a sick President: Roosevelt would die on 12 April. Nor was Roosevelt's successor, Harry S. Truman, in a hurry to reset relations. Incensed by the episodes at Stuttgart and (especially) the Val d'Aosta, Truman took the British side against de Gaulle in the final outburst of the Levant conflict, late in May. De Gaulle did, it is true, make a second visit to Washington, from 22 to 26 August 1945: he was received as a head of state and presented with a DC4 aircraft, and Monnet's negotiation of a $650 million loan for France was finalised.[51] But the German question, especially after Koenig's vetoes on the Allied Control Council, continued to obstruct any major improvement in relations.[52]

De Gaulle's foreign policy at the head of the GRPF worried leading diplomats. Hervé Alphand and Jean Chauvel, top officials at the French Foreign Ministry who enjoyed de Gaulle's trust, both wrote privately – Alphand in January 1945, Chauvel a year later – that de Gaulle had isolated France.[53] The Soviet alliance was grand but useless; Stalin was unrelentingly hostile to France's 'unrealistic' pretensions. Meanwhile France received American economic, and British diplomatic, support, without enjoying the stability of an alliance. Certainly, Germany was an issue which France, having sustained three invasions in a lifetime and been abandoned by its allies after 1919, was almost bound to view differently from the British and Americans in 1945. On other matters, though, there is a sense that de Gaulle was either out to provoke, or at least insensitive to the consequences of his assertiveness.

Pierre Messmer, de Gaulle's Defence Minister from 1960 to 1969, once summarised Gaullism as 'authority of the state and national independence'.[54] Re-establishing the authority of the state within France was a significant achievement of de Gaulle as head of the GPRF. In the world, however, he set out a template for what a policy of national independence would become, without the means to implement it;[55] the confrontational techniques of Free France no longer sufficed. The same could be said of de Gaulle's record in France's restless overseas territories.

Cracks in the Empire

The Brazzaville conference of January 1944 has gone down in Gaullist mythology as the start of a liberal trajectory which would bring almost all of France's overseas territories, including Algeria, to self-government and then independence by 1962.[56] Yet even de Gaulle's opening speech there had been cautious; and the conference's conclusions explicitly ruled out self-government. De Gaulle might understand the aspirations of colonised peoples; but his record to 1946 is, in general, far from liberal. Colonial officials on the ground generally used force when challenged; de Gaulle covered them; and the wartime line of the Free French, that they had to return France's Empire intact to the Republic, outlasted the end of hostilities.

Indochina, today's three states of Vietnam, Cambodia and Laos, was the wealthiest, most populous part of the French Empire. But it was not represented at Brazzaville and was out of Free French reach till 1945. Governed by Vichy-appointed officials from 1940, integrated into Japan's war economy, Indochina was then occupied by Japanese troops from 9 March 1945. They would surrender to British forces in the south and Chinese in the north. The French expeditionary force that finally arrived on 2 October 1945 (for the French depended entirely on Allied transport) thus encountered troops from three countries – Japanese, Chinese, and British – plus a powerful armed nationalist movement, the Viet Minh, created in 1941. Its leader, the Communist Ho Chi Minh, had declared Vietnam's independence on the day of the formal Japanese surrender, 2 September.

On 24 March 1945 the GPRF had reacted to the Japanese occupation with a declaration promising that 'The Indochinese Federation' would enjoy freedom within a '"French Union", whose external interests will be represented by France'. But the colonial division of Vietnam into three states – Tonkin to the north, Annam at the centre, and Cochinchina to the south – would be perpetuated – and there would still be a French-appointed Governor-General.[57] Pierre Messmer, parachuted into Indochina as a GPRF representative in summer 1945, later said that he 'never understood why General de Gaulle approved this disastrous declaration', viewed in Indochina as 'an unacceptable programme of recolonisation'. And when Henri Laurentie, architect of the Brazzaville conference, tried to put a liberal gloss on French policy there, de Gaulle personally disowned him.[58]

The GPRF attempted three policies in Indochina from October 1945: the military reconquest of the country by Leclerc's expeditionary force; setting up a new French administration under Governor-General Thierry d'Argenlieu; and negotiations with the Viet Minh conducted by France's representative in Tonkin, Jean Sainteny. These produced results of a sort. The Saigon area was recovered from the Viet Minh. British and Chinese troops were evacuated by the end of March 1946. Sainteny reached a provisional agreement with Ho Chi Minh on 6 March which referred to Vietnam as 'a free state within the Indochinese Federation and the French union' – leaving independence, and the unity of Vietnam, for future negotiation.[59] Indochina's later slide into a full-scale colonial war was not preordained when de Gaulle left. But both the declaration of 24 March 1945 and the priority de Gaulle placed on recovering territory rather than offering new perspectives meant that trust between the French and the Viet Minh remained fragile. Events, tragically, would bear that out.[60]

Uncertain in Indochina, de Gaulle's legacy was frankly disastrous in Algeria – despite several liberal gestures there. At Constantine on 12 December 1943, he had promised more economic development, greater recruitment of Moslems to the civil service, and full citizenship for 'tens of thousands' of Moslems – which duly materialised, for 70,000, in the *ordonnance* of 7 March 1944.[61] But on departing for mainland France on 17 August 1944, he left orders that Algerian nationalism must be monitored and if necessary repressed.[62] It was. In his *Memoirs* he would write that 'In Algeria, an insurrection began in the Constantinois and synchronized with the Syrian riots in May, was put down by Governor General Chataigneau.'[63] Inaccurate in detail, this statement grossly understated both the bloodiness and the historic importance of what really happened.

Granting French citizenship to some 0.9% of the Moslem population was never going to satisfy Algeria's nationalists. In March 1945 Ferhat Abbas, a pharmacist from the eastern town of Sétif, founded a moderate nationalist movement, the Amis du Manifeste et de la Liberté (AML), calling for Algerian self-government under French sovereignty. But pro-independence radicals rapidly took the AML over. Their leader, Messali Hadj, was soon arrested by the French and deported. Demonstrations marking 1 May – quiet in many towns, fiercely repressed in Algiers and Oran – then called for Messali's release. Faced with this unrest, the liberal governor of Algeria, Yves Chataigneau, was recalled to Paris for consultations, leaving the field open for less scrupulous officials.

On 8 May 1945, parades celebrated the Allied victory against Germany, in Algeria as in mainland France. For many Algerian Moslems, especially veterans, it was not just France's victory but theirs, and that of the values, enshrined in the Atlantic Charter, for which the Allies had fought. In Sétif Algerian flags suddenly appeared among those of the Allies. Banners called for Messali's release and for independence. And the local police opened fire, killing an unknown number of Algerians. The crowd in Sétif, and then surrounding villages, began attacking Europeans; by the end of 11 May some 102 lay murdered, many mutilated.

Ghastly though these acts were, they were dwarfed by the ensuing reprisals. These affected not only the Sétif area but also Guelma, 100 miles away, where no massacre of Europeans had taken place – but where the sub-prefect quickly organised white vigilante groups. Now the full panoply of French techniques later used during the Algerian war, including torture, summary executions, and air attacks on villages, was deployed in a succession of massacres lasting well into June. According to French civilian authorities, 1,500 Algerians died; but the military estimate was 8,000. Other sources put the total at 20,000; the Algerian government figure is 80,000.[64]

Was de Gaulle responsible? There is no smoking gun, though two authors write of a telegram sent on 11 May, apparently at de Gaulle's behest, ordering 'all possible means' to put down the unrest – which officials on the ground could take as declaring open season on Algerian Moslems.[65] It is clear that afterwards, de Gaulle wanted the affair buried. An official enquiry set up at Interior Minister Tixier's recommendation on 19 May was cut short. Tixier, under pressure from de Gaulle, played down the killings as exaggerated by the British and Americans. The Consultative Assembly was no more curious, ascribing all loss of life to the Algerian nationalists.[66]

An enlightened policy on Algeria, treating moderates like Ferhat Abbas as partners, might conceivably have allowed peaceful evolution there. After Sétif and Guelma that was impossible. Both towns were central to the independence struggle from 1954; Algeria's wider Moslem population neither forgave nor forgot.[67] If de Gaulle can be credited with ending the Algerian war in 1962, he also bears some responsibility for its beginning. And his dismissal of the massacres, suggesting 'synchronisation' with riots in Syria (and by implication, British involvement), is unworthy of his *War Memoirs*.

Syria was, indeed, the scene of another massacre of Arabs by French forces – and of confrontation with the British – late in May 1945. Little had changed politically there since the crisis of November 1943, other than the forced departure of Spears, *bête noire* of the French (and increasingly of the British Foreign Office). The French authorities, now headed by General Paul Beynet, would not work with the Syrian and Lebanese governments, or hand over to them command of the 24,000 or so *troupes spéciales*, locally recruited auxiliary forces. Indeed, many of the French were aiming to reverse the humiliation of the last crisis.[68]

Although France's justification for delaying Syrian and Lebanese independence ended with the war in Europe, De Gaulle was still resolved to guarantee by treaty French military and cultural predominance in the two new states. Amid the nationalist wave that swept the Middle East at the war's end, however, *any* treaty with the French was unwelcome to the Syrian and Lebanese governments.[69] The British, as usual, were caught between two incompatible priorities: not losing favour with the Arabs by backing France's neo-imperialist design; but avoiding the humiliation of their French allies. For the moment, they warned against any French show of force as the treaties were presented.

The warnings went unheeded. De Gaulle, against the advice both of Beynet and of his Foreign Minister Bidault, was determined to impose a treaty if necessary.[70] On 6 May French reinforcements, some 2,500 troops, began arriving in Beirut. Then Beynet presented France's treaty terms: 'extensive commercial and cultural concessions, transport facilities, military bases, naval bases and control of the *Troupes Spéciales*'.[71] The Syrians and Lebanese broke off negotiations on 21 May. Civil unrest began, including, in Syria, strikes, violent anti-French demonstrations, and clashes between Arabs and the army. On 29 May the French commander in Damascus, General Oliva-Roget, responded: across Syria, French troops fired indiscriminately on crowds; in Damascus, the Syrian Parliament building and the Foreign Ministry were shelled, then sacked.[72]

Thus far the British had stood aside. But on 30 May, under pressure from Parliament, Churchill instructed General Paget, British commander in the Middle East, to restore order in Syria, and told France's ambassador to London of his decision. De Gaulle told Beynet to order a cease-fire in Syria that same night but the violence continued on 31 May. The death toll from these days is estimated at 1,000.[73] Paget's orders were to 'assume command of all Allied troops in the Levant and oblige the French to retire to barracks'.[74] He reached Damascus on 31 May; that afternoon, Foreign Secretary

Eden informed the Commons of the British intervention – *before* a letter from Churchill outlining its purpose had reached de Gaulle.

Greeted as liberators by the Lebanese and Syrian governments, the British Ninth Army proceeded to strip the French administration of most of its remaining prerogatives, notably its control of the Wheat Office, before handing responsibility for order to the Lebanese and Syrian authorities. The *troupes spéciales* were transferred to the Lebanese and Syrians in August. All residual French authority now melted away. In June 1945 French homes in Syria were looted, and most of the (small) French civilian population fled to Beirut and sought repatriation; according to the French trade attaché, any Frenchman venturing unescorted in Damascus, Homs, Hama, or Aleppo risked being murdered.[75] British and French troops coexisted uneasily until a United Nations Security Council resolution, requested by the two Levantine governments, led to their evacuation from the Levant by 17 April 1946. For France, a foreseeable departure had become a humiliation.

De Gaulle believed that the British had organised the whole episode to further their designs on the Levant, and was correspondingly bitter.[76] On 4 June he told the British ambassador, Duff Cooper, that he would have opened hostilities but for France's weakness.[77] The British, he claimed, had armed protesters (including Syrian and Lebanese police forces) to have the French driven out; only when the French had restored order and achieved a cease-fire, on 31 May, did the British 'stage a tableau prepared in advance in order to inflict a public humiliation upon France'.[78] But no effective cease-fire was holding on 31 May. And his account minimises or ignores casualties caused by the French.[79] It misreads the intentions of the British who, though always worried about the repercussions for them of events in the Levant, faced enough difficulties in Egypt, Iraq, Palestine, or Transjordan, without trying to take over Syria and Lebanon as well. It interprets the Arab nationalist movement as the product of British manipulation.[80] Surprising in a man for whom nations were the primary reality of international politics, de Gaulle's own failure to get the measure of Arab nationalism contributed both to tragic loss of life in Syria and Algeria, and to an unnecessary humiliation for France in the Levant.

In the French protectorates of Morocco and Tunisia, events were less dramatic – though Morocco had seen rioting and repression in early 1944, and Tunisia the deposition of Bey Moncef in 1943. Morocco's young Sultan Mohammed V was received with pomp in Paris on 18 June 1945; so was Sidi Lamine, Moncef's successor as Bey, on 14 July. De Gaulle promised both (titular) sovereigns future talks about greater self-rule (Roosevelt had talked of independence to Mohammed V). But no contact was made with the moderate Tunisian nationalist leader Habib Bourguiba, and practical reforms reinforced the French 'residents' (in effect heads of government) in the two protectorates. The best that can be said of de Gaulle's policy here is that it did little serious damage.[81]

Later events would show that de Gaulle was no dyed-in-the-wool imperialist and understood the force of other peoples' nationalisms. But his record at the head of the GPRF frequently appears both inept and in contradiction with his often liberal discourse. Clearly his ideas changed between 1946 and 1958. But another key to his record may be that he saw liberalism as 'the prerogative of the strong'. As President of the Fifth Republic, he could afford to give colonies full independence; as president of the GPRF, de Gaulle headed a weakened France and was reluctant to contemplate even limited autonomy.[82]

Departure, January 1946

Without its dramatic stage-management (a Cabinet meeting summoned for *Sunday* 21 January 1946; a brief announcement to the astonished ministers; then away),[83] de Gaulle's resignation might have caused little surprise. As we have seen, trouble had been brewing since the October elections; the only problem is an overabundance of explanations.

Fatigue should not be overlooked. The de Gaulles' family holiday at Cap d'Antibes (4–14 January) was their first since before the war, a necessary rest after a gruelling five-and-a-half years which included two bouts of malaria.[84] But de Gaulle would not have resigned if the politics had been going well. They were not. Beyond even the fundamental disagreement about how the country should be governed, de Gaulle had come to hold most of France's political class in contempt. That included what he derided as 'la résistance politicienne' – anti-nazi, anti-fascist, but not in his view 'national', and whose congresses he carefully avoided.[85] A man who could take this view of the Resistance – which had, whatever their differences, shared the ideals of Free France for four years – faced serious difficulty maintaining the national unity he had discerned (with some wishful thinking) in August 1944.

Another politician might have created his own party before the elections. But that, for de Gaulle, meant renouncing his mission to represent *all* of France. For the same reason, he had no wish to lead a majority coalition built from existing parties.[86] Besides, he had reasons for disliking each of them. His suspicions of France's Communists were well founded; they were determined to get rid of him and would express great private satisfaction at his departure.[87] The Socialists still suspected de Gaulle's republican credentials, and de Gaulle considered their aims to be too partisan and insufficiently national. The MRP's social Catholic sensibility was probably closest to his own, and it presented itself as the party most loyal to him; yet its leaders still criticised aspects of his policy, and behaved as if *he* should be loyal to *them*. The Right and (many of) the Radicals, finally, had compromised with Vichy.[88] His ideal would have been to prolong 'the sort of monarchy which I had recently assumed and which general consent had subsequently ratified', but he knew that he could not impose such a regime on an unwilling people.[89] The unanimous vote his government received from the Constituent Assembly on 23 November 1945 was a last, symbolic, acknowledgement by the parties of his wartime role; but it secured him no stable basis of parliamentary support.

On some issues, de Gaulle and the parties made policy without reference to one another. De Gaulle's stance on Syria had left him isolated from his own ministers and from parliamentarians, as he himself acknowledged.[90] After the elections the Assembly delegated a committee to draft a new constitutional text; when de Gaulle dared ask about its progress, his own former Justice Minister, François de Menthon, told him it was none of his business as he had not been elected by the French people.[91]

Later, de Gaulle would say that he had 'put the train back on the rails' and then resigned to allow the Constituent Assembly to get on with its work.[92] Duff Cooper's less flattering interpretation is that he left 'because all was going wrong'.[93] In Germany, in Syria, in Indochina, de Gaulle's policies were blocked. At home, on 26

December 1945, the franc was devalued by 60% and bread rationing, suspended earlier in the year, reintroduced.[94] Setbacks here, at the heart of ordinary people's material concerns, damaged the government's popularity – and de Gaulle's.[95] As a result, the parties in the Assembly felt freer to raise their concerns. Why, asked the Socialists (soon joined by the Communists) at the year's end, should defence represent 28% of government spending when the war had ended?[96] Could it not be reduced by a fifth, freeing desperately needed funds for civilian uses?

For de Gaulle, the question was triply unacceptable. High military spending was essential to secure France's position in the world; defence was the head of government's responsibility; and the Assembly had no business meddling with the budget and preventing the government from governing. On 1 January 1946 he chided the Assembly with ignoring the lessons of recent French history about overmighty parliaments; this, he added, was probably his last appearance in the Chamber.[97] His budget survived, but he knew, as he left for Cap d'Antibes, that the Assembly would go on challenging him. He took his decision on 13 January – 'to get out before being thrown out or used up', as Hoffmann writes.[98]

There was every indication that he expected to be called back speedily.[99] Meanwhile, with Colombey still under repair after the Germans' depredations, he retired to Marly, 17 miles outside Paris, renting a hunting lodge with peeling wallpaper and faulty heating. He told visitors that he was well out of it all, and began writing his memoirs. After five months, boredom, and anxiety over the state of France, brought him back to the public arena.

De Gaulle's departure says three things about him as a politician. First, he was enough of a democrat to leave if the French did not want him; he would not force himself upon them as a dictator. A poll late in January showed that just 27% of the French wanted him back; 52% did not.[100] Second, he might be a realist but he was no more a compromiser in domestic politics than he had been towards his wartime Allies. He wanted power on his own terms or not at all. Third, he was a risk-taker, more inclined to walk away than to make concessions to his adversaries. This time the risk did not pay off. Years later he called his resignation a 'political error'.[101] Instead of the expected brief interval, he would wait 12 years, 4 months, and 9 days before being called back.

Conclusion

Duff Cooper's verdict on de Gaulle's resignation was probably closest to the truth. His foreign policy had placed excessive hopes in the Soviet Union and unnecessarily complicated relations with the Western Allies; his successors would have to negotiate a rapprochement with the United States and accept a resurrected West Germany. In 'overseas France', the record ranged from indifferent (in Morocco, Tunisia, or Indochina) to unnecessarily humiliating (in Syria), while in Algeria the horrors of Sétif and Guelma set the scene for the conflict to come. At home, the measures of December 1945 were an acknowledgement of the government's failure to bring the economy under control. And despite the importance that France's institutions held for him, de Gaulle found himself excluded from the developing constitutional debate after November 1945. On this basis he resembles Churchill, who had lost office on 26 July 1945 after Labour's historic election victory: a great wartime leader unable to make the transition to peacetime politics.

De Gaulle's record is nevertheless better than that. First, although he probably did not save France from a Communist coup (both the PCF and Stalin were too prudent to try one), his achievement in restoring a state out of the confusion of the Liberation period should not be underestimated. Second, although he lacked the means to implement it, the grand design that he would try to achieve from 1958 was there, in outline, in 1945. Third, his government's social and economic reforms set the framework for 40 (mostly successful) years of post-war French history. He shares the credit for them with the left-wing parties; in some respects he moderated the reforms; but they remain, in part, his, and buttressed his claim to be a leader who looked beyond the divisions of Left and Right.

Not that that made much difference in the short term. For during a 'crossing of the desert' that lasted until his return to power in May 1958, de Gaulle would most frequently pass for a figure of the reactionary Right.

Notes

1 Claude Mauriac, *Un autre de Gaulle* (Paris: Hachette, 1970), p. 160.

The Liberation Government

2. Philippe Buton, *Les Lendemains qui déchantent: le Parti communiste français à la Libération* (Paris: Presses de Sciences Po, 1994), pp. 180–90.
3. Philip Williams, *Crisis and Compromise: Politics in the Fourth Republic* (London: Longman, 1964), pp. 22, 502–3.
4. On 17 November. *DM*I, p. 650.
5. Sudhir Hazareesingh, *Political Traditions in Modern France* (Oxford: Oxford University Press, 1993), p. 82.
6. *WM*III, p. 130.
7. Speech to Consultative Assembly, 2 March 1945, *DM*I, p. 529.
8. William I. Hitchcock, *France Restored: Cold War Diplomacy and the Quest for Leadership in Europe, 1944–1954* (Chapel Hill: University of North Carolina Press, 1998), p. 37.
9. *WM*III, p. 100.
10. Speech of 2 March 1945, *DM*I, p. 528.
11. Herrick Chapman, 'France's Liberation Era, 1944–1947: A Social and Economic Settlement?', in Andrew Knapp (ed.), *The Uncertain Foundation: France at the Liberation, 1944–1947* (Basingstoke: Palgrave, 2007), pp. 102–20.
12. Peter Novick, *The Resistance versus Vichy: The Purge of Collaborators in Liberated France* (London: Chatto & Windus, 1968), p. 219.
13. Olivier Wieviorka, 'Replacement or Renewal? The French Political Élite at the Liberation', in Knapp (ed.), *The Uncertain Foundation*, pp. 75–86: pp. 77–8.
14. Mauriac, *Un autre de Gaulle*, p. 75.
15. *WM*III, p. 109.
16. Jean Lacouture, *De Gaulle*, vol. II: *Le Politique, 1944–1959* (Paris: Le Seuil, 1985), pp. 150–2.
17. Éric Roussel, *Charles de Gaulle* (Paris: Gallimard, 2002), p. 515.
18. Novick, *Resistance*, p. 188.
19. Roussel, *de Gaulle*, p. 490.
20. Novick, *Resistance*, p. 187.
21. Henri Weber, *Le Parti des patrons. Le CNPF, 1946–1990* (Paris: Le Seuil, 1991), p. 83.
22. Mauriac, *Un autre de Gaulle*, p. 11.
23. Danièle Voldman, *La Reconstruction des villes françaises de 1940 à 1954. Histoire d'une politique* (Paris: L'Harmattan, 1997), pp. 33–5.
24. *DM*I, pp. 522–3; *WM*III, pp. 7–9; Frances Lynch, *France and the International Economy: From Vichy to the Treaty of Rome* (London: Routledge, 1997), pp. 7, 31, 49, 98, 155; Weber, *Patrons*, p. 87.
25. Lacouture, *De Gaulle* II, p. 116.
26. *WM*III, p. 120; for *Le Fil*, cf. above, p. 18.
27. *WM*III, p. 229.
28. *WM*III, pp. 178–9.
29. *WM*III, pp. 83–4.
30. *WM*III, p. 132.

31 Lacouture, *De Gaulle* II, pp. 64–6; Hervé Alphand, *L'Étonnement d'être* (Paris: Fayard, 1977), p. 182.
32 Lacouture, *De Gaulle* II, pp. 68–75.
33 Julian Jackson, *A Certain Idea of France: The Life of Charles de Gaulle* (London: Allen Lane, 2018), pp. 356–8.
34 *DM*I, p. 476.
35 *DM*I, p. 388.
36 *DM*I, p. 518; Lacouture, *De Gaulle* II, pp. 80–4; J. Chauvel, *Commentaire*, vol. II: *D'Alger à Berne, 1944–1952* (Paris: Fayard, 1972), pp. 162–4.
37 Jean-Laloy, 'France-URSS: la belle et bonne alliance', in Maurice Vaïsse (ed.), *De Gaulle et la Russie* (Paris: CNRS Éditions, 2012 [2006]), pp. 132–40; Hélène Carrère d'Encausse, *Le Général de Gaulle et la Russie* (Paris: Fayard, 2017), pp. 60–2.
38 *WM*III, pp. 63–82.
39 Alexander Werth, *De Gaulle* (Harmondsworth: Penguin Books, 1965), p. 182.
40 Lacouture, *De Gaulle* II, pp. 87–95.
41 *Le Monde*, 19 December 1944.
42 Press conference, 9 September 1968, *DM*V, pp. 332–3.
43 *WM*III, p. 89.
44 John Young, *Britain, France, and the Unity of Europe, 1945–1951* (Leicester: Leicester University Press, 1984), p. 8; Anne Deighton, *The Impossible Peace: Britain, the Division of Germany, and the Origins of the Cold War* (Oxford: Oxford University Press, 1990), p. 40.
45 Broadcast of 5 February 1945 (*DM*I, pp. 515–19), and press conferences of 25 January 1945 (*DM*I, p. 504) and 12 October 1945 (*DM*I, pp. 630, 634–5).
46 *Le Monde*, 4 and 6 October 1945.
47 Hitchcock, *France Restored*, pp. 51–3.
48 Hitchcock, *France Restored*, p. 54.
49 John S. Hill, 'Germany, the United States, and De Gaulle's Strategy for Economic Reconstruction, 1944–1946', in Robert O. Paxton and Nicholas Wahl (eds), *De Gaulle and the United States: A Centennial Reappraisal* (Oxford: Berg, 1994), pp. 103–15.
50 *WM*III, pp. 90–1.
51 Charles Williams, *The Last Great Frenchman* (New York: John Wiley, 1993), p. 309.
52 Irwin Wall, 'Harry S. Truman and Charles de Gaulle', in Paxton and Wahl (eds), *De Gaulle and the United States*, pp. 117–39: pp. 127–8.
53 Alphand, *L'Étonnement*, p. 183; J. Chauvel, *Commentaire* II, pp. 162–4.
54 Interview with the author, 17 April 1991.
55 Stanley Hoffmann, *Decline or Renewal? France since the 1930s* (New York: Viking Press, 1974), p. 94.

56 Press conference, 25 October 1944, *DM*I, p. 464; Charles de Gaulle, *Memoirs of Hope*, tr. Terence Kilmartin (London: Weidenfeld & Nicolson, 1971), p. 12.
57 Martin Shipway, *Decolonization and its Impact: A Comparative Approach to the End of the Colonial Empires* (Oxford: Blackwell, 2008), p. 90.
58 Pierre Messmer, *Les Blancs s'en vont. Récits de décolonisation* (Paris: Albin Michel, 1998), pp. 40–3.
59 Shipway, *Decolonisation*, p. 91.
60 Lacouture, *De Gaulle* II, pp. 154–67.
61 *DM*I, pp. 351–4.
62 Martin Evans, *Algeria: France's Undeclared War* (Oxford: Oxford University Press, 2012), p. 79.
63 *WM*III, p. 220.
64 Lacouture, *De Gaulle* II, pp. 180–2; Jackson, *A Certain Idea*, p. 361.
65 Roger Benmebarek, 'Le Général de Gaulle et les événements de mai 1945 dans le Constantinois', in Maurice Vaïsse (ed.), *De Gaulle et l'Algérie, 1943–1969* (Paris: Armand Colin/Ministère de la Défense, 2012), pp. 39–40; Mahfoud Kaddache, 'De Gaulle et les nationalistes algériens (1940–1962)', in Institut Charles de Gaulle, *De Gaulle en son siècle*, vol. VI: *Liberté et dignité des peuples* (Paris: Plon, 1992), p. 97.
66 Evans, *Algerian War*, pp. 87–9; Jean-Pierre Peyroulou, 'La Politique algérienne du général de Gaulle 1943–1946', in Vaïsse (ed.), *De Gaulle et l'Algérie*, pp. 34–6.
67 Bernard Droz and Évelyne Lever, *Histoire de la guerre d'Algérie, 1954–1962* (Paris: Le Seuil, 1991 [1982]), pp. 32–3.
68 A.B. Gaunson, *The Anglo-French Clash in Lebanon and Syria, 1940–1945* (Basingstoke: Macmillan, 1987), pp. 156–9, 171.
69 Gaunson, *Clash*, p. 167.
70 Anne Bruchez, 'La Fin de la présence française en Syrie: de la crise de mai 1945 au départ des dernières troupes étrangères', *Relations internationales*, 122(2), January 2005, pp. 17–32: p. 30.
71 Gaunson, *Clash*, pp. 171–2.
72 Bruchez, 'La Fin', p. 22.
73 Lacouture, *De Gaulle* II, p. 173.
74 Gaunson, *Clash*, p. 174.
75 Bruchez, 'La Fin', pp. 25–8.
76 Press conference, 2 June 1945, *DM*I, pp. 558–72; *WM*III, pp. 184–93.
77 *WM*III, p. 192.
78 *WM*III, p, 189.
79 Bruchez, 'La Fin', p. 27.
80 Lacouture, *De Gaulle* II, p. 171.
81 Lacouture, *De Gaulle* II, pp. 177–8.
82 Jean Lacouture, 'Révision dans le désert, 1946–1958', in Institut du Droit de la Paix et du Développement de l'Université de Nice and

Institut Charles de Gaulle (eds), *De Gaulle et le Tiers Monde* (Paris: Pedone, 1984), p. 115.
83 Georgette Elgey, *La République des illusions, 1945–1951* (Paris: Fayard, 1965), p. 89.
84 Claude Guy, *En écoutant de Gaulle. Journal 1946–1949* (Paris: Grasset, 1996), pp. 35–42.
85 Mauriac, *Un autre*, pp. 97, 169.
86 Elgey, *Illusions*, p. 55.
87 Buton, 'Le Parti communiste', pp. 52–4; Buton, *Les Lendemains*, p. 215.
88 Lacouture, *De Gaulle* II, pp. 202–10, 249.
89 *WM*III, p. 233.
90 *WM*III, p. 194.
91 Elgey, *Illusions*, p. 75.
92 Speech at Bayeux, 16 June 1946, *DM*II, p. 7.
93 Jackson, *A Certain Idea*, p. 384.
94 Roussel, *de Gaulle*, p. 523.
95 Jean Charlot, *Le Gaullisme d'opposition, 1946–1958* (Paris: Fayard, 1983), pp. 42–4.
96 Roussel, *de Gaulle*, p. 523.
97 Elgey, *Illusions*, pp. 80–1; Charlot, *Opposition*, pp. 36–7.
98 Hoffmann, *Decline*, p. 101.
99 Elgey, *Illusions*, p. 94.
100 Charlot, *Opposition*, pp. 9, 43.
101 Lacouture, *De Gaulle* II, p. 249.

Further reading

Julian Jackson, *A Certain Idea of France* (London: Allen Lane, 2018), chapters 14–15, covers the period from August 1944 to December 1946. Jean Lacouture's *De Gaulle*, vol. II: *Le Politique, 1944–1959* (Paris: Le Seuil, 1985) opens with the Provisional Government.

The essays in Andrew Knapp (ed.), *The Uncertain Foundation: France at the Liberation, 1944–1947* (Basingstoke: Palgrave, 2007) cover France's 'long' liberation, including the Provisional Government.

De Gaulle's own account of the Provisional Government is in his *War Memoirs*, vol. III: *Salvation, 1944–1946*, tr. Richard Howard (London: Weidenfeld & Nicolson, 1960).

On de Gaulle's diplomacy, see John W. Young, *France, the Cold War and the Western Alliance, 1944–1949: French Foreign Policy and Post-War Europe* (Leicester: Leicester University Press, 1990); William I. Hitchcock, *France Restored: Cold War Diplomacy and the Quest for Leadership in Europe, 1944–1954* (Chapel Hill: University of North Carolina Press, 1998: also good on the post-war economy); and the essays by

Irwin Wall and John S. Hill in Robert O. Paxton and Nicholas Wahl (eds), *De Gaulle and the United States: A Centennial Reappraisal* (Oxford and Providence RI: Berg, 1994).

On France's Empire, see Martin Shipway, *Decolonization and its Impact: A Comparative Approach to the End of the Colonial Empires* (Oxford: Blackwell, 2008), A.B. Gaunson, *The Anglo-French Clash in Lebanon and Syria, 1940–1945* (London: Macmillan, 1987), and Anne Bruchez, 'La fin de la présence française en Syrie: de la crise de mai 1945 au départ des dernières troupes étrangères', *Relations internationales*, 122(2), January 2005, pp. 17–32.

Peter Novick, *The Resistance versus Vichy: The Purge of Collaborators in Liberated France* (London: Chatto & Windus, 1968) remains the standard work on the purges.

Philippe Buton, *Les Lendemains qui déchantent: le Parti communiste français à la Libération* (Paris: Presses de Sciences Po, 1994) covers the struggle between de Gaulle and the Communists.

Philip Williams, *Crisis and Compromise: Politics in the Fourth Republic* (London: Longman, 1964) opens with party strategies and the complex manoeuvrings over the future constitution that began under de Gaulle's Provisional Government.

7 A study in failure, 1946–1958

In the Gaullist narrative, the 'crossing of the desert' refers to the 12 years between the General's resignation in January 1946 and his return to power in May 1958. In his *Memoirs*, they are dismissed in barely a page: unsurprisingly, because they were years of failure. Above all, his attempt to create, in the Rassemblement du Peuple Français (Rally of the French People – RPF), a 'movement above parties' to sweep him back to power, merely added another political party to an already crowded field; by the time de Gaulle disowned it in 1953, the RPF had already disintegrated. It was a period when de Gaulle was especially prone to self-doubt. 'I've only ever gone from failure to failure, alone against everyone', he told Claude Mauriac in August 1946; 'Whatever I do, I feel as if I'm hitting an eiderdown', he said to his aide-de-camp Claude Guy on the very day he launched the RPF.[1]

His personal life, meanwhile, was marked by the tragic death of his beloved daughter Anne, on 6 February 1948, aged 20, of pneumonia. He suffered health difficulties of his own too. Convinced that he had cancer of the throat, he substituted chewing-gum for chain-smoking in December 1947; two difficult cataract operations in 1952 and 1953 left him permanently short-sighted. He turned 60 in 1950; colleagues said he had aged, even that he was 'finished'.[2]

The 'crossing of the desert' nevertheless deserves our attention, for four reasons. First, in 1946–1958, we see a more erratic de Gaulle than at any other time: his sense of timing, his intuition about world events, appeared, temporarily, to desert him. Second, though failing to bring de Gaulle back into power, the RPF still reached second place to the Communists in the 1951 parliamentary elections. So the period saw the crystallisation of Gaullism as an organised electoral force – which would revive from 1958 on. Third, failure can be productive. The de Gaulle of 1958 was not the de Gaulle of 1946; he had learnt from mistakes and changed his mind (sometimes more than once) on several issues, most notably the Soviet Union, Germany, and the colonies. Finally, this was when de Gaulle wrote the *War Memoirs*: deeply tendentious but superbly written, they created a heroic narrative for contemporaries and for history.

Constitution-making, 1946

De Gaulle's successor as Prime Minister was the Socialist Félix Gouin, who headed a *tripartiste* government. On 5 May 1946 a draft for the new Constitution, vesting political power in a single-chamber Assembly, was put to referendum. Backed by Communists and Socialists but opposed by MRP, Radicals, and conservatives, it was rejected by 53% of the voters. Elections to a second Constituent Assembly followed on 2 June: the *tripartiste* parties kept three-quarters of the vote between them, with the PCF steady on 26%, the Socialists falling back to 21%, and the MRP, with 28%, briefly becoming France's leading party. Its leader Georges Bidault succeeded Gouin as Prime Minister.

De Gaulle now ended nearly five months of silence. He was convinced that war was approaching between the Soviet Union and the West – an intuition he had had on the day of Pearl Harbor; he believed that the United States would seize North Africa and allow a Soviet occupation of France, and that the British would be of no assistance;[3] he considered France's political class incapable of supplying leadership to face the coming storm; and he aimed, by weighing on the constitutional debate, to be called back to power.

The half-hour speech delivered at Bayeux on 16 June, just over two years after his visit following the Normandy landings, set out de Gaulle's constitutional blueprint. It argued for a two-chamber Parliament, the upper house including representatives of local authorities (as under the Third Republic) but also of social and economic groups. More importantly, de Gaulle called for a strong president, elected, not by Parliament (as under the Third Republic), but by a big electoral college, including mayors and local councillors. No longer the creature of Parliament, and 'above political parties', the president would choose the government, including the prime minister, though the government would also need to reflect the majority in Parliament. The president (who would also be president of the French Empire, or Union) would be able to call new parliamentary elections if the situation required it, and to take full powers in a national crisis. It was clear that de Gaulle had himself in mind for the post.[4]

The Bayeux Constitution became the central Gaullist policy of the next decade. A revised version became the Constitution of the Fifth Republic in 1958. But this was 1946. De Gaulle expected the rapid support of the French people in general and of the MRP, the 'party of fidelity' to de Gaulle in the words of Maurice Schumann, in particular.[5] He was disappointed: strong personal leadership was always mistrusted in France's republican tradition, and never more so than in the wake of Pétain. So the Communists called de Gaulle a 'potential Bonaparte', the Socialists' Léon Blum wrote of an 'incompatibility of temperament' between de Gaulle and democracy, and the MRP wrote its own constitutional draft, which included the upper house of Parliament but not the strong president. De Gaulle attacked the MRP draft in August, and again in a speech at Épinal in September. His brother-in-law Jacques Vendroux left the MRP in October, signalling a final break. Privately, de Gaulle claimed that the MRP had 'betrayed' him – unfairly, as he had never shown any particular consideration for the party or for Bidault. A final broadside against the draft followed on 9 October, four days before the referendum on its adoption. It was not enough. Nine million voters backed what would become the Constitution of the Fourth Republic, against 7.8 million opposed and 8.2 million abstentions. De Gaulle had shifted an estimated 6 million votes to the 'Non' camp[6] – but he had lost his battle for Bayeux. Nor would he be reconciled to the new Republic: he contemptuously refused consolation offers – including the presidency, or promotion to five-star general – that seemed to lock him into the role of a national monument: 'One does not decorate France', he said.[7]

Instead, he told Claude Guy in February 1947, 'We'll have to start again from zero. Re-do Free France.'[8] Loyal Gaullists like Jacques Foccart and Pierre Lefranc had been preparing since autumn.[9] Four more – Guy, Gaston Palewski, Jacques Soustelle, and Michel Debré – met with de Gaulle and Vendroux on 5 February to plan what would become the RPF.[10] In private, de Gaulle was unenthusiastic, even reluctant.[11] But he went ahead anyway: from a sense of a growing national and international crisis (the Truman Doctrine, the clearest signal yet of the nascent Cold War, was announced on 12 March); from a growing demand (including 200 letters daily from supporters) to do more than sit in Colombey and await the call; and possibly, too, from simple impatience at being sidelined.[12] He could take some courage from the opinion polls. In October 1946, 35% of IFOP respondents said they would support a party under de Gaulle. But over half also said they saw him as a man of the Right, against 42% who regarded him as outside parties.[13] Both findings would be relevant in the coming months.

The RPF surge, 1947

De Gaulle went public on 30 March 1947. 'The day will come', he told an outdoor crowd of 50,000 on a windy Norman clifftop at Bruneval, scene of the first Resistance-assisted commando raid on occupied France six years earlier, 'when the French reject the parties' sterile games and rally to France.'[14] A second big speech followed, in Strasbourg, on 7 April, and a communiqué formalising the RPF's creation, under de Gaulle's leadership, a week later. Completing the sequence, he gave a press conference on 24 April: the RPF, he declared, was no more a party than Fighting France had been.[15] Attacking 'the parties' sterile games' was especially relevant at a time when differences over colonial and wages policies were tearing *tripartisme* apart: the Socialist Prime Minister, Paul Ramadier, would dismiss his Communist ministers on 4 May.

The 'companions' of Free France had dispersed since 1944, some into politics (Chaban-Delmas to the Radicals, Georges Gorse to the Socialists, Maurice Schumann to the MRP, René Pleven to the little Union Démocratique et Sociale de la Résistance (UDSR)), others to the civil service, business, or the military. Not all rallied to the RPF: Pleven and Schumann, René Cassin, Claude Bouchinet-Serreulles, Passy, Christian Pineau, Pierre Mendès-France, Alexandre Parodi, and Pierre Messmer all stayed away. But Foccart, Debré, Lefranc, Chaban, Palewski, Soustelle, General Catroux, Colonel Rémy, René

Capitant, Christian Fouchet, André Diethelm, and many other leading Free French figures did join. So did the philosopher and sociologist Raymond Aron, and the novelist, adventurer, and former Communist fellow-traveller André Malraux. There was no lack of talent at the top of the RPF.[16]

The RPF built its successes on a core narrative, repeated with variations in speech after speech, as much as on a set of policies. France had climbed out of the abyss of 1940 through her own efforts (under de Gaulle's leadership), was on the way to regaining her rank, but had been stalled by the re-emergence of divisive political parties and by a Constitution that left their activities unchecked. As a result, France was now in deadly danger, from internal fragmentation and decadence but also and most urgently from Communism, both external (the Red Army was only 500 kilometres away − 'two stages of the Tour de France') − and internal (the French Communists, henceforth referred to as 'separatists', were Moscow's agents within France: de Gaulle twice told the *New York Times* journalist Cyrus Sulzberger, in 1947 and 1951, that he intended to ban the Communist Party).[17] Fortunately, the narrative concluded, the RPF now stood ready to rally French people of every (non-Communist) political horizon, and to save France by sweeping the system aside, defeating Communism, and rebuilding the Republic under de Gaulle's guidance.[18]

The RPF's policies buttressed the core narrative − but also identified the RPF as a clearly right-wing organisation. The centrepiece was the Bayeux Constitution. Anti-Communism, meanwhile, translated into an ambitious call to modernise and expand the armed forces (de Gaulle welcomed the NATO treaty in 1949, on the condition that Europe made an effective contribution and had a real voice in the alliance). At home, it meant (undefined) measures to curb, or even 'liquidate', the PCF, but also an attempt to give workers greater involvement in their firms in the so-called *association capital-travail*, which looked to some observers like a remake of Vichy's corporatist model of industrial relations. Government spending needed curbing ('by a good third' de Gaulle said at Vincennes on 5 October 1947),[19] nationalised industries 'putting in order', and a greater role given in the economy to private business − with hints that firms like Renault might not be state-owned forever.[20] The decades-old question of whether the state should subsidise Catholic education would be resolved by the *allocation-éducation*, a system of vouchers which parents could redeem at state or Church schools. In Europe, so long as Germany remained fragmented and its capacity to harm removed, Western co-operation could and should take place. In the French Union, greater initiative might be given to the colonies, but 'leaving to the experience, the wisdom and the authority of France, the higher responsibilities for public order, foreign policy, external defence, and economic policies affecting the whole community'; and France's authority must be rigorously enforced there.[21] In many respects this was a clear rightward shift from the de Gaulle who brought Communists into his government ('to give them a chance to enter the national community', he said later), espoused *dirigisme*, and opened the Brazzaville conference.

Backing the narrative and the policies was an organisation rivalled only by the PCF's. People queued up to join. The RPF claimed 810,000 membership applications on 1 May 1947, and 1,500,000 members by 5 October; even on Jean Charlot's more realistic estimate of 400,000, this was extraordinarily impressive for a French right-wing party.[22] It allowed campaigning across the country in a grand style – fortunately, since de Gaulle was banned from the radio from April 1947. Rémy, a former film director, organised mass meetings in big locations like the Vincennes hippodrome or the Vieux Port at Marseille, typically with Cross of Lorraine banners, martial music, and Malraux as an incandescent warm-up speaker before de Gaulle's own triumphal appearance, still in military uniform. The organisational style, unsurprisingly, was top-down: as the RPF's president, de Gaulle chose its secretary-general, its executive committee, and its regional delegates, and 'therefore disposed of an absolute power over all the bodies of the RPF'.[23]

The RPF was carried forward by an exceptional leader, a strong narrative, and a mobilising capacity unusual (though not unprecedented) for a right-wing movement. The context, moreover, was uniquely favourable to its anti-Communist message. Excluded from government in May 1947, the PCF moved, at the behest of its Soviet masters, to open confrontation with all other parties from September. Along with the Communist leaders in the major trade union confederation, the CGT, the PCF in government had effectively promoted austerity; now, by contrast, it actively spurred on strikes in support of workers' pent-up wage demands. Fear of Communism, both at home and internationally, fed into the RPF's greatest electoral success. At the municipal elections of 19 and 26 October 1947, RPF-led lists won 38.7% of the vote in towns of over 9,000 inhabitants, against 28.9% for the PCF. Of France's 25 biggest towns, the Gaullists seized 13, mostly from Communists or Socialists, including Paris, where de Gaulle's brother Pierre now led the council. This was very different from an ordinary conservative vote. It was more urban (the RPF won 55.9% in Paris, but under 25% in small towns); it was more cross-class, with working-class support as high as the Socialists'; it was geographically original, strongest in the North and West of France, and weakest in the South and East, as if lingering Vichy influence had held back Gaullism in the former 'free zone'. As de Gaulle wanted, it drew support from all horizons, attracting seven in ten conservative voters, over half of MRP supporters, a quarter of Radicals and Socialists, and even one Communist in ten.[24] Above all, the Gaullist electorate was very large, especially for such a new formation. 'The wave has risen', de Gaulle told a press conference on 12 November. 'I can only pity those who don't want to understand ... their curses will have no more effect than spitting into the sea.'[25] The same day, the CGT opened a series of exceptionally tough strikes. Ramadier's government, apparently unable to cope, resigned a week later. De Gaulle's return to power suddenly looked possible, even likely.

Reflux, 1948–1953

But it was the Gaullists who ended up spitting into the sea. The first sign of the RPF's downward trajectory came on 7 November 1948, at elections (by a college of local councillors) to the upper house of Parliament: de Gaulle had hoped for 100 out of the 320 seats, but the RPF only managed 56. At the March 1949 cantonal elections, which chose councillors for France's *départements*, RPF support fell back to 31.3%.[26] At the parliamentary elections of 17 June 1951, the Gaullists managed 22.5% of the vote – 3.5% fewer than the Communists.[27] For an ordinary Fourth Republic party, this result would have been a success: with 120 seats, the RPF had the biggest group in the National Assembly. But for a party aiming to sweep away the system, it was a disaster: the system survived (temporarily) and the

RPF did not. At the municipal elections of spring 1953, it lost nearly two-thirds of its council seats in towns of over 9,000 inhabitants, and four-fifths in Paris, Lyon, and Marseille.[28] De Gaulle disowned his now-crumbling party, 'giving' the RPF parliamentarians a freedom which many, by supporting or joining governments from the mainstream parties, had already taken.[29]

Why did the RPF fail? De Gaulle's poor timing was a crucial factor. The RPF was created either too late or too early. A launch in early 1946 might have enabled de Gaulle to win the constitutional debate straight after his resignation. Alternatively, waiting till early 1951 could have given the RPF an aura of novelty when campaigning for the parliamentary elections.[30] But in 1947, the constitutional question had just been settled, however unenthusiastically, and the RPF's victory at the municipal elections was no automatic springboard to national power: de Gaulle might demand a dissolution of the National Assembly, but it was in no-one else's interest to heed him, and no national elections were due for another four years.

Over that long wait, events favoured de Gaulle less and less. The established parties coped in government, and undermined the RPF; and the RPF was prey to multiple organisational difficulties. Above all, de Gaulle as party leader showed minimal strategic sense, alienating supporters and potential coalition partners alike. The RPF, as Charlot observes, was de Gaulle's creation, and his failure.[31]

De Gaulle's forecasts of catastrophes that would precipitate his return proved consistently wrong. A new war, he thought, was inevitable; Stalin would kick Western forces out of Berlin and then Vienna; France was heading for financial meltdown, or else (as the 1948 cantonal elections were postponed by six months) about to abolish democracy; the Federal Republic of Germany would become a new and aggressive Reich.[32] That none of this happened damaged the prospects of a leader most attractive in times of crisis.[33]

The established parties, moreover, coped better than expected. With the Communists' departure from government in May 1947, a new, centrist, parliamentary majority emerged, incorporating Radicals as well as Socialists and MRP: the confusingly named 'Third Force' (between Communism and the Right). True, there were a dozen governments between de Gaulle's resignation and the 1951 elections. But the Third Force proved good at practical anti-Communism. At home, its governments ruthlessly halted the strike waves of autumn 1947 and 1948 by calling out troops and sacking strikers *en masse*. In the colonies, the Third Force governments prosecuted an anti-Communist colonial war in Indochina, and ferociously put down a rising in Madagascar in 1947. MRP Foreign Ministers Georges Bidault and Robert Schuman signed the 1948 Brussels Treaty and the 1949 North Atlantic Treaty, cornerstones of Western Europe's post-war security against the perceived Soviet threat; Schuman also signed the 1950 Paris Treaty creating the European Coal and Steel Community with West Germany, Italy, and the three Benelux countries – keeping West Germany's strong economic recovery within a peaceful European framework. It was Third Force governments, finally, which benefited from the influx of American Marshall Aid from 1948. In 1949–1950, inflation dropped below 10%, for the first time since the war; real wages, finally, rose. The sombre climate which had favoured the RPF's rise in 1947 thus slowly dissipated.[34]

Meanwhile, the Third Force's anti-Gaullism proved almost as resolute as its anti-Communism. De Gaulle opened the RPF as a 'movement above parties' which non-Communists could join while retaining their party allegiance too. But the Socialists and MRP banned double membership from 1947, the UDSR from 1949, and the Radicals from April 1951. The (Socialist) President of the Republic, Vincent Auriol, was relentlessly hostile to the RPF. De Gaulle was banned from the radio and denied military honours in mainland France. In May 1951, moreover, Henri Queuille's government modified the proportional system used for parliamentary elections to give extra seats to party lists prepared to join loose alliances, known as *apparentements*. Intended to reduce Communist representation, since no-one would team up with the PCF, *apparentements* also presented de Gaulle with a dilemma: whether to sign up for them with MRP, Radicals, or conservatives, thus joining the 'system' he denounced – or to refuse *apparentements* and sacrifice seats.

This difficult environment – a four-year wait for the big electoral showdown, a slowly improving political and economic situation, a hostile political establishment – faced the RPF with organisational and policy challenges. Organisationally, the RPF was a supercharged machine driven by its leader's exceptional stature and the mobilisation of tens of thousands of militants: good for a sprint to power, far less suited to the long haul of 1947–1951. Few activists could wait four years for recompense in the form of jobs, contracts, or simple emotional validation; by 1951, membership had dropped to 89,000.[35] Business funding, aside from a few committed backers like the aircraft manufacturer Dassault, dried up.[36] With its big meetings and heavily subsidised press, the RPF was always short of money; despite quite successful popular fundraising drives, it faced mounting debts by 1951.[37]

Unlike other parties, too, the RPF lacked deep roots in French society. It had too few *notables*. *Notables* were men (almost never women) whose prominence in business, the liberal professions, or major associations fed into roles as local councillors, mayors, and parliamentarians (sometimes simultaneously). The early RPF's new mayors and councillors were mostly unknowns: the talented Chaban-Delmas, who became boss of Bordeaux for half a century from 1946, was unusual in putting roots down very fast. Lacking reassuring *notables*, the RPF also suffered from its association with violence, with its meetings resembling far right-wing rallies from the start.[38] Fighting marked RPF campaigns from 1947 on, partly because Gaullists went into 'red' suburbs to challenge Communists, who responded with catapults and ball-bearings, or iron bars.[39] The RPF, in turn, recruited leather-jacketed toughs from the former Free French secret services and other, less reputable sources.[40] Some were armed; a Communist died of gunshot wounds at Grenoble on 22 September 1948, an incident which Interior Minister Jules Moch exploited politically to the full and which Charlot identifies as the start of the RPF reflux.[41] With the stain of violence came the accusation of fascism from the Communists and their sympathisers, and a wider sense that the RPF had become 'a nasty caricature of Free France'.[42]

Facing an increasingly difficult environment, organisational difficulties, and an image problem, the RPF badly needed clear strategic vision at the top. De Gaulle did not supply it. The RPF's policies slowly unravelled, or began to resemble the uneasy compromises of ordinary politicians. Promised budget cuts, however pleasing to the right-wing taxpayer groups drawn to the RPF, sat ill with commitments to spend on social policy, economic modernisation, and above all defence.[43] The *association capital-travail*, presented by de Gaulle as a means to 'abolish the wage-earning system',[44] was watered down by a sceptical RPF committee and by hostile business backers.[45] De Gaulle even seemed uncertain about eliminating the legacy of the Occupation, angrily rejecting Rémy's (published) view that Pétain had 'shielded' the French from its worst effects, but calling for clemency towards convicted Vichyites, Pétain first among them.[46] This combination probably alienated both Resistance loyalists and former Vichyites.[47]

His touch was no surer on mapping a route back to power. Certainly, he insisted on respecting democracy and the law.[48] But however much he might state, in speeches, that the Fourth Republic's problem was the system not the politicians, in private he spoke of his determination to 'crush' the parties, particularly the MRP, and their leaders.[49] Not surprisingly, the occasional contacts made in 1948–1949 with MRP leaders came to nothing; his expectation was still of his own return to power and the parties' unconditional surrender, although he lacked the parliamentary forces to achieve this.[50] This peremptory character of the RPF, and de Gaulle's verbal violence towards those who disputed his analyses, rendered negotiations with other parties impossible and put off many who had supported the Gaullism of Free France and the Liberation.[51]

Then there was the problem of candidate selection for the 1951 elections. RPF stalwarts might be trusted not to compromise with the 'system'; but they lacked name recognition, and the RPF label alone was less of a selling-point than in 1947. Well-known *notables*, if they could be recruited, were more attractive to voters – but prone to indiscipline. But the weaker the RPF brand, the more de Gaulle needed *notables*. And it was often they, rather than the committed activists, who were selected.[52] Once in the Assembly, they duly refused the iron discipline that de Gaulle expected.

A final dilemma for de Gaulle was how to respond to the trap laid by the Third Force parties with the *apparentements* system. Here too he showed uncertainty of touch. He refused *apparentements* in principle, thereby sacrificing seats; but he made exceptions in 13 *départements* where local RPF leaders like Chaban-Delmas had persuaded him of their usefulness, and lost ideological purity: the worst of both worlds.

The *apparentements* helped secure 396 of the Assembly's 627 seats for the Fourth Republic's mainstream parties – Socialists, MRP, UDSR, Radicals, and conservatives. Divided amongst themselves, they would, as usual, find it hard to govern. But with just 120 seats, the RPF was not indispensable to form a parliamentary majority. So when de Gaulle offered co-operation with other parties, if they accepted the Bayeux Constitution, he was ignored. Auriol was now intent on splitting the RPF's parliamentarians. In February 1952, for the first time since the war, he invited a conservative to form a government, calculating on such a figure attracting some RPF support. It worked. On 8 March, 27 RPF Deputies voted to support the new Prime Minister Antoine Pinay, opening a breach in the Gaullists' 'anti-system' stance from which the RPF never recovered. The 'dissidents', mostly *notables* who had borrowed the RPF ticket, were expelled after a stormy meeting of the RPF council on 6 July. De Gaulle now lost interest in his diminished party: he made just two speeches at RPF events in the second half of 1952, and none in 1953. A communiqué of 6 May 1953 dissociated de Gaulle from the RPF's electoral activity and insisted that parliamentarians taking part in the 'games, poisons, and delights' of the system did so on their own initiative and not as RPF representatives.[53] But his disengagement was still not quite complete.

Restless retirement, 1953–1958

The year 1953 marks a turning-point in the 'crossing of the desert'. In Volume II of his *Discours et messages*, the years 1946–1953 account for nearly 600 pages – and 1953–1957 for fewer than 90. After disowning the RPF's parliamentarians in May, de Gaulle gave just three press conferences – the last on 30 June 1955 – before his return to power in 1958. This steep decline in speeches and declarations is matched by that of the public's interest: in December 1955 only 1% of respondents to an IFOP poll wanted him to head another government.[54] Appearances, therefore, might suggest a retreat into private life. At La Boisserie, the house at Colombey-les-Deux-Églises, now renovated, and reoccupied since April 1946, he received his surviving children Philippe and Élisabeth and their growing families. When they were not visiting, he wrote: the three-volume *War Memoirs* were published in 1954, 1956 and 1959.

But this was no serene retirement. Sulzberger wrote in 1956 that 'De Gaulle impressed me more than ever by his arrogance, his obstinacy, his conceit, and his bitterness'.[55] And de Gaulle could never again be a simple private citizen: as Lefranc notes, he could never enter a shop.[56] He never lost hope of a return to power, but often despaired that his time was running out (he turned 65 in 1955). He kept the RPF on life-support. He received visitors – most frequently at the now almost deserted RPF headquarters in the rue de Solférino in Paris, more seldom at the Hotel La Pérouse, where he stayed during his weekly Paris visits, quite rarely at Colombey. He maintained and developed his personal networks, as did his supporters. And he travelled through France's Empire, where much of the next decade's history was to unfold.

He even, on 9 May 1954, made what might be construed as an attempt to return to power by popular acclaim when, in a 15-minute ceremony announced three weeks earlier, he laid a wreath at the tomb of the unknown soldier under the Arc de Triomphe. The timing was perfect, in principle: just two days earlier, the Viet Minh had overrun the French base at Dien Bien Phu, defeating France decisively in Indochina and adding to the Fourth Republic's discredit. But de Gaulle attracted a crowd of 10,000–15,000, fewer than had attended that morning's official VE-day anniversary commemorations. 'Not many people', he observed. If he was testing the water, the result was negative.[57]

The RPF parliamentarians, now rebranded Social Republicans, completed their integration into the abhorred 'system' by accepting ministerial posts, notably under Joseph Laniel and Pierre Mendès-France. But de Gaulle still would not decommission the RPF. He kept it going partly out of respect for the remaining activists, partly for possible future use, and partly as a vehicle for his last campaign of the Fourth Republic, against the treaty of 27 May 1952 integrating France's armed forces into a new European Defence Community (EDC). This worked: on 30 August 1954, the National Assembly rejected ratification of the treaty, with the Gaullist Deputies voting en bloc against it (ironically, alongside the Communists).[58]

By then, though, the RPF was moribund. The main task of Jacques Foccart, the secretary-general appointed by de Gaulle in 1953, was to pay off the movement's considerable debts (fortunately, many business backers wrote them off).[59] To RPF cadres, meeting in December 1954 at what resembled a wake, de Gaulle reiterated his – confusing – position: the RPF must be ready to become 'the vanguard of the nation' in the future, but in the meantime they should do nothing in its name or his.[60] Some used the RPF label anyway at the spring 1955 cantonal elections, whereupon de Gaulle, on 13 September 1955, all but closed the RPF down: it kept the Solférino headquarters (described by Sulzberger in 1956 as 'dilapidated and shabby'),[61] and Foccart as secretary-general, but all other party officers were suspended. Local delegates were simply told to keep their archives and membership lists – in case.[62]

Foccart had been responsible in the RPF for relations with the French Union, and had developed a network of contacts with army officers, business leaders, and even moderate African nationalists who sat in the Assembly of the French Union. He was the ideal choice to organise and accompany the four imperial tours de Gaulle undertook during his retirement: to West Africa, from Dakar to Tunis, in March 1953; to East Africa (including, exceptionally, Ethiopia), plus Madagascar and La Réunion, that October; to the Caribbean and Pacific colonies, and home via Djibouti and Algiers, in summer 1955, and finally to the Algerian Sahara, including atomic weapons research and oil-drilling facilities, in March 1957.[63] Here, even more than in France, he was very much more than a private citizen. He travelled in the DC4 that Truman had given him, with government-supplied aircrew, and was received with full military honours and an official visit to the Assembly of each territory. When Foccart tried to organise one meeting too many with his RPF networks in Africa, he provoked the crushing response that 'you're getting on my nerves with *your* RPF': de Gaulle was there, in his own view, representing France, not inspecting the remains of his party.[64]

As to visitors, as Jackson observes, 'For a hermit, de Gaulle managed to see a lot of people', with some 550 meetings at Solférino alone.[65] Aside from the Gaullist faithful, they included politicians (Pierre Mendès-France, the Prime Minister who got France out of Indochina, had a well-publicised meeting), business leaders, one or two Americans (Sulzberger, and the young academic Nicholas Wahl), the Soviet ambassador Sergei Vinogradov and his Tunisian counterpart Mohammed Masmoudi – and, especially after 1956, a growing number of senior army officers.[66]

De Gaulle talked of a possible *coup d'état*: hypothetically with Sulzberger, more practically with the military men. He even encouraged them to plan one. But he never committed himself to a project: although he knew that the military might assist his return, he also believed that to be sustainable, power must come from the people.[67] With other visitors he spoke more generally about French and world politics, on which his views never ceased to evolve. This was particularly true in two areas: the Soviet Union, which after Stalin's death in March 1953 he considered to have 'softened'; and the colonies. As he had called, on 7 April 1954, for an end to the war in Indochina, he unsurprisingly approved Mendès-France's liberal colonial policy – including the start of the process that would lead to the full independence of Tunisia and Morocco in 1956.[68] His last press conference before 1958, held on 30 June 1955, included a vision of North Africa where 'association' had taken the place of French 'domination'.[69] Algeria, where an anti-French rising had started on 1 November 1954, was a steadily more frequent subject of conversation. Both supporters and opponents of keeping Algeria French left de Gaulle thinking he shared their views. But the balance leant towards accepting the inevitability of decolonisation in some form. To the former RPF secretary-general Louis Terrenoire, he observed in 1955 that 'We are in the presence of a general movement in the world, a wave which is carrying every people towards emancipation' – a remark that foreshadowed Harold Macmillan's 'Wind of Change' speech of five years later. The colonies, including Algeria, would become independent – even if he, de Gaulle, might hang on to them for 10 to 15 years if returned to power.[70] These positions were, by 1954, much more liberal than those of Foccart and his colonial networks, or of imperialist zealots in the Gaullist diaspora like Debré or Soustelle or Léon Delbecque, former RPF delegate in northern France.[71]

Meanwhile de Gaulle's most devoted supporters organised themselves. Foccart was one of a group of so-called 'barons' of Gaullism who began lunching together weekly from the mid-1950s. The 'barons' included Foccart's two predecessors as RPF secretary-general, Soustelle and Terrenoire; Olivier Guichard, who had become de Gaulle's personal assistant from 1953; Edmond Michelet, Michel Debré, Roger Frey, Pierre Lefranc, Gaston Palewski, and Jacques Chaban-Delmas, all of whom had passed through Free France or the Resistance and the RPF; Malraux; and Georges Pompidou, a former secondary school teacher who had served on de Gaulle's staff at the Liberation and had headed his private staff from 1948 to 1953, when he left for a senior post with Rothschild's bank. The lunches were more than social events. This inner circle would play a crucial role during and after de Gaulle's return to power; it included three future prime ministers.[72]

The *War Memoirs* were de Gaulle's chief enterprise from 1953 to 1958. He wrote neither fast nor easily. Everything went through two manuscripts, then two typescripts (prepared by Élisabeth), each heavily annotated. He read excerpts to Vendroux, Pompidou, Malraux, or Aron, seeking to tighten his penchant for a full and pompous tone into something sharper. He even showed Vinogradov the passages covering his Moscow visit.[73] He had one assistant (unlike Churchill, who used an army of researchers for his six-volume *Second World War*) and was keen to offer incontestable facts (however tendentious his interpretations).[74] These painstaking efforts paid off. Sulzberger even claimed that 'he writes the best French of any living Frenchman'[75] – in a decade when Aragon, Camus, Duras, de Beauvoir, Giono, Sartre, Vian, and Yourcenar, among others, were all active. His very classical writing stays just on the right side of the ponderous; certain rhetorical techniques, like the ubiquitous ternary rhythm, have found many imitators but always sound *gaulliens*.

He deployed these formidable literary tools in the service of an enterprise intended to airbrush memories of the RPF out of the de Gaulle legend and instead focus on his historic – and heroic – services to his country. In the *Memoirs* as in the openings to so many RPF speeches, France begins to climb out of the abyss (Volume I), unifies in its defiance of the Germans (Volume II), and gives way to the fragmenting forces of the revived parties (Volume III) – but always with the hope of being 'revived, century after century, by the genius of renewal'.[76] Within this perspective, as Sudhir Hazareesingh observes, de Gaulle himself appears as the only expression of France's national will in the face of defeat; as the unifier of the Resistance in 1943–1944; as the defender of French sovereignty against Allies seeking to 'vassalise' France; and as France's ultimate recourse in case of need.[77]

From the wartime speeches, however, the *Memoirs* differ strongly, in two ways. First, whereas in the speeches, he claims the support of 'all French people worthy of the name',[78] the better to buttress his claim to represent France, in the *Memoirs*, he underlines the loneliness of his enterprise, the better to emphasise its heroism.[79] Second, where the speeches only mention his difficulties with the Allies sparingly, and in diplomatic terms, the same conflicts are a central theme of the *Memoirs*. Both British and Americans had, of course, given de Gaulle plenty of material. But he consistently placed the worst imaginable interpretation on their actions, and saw deliberate malice towards Free France where there was more frequently tactlessness, indifference, and cavalier duplicity. However courteous his praise of Allied leaders as individuals, and of Allied armies and peoples, no reader of the *Memoirs* could be in much doubt as to the difficulties the 'Anglo-Saxons' would face at his hands if ever he returned to power.

The *War Memoirs* were not, of course, simply memoirs about the war. 'Timeless and topical', they offer moral lessons about the whole sweep of French history.[80] The contrast between the greatness that appears, at the first page, as France's rightful status, and the 'ferments of dispersion' that constantly threaten not only that status but the nation itself is their constant theme. So is the need for strong leadership exercised through a strong state.[81] For these are also memoirs for the future: hence the 'Old man ... always watching in the shadows for a gleam of hope' that closes them.[82]

The *Memoirs* were a literary and commercial success: Volume I sold 100,000 in a month,[83] all proceeds from all volumes going to the Fondation Anne de Gaulle for handicapped girls. They were therefore a political success too. As the Algerian War plunged the Fourth Republic deeper into crisis, de Gaulle the divisive RPF leader could fade away, and de Gaulle France's wartime saviour return to the stage.

Conclusion

The legacy of the 'long' crossing of the desert, from 1946 to 1958, is of two great enterprises. The more lasting has been the *War Memoirs*, republished in the prestigious *La Pleiade* series in 2000. The other, the RPF, might appear to have left little trace: surging into French politics in spring 1947, it practically disappeared as a major force within six years. Not, though, without leaving a strong impression. Certainly right-wing, this first manifestation of partisan

Gaullism was, in its electorate, more northern, more urban, more cross-class than traditional conservatism; organisationally, more centrally controlled (though de Gaulle would never again stoop to be a party leader); ideologically, nationalist but reaching far beyond the confines of the existing Right: 'Every French person was, is or will be "Gaullist"', de Gaulle optimistically told a press conference on 10 March 1952.[84] And the RPF also planted its elites, barons and others, in French politics: committed, energetic, and now experienced, men in the prime of life, still available for future service. As Guichard remarks, without the RPF they could not have (re-)built a Gaullist party, apparently from nothing, over just three months in 1958.[85]

For de Gaulle himself, the RPF was a political apprenticeship. Far less of a natural as politician than as war leader, he nevertheless learnt from the experience. His elephantine memory assimilated, from criss-crossing France in an ageing Citroën on gruelling campaign trips, every detail of France's electoral geography and the *notables* in every locality. He repeated and perfected, to the despair of his security men, his technique of plunging into the crowds. And he determined to keep anything resembling a Gaullist party at arm's length in future.

The policies are a further legacy of the period – developing from Bayeux in 1946 to the RPF, the post-1953 years, and ultimately the de Gaulle presidency. Some were relatively constant: most obviously the constitutional blueprint, but also the (always vague) *association capital-travail*, as well as financial support for Catholic schools, the insistence that European powers must be equal partners in the Atlantic Alliance, with the corresponding demand to modernise the armed forces (he first voiced the ambition for France to become an 'atomic power' in 1954)[86] and the call – albeit in many different forms – for a European confederation under French leadership: it was in 1950 that de Gaulle first spoke – as he would during the presidency – of a 'Europe from the Atlantic to the Urals', transcending Cold War divisions.[87] Other policies changed significantly over the period. Dire warnings about the dangers of a German Reich gave way, from 1950, to guarded acceptance of the Federal Republic, henceforth seen as partners in Europe. The Soviet Union was a bogeyman in 1947; by the mid-1950s de Gaulle had decided – too early – that Soviet Communism was a spent force.[88] Above all, the insistence, through most of the RPF years, on repressing any challenges to French rule in the colonies, slowly gave way to a greater acceptance of the aspirations of colonised peoples. How great? No-one was quite sure. De Gaulle's last public declaration before 1958 was a terse communiqué dissociating himself from statements attributed to him in the press. When he had something to say, ran the communiqué, he would say it himself, and publicly. 'This applies notably', it concluded, 'to the subject of Algeria.'[89]

Notes

1 Claude Mauriac, *Un autre de Gaulle: Journal 1944–1954* (Paris: Hachette, 1970), p. 229; Claude Guy, *En écoutant de Gaulle. Journal 1946–1949* (Paris: Grasset, 1996), pp. 391–2.
2 Georges Pompidou, *Pour rétablir une vérité* (Paris: Flammarion, 1982), p. 133.
3 Mauriac, *Un autre de Gaulle*, p. 226.
4 Olivier Guichard, *Mon Général* (Paris: Grasset, 1980), p. 204; *DM*II, pp. 5–11.
5 Jean Lacouture, *De Gaulle*, vol. II: *Le Politique, 1944–1959* (Paris: Le Seuil, 1985), p. 207.
6 Philip Williams, *Crisis and Compromise: Politics in the Fourth Republic* (London: Longman, 1964), p. 23.
7 Julian Jackson, *A Certain Idea of France: The Life of Charles de Gaulle* (London: Allen Lane, 2018), p. 385.
8 Guy, *En écoutant*, p. 241.
9 Lacouture, *De Gaulle* II, pp. 288–9.
10 Jackson, *A Certain Idea*, p. 393.
11 Mauriac, *Un autre de Gaulle*, pp. 258, 261–5; Guy, *En écoutant*, p. 282.
12 Lacouture, *De Gaulle* II, p. 286; Jean-Louis Matharan, 'Charles de Gaulle à Strasbourg: Refonder le sentiment d'appartenance', in Fondation Charles de Gaulle, *De Gaulle et le RPF, 1947–1955* (Paris: Armand Colin, 1998), pp. 36–47.
13 R.W. Johnson, *The Long March of the French Left* (London: Macmillan, 1981), p. 74.
14 Éric Duhamel, 'L'Accueil du RPF au printemps 1947', in Fondation Charles de Gaulle, *De Gaulle et le RPF*, p. 51.
15 *DM*II, pp. 41–73.
16 Lacouture, *De Gaulle* II, pp. 337–8.
17 Speech at Rennes, 27 July 1947, *DM*II, pp. 97–103; C.L. Sulzberger, *A Long Row of Candles: Memoirs and Diaries, 1934–1954* (London: McDonald, 1969), pp. 328, 549.
18 Guichard, *Mon Général*, pp. 270–1.
19 *DM*II, p. 124.

20 Press conference, 12 November 1947, *DM*II, pp. 138–60.
21 Strasbourg speech, 7 April 1947, *DM*II, pp. 48–55. Jean Touchard, *Le Gaullisme, 1940–1969* (Paris: Le Seuil, 1978), p. 100.
22 Touchard, *Le Gaullisme*, p. 100; Jean Charlot, *Le Gaullisme d'opposition, 1946–1958* (Paris: Fayard, 1983), pp. 86–9.
23 Christian Purtschet, 'L'Organisation nationale: les rouages', in Fondation Charles de Gaulle, *De Gaulle et le RPF*, pp. 67–77.
24 Johnson, *The Long March*, p. 75.
25 *DM*II, p. 139.
26 Charlot, *Opposition*, pp. 134–5, 138.
27 Lacouture, *De Gaulle* II, pp. 364–75; Williams, *Crisis and Compromise*, p. 502.
28 Charlot, *Opposition*, p. 294.
29 On 6 May 1953: *DM*II, pp. 580–2.
30 Pierre Lefranc, 'La Création et les grandes étapes du RPF. Rapport de synthèse', in Fondation Charles de Gaulle, *De Gaulle et le RPF*, pp. 28–36: pp. 32, 48; Pierre Lefranc, *Avec de Gaulle* (Paris: Plon, 1989), p. 86.
31 Quoted in Lacouture, *De Gaulle* II, p. 336.
32 Mauriac, *Un autre de Gaulle*, pp. 308–9, 315, 322, 326; Pompidou, *Vérité*, p. 73; Guichard, *Mon Général*, p. 267.
33 Charlot, *Opposition*, pp. 424–5.
34 Charlot, *Opposition*, pp. 174–8, 424–5.
35 Bernard Lachaise, 'Qu'est-ce qu'un compagnon?', in Serge Berstein, Pierre Birnbaum, and Jean-Pierre Rioux (eds), *De Gaulle et les élites* (Paris: La Découverte, 2008), pp. 62–74: p. 66.
36 Richard Vinen, *Bourgeois Politics in France, 1945–1951* (Cambridge: Cambridge University Press, 1995), pp. 218–19, 223.
37 Guichard, *Mon Général*, p. 239; Charlot, *Opposition*, p. 243.
38 Mauriac, *Un autre de Gaulle*, p. 284.
39 Lefranc, *Avec de Gaulle*, p. 88; *Le Monde*, 28 September 1948.
40 Frédéric Turpin, *Jacques Foccart. Dans l'ombre du pouvoir* (Paris: CNRS editions, 2015), p. 141; Vinen, *Bourgeois Politics*, p. 225.
41 Mauriac, *Un autre de Gaulle*, pp. 331–2; Charlot, *Opposition*, p. 359.
42 Alexander Werth, *De Gaulle* (Harmondsworth: Penguin Books, 1965), pp. 203–5; *Le Monde*, 28 September 1948; Lacouture, *De Gaulle* II, p. 336.
43 Vinen, *Bourgeois Politics*, p. 226.
44 Speech at Bordeaux, 25 September 1949, *DM*II, p. 307.
45 Patrick Guiol, 'L'Action ouvrière et l'Association capital-travail dans la stratégie de conquête du pouvoir', in Fondation Charles de Gaulle, *De Gaulle et le RPF*, pp. 399–428.
46 Guichard, *Mon Général*, pp. 241–2.
47 Bordeaux, 25 September 1949, *DM*II, p. 307; Jackson, *A Certain Idea*, p. 420.

48 Bernard Lachaise, 'La Création du Rassemblement du peuple français', in Serge Berstein and Pierre Milza (eds), *L'Année 1947* (Paris: Presses de Sciences Po, 2000), pp. 327–37: pp. 335–6.
49 Speeches at Saint-Étienne, 4 January 1948, and Saint-Maur, 6 July 1952, *DM*II, pp. 127 and 534–5; Mauriac, *Un autre de Gaulle*, p. 345.
50 Jackson, *A Certain Idea*, pp. 403–6; Lacouture, *De Gaulle* II, p. 266.
51 Touchard, *Le Gaullisme*, p. 133.
52 Charlot, *Opposition*, pp. 134–5; Lefranc, *Avec de Gaulle*, p. 111; Guichard, *Mon Général*, p. 262.
53 Declaration, 6 May 1953, *DM*II, pp. 580–2.
54 Touchard, *Le Gaullisme*, p. 146.
55 C.L. Sulzberger, *The Last of the Giants* (London: Weidenfeld & Nicolson, 1970), p. 80.
56 Lefranc, *Avec de Gaulle*, p. 129.
57 Éric Roussel, *Charles de Gaulle* (Paris: Gallimard, 2002), p. 564; Guichard, *Mon Général*, p. 504.
58 Williams, *Crisis and Compromise*, p. 43.
59 Turpin, *Foccart*, p. 87.
60 *DM*II, p. 628.
61 Sulzberger, *Giants*, p. 80.
62 Turpin, *Foccart*, p. 86.
63 Jackson, *A Certain Idea*, pp. 438–9.
64 Jacques Foccart, *Foccart parle. Entretiens avec Philippe Gaillard 1* (Paris: Fayard/Jeune Afrique, 1995), p. 103; Turpin, *Foccart*, pp. 63–4, Guichard, *Mon Général*, p. 310.
65 Jackson, *A Certain Idea*, p. 443.
66 Lacouture, *De Gaulle* II, p. 433.
67 Sulzberger, *Giants*, pp. 29–32; Roussel, *de Gaulle*, pp. 565–7.
68 Foccart, *Foccart parle 1*, pp. 116–17; *DM*II, pp. 613–14.
69 *DM*II, p. 638.
70 Touchard, *Le Gaullisme*, pp. 147–9.
71 Turpin, *Foccart*, pp. 94–8.
72 Charlot, *Opposition*, pp. 322, 372; Lefranc, *Avec de Gaulle*, pp. 254–5.
73 Roussel, *de Gaulle*, p. 573.
74 Sudhir Hazareesingh, *In the Shadow of the General: Modern France and the Myth of de Gaulle* (New York: Oxford University Press, 2012), p. 42; Serge Berstein, *Histoire du gaullisme* (Paris: Perrin, 2002, pp. 176–7; Charlot, *Opposition*, pp. 317–18.
75 Sulzberger, *Giants*, p. 80.
76 Charles de Gaulle, *War Memoirs*, vol. III: *Salvation*, tr. Richard Howard (London: Weidenfeld & Nicolson, 1960), p. 284.
77 Hazareesingh, *Shadow*, pp. 40, 56.
78 Broadcast, 31 December 1941, *DM*I, p. 151.
79 'In short, limited and alone though I was, and precisely because I was so, I had to climb to the heights and never then to come down.' Charles

de Gaulle, *War Memoirs*, vol. I: *The Call to Honour 1940–1942*, tr. Jonathan Griffin, (London: Collins, 1955), p. 89.
80 Hazareesingh, *Shadow*, p. 42.
81 Julian Jackson, *De Gaulle* (London: Haus Publishing, 2003), pp. 60–2.
82 *WM*III, p. 284. By the time these words were published, they were already out of date: de Gaulle had been President for over nine months.
83 Jackson, *A Certain Idea*, p. 438.
84 *DM*II, p. 513.
85 Guichard, *Mon Général*, p. 298.
86 Press conference, 7 April 1954, *DM*II, p. 606.
87 Press conference, 16 March 1950, *DM*II, p. 354; Touchard, *Le Gaullisme*, p. 211.
88 Sulzberger, *Giants*, pp. 42–3.
89 Communiqué, 12 September 1957, *DM*II, p. 654.

Further reading

Julian Jackson, *A Certain Idea of France* (London: Allen Lane, 2018), chapters 16–17, covers the period of the RPF and the 'crossing of the desert'.

The standard analytical work on Fourth Republic politics remains Philip Williams, *Crisis and Compromise: Politics in the Fourth Republic* (London: Longman, 1964).

The key study of the RPF is Jean Charlot's *Le Gaullisme d'opposition, 1946–1958* (Paris: Fayard, 1983). In English, both Malcolm Anderson, *Conservative Politics in France* (London: George Allen & Unwin, 1974) and Richard Vinen, *Bourgeois Politics in France, 1945–1951* (Cambridge: Cambridge University Press, 1995) have good relevant chapters.

Sudhir Hazareesingh's excellent *Political Traditions in Modern France* (Oxford: Oxford University Press, 1993) sets Gaullism in its ideological context, especially in opposition to mainstream French republicanism.

The period 1946–1958 is practically absent from de Gaulle's memoirs. His own words appear in his *Discours et Messages*, vol. II (Paris: Plon, 1970) and in other people's recollections: in English, C.L. Sulzberger's *A Long Row of Candles: Memoirs and Diaries, 1934–1954* (London: Macdonald, 1969) and *The Last of the Giants* (London: Weidenfeld & Nicolson, 1970); in French, most notably Claude Mauriac, *Un autre de Gaulle: Journal 1944–1954* (Paris: Hachette, 1970), Jacques Foccart, *Foccart parle. Entretiens avec Philippe Gaillard 1* (Paris: Fayard/Jeune Afrique, 1995), and Olivier Guichard, *Mon Général* (Paris: Grasset, 1980).

8 The return, 1958

On the evening of Thursday 29 May 1958 René Coty, Auriol's successor as President of France, invited Charles de Gaulle to form a government. De Gaulle appeared before the National Assembly shortly after 3pm on Sunday 1 June, gave a 633-word speech and left the parliamentarians to decide whether to accept him. They did, and went on to vote him special powers to settle the Algerian question and to draft a new Constitution. The following day they adjourned their sitting *sine die*. The de Gaulle government, the twenty-second of the Fourth Republic, would be its last.

Outwardly, due process was observed. For de Gaulle's adversaries, his return to power was nevertheless tainted: it had taken place under intense pressure from the army. François Mitterrand, former Fourth Republic minister (and future President), attacked the regime founded in 1958 as a 'Permanent *coup d'état*'.[1]

Gilding a violent power grab with the forms of due process is typical of a successful coup: how else to lend it the legitimacy of a fresh constitutional start, to transform its author from upstart to founding father? But the de Gaulle case is more complex. There was no violent seizure of power. One was planned, but not by de Gaulle. Still, the army had, on 13 May, mounted an insurrection in Algiers, in which de Gaulle's supporters were implicated, and which called for de Gaulle's return. De Gaulle himself was kept informed of plans to extend the rebellion to mainland France. And Coty's invitation to form a government was made to prevent such an operation – by conceding its main purpose.

How legitimate, then, was de Gaulle's return to power? To whom, if anyone, did he owe it? Although the transition was played out, in the end, in Paris, we must first look to Algeria for answers. It was Algeria that involved the army in politics, and Algeria that had made the Fourth Republic ungovernable.

Algeria: the jewel in the crown?

With Indochina lost, Algeria in 1954 was France's largest, most populous overseas territory. It was no ordinary colony. A 24-hour boat trip from Marseille, it was home to nearly a million white settlers, against 8.85 million Algerian Moslems. Falling under the jurisdiction of the Interior, not the Colonial Ministry, its three French-style *départements* (Oran, Algiers, Constantine) sent Deputies to the National Assembly in Paris. France had long benefited from the agricultural produce of the northern coastal strip. In the 1950s the Algerian Sahara revealed new potential. Oil was discovered in January 1956. France established a missile testing facility at Colomb-Béchar from 1953, and an atomic weapons test base at Reggane from 1957.

Being 'part of France' did not ensure respect for the Republican ideal of Liberty, Equality, and Fraternity in Algeria. Any sense of shared community had been wrecked by the Sétif and Guelma massacres in 1945. For voting purposes, the population was divided into two electoral colleges, one of 470,000 Europeans, plus the 70,000 Moslems enfranchised in 1944, the other of 1.4 million Moslem men. Numerically unequal, each college nevertheless elected the same numbers of representatives to the National Assembly in Paris and to the Algerian Assembly, established in 1947. Elections to 'native' seats in both were generally rigged; hundreds of preventive arrests had preceded the first Algerian Assembly elections, in 1948. French Algeria's political institutions had forfeited the confidence of most Algerian Moslems well before the Assembly was abolished in 1956.[2]

Flagrant in politics, inequality was even more marked in Algerian society. A small, cohesive elite of big landowners, the *colons* (2% of the agricultural population possessed a quarter of the land), and of major business owners and managers, typically in food processing and import-export, controlled the press and most political representation. Below them were the mass of the white population (known as *pieds-noirs*), consisting of small farmers, minor civil servants, and shopkeepers. Their somewhat lower living standards than those of metropolitan France made them all the more attached to *Algérie française*, which ensured them a superior social and political status. They coexisted uneasily with some 2 million Algerian Moslems whose living standards approached European levels. But the mass of Algeria's population was Moslem, rural, and very poor. Agriculture occupied one in ten of the whites but three-quarters of the Moslems. For two-fifths, that meant subsistence agriculture. European commercial farms, just 22,000 of them, covered 2,726,000 hectares, including three-quarters of Algeria's irrigated land, and most of the fertile coastal belt. Moslem farms numbered 630,000, and covered 7,350,000 hectares of smallholdings, suitable only for low-yield cereals, olives, figs, and grazing, and less and less productive. Since 1900, grain yields had fallen by a quarter, the sheep population from 9 million to 5 million – while the Moslem Algerian population had more than doubled.[3] Land hunger, or simply hunger, forced men into towns, in Algeria or France, where their lack of qualifications (only one Moslem boy in eight was schooled) placed them at the very bottom of the employment market.

The British intelligence officer Norman Lewis has given a vivid description of the poverty he saw in Algeria in 1943:

> Most of the males observed on our arrival wore garments made from sacks, on which in many cases the stencilled mark of whatever produce they had contained was still visible. A woman forced for any reason to leave her village and go into town might only be able to make this journey after several neighbours had clubbed together to provide her with sufficient clothing.[4]

Into this cruel – and extremely beautiful – landscape, on 1 November 1954, stepped Algeria's Front de Libération Nationale (FLN), with co-ordinated attacks on 70 separate targets associated with French rule. Ten people died, including a 23-year-old French schoolteacher who had arrived days earlier; his wife was wounded.

A dirty war, 1954–1958

The FLN was formed of dissidents from earlier nationalist movements, who had reacted to the French authorities' post-1945 repression of peaceful nationalism by espousing violence. Fewer than a thousand strong in 1954, they had barely 50 men in Algiers and Oran, but 450 in Kabylie, east of Algiers, and 350 in the Aurès mountains further south-east. These two regions would be central to the developing Algerian war. The FLN's goal, set out in a proclamation on 1 November, was complete independence. Its leaders, men like Ahmed Ben Bella, Mohammed Boudiaf, Hocine Aït Ahmed, Mohammed Khider, or Krim Belkacem were nationalists, not democrats. They would not submit their belief that they alone represented the Algerian nation to a popular vote – for they had seen how the French subverted and manipulated democratic processes. They therefore relied primarily on armed force, on terrorism. FLN violence targeted four groups. Attacks on the French military aimed to provoke reprisals that would bring more Algerians into the independence struggle. Attacks on the wider *pied-noir* population sought to provoke their departure. Attacks on rival nationalist groups, particularly Ferhat Abbas's Union Démocratique du Manifeste Algérien (UDMA) and Messali Hadj's Mouvement National Algérien, aimed at their elimination and the incorporation of their activists into the FLN. Attacks on the wider Moslem population served to compel support in the form of food, shelter, arms caches, and the other requirements of a guerrilla army. The FLN's internal faction-fighting was equally violent.

To the wider world, the FLN presented a less sanguinary face. From the start it aimed to internationalise the conflict, especially in the Arab world, in the international non-aligned movement, and in the United Nations. Installed there from 1955, intelligent and cultivated spokesmen like M'hamed Yazid and Abdelkader Chanderli placed the conflict before the General Assembly, and thence world opinion.

By 1958 the FLN had achieved notable successes. Its armed wing, the Armée de Libération Nationale (ALN), had grown to 20,000 with perhaps 40,000 lightly armed auxiliaries, capable of organising 'terrorist incidents' by the thousand each month and possessing 6,000 heavy weapons.[5] In August 1955, attacks in 30 towns in the Constantine-Philippeville-Guelma triangle, though unsuccessful in themselves, had provoked the escalation of the war by the French, who had committed 190,000 soldiers to the colony by early 1956 and over 400,000, half of them conscripts, by 1958. It had carried the fight into Algeria's cities: in September 1956 ALN bombs tore apart the Milk Bar and the Cafeteria, favoured meeting-places of young whites in Algiers. It harassed French forces from cross-border bases in Morocco and (especially) Tunisia. It had forced the dissolution of the UDMA, whose moderate leader Ferhat Abbas became the FLN's figurehead for world opinion. At the Soummam conference of August 1956, it had formed a quasi-government, and reaffirmed the principle that recognition of Algerian sovereignty was a precondition for any peace talks. Meanwhile the FLN had secured support within the Arab world, notably from Gamal Abdel Nasser's Egypt, sent observers to the 1955 Bandung conference of non-aligned nations, and brought the Algerian conflict to the United Nations General Assembly. In 1957, US Senator John F. Kennedy had called for the international community to help secure a settlement.

There had also been reverses. French paratroopers had ejected the FLN from Algiers in 1957, forcing its headquarters to Tunis, and thence to Cairo. In the countryside, the French Commander-in-Chief general Raoul Salan's strategy of *quadrillage* – dividing Algeria into zones and committing forces to hold each of them – had forced the ALN into its mountain hide-outs, able to move only at night. Along the frontiers, thousands of kilometres of barbed wire and radar defences hampered cross-border raids. Undefeated, the FLN had nevertheless been fought to a near-standstill.

The *pieds-noirs*, the Moslem population, and the FLN were three protagonists in the war. The fourth was the French army. On 1 June 1958, there were 429,300 French servicemen in Algeria, of whom 412,000 were ground troops, including 265,000 conscripts. This was half the French army's total manpower, more than half of its operational capacity. Equipment was largely American.[6] The 17,000 officers were the most political element. For many of them, at war almost continuously since 1939, winning had become a ruling passion, for three reasons. First, they sought to salvage the honour of an army damaged by the defeat of 1940, the stain of Vichy, and the humiliation of Dien Bien Phu. Second, they believed they were in the front line of the West's worldwide struggle against 'Communism' – a misleading characterisation of the FLN's Islamic nationalism, barely supported from Moscow. Third, having given undertakings of France's permanent presence in Algeria to Moslems whose co-operation they sought against the FLN, they considered anything less as a betrayal. To these sensitivities were added a belief that politicians had failed to back them politically (especially in Indochina) and materially: low pay was a persistent humiliation.[7]

The army's mindset in Algeria had two consequences. The first was a willingness to use any dirty technique to win: air raids (some employing napalm) against rebel-held territory; the creation of free-fire zones, resulting in the forced displacement of populations into concentration camps; summary executions; and the routine torture of 'suspects'. Torture was systematic in the so-called 'battle of Algiers' waged against the FLN from January to October 1957, during which 3,000 suspects died in custody.[8] But it extended far beyond the capital, as even an official report revealed in 1957.[9] Against this background, the efforts of idealistic younger officers in the 600 or so *Sections Administratives Spéciales* (SAS), centres created from 1955 in rural, and later urban Algeria to offer basic healthcare and support for building projects and craft-based industry, could win few hearts and minds. Secondly, the army's mindset increasingly led it to intervene in politics.

A crisis of ungovernability

The fifth player in the conflict was the government, or rather governments, of the Fourth Republic, constantly trying, and failing, to keep pace with events. The Algerian war corroded French politics in five ways. First, it added an extra division to the already complex party system. Algeria overlaid the pre-existing divisions between Socialists and Radicals, MRP, UDSR, and conservatives, dividing each party within itself and rendering government still more unstable. Before de Gaulle came to power, it had toppled six prime ministers: Pierre Mendès-France (February 1955), Edgar Faure (January 1956), Guy Mollet (May 1957), Maurice Bourgès-Maunoury (September 1957), Félix Gaillard (April 1958) and Pierre Pflimlin (May 1958). In the year following Mollet's fall, France was without a government for 78 days.[10] Second, policy paralysis resulted. Governments tried to reform Algeria just enough to satisfy international opinion, hoping that new (and overdue) economic and social development projects would bring the population round while maintaining French dominance.[11] But conservatives in each party blocked each reform attempt. Alternatively, like Mollet, the politicians attempted a three-stage approach – military 'pacification', elections from which it was hoped moderate Algerians would emerge, then negotiation. But that option relied on an always-elusive 'pacification'. Third, their tolerance of torture cost governments their moral authority. Fourth, their impermanence cost governments' capacity to command the obedience of the civil servants and military on the ground, who increasingly felt free to obstruct or sabotage policies decided in Paris. A prime example was the effective kidnapping of the FLN leadership, whose aircraft was forced down by the French Air Force as it flew from Rabat to Tunis on 22 October 1956. Ben Bella and his colleagues remained prisoners for the rest of the war. They were quickly replaced; but the main, and intended, result was to wreck secret preliminary talks undertaken by the Mollet government with the FLN. The government was so weak, moreover, that it felt obliged to 'cover' the action of the military.[12] Fifth and finally, by 1958 the French population was weary of a war that was claiming an eighth of the national budget and 30 months of the lives of young conscripts, and to which no end was in sight. This did not entail a consensus for withdrawal; it did mean disenchantment with the regime.[13]

The Fourth Republic's general malaise was such that President Coty told his advisers, straight after his election by Parliament in December 1953, that he might, one day, send for de Gaulle.[14] De Gaulle and the Gaullists were the final set of actors in the events of May 1958. But there was no command post from which orders emanated to a disciplined team: Colombey had a single telephone under the stairs, which de Gaulle avoided if he could. During the 'crossing of the desert' he had avoided committing himself to any policy on Algeria. This would greatly enhance his freedom of manoeuvre in the crisis. But he had no preconceived plan to return, appeared aged and tired out to many visitors, and only intermittently believed in his chances before February 1958. As his prospects improved that spring, so he revived physically.[15]

His two key aides during the crisis were his chief of staff Olivier Guichard, who was in regular contact with Coty and leading politicians; and the secretary-general of the residual RPF, Jacques Foccart, who worked both RPF networks and army contacts (he was a reservist with the *11e choc*, an elite paratroop regiment with secret service connections). Assisting this pair was Pierre Lefranc, who in May 1958 created an Association for de Gaulle's Legal Return to Power. Jacques Chaban-Delmas provided invaluable assistance as Defence Minister in the outgoing Gaillard government (which stayed on in a caretaker capacity till 14 May). On his appointment in November 1957, Chaban had created a personal 'antenna' in Algiers, headed by the former RPF delegate for northern France, Léon Delbecque. This allowed Chaban to visit Algiers and preach the need for de Gaulle's return to power to senior army officers. Meanwhile Delbecque established his own links, independent of the Defence Ministry, with army officers, with the various right-wing, pro-*Algérie française* movements present in Algiers, and with the remnants of the 200 or so conspirators who had briefly taken the city for the Allies on 8 November 1942.

These men sometimes took de Gaulle's orders during the crisis, but quite often they guessed them.[16] Foccart observed that when he was told to do nothing, what was really meant was to do nothing that would directly implicate de Gaulle.[17] Perhaps fortunately, de Gaulle's most fiercely pro-*Algérie française* associates played relatively minor roles: Michel Debré was suffering from sciatica, and Jacques Soustelle, former RPF secretary-general, former governor of Algeria, was banned from travelling by the government, and largely marginalised by fellow Gaullists when he broke free. De Gaulle himself spent much of May 1958 shuttling between Colombey and Paris, a slow 150-mile car journey. Perhaps that offers the best metaphor for his role in this complex crisis: part of events, but detached – and alone.

Sakhiet and after, February–May 1958

On 29 January 1958, Félix Gaillard's government approved the army's request for air raids against ALN camps in Tunisia. Unwisely, because such raids promised few military advantages without ground support, and carried the risk of further internationalising the conflict – which the FLN wanted and France did not. This duly occurred on 8 February, when an attack on the Tunisian border village of Sakhiet-Sidi-Youssef left 78 dead and over 100 wounded. A Red Cross lorry was hit. So was a school, killing a dozen pupils. President Habib Bourguiba recalled Tunisia's ambassador, Mohammed Masmoudi, blockaded France's Tunisian bases, and complained formally to the United Nations Security Council. The UN created a good offices mission under Anglo-American auspices to settle Franco-Tunisian differences, which the French, still dependent on American loans (the last one dated from January), accepted. Led by Robert Murphy (Roosevelt's envoy in Algiers in 1942–1943), the mission fully backed Bourguiba's demands: compensation to be fixed by the Red Cross, and the evacuation of French bases in Tunisia, except the naval installation at Bizerte. Gaillard accepted this humiliating plan on 13 April, but fell victim to the Right (and the Communists) in the ensuing National Assembly debate. His government's resignation on 15 April, though it remained in a caretaker role till 14 May, opened the Fourth Republic's final crisis. The Sakhiet attack (carried out with American-made bombers, earmarked for NATO use) also destroyed the Americans' confidence in the regime's North African policies. President Eisenhower would not come to the Fourth Republic's help.[18]

De Gaulle now tiptoed back onto the political stage by receiving Masmoudi at Colombey (a rare privilege) on 9 February. Masmoudi's ensuing statement played up the contrast between the regime's adventurism and 'the liberator de Gaulle, the man of Brazzaville, France's true conscience'; de Gaulle's own presidential-sounding communiqué stressed the importance of good Franco-Tunisian relations.[19] A small flurry of press speculation followed: Georgette Elgey in *Paris-Presse*, Raymond Tournoux in *Combat*, and the Sorbonne professor Maurice Duverger in *Le Monde* all wondered when de Gaulle would return.[20] He was now favoured by 13% of the French to succeed Gaillard as Prime Minister – hardly a spectacular total, but ahead of anyone else.[21] Meanwhile the Gaullist networks were quietly activated and de Gaulle started receiving visitors in Paris – over 50 in the next two months. To most of them, however, he appeared pessimistic about any possible return to power.[22]

Delbecque came on 6 March, and told de Gaulle of his plans to create a 'Vigilance Committee' of existing *Algérie française* groups – and to promote his return. De Gaulle told him to 'act for the best', to keep Foccart informed, and to stay out of prison.[23] On 26 April, after Coty had asked René Pleven, who was prepared to talk to the FLN, to form a government, Delbecque helped organise a demonstration of 30,000 people in Algiers against such 'treason'. The next day, at Colombey again, he asked de Gaulle how he would react to an insurrection in Algiers. De Gaulle replied that he would 'take his responsibilities' but never as the army's creature, and never without the French people's endorsement.[24]

The next approach, though indirect, came from the President: on 5 May Coty sent a staff officer to sound out Foccart and Guichard about a de Gaulle government. He was acting on information from Raoul Salan, Commander-in-Chief in Algeria, that the army was preparing a rising and the creation of a Committee of Public Safety – an expression borrowed from the extreme phase of the French Revolution. De Gaulle responded that it was too soon to answer. Events had not yet moved decisively in his favour.[25]

On 8 May Coty turned to the Christian Democrat Pierre Pflimlin, another partisan of direct talks with the FLN. This provoked the resignation of Robert Lacoste, Minister Resident in Algeria, who talked of a 'diplomatic Dien Bien Phu'. The next day the FLN announced that it had killed three French prisoners in retaliation for the earlier execution of three FLN activists. These two events prompted Salan to send Coty a telegram underlining the army's concerns, which, he claimed, only the appointment of a government determined to keep Algeria French would allay. This was an unprecedented attempt by the military to dictate the composition of the government of the Republic. The message made no mention of de Gaulle, but was still supported by Foccart, Delbecque, Soustelle and Debré.[26] And on 11 May Alain de Sérigny, editor of the influential *Écho d'Alger*, used his newspaper to call on de Gaulle to 'speak out quickly'. De Gaulle still remained silent. The stage was now set for an army insurrection; what was not clear was how far the Gaullists could turn it to their advantage.

Insurrection, 13–19 May

The demonstration of 13 May at the Forum, the main square in Algiers, ostensibly in memory of the three French soldiers, was Delbecque's initiative. It got out of hand when Pierre Lagaillarde, lawyer, army reservist, and leader of an extreme right-wing students' association, drove an army lorry through the barriers protecting the Governorate-General. *Algérie française* protesters poured into the offices, throwing files out of the windows, then took other key buildings. The army joined them and moved into the

Governorate-General, whose balcony now became a stage for the unfolding drama. Salan appeared on it and was copiously booed, as insufficiently *Algérie française*. Jacques Massu, commander of France's paratroops in Algiers, fared better, announcing the formation of a Committee of Public Safety at 8.40pm, and calling for the formation of a Government of Public Safety in Paris under de Gaulle. Delbecque arrived and was made vice-president of the Committee. The outgoing Gaillard government, meanwhile, gave Salan, still not quite a part of the rebellion, full civil and military powers to deal with the situation in Algiers.

These were confirmed on 14 May by the Pflimlin government, voted into office in the early hours by 274 votes to 129 in the National Assembly. If Pflimlin had hoped thereby to secure obedience from the Algiers generals, he failed: indeed, Salan used his powers to place senior officials opposed to the Committee under house arrest. The Committee, in its first formal communiqué, called for de Gaulle's return.

Salan did the same on 15 May, at Delbecque's prompting, at the end of his second speech from the Governorate-General balcony, and again in a telegram to Pflimlin. For the first time, the Commander-in-Chief in Algiers was demanding that the legitimate government of the Republic be replaced. And de Gaulle now made his first public declaration in three months, stating that, faced with the 'degradation of the state', he 'stood ready to assume the powers of the Republic'.[27] It was, as his left-wing opponents pointed out, an arrogant statement to make when France had a legitimate government, deserving of support against the army's rebellion. But it put de Gaulle at the centre of the unfolding game.

The government's response was swift: on 16 May it obtained the vote of a three-month state of emergency by 462 to 112 National Assembly votes. General Ély, the army Chief of Staff, resigned. Meanwhile Guy Mollet, leader of the Socialist Party and now vice-premier, asked journalists if de Gaulle would recognise Pflimlin's ministry as France's sole legitimate government, disown the Algiers rebellion, and – if ever he were called upon to form a government – present a programme for the Assembly's approval in the normal way. Mollet was a key player because de Gaulle would need at least some Socialist support to get a National Assembly majority. But the thrust of Mollet's questions was ambiguous. Was he aiming to block de

Gaulle's return – or to open a window that might enable it?[28] De Gaulle's response was to announce a press conference for 19 May.

In Algiers, demonstrations continued from 16 May with more or less forced displays, orchestrated to establish the legitimacy of the *Algérie française* cause, in which Moslems 'fraternised' with *pieds-noirs* and Moslem women removed their veils in public.[29] Meanwhile army officers in Algiers and Toulouse began planning a military takeover in Paris. Both Soustelle (by now smuggled to Algiers) and Debré were kept informed. Debré now spelt out to the army that such an operation should only be undertaken if Parliament refused a de Gaulle premiership, if there was a Communist takeover (never likely in 1958), or if there was a danger of civil war. Otherwise the army's preparations, and the carefully propagated rumours about them, should simply generate a state of tension that would facilitate de Gaulle's return.[30]

De Gaulle gave his press conference of 19 May to a packed room at the Palais d'Orsay hotel, which Interior Minister Moch had surrounded with police. He refused to answer Mollet's questions directly; but he did point out that he had restored the Republic, and civil liberties, in 1944, and had resigned when he and the newly elected Assembly came into conflict. 'Does anyone believe', he asked, 'that at 67 I am about to begin a career as a dictator?' No longer leader of the RPF, he could honestly say that he was identified with no party, had been politically inactive for five years, and was now 'a man alone ... I belong to no one and to everyone'. As for events in Algiers, de Gaulle would not condemn the army, claiming it was ensuring 'order' in Algiers, before warning that 'the army is normally the instrument of the state and should remain so ... but for that, there needs to be a state'. As to going through the normal processes of parliamentary approval to form a government, he refused to say. De Gaulle had teased a little, reassured republicans quite a lot, and given no-one any commitments. 'Now', he stated at the end of a bravura performance, 'I shall return to my village, and remain at the disposal of the country'.[31] He was not looking for power; it was for others to find him in Colombey if they wanted him.

Resurrection, 20–29 May

The week to 19 May had placed de Gaulle at the centre of France's crisis. The ensuing ten days brought him steadily closer to power.

Pflimlin resigned on 28 May. But opposition to a legal return remained, particularly among the Socialists. Meanwhile the military preparations advanced: on 29 May de Gaulle wrote to his son that 'an action from the south towards the north appears imminent'.[32] That afternoon, the outcome remained in the balance.

Colombey received more and more eminent visitors from 19 May. Two former prime ministers, Bidault, the very *Algérie française* MRP leader, and Pinay, the moderate conservative, rallied to de Gaulle on 22 May. Left-wingers, however, did not budge. Mollet was still opposed; so was Mendès-France, despite de Gaulle's best (if indirect) efforts to persuade him. Nevertheless, by 24 May de Gaulle felt sufficiently confident to ask Georges Pompidou to leave Rothschild's, to start assembling a staff team, and to prepare 'the necessary texts for him to take power legally'.[33]

That day saw further proof of the government's impotence as local activists (headed by a Deputy, Pascal Arrighi) plus elements of the *11e choc*, Foccart's regiment, took Corsica for the insurrectionists. Riot police sent from Nice promptly joined them.[34] Corsica confirmed many Socialists' suspicions of de Gaulle, but not all were ruling him out. Vincent Auriol, de Gaulle's implacable opponent during his presidency, now believed that France needed him back. On 26 May Auriol accordingly wrote to support de Gaulle's return to power, and a referendum on constitutional reform – if only he would disown the insurrection.[35]

As de Gaulle was aware, plans for operation 'Resurrection' – a code-word borrowed from his own press conference of 19 May, and signifying a *coup d'état* in Paris spearheaded by paratroopers from Algiers – were now well advanced. De Gaulle therefore approached Pflimlin directly, proposing a meeting to examine, in effect, a legal and peaceful transfer of power. The two men met secretly on the evening of 26 May, at the residence of the curator of the Parc de Saint-Cloud.[36] On de Gaulle's account, Pflimlin begged him to bring the army insurrectionists to heel, admitting that he himself could not. De Gaulle replied that this request proved 'the solution which the Republic requires' – a de Gaulle government.[37] But Pflimlin stayed put – for the moment.

De Gaulle now increased the pressure, announcing on 27 May that he had begun 'the regular process for the establishment of a Republican government capable of ensuring the unity and independence of the country' – and, crucially, enjoining 'the land, sea and air forces in Algeria to observe exemplary discipline under the orders of their commanders'.[38] Pflimlin was understandably infuriated: no such 'regular process' had been started. But both his chief of staff Michel Poniatowski and President Coty warned against issuing a denial. They understood from the message that de Gaulle knew a military operation to be imminent.[39] Operation Resurrection had, indeed, been planned for 28 May; de Gaulle's statement secured a postponement.

For the moment, however, neither Pflimlin nor the Socialists changed position. The Socialist Deputies voted 117–13 on 27 May against backing de Gaulle for Prime Minister until he denounced the Algiers insurrection. It was probably this which inspired de Gaulle to cable Salan the same day, requesting that an emissary come to inform him of Resurrection preparations.[40] At 10am on 28 May he duly heard the detailed plan for Resurrection, now scheduled to start in under 48 hours, from Salan's staff officer General Dulac at Colombey. Six hours earlier one major obstacle to de Gaulle's return had been removed: Pflimlin had resigned, just after winning a vote of confidence from the National Assembly, by 408–165. His Minister for Algeria could not go to Algeria, his Interior Minister did not control the police, and his National Defence Minister was defied by the armed forces; in these conditions even a big parliamentary majority was useless.

To Dulac, de Gaulle approved Salan's actions, but was critical of the Resurrection plan, refused to commit himself to a specific Algerian policy, and stressed his preference for a legal return to power.[41] Did he also signal his acceptance of a coup if that failed? Dulac claimed that he did. So did General Nicot of the Air Force staff, who stated that at a meeting with leading Gaullists held at 11am on 29 May at Solférino, Lefranc received de Gaulle's approval for Resurrection by telephone from Colombey.[42] Lefranc and the others present denied Nicot's claim.[43] What appears certain, however, is that de Gaulle did not exclude military action unconditionally, and that the military *believed* that they had his backing for Resurrection if events required. Hence, in particular, the telegram sent by Nicot's assistant Major Robert Vitasse to Algiers confirming de Gaulle's agreement for an operation beginning early on 30 May.[44]

The military option remained live because the political situation was still not moving. On the afternoon of 28 May, François Mitterrand, Édouard Daladier, and André Philip led an estimated 150,000 people on a march 'in defence of the Republic' – and against de Gaulle's return. That night, at Coty's suggestion, a second meeting at Saint-Cloud brought together de Gaulle and the presidents of the two houses of Parliament, Gaston Monnerville and André Le Troquer. De Gaulle was uncompromising, insisting that the National Assembly should vote him into office *in absentia* and without debate; that he should receive powers to govern without Parliament for a whole year; and that his constitutional reform should go to referendum directly, by-passing Parliament.[45] Monnerville accepted, but Le Troquer refused the whole package. De Gaulle returned to Colombey; Foccart drove Monnerville and Le Troquer to report to Coty at the Élysée Palace.[46]

What helped unblock the politics, on 29 May, was de Gaulle's reply to Auriol. France, he wrote to the former President, faced the threats of military action from Algiers, anarchy and civil war; he, de Gaulle, could save the Republic by heading a government committed to constitutional reform; and if the Socialists' 'incomprehensible sectarianism' prevented him, they would bear a heavy responsibility. 'As for me', he concluded, 'it will only be left to remain with my grief until death.' This appeal convinced Auriol; with de Gaulle's agreement he made it public – which helped switch enough Socialist parliamentarians in de Gaulle's favour.[47]

No-one, though, had yet asked de Gaulle to form a government. And so at 3pm on 29 May, six Douglas Dakotas were ordered to bases in south-west France, where troops were waiting to embark for Paris. Operation Resurrection had begun, though on a modest scale: a Dakota carries just 30 men. After barely an hour, however, they were turned back. Coty had finally issued his invitation.[48]

Endgame, 29 May 1958 – 8 January 1959

Coty announced his decision with unprecedented solemnity. In an official message, read out to each house of Parliament under Article 37 of the Constitution, he stated that if Parliament did not accept de Gaulle, the 'most illustrious of Frenchmen', as Prime Minister, he himself would resign. De Gaulle himself arrived at the Élysée a little before 8pm, re-emerging shortly after having agreed to lead a government.

From 30 May, as was customary under the Fourth Republic (and as Coty had insisted), de Gaulle consulted with party leaders. With the Socialists, he turned on the charm, receiving Mollet, Auriol, and Maurice Deixonne, chairman of the Socialist parliamentarians, at Colombey. Auriol needed no persuasion, but Mollet and Deixonne were now converted too; so, the next day, was a narrow majority of the Socialist group in the National Assembly. On 31 May de Gaulle met the heads of the other parties, except the Communists, in Paris, and made a formal concession to Coty: he would, after all, state his case before the parliamentarians – but only in a short declaration, after which he would leave them to their debate.

By Sunday 1 June de Gaulle's government was formed – with almost no Gaullists. The only true believer was Michel Debré – though he did take a key position as Justice Minister, in charge of getting the new Constitution drafted. Other appointments reflected de Gaulle's aspiration to national unity (Communists excepted): a Socialist (Mollet), an MRP (Pflimlin) and a conservative each had a top-ranking post as Minister of State, as did a representative of the French Union, Félix Houphouët-Boigny of Côte d'Ivoire. Interior, Defence, and Foreign Affairs went to non-political technicians, while the reassuring conservative Pinay got Finance. The only army officer was de Gaulle.

De Gaulle's speech to the National Assembly that same Sunday, 1 June, lasted just seven minutes – a record for brevity. Having outlined the gravity of the situation, he stressed that he needed, not just a vote of confidence and (like his predecessors) special powers to deal with Algeria but also powers to govern without Parliament for six months (the term initially envisaged was thus cut by half), and to draw up a new Constitution to be submitted to referendum. To reassure the parliamentarians, he promised that the new text would respect the sovereignty of the people and that the government would be responsible to Parliament.

The National Assembly voted de Gaulle in by 329 votes to 224, the opposition including all the Communists, nearly half the Socialists, and most of Mendès-France's supporters. By 10pm the new Prime Minister and his government were at the Élysée, with Coty in the chair, finalising the bills that would give them special powers.

The National Assembly began debating these from 10.30pm that night, and forced the government into a concession (granted when de Gaulle had already gone to bed): the constitutional text would go to a Parliamentary Consultative Committee before being put to the people. The debate continued on Monday 2 June, and now de Gaulle appeared in the Assembly to press his case. Warning the parliamentarians that he needed their votes that same night, he also resorted to flattery, referring to 'the pleasure and the honour I feel at being in your midst'. That night, the Assembly voted special powers by 350 to 163; the following day, Tuesday 3 June, the upper house adopted them by 236 votes to 30. Returning to the Hôtel La Pérouse, de Gaulle allowed himself a rare moment of self-congratulation: 'Albert, I've won!', he told the liftman.[49]

The Constitution of the Fifth Republic, drafted over the summer, was modelled on Bayeux. Its major innovations were fourfold. The president of the Republic, to be elected not just by Parliament, but by a college of some 80,000 mayors and local councillors, would have enhanced powers – in particular, to call new parliamentary elections, or a referendum, and to take special powers in a national emergency. The government was given a far stronger procedural capacity to get its policies through Parliament, and therefore, in principle, far greater stability than under the Fourth Republic. A Constitutional Council was created, a sort of Supreme Court empowered to judge on the constitutionality of new legislation. And the French Union was replaced by a new, looser structure, the French Community, from which colonies were in principle allowed to secede.

At the referendum of 28 September 1958, the text was backed by 79.2% of valid votes cast, with 16.2% abstentions. The vote was more about whether the electorate wanted de Gaulle to stay or leave than about constitutional details; it was still vastly more decisive than the referendum that had brought the Fourth Republic into being. Elections to a new National Assembly followed, on 23–30 November. The proportional electoral system in force since 1945 was replaced by a single-member-constituency system, with two ballots a week apart, which benefited larger parties able to make electoral alliances. And by this time a new Gaullist party, the Union pour la Nouvelle République (UNR), existed. It won 20.6% of the vote and 206 out of 579 seats – far from a majority, but a solid basis of Gaullist support. De Gaulle then easily won the first presidential election under the new system, with 78.5% of the electoral college votes on 21 December. On 8 January 1959, the last prime minister of the Fourth Republic became the first president of the Fifth; he would remain in office for ten years and (nearly) four months. On the same day, de Gaulle appointed Michel Debré Prime Minister: he held the post for over three years till 14 April 1962 – far longer than any Fourth Republic premier. France had entered a new political world.

Conclusion: *coup d'état* or democratic transition?

As Lacouture observes, de Gaulle had played like a virtuoso, transforming himself in three weeks from a sage in seclusion to a head of government endowed by Parliament with sweeping powers.[50] He had done so, moreover, without a party behind him, and with great economy of effort. He made just six public statements during the crisis: the communiqué of 15 May, the press conference of 19 May, the declaration of 27 May, the speeches to the Assembly and the upper house of 1, 2, and 3 June. Between them, his silence kept other players guessing, and he quietly deployed powers of persuasion, dissuasion, and even charm, to visitors at the La Pérouse, at Saint-Cloud, and at Colombey. The contrast between the battering-ram efforts of the RPF days could not be greater. In part this was because his hour had come: 12 years of diatribes against the regime's weakness were now amply and visibly justified. But he had also clearly drawn lessons from his years as an unsuccessful party leader.

A virtuoso performance, but not an unaccompanied one. Of the many plotters in May 1958, the Gaullists had the clearest aims and the best-developed networks. They won the confidence, for the time necessary, of both the military insurrectionists and the quasi-fascists in Algiers who supported them, and of politicians in Paris, including left-wingers like Mollet and Auriol. The chief orchestrators, Foccart, Guichard, and Delbecque, played a crucial role.

The Gaullist orchestrators are also central to the accusation that de Gaulle's return was achieved by a *coup d'état*. Five elements support such a claim. First, Gaullists had helped create a pre-insurrectionary context. Soustelle and Debré both helped found extreme

Algérie française groups. Debré's monthly, the *Courrier de la colère*, launched in 1957, not only called for de Gaulle's return but claimed that a rising to defend French Algeria was legitimate.[51] Second, Delbecque organised the Algiers demonstrations of 26 April and 13 May – the latter leading to the military insurrection which he then canalised in a Gaullist direction. Third, senior officers in Algiers were in touch with leading Gaullists, including Foccart, Soustelle, Guichard, and Debré *before* 13 May.[52] Fourth, Gaullists took an active part in the seizure of Corsica, and the storming of a prefecture. Fifth, de Gaulle himself had direct and (more frequently) indirect contact with the Algiers insurrectionists and never denounced their action, using it instead as leverage with politicians from the President and Prime Minister down. He may even have approved, on 28–9 May, a violent coup against France's legitimate institutions if all else failed. Only when Coty conceded the insurrectionists' main demand, de Gaulle's return, was it called off.

But the Gaullists did not conjure a coup, or the threat of one, out of thin air. The regime's weakness and instability were manifest in spring 1958. By then, Algiers lacked neither rebellious officers nor hot-headed *Algérie française* activists. And the army would prove in 1961 that it could attempt a coup not only without, but against de Gaulle. With or without encouragement from de Gaulle's supporters, therefore, an attempt would surely have been made in 1958: if not at Pflimlin's appointment, then at the moment that he tried serious negotiation with the FLN. If de Gaulle had stayed at home, such an attempt would have led to serious bloodletting, a military or extreme right-wing *Algérie française* government, or both. The peaceful outcome of May 1958, after all, was far from preordained. And as Foccart observed, 'the threat of Resurrection was a lever which facilitated de Gaulle's return to power. Its execution would have been an irreparable catastrophe'.[53] In the event, France was given, in Charlot's words, 'a revolution that was legalised as it unfolded' – starting with the full powers granted to Salan, not by de Gaulle, but by Gaillard and then by Pflimlin.[54] And the voters' verdict at the referendum of September 1958, though partly obtained by a campaign heavily loaded in the Gaullists' favour, was still convincing enough to complete the process of legitimation.[55]

In the end, the manner of his return is illustrative of de Gaulle's attitude to democracy. He was not, or not always, a stickler for due process of law. But it was inconceivable for him to come to power in the baggage of a group of generals; to govern, he needed the explicit consent of the French people. The referendum of September 1958 satisfied him that he had it.

For a few weeks, de Gaulle created a unity among the French not seen since August 1944. But it was achieved by being all things to all men: to parliamentarians, the saviour of the Republic from the Algiers colonels and fascists; to the Algiers insurrectionists, the saviour of *Algérie française* from a Republic prepared to sell out to the FLN. He could not indefinitely ride both these horses. The resulting difficulties would dominate the second half of the Algerian war.

Notes

1 François Mitterrand, *Le Coup d'État permanent* (Paris: Plon, 1964).
2 Irwin M. Wall, *The United States and the Algerian War* (Berkeley, London: University of California Press, 2001), p. 11.
3 Bernard Droz and Évelyne Lever, *Histoire de la guerre d'Algérie, 1954–1962* (Paris: Le Seuil, 1991 [1982]), pp. 39–41; Pierre Bourdieu, *Sociologie de l'Algérie* (Paris: Presses Universitaires de France, 1961), pp. 108–12.
4 Norman Lewis, *Jackdaw Cake* (Harmondsworth: Penguin, 1987 [1985]), p. 143.
5 Jean-Paul Angelier, 'Témoignage', in Jean-Paul Thomas, Gilles Le Béguec, and Bernard Lachaise (eds), *Mai 58. Le Retour du général de Gaulle* (Rennes: Presses Universitaires de Rennes, 2010), pp. 89–90.
6 Jacques Frémeaux, 'L'Armée et le 13 mai', in Thomas, Le Béguec, and Lachaise, *Mai 58*, pp. 59–68.
7 Alistair Horne, *The French Army and Politics, 1870–1970* (London: Macmillan, 1984), p. 74.
8 Martin Alexander and J.F.V. Keiger (eds), *France and the Algerian War, 1954–1962: Strategy, Operations and Diplomacy* (London: Frank Cass, 2002), p. xii.
9 Raphaëlle Branche, *La Torture et l'armée pendant la guerre d'Algérie, 1954–1962* (Paris: Gallimard (Folio), 2011 [2001]); Paul-Marie de la Gorce, 'De Gaulle en 1958: chances de succès, risques d'échecs', in Fondation Charles de Gaulle, *L'Avènement de la Ve République. Entre nouveauté et tradition* (Paris: Armand Colin, 1999), p. 38.
10 Jean Charlot, *Le Gaullisme d'opposition, 1946–1958* (Paris: Fayard, 1983), p. 324.
11 Wall, *United States*, p. 2.
12 Alistair Horne, *A Savage War of Peace: Algeria 1954–1962* (London: Pan Books, 2002 [1977]), p. 159; Wall, *United States*, pp. 51–5.

13 Philippe Buton, 'L'Opinion publique en 1958 selon les rapports de préfets', in Fondation Charles de Gaulle, *L'Avènement*, pp. 203–18.
14 Francis de Baëcque, 'Témoignage', in *ibid.*, pp. 60–1.
15 Jean Lacouture, *De Gaulle*, vol. II: *Le Politique, 1944–1959* (Paris: Le Seuil, 1985), pp. 454–5.
16 Pascal Girard, 'Les Complots, les mythes et les présomptions du 13 mai', in Thomas, Le Béguec, and Lachaise, *Mai 58*, pp. 145–67; Jérôme Pozzi, 'Les Entourages et les initiatives gaullistes du début de 1958', in *ibid.*, pp. 101–12.
17 Jacques Foccart, *Foccart parle. Entretiens avec Philippe Gaillard*, vol. I (Paris: Fayard/Jeune Afrique, 1995), p. 141.
18 Lacouture, *De Gaulle* II, p. 444; Wall, *United States*, pp. 114–15, 130–4; Matthew Connelly, *A Diplomatic Revolution: Algeria's Fight for Independence and the Origins of the Post-Cold War Era* (Oxford: Oxford University Press, 2002), pp. 248–58.
19 *Le Monde*, 11 and 12 February 1958.
20 Lacouture, *De Gaulle* II, pp. 442–3.
21 Roland Sadoun, 'L'Opinion publique française en 1958', in Fondation Charles de Gaulle, *L'avènement*, pp. 200–3.
22 Julian Jackson, *A Certain Idea of France: The Life of Charles de Gaulle* (London: Allen Lane, 2018), pp. 455–7.
23 Patrick and Philippe Chastenet, *Chaban* (Paris: Le Seuil, 1991), pp. 233–4.
24 Lacouture, *De Gaulle* II, pp. 454–6; Charles Williams, *The Last Great Frenchman* (New York: John Wiley, 1993), p. 367.
25 Williams, *Last Great*, p. 370; Charlot, *Opposition*, pp. 332–3.
26 Wall, *United States*, p. 137.
27 *DM*III, p. 3.
28 Charlot, *Opposition*, pp. 344–5; *Le Monde*, 19 May 1958.
29 Droz and Lever, *Guerre d'Algérie*, pp. 177–8; Malika Rahal, 'Les Manifestations de mai 1958 en Algérie ou l'impossible expression d'une opinion publique "musulmane"', in Thomas, Le Béguec, and Lachaise, *Mai 58*, pp. 39–58.
30 Guy Pervillé, '"Résurrection" ou "entreprise d'usurpation"? Le Retour de la légalité républicaine en Algérie', in Fondation Charles de Gaulle, *L'Avènement*, pp. 95–105: pp. 99–101.
31 *DM*III, pp. 4–10.
32 *LNC*II, pp. 1282–3.
33 Georgette Elgey, *La République des Tourmentes*, vol. III: *La Fin* (Paris: Fayard, 2008), p. 808.
34 Charlot, *Opposition*, p. 352.
35 Lacouture, *De Gaulle* II, p. 475.
36 *LNC*II, p. 1279; Elgey, *La Fin*, p. 816.
37 *MH*, p. 24.
38 *MH*, p. 25.
39 Michel Poniatowski, 'Témoignage', in Fondation Charles de Gaulle, *L'Avènement*, pp. 61–3.

40 *LNC*II, pp. 1280–1281.
41 Olivier Guichard, *Mon Général* (Paris: Grasset, 1980), pp. 352–4.
42 Lacouture, *De Gaulle* II, p. 483.
43 Georgette Elgey, *La République des Tourmentes*, vol. IV: *De Gaulle à Matignon* (Paris: Fayard, 2012), p. 30; Olivier Guichard, *Mon Général* (Paris: Grasset, 1980), pp. 352–4; Foccart, *Foccart parle* I, pp. 147–8; Lacouture, *De Gaulle* II, p. 484; Pierre Lefranc, *Avec de Gaulle* (Paris: Plon, 1989 [1979]), pp. 152–4.
44 Edmond Jouhaud, *Serons-nous enfin compris?* (Paris: Albin Michel, 1984), p. 53.
45 Jean Touchard, *Le Gaullisme, 1940–1969* (Paris: Le Seuil, 1978), p. 160.
46 Elgey, *De Gaulle à Matignon*, pp. 28–32.
47 *LNC*II, p. 1281; Elgey, *De Gaulle à Matignon*, p. 33; Touchard, *Le Gaullisme*, p. 161.
48 Elgey, *De Gaulle à Matignon*, p. 35.
49 Elgey, *De Gaulle à Matignon*, pp. 58–75; Lacouture, *De Gaulle* II, pp. 497–501.
50 Lacouture, *De Gaulle* II, pp. 469.
51 Christophe Nick, 'Débat', in Fondation Charles de Gaulle, *L'Avènement*, pp. 63–4.
52 Guichard, *Mon Général*, pp. 349–50.
53 Foccart, *Foccart parle* I, p. 147.
54 Charlot, *Opposition*, p. 358.
55 Philip Williams, *French Politicians and Elections, 1951–1969* (Cambridge: Cambridge University Press, 1970), pp. 96–100.

Further reading

Julian Jackson, *A Certain Idea of France* (London: Allen Lane, 2018), chapters 18–19, covers de Gaulle's return and the last months of the Fourth Republic.

Charles de Gaulle, *Memoirs of Hope: Renewal 1958–1962; Endeavour 1962–*, tr. Terence Kilmartin (London: Weidenfeld & Nicolson, 1971) begins with the return to power. His speeches from 1958 onwards appear in his *Discours et Messages*, vol. III (Paris: Plon, 1970).

On the Algerian War, see the classic Alistair Horne, *A Savage War of Peace: Algeria 1954–1962* (London: Pan/Macmillan, 1996 [1977]), and the more recent Martin Evans, *Algeria: France's Undeclared War* (Oxford: Oxford University Press, 2012).

The numerous detailed accounts of de Gaulle's return to power are in French. They include Fondation Charles de Gaulle, *L'Avènement de la Ve République. Entre nouveauté et tradition* (Paris: Armand Colin, 1999); Christophe Nick, *Résurrection. Naissance de la Ve République, un coup d'État démocratique* (Paris: Fayard, 1998); Jean-Paul Thomas,

Gilles Le Béguec, and Bernard Lachaise (eds), *Mai 58. Le retour du général de Gaulle* (Rennes: Presses Universitaires de Rennes, 2010); and the last two volumes of Georgette Elgey's incomparable *Histoire de la Quatrième République: La fin* (Paris: Fayard, 2008) and *De Gaulle à Matignon* (Paris: Fayard, 2012).

9 Setting an example? De Gaulle, decolonisation, and the Third World

De Gaulle the decoloniser and friend of the Third World is a major component of the larger de Gaulle myth, along with de Gaulle the liberator and the constitution-maker. 'Since Brazzaville', he claimed in 1961, 'I have never ceased to say that the peoples of our dependencies should have the right of self-determination.'[1] Yet his 1944 Brazzaville speech only mentioned colonised peoples gradually 'taking part in the management of their own affairs;'[2] and his policies as head of the provisional government, and as RPF leader, were noticeably hard-line. Early decolonisation happened despite de Gaulle (in the cases of Syria and Lebanon in 1945) or without him (in those of Indochina, after Dien Bien Phu, in 1954; and of Tunisia and Morocco, in relatively peaceful conditions, in 1956). It was a Socialist minister, Gaston Defferre, who drafted a framework law giving greater autonomy to France's colonies in sub-Saharan Africa in 1956.

Yet the 'Brazzaville narrative' has a kernel of truth. De Gaulle personally evolved towards more liberal colonial positions after 1953.[3] Decolonisation, especially France's excruciating severance from Algeria, dominated his early presidency; by 1962 almost all of France's vast African empire had won independence. And without inventing decolonisation, de Gaulle embraced it as part of France's *grandeur* as an open, generous, freedom-loving power. France's relations with the emerging Third World, long crippled by Algeria, were reset on this basis: the French way, de Gaulle claimed, offered developing countries an exemplary alternative to superpower domination in the bipolar Cold War world.

How far did the de Gaulle spin correspond to the reality of French decolonisation and to postcolonial relations with former colonies, and with the wider Third World? And how successfully did he extract France from the Algerian imbroglio? For resolving Algeria was the essential preliminary for de Gaulle's wider undertakings on the world stage.

Algeria: a five-stranded narrative

De Gaulle's colossal moral stature, and, soon, the Fifth Republic Constitution, gave him more freedom of policy-making manoeuvre in Algeria than his predecessors had enjoyed. He still faced formidable constraints. The insurrection that helped him to power in May 1958 was intended to keep Algeria French. The FLN, by contrast, was committed to complete independence for Algeria, and the recognition of itself as sole representative of the Algerian people. Between these positions, no compromise was possible.

De Gaulle wrote later that while he had no 'pre-determined plan', he was clear about 'the main outlines' of a settlement. France should not suffer humiliation as it had in Indochina; French forces must therefore become 'masters of the battlefield'. But *Algérie française* could not last. As he observed to the young Gaullist Deputy Alain Peyrefitte, integrating the fast-growing Moslem population into the Republic, as the *Algérie française* lobby now said it wanted, would transform France out of recognition: his village of Colombey-les-Deux-Églises would become 'Colombey-les-Deux-Mosquées'.[4] Instead, Algeria's future relations with France should be based on free association not French domination – and should be decided by the Algerians.[5]

Such ideas were anathema to *Algerie française* ministers like Soustelle, and to the Gaullists' temporary allies of May 1958 – the officer corps in Algeria, and the militant *pieds-noirs*. So de Gaulle could not simply announce a plan for Algerian independence, or even autonomy, that June. Rather, in the Gaullist narrative, he had to proceed like the skipper of a sailing vessel, tacking slowly into a headwind towards his objective.

Table 9.1 gives a chronology of the journey towards Algerian independence. The story has five interwoven strands. The first is military. In August 1958 de Gaulle escalated the war. Raoul Salan, Commander-in-Chief in Algeria, got 80,000 reservists as reinforcements, taking the French military headcount there above 500,000.

Table 9.1 The Algerian War, 1958–1962

4–7 June 1958	De Gaulle visits Algeria and announces one person, one vote for the colony. 'Vive l'Algérie française!' at Mostaganem (6 June).
Summer 1958	Secret, indirect, contacts with FLN via Abderrahmane Farès.
19 September 1958	The FLN, based in Cairo, announces a 'Gouvernement Provisoire de la République Algérienne' under Ferhat Abbas.
3 October 1958	De Gaulle announces Constantine Plan for Algeria's economic development.
23 October 1958	De Gaulle proposes '*paix des braves*' cease-fire, which FLN rejects.
23–30 November 1958	Elections in France and Algeria. No major Algerian 'third force' emerges between *Algérie française* and FLN.
11 December 1958	UN General Assembly resolution calling on the French government and the FLN to negotiate falls one vote short of a two-thirds majority.
19 December 1958	Raoul Salan replaced as Commander-in-Chief in Algeria by Maurice Challe. Paul Delouvrier becomes delegate for civil affairs.
February 1959	Start of two-year offensive against FLN ('Challe Plan').
April 1959	Municipal elections.
May 1959	Senatorial elections.
Spring, summer 1959	Georges Pompidou in secret talks with FLN.
27–31 August 1959	De Gaulle visits army in Algeria.
16 September 1959	De Gaulle's self-determination speech.
October 1959	Failure of *Algérie française* supporters' attempts to block self-determination plan in National Assembly and in Gaullist Party.
10 November 1959	De Gaulle renews invitation to FLN to talks. On 20 November, FLN names its imprisoned leaders as its negotiating team. De Gaulle refuses.
12 December 1959	A further UN resolution calling for negotiations wins 35 votes to 18. US abstains.
24 January – 1 February 1960	Barricades Week rebellion in Algiers.

(*continued*)

Table 9.1 (continued)

February 1960	Further Pompidou–FLN contacts.
3–5 March 1960	De Gaulle visits army in Algeria.
May 1960	Cantonal elections.
10 June 1960	De Gaulle receives secret visit of Médéa group of leading FLN combatants.
14 June 1960	De Gaulle's speech mentioning 'Algerian Algeria', and inviting the FLN to talks.
25–29 June 1960	Melun talks with FLN.
4 November 1960	In a broadcast, de Gaulle refers to 'an Algerian Republic, which will one day exist'.
16 November 1960	Announcement of referendum on self-determination.
22 November 1960	Creation of a Ministry for Algerian Affairs under Louis Joxe.
9–13 December 1960	De Gaulle's final visit to Algeria. Big pro-FLN demonstrations.
19 December 1960	UN General Assembly vote recognises Algeria's 'right to independence', by 63 votes to 27 abstentions.
8 January 1961	Referendum on self-determination: 75% Yes vote.
February 1961	Pompidou talks with FLN in Lucerne.
March 1961	Beginning of OAS activity in Algeria.
31 March 1961	FLN pulls out of planned talks after Joxe invites rival Mouvement National Algérien to take part.
11 April 1961	De Gaulle in press conference underlines the cost of Algeria to France, and states expectation of an Algerian state, 'sovereign within and without', but associated with France.
22–5 April 1961	Generals' Putsch. OAS attacks in Algeria and mainland intensify after failed coup attempt.
May–August 1961	Unilateral cease-fire by French army.
20 May – 28 July 1961	Évian–Lugrin negotiations, which break down over status of Sahara.
5 September 1961	De Gaulle concedes that Sahara will be Algerian though insists on preservation of French interests there.

(continued)

Table 9.1 (continued)

October 1961	Secret meetings between French and FLN representatives in Basle.
December 1961 – February 1962	Further secret French–FLN meetings, including Joxe.
20 December 1961	UN General Assembly calls for resumption of negotiations.
12–18 February 1962	Les Rousses negotiations with FLN produce outline agreement.
5–18 March 1962	Final round of France–FLN negotiations at Évian.
19 March 1962	Cease-fire with FLN after final agreement at Évian.
8 April 1962	Referendum in France on Évian agreements: 90% Yes vote.
3 July 1962	De Gaulle recognises Algerian independence after Algerian referendum on Évian accords produces 99% Yes vote.

From March 1959, Salan's successor Maurice Challe launched a programme of aggressive operations rolling from west to east of the country against the FLN's mountain strongholds. The 'Challe Plan', which ran into 1961, reduced the Armée de Libération Nationale (ALN) to a mere 5,000 fully operational guerrillas, from nearly 30,000 in 1958. Large swathes of the country were 'pacified'.[6] But the ALN, never quite annihilated, was always liable to recruit, regroup, and attack again. So the war continued: during operations early in April 1961, for example, 79,000 French soldiers were transported in Algeria by helicopter.[7] Mostly confined to Algeria, conflict sometimes spread to mainland France. The FLN and its rival, Messali Hadj's Mouvement National Algérien (MNA), fought a nasty internecine struggle in France, the 'café wars', leaving some 4,000 dead. The FLN began killing French gendarmes in 1961. An unauthorised pro-FLN demonstration that 17 October left at least 100, possibly 200, Algerians dead, most of them thrown into the Seine by Maurice Papon's police. The French authorities hushed up the killings.[8] Military activity of various sorts was thus a constant until the final cease-fire of 19 March 1962.

The second strand was diplomatic. By late 1956 the FLN had world-wide offices, most importantly in New York. It capitalised on events like the bombing of Sakhiet, and undertook its own spectacular initiatives – most notably constituting the Provisional Government of the Algerian Republic (GPRA – a term deliberately reminiscent of 1944 and de Gaulle's Algiers-based GPRF), in September 1958.[9] The key diplomatic forum was the United Nations, where every December the General Assembly debated a resolution calling for negotiations, or (in 1960) declaring Algeria's right to independence. From 1956 to 1959, the resolutions fell just short of the two-thirds majority needed to pass; that of 1960, however, was adopted. This infuriated the French, who saw Algeria as an internal matter, and especially resented the American habit of abstaining rather than supporting France. France's Foreign Ministry tried to take measures against FLN diplomats; the secret services, inspired by de Gaulle's adviser Jacques Foccart, assassinated several.[10] To no avail. As France's ambassador to the UN knew, the FLN's diplomatic gains more than compensated for its military setbacks.[11] De Gaulle might rail against the 'so-called' UN and the 'mostly improvised' Third World nations who dared to challenge France there.[12] But he timed several major initiatives for the autumn, with the impending UN debate in mind. He knew that the annual December humiliations prevented the global acceptance of France as a great power with a universal mission – which he craved – and that the only remedy lay in an Algerian settlement.[13]

A third strand was electoral. At Algiers on 4 June 1958 de Gaulle announced that all Algerians would henceforth vote in a single electoral college, on the basis of one person, one vote. This, he hoped, would allow a 'third force' of moderate Algerians, less intransigent than the FLN, to emerge. So Moslem Algerians voted, in varying numbers, in the referendums of 28 September 1958 and 8 January 1961, in elections to the French National Assembly in November 1958 and to Algerian local authorities in April 1959 and May 1960. Significant numbers of Moslems were elected to local authorities. But army and FLN hostility denied them significant influence on events. The army, despite written, public instructions from de Gaulle to make the November 1958 elections free and fair, forced the withdrawal of Moslem candidates who did not support its *Algérie française* positions. It did the same, albeit less effectively, at local elections. The FLN, meanwhile, boycotted elections and tried with some success to get the population to do the same. The major referendums, however, were successful – not so much in Algeria as in France. In January 1961 three-quarters of voters endorsed de Gaulle's plan to give Algeria self-determination; in April 1962, over 90% backed the independence agreement reached that March. When Algerians voted, in July 1962, they were 99% in favour of independence. These were solid democratic ramparts against de Gaulle's opponents in France.

The *Algérie française* opposition is a fourth strand in the narrative. In his Algerian visit of 4–7 June 1958, de Gaulle gave army and *pieds-noirs* alike reasons to doubt that he was really 'their' head of government. He told them gnomically that he 'understood' them. He pronounced the words *Algérie française* only once, and then after hesitation, in Mostaganem. And he ordered officers to leave the Committees of Public Safety set up in May 1958. In December, he replaced Salan with Challe. Disaffection in the *Algérie française* community, military and civilian, was widespread by spring 1959; it became systemic when de Gaulle offered Algeria self-determination on 16 September 1959. Its first clear manifestations, in October 1959, fell (just) within the domain of conventional politics: an attempt in the National Assembly to force the government to change policy, and a bid by Soustelle to win control of the Gaullist party for its *Algérie française* faction. Both failed.

More dangerous were two outright rebellions in Algiers – 'Barricades Week' in late January 1960 and the 'Generals' Putsch' in April 1961. 'Barricades Week' began as a demonstration against the transfer to Europe of Jacques Massu, the charismatic paratroop general and leader of the May 1958 revolt. It quickly became a rebellion by armed civilians who installed themselves behind barricades in the city centre and fired on the gendarmes who advanced on them, killing 14 and wounding 123. They were supported by at least one parachute regiment and most of the white Algiers population. De Gaulle gave one ineffectual radio broadcast on 24 January, before finding his style (and full military uniform) five days later in a televised speech. This, plus heavy rain, flushed out the rebels; a minor purge of the officer corps followed, and Challe, whose response to the rising de Gaulle considered weak, was replaced in April.

The second *Algérie française* rising against de Gaulle, the 'Generals' Putsch' of 22–25 April 1961, was a coup attempt led by the two sacked Commanders-in-Chief, Salan and Challe, plus two former Chiefs of Staff, Edmond Jouhaud (air force) and André Zeller (army), and involving some 14,000 officers and men.[14] It failed swiftly thanks to its own poor organisation, to timely government precautions (leading backers in mainland France were arrested, and transport aircraft removed from Algeria),[15] and to effective government communication: Prime Minister Michel Debré's two broadcasts, and de Gaulle's speech of 23 April, in which he poured scorn on the 'quartet of retired generals' and the 'partisan, fanatical, ambitious officers' behind the putsch, and activated Article 16 of the Constitution, empowering him to 'take all measures required by the circumstances'.[16] Conscripts in Algeria heard it on their personal transistor radios; some reacted by arresting their own (pro-putsch) officers.[17] The putsch fizzled out, Challe gave himself up on 25 April, Zeller followed two weeks later, and Salan and Jouhaud went underground. Supported among both Debré's and de Gaulle's military staffs, however, the putsch had been dangerous: Foccart and Lefranc, both members of de Gaulle's innermost circle, spent four nights in the Élysée with their side-arms in case insiders tried to kidnap the President.[18] A much larger purge of the officer corps than in 1960 followed.[19]

The most poisonous manifestation of *Algérie française* opposition, however, was the Organisation de l'Armée Secrète (OAS), a white terrorist organisation active from March 1961 and headed from May by Salan. By the year's end it had 1,500 operatives and 15,000 logistical helpers, overwhelming *pied-noir* support, and the capacity to detonate 30 charges of plastic explosive in Paris, and kill 20 people in Algiers, every day.[20] On 8 September 1961 OAS operatives tried to kill de Gaulle with a roadside bomb at Pont-sur-Seine. On 9 February 1962, the Paris police, which counted numerous OAS supporters, attacked a Communist-organised anti-OAS demonstration in Paris, crushing to death four men, three women, and a boy of 16 at the Charonne metro station.[21] Aiming to block any peace negotiations, to secure *Algérie française* permanently, or even to kill de Gaulle and install a Spanish-style dictatorship in Paris, OAS violence imitated the FLN's – but had the opposite effects to those intended, pushing de Gaulle to settle with the FLN.

The Évian accords, which technically ended the war on 19 March 1962, did not stop OAS violence. A pitched battle with the French army in the rue d'Isly in Algiers, on 27 March 1962, left 46 OAS supporters dead.[22] Thereafter the OAS aimed simply to kill educated Moslems and to wreck any asset, like Algiers university library, that might serve the new Algerian regime: unofficial estimates put OAS-caused deaths at 2,200 between 20 April and 30 June, when an agreement with the FLN ended OAS activity in Algeria.[23]

The final, and most complex, strand in the Algerian narrative consists of de Gaulle's own initiatives, punctuated by contacts with the FLN, open and secret, and underpinned by a sustained effort at communication with the public through speeches, broadcasts, and press conferences, as well as visits to Algeria. The direction of travel is clear. De Gaulle moved from statements that might be interpreted, in June 1958, as favourable to *Algérie française* ('Come to France! She will not betray you!', to a crowd in Bône on 5 June)[24] to endorsing full Algerian independence, with the support of nine French voters in ten. But the road was tortuous. This was due not only to outside constraints but also to de Gaulle's own reluctance to concede more than he had to, or to appear to act under pressure.

His first initiative, in summer 1958, was to invite Abderrahmane Farès, former president of the defunct Algerian Assembly, to join his government. The FLN, sounded out by the prudent Farès, said no; so, then, did Farès. That, and the GPRA's formation in September, convinced de Gaulle that speedy negotiations were not on the FLN's agenda. Thus when, during his press conference of 23 October, he made the '*paix des braves*' invitation to the FLN to lay down its arms and talk under the white flag of parley, he was not offering full peace talks; indeed, he instructed Salan to take any FLN negotiators, should they appear, to an quiet provincial spot to discuss a cease-fire, not a political settlement.[25] The FLN, considering the offer an invitation to surrender, refused it. But de Gaulle's '*paix des braves*' rhetoric still crossed a threshold by acknowledging that the FLN were not mere bandits but fighters for a cause. Similarly, although his social and economic development plan for Algeria, unveiled at Constantine on 3 October, was a rehash of measures announced under the Fourth Republic, it did implicitly acknowledge the rebellion's roots in long-term deprivation. And de Gaulle was more serious than his predecessors about implementing it; the Constantine Plan was central to the brief de Gaulle gave to Paul Delouvrier, appointed as his civilian delegate in Algeria that December.

The political situation, however, remained deadlocked into 1959. This was partly because de Gaulle wanted to give war a chance: hence the Challe Plan. Even then, though, he was clear that Algeria had to change – that 'l'Algérie de papa' was dead, as he told an Oran newspaper in March 1959, much to the annoyance of *pieds-noirs*.[26] And that spring and summer he despatched Georges Pompidou, who had returned to Rothschild's Bank but remained available for special missions, to sound out FLN representatives about a new political departure.[27]

The result, after de Gaulle had also consulted President Eisenhower (who was pressing for a new initiative), as well as his own full cabinet, was the broadcast speech of 16 September 1959 offering Algeria self-determination. Algerians, he said, would choose at a referendum between the options of independence (which de Gaulle called 'secession' and considered disastrous); 'Francisation', or the full integration of Algeria into a French Republic stretching 'from Dunkirk to Tamanrasset'; or 'the government of Algerians by Algerians, backed by French aid and in close union with France for the economy, education, defence and foreign relations', on a 'federal model'. It was clear that his preference lay with this model of 'independence-association'.[28]

Certainly, there were prerequisites for the referendum: four years of peace, defined as no more than 200 deaths per year from civil strife, and a disarmed FLN ready to accept an open democratic process. Nevertheless, by declaring that 'the fate of Algerians belongs to Algerians' and that independence was available if the majority wanted it, de Gaulle had taken a decisive step. On 10 November he renewed his invitation to the FLN to talk.

Ferhat Abbas cautiously welcomed the initiative in the FLN press. Then his colleagues backpedalled. In November, the FLN chose Ben Bella and its other leaders detained since 1956 as its negotiating team – which it knew de Gaulle would not accept. Politics stalled again. Indeed, de Gaulle's Barricades Week television broadcast of 29 January 1960 sounded like a move backwards. Without dropping self-determination, he invited the army to 'liquidate' ALN forces, and enjoined the *pieds-noirs* not to believe claims that he planned to 'abandon' them and hand over Algeria to the FLN.[29] To army officers in March, he promised (off the record) that he would never negotiate with the FLN. Self-determination, the press concluded, had been dropped, or delayed.[30]

They were wrong. In June 1960 de Gaulle even received three ALN commanders from the Médéa district, south of Algiers, in the Élysée. Hard-pressed militarily, they were trying to extend peace feelers without, however, going behind the FLN leadership. The top-secret meeting reached no definite results, and all three men had been killed (one by the FLN, two by the French) within 14 months. But de Gaulle probably concluded that the FLN would be receptive to a new peace offer. This followed in his speech of 14 June, which he opened with a nostalgic reference to bygone days of 'oil lamps and sailing fleets' the better to underline France's need to modernise, before calling for 'the transformation of an Algerian Algeria into a modern and fraternal country'. The 'Algerian Algeria' reference was new, and for the first time the FLN agreed to talks.

They opened at the prefecture of Melun, south-east of Paris, on 25 June 1960. But the two sides were talking at cross-purposes. The Algerian delegates expected to arrange a summit for de Gaulle and Ferhat Abbas to discuss independence. But de Gaulle, perhaps misled by the Médéa trio into believing the FLN on its knees, had instructed his negotiator Roger Moris to limit talks to a cease-fire, disposal of weapons, and treatment of combatants. When the FLN refused this agenda, de Gaulle shut down discussions after four days, though even Debré thought they were worth continuing. The aftermath was predictable: the FLN announced that no further talks were planned and de Gaulle, in his 5 September press conference, vehemently excluded full negotiations with the FLN as long as it continued to commit atrocities.[31]

There matters rested until a dense sequence of events opened late in 1960. First, in his broadcast of 4 November, while still attacking the FLN's claims to negotiate its way into government without a cease-fire, de Gaulle crossed a new threshold by referring to 'an Algerian Republic, which has never existed but which will exist one day' – suggesting he now viewed independence as likely.[32] Second, he announced a referendum on the principle of self-determination. Third, he created a full Ministry of Algerian Affairs, directly responsible to him, under Louis Joxe, former CFLN secretary-general in Algiers in 1943. Fourth, in December de Gaulle made his last visit to Algeria, where white crowds were now overwhelmingly hostile and the Moslems not: their mass demonstrations behind the FLN flag dispelled any doubts de Gaulle had had about the FLN's majority support among Moslems. Conversely, the visit was cut by a day, and Algiers by-passed, because of the risk of assassination by the *Algérie française* opposition. Back in Paris, he set the referendum for 8 January, then stressed in broadcasts that a negative or luke-warm result would trigger his immediate resignation. Having won the referendum, he despatched Pompidou to Lucerne to prepare negotiations with FLN emissaries at two difficult secret meetings, on 20 February and 5 March 1961.[33]

New talks were fixed for April – until Joxe, at de Gaulle's behest, tried to bring in Messali Hadj's MNA. The FLN had always insisted on being France's sole negotiating partner and was the MNA's implacable enemy: it therefore withdrew from talks on 31 March. Talking to the MNA without the FLN was pointless: the FLN had to be brought back. De Gaulle tried in a speech of 11 April 1961, which gave the strongest statement yet of his plans: 'decolonisation is our interest and is therefore our policy'; 'Algeria costs us more than she brings in, to say the least'; the future Algeria would be 'sovereign within and without'; and if the Soviet Union or the United States tried to take France's place in Algeria, he wished them 'every joy of it'.[34] The cynicism of some passages led Challe to join the Generals' Putsch, which delayed negotiations further; they finally began on 20 May at Évian, on Lake Geneva. The FLN delegation arrived daily from Switzerland.

De Gaulle had made two big concessions: the FLN would be sole negotiating partner, and without a preliminary cease-fire (the French observed one unilaterally, from May to August 1961). The two rounds of negotiations, at Évian (20 May – 13 June 1961), and Lugrin (20–28 July), discussed substantive questions such as the transition regime from cease-fire to self-determination and possible independence, the continuity of essential services, the future of Moslems who wanted to stay French, future co-operation, and defence issues.[35] But they broke up over two main points. One was the future of the *pieds-noirs*. Joxe sought to guarantee their representation, and their own judicial and educational systems, within the new institutions; the Algerians, led by the GPRA's Foreign Minister Krim Belkacem, stressed the 'unity of the Algerian people', without privileges for any group. The second issue was the status of the Sahara. For de Gaulle, the Sahara's oil and gas reserves, discovered by the French, should be exploited under French leadership by all surrounding states. For the Algerians, the Sahara, home to 400,000 (mostly nomadic) Algerians, was part of Algerian national territory under the UN resolution of December 1960.[36]

This was the key sticking point, but not for long: de Gaulle conceded the Sahara in his press conference of 5 September 1961. Saad Dahlab, Krim's most senior colleague, said later that only this finally convinced the FLN of de Gaulle's serious intentions.[37] Certainly, de Gaulle also talked about the FLN negotiators' bad faith, about partitioning Algeria to reserve territory for *pieds-noirs*, and about safeguarding vital French oil and gas interests – but he rightly acknowledged that all Algerians considered the desert Algerian.[38] Debré, by-passed as usual from policy-making on Algeria, contemplated resignation. Pompidou remarked that with the Sahara concession he could have secured an agreement at Lucerne the previous March.[39]

Instead, the war dragged on another six months. Autumn 1961 saw one of the FLN's periodic leadership upheavals, as Ben Youssef Ben Khedda replaced Ferhat Abbas at the head of the GPRA, Saad Dahlab took over from Krim as GPRA Foreign Minister – and, crucially, the hard-liner Houari Boumediene consolidated his power base as head of the ALN, based outside Algeria. It was above all Boumediene who stalled negotiations after September 1961. In December, however, Joxe, having re-established contacts with Saad Dahlab, exchanged written proposals, and finally undertook a new round of talks (12–18 February) near the Alpine resort of Les Rousses, in a concrete bunker chiefly used for snow ploughs. This time, thanks to the OAS, de Gaulle was eager to conclude. On 18 February he urged Joxe to finish that very day: agreeing, he said, was more important than 'holding a little longer certain things which, anyway, we do not reckon to hold forever'.[40] Outline accords were sent to the French government and the FLN leadership on 19 February. Concluding talks opened at Évian on 5 March; the two sides finally signed a 93-page document on 18 March. A cease-fire came into force next day at noon. The referendums of 8 April and 1 July 1962 confirmed the agreements, and Algerian independence, on each side. But 19 March is still remembered in France as the day the war ended.

The Évian accords meant full Algerian independence, not 'independence-association'. Instead of a four-year interval from cease-fire to referendum, Algeria would vote within barely three months. French troops would be cut to 80,000 within a year and zero within three. The GPRA would become the real government of Algeria without elections; the Sahara would be Algerian. Notwithstanding independence, the French would continue the Constantine Plan as aid till 1964, and provide longer-term technical and financial assistance to the new republic.

The French did, it is true, salvage something from the wreckage of French Algeria. The big Mers-el-Kébir base remained French on a 15-year lease. So did aerodromes and refuelling facilities in the Sahara, and nuclear and missile testing sites for five years. French firms got preferential treatment in oil and gas prospecting for six years. The French could pay for Algerian petroleum products not in dollars but in francs, which would be recycled to buy French goods. And thanks to Joxe's efforts, the *pieds-noirs* would retain dual nationality for three years, after which they would choose between Algerian citizenship and the status of 'privileged foreign residents'. Their property rights were guaranteed, as were political representation proportional to their numbers, and control of the two most European towns, Algiers and Oran. This was very much less than what de Gaulle, let alone the *pieds-noirs*, might have hoped for in 1958 or 1959. But it was not a complete rout – on paper.[41]

An Algerian balance-sheet

The most upbeat assessment of de Gaulle's record in Algeria is given by the American journalist Cyrus Sulzberger, who writes that

> with courage, skill, and mastery of ruse, he restored firm discipline over an unruly army, squashed secret terrorist movements aiming at his downfall, and, at a moment when their actual military insurrection had been defeated in the field, gave the Algerians freedom – and made the French like it.[42]

For Debré, 'It was a miracle we didn't collapse into civil war after Algeria; and this we owed to de Gaulle.'[43] Perhaps an army coup in mainland France would not have got very far, but part of the officer corps was certainly willing to try – and de Gaulle was instrumental in facing down their challenges. The 'café wars', gendarme killings, and OAS attacks aside, the war was kept away from mainland France.

De Gaulle avoided not only civil war but also national humiliation. His broadcasts and press conferences 'presented the ordeal as a victory for France's national interest, as a fulfilment of France's own liberal ideals, as a precondition for modern action on the world stage'.[44] The army was not defeated. The referendums of 1961 and 1962 established a consensus that simply closed France's political debate on Algeria by late 1962. And de Gaulle ensured that state-to-state relations between France and independent Algeria were 'exemplary': the French respected their commercial and aid obligations under Évian, and left their bases and Saharan facilities, freely, earlier than planned.

Yet there was a massive negative side to the balance-sheet, in three respects. The first is the four years it took to end the war. For de Gaulle, this was the time required before 'common sense broke through the mists'.[45] The record, however, suggests that he himself contributed to the delay. No peace was possible without the FLN, bloodthirsty and undemocratic though it was; yet political talks with this inescapable negotiating partner began fully three years after de Gaulle's return to power. One likely reason was that de Gaulle was less clear about his final objective than his memoirs claim. His son Philippe even writes that in 1958 he still thought *Algérie française* a serious possibility.[46] His model of 'independence-association', was, at least initially, that of the French Community, built into the Fifth Republic Constitution.[47] This was light years away from the full independence the FLN demanded. The attempt to by-pass or domesticate the FLN by opening up a democratic process from which moderate representative Moslems might emerge was no more realistic in 1958 than when Mollet had tried it in 1956. The idea of partitioning Algeria, of creating a separate *pieds-noirs* zone, touted in speeches and in the articles he encouraged Peyrefitte to write in 1961,[48] was another blind alley. Such an enclave would be anathema to the FLN and as needy of military protection, and as vulnerable to UN censure, as French Algeria. Even conceding the logic of waiting for common sense to prevail, allowing talks to break down over the Sahara on 28 July 1961, only to concede the point less than six weeks later, appears wholly unnecessary.

From this perspective, de Gaulle's speeches on Algeria appear, not as a patient effort to get the French to accept the inevitability of independence, but rather as a series of improvisations, feints, and forced concessions from a leader determined to try anything to avoid that outcome. That, certainly, is how it looked to the FLN. And gambits like partition played into the hands of Boumediene and other hard-liners.[49]

Secondly, the cease-fire of 19 March 1962 did not end the conflict. Over 150,000 people, overwhelmingly Moslems, died in the months after the Évian agreements.[50] During this period the French government failed two groups to which it owed a duty of care. The first was the *pieds-noirs*, of whom 2,885 disappeared between 19 March 1962 and 30 September 1963 (1,219 were found alive, but 1,676 were killed or missing).[51] Faced with a straight handover of power to the FLN, mistrusting guarantees offered at Évian, and certain, at least from Salan's arrest on 20 April, that the OAS could not stop independence, the *pieds-noirs* migrated massively to mainland France. By 19 August, government figures showed 533,000 *pieds-noirs* there; by 12 September, 750,000; by 23 November, just 180,000 were left in Algeria out of over a million. Another 80,000 left in 1963.[52] These numbers overwhelmed government plans, based on a possible 350,000 arrivals from all of North Africa over five years, and available shipping: most *pieds-noirs* were allowed to bring just two suitcases to France. They also made the Évian safeguards irrelevant: Algeria's remaining *pieds-noirs* were scattered individuals, not a group. In France, *pieds-noirs* received practical help such as free transport, cheap loans, and assistance finding employment and housing – amounting, in 1963, to 4.4% of total central government spending. France's booming economy of the 1960s absorbed them remarkably smoothly. But there was no compensation for goods lost, nor any symbolic gesture of reconciliation: de Gaulle considered that their support for the OAS had sabotaged the Évian agreements and that France, having borne the burden of the war over eight years, owed them no more.[53] Mostly settled in south-eastern France, the *pieds-noirs* returned the favour by providing a reservoir of anti-de Gaulle votes, morphing, for many, into support for the far-Right Front National from the 1980s.

If the *pieds-noirs* were (arguably) sold short, the Algerian Moslems who fought on the French side, known as *harkis*, were treated far worse.[54] Their numbers had been doubled, to some 60,000, at the start of the Challe Plan, because of their knowledge of local terrain, and of the enemy (some having defected from the FLN). But every *harki* became a potential target for post-war FLN reprisals.

In 1961 the Algerian Affairs Committee, chaired by de Gaulle, had considered that the arrival in France of many Moslems was 'not to be foreseen, or wished, still less encouraged', and that the *harkis*' safety was best secured by guarantees in the peace agreement. A decree of 20 March 1962 offered them three choices: redundancy with a lump sum, joining the army, and a six-month civilian contract with the army.[55] But *harkis* were generally encouraged to take redundancy and return to their villages, on the assumption that the FLN would respect the Évian agreements.[56] They did not. Killings carried out by ALN fighters, or by last-minute FLN supporters, are estimated at up to 150,000. Some *harkis* attracted retribution for crimes they had committed alongside the French; but family members were also murdered, with every imaginable atrocity and mutilation to the living and the dead.[57]

Harkis seeking to reach France were treated like any other Algerian Moslems: they had to submit a form at a prefecture, with a certificate proving that someone would house them. When the killings began, the army engaged special procedures to settle Algerians such as *harkis*, civil servants or elected officials in France. Some 26,000, mostly *harkis*, thus reached France with army help; a further 25,000–35,000 fled by their own means. Through the spring, however, ministers insisted that only official channels be used: Interior Minister Christian Fouchet advised prefects in Algeria to oppose departures. Joxe, questioned in the Assembly on 29 June, claimed the government's plan would cover all necessary eventualities.[58] De Gaulle's limpid instruction of 26 July 1962 brutally summed up the official position: 'The Harkis were recruited in the past from among down-and-outs, and they want it to continue at the expense of the French. This is a bad joke that has gone on long enough.'[59] The prime responsibility for the *harki* massacres belongs to the FLN, but the President and France's government bear a share.[60] The minority of *harkis* who did reach France, excluded from assistance measures designed for whites, were parked for a generation in 1930s camps built to house Spanish Republican refugees, then re-used by Vichy for internees.[61]

The greatest negative in de Gaulle's Algerian balance-sheet, however, was the destruction visited upon the land and people of Algeria by his pursuit of military victory. The Challe Plan represented 'the largest military operations of the war'.[62] It deployed French troops plus 60,000 *harkis*, along with 700 fixed-wing aircraft and 200 helicopters, plus 120 Observation Corps planes, to seek out and destroy ALN units in their mountain hide-outs, day and night.[63] In its own terms, the plan was devastatingly effective. In 1959 it cost the ALN 26,000 dead, 10,000 prisoners, and 20,800 arms taken.[64] But it also destroyed any residual prospect of the kind of settlement de Gaulle wanted, because of the means it used. More specifically, the Challe Plan extended and intensified military practices expressly forbidden under the Fourth Geneva Convention, signed by France in 1949 and ratified in 1951, and which would today count as war crimes.[65]

The first of these was torture and summary executions, common practices among the French military since (at least) the Indochina war, practised systematically in the 1957 Battle of Algiers, and prohibited 'at any time and in any place whatsoever' under the Geneva Convention. De Gaulle never approved of either. On the contrary, he created a commission to investigate allegations related to them, and ordered the perpetrators punished whenever individual cases came to his notice.[66] But the task he assigned the army helped preserve a long-standing culture of impunity. The Challe Plan depended on intelligence, and the intelligence units, which routinely used torture, saw their role expanded, with the approval of Defence Minister Pierre Guillaumat. Torture therefore spread out from Algiers and other cities across the country.[67] Challe, presented with an instruction from Debré's office banning the use of torture, replied 'I've got a war to fight!' Government instructions on the humane treatment of prisoners were almost impossible to get distributed, let alone acted upon.[68] Impunity also covered rape – the FLN used more and more women in its political organisation from 1958–1959, and female suspects were invariably raped if arrested – and summary executions, sometimes with the public display of bodies; 1,000 summary executions were recorded in the first eight months of 1960 – certainly fewer than the true total.[69]

Also germane to the Challe Plan was the creation of free-fire zones where, as one airman who flew over them put it, 'everything that moved was an enemy, most often the donkeys and other quadrupeds that served as transport or food reserves for the rebels; our job was to ... make life there impossible'. The air force weapon of choice for this work was napalm.[70] Civilians living in free-fire zones were removed and placed in what the British, using similar techniques in South Africa 60 years earlier, had called concentration camps. With their villages left empty, bombed, or burnt down, their crops abandoned, their livestock often dispersed, rural Algerians became wholly dependent on whatever shelter and hand-outs the French gave them. The total 'resettled' population rose from 237,231 early in 1958 to between 1.8 and 2 million by October 1960: nearly half the rural population of Algeria was parked in some 1,800 centres. A handful were model villages with running water, electricity, a nurse, and a school. Many more were tent encampments infested with malnutrition and disease. Even humanely managed, forced displacement meant, as the sociologist Pierre Bourdieu found, that 'The whole economic and social fabric of vast swathes of rural Algeria was overturned to the point of destruction.' Napalm, and the little incendiaries called 'chocolats', destroyed wood and agricultural land that would take three generations to recover. The impact of resettlement was known at least by March 1959, when a report to Delouvrier (by future Prime Minister Michel Rocard) was leaked to *Le Monde*.[71] But the displacements went on well into 1960.

Nor did this colossal destruction produce decisive military results – certainly not the victory in six months de Gaulle demanded.[72] Down but not out, the ALN maintained a capacity for low-level attacks that left Delouvrier's office worried by its ability to bounce back.[73] Moreover, as de Gaulle could not risk another Sakhiet, the Challe Plan could not touch the FLN's Army of the Frontiers, 80,000 strong, massed along the borders of Tunisia and Morocco under Boumediene. Just in March 1961, the ALN crossed over from Tunisia five times; and it now possessed weapons capable of bringing down French aircraft.[74]

Falling short of its military goals, the Challe Plan quite failed in its political aim, to enable France to negotiate a settlement from strength. In September 1959, de Gaulle was apparently confident that the FLN would join peace talks 'on their knees'.[75] On 12 July 1961 he announced that France's army had 'won on the ground, so that France could retain complete freedom in her own decisions and acts'.[76] But the torture and summary executions (which the FLN also practised widely) made a nonsense of any attempt by de Gaulle to create a 'middle group' of moderate, pro-French Algerians, and the uprooting of Algeria's rural population ensured the FLN a ready reception in the camps. As for the million or so men thrown into unemployment by the forced resettlement policy, perhaps 200,000 became migrant workers in France, and contributors (willing or not) to FLN funds.[77]

Moreover, weakening the ALN, and the FLN's 'political-administrative organisation' within Algeria which was a particular target for Challe, shifted the balance of power within the FLN towards groups based outside Algeria, especially, from late 1959, to the intransigent Boumediene.[78] Military setbacks, however grave, did not bring the FLN to the negotiating table. It was de Gaulle's preliminary concession of the FLN's core demands, that Algeria would be independent and under FLN control, that allowed serious negotiations to begin; it was only his further concession of the Sahara that allowed them to conclude. In the international arena, finally, as long as military operations continued, so would the hostile votes at the United Nations, leaving France's diplomacy half-paralysed.

In the end, the futility of military action was best expressed by de Gaulle himself. 'If the army did win, where would that get us?' he asked Pierre Laffont of *L'Écho d'Oran*, in November 1960. 'We'd have to start all over again in five years, ten years, when there'll be even more Moslems than there are now.'[79] Although the army had rendered an FLN victory impossible, he later wrote, 'resistance could and would be indefinitely prolonged and renewed in appropriate areas thanks to the widespread collusion of the population'.[80]

Counterproductive against the FLN, did war-making serve any other political purpose? Lacouture suggests that the Challe Plan was also intended to divert the army from politics by reinvigorating its military mission;[81] in other words, that de Gaulle inflicted horrific destruction on Algeria in order to solve a French political problem.

But this hardly worked either. The more the army believed it was winning, the more de Gaulle's political concessions appeared as a betrayal of France's dead. And the more the military used *harkis*, the more they felt obliged to reassure them that France would stay. These frustrations boiled over into the 1961 putsch.

In retrospect, even the loyal Chaban-Delmas called seeking military victory before negotiation a 'pure utopia' which ignored the obvious lessons of the French Resistance about how and why nationalists fight.[82] Was de Gaulle's preferred outcome an Algeria within the French Community where Moslems lived cheek by jowl with *pieds-noirs*? Supposing such a dream still possible in 1958, the Challe Plan destroyed it forever. Or did de Gaulle believe all along that independence was inevitable? In that case, the Challe Plan merely forced Algerians to pay an unimaginable price so that French opinion could believe that France, having 'won', had generously conceded Algeria its freedom.

The French Community and its failure

Compared with Algeria, decolonising sub-Saharan Africa was easy. France's sub-Saharan territories included French Equatorial Africa (consisting of the Congo, Oubangui-Chari (now Central Africa), Chad, and Gabon); French West Africa (Guinea, Senegal, French Sudan (now Mali), Côte d'Ivoire, Dahomey (Benin), Niger, Upper Volta (Burkina Faso), and Mauritania); plus Madagascar, and Togo and Cameroon, former German colonies which became French mandates after 1918. De Gaulle built on the greater autonomy given these colonies under the Defferre Law of 1956 to create the French Community, incorporated into the Constitution of 1958. But the Community did not satisfy its members' aspirations, and de Gaulle quickly conceded them full independence. In nearly all cases, a close, co-operative relationship with France, a major supplier of aid, followed. With Tunisia and Morocco, both fully independent since 1956, relations were more difficult.

This generally benign narrative has a dark side: a pattern of neo-colonial dependency, personal favours, corruption, and periodic violence, encapsulated in the expression *Françafrique*.[83] Not every trait of *la Françafrique* dates from the de Gaulle years; but most of the foundations were there by 1969.

Under Articles 77–87 of the 1958 Constitution, the French Community federated autonomous African states – former colonies – around France. Their autonomy dated from the *ordonnance* of 26 July 1958, under which each state's head of government became an African prime minister, not a French-appointed official. Each state sent delegates to the Community's executive and representative institutions. But the president of France would always be the Community's president, and central Community competences would include foreign and defence policy, the economy, finance and the currency, strategic raw materials, telecommunications, and higher education. These centralising provisions represented little real progress from Defferre. Hence the disappointment of African leaders when they saw the first draft of the Constitution on 25 July. They were in a position to demand changes: one, Félix Houphouët-Boigny of Côte d'Ivoire, was a Minister of State in de Gaulle's government, and four more sat on the Constitutional Consultative Committee. Within two weeks de Gaulle had conceded their right, if they wished, to secede from the Community.[84] Campaigning for the new Constitution on an African tour from 20 August, he made clear that any territory voting No would also be leaving the Community and claiming full independence. His reception, warm in Tananarive (Madagascar), Brazzaville (Congo), and Abidjan (Côte d'Ivoire), was mixed in Dakar (Senegal), and clearly hostile in Conakry (Guinea), where the left-wing Prime Minister Sékou Touré had mobilised his supporters to vote No. On 28 September, all the sub-Saharan territories (as well as Algeria) voted Yes to the Constitution, usually with large majorities – except for Guinea, which French military and civilian personnel began evacuating the next day, and which was declared independent on 2 October.

In public, de Gaulle praised the Community as an example to the world, as an update of France's former 'civilising mission', offering its members development, security, and co-operation.[85] In private, even in August 1958, he called it 'hogwash' and predicted that 'as soon as these people [African leaders] are in it, they'll only be thinking of one thing – getting out'.[86] This proved prescient: with Guinea fully independent, Sékou Touré acclaimed at the UN, and Algeria promised self-determination in September 1959, the African leaders found it impossible to resist the pull towards independence, guaranteed as a right under Article 86 of the Constitution. In two speeches in Senegal on 12 and 13 December 1959 de Gaulle gracefully recognised that the African states' independence was both possible and imminent, and began to make the rhetorical transition from 'Community' to 'co-operation'.[87] The Community's Executive Council held its seventh and last session on 21 March 1960; its Senate, inaugurated only on 15 July 1959, enjoyed 'a few useless months of existence'.[88] By the end of 1960 the Community no longer existed. A little before their British counterparts, all of its member states, plus Cameroon and Togo, were independent.

Why did de Gaulle find it so easy to grant independence (he called it 'international sovereignty') to France's sub-Saharan African territories? First, there was no large settler population to resist decolonisation, no army with an emotional investment in French Africa. Second, leaders like Houphouët, or Léopold Senghor of Senegal, or Philibert Tsiranana of Madagascar, were vastly more Francophile negotiating partners than the FLN. Third, de Gaulle could be confident that France's vital interests would remain intact even after independence. That was part of the point of the 'co-operation' which de Gaulle announced as France's 'historic vocation' in December 1962.[89]

'Co-operation' and *Françafrique*

De Gaulle stopped visiting Africa after 1960, but followed African affairs very closely. He created a Ministry for Co-operation, and Jacques Foccart, his adviser for Africa from 1960, was among his closest political confidants. France's relations with the new African states remained symbiotic.

They took the form, firstly, of aid. In 1963 France ranked second among the world's aid suppliers, contributing 14.5% of the world total. Civilian aid to independent states represented 0.35% of French GNP in 1965. Of this, some 70% (and 32,000 out of 46,000 personnel) consisted of educational assistance, the rest being technical (expertise for transport or telecoms projects), or administrative (building civil services on a French model). Aid was very unequally distributed, with Algeria (furthering the 'exemplary' post-independence policy) getting four times as much per capita as sub-Saharan Africa, which itself received twice as much as Morocco and Tunisia.[90]

Development aid was complemented by a French military and secret service presence. France spent some 0.28% of GDP on military aid in the 1960s, with seven bases in continental Africa and an eighth in Madagascar. Troop numbers, it is true, fell rapidly, from 58,500 in 1962, to 21,300 in 1964 and 6,420 in 1970. But France's light, mobile forces were still there – as Defence Minister Messmer stated in 1963 – to help keep internal order, and to man permanent command, communications and intelligence systems.[91] In each capital, the head of station for French intelligence services had direct access to the head of state and his staff.[92]

These state-to-state relations were highly personal. As de Gaulle recalled, 'In order that these new relations should be sealed at the summit and should accord with what was for me a duty, an honor and a pleasure, I maintained friendly personal relations with the Heads of State.'[93] In private, on a bad day, he was less flattering: 'Will you bugger off with your blacks?', he swore at Foccart one autumn day in 1968. 'It makes a very bad impression, people see nothing but blacks at the Élysée, day after day.'[94] In practice, Foccart handled day-to-day relations, with extreme care, as his diaries show, and usually sidelining the Ministry for Co-operation and the Foreign Ministry. He was normally available to African heads of state by telephone day and night; no fewer than eight of them attended his funeral in 1997.[95]

What France got in return for this outlay was prestige – the gross aid figures reflected de Gaulle's idea of the generous face France should show to the world – and relatively stable, friendly regimes in a region on which France relied for vital raw materials. France had first refusal on sales of oil (above all from Gabon) plus minerals such as uranium, lithium, beryllium, and thorium, facilitated by the former colonies' sharing a currency, the 'franc CFA', which was pegged to the French franc. In addition, a slice of French aid went to heads of state personally, who returned the favour by making donations to the Gaullist party – a practice Foccart mentioned explicitly in his diary for 1972, but in a manner that suggests it started much earlier.[96] Economically, politically, and militarily, therefore, Francophone Africa became France's special preserve, with the approval, in the name of anti-Communism, of the United States.

Stability, however, could not be guaranteed in a coup-ridden region. Certainly, Houphouët in Côte d'Ivoire and Senghor in

Senegal survived well beyond de Gaulle. In oil-rich Gabon the French foiled a coup attempt against Léon Mba in 1964, then groomed Omar Bongo for a smooth succession in 1967; in Chad, they protected Ngarta Tombalbaye against northern rebels in 1968. But elsewhere French military help was withheld, by accident or design. In Congo, Fulbert Youlou was overthrown in August 1963 (Foccart was away deep-sea fishing); between December 1965 and January 1966, three coups in two weeks in Dahomey, Central Africa, and Upper Volta went unopposed by France, on de Gaulle's decision; so did a further coup in Dahomey in 1967.[97] Successful coup leaders were generally welcomed into Foccart's orbit after a probationary period; this applied even to Jean-Bedel Bokassa, the former NCO who took control of Central Africa in January 1966, whom de Gaulle rightly considered unfit for office.

The French did not, according to Foccart, engineer coups.[98] But against Sékou Touré's Guinea they used mercenaries to destabilise the regime. Sékou Touré's one-party state survived; he even sought a reconciliation by repeatedly sending de Gaulle books and letters. But for de Gaulle, he had insulted France in September 1958 – and this was more important than the abundant bauxite reserves to which better relations would have given France access.[99] In Cameroon, meanwhile, the French undertook a far more brutal, Algerian-style intervention, deploying troops and aircraft in the Bamileke War against Marxist insurgents in the north of the country. The French army killed the insurgents' leader Ruben Um Nyobé; the secret services then murdered his successor, Félix Moumié, on Foccart's orders.[100]

De Gaulle's preference for stability in Africa did not extend beyond France's client states. In 1960, he supplied secret support, including mercenaries, to Moïse Tschombe's attempt to detach the mineral-rich southern province of Katanga from the rest of the former Belgian Congo, and rejected the UN's intervention.[101] Eight years later, he agreed to assist the breakaway Nigerian state of Biafra with both open humanitarian aid and covert arms, via Côte d'Ivoire, in an operation co-ordinated through Foccart and strongly opposed by Foreign Minister Couve de Murville and Defence Minister Messmer (who was instructed to deny any French involvement).[102] Ironically given this record, de Gaulle nevertheless invoked the principle of non-intervention when he refused to condemn South Africa's apartheid regime (to which France sold Mirage aircraft, helicopters, armoured vehicles, warships, and ground-air missiles), or white-ruled Rhodesia's Unilateral Declaration of Independence of 1965.[103]

The countries of North-West Africa were never part of the *Françafrique* constellation. Algeria was obviously a special case. Morocco under Kings Mohammed V (until 1961) then Hassan II, and Tunisia under Habib Bourguiba, were moderate, pro-Western regimes, independent since 1956, with which good relations should have been straightforward. De Gaulle swiftly resolved France's post-Sakhiet dispute with Tunisia, agreeing in 1958 to evacuate all French bases except Bizerte within four months; with Morocco too a settlement on bases was reached.[104] Yet for much of the de Gaulle presidency relations were troubled, and the aid they received per inhabitant was one-third that prevailing in sub-Saharan Africa. Both countries were too friendly with the United States for de Gaulle's liking; both undertook land reform programmes at the expense of French *colons*. Other reasons for the malaise were more specific.

The Tunisian case was the more dramatic. Bourguiba, seeking to reinforce his standing within the Arab world, wrote to de Gaulle on 6 July 1961 demanding France's withdrawal from Bizerte and from 'our territories in the south' – apparently seeking a slice of Algeria's oil-rich Sahara. But Bizerte remained an important French base during the Algerian war, and Bourguiba's letter provoked a stern warning from Paris. This the Tunisians ignored, blockading and shelling the Bizerte base on 19 July. De Gaulle's response was brutal: carrier-based aircraft and 7,000 paratroopers secured the base, leaving at least 630 Tunisian dead. Bourguiba received no US support as he had after Sakhiet in 1958.[105] For de Gaulle, the fact that he was already resolved to end the Algerian war, and planned to evacuate Bizerte soon thereafter, was immaterial: 'I could not permit France to be flouted', he wrote later.[106] Relations with Tunisia never fully recovered during his presidency.

French relations with Morocco worsened after October 1964 owing to land reforms and restrictions on international capital transfers, but the major damage was done in 1965 by the kidnapping on a busy Paris street, and subsequent murder, of the Moroccan opposition leader Mehdi Ben Barka. De Gaulle was as outraged by the Ben Barka affair as by the Bizerte incident – all the more so as General Oufkir's Moroccan security services, responsible for the kidnap, appeared to have had accomplices among their French counterparts. France's ambassador to Rabat was recalled, and, again, relations barely recovered in the de Gaulle presidency.[107]

De Gaulle was as proud of his record as a decoloniser as he was of France's past colonial 'civilising mission' and post-(or neo-) colonial role from 1960. But he was clear that new nations needed independence with, not against, their former masters: anything else was 'absurd and ruinous'.[108] To Peyrefitte, he claimed in February 1963 that France 'is distinguished from others in that its vocation is more disinterested and more universal than that of any other'.[109] That was setting the bar high. In public, de Gaulle could be more down-to-earth and conventional: French aid, he said in 1965, was a good investment which paid off in terms of prestige and export markets.[110]

The most impressive feature of de Gaulle's relations with sub-Saharan Africa is the speed with which he accepted that the Community was useless and independence inevitable. But disinterestedness is not the salient feature of France's record. And indeed, the benefits of French aid to sub-Saharan African countries, whose economies tended to stagnate in the 1960s, were barely apparent.[111] But that was not the primary concern of Foccart, who ran the policy. As his diaries show, his focus was always on keeping the heads of state contented, secure, and loyal to France. The occasional coup aside, France's record in sub-Saharan Africa was a success in Foccart's terms, defined above all by *realpolitik*. But it was in the idealised terms of his remarks to Peyrefitte that de Gaulle attempted to sell France to the wider Third World.

France and the wider Third World

Few statesmen expressed as eloquently as de Gaulle – even as he unleashed the Challe Plan on Algeria – the injustice of global inequality. The only 'worthy quarrel', he told a press conference on 25 March 1959, alluding to *Hamlet*, was that of 'man, man who must be saved, allowed to live, to develop' – before proposing that developed countries of West and East contribute part of their industrial and agricultural produce, but also infrastructure and scientists, to lift two billion people of the Third World out of misery.[112] Global inequality, he added in speeches to the UK Parliament and to the US Congress in April 1960, threatens global peace.[113]

This discourse made little impression as long as the Algerian war lasted and de Gaulle poured scorn on the UN.[114] But Algerian independence signalled a major turning-point. His co-operation with this radical new state, which he touted as 'an example to the world', was intended as the 'narrow door' for French penetration of the whole Third World.[115]

The first target of de Gaulle's grand Third World design was Latin America. In 1964, he became the first French president to visit Mexico (15–19 March) and then South America (taking in Venezuela, Colombia, Ecuador, Peru, Bolivia, Chile, Argentina, Paraguay, Uruguay, and Brazil, from 20 September to 16 October). These countries, reasoned de Gaulle, longed to shake off US hegemony; France, as another 'Latin' nation, could help; and South America had supported the Free French after 1940.

These were gruelling tours, undertaken with energy and aplomb by the 73-year-old de Gaulle, and offered some of his presidency's grandest moments, such as the 'Let us walk together hand in hand', declaimed in Spanish to a huge crowd in Mexico City. But he did not always hit the right note. Speeches about a common Latin heritage left South American Indians indifferent; attacks on US hegemony could grate on pro-American elites. The tours secured a valuable contract to build the Mexico City metro, and the foundation of a French lycée in Buenos Aires, but did not detach Latin America from the United States, or tie it more closely to France.[116] Their success lay largely in demonstrating France's willingness to challenge US dominance in Washington's own 'back yard'.

The same was broadly true of de Gaulle's policies in East Asia. On 27 January 1964 France recognised the People's Republic of China, a decision at least two years in the making. No doubt he sought, partly, to irritate the United States, which had withheld recognition since the Communists took Beijing in 1949. De Gaulle believed that the Americans had a misguided, ideological, and monolithic view of 'world Communism', that his own nation-based view of world politics was correct, and that the Sino-Soviet split, open since at least 1960, was about national interests not ideology.[117] To this was added a conviction that a country of 700 million people should not be left outside the international community, and a cautious interest in (very) long-term commercial advantage.[118]

Divergence with the United States over China was echoed, more intensely, over south-east Asia. For most of the RPF years, de Gaulle had strongly supported France's (American-backed) war against the Viet Minh insurgency in Indochina. During his presidency, however, de Gaulle campaigned with the zeal of a convert to end US military involvement in Vietnam. As early as September 1959, he warned Eisenhower to withdraw his few hundred military advisers, arguing that a government with such visible foreign backing would lose popular support.[119] Kennedy got similar advice. Following Lyndon Johnson's escalation of the war, Foreign Minister Couve de Murville used the (formerly derided) UN General Assembly to voice France's criticisms of the war, on 29 September 1965.[120] But the climax of de Gaulle's Vietnam campaign was his own speech to a crowd of 100,000 in the Cambodian capital Phnom Penh on 1 September 1966. Citing France's departure from Algeria as an example, he called for an immediate withdrawal of American forces and an international peace conference, in the interests of Vietnam, of world peace, and of the United States.[121] In his press conference of 28 October, he referred to 'the bombing of a small people by a large one' as 'detestable', and in June 1967 squarely blamed the US for starting the war.[122] The Phnom Penh speech was instrumental in winning the trust of Ho Chi Minh and thence the choice of Paris as the location for negotiations between the United States and North Vietnam. This too was consistent with de Gaulle's view of France's universal mission. Unfortunately, as talks started in May 1968, Paris was attracting the world's attention for other reasons.[123]

The final area in which de Gaulle distanced France from mainstream Western policies was the Middle East. France under the Fourth Republic had been closely tied to Israel, particularly during the ill-fated Suez expedition of 1956. Israel bought Dassault jets. The two countries even undertook joint research on nuclear weapons. De Gaulle's policy was different. He ended nuclear co-operation with Israel (and Italy, and Germany) in 1959, and refused a formal offer of alliance made by Prime Minister David Ben Gurion in 1961. After the Évian accords, he sought improved relations with the Arab states, re-establishing diplomatic relations (broken after Suez) with Jordan, Syria, Saudi Arabia, and Iraq. In exchange for further improvement, the Arabs demanded that France be 'more reserved' towards Israel.[124] De Gaulle needed little persuading. He increasingly viewed Israel as fundamentally expansionist; crucially, too, by 1966 Arab countries supplied four-fifths of France's ever-growing oil needs, and offered export markets 20 times bigger than Israel's. Lacking the well-established sources of British and American oil firms, France needed good political relations for secure supplies. But being reserved towards Israel did not mean hostility; and Israel still shopped at Dassault.[125]

De Gaulle's pro-Arab pivot came into sharper focus during the 1967 Arab-Israeli war. His warning to all parties, as the crisis built in May, not to shoot first – delivered personally to Israeli Foreign Minister Abba Eban on 24 May – appeared as a rather pro-Arab form of impartiality since Egypt was doing most of the (visible) provocation. So did the embargo on arms sales to Israel and seven Arab countries announced by France on 2 June: Israel was France's biggest customer in the region.

At dawn on 5 June the Israelis used their Dassault Mirage jets to destroy the Egyptian air force on the ground in a surprise attack. By the time of the cease-fire on 10 June, Israel had comprehensively beaten the armed forces of Egypt, Syria, and Jordan, and seized the West Bank of the Jordan, Sinai, the Gaza Strip, and the Golan Heights. De Gaulle never quite forgave Israel for ignoring his warnings.[126] After the war, as before, he called for an international conference to resolve Middle Eastern issues; but President Johnson and Soviet Premier Kosygin preferred to meet one-to-one at Glassboro in the United States. He also believed that Israel should leave all of the newly occupied territories in return for recognition by the Arab states. France supported a Yugoslav resolution to that effect in the UN – taking a position on this vote that was closer to those of the Soviet bloc and the Arab countries than to the West's.[127] This reaped benefits for France in terms of an exemption from the first sanctions the Arab oil-producing countries attempted to apply to the West.[128]

De Gaulle went further at a press conference of 27 November 1967, when he referred to the Jews as 'since time immemorial an elite people, self-assured and domineering' and to the State of Israel as 'warlike and expansionist'.[129] These remarks, unsurprisingly, were widely considered anti-Semitic. Certainly, the charge of anti-Semitism hardly sticks if de Gaulle's whole career is taken into consideration. Only one anti-Semitic remark appears in his correspondence – from 1919: an unusually thin record for a man of his generation and milieu.[130] As eminent a figure as René Cassin testified to de Gaulle's resolutely liberal attitude towards Jews in 1940–1941.[131] He restored the French citizenship of Jews in Algeria in 1943, and condemned Vichy's persecution of Jews three times in Volume II of the *War Memoirs*.[132] Three months before the press conference, he had visited Auschwitz. It is a measure of his stature, and perhaps of the less fierce sensitivities of the time, that de Gaulle's remarks provoked, not outrage, but a firm but respectful riposte from Raymond Aron and a tough but courteous exchange of letters with Ben Gurion.[133] To Ben Gurion, he stated that he had meant to underline the qualities that had enabled the Jewish people to survive 19 centuries of persecution. To his son, he said he wished he could apply the same expression to the French.[134] But the press conference was still very damaging. At his last referendum, in April 1969, de Gaulle lost almost the whole Jewish vote.[135]

De Gaulle's Third World initiatives display a determination, consistent with his belief in France's universal mission, to place France at the heart of world affairs. They were also informed by clear economic interests (Middle East oil) and by a conviction, contrary to what he viewed as America's Cold War mindset, that nationalisms, not ideologies, drove world conflicts. In Asia and the Middle East, at least, de Gaulle's intuitions were mostly sound. France's recognition of the PRC preceded the normalisation undertaken by Richard Nixon for the United States eight years later. The Vietnam War, as de Gaulle warned, damaged US interests as well as bringing untold suffering to the Vietnamese. And his prediction that Israeli occupation of territories conquered in 1967 would start a vicious circle of repression and resistance proved wholly accurate.

All de Gaulle's initiatives and tours, finally, resonated in the Third World far beyond their immediate, concrete effects. Thus, for example, the French filmmaker in a remote region of India being welcomed by a group of Marxist guerrillas crying 'De Gaulle-Phnom Penh'; or the Palestinian leader Yasser Arafat constantly wearing the Cross of Lorraine pendant de Gaulle had given him.[136] On de Gaulle's death in 1970, the left-wing journalist Jean Daniel wrote that during his presidency 'France was practically clothed in light for millions of rebels across the world'.[137] De Gaulle had transformed France from the target of hostile UN votes over Algeria to a Third World standard-bearer. Rhetorically at least, this was a tour de force.

Conclusion

March 1962 was clearly a turning-point for France's relations with the Third World. Before the Évian accords, no effective policy was possible; afterwards, one took off with remarkable speed. But the chronology is far from the whole story. As we have seen, de Gaulle pleaded eloquently for solidarity with the Third World as he launched the Challe Plan; and the man of Phnom Penh still employed Jacques Foccart to keep France's African client states in order.

As Paul Isoart has argued, de Gaulle really had two visions of the Third World. On the one hand was a clear realisation that colonised peoples sought emancipation and that wealthy countries should grant it, and contribute more to the development of poor ones. In addition, his insistence that a multipolar world of independent nations was preferable to a bipolar world dominated by the two superpowers chimed well with Third World aspirations. Hence, for example, the approval of Third World countries for de Gaulle's withdrawal of France from the NATO command in 1966. At the same time, however, he retained a hierarchical view of nations and considered that while a bipolar world might be dysfunctional, the circle of great powers with global responsibilities could hardly be much wider than the five permanent members of the UN Security Council.[138] Though he effectively preached non-alignment to Third World countries, de Gaulle never joined the non-aligned movement and never met its leaders like Nehru, Nasser, Nkrumah, or Tito.[139] And he had no patience with a demanding, militant, or even anti-colonial Third World when it challenged French interests. Hence his brutal handling of the Bizerte crisis; hence *la Françafrique*, a system built to ensure compliance more than emancipation among France's client states in sub-Saharan Africa; hence, above all, his pursuit of the chimera of victory over the FLN, at enormous human and material cost to France and more particularly to Algeria.[140] The fact that it was de Gaulle who ended the Algerian war, the apparent generosity of France's aid budget, even the warmth and conviction of his speeches, should not obscure the horrors of France's record as a late colonial power, nor its sometimes less than exemplary behaviour as a postcolonial one.

Notes

1. Press conference, 11 April 1961, *DM*III, pp. 286–304: p. 289.
2. See above, pp. 114–5.
3. Jean Lacouture, 'Révision dans le désert, 1946–1958', in Institut du Droit de la Paix et du Développement de l'Université de Nice and Institut Charles de Gaulle (eds), *De Gaulle et le Tiers Monde*, actes du colloque de Nice, 25–6 février 1983 (Paris: Pedone, 1984), pp. 114–21.
4. Alain Peyrefitte, *C'était de Gaulle*, vol. I (Paris: Éditions de Fallois/Fayard, 1994), p. 52.
5. *MH*, pp. 44–7.
6. Antoine Prost, 'Témoignage', in Maurice Vaïsse (ed.), *De Gaulle et l'Algérie, 1943–1969* (Paris: Armand Colin/Ministère de la Défense, 2012), pp. 338–9.
7. Pierre Miquel, *La Guerre d'Algérie* (Paris: Fayard, 1993), pp. 475–6.
8. Martin Evans, *Algeria: France's Undeclared War* (Oxford: Oxford University Press, 2012), p. 308; Julian Jackson, *A Certain Idea of France: The Life of Charles de Gaulle* (London: Allen Lane, 2018), pp. 537–8. For Papon, Paris Prefect of Police (1958–1967), see above, p. 155.
9. Benjamin Stora, *De Gaulle et la guerre d'Algérie* (Paris: Fayard, 2012 [2009]), pp. 82–4; Matthew Connelly, *A Diplomatic Revolution: Algeria's Fight for Independence and the Origins of the Post-Cold War Era* (Oxford: Oxford University Press, 2002), p. 345.
10. Connelly, *Diplomatic Revolution*, pp. 304–8; Frédéric Turpin, *Jacques Foccart. Dans l'ombre du pouvoir* (Paris: CNRS editions, 2015), p. 120.
11. Miquel, *La Guerre d'Algérie*, p. 374.
12. Press conference, 11 April 1961, *DM*III, pp. 286–304: p. 296; Jean Touchard, *Le Gaullisme, 1940–1969* (Paris: Le Seuil, 1978), p. 198.
13. Irwin M. Wall, *The United States and the Algerian War* (Berkeley, London: University of California Press, 2001), p. 186.
14. Alistair Horne, *The French Army and Politics, 1870–1970* (London: Macmillan, 1984), p. 82.
15. Pierre Messmer, *Après tant de batailles ... mémoires* (Paris: Albin Michel, 1992), p. 274; Jacques Chaban-Delmas, *Mémoires pour demain* (Paris: Flammarion, 1997), p. 320.
16. *DM*III, pp. 306–8.
17. Miquel, *La Guerre d'Algérie*, pp. 486–90.

18 Chaban-Delmas, *Mémoires*, pp. 315–17; François Flohic, *Souvenirs d'Outre-Gaulle* (Paris: Plon, 1979), pp. 51–2; Turpin, *Foccart*, p. 164; Jacques Foccart, *Foccart parle. Entretiens avec Philippe Gaillard*, vol. I (Paris: Fayard/Jeune Afrique, 1995), pp. 350–6.
19 Maurice Vaïsse and Patrice Buffotot, 'Les Élites de la Défense nationale', in Serge Berstein, Pierre Birnbaum, and Jean-Pierre Rioux (eds), *De Gaulle et les élites* (Paris: La Découverte, 2008), pp. 112–27.
20 Miquel, *La Guerre d'Algérie*, p. 499; Horne, *Savage War*, p. 531.
21 Connelly, *Diplomatic Revolution*, pp. 388–9; Horne, *Savage War*, p. 504.
22 Connelly, *Diplomatic Revolution*, p. 400; Roger le Doussal, 'De Gaulle contre l'OAS', in Vaïsse, *De Gaulle et l'Algérie*, pp. 229–45: p. 236.
23 Charles-Robert Ageron, 'L'OAS-Algérie-Sahara', in Christian Bidégaray and Paul Isoart (eds), *Les Droites et le Général de Gaulle* (Paris: Economica, 1991), pp. 145–57; Connelly, *Diplomatic Revolution*, p. 401; Evans, *Undeclared War*, pp. 319–20.
24 *Le Monde*, 7 June 1958.
25 *DM*III, pp. 51–60: p. 55; de Gaulle to Salan, 24 October 1958, *LNC*III, pp. 78–9.
26 *L'Écho d'Oran*, 29 April 1959, quoted in *MH*, p. 70.
27 Alain de Boissieu, *Pour servir le Général* (Paris: Plon, 1982), pp. 119–20.
28 *DM*III, pp. 117–23.
29 *DM*III, pp. 162–6.
30 Julian Jackson, *A Certain Idea*, pp. 522–3; Jean Lacouture, *De Gaulle*, vol. III (Paris: Le Seuil, 1986), pp. 111–15.
31 *DM*III, pp. 234–51: p. 243.
32 *DM*III, pp. 256–62.
33 Georges Pompidou, *Lettres, notes et portraits 1928–1974* (Paris: Robert Laffont, 2012), pp. 319–28.
34 *DM*III, pp. 286–304; pp. 292–3.
35 Bernard Tricot, *Les Sentiers de la paix: Algérie 1958–1962* (Paris: Plon, 1972), p. 271; Lacouture, *De Gaulle* III, p. 191.
36 Connelly, *Diplomatic Revolution*, p. 363; Redha Malek, 'Témoignage', in Institut Charles de Gaulle, *De Gaulle en son siècle*, vol. VI: *Liberté et dignité des peuples* (Paris: Plon, 1992), p. 152.
37 Lacouture, *De Gaulle* III, p. 203.
38 *DM*III, pp. 333–49: p. 340.
39 Michel Debré, *Gouverner. Mémoires, 1958–1962* (Paris: Albin Michel, 1988), pp. 296–7.
40 Alistair Horne, *A Savage War of Peace: Algeria 1954–1962* (London: Pan Books, 2002 [1977]), pp. 512–14.
41 Maurice Vaïsse, *La Grandeur. Politique étrangère du général de Gaulle, 1958–1969* (Paris: Fayard, 1998), pp. 77–8.
42 C.L. Sulzberger, *The Last of the Giants* (London: Weidenfeld & Nicolson, 1970), p. 68.

43 Horne, *Savage War*, p. 548.
44 Stanley Hoffmann, *Decline or Renewal? France since the 1930s* (New York: Viking Press, 1974), p. 293.
45 *MH*, p. 47.
46 Philippe de Gaulle, *De Gaulle mon père. Entretiens avec Michel Tauriac*, vol. I (Paris: Plon, 2003), pp. 154–5, 183–4.
47 Speech of 8 January 1959, *DM*III, pp. 71–3; Chaban-Delmas, *Mémoires*, p. 311.
48 Press conferences, 11 April and 5 September 1961, *DM*III, pp. 293, 341; Peyrefitte, *C'était de Gaulle* I, pp. 76–86; Debré, *Gouverner*, p. 293.
49 Mahfoud Kaddache, 'De Gaulle et les nationalistes algériens (1940–1962)', in Institut Charles de Gaulle, *De Gaulle en son siècle* VI, pp. 93–107: pp. 102–5; Connelly, *Diplomatic Revolution*, p. 380.
50 Martin Alexander and J.F.V. Keiger (eds), *France and the Algerian War, 1954–1962: Strategy, Operations and Diplomacy* (London: Frank Cass, 2002), p. xvii.
51 Jacques Frémeaux, 'De Gaulle et les pieds-noirs (1962–1969)', in Vaïsse (ed.), *De Gaulle et l'Algérie*, pp. 248–63: p. 251.
52 Tricot, *Sentiers*, p. 327; Peyrefitte, *C'était de Gaulle* I, pp. 203–7, 249–55; Éric Roussel, *Charles de Gaulle* (Paris: Gallimard, 2002), p. 723.
53 Tricot, *Sentiers*, p. 326; Frémeaux, 'De Gaulle et les pieds-noirs', pp. 251–8; Peyrefitte, *C'était de Gaulle* I, pp. 254–5.
54 Strictly speaking, the *harkis* were only one type of auxiliary employed by the French forces, alongside other defence personnel ranging from regular soldiers to village defence groups. But the term *harkis* has come to stand for them all. Cf. Abd-El-Aziz Méliani, *Le Drame des harkis* (Paris: Perrin, 1993), pp. 18–27; *Le Monde*, 20 March 1962.
55 François-Xavier Hautreux, 'De Gaulle face au problème des harkis', in Vaïsse (ed.), *De Gaulle et l'Algérie*, pp. 264–77: p. 268.
56 Méliani, *Le Drame des harkis*, p. 66.
57 Horne, *Savage War*, p. 538; Martin Evans, 'The *Harkis*: The Experience and Memory of France's Muslim Auxiliaries', in Martin Alexander, Martin Evans, and J.F.V. Keiger (eds), *The Algerian War and the French Army, 1954–1962: Experiences, Images, Testimonies* (Basingstoke: Palgrave Macmillan, 2002), pp. 117–33: p. 127.
58 Hautreux, 'De Gaulle face au problème des harkis', pp. 269–70.
59 Jackson, *A Certain Idea*, p. 545.
60 Pierre Messmer, *Les Blancs s'en vont. Récits de décolonisation* (Paris: Albin Michel, 1998), pp. 173–4.
61 Méliani, *Le Drame des harkis*, pp. 126, 145; Hautreux, 'De Gaulle face au problème des harkis', pp. 264–77; Messmer, *Les Blancs*, pp. 171–2.
62 Martin Alexander and J.F.V. Keiger, 'France and the Algerian War, 1954–1962: Strategy, Operations and Diplomacy' in Alexander and Keiger, *France and the Algerian War, 1954–1962: Strategy, Operations and Diplomacy* (London: Frank Cass, 2002), pp. 1–32: p. 16.

63 Alexander and Keiger, 'France and the Algerian War', pp. 12–13.
64 Benjamin Stora, *De Gaulle et la guerre d'Algérie* (Paris: Fayard, 2012 [2009]), p. 76.
65 Fourth Geneva Convention, https://ihl-databases.icrc.org/ihl/INTRO/380, particularly Art. 32; Rome Statute of the International Criminal Court, 1998, from https://www.icc-cpi.int/resource-library/Documents/RS-Eng.pdf, particularly Art. 8, accessed 4 July 2019.
66 Maurice Vaïsse, 'De Gaulle face à l'armée', in Vaïsse, *De Gaulle et l'Algérie*, pp. 166–80: p. 169.
67 Raphaëlle Branche, *La Torture et l'armée pendant la guerre d'Algérie, 1954–1962* (Paris: Gallimard, 2011 [2001]), pp. 319–22.
68 Debré, *Gouverner*, pp. 213–14; Branche, *La Torture*, pp. 490–1.
69 Branche, *La Torture*, pp. 396–8, 423–9, 491.
70 Lucien Robineau, 'Chasse lourde sur les Djebels', *Revue Historique des Armées*, 187, 1992, pp. 59–65.
71 Keith Sutton, 'Army administration tensions over Algeria's Centres de Regroupement, 1954–1962', *British Journal of Middle Eastern Studies*, 26(2), November 1999, pp. 243–70: pp. 255–8; Evans, *Undeclared War*, pp. 250, 254; Miquel, *La Guerre d'Algérie*, pp. 366, 455; Branche, *La Torture*, p. 390; *Le Monde*, 18 April 1959.
72 Evans, *Undeclared War*, p. 245.
73 Connelly, *Diplomatic Revolution*, p. 313; Stora, *De Gaulle et la guerre d'Algérie*, pp. 100–1.
74 Miquel, *La Guerre d'Algérie*, pp. 475–6.
75 Raymond Tournoux, quoted in Stora, *De Gaulle et la guerre d'Algérie*, p. 121.
76 *DM*III, pp. 327–32: p. 330.
77 Stora, *De Gaulle et la guerre d'Algérie*, pp. 76–9; Miquel, *La Guerre d'Algérie*, pp. 366–7.
78 Horne, *Savage War*, p. 535; Evans, *Undeclared War*, p. 248.
79 Lacouture, *De Gaulle* III, p. 136.
80 *MH*, p. 73.
81 Lacouture, *De Gaulle* III, pp. 34–5.
82 Chaban-Delmas, *Mémoires*, p. 295.
83 François-Xavier Verschave, *La Françafrique: le plus long scandale de la République* (Paris: Stock, 1998).
84 Jean Lacouture, *De Gaulle*, vol. II: *Le Politique, 1944–1959* (Paris: Éditions du Seuil, 1985), pp. 571–3.
85 Albert Mabileau and Patrick Quantin, 'L'Afrique noire dans la pensée politique du général de Gaulle', in Centre Bordelais d'Études Africaines, Centre d'Étude d'Afrique Noire, Institut Charles-de-Gaulle (eds), *La Politique africaine du général de Gaulle (1958–1969)* (Paris: Pedone, 1980), pp. 145–66: pp. 150–1. Cf. also de Gaulle's speech at Tananarive, 8 July 1959, *DM*III, pp. 53–73.
86 Lacouture, *De Gaulle* II, p. 578.

87 Raymond Triboulet, 'Les Moyens d'action du général de Gaulle', in *De Gaulle et le Tiers Monde*, pp. 143–7; Paul Isoart, 'Le Général de Gaulle et le Tiers monde: 1958–1962', in *ibid.*, pp. 122–42.
88 Messmer, *Les Blancs*, pp. 155–6.
89 Message to National Assembly, 11 December 1962, *DM*IV, pp. 46–9: p. 49.
90 Huguette Durand, 'L'Aide française aux pays en voie de développement', *L'Actualité économique*, 412, 1965, pp. 205–25: p. 212.
91 Pierre Dabezies, 'La Politique militaire de la France en Afrique noire sous le général de Gaulle', in *La Politique africaine*, pp. 229–62: pp. 239–40.
92 Turpin, *Foccart*, p. 156.
93 *MH*, p. 67.
94 Jacques Foccart, *Le Général en Mai. Journal de l'Élysée – II, 1968–1969* (Paris: Fayard/Jeune Afrique, 1998), p. 427. Four days later, however, Foccart persuaded de Gaulle to lunch with President Bongo of Gabon.
95 Turpin, *Foccart*, pp. 147, 186; Jacques Foccart, intervention, in *La Politique africaine*, p. 403.
96 Turpin, *Foccart*, pp. 212–13, 219, 224–5.
97 Turpin, *Foccart*, pp. 203–5.
98 Jacques Foccart, intervention in *La Politique africaine*, pp. 274–5.
99 Jackson, *A Certain Idea*, p. 609; Turpin, *Foccart*, pp. 147, 206; Foccart, *Le Général en Mai*, p. 388; Jean Méo, 'De Gaulle et le problème pétrolier', in *De Gaulle et le Tiers Monde*, pp. 236–8.
100 Turpin, *Foccart*, pp. 206–7; Thomas Deltombe, Manuel Domergue and Jacob Tatsitsa, *Kamerun! Une guerre cachée aux origines de la Françafrique (1948–1971)* (Paris: La Découverte, 2011).
101 Turpin, *Foccart*, pp. 199–200.
102 Vaïsse, *La Grandeur*, pp. 496–7; Foccart, *Foccart parle* I, pp. 342–7; Turpin, *Foccart*, p. 212; Messmer, *Les Blancs*, pp. 94–5.
103 Jackson, *A Certain Idea*, p. 692; Claude Wauthier, 'Jacques Foccart et les mauvais conseils de Félix Houphouët-Boigny', *Les Cahiers du Centre de Recherches Historiques*, 30, 2002, http://journals.opendition.org/ccrh/512, accessed 10 November 2019.
104 Elgey, *De Gaulle à Matignon*, p. 263.
105 Connelly, *Diplomatic Revolution*, pp. 374–7.
106 *MH*, p. 124.
107 Mohsen Toumi, 'De Gaulle et le Maghreb', in *De Gaulle et le Tiers Monde*, pp. 349–57: p. 353.
108 Press conference, 5 September 1960, *DM*III, pp. 234–51: p. 237.
109 Peyrefitte, *C'était de Gaulle* I, p. 283.
110 Interview with Michel Droit, 14 December 1965, *DM*IV, pp. 422–32: pp. 430–1.
111 Vaïsse, *La Grandeur*, p. 500.
112 *DM*III, pp. 82–96: pp. 86–7.

113 *DM*III, pp. 182,199.
114 Press conference, 11 April 1961, *DM*III, pp. 286–304: p. 296; Touchard, *Le Gaullisme*, p. 198.
115 *DM*III, pp. 395–7; p. 397; Charles-Robert Ageron, 'La Coopération avec l'Algérie Indépendante', in Institut Charles de Gaulle, *De Gaulle en son siècle* VI, p. 216; Isoart, 'De Gaulle et le Tiers monde', p. 141; Connelly, *Diplomatic Revolution*, p. 405.
116 Jackson, *A Certain Idea*, pp. 605–7.
117 *DM*III, pp. 162–82; pp. 178–9.
118 Jackson, *A Certain Idea*, pp. 602–3; Alain Peyrefitte, *C'était de Gaulle*, vol II (Paris: Éditions de Fallois/Fayard, 1997), pp. 485–94.
119 Claude Lebel, 'Les Politiques française et américaine en Indochine', in *De Gaulle et le Tiers Monde*, pp. 329–30.
120 Maurice Couve de Murville, *Une Politique étrangère, 1958–1969* (Paris: Plon, 1971), pp. 459–60; Philippe Devillers, 'De Gaulle et l'Asie', in *De Gaulle et le Tiers Monde*, pp. 299–327: pp. 311–12.
121 *DM*V, pp. 74–8. In Algeria, France neither withdrew its troops before negotiating, nor accepted an international conference.
122 *DM*V, pp. 96–117; p. 99; *LNC*III, p. 902; Philippe Devillers, 'De Gaulle et l'Asie', pp. 315–16.
123 Jean Lacouture, in *De Gaulle et le Tiers Monde*, pp. 331–2.
124 Isoart, 'De Gaulle et le Tiers monde', pp. 138–9.
125 Jackson, *A Certain Idea*, pp. 681–2; Paul Balta and Claudine Rulleau, *La Politique arabe de la France, de De Gaulle à Pompidou* (Paris: Éditions Sindbad, 1973), pp. 65–6, 69, 73–4.
126 Lacouture, *De Gaulle* III, p. 501.
127 Jackson, *A Certain Idea*, p. 684.
128 Balta and Rulleau, *La Politique arabe*, pp. 96–8.
129 *DM*V, pp. 227–47: p. 232.
130 See above, p. 11.
131 René Cassin, *Les Hommes partis de rien: le réveil de la France abattue (1940–1941)* (Paris: Plon, 1975), p. 138.
132 *WM*II, pp. 42, 93, 174.
133 Lacouture, *De Gaulle* III, p. 50.
134 *LNC*III, pp. 942–4; Philippe de Gaulle, *De Gaulle mon père. Entretiens avec Michel Tauriac*, vol. II (Paris: Plon, 2003), p. 323.
135 Touchard, *Le Gaullisme*, p. 231.
136 Sudhir Hazareesingh, *In the Shadow of the General: Modern France and the Myth of de Gaulle* (New York: Oxford University Press, 2012), pp. 154, 171.
137 Isoart, 'De Gaulle et le Tiers monde', p. 142.
138 Hoffmann, *Decline or Renewal?*, pp. 189–90, 208.
139 Edmond Jouve, commentaire, in *De Gaulle et le Tiers Monde*, p. 150
140 Isoart, 'De Gaulle et le Tiers monde', p. 142; Charles Zorgbibe, 'De Gaulle et le Tiers monde: orientations générales', in *De Gaulle et le Tiers Monde*, pp. 161–6.

Further reading

Julian Jackson, *A Certain Idea of France* (London: Allen Lane, 2018), chapter 20, covers Algeria and decolonisation. A lengthier treatment is given in Jean Lacouture, *De Gaulle*, vol. III: *Le Souverain* (Paris: Le Seuil, 1986), chapters 1–10 (for Algeria), and 15–16 (for other colonies, and subsequent relations with the Third World).

De Gaulle's *Memoirs of Hope*, tr. Terence Kilmartin (London: Weidenfeld & Nicolson, 1971), chapters 2–3, present his own case on decolonisation. His *Discours et Messages*, vol. III (Paris: Plon, 1970) cover the period.

On decolonisation generally, see Martin Shipway, *Decolonization and its Impact: A Comparative Approach to the End of Colonial Empires* (Oxford: Blackwell, 2008).

On Algeria, in addition to works mentioned for Chapter 8, see Matthew Connelly, *A Diplomatic Revolution: Algeria's Fight for Independence and the Origins of the Post-Cold War Era* (Oxford: Oxford University Press, 2002); Irwin M. Wall, The *United States and the Algerian War* (Berkeley, London: University of California Press, 2001); Martin Alexander, Martin Evans, and J.F.V. Keiger (eds), *The Algerian War and the French Army, 1954–1962: Experiences, Images, Testimonies* (Basingstoke: Palgrave Macmillan, 2002); and Martin Alexander and J.F.V. Keiger (eds), *France and the Algerian War, 1954–1962: Strategy, Operations and Diplomacy* (London: Frank Cass, 2002).

On torture, see Marnia Lazreg, *Torture and the Twilight of Empire* (Princeton: Princeton University Press, 2008), and Raphaëlle Branche, *La Torture et l'armée pendant la guerre d'Algérie, 1954–1962* (Paris: Gallimard (Folio), 2011 [2001]). On *Centres de regroupement*, see Keith Sutton, 'Army administration tensions over Algeria's Centres de Regroupement, 1954–1962', *British Journal of Middle Eastern Studies*, 26(2), November1999, pp. 243–270.

Institut Charles de Gaulle, *De Gaulle en son siècle*, vol. VI: *Liberté et dignité des peuples* (Paris: Plon, 1992) contains valuable essays and first-hand accounts on Algeria and relations with the Third World.

Vivid contemporary insights into de Gaulle's policies appear in C.L. Sulzberger, *The Last of the Giants* (London: Weidenfeld & Nicolson, 1970), and Alain Peyrefitte, *C'était de Gaulle*, vol. I (Paris: Éditions de Fallois/Fayard, 1994).

10 De Gaulle's Constitution and the politics of presidential primacy

De Gaulle cared far more about France than about democracy. His evocations of France's hours of grandeur took in the old monarchy, the revolutionary republic, Napoleon's Empire, and the Third Republic without distinction. In this he differed from a certain right-wing tradition, according to which France had achieved nothing good since 1789, and from a left-wing one, which saw nothing worthwhile before. 'I don't love the Republic for the Republic', he told Peyrefitte. 'But since the French are attached to it, I have always thought there was no other choice'.[1]

For de Gaulle, however, his legitimacy – his right to lead the French – sprang not from republican institutions or processes but from his actions from June 1940 on. And his conception of the institutions that France needed in order to take her deserved place at the 'front rank' of nations was far removed from France's parliament-centred republican tradition. For de Gaulle, institutions needed to allow the exercise of leadership. This was the core message of the Bayeux speech of 1946, and the main thrust of the Constitution adopted by 79.25% of the vote on 28 September 1958. Few voters, however, had read it in detail. Many had not read it at all. Embedding Gaullist constitutional principles into French political practice was always going to take more than a single referendum, however decisive.

This chapter concerns de Gaulle's exercise of power from his inauguration as President on 8 January 1959 to his resignation on 28 April 1969. What were the sources of his power, constitutional and political? And how did he deploy them to establish a degree of presidential primacy scarcely present in the constitutional text, and which his successors would, broadly, perpetuate?

The sources of presidential power

Presidential power was grounded in the Constitution adopted on 28 September 1958 and amended on 6 November 1962. But as de Gaulle remarked, a Constitution, more than a text, is 'a spirit, a set of institutions, and day-to-day practice'.[2] As founding President of the Fifth Republic, de Gaulle was uniquely placed to mould the office to his preferences. He did so with the help of his exceptional personal legitimacy; of a much-expanded staff; and of the Gaullist party and its parliamentary majority.

The Constitution of 1958: rationalised parliamentarianism versus republican monarchy

The Constitution of 1958 was not born presidential; it became it. The text devotes three times as much space to relations between government and Parliament as to the presidency. Indeed, when Michel Debré, Justice Minister in the 1958 de Gaulle government, presented it to Parliament on 27 August, he entitled his speech 'Giving France a parliamentary regime'. Debré, who co-ordinated the drafting process, admired the stability of Westminster politics. But this, he believed, depended on disciplined political parties, which France lacked. He therefore set out to give France a stabilised, or 'rationalised', parliamentary regime through constitutional means.

The new Constitution reinforced the government's powers at the expense of Parliament, and especially its lower house, the National Assembly. Parliamentary sittings were shortened, as were debates on finance bills; the scope of parliamentary legislation was restricted to general principles, leaving details to government decrees; government bills had priority on the parliamentary agenda; the government could ask Parliament to delegate legislative powers to it (Article 38), or require a package vote on its own version of a bill (Article 44). And the government could make any bill a question of confidence, to be deemed passed unless an absolute majority of parliamentarians voted a motion of censure (no-confidence) against the government (Article 49–3). These were all bulwarks against the parliamentary sniping that had brought down successive governments under the Third and Fourth Republics. It was for the government, under the Constitution, to 'determine and conduct the policy of the Nation' (Article 20). To remain (theoretically) untroubled by base constituency interests, its members could not sit as parliamentarians. And the new Constitutional Council could strike down bills it deemed unconstitutional, in case, for example, Parliament overstepped its role.

These 'Debré sections' of the 1958 Constitution, roughly titles III to V, embody a rationalised, stabilised, but still parliamentary regime. But they coexist with a 'de Gaulle section', roughly title II, which reinforces presidential powers.

Some of these were quite new. Under Article 11, the president may call a referendum on any matter concerning the 'organisation of the public authorities'. He can take emergency powers under Article 16. And Article 5 made him the 'guarantor of national independence, territorial integrity and due respect for Treaties', stating that he 'shall ensure, by his arbitration, the proper functioning of the public authorities and the continuity of the State' as well as 'due respect for the Constitution': words susceptible of very broad interpretation. Other, long-standing presidential powers were also reinforced, by removing the need for consultation or countersignature in their exercise. The president of the Fifth Republic can dissolve the National Assembly, triggering new elections, alone. He can appoint any prime minister he chooses – even from outside Parliament. And he is Commander-in-Chief of the armed forces, not just in title but in fact. Finally, the president ceased to be a creature of Parliament; he was no longer elected by the National Assembly and the Senate, but by a college of some 80,000 mayors and local councillors, among whom parliamentarians were a small minority. On 21 December 1958 the college elected de Gaulle to the presidency by 78.5% of the vote, against 13% for a Communist and 8.5% for another left-winger.

These articles reflected the principles de Gaulle had outlined at Bayeux 12 years earlier.[3] Far more than the 'Debré sections', this much presidentialism challenged republican constitutional tradition.

Second foundation, 1962

The Constitution of 1958 was thus balanced between its presidential and its (rationalised) parliamentary components. For four years, most parliamentarians were willing to lend the President exceptional powers to handle Algeria. Then, after the Évian accords, they wanted them back. De Gaulle's first clear indication that he would not oblige them came on 14 April 1962, when he replaced Debré as Prime Minister with Georges Pompidou, who had never been a parliamentarian. Five months later, he moved to ensure permanent presidential primacy.

He did so through the constitutional amendment of 6 November 1962, under which the president would be elected, no longer by an electoral college, but by direct universal suffrage, on two ballots 14 days apart. Direct election had been ruled out in 1958, partly so as not to diminish support for the new Constitution by offending traditional republican sensibilities, and partly, as Debré admitted, to avoid giving France's citizens in the African colonies a voice in choosing France's president.[4] But with the Constitution secured, decolonisation accomplished, and the citizenship rights of France's imperial subjects ended, these objections disappeared. De Gaulle stated his wish for a change in his press conference of 11 April 1961, and was set on it by late May 1962.[5] The ideal moment came after an OAS assassination attempt on de Gaulle, as his car travelled through the Paris suburb of Petit-Clamart on 22 August 1962. The attack was bungled: neither the General nor Yvonne, seated beside him, was hurt. But over 150 bullets had been fired and eight had pierced the Citroën's coachwork. There was no certainty that a future attempt would miss. Three weeks later a government communiqué stated that the President would put a constitutional amendment to the nation, by referendum.

De Gaulle explained the connection in two broadcasts, on 20 September and 4 October 1962. While he personally had an 'exceptional link' with the French, he said, because of 'all that we have lived through and achieved together', his successor would not – and would need the full legitimacy that only direct election could provide. 'From the start', he added, 'I knew that I would have to propose to the nation that it should be so', and concluded that his remaining in power would depend on a favourable result.[6]

By October the initiative had provoked a full-scale confrontation with both houses of Parliament, which still had non-Gaullist majorities. 'France is here and not elsewhere', former Prime Minister Reynaud declaimed in a National Assembly debate.[7] Parliamentarians correctly saw the planned reform as a bid to shift France's

De Gaulle and the presidential primacy

political system permanently towards presidentialism, and thus as an affront to French republican traditions.

If de Gaulle's aim challenged Parliament, so did his method. Article 11 of the Constitution states that the president may call a referendum on a bill if the government proposed it. This, however, was not just any bill, but a constitutional amendment. Under Article 89, constitutional amendments must be passed by both houses of Parliament *before* being put to referendum. The Constitutional Council advised de Gaulle of its view that his referendum project was unconstitutional – before declaring itself incompetent (under the Constitution) to reject a bill which Parliament had not yet passed.[8] One minister resigned over the issue; Pompidou himself considered (in private) the method of more than dubious legality.[9] Among parliamentarians, Gaston Monnerville, President of the Senate, referred to a 'wilful abuse of authority'. Unable to attack de Gaulle directly, the National Assembly passed a motion of no-confidence in his government on 5 October, obliging Pompidou to tender his resignation.

De Gaulle refused it, dissolved the National Assembly, and called new elections, effectively doubling the stake. The public cared little for constitutional niceties, and might, in the middle of the Cuban missile crisis, have felt particular reasons to back their President. At the referendum on 28 October, 62.3% of voters backed the amendment; at the parliamentary elections, the Gaullists won 32.1% of the first-round vote on 18 November; after the run-off a week later they had 233 out of 482 seats – which, with the 35 seats of their close conservative allies led by Finance Minister Valéry Giscard d'Estaing, was a stable majority.

De Gaulle's comprehensive victory constitutes a second foundation of the Fifth Republic, on two counts. First, the President could henceforth claim to be, alone, 'the nation's man', chosen by the whole French electorate, and not just a constituency. Second, France had, for practically the first time in its republican history, a stable parliamentary majority. These two developments made the French president in normal times uniquely powerful among Western leaders, combining the legitimacy through popular election of his American counterpart with the stable parliamentary support of a British prime minister. French commentators like Maurice Duverger began talking of a 'republican monarchy'.

Yet the Constitution remains deeply ambiguous. How, for example, to reconcile Articles 20, which states that the government 'has the armed forces at its disposal', 21, which identifies the prime minister as 'responsible for national defence', and 15, under which the president is Commander-in-Chief? And how would a prime minister fare who defied the president's wishes, since the president could appoint him, but not (as de Gaulle retrospectively regretted) sack him? How would the prime minister and government be chosen if the parliamentary majority was clearly opposed to the president, since they were appointed by the president but responsible before Parliament? For Odile Rudelle, these ambiguities were intentional compromises necessary to win the Constitution wide support.[10] Vincent Wright, more critically, calls the Constitution 'not a happy compromise but a constitutional mess ... The central question of any constitution – who rules? – is fudged'.[11] Whatever ambiguities there were, however, de Gaulle would always seek to resolve them in the President's favour.

Personal legitimacy

That he was able to do so depended in part on his special personal legitimacy. This was derived above all from his wartime leadership, but also from the discredit – which he had foreseen – of the Fourth Republic, and from the widely shared view that he alone could extricate France from Algeria. De Gaulle was quite explicit about his exceptional relationship with the French. In the broadcast of 29 January 1960, at the height of Barricades Week, for example, he appealed for the public's support 'By virtue of the mandate that the people have given me and *the national legitimacy which I have incarnated over the last twenty years.*'[12] To his aide-de-camp François Flohic, he declared that 'I shall incarnate legitimacy until I die.'[13] Remarkably for a man who bestrode his country's politics for three decades, de Gaulle only once, in 1965, stood at an election by direct suffrage. In Weber's terms, the leadership he exercised, initially at least, was neither traditional, as for kings, nor 'rational-legal', as for ordinary elected politicians, but *charismatic*, and unique to his person.[14]

Charismatic legitimacy is more complex and intuitive than that bestowed by election. Nor is it static. As Jean Charlot observes, for a decade before 1958 the French people felt no particular proximity de Gaulle; even thereafter, their support was neither unanimous nor consistent.[15] For de Gaulle, nurturing the relationship required constant contact with the people. His public actions – the broadcasts, the press conferences, the provincial visits – should be understood in this context. So should his repeated promises – or threats – to leave in the event of a reverse at the polls, directly linked to his presidential mandate or not. Even being forced into a second ballot at the 1965 presidential election, when he had expected to win over half the vote at the first, led him to conclude that his unique link with the French was broken, and to contemplate resignation. His advisers, plus the constitutional expert François Goguel, dissuaded him.[16] But in a sense, his doubts were well founded: his charismatic authority, better suited to moments of national peril than to the more humdrum context of the mid-1960s, became 'routinised' in 1965, mutating into the rational-legal authority of ordinary – and mortal – politicians.

The Élysée staff

De Gaulle's presidency depended from day to day on his staff at the Élysée Palace. By the mid-1960s de Gaulle had a total of 100 or so advisers, official and unofficial. Small compared with Washington, this staff was still four to five times the typical Fourth Republic total, big enough to work as the President's eyes and ears, to engage the presidency with the main machinery of government (which still ran largely from the Prime Minister's office in the Hôtel Matignon) and to organise his many domestic and foreign trips.[17] Most staffers were senior civil servants, on temporary secondment from their ministries. The 'big four', whom de Gaulle saw successively at the end of each working day when in Paris, were the secretary-general of the presidency, who handled relations with the government; the *directeur de cabinet*, responsible for audiences, travel, relations with the press and the country generally (including the prefects in provincial France); the head of the personal military staff; and Jacques Foccart, for relations with Africa and with the Gaullist party.

These were among de Gaulle's most trusted associates. Of the three secretaries-general, the first, Geoffroy de Courcel, had been de Gaulle's aide-de-camp when he flew to London on 17 June 1940; his successor, Étienne Burin des Roziers, had joined the Free French in 1942; the third, Bernard Tricot, had helped draft the Constitution and negotiate the Évian accords. Foccart had been a close confidant since RPF days. Far more than administrators, they fed de Gaulle's thinking, meeting his frequent requests for information and acting as sounding-boards to test ideas. De Gaulle might *take* decisions alone, but in their *preparation*, often a lengthy process, the Élysée staff played a crucial role. For decision to be translated into action, moreover, it was the regular meetings between the Élysée secretary-general and the Matignon-based secretary-general of the government, and more generally between Élysée staff members and those of the Prime Minister and other ministers, which allowed the presidency to lock onto and direct the main government machinery – as de Gaulle's Fourth Republic predecessors had never aspired to do.

A presidential party

Presidential leadership also required a strong presidential party. Yet parties were de Gaulle's *bêtes noires*, blamed, even as he vaunted the merits of his new Constitution in Paris on 4 September 1958, for the division and weakness of previous regimes.[18] They might, under Article 4 of the Constitution, 'contribute to the exercise of suffrage', but they still, for de Gaulle, represented selfish, sectional interests, not the indivisible, national interest that he claimed to incarnate.

Even a Gaullist party, after the unhappy experience of the RPF, was suspect. The Union pour la Nouvelle République (UNR) was formally launched on 1 October 1958, not by de Gaulle, but by Foccart and Guichard. 'A strange party', wrote Charlot, 'whose raison d'être, General de Gaulle, wants nothing to do with it, on principle, which achieved power while still in the cradle and won an electoral triumph without having time to organise itself'.[19] A month before the November 1958 parliamentary elections, de Gaulle told voters that 'my name, even in the form of an adjective, should not be used as a label by any group or by any candidate'.[20] The strong UNR performance on 23–30 November was a surprise, but one which supplied him, through the tumultuous Algerian years, with a solid phalanx of (largely) faithful parliamentarians.

In November 1962 de Gaulle was somewhat less coy. Following the Yes vote at the referendum on direct election of the president, he coined the UNR campaign slogan – 'Make sure your YES is respected', and publicly expressed the wish that the parliamentary elections would confirm the referendum result.[21] They did. But the UNR was still sidelined from the first presidential election under universal suffrage, held on 5 and 19 December 1965. De Gaulle waited till 4 November before saying he would run, at the age of 75. He then refused to campaign, limiting himself, initially, to three brief and wooden television broadcasts. In the next six weeks, his voting intentions dropped 20%, as other candidates – Jean Lecanuet for the Christian Democrats, François Mitterrand for the Left, even Jean-Louis Tixier-Vignancour for the far Right – made the most of their allotted television appearances. De Gaulle's results – 44.7% at the first ballot, then 55.2% against Mitterrand at the run-off – were excellent for a conventional politician, disappointing for a national legend. Only his three informal television interviews with the (sympathetic) journalist Michel Droit, on 13–15 December, ensured the strong second-ballot result. But the UNR was almost invisible.

The effect of 1965, according to Peyrefitte, was decisive.

> De Gaulle had believed – as I had, and we were both wrong – that the fact of being elected by universal suffrage, and, for him, of being a historic figure, made a party unnecessary for the president. The 1965 election opened his eyes. It was the end of a myth according to which the president and the people maintained a continuous dialogue beyond parties.[22]

This reflected the state of French opinion: in a November 1965 poll, most people thought the president should be a non-partisan figure but most also thought de Gaulle was not one.[23] The last two parliamentary elections of his presidency can only have confirmed this view. In March 1967, he was active in preparing the elections and choosing candidates, and gave a broadcast underlining the risks of a non-Gaullist Assembly.[24] On 29 June 1968, having called new elections in the wake of the dramatic May 'Events', he called for 'a Parliament capable of supporting, with a strong, constant and coherent majority, the necessary policy'.[25]

Over the decade, the Gaullists settled as France's 'natural' majority party: the biggest National Assembly group of 1958 (with 20.6% of the first-ballot vote) became, with Giscard d'Estaing's

Independent Republicans, the parliamentary majority of 1962 (32.1% of the first-round vote); the majority was maintained, by a whisker (and 31.4% of the first-round vote, or 38.5% with the allies), against a strong left-wing challenge in 1967; in 1968, thanks to a landslide conservative backlash against the May 'Events', the Gaullists, with 37.3% of the first-round vote, won 293 out of 487 seats, the first-ever single-party majority in French republican history. The figures for re-elected Deputies (National Assembly members) reflect the Gaullist consolidation. In the upheaval of 1958, only a quarter of sitting Deputies who stood again were re-elected; in 1962 it was half; in 1967 it was two-thirds – most of them Gaullists.[26]

Who supported de Gaulle and 'his' party? They certainly attracted classic conservative groups – practising Catholics, peasants, older voters, and women (who in the mid-1960s still went to Church more and to work less than men: the minority of young, educated, working women, however, often leaned Left). But the Gaullists were also more urban and more working-class than a classic conservative electorate: de Gaulle won 42% of the blue-collar vote in 1965. These tendencies were more marked for de Gaulle personally than for the party, but even the UNR could attract the support of 30% of blue-collar and 35% of white-collar workers in 1967. This did not amount to a cross-section of French society – the 'metro crowd at rush-hour' as Malraux had called the RPF; nor was it really the 'dominant' party evoked by Charlot.[27] But the UNR was still something new in French politics: a centre-right party with no major regional or social 'blind spots', capable in favourable conditions of winning a parliamentary majority alone.

As the UNR consolidated its positions, so its relationship with de Gaulle changed. Its second secretary-general, Albin Chalandon, might observe in 1959 that 'We are his creature, he is not ours',[28] but in the 1960s the General and the party needed each other. Of course the UNR (or Union des Démocrates pour la République (UDR), as it was renamed in 1968) benefited from having de Gaulle as its locomotive. But de Gaulle also depended on the party to govern. The UNR supplied most government ministers, especially after the departure from government of the Socialists in January 1959 and the Christian Democrats in 1962. When ministers like Couve de Murville or Messmer, appointed as non-party 'technicians', ran for parliamentary seats, as they did in 1967, they did so on the UNR ticket. And above all, the UNR was the heart of the parliamentary majority which de Gaulle and Pompidou needed to get bills and budgets adopted. Pompidou fully accepted this: 'The General needs to give up his unanimist utopia', he told Peyrefitte. 'Of course he is the president of all the French, but thanks to a majority and in spite of a minority'.[29]

De Gaulle, by contrast, always aimed to lead the party without ever appearing to. He never, for example, remotely contemplated addressing a party congress. Control was exercised through close aides like Guichard, Lefranc, and above all Foccart. Much was done by implicit understandings, but some interventions were more direct. De Gaulle insisted that no-one had the title of president of the UNR. The party's successive secretaries-general were all vetted by him. So were the UNR parliamentary candidates, at least from 1967, and de Gaulle suggested financial help for campaigns in particular constituencies. He even discussed UNR candidates for the municipal elections of 1965 with Foccart, no fewer than 28 times, between January and March that year – while protesting that a president should not be troubled with such matters. Similarly, he encouraged the UNR to hold a major congress at Lille in November 1967, then criticised it in private for seeking to prepare the succession prematurely, before giving it his very cautious public approval in his press conference of 27 November 1967.[30] The tensions in de Gaulle's attitude to his party lie at the heart of the office he created: how to avoid being seen as a party man, to measure up to the Olympian status assigned to a Fifth Republic president, while keeping control of his most precious political asset.

The practice of presidential primacy

How did de Gaulle use the resources of Constitution, charisma, staff, and party to construct the Fifth Republic presidency? First, he made sure that the wings of Parliament were clipped even more than the Constitution prescribed. Second, he asserted presidential pre-eminence rhetorically and practically, using every power the Constitution gave him, new and old, to the full and clearly overshadowing his prime ministers. Third, with the aid of leading Gaullists he carved out a so-called 'reserved domain' of presidential policy-making. Fourth, he placed the president at the centre of the political process through a varied palette of communication techniques.

Curbing Parliament

'Under the new regime', wrote Philip Williams, 'the Parliament of France, once among the most powerful in the world, became one of the weakest'.[31] De Gaulle complained that Parliament's 'morose mechanization ... inspired in me a certain melancholy'.[32] But the weakening of Parliament was an intended consequence of his Constitution and the way in which de Gaulle and his governments worked it.

Its manifestations were fourfold. First, de Gaulle took care to show that the prime minister and the government were the president's choice, not Parliament's. Hence his appointment of Pompidou, who had never held elective office, as Prime Minister in April 1962; hence his refusal of Pompidou's resignation, after the National Assembly had passed a vote of censure in October 1962; hence, too, Pompidou's refusal (with de Gaulle's backing), when reappointed in January 1966 after the presidential elections, to seek the confidence of the National Assembly in the traditional manner. We cannot tell what de Gaulle would have done had the Left won a parliamentary election, but to Peyrefitte he stated that he would never appoint a government simply to appease a hostile National Assembly majority.[33]

Second, the governments of Debré, Pompidou and (from 1968) Maurice Couve de Murville used the new Constitution's provisions to press legislation through a sometimes unwilling Assembly. Article 44–3, allowing the government to require a package vote on its preferred version of a bill, was invoked 23 times in the 1958–1962 Assembly, 68 times in that of 1962–1967, 17 times in 1967–1968, and 13 times in 1968–1973. Article 49–3, allowing the government to make a bill a question of confidence, was activated seven times on four bills in 1958–1962 and three times on one bill in 1967–1968.[34] These instances included, in 1960, the laws authorising and financing France's independent nuclear deterrent.[35] And in 1967, the government, with a wafer-thin majority, managed to pass several highly contentious changes to the Social Security system by *ordonnance* under Article 38, postponing detailed debate until after the measures were in place.

Third, when, in March 1960, a majority of the National Assembly demanded a special session, under Article 29 of the Constitution, to discuss agricultural problems, de Gaulle refused, claiming that the demand was made 'for reasons of electoral propaganda' and that his own agreement was necessary for a special session – a highly tendentious reading of Article 30.[36] Finally, one of the essential functions of a legislature – holding the executive to account – was hindered or blocked by successive governments. Ministers, under Article 23, could not be parliamentarians; and their presence in the National Assembly to answer questions was rare. For example, a question about the complicity of members of the French secret services in the kidnap and murder of Mehdi Ben Barka, put down in November 1965, received a perfunctory answer only in May 1967.[37] Even UNR Deputies, after a few months in the Assembly, began talking of de Gaulle's 'contempt' for them.[38]

The Constitution in practice did its job of protecting governments from the instability of earlier regimes: according to Williams and Harrison 'there were at least seven occasions when a Fourth Republican government would have fallen' between 1958 and late 1962. France was also spared the interminable budget debates and clientelistic micro-legislation of former times. And the unexpected emergence of stable parliamentary majorities reinforced stability further. Whether Parliament was able, in the annual 120 days accorded it, to fulfil the essential functions of a legislature, was another matter.

Asserting presidential primacy

Resolved to end Parliament's preponderance, de Gaulle was equally determined to establish and reinforce presidential primacy. Until the Constitution was in force he was fairly muted on the subject. To the Constitutional Consultative Committee, he stressed the president's *arbitre* role, as if he meant a neutral referee who would 'ensure the regular functioning of the public authorities'. In his big speech of 4 September 1958, he again talked of the president as an *arbitre* and the nation's recourse in times of peril.[39] With the Constitution adopted, however, he grew bolder. 'As France's guide and head of the republican state', he said in a broadcast on 28 December, 'I shall exercise supreme power to the full extent that it will henceforth embody.'[40] Perhaps the fullest statement of his presidentialist vision came in the press conference of 31 January 1964: 'It must of course be understood', he declared, 'that the indivisible authority of the State is entrusted in its entirety to the President by the people who have elected him, that no other authority exists, neither ministerial nor civil nor military nor judicial, which is not conferred and maintained by him ...'[41] Presidential supremacy became an endlessly expounded theme of speeches and of press conferences, including the last.[42]

As much practical as rhetorical, de Gaulle's assertion of presidential primacy found expression, firstly, in a full use of new constitutional powers. He called four referendums after 1958 – in 1961 on Algerian self-determination, in 1962 on Algerian independence, in 1962 (again) on the direct election of the president, and in 1969 over reforms to the Senate and to France's regions. He dissolved Parliament and called new elections twice, in October 1962 and May 1968. And in April 1961, the Generals' Putsch in Algiers gave him an opportunity to invoke emergency powers under Article 16. The fact that the putsch collapsed after four days did not prevent him from keeping Article 16 in force for five months.

De Gaulle also took a very activist view of powers that his predecessors had only exercised formally. He chose France's most important officials directly (not all were Gaullists – he trusted competence and what he called 'the sense of the State' more than political loyalty). As chair of the Council of Ministers, controlling its agenda, he transformed its weekly meetings into dull affairs where decisions taken in committees were rubber-stamped and generally banal reports heard (if not listened to). Exceptionally, ministers might be told in advance of an issue to be discussed, and instructed to prepare recommendations. Each then spoke in turn at the meeting, after which de Gaulle would announce the 'collective' decision, which ministers had to support or resign. Examples included self-determination for Algeria, Church school subsidies, and tax reform (in 1959); the Évian accords and the presidential election reform (in 1962); the May disorders and education reform (in 1968); and regionalisation and Senate reform (in 1969). De Gaulle delegated the chair to Pompidou just three times, once when in hospital and twice when abroad.[43] De Gaulle also chaired other important committees such as the Defence Council and the Algerian Affairs Committee, and summoned ad hoc committees on specific issues at an average rate of just under once a week.[44]

At the heart of de Gaulle's activism lay the new relations between the president and his prime ministers. Under the Fourth Republic, the prime minister (officially, President of the Council of Ministers) was France's chief political leader, and a reflection of the parliamentary majority. Under the Fifth, the prime minister became the president's choice and his subordinate; de Gaulle only regretted not having built the right to sack him into the Constitution. According to Peyrefitte, de Gaulle circumvented this obstacle, at least from January 1966, by requiring Pompidou on his reappointment to give him an undated letter of resignation.[45] So long as the parliamentary majority supports the president, indeed, Fifth Republic prime ministers who lose the president's confidence have no choice but to resign.

De Gaulle often compared the prime minister's role to the president's, invariably to the latter's advantage. The prime minister's role, he said in 1968, is 'to translate into actions of the moment the overall directives given by the president'. His tenure in office corresponds to a 'phase' of the president's action; it is for the president to 'fix the objectives, the direction, and the rhythm of policy'.[46] In his memoirs he likened the prime minister to the first officer alongside the captain of a ship. The fact that his task was 'more onerous and exhausting than any other' – because everything lands on the prime minister's desk, whereas the president can intervene selectively in policy – also justified the prime minister holding office only for a 'specified period'.[47] To Peyrefitte, his words were even starker. 'The government', he said,

> has no substance outside of me ... The head of government is me. The prime minister is the first among ministers, *primus inter pares*, he co-ordinates their action, but he does so under the responsibility of the president of the Republic, who alone directs the executive.[48]

That a large part of the specialised committee system that underpins the Council of Ministers remained under the organisation of

Matignon, or that the prime minister in practice ran large sectors of domestic policy, as well as the government's relations with Parliament, did not alter his subordinate role. One illustration of this was the fate of the *conseil de cabinet* – in effect, government meetings, chaired by the prime minister, without the president. Debré held seven or eight of these during his premiership; Pompidou managed just one. Then de Gaulle stopped them, permanently.

The prime ministers

De Gaulle's prime ministers, however, were not interchangeable executants but individuals with distinct conceptions of the role. Michel Debré (January 1959–April 1962) was the ultimate de Gaulle loyalist, charged from 1943 with preparing a skeleton Free French administration for liberated France, and as Justice Minister in 1958 with drafting the Constitution. Debré's strong *Algérie française* sympathies 'covered' de Gaulle on the Right as he slowly moved towards Algerian independence. Deeply pained by this policy shift, Debré offered his resignation several times; de Gaulle refused it until the Algerian conflict was over and Debré's usefulness exhausted. After leaving office Debré would complain at having been bypassed by de Gaulle's direct contacts with ministers behind his back, and his failure to consult him on major policy changes such as the Saharan concession to the FLN in September 1961.[49] He returned to government as Finance Minister in 1967 – and was again circumvented in 1968.

Georges Pompidou (April 1962–July 1968) was the longest-serving prime minister of French republican history. A former literature teacher in two of France's most prestigious *lycées*, he joined de Gaulle's staff in 1944 and ran his private office during the RPF years before leaving in 1952 to join Rothschild's Bank. De Gaulle showed his trust by giving him three tasks: to run the Fondation Anne de Gaulle, named after his late daughter; to return as his *directeur de cabinet* during the crucial months of 1958 when the Fifth Republic was constructed; and to undertake secret negotiations with the FLN. A more relaxed personality than Debré, Pompidou saw his role as taking problems off de Gaulle's hands. At his appointment in 1962 he was a political novice, and an indifferent parliamentary and television performer. By 1964, however, he was a figure of authority within the government and enjoyed some popularity in the country at large.

Growing into the job, Pompidou also grew in autonomy – and appeared as the likely successor. A pro-business conservative, he was sceptical about de Gaulle's plans for employees' 'participation' in running firms. After the 1965 presidential election, moreover, he took the UNR in hand, convinced that only the party could perpetuate Gaullism after the General's departure – and, incidentally, deliver a Pompidou succession.[50] None of this was agreeable to de Gaulle, who wanted to replace Pompidou with Maurice Couve de Murville after the 1967 legislative elections. But the plan backfired when Couve stood for election in a Paris parliamentary constituency and lost. So Pompidou stayed. To Foccart, de Gaulle's comments on Pompidou now grew more acid: 'He's wrong to set himself up as leader of the majority, the majority must form up around me', and later 'he's not implementing my policy' and even 'he's got no balls'.[51] The chance to dispose of Pompidou came just after the May 1968 'Events', when the worn-out Prime Minister offered his resignation and de Gaulle accepted – too eagerly for Pompidou's taste.[52]

Maurice Couve de Murville (July 1968–June 1969), de Gaulle's third and last Prime Minister, had been a senior civil servant under Vichy before joining the CFLN in Algiers in 1943 and then pursuing a post-war career as a diplomat, serving as ambassador in Bonn. He took on the premiership after ten successful years as de Gaulle's Foreign Minister. In this capacity he was very much a policy-implementer not a policy-maker, and he understood his role as Prime Minister in the same way, achieving none of Pompidou's independent political impact. He resigned on 20 June 1969, the day Pompidou took office as de Gaulle's successor.

The 'reserved domain'

Constitutionally, the 'reserved domain', in which the president is chief policy-maker, does not exist. The UNR's secretary-general Albin Chalandon coined the term at the party's national council in July 1959, referring to foreign policy, Algeria, and the French Community; Jacques Chaban-Delmas, President of the National Assembly, later added defence. As Couve de Murville observed, 'the president took a predominant role in foreign relations and defence, not at all because the constitutional text said he should, but because the president was General de Gaulle'.[53] These were areas, for Chaban and Chalandon, where the party should abstain from expressing a view – as distinct from an 'open sector' including most of domestic policy.[54] The truth, however, was less clear-cut. The prime minister could not be excluded from foreign policy. He had to defend it to Parliament and the press, and always held talks with visiting heads of state or government.[55] The president, meanwhile, might intervene, decisively, in domestic policy. As Peyrefitte put it, 'the president's reserved domain is any question he considers it his duty to take up because it involves the national interest'.[56] In other words, de Gaulle's constitutional practice, followed, more or less, by his successors, *allows* the president to intervene not only in foreign policy and defence, but anywhere he likes. Despite Article 20, it is *not* the government that 'determines and conducts' national policy, but the president. The president does not, however, intervene in everything all the time. A careful president will limit interventions, to avoid entanglement in policy details and blame for setbacks. De Gaulle usually achieved this, which helps explain the success of much of his presidency.[57] He was able thereby to present himself as looking after France's long-term interests, operating on a higher plane than the prime minister and government – thanks in part to an idiosyncratic but broadly effective communications policy.

Presidential communications

At half a century's distance, de Gaulle's communications strategy looks archaic in three ways. First, he paid little attention to opinion polls, which he saw as an American innovation. Second, his attitude towards the written press – 'barkers and vinegar-pissers', as he called them after 1962 – was usually contemptuous.[58] 'What you say is forgotten the next day', he told a New Year's press corps reception in 1967, '... having the press against me leaves me neither hot nor cold'.[59] Third, like the Fourth Republic governments, he used an Information Ministry not only for press relations but also to control state television and radio, whose news programmers got a daily briefing from the minister (Peyrefitte from 1962 to 1966) or his officials. The result was predictably servile: news bulletins were stuffed with 'close-ups of the spectators' exultant faces' as de Gaulle made another provincial (or, better, foreign) visit. De Gaulle still privately accused the broadcasters of being 'Sovietised' and 'against the state', and resisted Peyrefitte's (modest) attempts at liberalisation.[60]

Old-fashioned these practices might be, but de Gaulle, who owed his political existence to radio, still understood the value of powerful communication, summarised by Hoffmann as 'well-spaced and well-prepared public announcements, trips sublime or familiar', and 'always an attempt to enlist the French in a "great undertaking"'.[61] De Gaulle's first technique was the radio-television broadcast: he made 56 broadcast speeches from 1958 to 1969, as well as 80 major speeches abroad. He gave his first televised address in June 1958, weeks after returning to power, performed poorly, took advice on using make-up and speaking to camera, and became (almost) a natural. As 62% of French households had a television in 1968, up from 7% a decade earlier, more and more people could see as well as hear him. De Gaulle was not an orthodox television performer: given by anyone else, his speeches might have appeared grandiloquent, and full of over-ample gestures, for the small screen. Some – at the start of Barricades Week in 1960 and of the 1965 presidential election campaign, and on 24 May 1968, during the 'Events' – fell flat. But at his best he achieved, as Jackson observes, an intimate, personal encounter with viewers, reinforced by a 'genius for simplification': the speeches that brought an end to Barricades Week (29 January 1960), to the Generals' Putsch (23 April 1961), and to the May 1968 Events (a radio broadcast only, on 30 May 1968), were decisive political moments.[62] He also revealed, in his televised interviews with Michel Droit, a more relaxed, at times playful style, which helped ensure his comfortable second-ballot victory in 1965.

Alongside the big broadcasts, de Gaulle gave 17 press conferences from 1958 to 1968, usually one between January and May and a second in the autumn. They were like no others. There was no discussion, little improvisation or spontaneity, though he showed in Washington that he was capable of all three.[63] But he considered that his words 'committed the state', and preferred to prepare minutely. So he would choose (usually) four topics, order relevant briefings, spend a week in purdah at Colombey, write and memorise a text, get his press attaché to plant the right questions, and finally give the conference. Hostile questions were accepted – and then dismissed with an acid comment or a joke, before de Gaulle said what he had memorised, with external affairs generally predominating. Part of the purpose was to show the world's press the majesty of the French state, in the main gilded salon of the Élysée, with the whole government present and a president capable of speaking grandly but in detail, without using his notes, on several topics over 60–105 minutes. But the press conferences also served to place markers for future policy, such as the switch to direct presidential elections (in April 1961) or the withdrawal from the NATO integrated command (in February 1966) – and to announce immediate policy decisions, such as the move to self-determination for Algeria, the concession of the Sahara, or the two vetoes of British entry to the European Economic Community.[64]

The final form of communication with the French was the provincial visit. A de Gaulle road trip typically covered four or five *départements* in three to four days, stopping in prefectures, sub-prefectures and small towns, meeting mayors, farmers, and business leaders as well as prefects, and plunging into the crowd whenever possible. This was a complete break with the style of earlier presidents: the pace was faster, the travel by car (rarely train), and there were no lengthy banquets. Gruelling for organisers and staff, a nightmare for the security team, the trips always found de Gaulle, twice the age of most of them, happy, relaxed, and energetic. In 1965 he claimed to have visited 94 *départements* (out of 100) including overseas ones, seeing some 15 million French people, visited some 2,500 municipalities, including all the main ones, and spoken in 600 locations to the public.[65] For de Gaulle, provincial visits were a form of direct democracy, a means of drawing the nation together. And his 'crowd baths' were unprecedented among French leaders: sometimes, in echo of medieval kingship, people brought him sick or handicapped children, hoping for a cure.[66]

In many ways de Gaulle's communication summarised the qualities and failings of his presidency. It highlighted a strong leader in command of all major policy issues, able to take independent decisions on the basis of his conception of the national interest, and in close contact with his people. But it was all one-way.

Presidential primacy under de Gaulle: functional or flawed?

The machinery of government that de Gaulle built, on the basis of the new Constitution, certainly ran more smoothly than that of the Fourth Republic, or, for that matter, than the ramshackle constructions of the Free French in London and Algiers. It allowed de Gaulle to keep a normal routine, timed to the minute by his staff, that appears impossibly light for a modern president: morning appointments from 10am after a thorough consultation of French, German, British, and American newspapers; lunch (usually with guests) from 12.30 to 2.30; afternoon appointments (which the staff tried to squeeze into two afternoons a week) from 2.30 to 6.00; meetings with the 'big four' staff chiefs from 6.00; departure just before 8.00 to the private apartments for the television news, possibly the study of files or more television, and bed – with weekends at Colombey when possible. It was a rhythm that gave de Gaulle time to read, to consult, and to think hard about policy. In his press conference of 9 September 1965, he listed 505 meetings with the Prime Minister, over 2,000 with other ministers, over 100 with parliamentary committee chairmen, 1,500 with leading civil servants and pressure group representatives, as well as 600 hours of conversation with foreign heads of state or government.[67] To ministers and advisers, de Gaulle was a brilliant, extremely demanding listener who obliged his visitors to set their issue in a general and elevated context. De Gaulle's decision-making was almost invariably preceded by confronting his views vigorously with others. They could give opinions freely on anything – but would have to defend them against a withering cross-examination.[68]

The major defect of de Gaulle's system was its authoritarianism. This did not mean anything so vulgar as persecuting the political opposition (though the police were capable, during the Algerian war, of terrifying ferocity with pro-FLN or anti-OAS demonstrators). But three specific examples stand out. One was his treatment of the justice system in the wake of the Generals' Putsch. He first created a High Military Tribunal using his Article 16 powers, with nine judges appointed by himself, limited rights for the accused and no right of appeal; then, when it failed to condemn Salan to death for leading the Generals' Putsch and OAS activities, he replaced it with a Military Court of Justice. This court, too, was abolished after its sixth case when André Canal, convicted of organising plastic explosive attacks and facing the death penalty, successfully appealed to the Council of State, France's highest administrative court, which ruled that basic principles of law were being violated. With Article 16 no longer in force, de Gaulle, via the government, then had to go through Parliament to create a new State Security Court, with (thanks to Parliament) better rights for the accused and a right of appeal, which lasted until its abolition in 1981. The episode left the impression that de Gaulle's support for the constitutional separation of powers ended when the courts delivered verdicts or sentences that he did not like.[69]

A second illustration of the regime's authoritarianism was the frequency of prosecutions, under a law of 29 July 1881, for 'offences to the head of state'. Under the Third and Fourth Republics, they numbered 6; between 1959 and 1965, the total reached 300, for such dangerous gestures as shouting 'Retire!' as de Gaulle's car passed or caricaturing him on a restaurant tablecloth.[70] Government had become more authoritarian just as society was becoming less so.

Most importantly, de Gaulle's presidency offered firm government but too few safety valves and too few channels for peaceful opposition. As Williams and Harrison observe, 'Not once in his eleven years of power did the General expose himself publicly to free discussion or questioning'.[71] The one-way character of de Gaulle's communications with press and public narrowed the opportunities for public participation in politics at any other level than the vote. The constitutional separation of powers – meaning that the president never appeared before Parliament – and the government's cavalier attitude to parliamentary questions meant that Parliament ceased to play its essential role in calling the executive to account. Political parties were generally relegated to a minor role. Despite its impressive record of stability and growth, the de Gaulle presidency was punctuated by serious outbreaks of protest – farmers in 1961 and 1963, miners in 1963, and almost everyone in May 1968 – which the authorities quite failed to anticipate. Blocked or hindered in normal institutional channels, protest found its way onto the streets – and in 1968 shook the regime to its foundations.

Conclusion

The Constitution of the Fifth Republic was de Gaulle's single most tangible legacy. France's liberation in 1944, and Algerian independence, would have happened without de Gaulle (though no doubt differently and more painfully). But the Fifth Republic Constitution would never have been adopted without him. Nor would the presidentialist 'reading' of the Constitution have become so embedded without his decade-long practice as the founding president. The legacy was a difficult and ambiguous one: a semi-presidential regime, with a seven-year mandate for the president, unsynchronised with the five-year parliamentary term, and no obvious guidance as to how the system would work when the parliamentary majority opposed the president. That would only be resolved after three periods of 'cohabitation' between a president and a majority of opposed parties: in 2002, the presidential term was cut to five years, synchronised with the Parliament's, since when – so far – the parliamentary majority has always been on the President's side. However sensible, this reform still went directly against de Gaulle's conception of a president above politics, elected for long enough to concern himself with the long term, not the merely contingent.

In the short term de Gaulle and his Constitution brought France a stability which, while top-heavy, conservative and (to some) suffocating, allowed the return of 'normal', humdrum politics, which had been lacking almost throughout the Fourth Republic, and towards the end of the Third. But as R.W. Johnson observes, 'the very achievement of Gaullist stability left less and less room for the role or the image of the providential superman'.[72] De Gaulle's personal, charismatic authority had become 'routinised', institutionalised, and he did not like it. 'It's not much fun anymore. There's nothing difficult or heroic left to do', he told his aide-de-camp on 28 April 1968.[73] The following month, at least, would offer a break from routine.

Notes

1 Alain Peyrefitte, *C'était de Gaulle*, vol. II (Paris: Éditions de Fallois/Fayard, 1997), p. 534.
2 Press conference, 31 January 1964. *DM*IV, pp. 162–82; p. 163.
3 See above, pp. 176–7.

4 Michel Debré, 'The Constitution of 1958, its Raison d'être and How it Evolved', in William G. Andrews and Stanley Hoffmann (eds.), *The Fifth Republic at Twenty* (Albany: State University of New York Press, 1981), pp. 11–24: p. 18.
5 *DM*III, pp. 286–304: pp. 301–2; Alain Peyrefitte, *C'était de Gaulle*, vol. I (Paris: Éditions de Fallois/Fayard, 1994), pp. 177–9.
6 *DM*IV, pp. 19–24, 30–3.
7 Éric Roussel, *Charles de Gaulle* (Paris: Gallimard, 2002), p. 730.
8 Louis Favoreu, 'De Gaulle et le Conseil constitutionnel', in Institut Charles de Gaulle, *De Gaulle en son siècle*, vol. II: *La République* (Paris: Plon, 1992), pp. 499–512: p. 507.
9 Peyrefitte, *C'était de Gaulle* I, p. 233.
10 Odile Rudelle, intervention, in Institut Charles de Gaulle, Association Française de Science Politique, *De Gaulle et ses Premiers Ministres, 1959–1969* (Paris: Plon, 1990), p. 56.
11 Vincent Wright, *The Government and Politics of France*, 3rd edn. (London: Unwin Hyman, 1989), p. 12.
12 *DM*III, pp. 162–6: p. 166. My italics.
13 François Flohic, *Souvenirs d'Outre-Gaulle* (Paris: Plon, 1979), p. 195; see also *MH*, pp. 270–1.
14 Max Weber, 'Politics as a Vocation', lecture given in Munich, 28 January 1919, http://anthropos-lab.net/wp/wp-content/uploads/2011/12/Weber-Politics-as-a-Vocation.pdf, accessed 25 July 2019, p. 2.
15 Jean Charlot, *The Gaullist Phenomenon* (London: George Allen & Unwin, 1971), pp. 44–5.
16 Peyrefitte, *C'était de Gaulle* II, pp. 605–7.
17 Philip M. Williams and Martin Harrison, *Politics and Society in de Gaulle's Republic* (New York: Doubleday, 1972), p. 191.
18 *DM*III, p. 42.
19 Jean Charlot, *L'UNR. Étude du pouvoir au sein d'un parti politique* (Paris: Armand Colin, 1967), p. 23.
20 Press conference, 23 October 1958, *DM*III, pp. 51–60; p. 52.
21 Peyrefitte, *C'était de Gaulle* I, p. 266; Broadcast, 7 November 1962, *DM*III, p. 256.
22 Alain Peyrefitte, interview with the author, 10 July 1991.
23 Charlot, *L'UNR*, p. 264n.
24 Jacques Foccart, *Tous les soirs avec de Gaulle. Journal de l'Élysée – I: 1965–1967* (Paris: Fayard/Jeune Afrique, 1997), p. 533; Broadcast, 4 March 1967, *DM*V, pp. 147–9.
25 *DM*V, pp. 313–15.
26 Williams and Harrison, *Politics and Society*, p. 75.
27 Charlot, *Gaullist Phenomenon*, pp. 66, 71.
28 Charlot, *L'UNR*, pp. 85–6.
29 Peyrefitte, *C'était de Gaulle* I, p. 267.
30 Jacques Foccart, *Tous les soirs*, pp. 60–1, 75–6, 86, 95, 329, 427, 533, 750–1; Jacques Foccart, *Le Général en Mai. Journal de l'Élysée – II:*

1968–1969 (Paris: Fayard/Jeune Afrique, 1998), p. 169; *DM*v, pp. 227–47: p. 247.
31 Philip M. Williams, *The French Parliament, 1958–1967* (London: George Allen & Unwin, 1968), p. 21.
32 *MH*, p. 277.
33 Alain Peyrefitte, *C'était de Gaulle*, vol. III (Paris: Éditions de Fallois/Fayard, 2000), pp. 86–90.
34 Andrew Knapp and Vincent Wright, *The Government and Politics of France*, 5th edn (London: Routledge, 2006), p. 146.
35 Wilfrid H. Kohl, *French Nuclear Diplomacy* (Princeton, NJ: Princeton University Press, 1971), pp. 115–19. The UK's atomic weapons programme, initiated in 1946, was not debated in full Cabinet or in the House of Commons.
36 *MH*, p. 278.
37 Knapp and Wright, *Government and Politics*, p. 151.
38 Pierre Lefranc, *Avec de Gaulle* (Paris: Plon, 1989 [1979]), p. 254.
39 Jean Touchard, *Le Gaullisme, 1940–1969* (Paris: Le Seuil, 1978), p. 247; *DM*III, pp. 41–5: p. 44.
40 *DM*III, pp. 64–7.
41 *DM*IV, pp. 162–82: pp. 163–9.
42 Press conferences, 9 September 1965, *DM*v, pp. 372–92: p. 389; 27 November 1967, *DM*v, pp. 227–47: p. 246; 9 September 1968, *DM*v, pp. 318–35: p. 323.
43 William G. Andrews, 'The Collective Political Executive under the Gaullists', in Andrews and Hoffmann, *Fifth Republic*, pp. 25–56: pp. 35–6.
44 Andrews, 'Collective Political Executive', p. 43; Étienne Burin des Roziers, 'Les Rapports entre le président de la République et le premier ministre, janvier 1962 – juillet 1967', in *De Gaulle et ses Premiers Ministres*, pp. 81–9.
45 Peyrefitte, *C'était de Gaulle* III, pp. 90–1 and n.
46 Press conference, 9 September 1968, *DM*v, pp. 318–35: p. 323.
47 *MH*, p. 275.
48 Peyrefitte, *C'était de Gaulle* I, pp. 116–17.
49 Michel Debré, *Entretiens avec le général de Gaulle, 1961–1969* (Paris: Albin Michel, 1993), p. 55.
50 Lefranc, *Avec de Gaulle*, p. 306.
51 Foccart, *Tous les soirs*, pp. 361, 734–7.
52 Georges Pompidou, *Pour rétablir une vérité* (Paris: Flammarion, 1982), pp. 202–4.
53 Maurice Couve de Murville, intervention in *De Gaulle et ses Premiers Ministres*, p. 274.
54 Charlot, *L'UNR*, pp. 85–6.
55 Jacques Basso, 'Quelques aspects de la pratique de la Ve République', in *De Gaulle et ses Premiers Ministres*, pp. 265–70.
56 Peyrefitte, *C'était de Gaulle* II, p. 341.

57 Éric Roussel, *Georges Pompidou, 1911–1974*, 2nd edn (Paris: Jean-Claude Lattès, 1994), p. 149; Olivier Guichard, *Mon Général* (Paris: Grasset, 1980), p. 420.
58 Alain Peyrefitte, 'De Gaulle et la communication', in Institut Charles de Gaulle, *De Gaulle et les médias* (Paris: Plon, 1994), pp. 101–9: pp. 105–6.
59 Foccart, *Tous les soirs*, p. 538.
60 Jackson, *A Certain Idea*, p. 625; Peyrefitte, 'De Gaulle et la communication', pp. 101–9.
61 Hoffmann, *Decline or Renewal?*, p. 88.
62 Jackson, *A Certain Idea*, p. 622; *DM*III, pp. 162–6, 306–8; *DM*V, pp. 291–3.
63 On 23 April 1960. *DM*III, pp. 189–96.
64 Peyrefitte, 'De Gaulle et la communication', pp. 101–9; Gilbert Pérol, 'Les Conférences de presse', in Institut Charles de Gaulle, *De Gaulle et les médias* (Paris: Plon, 1994), pp. 271–80; interventions by Étienne Burin des Roziers, Gilbert Pérol, Alain Peyrefitte, and Maurice Delarue, in *ibid.*, pp. 83–6.
65 Press conference, 9 September 1965, *DM*IV, pp. 372–92: p. 391.
66 Lefranc, *Avec de Gaulle*, pp. 220, 225–6, 229; Philippe de Gaulle, *De Gaulle mon père. Entretiens avec Michel Tauriac*, vol. II (Paris: Plon, 2003), p. 119.
67 *DM*IV, pp. 372–92: pp. 389–92: p. 390.
68 Edgard Pisani, *Le Général indivis* (Paris: Albin Michel, 1974), pp. 120–2.
69 Williams and Harrison, *Politics and Society*, pp. 258–61.
70 Williams and Harrison, *Politics and Society*, p. 376n.
71 Williams and Harrison, *Politics and Society*, p. 377.
72 R.W. Johnson, *The Long March of the French Left* (London: Macmillan, 1981), p. 128.
73 Flohic, *Souvenirs d'Outre-Gaulle*, p. 172.

Further reading

Julian Jackson, *A Certain Idea of France* (London: Allen Lane, 2018), chapters 19, 21, 25, and 27, covers constitution-making and domestic politics.

De Gaulle's *Memoirs of Hope* (London: Weidenfeld & Nicolson, 1971), chapters 1, 7, and 8 give his vision of the president's role in the Fifth Republic. His *Discours et Messages*, vols III–V (Paris: Plon, 1970) cover the Fifth Republic.

For the Constitution and its workings, see William G. Andrews and Stanley Hoffmann (eds), *The Fifth Republic at Twenty* (Albany: State University of New York Press, 1981), including a remarkable contribution by Michel Debré; Philip M. Williams and Martin Harrison, *Politics and*

Society in de Gaulle's Republic (New York: Doubleday, 1972); and Andrew Knapp and Vincent Wright, *The Government and Politics of France*, 5th edn (London: Routledge, 2006). Jack Hayward (ed.), *De Gaulle to Mitterrand: Presidential Power in France* (London: Hurst, 1993) places the de Gaulle presidency in a longer context.

The broad sweep of de Gaulle's constitutional ideas appears in Institut Charles de Gaulle, *De Gaulle en son siècle*, vol. II: *La République* (Paris: Plon, 1992).

Philip M. Williams, *French Politicians and Elections, 1951–1969* (Cambridge: Cambridge University Press, 1970) covers elections during the period (and earlier).

Jean Charlot's *The Gaullist Phenomenon* (London: George Allen & Unwin, 1971) is the indispensable work on the Gaullist party at its peak. Charlot's *Les Français et de Gaulle* (Paris: Plon, 1971), easily decipherable to readers with basic French, covers de Gaulle's poll ratings exhaustively.

Stanley Hoffmann, *Decline or Renewal? France since the 1930s* (New York: Viking Press, 1974) is a deeply interpretative study focused chiefly on de Gaulle and his presidency.

Each of the three volumes of Alain Peyrefitte, *C'était de Gaulle* (Paris: Éditions de Fallois/Fayard, 1994, 1997 and 2000) contains revealing conversations about domestic politics.

11 Superpowers and bombs

No experience of de Gaulle's was more searing than that of his near-total dependence, as leader of Free France, on the British and Americans. And nothing was more important to him, after 1958, than restoring France's independence and 'rank' in the world. This did not mean isolation, or narrow nationalism, or economic autarchy. But it did mean the avoidance of lasting dependence on any other state.[1] So, for example, France's diplomats, invited by governments before 1958 to embrace American leadership of the West, were now instructed that France should never accept decisions that were not her own.[2] Diplomatic independence required military independence: a state's primary duty was to answer for national security. It followed that France's defences should be under national control and that foreign troops, even friendly ones, should not be stationed on French soil.[3] The resulting policy would entail a major upheaval in France's foreign relations.

In the jargon of international relations theorists, de Gaulle's approach to foreign policy was defined by 'realism'. The only international realities, for de Gaulle, were nation-states.[4] International politics was a constant battle: 'Politics isn't for choirboys' he told Alain Peyrefitte. 'You have to speak loud and firm to win respect. If you don't you'll always get screwed.' And 'in international relations, one does not have friends'.[5] As for international organisations like the UN, far from promoting international understanding and co-operation, de Gaulle saw them as 'festive forums in which the old game was pursued in decorous disguise'.[6] Even alliances were entangling: different national interests might converge, but convergence was usually temporary. International negotiations were 'too costly when one was weak, and often unnecessary when one was strong'.[7] So de Gaulle only negotiated two treaties as President: the Évian accords which closed the Algerian War, and the 1963 Élysée Treaty of friendship with West Germany. Ideologies, meanwhile, whether American-style capitalism or Soviet Communism, were mere cloaks for national ambition.[8] 'Communism will pass. But France will not pass.'[9] So he called the USSR 'Russia' nine times out of ten. It followed that for de Gaulle, the ideological division of the Cold War world, seen as permanent by many contemporaries, was also ephemeral.

The opening page of the *War Memoirs* carries de Gaulle's claim of a place for France 'in the first rank' among nations, to which he constantly returned. 'France must have a world policy because she is France', he told the French in his end-of-year broadcast on 31 December 1963.[10] This did not imply illusions of measuring up to the superpowers. 'It is because we are no longer a great power', he said in private, 'that we need a grand policy, because if we do not have a grand policy ... we will no longer be anything at all.'[11] Unable to dominate as under Louis XIV, France could be culturally strong, economically ambitious, and politically important. That could then raise the horizons of the French beyond their political conflicts and forge a new national consensus at home.[12]

The place in the 'front rank' was deserved, for de Gaulle, because France bore a universal mission for humanity, having spread enlightenment, human rights, and national freedom across the globe. 'France', he told Alain Peyrefitte, 'is the light of the world'.[13] When de Gaulle lauded national independence he claimed to mean it for everyone, not just France. There were certainly limits to this universalism. De Gaulle never believed in the equality of nation-states, and he regarded the former sub-Saharan African colonies as largely dependent on France in practice.[14] But it did add an idealistic, almost revolutionary twist to a view of the world otherwise bleakly selfish, realist, and Machiavellian.[15]

But how to operationalise de Gaulle's aspiration to independence in the world of the Cold War? In 1949, France had signed the North Atlantic Treaty, which committed its members (North America, most of Western Europe, later Greece and Turkey) to treating an attack on one as an attack on all and responding to the aggressor – assumed to be the USSR and its Eastern bloc satellites – by all means they saw fit. De Gaulle kept France in the alliance: 'France has chosen to be on the side of the free peoples, she has chosen to be with you', he told Congress in Washington, on 25 April 1960.[16] One of his last acts as President was to renew France's membership when the treaty reached its 20-year term in 1969.

It was the practicalities of the alliance, and particularly the military integration of the North Atlantic Treaty Organisation (NATO), that so irked de Gaulle. NATO headquarters were in Paris but France was a second- or third-rank member. All NATO troops in Europe fell under the command of an American general. Of the 13 regional NATO commands, Americans held seven, British generals five, and a Frenchman just one.[17] Of 326,000 American service personnel in Europe in 1959, 61,000 were in France, spread across eight US air bases, a home port for the Sixth Fleet at Villefranche-sur-Mer, headquarters and logistical facilities. US nuclear weapons were stockpiled in France without the French government knowing either their number or their location.[18] Many French people shared de Gaulle's misgivings about NATO. Late in 1956, only one in ten thought the Americans treated France as an equal alliance partner, and half (in 1958) and 58% (in 1960) viewed US military personnel in France negatively.[19]

Reserved about American military assets on French soil, de Gaulle disliked French troops serving under NATO command because he believed that troops only fought well for their own country.[20] Above all, he doubted the willingness of the United States to protect its allies – the very purpose of NATO. By 1958, the Soviets possessed hydrogen bombs and the missile technology to deliver warheads to the United States. Would the Americans risk sacrificing New York or Washington to save Berlin, Bonn or Paris from attack by the Warsaw Pact, the Soviet-led Eastern bloc alliance? De Gaulle thought not, telling the American journalist Cyrus Sulzberger in February 1958 that NATO did not defend France and was 'no longer an alliance. It is a subordination'.[21] De Gaulle returned to power determined to regain France's independence from NATO and to redefine her position in the Atlantic Alliance.

To do what? Not to fight the Cold War better, though de Gaulle was no friend of Communism. Nor, although he popularised the term *détente*,[22] did he aim to promote peaceful coexistence between the American and Soviet blocs. His long-term goal was more ambitious: the dissolution of the two-bloc system which, according to (misleading) Gaullist mythology, the Soviets and 'Anglo-Saxons' had agreed at the Yalta conference in February 1945. In international relations terms, he was a 'revisionist', seeking to transform the world system – but not by seeking more territory.[23] A multipolar world, in which superpowers were constrained, blocs dissolved, and smaller countries freer, would, in the Gaullist view, be more stable: states would normally pursue balance-of-power policies which would limit the domination of great powers; spheres of influence would be more decentralised; flashpoints of conflict more readily contained.[24] This would reduce the danger of nuclear war, which de Gaulle repeatedly stressed would be a 'disaster for everyone'.[25] But not all states would be equals in this multipolar vision. Rather, he imagined a hierarchy of nation-states in which leading powers (more than two; certainly fewer than ten) conferred regularly to maintain international law and order.[26] In the Cold War context, this was a highly subversive vision of the future. It was also, of course, one designed to ensure a prominent place for France.

Constraining though it was, the Cold War context of the 1960s offered opportunities to challenge the duopoly. First, the Soviet Union appeared less aggressive. Communism, de Gaulle told Sulzberger in December 1956, was 'finished';[27] in 1960, he thought the Soviet leader, Nikita Khrushchev, 'too old and too fat' to want a war.[28] Second, however, the Soviets' growing nuclear and missile capabilities meant that de Gaulle was not alone in querying America's readiness to use nuclear weapons on Europe's behalf.[29] Third, the Europeans therefore had good reason to try and assure more of their own defences – as they were better able to by 1958, having recovered much of their prosperity.[30] Fourth, the Non-Aligned movement, built in the wake of the 1955 Bandung Conference, demonstrated the resistance of leading Third World nations like India and Egypt to superpower domination. Fifth, the Soviet bloc itself looked less monolithic than a decade earlier: the 1956 Hungarian uprising had highlighted East European aspirations to greater independence, while the Sino-Soviet split was patent by 1960. For all these reasons, de Gaulle claimed in 1964 that the blocs were already breaking up.[31] This was premature; but the Cold War power structure offered de Gaulle's France enough loopholes to follow an original path.[32]

Western Europe offered the clearest opportunities for furthering de Gaulle's ambitions. As he told Peyrefitte, of the six member states of the European Economic Community,

> only France can have a foreign policy. The governments of Italy, Belgium, Holland and Luxembourg don't even imagine having one. Germany is infirm ... We are the only state able to face down the Americans. We are the spokesmen of 200 million silent people who are secretly grateful to us for speaking in their place.[33]

Europe, he claimed, suffered more than anywhere from Cold War divisions. Europe's unification 'from the Atlantic to the Urals', as de Gaulle put it 12 times during his presidency, on the initiative of the French-led Western group, would be the surest sign that the Cold War was over. 'Then Europe, no longer split in two by ambitions and ideologies that would become progressively out of date, would again be the heart of civilisation'.[34]

There was more than a touch of racism in this vision. 'Russia', he told Sulzberger in 1960, 'regardless of its present ideology, was essentially a white, European, and Western nation'.[35] At his press conference of 10 November 1959, Russia appeared as a 'white nation of Europe' holding back 'the yellow multitude that is China, innumerable and miserable'.[36] In 1962 he imagined 'a concord among the white people against the colored'.[37] In his memoirs, he wrote that 'Being all of the same white race, with the same Christian origins and the same way of life, linked ... by countless ties of thought, art, science, politics and trade, it was natural that [Europeans] should come to form a whole.'[38] Whatever his racist leanings, however, what drove the policy from day to day was geopolitics.

Personalities, finally, were of secondary importance in de Gaulle's grand scheme. His good relations with President Eisenhower, dating from the war, did little to ease early conflicts over NATO reform. There was a certain mutual admiration, at first, between de Gaulle and Eisenhower's successor John F. Kennedy, reinforced, for de Gaulle, by Kennedy's handling of the Cuban missile crisis in October 1962. But Franco-American relations still deteriorated. Kennedy met British Prime Minister Harold Macmillan seven times during his presidency, and de Gaulle just once. After a particularly difficult telephone conversation in December 1961, contacts between the two men were indirect or epistolary.[39] Paradoxically, it was late in the presidency of Lyndon Johnson, a leader whom de Gaulle held in near-contempt, that relations improved. On the Soviet side, neither the human contact established with Khrushchev during his 1960 visit to Paris nor increasingly cordial relations between the two Foreign Ministers, Maurice Couve de Murville and Andrei Gromyko, secured a privileged relation for France with the USSR. None of this should surprise. For a president who thought in terms of unchanging national interests and long cycles of history, individuals were a mere contingency.

This was the framework within which de Gaulle approached relations with the superpowers. But his approach also developed over four distinct periods of the presidency: the early years (1958–1962), constrained by the Algerian War; the more assertive second period (1962–1966), culminating in the withdrawal from NATO; the zenith of independence (1966–1968), highlighted by a spectacular Soviet visit; and a closing period (1968–1969) marked by setbacks at home and abroad.

Hoisting the colours, 1958–1962

Everyone seemed to come to Paris after de Gaulle's return to power. Macmillan visited in June 1958, US Secretary of State John Foster Dulles in July, while German Chancellor Konrad Adenauer was de Gaulle's guest at Colombey that September. Eisenhower made an official visit in September 1959; Macmillan returned, to the presidential château at Rambouillet, outside Paris, in March 1960, and was closely followed by Khrushchev, from 23 March to 3 April. That April de Gaulle made state visits first to the UK, where he addressed the Lords and the Commons in Westminster Hall, and then to Canada and to the United States, where he spoke to both houses of Congress. On 16–17 May 1960 he hosted a four-power summit in Paris. Kennedy visited a year later.

The trappings of great-power status, therefore, were certainly there. But de Gaulle could not claim at a stroke the independence he craved. His early attempts to reform NATO, to open a dialogue with the Soviet Union, or to enlist Western Europe in his projects, all failed. The Algerian War weighed like a millstone on his diplomacy, and the two international crises provoked by Khrushchev – over Berlin from 1958 to 1961, over Cuba in 1962 – demanded maximum Western solidarity, not challenges to the alliance. But by the end of 1962, with Algeria independent and France within reach of an independent nuclear deterrent, de Gaulle was ready for a more assertive second phase.

NATO and the memorandum of September 1958

De Gaulle's complaints about NATO and US policy echoed those of his predecessors, but were much more systematically pressed. NATO needed reforming, he told Couve de Murville, Defence Minister Pierre Guillaumat, and armed forces Chief of Staff Paul Ély, on 17 June 1958. No US warheads should be stockpiled in France without French consent; and France should take part in NATO nuclear planning.[40] On 5 July he refused Dulles's offer of tactical nuclear warheads because France would not have complete control of their use; and he pointedly questioned America's willingness to defend Western Europe.[41] De Gaulle's mistrust of his allies was reinforced when Britain and the United States sent troops respectively to Jordan and to Lebanon (traditionally a French area of influence) in July 1958, and when the United States threatened nuclear war against Communist China for bombing the islands of Quemoy and Matsu in August – all without consulting France.[42]

Describing his first major NATO initiative, de Gaulle borrowed an expression he had used of the *Appel du 18 juin*: 'I hoisted my colours'.[43] He did so in a 533-word, four-point memorandum addressed to Eisenhower and Macmillan on 17 September 1958.[44] The 1949 NATO structure, it said first, was out of date: security concerns had arisen far outside the NATO area of Europe. Second, France had global interests stretching beyond this area: so did the UK and the USA. Third, the effective delegation to the USA of the decision to use atomic weapons, logical when only one NATO power possessed them, was also, now, out of date when Britain had the Bomb and France nearly did. Fourth, therefore, a triumvirate (the United States, Britain, and France – but not Germany) should jointly plan on the deployment and eventual use of NATO forces, including nuclear forces, across the globe.[45]

What did de Gaulle aim to achieve with the NATO memorandum? One view was that he sought parity with Britain in NATO, to replicate the UK's 'special relationship' with the USA, notably with respect to nuclear weapons. 'I ... proposed that the alliance should henceforth be placed under a triple rather than a dual direction', he wrote in his *Memoirs*.[46] The problem was that there was not really a 'dual' direction: no American president would share decisions on using nuclear weapons with anyone, not even the British.[47] Or was de Gaulle seeking a triumvirate of equals – tantamount to a French (and British) veto on the use of any NATO nuclear weapons, including American ones? The US State Department thought he did; so did General Lauris Norstad, NATO's Supreme Commander in Europe.[48] De Gaulle's Grenoble speech of 7 October 1960 appeared to offer confirmation: no atomic weapon, he said, should be launched from anywhere in the free world without France's agreement, nor any from France except on France's decision.[49] To the Americans, such a claim appeared exorbitant and unrealistic.

A third interpretation was that, precisely, de Gaulle never expected his memorandum to be accepted, and simply wanted an excuse to pull out of NATO. 'I asked for the moon. I was sure they wouldn't give it to me', he told Peyrefitte; Eisenhower and Macmillan, he wrote in his memoirs, 'replied evasively. So there was nothing to prevent us from taking action.'[50] Yet as late as 11 January 1962, de Gaulle was still pressing the idea of a three-power directorate on Kennedy.[51] That suggests he took his memorandum more seriously than his later accounts imply.

The view of Kennedy's National Security Adviser McGeorge Bundy is probably the most accurate:

> What de Gaulle wanted was a place at the table where decisions that could mean life or death for France would be made. I do not assert that the demand was realistic, or even that de Gaulle was optimistic about its chance of success. I do conclude that he thought it right to try.[52]

When he did not succeed, he went on trying, for three years. But he also started to scale down France's participation in NATO: a two-track approach characteristic of de Gaulle.

Eisenhower's formal reply, dated 20 October, rejected each of de Gaulle's proposals. The United States did not plan to use NATO alone to fight world Communism; extending the NATO area beyond Europe presented difficulties; a three-power directorate would offend smaller states (or, as Norstad put it, 'We can't ... have three big top powers dictating to the West').[53] The other European NATO states, when news of the memo leaked out, agreed, preferring to be 'equally unequal' than to give France special status.[54] Eisenhower did not reject lower-level consultation between the big three – what de Gaulle dismissively called 'secret dinners organised from time to time by embassy counsellors' – but even this annoyed other NATO members.[55]

De Gaulle's severance of NATO links, however, began swiftly, with the withdrawal of France's Mediterranean Fleet in March 1959. It made little practical difference. The French ships, merely 'earmarked' in peacetime, continued to participate in joint exercises.[56] But the move's symbolic importance was greater. Couve asserted 'France's exclusive right to control her communications with North Africa', de Gaulle that NATO should be about cooperation not integration; both irritated Americans (who responded by cancelling plans to sell France a nuclear reactor for submarines) and smaller NATO states.[57] Then de Gaulle told Eisenhower, in letters dated 25 May and 6 October 1959, to allow France a voice in the use of US nuclear weapons based in France – or withdraw them from French soil. With no agreement reached, 200 Super Sabre fighter-bombers had to be removed from France to the UK and Germany, with their nuclear weapons, from 1959 onwards.[58]

Privately, meanwhile, de Gaulle irritated first Eisenhower, then Kennedy, by repeatedly questioning the viability of the US 'nuclear umbrella' for Europe.[59] Publicly, he effectively revealed the contents of the memorandum in his press conference of 5 September 1960.[60] But by February 1962, after giving Kennedy a year to consider the memorandum, he abandoned it. His next initiatives would be centred on Europe – and on France's own bomb.

Hourra pour la France![61] France's bomb, 1960–1962

On 18 October 1945, 74 days after an atomic bomb was dropped on Hiroshima, de Gaulle founded France's Atomic Energy

Commissariat – 'to create the Bomb', he told Peyrefitte in 1966.[62] Successive governments of the Fourth Republic continued the enterprise. On 11 April 1958 the Gaillard government decided to aim for an atomic test early in 1960.[63] But Fourth Republic governments had imagined a French bomb within NATO; for de Gaulle, by contrast, as he told the École Militaire on 3 November 1959, 'The defence of France must be French.'[64] And it was under de Gaulle that France's first bomb was exploded, at Reggane in the Algerian Sahara, on 13 February 1960. 'Hurrah for France!', de Gaulle telegraphed to Guillaumat. 'From this morning she is prouder and stronger.' The official communiqué added the improbable argument that France joining the nuclear club, as its fourth member, would facilitate agreements between nuclear powers and promote nuclear disarmament.[65]

Developing a viable deterrent, however, was another matter. France was at least 15 years behind the United States; access to American know-how would make a French deterrent quicker and cheaper to create. The early de Gaulle presidency therefore saw France attempt to obtain American help in nuclear technology, but without strings attached.[66] These were generally unsuccessful. Congress voted in February 1960 against making France an exception to the general US ban on sharing nuclear secrets.[67] When a French military delegation went shopping in Washington in March 1962, the Americans wanted to improve their balance of payments by selling conventional weapons which the French did not want, while the French sought enriched uranium and centrifuges which the Americans would not sell. The only deal reached was for France's purchase of a dozen KC-135 tanker aircraft, surplus to American requirements but necessary to refuel the Mirage-IV aircraft set to carry the French bomb.[68] Kennedy discussed loosening American nuclear policy with his inner circle on 16 April 1962, but decided not to. American assistance, he reasoned, would not bring de Gaulle back into the NATO mainstream.[69]

De Gaulle's efforts to obtain American nuclear secrets through espionage also met with little success.[70] So de Gaulle's France would go it almost alone, slowly and expensively. The first nuclear programming law, tabled on 18 July 1960, allocated 3.9 billion francs to military nuclear research, one billion to Mirage-IV bombers, 770 million to missile research, and 250 million to start work on a nuclear submarine. Opposed by most non-Gaullist forces, it took nearly five months to get through Parliament, even though the Debré government thrice made it a question of confidence. The Senate was consistently opposed. But by the time of its promulgation, on 10 December 1960, there had been a real political debate – which the British had been denied a decade earlier.[71] In May 1962, de Gaulle was able to tell Peyrefitte that 'From September next year, every month we will make a Mirage and its bomb. By the end of next year we will have enough to kill 20 million men within two hours of the start of an attack.' But 'we won't kill them, because it will be known that we can.'[72]

De Gaulle and the USSR: sketching détente

Communism being a spent force, reasoned de Gaulle, France should reset the relationship with the USSR on the basis of national interest, not ideological conflict. This was difficult because of the long crisis over Berlin, which lasted from 1958 until the building of the Berlin Wall in 1961. Berlin, under four-power (American, British, French, and Soviet) control since 1945, was situated in the middle of Communist East Germany. On 27 November 1958, Khrushchev addressed an ultimatum to Western leaders, demanding their agreement that it become a free and demilitarised city under international supervision. Failing such an agreement within six months, the USSR would sign a treaty with East Germany. The implicit threat was of East Germany then cutting road and rail links between West Germany and West Berlin. Khrushchev hoped for a variety of diplomatic gains from this initiative, including the division of the Western powers. But his ultimatum was dangerous because the isolation of West Berlin could be viewed by the West as a *casus belli*.

De Gaulle thought Khrushchev was bluffing and would not risk war. Where Eisenhower, Kennedy, and especially Macmillan favoured negotiation on Berlin, de Gaulle did not – a position that also reinforced his standing with Adenauer. Khrushchev's deadline passed without incident. In 1960 the Western leaders agreed to meet him in Paris. Two weeks before the summit was due to open on 16 May, an American U2 spy aircraft was shot down in Soviet airspace. Khrushchev came to Paris determined to exact a humiliating apology from Eisenhower. De Gaulle advised Eisenhower to stand firm, and reminded Khrushchev that Soviet satellites regularly overflew France.[73] Khrushchev walked out of the summit almost before it had begun, but de Gaulle was widely praised for his calm but firm handling of it.[74] No substantive negotiations over Berlin took place.

It was Khrushchev who closed the Berlin crisis, even more brutally than he had opened it. The construction of a wall dividing East from West Berlin, from Sunday 13 August 1961, was timed to catch Macmillan on a Scottish grouse moor and Kennedy on a boat off Hyannis Port. No three-way consultation was possible, and de Gaulle later claimed that had he been listened to, no wall would have been built.[75] East Germans could no longer migrate westwards; but West Berlin was now left alone. On 17 October Khrushchev withdrew his ultimatum.[76]

Alongside this firmness, however, de Gaulle worked to improve longer-term relations with the Soviets. An agreement on Franco-Soviet cultural exchanges was signed in January 1959; France's new jet airliner, the Caravelle, was presented in Moscow on 25 May; Soviet press coverage of de Gaulle, initially very hostile, became less so from March 1959 as de Gaulle began to cut ties with NATO. Above all, in March 1960 Khrushchev became the first Russian leader to visit France since Tsar Nicholas II in 1896. On a human level, the visit was successful.[77] And de Gaulle was able to support the Soviet position that Germany's eastern border should remain at the Oder–Neisse line, fixed in 1945; to show Khrushchev that France was an independent member of the Western camp; and to try and convince him that West Germany posed no threat to the USSR.[78]

The Americans, too, had hosted Khrushchev for a successful visit in 1959. But, unlike them, de Gaulle also insisted – on 31 May 1960, just two weeks after the failed Paris summit – that 'no direct dispute' opposed French interests to Russia's, and that (thinking, no doubt, of the pre-1917 Russian alliance) the Russian people had a 'traditional appeal' for the French.[79] And his repeated references – five times in speeches between 1959 and 1962 – to a Europe 'from the Atlantic to the Urals' also set him apart from his allies. The expression left Hervé Alphand, a long-term Gaullist and France's ambassador to Washington, bewildered: it appeared to cut the Soviet Union in half, and he worried that it could 'create misunderstandings and generate suspicions without anything beneficial to show for it'.[80] Khrushchev, indeed, would later admit both incomprehension and suspicion: after all, he said, Hitler had wanted to get to the Urals.[81] De Gaulle would go on using it as a sort of shorthand for a dream of a post-Cold War Europe, reunited and stretching to its fullest dimensions. But in the short term at least, his attempt to reset relations with the USSR yielded limited results.

Conclusions from Cuba, 1962–1963

On 22 October 1962 Kennedy's personal envoy Dean Acheson briefed de Gaulle at the Élysée on the presence of Soviet missiles in Cuba. De Gaulle (unlike Macmillan, who was also briefed) did not ask for evidence. 'If there was a war', he told Acheson, 'France will be with you. But there will be no war.'[82] Events proved him right. Kennedy's naval blockade of Cuba secured the withdrawal of the Soviet missiles at the end of the tensest week in Cold War history, without a shot being fired.

Cuba reinforced Washington's belief that NATO nuclear policy had to be centralised; such a crisis offered no time for long consultations among allies.[83] De Gaulle's conclusions were almost diametrically opposed. First, Acheson, however courteously, had not consulted him as an ally but merely informed him of America's intentions; and (as he said in his press conference of 14 January 1963), the United States had risked nuclear war for its own interests, not Europe's.[84] Second, Khrushchev's climb-down demonstrated that the Soviet Union was *not* willing to risk war, either for Cuba or for Berlin; and therefore that the United States, as the more powerful of the two superpowers, was the more dangerous.[85] Third, the establishment of a hot line and other signs of US–Soviet détente after Cuba raised the spectre of a 'new Yalta' with the two superpowers co-operating at Europe's expense.[86] All of this confirmed de Gaulle's belief in the need to develop France's independent nuclear deterrent, and an independent diplomacy directed towards Western Europe but also towards the USSR itself.

Developing independence, 1962–1966

'Now we have given our colonies their independence', de Gaulle told Peyrefitte in January 1963, 'it is time to claim our own' – from the 'American protectorate'.[87] Three elements reinforced his assertiveness. The Algerian War was over; the referendum and elections of autumn 1962 had reinforced his domestic position; the Soviet challenge, and thus the need for Western solidarity, had weakened since the Cuban crisis. The ensuing three years saw a crystallisation of fundamental differences over nuclear doctrine with the Americans but also, to a degree, with France's European allies; a clear challenge thrown down to the Anglo-Saxons, chiefly over these differences, at the press conference of 14 January 1963; a failed attempt to win Germany over to France's side of the dispute; a new economic dimension to the confrontation with the United States; a corresponding further deterioration in relations with Washington; and finally, on 7 March 1966, the announcement of France's withdrawal from NATO.

Nuclear doctrines: force de frappe, flexible response, and Multilateral Force

For de Gaulle, France's nascent nuclear strike force – *force de frappe* – was an all-or-nothing weapon. Even with many fewer megatons than the superpowers, France's capacity to destroy, say, Kiev and Leningrad and to kill their inhabitants, sufficed to deter a Soviet attack. In his press conference of 23 July 1964, de Gaulle called it the deterrence of the weak against the strong.[88]

This ran directly counter to Washington's thinking. To face the Soviets' new technological capacity to destroy targets across the globe – including American ones – highlighted by the 1957 Sputnik satellite launch, American administrations developed, and NATO formally adopted (in January 1968), the doctrine of 'flexible response'.[89] Under 'flexible response', Warsaw Pact aggression with conventional weapons would trigger a conventional riposte; only after due warning would NATO use small, 'tactical', nuclear weapons – against military targets, not cities; and a further pause would follow before any all-out nuclear exchange. Designed to limit the danger to the American heartland, flexible response would also encourage the Europeans to invest more in their own conventional defence, notably by buying American weapons. This would in turn reduce America's trade deficit.[90]

For de Gaulle, flexible response merely proved his claim that the US strategic deterrent would never be used in Europe's defence. As he wrote to Pompidou and Couve on 27 October 1963,

> Rather than indefinitely increasing her conventional forces, without any hope of bringing them to a higher level than the Soviets, she [by which de Gaulle meant Europe, for which he claimed to speak] considers it necessary that in case of Soviet aggression, nuclear weapons should be used immediately for her defence. There is therefore an essential divergence between the American and European points of view on strategy. This should not prevent an 'alliance'. But it makes 'integration' impossible to justify.[91]

A second American initiative, the Multilateral Force (MLF), reinforced de Gaulle's mistrust. The MLF was imagined as a truly NATO nuclear force, whether airborne or consisting of submarines or surface vessels equipped with American Polaris missiles and carrying multinational crews. Each participating nation would have a veto on using the MLF's nuclear weapons.[92] But the corollary of the MLF was that no European state should have its own deterrent. As Kennedy's Defense Secretary Robert McNamara explained on 9 July 1962, 'limited nuclear capabilities, operating independently, are dangerous, expensive, prone to obsolescence, and lacking in credibility as a deterrent'.[93] For the Americans, the *force de frappe* and de Gaulle's all-out nuclear doctrine risked wrecking the delicate scenarios of flexible response and might even be used to 'trigger' American nuclear weapons. A French deterrent, moreover, risked leading to nuclear proliferation, and especially emulation by West Germany.[94]

Though rather favoured by those European countries, especially Italy and Germany, that lacked nuclear weapons, MLF was unattractive to Europe's two nuclear powers, Britain and France. Macmillan privately called it 'a racket of American industry'.[95] De Gaulle, at his press conference of 14 January 1963, rejected it outright for France.[96] He went on to lobby against MLF in principle, claiming it would reinforce West Germany's dependence on the United States – and possibly its appetite for nuclear weapons.[97] In the end, the MLF project collapsed late in 1965. The British did not want it, the French opposed it, and support for it within the Johnson administration steadily declined.[98] But the clash over nuclear doctrine had created what Bundy called an 'unpleasant split' between de Gaulle and the US administration by summer 1962.[99]

Polaris and its fall-out

The Polaris episode widened the split. On 18–21 December 1962, Macmillan met Kennedy at Nassau, in the Bahamas, and secured the purchase of American Polaris missiles, which would be fired with British warheads from British submarines. Normally the submarines would fall under NATO command, within the MLF, on a dual-key system; but Kennedy agreed that Britain could use them independently if 'supreme national interests' were at stake. For Macmillan, the agreement saved Britain's nuclear deterrent, threatened by the obsolescence of Britain's existing 'V-bomber' fleet and the cancellation of the earlier Blue Streak and Skybolt systems intended to replace it. On paper, it was also a victory against McNamara's vocal opposition to independent nuclear forces.[100] But it confirmed de Gaulle's views that Britain was an American satellite, especially as barely a week earlier, at Rambouillet on 15–16 December, Macmillan had turned down his suggestion of a joint Anglo-French missile project. This would be de Gaulle's pretext to veto Britain's entry into the European Economic Community (EEC).[101]

Kennedy did offer Polaris, on identical terms, to de Gaulle, who refused – again on 14 January 1963 – on grounds both technical (France lacked submarines and warheads to use Polaris) and political (de Gaulle refused to place French nuclear weapons under NATO command, even partially).[102] That Kennedy's offer appeared to have come as an afterthought following Nassau no doubt contributed to the refusal.[103] But fundamentally, as Bundy recognised, 'de Gaulle's decision was rooted in conviction'.[104]

Kennedy's reaction was both angry ('those bastards just live off the fat of the land and spit on us every chance they get')[105] and bewildered. 'What does de Gaulle want?', he asked, having mistakenly believed he wanted parity with Britain.[106] He considered de Gaulle's France as a free-rider, drawing the benefits of NATO without the corresponding solidarity, and de Gaulle as a hypocrite who counselled firmness on Berlin to win Adenauer's friendship but failed to contribute to NATO forces defending the city.[107] In practical terms, he directed the CIA to find out if de Gaulle was preparing a deal with the Soviet Union (he was not) and to influence European opinion against him.[108] Hence Couve's assessment that the first half of 1963 saw the worst crisis in Franco-American relations of de Gaulle's presidency.[109]

Kennedy reached out just once more to de Gaulle, to seek French support for the Partial Nuclear Test Ban Treaty signed in Moscow on 5 August 1963. In return for a French signature, he offered technical information on underground nuclear testing (not covered by the treaty) and US testing sites for French weapons. De Gaulle again refused, pointing out in his press conference of 29 July 1963 that the treaty was pointless as the two superpowers already had enough weapons to destroy the world several times over.[110] Over 100 countries, including the UK, the USA, and the USSR, still signed it; as a non-signatory, France was in the company of Cuba, Communist China, and Albania. De Gaulle did, it is true, make a counter-proposal, never accepted, that the superpowers' missiles be placed under international control and new ones banned.[111] And France did sign other treaties which de Gaulle thought useful – on keeping Antarctica demilitarised in 1959, and banning nuclear weapons from space in 1967. But the non-signature of the PTBT halted any prospect of Franco-American nuclear co-operation for at least five years.[112]

West Germany and the Élysée Treaty, 1963–1964[113]

De Gaulle attempted, in 1960, to enlist the other five EEC countries – West Germany, Italy, the Netherlands, Belgium, and Luxembourg – in a bid to create a West European confederation that would effectively replace the EEC and reform the Atlantic Alliance. Known as the Fouchet Plan, this initiative collapsed in April 1962. De Gaulle then turned his attention exclusively to West Germany, which became a major stake of Franco-American tensions. On 22 January 1963 he signed a Treaty of Friendship and Co-operation (the Élysée Treaty) with Adenauer. Like the Fouchet Plan but between France and West Germany only, it promised regular consultation on diplomatic, defence, cultural, and economic matters – and, crucially, made no mention of NATO or the EEC. Its signature came just eight days after de Gaulle had refused Polaris and the MLF and vetoed Britain's EEC application.

Kennedy would not tolerate the West's chief front-line state in the Cold War falling into de Gaulle's lap. He therefore lobbied (indirectly) in Bonn to ensure that the treaty would not detach West Germany from NATO. When the Bundestag, West Germany's lower house of Parliament, ratified the treaty unanimously on 15 June, it duly added a preamble stating that the treaty did not affect existing NATO commitments. This, for de Gaulle, emptied the treaty of its essential purpose – to cut West Germany loose from the United States and anchor it to France. The treaty survived, but the first meeting under its auspices, on 4–5 July 1963 in Bonn, was a low-key affair. De Gaulle would meet Adenauer as Chancellor just once more, at Rambouillet in September. The following month Adenauer's party retired him, aged 87, ending the closest relationship de Gaulle ever had with the head of a foreign government.

Adenauer's successor was the more 'Atlanticist' Ludwig Erhard. Through 1964 de Gaulle tried to turn Erhard around – and away from his interest in the MLF, which Pompidou warned was incompatible with the Élysée Treaty.[114] The MLF would collapse, partly thanks to de Gaulle's efforts; and the de Gaulle–Erhard partnership had, if anything, a negative record of achievement. When they met in Bonn on 3–4 July 1964, de Gaulle refused Erhard's request to share France's *force de frappe* as a European weapon. De Gaulle might claim that the *force de frappe* offered better protection for Western Europe (and West Germany in particular) than America's nuclear umbrella because France's fate was inextricably bound to Europe's, but there could be no question of shared control.[115] For West Germany's political and military establishment, in any case, the *force de frappe* appeared useless militarily and unrealistic politically, given the Federal Republic's long-term choice for Atlantic integration.[116] Less than two years after its signature, therefore, the Élysée Treaty was practically on ice.

Challenging the dollar, 1965

Trade was the least fraught side of Franco-American economic relations in 1962–1964. In particular, the Kennedy Round of negotiations, under the auspices of the General Agreement on Tariffs and Trade, began successfully in May 1964 around a central proposition of across-the-board tariff cuts of 50%, with France broadly accepting the EEC position.[117] US inward investment to France was, however, another matter. Welcomed early in the presidency, it was increasingly restricted from 1962 owing to worries that Americans were acquiring French firms considered economically strategic. Only from 1966 was the regime liberalised.[118]

De Gaulle picked a more serious quarrel, however, over the international monetary system. The Bretton Woods conference of 1944 had given the US dollar a unique place among the world's currencies, fixing its value permanently at $35 an ounce of gold. The currencies of all other states in the system had set rates against the dollar. These might be devalued or revalued with the agreement of governments, if a country's economic prospects – for example, inflation or the balance of trade – deteriorated or improved. The French franc had been repeatedly devalued after 1945, and again in December 1958 – after which de Gaulle aimed to avoid any repetition. The United States, by contrast, could not devalue, however much its balance of payments deteriorated. And it could, in theory, print as many dollars as it liked, all redeemable in gold.

From the 1950s, a big US trade deficit developed, chiefly owing to high military spending overseas. US presidents from Eisenhower on blamed the Europeans, for not contributing enough to Western defence. De Gaulle, by contrast, considered it scandalous that the Americans could print dollars, thus exporting inflation, which financed their corporations' takeovers of French businesses, and later, the Vietnam War.[119] As early as 1963, he told Peyrefitte that the dollar was the most insidious form of US imperialism.[120]

His short-term response, from 1961, was to sell dollars and buy gold. In 1957, France's gold reserves had amounted to 500 tons; by 1966 the figure was 4,650 – which he insisted were physically kept in France, not the United States.[121] At his press conference of 4 February 1965 he went further, calling for an end to the dollar's privileges. The pre-war Gold Standard, he said, should replace the Bretton Woods Gold Exchange Standard: gold 'mirrored the requirements of a healthy international order, meaning a multipolar world system based on interdependence without hegemony, where everyone obeys the same rules'.[122]

To succeed, however, de Gaulle would (at least) have needed to enlist his European partners in the challenge. But that would have entailed a degree of dependence on West Germany (home to Western Europe's strongest currency, the deutschmark) which he was unlikely to accept. In any case, the Europeans had no collective will to impose another system. Correct in analysing how unbalanced the Bretton Woods system had become, de Gaulle could offer no practicable remedy. His stance further irritated not only the US government, which decided to stop selling France supercomputers, but also the American public, whose earlier high regard for de Gaulle gave way to a perception that he was attacking their wallets.[123]

Leaving NATO, 1966

In a sense the announcement, in March 1966, of France's complete withdrawal from NATO was long-expected. France was already semi-detached. The Mediterranean fleet had been withdrawn in 1959, the Atlantic fleet in 1963. Army units repatriated from Algeria were not returned to NATO command. Under France's three-level defence posture unveiled in 1963, both the top-level strategic nuclear forces and the Operational Territorial Defence (a home defence force, in case enemy troops reached France), were independent. And even the intermediate 'inter-service intervention force', most closely associated with the alliance, retained six divisions under national command against two for NATO. Within NATO, French troops were treated as a reserve force. Meanwhile US troops in France had been cut from 57,400 to 28,700 since 1962.[124]

Ready to leave NATO from January 1965[125] de Gaulle still waited another 14 months, settling most outstanding differences with his EEC partners and winning re-election as President. Two press conferences, on 9 September 1965 and 21 February 1966, made his intentions clear. In September he stated that at the latest in 1969, when the Atlantic Treaty came up for renewal, 'the subordination known as "integration" that NATO entails and which puts our destiny under foreign authority will cease as far as we are concerned'. In February he called NATO a 'protectorate', though making a distinction between the alliance and the integrated military structure.[126] In addition, a State Department mole in the

Quai d'Orsay informed Washington about the imminence of withdrawal.[127]

In principle, then, de Gaulle's letter to Johnson of 7 March 1966, stating that 'France proposes to recover full sovereignty over its territory ... and no longer to place its forces at NATO's disposal', merely confirmed what everyone knew. Johnson's reaction was measured: with France's veto power gone, he could concentrate on reasserting American leadership in NATO.[128] The practical difference, too, was limited: in peacetime, NATO troops fell under national command anyway, and many outstanding issues such as overflights were settled in 1966–7.

Yet however much de Gaulle had trailed it, the announcement was sudden and brutal. Even France's ambassador to Washington was not warned.[129] De Gaulle's tight programme meant that NATO had a single year to empty some 30 bases, evacuate 27,000 servicemen and 37,000 dependents, and remove 700,000 tons of equipment, with an extra six months to move headquarters to Brussels.[130] Even though French forces on the ground remained in position, NATO planners could not know from 1 July 1966 which, if any, might be available in a war.[131] And even if NATO managed to limit the damage, it was clear that if every ally (the West Germans, for example) imitated de Gaulle, the Atlantic Alliance would be finished.[132]

This inspired little respect among the NATO allies. The British defence expert Sir Michael Quinlan later recalled that British policymakers viewed their French counterparts with sentiments bordering on contempt.[133] Johnson's restrained reaction was shaped by his calculation that de Gaulle would not last forever and Franco-American relations could be placed on hold in the meantime. The West Germans, meanwhile, were irritated at not having been consulted under the provisions of the 1963 treaty, and by the uncertainty surrounding the presence of French troops on German soil.[134]

France's relations with the major Western allies had hardly been set fair before 1966, but the NATO withdrawal further isolated de Gaulle from them. But the withdrawal also enhanced his standing with the Third World at a time of American unpopularity owing to Vietnam; and it suggested to Moscow that France was an independent power with which the Soviets could do business.[135] In the next phase of his grand design, de Gaulle was looking East.

The zenith, 1966–1968

The following two years saw de Gaulle's independent foreign policy at its zenith. The Cold War, de Gaulle claimed in a broadcast of 31 December 1966, was 'in process of disappearing', opening up new opportunities for 'détente, and then entente and finally co-operation', which would place Europe 'once more at the forefront of human progress'.[136] De Gaulle had talked to Peyrefitte of a pivot to the USSR, in reaction to American hegemony, in October 1964.[137] Now it happened, in a series of diplomatic initiatives and visits. At the same time he called, with a singular lack of tact, for Canada's francophone province of Quebec to secure its independence. Even while preaching détente, however, de Gaulle pressed ahead with France's independent nuclear deterrent; indeed, that, in his eyes, was central to the credibility of his enterprise.

Completing the deterrent

An effective deterrent required more than a bomb and some Mirages. Creating one, over the 1960s, mobilised the efforts of some 10% of France's scientists, 60% of its electronics industry, and 70% of its aerospace industry.[138] French researchers grappled with missile propulsion, guidance systems, the miniaturisation and hardening of warheads, as well as reactors and noise concealment systems for submarines.[139] Real spending on nuclear weapons in 1967 was ten times that of 1960 and amounted to 40% of the military programme law covering 1965–1971.[140] The law's aims were, broadly, fulfilled. All 62 of the atom-bomb-equipped Mirage IVs were deployed by 1967. Land-based ballistic missiles were sited on the Plateau d'Albion in Provence from 1971. France's first nuclear submarine, the *Redoutable*, launched on 29 March 1967, entered service in December 1971; three others had followed by 1976.[141] France's first hydrogen bomb was detonated on 24 August 1968. By then French nuclear testing had moved from Algeria to the Fangataufa and Mururoa atolls in the Pacific. 'Mururoa', de Gaulle told Peyrefitte during their visit there in September 1966, 'means invulnerability and therefore peace. It sums up everything we have been trying to do for twenty-six years.'[142]

Not quite independent, France's nuclear deterrent was still built (unlike the British) with minimal American help: 180 kilograms of uranium 235 under a 1959 agreement, some measuring instruments, a single supercomputer, and KC-135 refuelling aircraft – no more.[143] And nuclear weapons were absent from the agreements negotiated with NATO after 1966 – notably the Ailleret–Lemnitzer accords, under which France's two divisions continued covering 'their' sector in Germany and might come under NATO operational command in the event of war.[144]

The deterrent was also underpinned, albeit briefly, with an independent doctrine, the notorious *tous azimuts* (multi-directional defence, or all-horizon defence) outlined by Chief of Staff Charles Ailleret, with de Gaulle's blessing, in the *Revue de la Défense Nationale* in December 1967.[145] This meant, officially, a capacity to inflict unacceptable damage on *any* power on the globe, not just the Soviets. It would deter not only aggressors, but any 'abusive protector' – meaning the Americans, as de Gaulle told Peyrefitte in May 1962; it would ensure, he added in December 1966, that if the 'Germans, the Algerians and the Tunisians ever want to cause us trouble, we'll be able to crush them, easily'.[146] De Gaulle also underlined France's independence by refusing to join the nuclear non-proliferation treaty, signed on 1 July 1968 by the two superpowers, the United Kingdom, and 53 other states. The treaty, he argued, simply froze an unjust balance of forces – but added that France would not share secrets and would behave as if he had signed.[147]

Was France's nuclear deterrent worth it? For de Gaulle, as the American nuclear umbrella was unreliable, nuclear weapons gave France 'her only means of ensuring that no one could attempt to destroy her without the risk of self-destruction'.[148] In addition, they were a guarantee against a resurgent Germany, enhanced France's standing in the Atlantic Alliance, and offered spin-offs in terms of nuclear energy.

Critics argue that France could not afford the deterrent, even that de Gaulle 'sacrificed the economic and educational well-being of a generation of French students and workers'.[149] This ignores the unique window of affordability of the 1960s. Between 1960 and 1969, high economic growth, plus an Algerian 'peace dividend' that cut the military headcount from over a million to 568,000, meant that defence spending in the 1960s as a percentage of France's GDP *fell* from 6.34% to 4.17% – a proportion lower than that of the

United Kingdom and barely higher than that of non-nuclear West Germany. Nor were conventional forces wholly starved. Twenty-five new warships were laid down in the 1960s, and 600 new 30-ton tanks delivered to the army, along with 130 Puma and 68 Alouette helicopters.[150] Education spending, meanwhile, tripled in real terms.[151]

Other criticisms carry more weight. The deterrent absorbed large slices of France's scarce technological know-how. Above all, the capacity of the *force de frappe* to inflict unacceptable damage on an enemy – the very essence of deterrence – was doubtful. The earliest version, which involved Mirages having to be refuelled in mid-air by KC-135s and then fly to their targets at tree height, at twice the speed of sound, to avoid Soviet radar, was clearly the least credible.[152] More surprisingly, Howorth considered the much more sophisticated deterrent of the mid-1980s of doubtful utility.[153] The *force de frappe* also relied on constant access to NATO's early warning system, NADGE, negotiated in 1967 in return for the right of NATO aircraft to use French airspace.[154] As Johnson's National Security Adviser Walt Rostow argued, 'The *force de frappe* is deaf, dumb and blind without our help.'[155] His predecessor Bundy, writing in 1990, was more brutal still: 'No neighbour is awed by [France's nuclear weapons], and no ally made more respectful.'[156]

Fortunately, the *force de frappe* has never been tested in use. Its power as a deterrent cannot be quantified. Nor can de Gaulle's claim that it somehow loosened Cold War tensions in Europe.[157] We are left with justifications based more on internal politics, or even psychology, than on deterrence. For de Gaulle, how could France be 'in the first rank' without nuclear weapons? And how could he, having lived through June 1940, not equip France with the most powerful defences available? More broadly, argues Cerny, nuclear weapons 'enhanced not so much French prestige abroad but Gaullist prestige at home', giving the armed forces a new post-Algeria mission and releasing the French from a sense of dependence on US science and technology.[158] Perhaps Bundy put it most simply, though also most subjectively, when he wrote that for the British and the French, the chief aim was 'to have a kind of power without which these two ancient sovereign powers could not truly be themselves'.[159]

Soviets and satellites

De Gaulle's press conference of 23 July 1964 effectively put the Élysée Treaty with West Germany on hold. Weeks later he began France's pivot towards the USSR and its satellites.[160] Finance Minister Valéry Giscard d'Estaing signed a trade agreement with the Soviets on 30 October 1964. In March 1965, after Peyrefitte had visited Moscow, the Soviets sent Valerian Zorin, a Communist Central Committee member, as ambassador to Paris, and adopted the French SECAM colour television system in preference to the German-developed PAL. Soviet Foreign Minister Andrei Gromyko visited France in April 1965, and Couve de Murville returned the visit in the autumn. On 31 March 1966, just after the NATO withdrawal, French Communist leader Waldeck Rochet even got de Gaulle's name applauded at the PCF congress.[161] Meanwhile the foreign ministers of all the Eastern bloc satellites, plus the Polish President and the Romanian Prime Minister, visited Paris in 1964 and 1965, and Couve visited Bucharest, Sofia, Warsaw, Prague, and Budapest, in April–July 1966.[162] The climax of this Eastern bloc honeymoon was de Gaulle's state visit to the Soviet Union between 20 June and 1 July 1966, followed by trips to Poland in September 1967 and Romania in May 1968.

Underlying these initiatives lay four beliefs, repeatedly expressed in public and in private by de Gaulle. Communism as a dynamic ideology was finished; the USSR would eventually slacken its grip on its own people and on the satellites; Soviet efforts to loosen up would need encouraging, starting with cultural, economic, technical, scientific, and touristic exchanges; and the Soviets needed reassurance that the West, especially West Germany, did not threaten their security.[163] That would allow the Gaullist triptych of 'détente, entente, cooperation' to operate. The Soviets would release their satellite states, reuniting both Europe and, finally, Germany; US troops would leave Europe, though the United States would remain as an ultimate underwriter of European security. And France would play a central role in the process – as guarantor of Soviet good behaviour to the Germans, and of Germany's peaceful intentions to Moscow.[164]

Not that de Gaulle expected a speedy transformation. There was certainly common ground with the Soviets on Vietnam, on the need for a non-nuclear Germany with its eastern border on the Oder–Neisse line, or even on the unwisdom of any rush to German unification.[165] But his ambitions for 1966 were limited: 'I shan't refuse their polite gestures', he told Adenauer in March, 'but I shan't reach any fundamental political agreement with them. We'll probably improve scientific and cultural relations.'[166]

His caution was justified. The trio who had toppled Khrushchev in 1964 (Leonid Brezhnev, Alexei Kosygin, and Nicolai Podkorny) had no interest in de Gaulle's ambitions for a new international order.[167] But they did seek to ease the Americans out of Europe; to develop technology transfer from Western countries; to win international recognition for East Germany; and to convene a European conference on security and co-operation, without the Americans. From this perspective, France was an attractive partner: semi-detached, apparently, from the Atlantic Alliance, firm on Oder–Neisse and on Germany's non-nuclear status, and distinctly cooler towards West Germany than in 1963.[168] The Soviets also expected propaganda gains from de Gaulle's visit: to maximise Franco-Soviet convergences, to contrast warm Franco-Soviet relations with the hostile 'Atlanticist' project, and to highlight social forces in France led by the PCF as the motor of de Gaulle's policy.[169]

De Gaulle was therefore treated to a spectacular visit to the USSR. He slept at the Kremlin, visited the Baïkonour cosmodrome, gave a speech at Lomonossov University, and spoke live on Soviet television – all unprecedented privileges for a Western leader.[170] At the university, he called for a 'new alliance between France and Russia' based on 'Culture, science and progress'.[171] Twice, on 30 June, he referred publicly to 'the union of our whole Europe' or 'the union of our Europe from one end to the other'.[172] As usual, he spoke without notes, and added a few carefully rehearsed sentences in his hosts' language. Contacts with ordinary Russians were warmer than in 1944. But he disappointed his hosts. The United States, he insisted, must be party to a German settlement; any conference on European security therefore required US participation. He would neither recognise East Germany, which he considered an artificial creation, nor sign a formal treaty, though the Soviets had one ready.[173]

The visits to Eastern Europe produced similarly muted results. In Poland in September 1967, where 48 years earlier he had helped fight the Russians, de Gaulle was greeted by enthusiastic crowds – which the authorities tried to keep away. When he talked of Poland 'regaining the full disposal of herself' in international relations,

Communist First Secretary Wladislav Gomulka pointedly replied that 'the Soviet alliance is the cornerstone of Poland's policy'.[174] His repeated insistence on the Oder–Neisse border pleased the Poles but irritated the Germans, while the Soviets feared that de Gaulle had encouraged Polish anti-Communists.[175] The visit to Romania on 14–18 May 1968 was also a popular success with few diplomatic results. Romania's dictator, Nicolai Ceausescu, had distanced himself from Moscow more than any other Warsaw Pact leader; but at a time of great tension in the Eastern bloc as speculation grew about Soviet reactions to the 'Prague spring', both he and de Gaulle refrained from talking about demolishing the Iron Curtain.[176]

In the short-to-medium term, de Gaulle's eastern approaches therefore yielded modest outcomes. University and cultural exchanges developed after the Soviet visit.[177] Eastern bloc countries, like the Soviets, adopted SECAM. France was the Soviets' prime Western space partner till the 1980s.[178] Franco-Soviet trade trebled between 1966 and 1974. But the cultural exchanges were soon emulated by other countries, especially the United States. Franco-Soviet exchanges seldom exceeded 2% of total French foreign trade.[179] And Italian Fiats, not French Renaults, were mass-built under licence in the Soviet Union.

As for the political fall-out, the 1966 Soviet visit was a climax, not a beginning.[180] Certainly, French and Soviets shared broadly pro-Arab positions during and after the Six-Day War, and Couve, Pompidou, and Messmer all visited Moscow in the ensuing year. But the French did not support the Soviet UN resolution naming Israel as the aggressor, nor the Soviets France's call for a four-power conference. Certainly, détente seemed to be on everyone's lips after de Gaulle's Soviet visit. Lyndon Johnson placed it at the heart of a speech given on 7 October 1966; the Harmel Report, adopted unanimously by the Atlantic Council on 14 December 1967, enshrined it as part of NATO strategy. Willy Brandt, as West German Foreign Minister from November 1966, opened a new *Ostpolitik* that built closer relations with Eastern bloc countries. And a conference on European Security and Co-Operation, including the United States and Canada, concluded the historic Helsinki Accords in 1975. But these initiatives did not simply flow from de Gaulle's. He was not alone in pursuing détente, and the type of détente they embodied was emphatically not his. The role of guarantor to both Germans and Soviets that he sought for France never attracted either potential partner, and by mid-1967 the Soviets viewed the United States and West Germany as more useful interlocutors. De Gaulle had sought the dissolution of blocs; the Helsinki Accords confirmed bipolarity by aiming at the reduction of tensions between blocs rather than their disappearance.[181]

A new front: Quebec, 24 July 1967

De Gaulle made his most extravagant foreign policy gesture on 24 July 1967, during a visit to Quebec. There, in a 328-word speech to rapturous crowds from the balcony of Montreal Town Hall, he described the atmosphere on his triumphal drive along the banks of the St Lawrence river as 'similar to the Liberation', and closed with 'Vive le Québec Libre' – proposing, in effect, the secession of part of Canada's sovereign territory.[182] Canada's federal government, which he had implicitly compared to occupying Nazis, promptly cancelled de Gaulle's visit to Ottawa. He managed one more speech, at Montreal University on 26 July, in which he warned of 'a colossal neighbour, whose very size threatens your identity'.[183] Then he flew home, later telling Foccart that 'I'd rather die than go to Ottawa and drink a toast to the Queen of England.'[184]

An underdeveloped province, Quebec had lived under the sovereignty of British Canada since the Treaty of Paris of 1763. Its inhabitants' French language and heritage were barely recognised. During the war years the Québécois, unlike the Anglophone Canadians, were staunch Pétainists, associating de Gaulle with the British.[185] Visiting Canada in 1960, de Gaulle never raised the status of Quebec publicly.[186] Yet it was then, apparently, that he formed the view that 'Canada is split into two radically different ethnic communities', and that France had a two-centuries-old obligation to help the Québécois assert their French identity.[187] Over the following years the Quebec Prime Minister Jean Lesage was received in Paris with honours equivalent to those of a head of state; Quebec's representation there acquired quasi-diplomatic status. In 1963 de Gaulle was already telling Peyrefitte that Quebec would end up separating from 'English' Canada.[188] Lesage's successor Daniel Johnson visited Paris in May 1967 to prepare de Gaulle's trip – for which 300,000 French and Quebec flags would be distributed among the *Québécois*, but no Canadian ones.[189]

The Montreal speech was anything but improvised. 'A calculated provocation', in Guichard's words, it had ambitious long-term aims.[190] De Gaulle quickly instructed Peyrefitte to establish a big education and research programme with Quebec.[191] He told his government that the Québécois were 'part of the French people' who needed France's help to change their relations with 'English' Canada. At his press conference of 27 November, he called for a 'complete reorganisation' of the federation of Canada to accommodate Quebec as an independent sovereign state.[192] Peyrefitte was charged with preparing a treaty with Quebec comparable to the Élysée Treaty with West Germany. This would treat Quebec as sovereign and create a fait accompli.[193]

The results fell well below these vaulting ambitions. Among de Gaulle's own ministers, assembled as usual at the airport to meet him on 27 July, most were doubtful about the speech. Couve said privately that it 'could only lead to disaster'; Pompidou compared de Gaulle to 'a child playing with matches'.[194] Daniel Johnson himself refused any treaty, considering that de Gaulle had shifted Quebec's position forward 20 years but was now moving too fast.[195] Quebec's ambition for cultural independence, supported by Johnson and surely reinforced by de Gaulle's visit, was fulfilled with the adoption of French as the province's sole official language in 1977. A Franco-Québécois youth office was established and Quebec's representatives began to participate in international francophone events alongside France's former African colonies. But the *Québécois* were twice given the opportunity to choose sovereignty by referendum, in 1980 and 1995, and twice refused.

Other Western leaders greeted the Montreal speech with resignation: de Gaulle would not last forever. Their view would doubtless have been reinforced if they had heard him tell Foccart, in May 1968, that France needed to 'take back' not just Quebec, but Mauritius, the Channel Islands and 'all the territories that England has filched from us'.[196]

Foreign policy at home

For much of his presidency, the French supported de Gaulle's foreign policy. IFOP polls indicated that 48% of respondents were satisfied with it on average in 1965, against just 19% dissatisfied (and 33% of Don't knows); in 1966 and 1967, the positive figure reached 51%, peaking at 57% (and only 12% dissatisfied) in June 1967. But then the approval rating dropped below 50%, and in February 1968 to 41%, with 32% dissatisfied.[197]

These ratings were high because de Gaulle was giving the French what they (mostly) wanted. From 1952 to 1957, relative or (increasingly) absolute majorities of poll respondents already wanted France to be on neither side in the Cold War – and American troops to leave France. The idea of a 'united Europe independent of the United States' also attracted clear pluralities or better between 1962 and 1967; in May 1967, only 29% of the French thought that France and the United States had common interests; 46% thought the opposite.[198]

Yet on specific aspects of de Gaulle's foreign policy the French showed scepticism. Asked in May 1964 if France should be a leading world power or play a more modest role, they divided evenly, 42% favouring each option.[199] Above all, they divided on the *force de frappe*, with narrow majorities or none at all, between 1962 and 1966, believing that France should have it.[200] A majority, too, was sceptical, at least in 1963, about whether France could afford it, and whether it really gave France security and independence.[201] And strong majorities opposed nuclear tests in Mururoa in 1966, 1967, and 1968.[202]

This pattern of broad approval of de Gaulle's foreign policy, with scepticism about specifics, gave way to a more general scepticism from 1967. Two events in mid-year tipped the balance. One was the Israeli-Arab War, the ensuing arms embargo, and the remarks about Jews in the November 1967 press conference, which only a small majority even of Gaullists approved.[203] The other was the Quebec speech, disapproved of by 45% in August 1967 and by smaller pluralities thereafter.[204] These appear to have broken the foreign policy spell. At the end of 1965, 46% of the French thought French policy could be politically independent, but this fell to 34% in January 1968; for economic independence, the figure fell from 41% to 26%, for military independence, from 31% to 28%.[205] For a president whose strongest suit was foreign policy, and who placed national independence at the heart of his ambition, these changes were damaging – as the year 1968 would demonstrate. Part of the explanation for that year's May events was that the French were 'no longer ready to make sacrifices' for de Gaulle's foreign policy.[206] But the events themselves also made an independent foreign policy much harder to pursue.

Returning to the fold? 1968–1969

The year 1968 began well. On 31 March President Johnson announced a halt to the bombing of North Vietnam and a willingness to negotiate with its government, an initiative de Gaulle immediately hailed as 'an act of reason and political courage'.[207] Peace talks started in Paris in May. But two events of 1968 dramatically undermined de Gaulle's foreign policy: the near-general strike of May, and the Warsaw Pact invasion of Czechoslovakia on 21 August. A pivot westwards followed from the autumn.

Paris and Prague, May–August 1968

The strikes of May 1968 caused short-term disruption and long-term costs for France's economy. Big wage rises (including 35% on the minimum wage) fuelled inflation and caused downward pressure on the franc, which had kept its exchange value since 1958. France had, in any case, suffered a major setback in the 'Gold War' after other European countries had accepted, against French preferences, the American introduction of a two-tier gold price in March 1968.[208] A third of France's gold reserves were spent defending the franc, leaving de Gaulle without the means to challenge the dollar.[209] Moreover, when the franc was directly threatened with devaluation in November 1968, it was the Americans who intervened in its favour; the West Germans' refusal to assist was a sign of growing German dominance within Europe's economy which the French would find hard to resist. The fall-out of May 1968 all but wrecked the bases for de Gaulle's independent economic and monetary policy.[210]

Wage rises and the need to divert spending to calm domestic discontents also squeezed the defence budget. Defence spending fell from 20% to 17.8% of France's total budget in 1969, leading to delays of a year to ongoing programmes and significant reductions to future ones including the development of intercontinental ballistic missiles.[211] Strategic revision went apace with the cuts: *tous azimuts* was quietly dropped, and something resembling the NATO doctrine of flexible response was rehabilitated.[212]

If May 1968 undermined de Gaulle's foreign and defence posture materially, events in Prague did so morally and strategically. Since January Alexander Dubček, Czechoslovakia's new Communist Party leader, had undertaken an ambitious process of liberalisation. Even de Gaulle felt Dubček was going too fast for comfort; and Soviet Defence Minister Gretchkov warned Messmer that contagion from what had become known as the Prague Spring risked breaking up the Warsaw Pact, which the Soviets could not accept.[213] Warsaw Pact troops duly invaded on 21 August, closing down the Prague Spring and deposing Dubček. De Gaulle reacted on 24 August with a tough communiqué attacking the invasion as contrary to international law, détente, national self-determination, and peace.[214] At his press conference of 9 September, he underlined his own absence from the Yalta conference, where, supposedly, Europe had been divided in two, but went on to state that in pursuing détente,

> We were indicating to the great Russian people – whom the French people has throughout history, for rational and emotional reasons, considered its appointed friend – that all of Europe expects from it something quite different and much better than seeing it shut itself in and chain its satellites behind the walls of a crushing totalitarianism.[215]

Prague notwithstanding, he concluded, détente would continue. The fact was, however, that while the invasion of Czechoslovakia did no long-term harm to Lyndon Johnson's type of détente – peaceful coexistence between two still-intact blocs – it effectively killed off de Gaulle's. A central tenet of his foreign policy – that the Soviets would loosen their hold over Eastern Europe – simply collapsed. Communism might be finished as an ideology, as de Gaulle claimed, but it was so woven into the structure of Soviet power internally, and of Soviet power over its satellites externally, that a challenge such as Dubček's represented an intolerable threat.

Suddenly, as Kolodziej remarks, the French became more concerned about retaining 'American military power as a deterrent to Soviet military or diplomatic expansion in Europe'.[216] A strategic approchement with the West followed. Talks even began with

NATO's supreme commander in Europe, General Lyman Lemnitzer, about co-ordinating future use of French and NATO tactical nuclear weapons.[217] In November 1968, the French redeployed naval vessels from the Atlantic in support of NATO against the Soviet naval build-up in the Mediterranean. And de Gaulle extended France's membership of the Atlantic Alliance on 4 April 1969.[218] These were practical steps. There were also symbolic ones.

American honeymoon, 1969

By early 1968, a vast, varied backlog of mistrust had accumulated between France and the United States. De Gaulle had undertaken a 'multiform and universal' challenge to US power – refusing the test ban and non-proliferation treaties, recognising Communist China, encouraging Latin America to break loose from US hegemony, disputing the anchor role of the US dollar, condemning the Vietnam War, leaving NATO, backing Quebec against Canada and the Arabs against Israel.[219] The French and the Americans bugged and spied on one another. De Gaulle called NATO a protectorate while relying (in the Americans' view) on NATO's protection.[220] These things were compounded by a cultural difference: de Gaulle played balance-of-power politics, while the Americans 'tended to consider foreign policy a matter of friendships and moral stances'.[221] Might the election of Richard Nixon, a president more attuned to balance-of-power politics, disperse some of the mistrust?

Franco-American relations did in any case improve slowly during 1968, helped by the suspension of American bombing of North Vietnam. Shortly after the devaluation crisis, de Gaulle and Johnson exchanged friendly telegrams for de Gaulle's 78th birthday.[222] But Nixon was different. De Gaulle had regularly received the former vice-president in the Élysée during his years out of office from 1961. Nixon, Kolodziej argues, was a 'Gaullist', who put national interest before ideology, avoided moralising in foreign affairs, recognised divergent national interests, did détente, and (eventually) ended US involvement in Vietnam.[223] His National Security Adviser Henry Kissinger would later refer to de Gaulle as 'a truly astonishingly great man'.[224] Nixon called his visit to France, from 28 February to 2 March 1969 the 'high point' of his opening European tour.[225] He saw de Gaulle's more self-confident France as an asset to US interests, and a loyal member of the Atlantic Alliance even outside NATO. The *force de frappe* was no longer a problem. Co-operation on nuclear weapons research even began after de Gaulle's departure.[226] Nixon actually asked de Gaulle for advice, or pretended to, on détente and on relations with China. And de Gaulle agreed to visit the United States, early in 1970.[227]

In fact he travelled to Washington at the end of March 1969, for Eisenhower's funeral. As usual, he dominated a room full of the world's heads of state and government.[228] But by then de Gaulle had less than a month left in power. Whether the improvement in relations could have survived Nixon's bombing campaign against Cambodia from 1969, or his destruction of the Bretton Woods system in 1971, supposing de Gaulle had survived politically and physically, is an open question.

Conclusion

At first sight de Gaulle's foreign policy looks like a catalogue of failures. The international system of the 1970s remained bipolar: he had failed to reconfigure the world, or Europe, or prise open the Soviet grip on the Eastern bloc. Nor did he achieve any fundamental reform of NATO, or turn Western Europe (or even West Germany) into French allies independent of the United States. He emancipated neither Quebec nor anywhere else. He neither stopped war nor achieved peace in the Middle East. He may not even have built a nuclear deterrent that deterred.

The achievements appeared largely negative. He helped block Soviet pressure on Berlin, helped wreck the MLF project, and kept the UK out of the EEC. Not all of these blocking actions had wholly negative results. But de Gaulle's fondness for secrecy, manoeuvre, obstruction, and surprise caused his partners lasting and often unnecessary irritation: more pragmatism and less drama might have achieved more of his stated aims.[229]

De Gaulle's failures owed much to his own miscalculations. The international system was more resilient than he thought, and France's power – especially France's economic power – to change it more limited. He overestimated the rise of nationalisms in Eastern Europe and in Quebec. His interpretation of Yalta, and his suggestion of an equivalence between NATO, a freely joined alliance, and the Warsaw Pact, a constrained one, were wrong.[230] Perspicacious in viewing Communist and liberal-capitalist ideologies as cloaks for national interests, he failed to see how easily his own claim of France's special moral standing in the world was interpreted by others in exactly the same way.

A more favourable interpretation is that de Gaulle was playing a long game. 'I am sowing seeds which may, with others, ripen in twenty or thirty years', he told Peyrefitte after visiting Poland.[231] From this perspective, Eastern Europe's (mostly) peaceful revolutions of 1989–1991 fulfilled his dreams.[232] He was clearly right to believe, as few of his contemporaries did, that the Cold War was not permanent. But the manner of Europe's transformation would surely have shocked de Gaulle. France was largely marginalised from it rather than playing the central role he had imagined. There was no convergence of two systems, but the triumph of one over the other, furthered not only by an enlightened Soviet leader but by a ruthless American arms build-up. Soviet Communism did not adjust but collapsed. The type of capitalism that prevailed, red in tooth and claw, was one that de Gaulle believed belonged in the past.[233] And the post-1989 multipolar world would become no less dangerous than the preceding bipolar one.

Perhaps de Gaulle's impact on the world, though assuredly more limited, was still real. As Kissinger observed, he had the merit of posing openly the difficult questions which would have been more damaging if left unresolved.[234] He was surely speaking for his neighbours as well as for France when he invited the United States to reassess US–European relations within NATO. He also inspired a range of politicians as diverse as Willi Brandt, Richard Nixon, Konstantin Karamanlis, Mario Soares, Bruno Kreisky, Yasser Arafat – and even Albania's Enver Hoxha.[235]

However illustrious his admirers, this seems a small result for such a vast deployment of energy. The focus shifts, however, if we turn to France itself. However meagre their results, de Gaulle's policy and gestures were palpably forceful and independent. France, in the words of one observer, was *'dé-ridiculisé'* and had to be taken seriously in the world.[236] Nor did this end with de Gaulle's departure. Charles Cogan's twenty-first-century study of French negotiating behaviour still finds it cast in a Gaullist mould.[237] De Gaulle founded a defence consensus based around France's role as a nuclear power, capacity to project military power across the globe, and readiness to act independently from the United States (most strikingly, in 2003, by refusing to take part in the invasion of Iraq).[238] For Alfred Grosser, he succeeded, at least partially, in transforming a 'nationalism of resentment' – typified by the far Right, from the anti-Dreyfusards to Vichy to the *Algérie française* movements – into a 'nationalism of pride'.[239]

Hence, for his American admirers, 'De Gaulle's most lasting achievement, finally, was a confident France'.[240] Perhaps most remarkably, Nixon, the foul-mouthed villain of Watergate, praised de Gaulle as 'a modern-day cathedral builder' – the cathedral being his idea of France and its acceptance by the French.[241] There are, however, three problems with this view. The first was the gap between the scope of de Gaulle's declared ambitions and the substance of their achievement. The polls suggest that the French were increasingly aware of this from 1967. The second was the amount of time and resources devoted to the ambition – at the expense, it was supposed (with some justification), of the living standards of the French. If forced to choose between them, the French preferred the latter. The third was the problem of Europe. To take on the world alone, as de Gaulle found in 1968, was beyond France's capacity. Europe was the obvious force multiplier. But to lead the Europe of the Six, France had to accept a limitation of sovereignty which negated the *raison d'être* of Gaullism.

Notes

1 'Brouillon d'un manifeste de politique générale', late 1966, *LNC*III, pp. 851–6: pp. 854–5; Stanley Hoffmann, *Decline or Renewal? France since the 1930s* (New York: Viking Press, 1974), pp. 191–2.
2 Étienne Burin des Roziers, 'Comment', in Robert O. Paxton and Nicholas Wahl (eds), *De Gaulle and the United States: A Centennial Reappraisal* (Oxford: Berg, 1994), pp. 422–3.
3 Alain Peyrefitte, *C'était de Gaulle*, vol. III (Paris: Éditions de Fallois/Fayard, 2000), p. 187 (9 March 1966).
4 Alain Peyrefitte, *C'était de Gaulle*, vol. I (Paris: Éditions de Fallois/Fayard, 1994), p. 297 (10 September 1962).
5 Peyrefitte, *C'était de Gaulle* I, p. 380 (13 February 1963); Jean-Marcel Jeanneney, 'Witness', in Paxton and Wahl, *De Gaulle and the United States*, p. 230.
6 Hoffmann, *Decline?*, p. 285.

7 Hoffmann, *Decline?*, p. 312.
8 Press conference, 29 July 1963, *DM*IV, pp. 112–30: p. 125.
9 *WM*I, p. 271.
10 *DM*IV, pp. 152–5: p. 155.
11 Quoted in Frédéric Bozo, *French Foreign Policy since 1945: An Introduction* (Oxford: Berghahn, 2016), p. 1.
12 Edward A. Kolodziej, *French International Policy under de Gaulle and Pompidou: The Politics of Grandeur* (Ithaca, NY: Cornell University Press, 1974), p. 28.
13 Peyrefitte, *C'était de Gaulle* I, p. 284.
14 Garret Joseph Martin, *General de Gaulle's Cold War: Challenging American Hegemony, 1963–1968* (New York and Oxford: Berghahn, 2013), pp. 81–2; Alain Peyrefitte, *C'était de Gaulle*, vol. II (Paris: Éditions de Fallois/Fayard, 1997), pp. 462–3.
15 Martin, *Cold War*, p. 194.
16 *DM*III, pp. 196–200: p. 198. Cf. also Hervé Alphand, *L'Étonnement d'être* (Paris: Fayard 1977), p. 351.
17 Philip G. Cerny, *The Politics of Grandeur: Ideological Aspects of de Gaulle's Foreign Policy* (Cambridge: Cambridge University Press, 1980), p. 187.
18 Jean Lacouture, *De Gaulle*, vol. III: *Le Souverain* (Paris: Le Seuil, 1986), p. 466; *MH*, pp. 257–8.
19 Jean Charlot (ed.), *Les Français et de Gaulle* (Paris: Plon, 1971), pp. 262–3.
20 Maurice Couve de Murville, Serge Maffert, and Maurice Vaïsse, 'Entretien avec Maurice Couve de Murville', in Institut Charles de Gaulle, *De Gaulle en son siècle*, vol. IV: *La Sécurité et l'indépendance de la France* (Paris: Plon, 1992), pp. 221–6: p. 222.
21 C.L. Sulzberger, *The Last of the Giants* (London: Weidenfeld & Nicolson, 1970), p. 61.
22 The word détente started out as *Entspannung* in German, and was popularised by de Gaulle before being adopted by the Americans. Cf. Timothy Garton Ash, *In Europe's Name: Germany and the Divided Continent* (London: Vintage Books, 1994 [1993]), p. 37.
23 Hoffmann, *Decline?*, p. 28.
24 Hoffmann, *Decline?*, p. 285; Cerny, *Grandeur*, pp. 139–40.
25 McGeorge Bundy, *Danger and Survival: Choices about the Bomb in the First Fifty Years* (New York: Vintage Books, 1990), p. 477; broadcast, 31 May 1960, *DM*III, pp. 225–8.
26 Cerny, *Grandeur*, p. 131.
27 Sulzberger, *Giants*, p. 48.
28 Lacouture, *De Gaulle* III, p. 387.
29 Denis Healey, *The Time of My Life* (London: Michael Joseph, 1989), p. 308.
30 Frédéric Bozo, *Two Strategies for Europe: De Gaulle, the United States, and the Atlantic Alliance* (Lanham, MD: Rowman & Littlefield, 2001), p. xvi.

31 Press conference, 23 July 1964, *DM*IV, pp. 222–37: pp. 226–9.
32 Cerny, *Grandeur*, p. 157.
33 Peyrefitte, *C'était de Gaulle* II, p. 20.
34 Broadcast, 31 May 1960, *DM*III, pp. 216–21: pp. 220–1.
35 Sulzberger, *Giants*, p. 51.
36 *DM*III, pp. 129–47: p. 130.
37 Sulzberger, *Giants*, p. 64.
38 *MH*, p. 171.
39 Frank Costigliola, 'Kennedy, De Gaulle, and the Challenge of Consultation', in Paxton and Wahl, *De Gaulle and the United States*, pp. 169–94: p. 172.
40 Bozo, *Two Strategies*, p. 10.
41 Frank Costigliola, *France and the United States: The Cold Alliance since World War II* (New York: Twayne, 1992), p. 122.
42 Maurice Vaïsse, *La grandeur. Politique étrangère du général de Gaulle, 1958–1969* (Paris: Fayard, 1998), pp. 116–17.
43 *MH*, p. 202; *WM*I, p. 89.
44 *LNC*III, pp. 52–4.
45 Richard Challener, 'Dulles and De Gaulle', in Paxton and Wahl, *De Gaulle and the United States*, pp. 143–68: pp. 155–7.
46 *MH*, p. 202.
47 Bundy, *Danger*, pp. 479–81.
48 Costigliola, 'Kennedy, De Gaulle', p. 173.
49 *Le Monde*, 10 October 1960.
50 Peyrefitte, *C'était de Gaulle* I, p. 352 (16 January 1963); *MH*, p. 203.
51 Costigliola, 'Kennedy, De Gaulle', p. 174; *LNC*III, pp. 444–6.
52 Bundy, *Danger*, p. 482.
53 Sulzberger, *Giants*, pp. 586–7.
54 Kolodziej, *French International Policy*, p. 74.
55 Vaïsse, *La Grandeur*, pp. 123–4; Challener, 'Dulles and de Gaulle', pp. 159–61.
56 Bozo, *Two Strategies*, pp. 44–5.
57 Maurice Couve de Murville, *Une Politique étrangère, 1958–1969* (Paris: Plon, 1971), p. 77; *DM*III, pp. 82–96: pp. 92–3; Sulzberger, *Giants*, p. 551; Vaïsse, *La Grandeur*, p. 130.
58 *LNC*III, pp. 148–50, 173–5; Bozo, *French Foreign Policy*, p. 51.
59 Vaïsse, *La Grandeur*, p. 133; Bozo, *Two Strategies*, pp. 37, 66.
60 *DM*III, pp. 234–51: pp. 248–50.
61 *Le Monde*, 15 February 1960.
62 Alain Peyrefitte, *C'était de Gaulle*, vol. III (Paris: Éditions de Fallois/Fayard, 2000), p. 101.
63 Vaïsse, *La Grandeur*, p. 56; Wilfrid H. Kohl, *French Nuclear Diplomacy* (Princeton, NJ: Princeton University Press, 1971), p. 19.
64 *DM*III, pp. 125–9.
65 *Le Monde*, 15 February 1960.

66 Vincent Jauvert, *L'Amérique contre de Gaulle. Histoire secrète, 1961–1969* (Paris: Le Seuil, 2000), pp. 49–55.
67 Kohl, *Nuclear Diplomacy*, pp. 106–7.
68 Bozo, *Two Strategies*, pp. 73–5, 77; Frank Costigliola, 'Kennedy, de Gaulle et la consultation entre alliés', in Institut Charles de Gaulle, *De Gaulle en son siècle* IV, pp. 254–66: p. 260.
69 Jauvert, *L'Amérique*, pp. 49–50.
70 Jauvert, *L'Amérique*, pp. 97–9.
71 Pierre Messmer, *Après tant de batailles ... mémoires* (Paris: Albin Michel, 1992), pp. 304–6; Pierre Messmer, 'De Gaulle's Defence Policy and the United States from 1958–69', in Paxton and Wahl, *De Gaulle and the United States*, pp. 351–9: pp. 352–3.
72 Peyrefitte, *C'était de Gaulle* I, p. 164.
73 Lacouture, *De Gaulle* III, p. 391.
74 Peter Mangold, *The Almost Impossible Ally: Harold Macmillan and Charles de Gaulle* (London: I.B.Tauris, 2006), p. 137.
75 Jauvert, *L'Amérique*, pp. 41–2; Peyrefitte, *C'était de Gaulle* II, p. 19.
76 Hélène Carrère d'Encausse, *Le Général de Gaulle et la Russie* (Paris: Fayard, 2017), pp. 152–5.
77 *MH*, pp. 220–34.
78 Carrère d'Encausse, *De Gaulle et la Russie*, pp. 134–44.
79 *DM*III, pp. 216–21: pp. 217–18.
80 Alphand, *L'Étonnement*, p. 385.
81 Nikita Khrushchev, *Memoirs*, vol. III: *Statesman*, ed. Sergei Khrushchev (University Park, PA: Pennsylvania State University, 2007), pp. 214–15.
82 Alistair Horne, *Macmillan 1957–1986* (London: Macmillan, 1989), p. 383.
83 Bozo, *French Foreign Policy*, p. 59.
84 *DM*IV, pp. 61–79: p. 73; Bozo, *Two Strategies*, p. 87; Costigliola, 'Kennedy, de Gaulle', in Institut Charles de Gaulle, *De Gaulle en son siècle*IV, p. 265.
85 Cerny, *Grandeur*, p. 173.
86 Peyrefitte, *C'était de Gaulle* I, p. 380 (13 February 1963).
87 Peyrefitte, *C'était de Gaulle* II, p. 15.
88 *DM*IV, pp. 222–37: p. 233.
89 Denis Healey, *The Time of My Life* (London: Michael Joseph, 1989), p. 310.
90 Bozo, *Two Strategies*, p. 61.
91 Bozo, *Two Strategies*, pp. 123–5; *LNC*III, p. 589.
92 Bozo, *Two Strategies*, p. 110.
93 Robert McNamara, Commencement speech, University of Ann Arbor, Michigan, 9 July 1962: www.atomicarchive.com/Docs/Deterrence/Nocities.shtml, accessed 20 April 2018.
94 John Newhouse, *De Gaulle and the Anglo-Saxons* (London: André Deutsch, 1970), pp. 161–3; Hoffmann, *Decline?*, p. 298; Costigliola, *France and the United States*, p. 130.

95 Horne, *Macmillan 1957–1986*, pp. 329–30.
96 *DM*IV, pp. 61–79: p. 77.
97 Vaïsse, *La Grandeur*, pp. 372–3.
98 Bozo, *Two Strategies*, pp. 118–22; Bundy, *Danger*, p. 494; Vaïsse, *La Grandeur*, p. 151; Costigliola, 'Kennedy, De Gaulle', in Paxton and Wahl, *De Gaulle and the United States*, p. 186.
99 Bundy, *Danger*, pp. 484–7.
100 Horne, *Macmillan 1957–1986*, pp. 430–2.
101 Peyrefitte, *C'était de Gaulle*I, p. 363; Costigliola, 'Kennedy, De Gaulle', in Paxton and Wahl, *De Gaulle and the United States*, p. 185.
102 *DM*IV, p. 75; Éric Roussel, *Charles de Gaulle* (Paris: Gallimard, 2002), p. 740; Vaïsse, *La Grandeur*, p. 156.
103 Couve de Murville, *Une Politique étrangère*, p. 63.
104 Bundy, *Danger*, p. 493.
105 Martin, *Cold War*, p. 3.
106 Bozo, *Two Strategies*, p. 104.
107 Bozo, *Two Strategies*, p. 108.
108 Jauvert, *L'Amérique*, pp. 111–18.
109 Couve de Murville, *Une Politique étrangère*, pp. 106–7.
110 *DM*IV, pp. 112–30: p. 126.
111 *MH*, pp. 205–6.
112 Bozo, *Two Strategies*, p. 114.
113 See also below, pp. 343–4.
114 Kohl, *Nuclear Diplomacy*, pp. 290–3.
115 Kohl, *Nuclear Diplomacy*, p. 295.
116 Kohl, *Nuclear Diplomacy*, p. 302n; Pierre Maillard, *De Gaulle et l'Allemagne. Le Rêve inachevé* (Paris: Plon, 1990), pp. 230–1.
117 Martin, *Cold War*, p. 26.
118 Alfred Grosser, *Affaires Extérieures: La politique de la France, 1944/1984* (Paris: Flammarion, 1984), p. 224; Richard F. Kuisel, 'The American Economic Challenge: De Gaulle and the French', in Paxton and Wahl, *De Gaulle and the United States*, pp. 195–212: pp. 205–12.
119 Costigliola, *France and the United States*, pp. 119–20; André de Lattre, 'Investissements étrangers et indépendance nationale', in Institut Charles de Gaulle, *De Gaulle en son siècle* IV, pp. 149–51.
120 Peyrefitte, *C'était de Gaulle* II, pp. 74–5 (27 February 1963).
121 Jean-Maxime Lévêque, 'Les Conditions économiques, financières et monétaires', in Institut Charles de Gaulle, *De Gaulle en son siècle*IV, pp. 147–9.
122 *DM*IV, pp. 325–42: p. 333.
123 Jauvert, *L'Amérique*, pp. 142–3; Robert Paxton, 'Comment', in Paxton and Wahl, *De Gaulle and the United States*, pp. 417–20; Alphand, *L'Étonnement*, p. 447.
124 Couve de Murville, *Une Politique étrangère*, p. 78; Bozo, *Two Strategies*, pp. 130–4.
125 Alphand, *L'Étonnement*, p. 444 (3 January 1965).

126 *DM*IV, pp. 372–92: pp. 383–4; *DM*V, pp. 6–23: pp. 18–19.
127 Jauvert, *L'Amérique*, pp. 144–53.
128 Bozo, *Two Strategies*, p. xv.
129 *LNC*III, pp. 789–90; Martin, *Cold War*, p. 100.
130 Bozo, *Two Strategies*, pp. 165–6; Vaïsse, *La Grandeur*, p. 391.
131 Henry Kissinger, 'Dealing with De Gaulle', in Paxton and Wahl, *De Gaulle and the United States*, pp. 331–41: p. 337.
132 Grosser, *Affaires Extérieures*, p. 218.
133 Interview with the author, 10 October 2001.
134 Maillard, *De Gaulle et l'Allemagne*, pp. 232–3.
135 Cerny, *Grandeur*, pp. 215, 223; Hoffmann, *Decline?*, pp. 319–20.
136 *DM*V, pp. 128–31.
137 Peyrefitte, *C'était de Gaulle* II, p. 58 (28 October 1964).
138 Edward L. Morse, *Foreign Policy and Interdependence in Gaullist France* (Princeton, NJ: Princeton University Press, 1973), p. 33.
139 Messmer, *Après tant de batailles*, pp. 297–8.
140 Messmer, *Après tant de batailles*, pp. 316–17; Messmer, 'De Gaulle's Defence Policy', p. 354.
141 François Maurin and François Valentin, 'Les Instruments de la défense', in Institut Charles de Gaulle, *De Gaulle en son siècle* IV, pp. 154–60.
142 Peyrefitte, *C'était de Gaulle* III, p. 148 (12 September 1966).
143 Messmer, *Après tant de batailles*, p. 325.
144 Cerny, *Grandeur*, pp. 233–5.
145 Lacouture, *De Gaulle* III, pp. 476–80.
146 Peyrefitte, *C'était de Gaulle* I, p. 290 (9 May 1962) and III, p. 169 (5 December 1966).
147 Cerny, *Grandeur*, pp. 239–40; Bozo, *Two Strategies*, pp. 198–200.
148 *MH*, p. 258; Wolf Mendl, 'De Gaulle et la politique nucléaire', in Institut Charles de Gaulle, *De Gaulle en son siècle* IV, pp. 186–96: pp. 187–8.
149 Irwin M. Wall, *The United States and the Algerian War* (Berkeley, London: University of California Press, 2001), p. 205.
150 Maurin and Valentin, 'Les Instruments de la défense', pp. 154–60.
151 Messmer, *Après tant de batailles*, pp. 261–3, 440; Roger Rhenter, 'Les Données budgétaires', in Institut Charles de Gaulle, *De Gaulle en son siècle* IV, pp. 125–6.
152 Kolodziej, *French International Policy*, p. 82; Jauvert, *L'Amérique*, p. 55; Peyrefitte, *C'était de Gaulle* I, p. 360 (16 January 1963).
153 Jolyon Howorth, 'Consensus and Mythology: Security Alternatives in post-Gaullist France', in Robert Aldrich and John Connell (eds), *France in World Politics* (London: Routledge, 1989), pp. 16–34: pp. 17–18.
154 Bozo, *Two Strategies*, pp. 208–12.
155 Costigliola, *France and the United States*, p. 146.
156 Bundy, *Danger*, p. 501.

157 In his press conference of 28 October 1966: *DM*v, pp. 96–107: p. 105.
158 Cerny, *Grandeur*, pp. 125, 200–1.
159 Bundy, *Danger*, pp. 501–2.
160 *DM*IV, pp. 222–37: p. 230; Jean-Paul Bled, 'Le Général de Gaulle et le triangle Paris-Bonn-Moscou', in Maurice Vaïsse (ed.), *De Gaulle et la Russie* (Paris: CNRS Éditions, 2012 [2006]), pp. 317–25: pp. 320–1.
161 Vaïsse, *La Grandeur*, pp. 420–5.
162 Martin, *Cold War*, p. 105.
163 Broadcast, 31 December 1963, *DM*IV, pp. 152–5: p. 155; 'Réflexions au sujet d'un choix politique et social adapté à la France', July 1964, *LNC*III, pp. 654–5; press conference, 4 February 1965, *DM*IV, pp. 327–42; pp. 341–2; and his conversation with Harold Wilson, 3 April 1965, in Vaïsse, *La Grandeur*, p. 418; Couve de Murville, *Une Politique étrangère*, p. 194; Mendl, 'De Gaulle et la politique nucléaire', p. 189.
164 Grosser, *Affaires Extérieures*, pp. 205–6; Martin, *Cold War*, pp. 107–8; Maillard, *De Gaulle et l'Allemagne*, pp. 249–50; Kolodziej, *French International Policy*, p. 367.
165 Vaïsse, *La Grandeur*, p. 420.
166 *LNC*III, pp. 794–8: p. 797.
167 Mikhail Narinsky, 'Le Retrait de la France de l'organisation militaire de l'OTAN, vu de Moscou', in Vaïsse, *De Gaulle et la Russie*, pp. 257–69.
168 Marie-Pierre Rey, 'De Gaulle, l'URSS et la sécurité européenne, 1958–1969', in Vaïsse, *De Gaulle et la Russie*, pp. 339–64.
169 Carrère d'Encausse, *De Gaulle et la Russie*, p. 195.
170 Jauvert, *L'Amérique*, p. 157.
171 *DM*v, pp. 47–8.
172 *DM*v, pp. 56–8.
173 Carrère d'Encausse, *De Gaulle et la Russie*, p. 201.
174 Speech to Polish Parliament, 11 September 1967, *DM*v, pp. 211–15: p. 212 and n; *Le Monde*, 12 September 1967.
175 Martin, *Cold War*, pp. 155–7.
176 *Ibid.*, pp. 177–8. And see below, p. 317.
177 Hélène Carrère d'Encausse, 'La Russie dans la géopolitique de Charles de Gaulle', in Vaïsse, *De Gaulle et la Russie*, pp. 439–50: p. 449.
178 Jacques Blamont, 'Le Général de Gaulle et la coopération spatiale franco-soviétique', in *ibid.*, pp. 405–23.
179 Hubert Bonin, 'L'Émergence de la coopération industrielle, bancaire et commerciale franco-soviétique dans les années 1960', in *ibid.*, pp. 365–403: pp. 396–7.
180 Cerny, *Grandeur*, p. 182.
181 Rey, 'De Gaulle, l'URSS et la sécurité européenne, 1958–1969', pp. 357–64.
182 *DM*v, pp. 191–2.
183 Grosser, *Affaires Extérieures*, p. 210.

184 Jacques Foccart, *Tous les soirs avec de Gaulle. Journal de l'Élysée – I, 1965–1967* (Paris: Fayard/Jeune Afrique, 1997), p. 685.
185 Peyrefitte, *C'était de Gaulle* III, p. 348.
186 *DM*III, pp. 184–6; *Le Monde*, 21 April 1960.
187 *MH*, pp. 239–40; Vaïsse, *La Grandeur*, p. 653; Bernard Tricot, 'Witness', in Paxton and Wahl, *De Gaulle and the United States*, pp. 234–5.
188 Peyrefitte, *C'était de Gaulle* III, pp. 303, 307 (7 May 1963).
189 Peyrefitte, *C'était de Gaulle* III, pp. 332–6.
190 Olivier Guichard, *Mon Général* (Paris: Grasset, 1980), p. 419.
191 Peyrefitte, *C'était de Gaulle* III, p. 341.
192 *DM*V, pp. 227–47: p. 239.
193 Peyrefitte, *C'était de Gaulle* III, pp. 356–7.
194 Peyrefitte, *C'était de Gaulle* III, pp. 338–9, 349–50 (27 July 1967).
195 Peyrefitte, *C'était de Gaulle* III, pp. 364, 371.
196 Jacques Foccart, *Le Général en Mai. Journal de l'Élysée – II, 1968–1969* (Paris: Fayard/Jeune Afrique, 1998), p. 92.
197 Charlot, *Les Français*, pp. 260–1.
198 Jean Charlot, *The Gaullist Phenomenon* (London: George Allen & Unwin, 1971), p. 58; Charlot, *Les Français*, pp. 262–7.
199 Vaïsse, *La Grandeur*, pp. 355–6.
200 Charlot, *Les Français*, p. 273.
201 Morse, *Foreign Policy and Interdependence*, p. 175; Charlot, *Les Français*, p. 274.
202 Charlot, *Les Français*, pp. 273–4.
203 Charlot, *Les Français*, p. 281; Vaïsse, *La Grandeur*, p. 353. See above, pp. 249–50.
204 Charlot, *Les Français*, p. 281.
205 Charlot, *Les Français*, p. 88.
206 Martin, *Cold War*, p. 191.
207 *LNC*III, p. 969.
208 Martin, *Cold War*, p. 184.
209 Alain Prate, 'L'Indépendance monétaire', in Institut Charles de Gaulle, *De Gaulle en son siècle* IV, pp. 151–3.
210 Grosser, *Affaires Extérieures*, p. 227.
211 *Le Monde*, 1 November and 7 December 1968; Kohl, *Nuclear Diplomacy*, pp. 148, 199.
212 Kolodziej, *French International Policy*, p. 142.
213 Martin, *Cold War*, p. 176; Lacouture, *De Gaulle* III, p. 547.
214 *LNC*III, pp. 990–1.
215 *DM*V, pp. 318–35: pp. 332–5.
216 Kolodziej, *French International Policy*, p. 145.
217 Andrew J. Pierre, 'Conflicting Visions: Defense, Nuclear Weapons, and Arms Control in the Franco-American Relationship during the De Gaulle Era', in Paxton and Wahl, *De Gaulle and the United States*, pp. 279–93: pp. 289–90.

218 Carrère d'Encausse, *De Gaulle et la Russie*, p. 244.
219 Vaïsse, *La Grandeur*, p. 363.
220 *Ibid.*, p. 370.
221 Robert O. Paxton, 'Foreword: De Gaulle and the Americans since 1940', in Paxton and Wahl, *De Gaulle and the United States*, pp. 1–9: p. 5.
222 *LNC*III, p. 1004.
223 Edward A. Kolodziej, 'Charles de Gaulle et Richard Nixon: l'exercice du pouvoir et la recherche de la légitimité', in Institut Charles de Gaulle, *De Gaulle en son siècle* IV, pp. 282–98: p. 283.
224 Kissinger, 'Dealing with De Gaulle', p. 333.
225 Costigliola, *France and the United States*, p. 163.
226 Bozo, *Two Strategies*, p. 246; Robert O. Paxton, 'Foreword', p. 6.
227 Vaïsse, *La Grandeur*, pp. 410–11.
228 Henry Kissinger, 'Dealing with De Gaulle', pp. 332–3.
229 Vaïsse, *La Grandeur*, p. 680.
230 *Ibid.*, pp. 675–9.
231 Peyrefitte, *C'était de Gaulle* I, p. 47.
232 Pierre Mélandri, 'Comment', in Paxton and Wahl, *De Gaulle and the United States*, p. 319; Carrère d'Encausse, *De Gaulle et la Russie*, p. 250.
233 Sulzberger, *Giants*, p. 715; 'Réflexions au sujet d'un choix politique et social adapté à la France', July 1964, *LNC*III, pp. 654–5.
234 Henry Kissinger, in Institut Charles de Gaulle, *De Gaulle en son siècle*, vol. I: *Dans la mémoire des hommes et des peuples* (Paris: Plon, 1991), p. 60.
235 Martin, *Cold War*, p. 198; Institut Charles de Gaulle, *De Gaulle en son siècle*, vol. I: *Dans la mémoire des hommes et des peuples* (Paris: Plon, 1991), p. 5; Sudhir Hazareesingh, *In the Shadow of the General: Modern France and the Myth of de Gaulle* (New York: Oxford University Press, 2012), p. 154.
236 Hoffmann, *Decline?*, p. 331.
237 Charles Cogan, *French Negotiating Behavior: Dealing with La Grande Nation* (Washington, DC: United States Institute of Peace Press, 2003), pp. 14, 87.
238 Jolyon Howorth, 'Le "consensus" gaulliste en matière de défense et l'avenir de la stratégie européenne: un héritage à double tranchant', in Institut Charles de Gaulle, *De Gaulle en son siècle* IV, pp. 196–206: p. 197.
239 Cerny, *Grandeur*, p. 80.
240 Paxton, 'Foreword', p. 9.
241 Richard Nixon, *Leaders: Profiles and Reminiscences of Men Who Have Shaped the Modern World* (New York: Warner Books, 1982), p. 79.

Further reading

Julian Jackson, *A Certain Idea of France* (London: Allen Lane, 2018), chapters 22, 23, and 26, covers foreign policy, as does Jean Lacouture's *De Gaulle*, vol. III, chapters 13–14 and 17–20.

De Gaulle's *Memoirs of Hope* (London: Weidenfeld & Nicolson, 1971), chapter 6, outlines his vision for France's foreign policy. His *Discours et Messages*, vols III–V (Paris: Plon, 1970) cover the Fifth Republic. Maurice Couve de Murville, impeccably loyal to his President, covers the whole presidency from the official viewpoint in *Une Politique étrangère, 1958–1969* (Paris: Plon, 1971).

Studies of de Gaulle's foreign policy are legion. A good (pro-Gaullist) starting-point is Frédéric Bozo, *French Foreign Policy since 1945: An Introduction* (Oxford: Berghahn, 2016), which sets the de Gaulle period in context. Fuller coverage is given in Philip G. Cerny, *The Politics of Grandeur: Ideological Aspects of de Gaulle's Foreign Policy* (Cambridge: Cambridge University Press, 1980), and Edward A. Kolodziej, *French International Policy under de Gaulle and Pompidou: The Politics of Grandeur* (Ithaca, NY: Cornell University Press, 1974), while Maurice Vaïsse's massive *La Grandeur. Politique étrangère du général de Gaulle, 1958–1969* (Paris: Fayard, 1998) is the most complete general work.

Relations with the United States are covered in Frank Costigliola, *France and the United States: The Cold Alliance since World War II* (New York: Twayne, 1992); Frédéric Bozo, *Two Strategies for Europe: De Gaulle, the United States, and the Atlantic Alliance* (Lanham, MD: Rowman & Littlefield, 2001); Garret Joseph Martin, *General de Gaulle's Cold War: Challenging American Hegemony, 1963–1968* (New York and Oxford: Berghahn, 2013); and Robert O. Paxton and Nicholas Wahl (eds), *De Gaulle and the United States: A Centennial Reappraisal* (Oxford, Providence RI: Berg, 1994).

French nuclear weapons are covered in Wilfrid H. Kohl, *French Nuclear Diplomacy* (Princeton, NJ: Princeton University Press, 1971) and, more briefly but excellently, in McGeorge Bundy, *Danger and Survival: Choices about the Bomb in the First Fifty Years* (New York: Vintage Books, 1990); and Institut Charles de Gaulle, *De Gaulle en son siècle*, vol. IV: *La Sécurité et l'indépendance de la France* (Paris: Plon, 1992).

For Franco-Soviet relations, see Hélène Carrère d'Encausse, *Le Général de Gaulle et la Russie* (Paris: Fayard, 2017) and Maurice Vaïsse (ed.), *De Gaulle et la Russie* (Paris: CNRS Éditions, 2012 [2006]).

12 De Gaulle's Europe

'Making Europe', in one or another form, was a recurrent Gaullian theme, from his speech to the CFLN's Consultative Assembly on 18 March 1944 right through the RPF period and into the presidency.[1] A 'European federation' featured in the RPF's 14-point programme for the June 1951 elections; six months later, two of de Gaulle's trusted lieutenants proposed a European confederation in the National Assembly.[2]

What did he mean? In 1951 de Gaulle described his Europe as 'a confederation of states which would constitute among themselves a confederal power to which each would delegate part of its sovereignty' in economic, defence, and cultural policy – to which foreign policy was sometimes added.[3] Initially the confederation would cover Western Europe, but the long-term ambition extended from Gibraltar to the Urals.[4] Britain, initially viewed as vital, became less so; the Federal Republic of (West) Germany, and its Chancellor Konrad Adenauer, soon became the indispensable partners, whose policies would thereby be safely constrained within a wider entity.[5] A council of heads of government, underpinned by a secretariat and a deliberative assembly, would lead the confederation; a referendum in all member states would ratify its creation.[6] It would be independent of but allied to the United States.[7] And France, inevitably, would take the leading role within it.[8]

Meanwhile another European project was taking shape. It would bear fruit, above all, in the 1957 Treaty of Rome and the creation of the European Economic Community by the 'Six' – France, West Germany, Italy, Belgium, the Netherlands, and Luxembourg. De Gaulle's relations with Western Europe from the RPF period to the end of his presidency were to a great extent his relations with this mainstream, integrationist project: his opposition to it in the 1950s, and acceptance of it, with reservations, in 1958; his failed bid to replace it with his own confederation plan between 1960 and 1962; and his rather more successful attempt to draw from the EEC the maximum economic benefit for France while blocking its challenges to national sovereignty. Each of these initiatives, and especially the last, had a durable effect on European institutions and policies. So did his relations with the neighbouring European powers: with West Germany, committed from 1963 to a bilateral treaty with France; and the United Kingdom, quarantined by de Gaulle on Europe's periphery.

De Gaulle and European integration, 1950–1958

The process of European integration began in 1950. It proceeded unevenly, thanks in part to fierce combined (though not co-ordinated) opposition, in France, from Communists and Gaullists. The first initiative, the European Coal and Steel Community between the Six, was signed in April 1951. Ratified in France that December, it came into operation in spring 1953. The second, the European Defence Community (EDC), a plan for a European (including West German) army covering the same six nations, was defeated in France's National Assembly on 30 August 1954. De Gaulle objected to the ECSC because its High Authority, chaired by the ECSC's architect Jean Monnet, was a clearly 'supranational' body, with powers to issue decisions binding on national governments; and to the EDC because no European authority, in his view, had the moral legitimacy to send men into combat.[9] Both projects therefore entailed constraints on national sovereignty unacceptable to de Gaulle. European federalists, he claimed, sought to standardise Europe's varied tapestry of nations: Châteaubriand, Goethe, Byron, or Tolstoy, he told a press conference on 12 November 1953, would have been nothing if they had written in Esperanto or Volapük.[10] On Germany, meanwhile, he remained ambiguous. Broadly favourable, unlike many opponents of EDC, to West German rearmament, he could still launch into anti-German tirades, attacking the EDC on the grounds that it 'leads directly to the political and military hegemony of the Reich in Europe'.[11]

The third, most important, European initiative saw the signature by the Six, on 25 March 1957, of the twin Treaties of Rome. These created the European Atomic Energy Community (Euratom) and, more importantly, the EEC. Both were comfortably ratified by France the following July. The EEC's chief purpose was freer trade through a decade-long build-down of tariffs between the Six. France's government under Guy Mollet had had major reservations, notably about the economic competition France would face. But the treaty accommodated many of Mollet's concerns. The EEC would not be a simple free trade area but a customs union, with a common external tariff; it would include a common agricultural policy; there would be special arrangements for France's colonies; and any state that suffered excessively from economic competition might temporarily suspend the treaty's operation. Moreover, supranationalism, represented by the EEC's Commission, whose members were appointed by member states but required to represent Europe as a whole, was balanced by intergovernmentalism, in the form of the Council of Ministers, who directly represented their national governments; the Commission proposed measures but the Council could agree or reject them. In due course, a system of qualified majority voting (QMV) would apply on the Council, with member states' votes weighted roughly according to population, and a supermajority (of about 70%), being required to pass a proposal. But at first, unanimity would apply on the Council of Ministers: each member state, in other words, possessed a veto.

De Gaulle was initially as hostile to these treaties as to their predecessors, telling Michel Debré in 1957 of his intention to destroy them once in power. Debré himself, in the parliamentary debate, said they meant 'the disappearance of the nation'.[12] But de Gaulle's criticisms were more muted than those directed at the other treaties: though he disliked the supranational provisions, he knew the French economy needed modernisation through competition.[13]

The Rome Treaties came into force on 1 January 1958, with the first tariff reductions due a year later. But an alternative proposal had been floated in February 1957 by the British, within the Organisation for European Economic Co-Operation, the grouping of European states in receipt of US Marshall Aid from 1948. This was a European Free Trade Area (FTA), covering more countries than the Six but with neither agriculture nor a common external tariff – and without the supranational provisions that de Gaulle disliked. The FTA proposal, developed by a committee chaired by Britain's Reginald Maudling, was favoured by the powerful West German Economics Minister, Ludwig Erhard, and, to a degree, by the Benelux countries and Italy.

Whether the Rome Treaties would survive de Gaulle's return to power, on 1 June 1958, therefore remained uncertain. The British, who had stayed out of the EEC, hoped his dislike of supranationalism would lead him to prefer the FTA. They were wrong. Euratom, it is true, was gradually marginalised, all the more easily as none of the Six was frankly enthusiastic about it.[14] But de Gaulle backed the EEC, believing that the Commission could be tamed, that France's economy could and should face international competition, and that French agriculture needed the export opportunities which the EEC offered and the FTA did not. Two visits – Adenauer's to Colombey-les-Deux-Églises in September 1958, de Gaulle's to Bad Kreuznach in November – sealed an agreement with the Germans: France would implement the EEC Treaty if the FTA project was dropped.[15] Pierre Pflimlin, de Gaulle's predecessor as Prime Minister, had raised doubts about France's ability to cope with tariff reductions on the agreed date; de Gaulle's France, thanks to a 17.5% devaluation of the franc in December 1958, and the tough measures known as the Rueff-Pinay plan, was ready.[16]

In its most basic aim, to increase trade among its members, the EEC during de Gaulle's presidency was a resounding success. Between 1957 and 1969, exports to other member states were multiplied by over 4.6 for the Benelux countries and West Germany, by 7.9 for Italy, and by 5.6 for France.[17] As de Gaulle said in 1965, 'I didn't make the treaty of Rome, and would have done it differently, but we made the best of it.'[18]

But trade was only part of the European project. European federalists like Monnet wanted the EEC to develop into the 'ever-closer union between the peoples of Europe' promised in the preamble to the Rome Treaty, in which national governments ceded steadily more powers to supranational, European institutions, and a federated Europe became a partner with the United States in an Atlantic community. De Gaulle's European ideal was very different: less supranational, robustly independent from the United

States, ready to join with eastern states when, as de Gaulle expected, the Cold War division of Europe ended.[19] More crudely, he also saw Europe as a force multiplier for France. 'What', he asked Peyrefitte in 1962,

> is the purpose of Europe? The Six together could do as well as either of the superpowers. And if France can manage to be the first of the Six, which is within our grasp, she could use this as a lever of Archimedes. She could lead the others. Europe is the means for France to become what she has not been since Waterloo – the first nation in the world.[20]

Such ambitions brought de Gaulle into a series of bruising conflicts with his European partners, as he strove to realise his vision of a French-led political Europe; as he tried to develop a special relationship with West Germany that would detach it from the United States; as he fought to get the agricultural provisions of the Rome Treaty implemented and the supranational ones jettisoned; as he blocked the entry of the country he saw as his most dangerous rival for European leadership, the United Kingdom. These conflicts and their outcomes shaped the future of Europe – but not always as de Gaulle intended.

A strong Europe with weak institutions: the Fouchet Plan, 1960–1962

Transforming Western Europe might have been, with decolonisation, the major achievement of de Gaulle's first presidential term. In his broadcast of 31 May 1960 he gave a broadcast outlining an 'imposing confederation', starting with the EEC Six, which would eventually spread from the Atlantic to the Urals.[21] At a press conference on 5 September 1960, he proposed intergovernmental co-operation between West European states in politics, economics, culture, and defence, underpinned by a small administrative cadre and an assembly delegated from national parliaments, the whole inaugurated by a 'solemn European referendum' to give the new structures 'popular support and conviction'.[22] In his end-of-year message to the French, he declared that France would help make Europe 'the greatest political, economic, military and cultural power that has ever existed'.[23] But within 18 months the project had collapsed.

It was not for want of trying to convince his European partners, initially at least. He had talked of the project both to Adenauer and to Italian Prime Minister Amintore Fanfani in 1958 and 1959. He had fleshed it out in a nine-point handwritten memo for Adenauer, after talks at Rambouillet on 29–30 July 1960, and secured Adenauer's guarded assent. He had despatched Couve de Murville to Europe's capitals that autumn. At a summit on 11 February 1961, he persuaded the Six to charge a committee chaired by Christian Fouchet, France's ambassador to Denmark and Free French veteran, with developing the project.

From these promising beginnings spun out 14 months of tortuous, and ultimately fruitless, negotiations. The Fouchet Committee reported on 15 May 1961. A summit of the Six at Bad Godesberg approved its plan in principle on 18 July, and the French unveiled a draft treaty on 19 October, which the Fouchet Committee approved on 2 November. Faced with new Dutch and Belgian objections, the French diplomats revised the draft again on 13 January 1962. Then de Gaulle undertook his own personal revision, wrenching the plan back towards his original project. The Fouchet Committee rejected this draft on 18 January.[24] At a meeting with Adenauer on 15 February, de Gaulle reinstated some of France's earlier concessions, but two meetings of the Foreign Ministers of the Six, on 20 March and 17 April, failed to reach agreement. De Gaulle now withdrew France's support for the committee sitting again. At his press conference of 15 May 1962 he re-used the Esperanto/Volapük jibe of 1953, mocking the ambitions of European federalists, and by implication his partners – and provoking the resignation of five Christian Democratic ministers from the government that Georges Pompidou had painstakingly assembled just a month earlier.[25] The Fouchet Plan was now dead.

It failed because there was insufficient common ground between de Gaulle's ambitious project and the much more cautious approach of the other five states. The Five did not object, in principle, to cooperation, through regular summits, on education, culture, research, and even foreign and defence policy – areas not covered by EEC institutions. This, however, did not amount to a confederation, and there was no enthusiasm for a referendum across the Six to create one. Moreover, none of the Five, not even Adenauer, wished to undermine either NATO or the EEC. Nor did they wish to fall in behind a French-led foreign policy.

Yet these were precisely de Gaulle's aims in the plan. In his note to Adenauer he had already urged that Europe be 'reorganised' around its states; that the EEC Commission be limited to purely technical functions; and that the Europeans 'put an end to the American "integration", which is what the Atlantic Alliance currently consists of and which is contradictory with the existence of a Europe possessing its own personality and responsibility on the international stage'.[26] These ideas reappeared in the September press conference and the December broadcast. More than a plan for co-operation, therefore, this was a bid to enlist his EEC partners in a drive to transform both the EEC and the Atlantic Alliance. In private, meanwhile, he repeatedly told Peyrefitte that among Europeans, 'only France can have a foreign policy', or that 'It is in the nature of things that we should be the first in Europe'.[27]

When, therefore, the negotiations dealt with the remit of the new institutions – whether or not it should include the economy (covered by the EEC) or defence (covered by NATO) – as well as the inclusion, or not, of positive references to the EEC and NATO in the founding text – they revealed a yawning gulf between two radically different approaches. Two other issues further complicated the process. One was majority voting in the new institutions, whether immediately or through a possible later revision. De Gaulle wanted unanimity to be the rule; some of the Five, particularly Italy, the Netherlands, and Belgium, preferred voting by a 5–1 majority. This corresponded to their more supranational preferences – and could make it possible for the Five actually to overrule France if necessary. The other issue was the UK's inclusion in the new grouping, particularly desired by the Dutch, the most Anglophile of the Five, often by the Belgians too. If the new institutions were to cover defence, they reasoned, it made sense to include both of Western Europe's nuclear powers – especially as the UK had declared an interest in joining the EEC in July 1961. This, of course, was hardly compatible with de Gaulle's vision of a French-led confederation.

The final issue that wrecked the negotiations was trust. Joseph Luns, the Dutch Prime Minister, usually backed by his Belgian counterpart, former NATO secretary-general Paul-Henri Spaak, repeatedly sabotaged otherwise agreed texts by demanding the UK's inclusion, irritating the French in particular, who considered he was acting as a British stooge.[28] Inclusion of the British was the issue that broke the final talks on 17 April 1962.[29] De Gaulle, for his part, deliberately hardened the French version of the text in mid-January 1962 by bringing economic affairs back in and removing positive references to the EEC and the Atlantic Alliance. When he sought to compromise again, in February and again in early April, the French position had lost credibility.

De Gaulle later mocked the Five for wanting contradictory things – more supranationality, through majority voting, than the French wished to concede, but also the inclusion of the United Kingdom, of all states the most committed to national sovereignty.[30] But the Five acted largely out of suspicion: either of these options would serve to avoid domination of the new institutions by the French. As Spaak said in the crucial meeting of 17 April 1962: either have a Community without the British, in which case (at least) the way should be open to revise the new treaty in a supranational direction; or have a wholly intergovernmental community, in which case include the British.[31]

De Gaulle's own position was at least as contradictory as those of his partners. He wanted a strong, ambitious Europe, playing a leading role on the world stage, but without the central institutions normally associated with a great power. The only way to square this circle would be for the Five to follow wherever the French led. But the Five ultimately preferred the United States, powerful and distant, as their protector, to France, relatively powerless (still not equipped with a nuclear strike force, let alone committed to using it to protect Europe) and close.[32]

'The General completely failed to realise', writes Vaïsse, 'that this Europe of his dreams was a chimera because France's partners would refuse to join it.'[33] Was de Gaulle deluded, as Vaïsse suggests, or was he playing to a domestic audience, presenting himself as a 'good European' but with little expectation of a successful outcome?[34] Certainly one close collaborator of de Gaulle said that he never mourned the plan's failure; for Debré, Luns even did de Gaulle a favour by torpedoing it. And perhaps de Gaulle came to realise that Fouchet-style institutions would tie his hands: it is hard to imagine him consulting the Five before, say, withdrawing from NATO, as the draft treaty would have obliged him to do.[35] But most evidence still suggests that de Gaulle wanted to succeed: the tone of the internal notes, the appointment of a trusted lieutenant, Fouchet, to head the committee, and even the apparent efforts to make new concessions from February 1962. Why bother otherwise?

If de Gaulle was sincere, however, his negotiating behaviour was highly erratic. He first outlined to Adenauer a maximalist project that stood very little chance of winning acceptance by West Germany, let alone the other Four. Over the next 18 months he allowed it to be watered down, until, on 17 January 1962, when agreement seemed in reach, he hardened his position. After the revised plan's rejection by the Five, de Gaulle embarked on another round of concessions, by which time he had lost his partners' trust. One possible reason for this see-saw performance may be Algeria. The endgame of the Fouchet Plan, early in 1962, coincided with that of the more pressing Les Rousses/Évian negotiations, which absorbed much of de Gaulle's attention. Another interpretation is that while de Gaulle would have liked the Fouchet Plan to succeed on his terms, he always had a Plan B: to focus on Germany on the assumption that others would follow. This was the course he chose in 1962.

France–Germany: the troubled partnership

Adenauer's historic visit to Colombey on 14–15 September 1958 is readily presented as opening an idyll of Franco-German reconciliation. The truth is more nuanced. Franco-German reconciliation began with Jean Monnet, Robert Schuman, and the ECSC in 1950, not de Gaulle in 1958; and Franco-German relations, sometimes strained during Adenauer's chancellorship, were often poor thereafter. Short-lived though it was, however, the idyll had a transformative impact. At Colombey and in the great exchange of visits of 1962, de Gaulle gave reconciliation a powerful symbolic dimension it had hitherto lacked, while the Élysée Treaty of 22 January 1963 gave Franco-German relations a unique and lasting institutional framework.

Since his youth, and his years as a prisoner-of-war, de Gaulle had been familiar with Germany's language, culture, and history. But he retained a deep suspicion of German power, expressed in *Vers l'Armée de métier* and his post-war speeches. After June 1958, therefore, German policymakers feared the worst.[36] The governments of the Fourth Republic, after all, had resolved several outstanding issues: German rearmament was fully accepted, the Saar had returned to German sovereignty, the ECSC was in full force and the EEC about to be. By contrast, de Gaulle's first act on returning to power had been to cancel plans for Franco-German–Italian nuclear co-operation. Colombey, therefore, was a welcome surprise for Adenauer: not just for the cordiality of de Gaulle's welcome but for his acceptance of West Germany as a partner.[37]

De Gaulle's rapport with Adenauer appears to have been an exception to the rule that personal relations were irrelevant to his statecraft: he would not have gone as far with another Chancellor. Between 1958 and 1963 they met one-to-one 15 times and exchanged some 40 letters; they also met after Adenauer left office.[38] To a degree, their characters were complementary. Adenauer's down-to-earth realism, understated manner, and determination (necessary in the light of German history) to remain predictable and thus trustworthy were a foil for de Gaulle's heroic projects and grandiloquent language. And they found much to agree about, beginning with a shared suspicion of Germany's dark side.[39] A close relationship with de Gaulle's France was an asset to Adenauer's ongoing project of Germany's recovery, security, and co-operation within the community of nations; de Gaulle knew that French leadership in Europe required German support to be accepted. Adenauer supported de Gaulle on Algeria for fear of Communism in Africa; de Gaulle fully backed Adenauer's firm stand on Berlin.[40]

Yet there were also many reasons to differ. First, each country was suspicious of any friendly approach by the other towards the USSR (for example, Khrushchev's long visit to France in 1960): such *démarches* provoked sinister memories, of the encircling pre-1914 Franco-Russian alliance (for Germany) and the 1939 Molotov–Ribbentrop Pact (for France). And whereas de Gaulle viewed the USSR as a potential long-term partner for détente, Adenauer, leading the West's chief front-line state in the Cold War, saw it as an immediate and existential threat. Of this, de Gaulle took little account.[41]

Second, it followed that Adenauer, whatever his misgivings about individual American leaders (especially Kennedy) or strategies (such as flexible response), could never countenance the semi-detached relationship with the United States which de Gaulle sought for France and for Europe. The French might back de Gaulle in seeing the United States as an overbearing hegemon; behind Adenauer, by contrast, was a post-war generation of Germans whose experiences since 1945 cast the United States in the role of benign protector. Disagreeing with such an ally was possible; picking fights, as de Gaulle did, was not – and de Gaulle's tendency to pick them without consulting or informing his German friends, as with the memorandum of September 1958 or the withdrawal of the Mediterranean fleet from NATO in 1959, was an irritant.

Third, there was a wide range of differences on Europe. The Germans were in no hurry to implement provisions in the Rome Treaty for the Common Agricultural Policy, or for association agreements with (mostly French) former colonies – both important for France. And whereas, as Couve would write, the EEC was the 'alpha and omega' of any French free-trading policy, the Germans were always more inclined than the French to look further, whether towards EEC enlargement or to new tariff reductions within the General Agreement on Tariffs and Trade (GATT).[42]

Tensions arose, fourthly, from de Gaulle's determination to maintain West Germany in an inferior position. Most obviously, de Gaulle was determined that the Germans should not have nuclear weapons, even if shared with other NATO powers within the proposed American-led Multilateral Force (MLF), which Adenauer and Erhard viewed with interest but the French opposed. From time to time, it is true, the French indulged in 'nuclear teasing', hinting at a revival of Franco-German nuclear co-operation or, more publicly (Messmer in an article in 1963, Pompidou to the National Assembly in 1964), suggesting that the *force de frappe*, though under French control, would 'automatically' be used to defend Western Europe.[43] But de Gaulle remained uncommitted, and the Germans, understandably, unimpressed.[44]

De Gaulle's assignment of second-class status to the Federal Republic had other manifestations, too. Berlin aside, he was lukewarm about things that mattered to the West Germans. While he stated at his press conference of 25 March 1959 that reunification was the 'normal destiny of the German people', he was in no hurry: 'France', writes Garton Ash, 'although sporadically interested in overcoming the division of Europe, was also the Western power least interested in overcoming the division of Germany'.[45] In the same press conference, de Gaulle also declared that Germany's eastern frontier should remain at the Oder–Neisse line, which the West Germans had not accepted.[46] Finally, his foreign policy style, marked by surprises, vetoes, and psychological pressure, provoked a sense of insecurity rather than partnership among the Germans.[47]

Adenauer personally showed great patience with the demanding conditions that de Gaulle placed on France's friendship. He probably accepted that unification was a distant goal, to be achieved within the Oder–Neisse frontier, though he could not say so publicly. Having being ejected by the British from his post as mayor of Cologne in 1945, he was never enthusiastic about the United Kingdom's application to join the EEC.[48] He viewed both Macmillan and Kennedy as soft on Berlin. He worried about flexible response. All this disposed him to a partnership, albeit not an exclusive one, with France. But Erhard, President Heinrich Lübke, the Foreign Ministry, and many within Adenauer's party, the Christian Democratic Union, preferred a straightforward pro-American Atlanticism to Adenauer's 'Gaullist' views. And the Atlanticists' strength grew. When the elections of 17 September 1961 ended his CDU party's absolute parliamentary majority, Adenauer was forced to appoint an Atlanticist, Gerhard Schröder, as his new Foreign Minister, and to promise to leave office himself in two years, by which time he would be 87.[49] If Adenauer wished to seal a lasting partnership with France, therefore, he had to act fast.

The honeymoon, 1962–1963

Nine days after the Fouchet Plan's rejection, de Gaulle invited Adenauer to France for an official visit. This took place on 2–8 July 1962. De Gaulle's aim was 'to consecrate Franco-German friendship'. The tour included a joint parade of French and German troops and armoured vehicles at Mourmelon, and a shared Mass at Reims cathedral, where France's kings had traditionally been crowned. Adenauer was delighted, and even the French public warmed to him a little more than during his previous visit in 1950.[50] During their talks Adenauer accepted in principle de Gaulle's proposal of a bilateral 'political union' comparable to the Fouchet Plan, with the option, set out in a note of 15 July, of a later agreement between the Six.[51] De Gaulle's return visit took place on 4–9 September, just after the Petit-Clamart assassination attempt. In six memorised speeches in German – to Thyssen steelworkers, to crowds in Bonn, Düsseldorf, Hamburg, and Munich, to young people in Ludwigsburg – he praised the qualities of the German people.[52] To officers at the Hamburg military school, he stressed military co-operation with France; to German youth, the change of generations following the 'culpable acts' of the past.

Ten days later, Adenauer received a draft memorandum of agreement, which became the basis of negotiations undertaken in Bonn on 11–12 January 1963.[53] Shortly afterwards Adenauer proposed, not a simple joint declaration, but a full treaty. A treaty, he reasoned, would require ratification by the Bundestag, and would then stand a better chance of surviving beyond his own chancellorship.[54] On the pattern of the Fouchet Plan for which it was a substitute, what became known as the Élysée Treaty provided for twice-yearly summits between President and Chancellor as well as quarterly meetings of defence and foreign ministers, an interministerial committee in each country for European affairs, and commitments to share military doctrines and personnel, to manufacture arms jointly, and to set up a joint youth and education office.[55] The economy, a bone of contention in the Fouchet negotiations, was largely excluded; so, pointedly, were references to NATO and the EEC. The French intention was to leave potential for Franco-German relations to develop and eventually render the older organisations superfluous. The signature ceremony on 22 January 1963 was marked by an unexpected embrace between the two principals – the last big symbol of reconciliation.

The preamble and after, 1963–1969

Kennedy called the treaty a 'very unfriendly act', correctly reading it as an attempt to draw West Germany away from the Atlantic Alliance as it stood.[56] He therefore enlisted (among others) Acheson, Monnet, Erhard, and the mayor of West Berlin, Willy Brandt, to ensure the insertion of a preamble. Adenauer agreed to one so as to ensure the treaty's ratification, which the Bundestag voted, almost unanimously, on 16 May 1963.[57] The German preamble stipulated that the treaty aimed at 'a particularly close co-operation between Europe and the United States' and at 'the common defence within the NATO framework and the integration of forces of countries belonging to this alliance, the unification of Europe following the path opened by the creation of the European Communities and including Great Britain'.[58] Publicly, de Gaulle raised no objection. But he told Peyrefitte that the preamble emptied the treaty of its purpose, and that German politicians deserved for France to switch alliances towards Moscow.[59] In June, meanwhile, Kennedy made a triumphant visit to West Germany, and to Berlin, to show West Germans where their interests really lay.[60] Then the Élysée Treaty 'lay fallow for some four years after its ratification before becoming the basis of Franco-German relations'.[61] And Adenauer left office on 11 October.

De Gaulle speedily played down the treaty. Like roses and young girls, he said in July, treaties only last as long as they last.[62] 'Our alliance', he told Sulzberger on 12 December, 'should not be exaggerated ... This was primarily an arrangement to end a historic quarrel. And this has been done.'[63] By then Erhard was Chancellor – and unlike Adenauer, as two of his ministers warned Peyrefitte, Erhard wanted parity in the partnership with France, German unification as an urgent objective, and access to nuclear weapons.[64] His meeting with de Gaulle in February 1964 was frosty: France's recognition of Communist China two weeks earlier, without any consultation, was a clear infringement of the treaty on an issue to which the Germans remained sensitive.

But the main showdown took place in July 1964. 'I'm off to bawl out the Germans', de Gaulle had told Peyrefitte. In Bonn, his lengthy talk with Adenauer kept the Chancellor waiting: 'I didn't see the time pass', he told Erhard, fooling no one.[65] He then tried to make Erhard choose between allegiance to the United States, symbolised by participation in the MLF, and co-operation with France. But when Erhard tried to press him on whether this meant the sort of nuclear co-operation that the MLF offered, de Gaulle remained non-committal.[66] At his press conference of 23 July, he observed that on a long list of topics – NATO, Eastern Europe, China, the Third World, defence questions, Vietnam, the Common Agricultural Policy (CAP), the future of the EEC – French and German policies differed, because the Germans were insufficiently 'European and independent'.[67]

It was psychologically and politically unrealistic to expect Germany to loosen ties with NATO in return for vague promises of access to a primitive prototype nuclear deterrent.[68] But the 'big sulk' towards Erhard that de Gaulle had promised Peyrefitte lasted the rest of Erhard's chancellorship. The Germans, he told Peyrefitte in November 1965, 'were my great hope. Now there are my great disappointment.'[69] By early 1966 he had decided that it was 'difficult to conceive and to apply a Franco-German policy', and even that West Germany might not be worth defending against any Soviet attack that the Germans 'provoked'.[70] At his press conference of 28 October 1966 he claimed that the Germans had practised, not the 1963 Treaty, but 'a unilateral preamble which changed [its] whole meaning'.[71] His ministers' verdicts were no more positive. Couve considered that by December 1966, the treaty had not laid down the bases for a constructive dialogue, still less for common policies.[72] Messmer recalled, of the regular defence ministers' meetings, that 'we swam in banalities and indulged in military tourism to kill time'.[73]

Erhard fell from office in November 1966. Relations with his successor, Kurt Georg Kiesinger, were superficially better. Kiesinger and Willy Brandt, now Foreign Minister, embarked on an opening towards Eastern Europe, soon christened *Ostpolitik*, which, initially, could be seen as inspired by de Gaulle's vision of détente; at their meeting in January 1967, de Gaulle held out the possibility of a joint negotiation with Moscow on the German question.[74]

Meanwhile, some of the Treaty's humdrum provisions took root. The Franco-German Youth Office began operating youth exchanges which benefited some 7 million young French and German people over the first 40 years, laying the basis for a profound improvement in the two countries' mutual perceptions.[75] Trade between the two countries grew sharply. The treaty-based ministerial meetings continued and developed confidence and a habit of co-operation between, at least, civil servants. Even defence co-operation developed, albeit not at the hoped-for level, through exchanges of units, training, and staff. Outside the treaty framework, after a difficult patch following France's NATO withdrawal, an agreement to keep French troops in the NATO line, albeit not under direct NATO command, reassured the Germans.[76]

These were developments in depth that prepared the long-term partnership. But relations still marked time at the summit. In

February 1968, Brandt attacked 'the rigid, anti-European conceptions of a Head of State [de Gaulle] with a thirst for power'.[77] The following September, de Gaulle blamed German business investments in Eastern Europe for arousing Soviet suspicions and provoking the Soviet invasion of Czechoslovakia.[78] The Germans gave no help during France's devaluation crisis of November 1968. More than any year since the war, 1968 highlighted the Federal Republic's growing economic power and political independence. The following February, Henry Kissinger asked de Gaulle how he proposed to prevent German domination of Europe. 'Through war', de Gaulle replied.[79] Intended seriously or not, it was a sobering comment on the success of his enterprise of Franco-German reconciliation.

The CAP wars and the Empty Chair

French and Germans disagreed not only on the high politics of diplomacy and defence but on the low politics of agriculture. The EEC, still in its formative years, experienced crises over its own development in 1961–1962 and 1965–1966, and over enlargement in 1963 and 1967. Agriculture played a major role in all of these. For de Gaulle was determined to implement fully, and then to defend, the EEC's Common Agricultural Policy.

The CAP, 1958–1964

The CAP took up fewer than 5 pages out of 80 in the Rome Treaty. But by the end of the 1960s, thanks to de Gaulle's persistence, it had become the EEC's major integrated policy, accounting for some 90% of its budget and its legislation.[80] De Gaulle had argued for a CAP in Europe since the 1940s.[81] The issue became particularly important for France a decade later, not just because there was a big French farm sector (20% of employment, still, by 1958), but because French agriculture was becoming vastly more productive, thanks to tractors and fertilisers, and in need of export markets. France's government, moreover, was spending more and more to subsidise its farmers.[82]

All European countries, including the UK, had subsidised agriculture since 1945 or earlier, out of concerns for food security. Creating a common market in farm produce therefore required not merely zero tariffs, as for manufactured goods, but also a Europe-wide system of subsidies. The CAP did this. Under the principles of the Rome Treaty, developed further at Stresa in July 1958, farmers would enjoy protection through a common external tariff, plus guaranteed prices and export subsidies, paid through a European Agricultural Guidance and Guarantee Fund (EAGGF) and financed by import duties. Such a system was inevitably more attractive to exporting countries (chiefly France and the Netherlands) than to net importing countries. As de Gaulle disarmingly put it to Peyrefitte on 8 September 1965, the CAP 'consists, for our partners, in paying a lot more for their food and paying taxes which are chiefly turned into subsidies for our farmers'.[83] Not that de Gaulle held French farmers, at least the prosperous ones who led France's biggest farm union, in high regard.[84] But he viewed the CAP as the quid pro quo for the export opportunities that the EEC offered for German manufacturing.

The countries that would have to pay for it – chiefly Germany – nevertheless tried to delay the CAP's implementation: hence, for de Gaulle, 'we were obliged to put up a literally desperate fight, sometimes going so far as to threaten to withdraw our membership'.[85] He had an ally in the EEC Commission, keen to activate one truly European policy. It was the Agriculture Commissioner Sicco Mansholt, a Dutchman, who in December 1960 secured the agreement of the Six to replace national tariffs and subsidies by European-level common tariffs, minimum prices, and export subsidies.[86]

There followed three steps, during each of which de Gaulle countered his partners' foot-dragging with threats. On 22 December 1961 he told Adenauer he would delay the second stage of the EEC's implementation (including internal tariff reductions, which the Germans wanted) unless agreement was reached on the external tariff, on the creation of the EAGGF, and on the system of guaranteed prices for agricultural products which the EAGGF would finance; agreement followed on 14 January 1962.[87] In autumn 1962, France blocked internal EEC negotiations to prepare the latest round of GATT tariff cuts until, on 23 December 1963, some 300 common rules relating to the CAP, as well as a joint system governing the exchange and marketing of products, were adopted.[88] In October 1964, an official government communiqué announced that France would leave the EEC unless the common prices for cereals and related products, necessary to make CAP operational, were fixed: negotiations were successfully concluded on 15 December. This was immensely positive for the French, who in 1964–1965 contributed a quarter of the EAGGF budget but received three-quarters of its payments, and whose farm exports to the Five quintupled between 1961 and 1969.[89] It was also a major achievement for the Commission, which emerged with enhanced authority and more staff. But it was the last instance during de Gaulle's presidency when France and the Commission worked together.[90]

Hallstein, the Empty Chair, and the Luxembourg Compromise, 1965–1966

The biggest of the CAP wars, however, concerned its long-term finances. Walter Hallstein, President of the Commission, saw here an opportunity to reinforce the EEC's supranational institutions. His Commission's proposals of 31 March 1965 proposed that revenue from *all* customs duties, industrial and agricultural, arising from the EEC's common external tariff should go into EEC, not national, coffers. The resulting budget, moreover, should be controlled by the Commission and the EEC's Assembly (composed of delegates from national parliaments); the member states, via the Council of Ministers, would take a secondary role only. This significant step towards supranationality would coincide, moreover, with the EEC's third phase of implementation from 1 January 1966, during which the national veto would disappear in certain policy areas, including the CAP, as QMV came into force. Hallstein hoped that the French wanted a long-term agricultural settlement sufficiently to accept his plans. He was wrong.[91]

De Gaulle mistrusted Hallstein, whose fondness of the 'trappings of sovereignty' reflected his eagerness to turn the EEC into a federal state with the Commission as government.[92] The French accordingly tried to detach Hallstein's financial proposals from his institutional ones – and faced German, Italian, and Dutch opposition, on the principle that Hallstein had offered an indivisible package. Couve then applied, at the Council of Ministers, the advice he had earlier given to Agriculture Minister Edgard Pisani: to be ready to break negotiations if French interests were not satisfied, and never to trust Brussels.[93] It was Couve who suggested the idea of the empty chair. When the deadline for a settlement passed on 30 June 1965, he not only halted negotiations but suspended France's participation in Community institutions, particularly the Council of Ministers, leaving them, since the unanimity principle still applied, paralysed in principle. 'We must maintain a terrifying silence', de Gaulle told Peyrefitte in July, with the aim of securing not only an acceptable financial settlement but also the weakening or even liquidation of the Commission.[94]

De Gaulle did not long remain silent. At his press conference on 9 September 1965 he called the Commission a 'technocratic, stateless and irresponsible assembly', and its planned financial settlement a 'usurpation', and compared European integration to the projects of Napoleon, Hitler, or Stalin. There was to be no question of QMV coming into force on 1 January as article 43.2 of the Rome Treaty stated it should. This challenge went well beyond opposition to Hallstein's proposals; it now concerned the EEC's whole structure and functioning.[95]

His rhetoric, in fact, overstepped reality; the makings of a settlement took shape late in 1965. From this, the Commission was largely marginalised. If the Five disliked de Gaulle's uncompromising intergovernmentalism, they increasingly felt that Hallstein had overreached himself.[96] The French, meanwhile, were more conciliatory than they looked. French civil servants in Brussels, and the government's European secretariat in Paris, both softened the impact of the Empty Chair.[97] Then again, delay or disunity in the ongoing GATT negotiations was in no one's interest. The 1965 presidential election, meanwhile, had shown a strong challenge from the pro-European Christian Democratic candidate Jean Lecanuet, suggesting a need to mend fences with centre-Right voters. And de Gaulle probably wished, as he prepared to leave NATO, to avoid a fight on two fronts.[98] All this pointed to a compromise.

Resolution came on 29 January 1966, after two meetings of the Council of Ministers in Luxembourg. A draft settlement by Couve, toned down, led to the so-called Luxembourg Compromise: not a treaty change, but an informal and partial agreement in which the French got much but not all of what they wanted. The Commission, though not liquidated, was reined back, both in the text (which, notably, stopped it from publicising proposals for EEC legislation before delivering them to national governments) and in subsequent practice. Hallstein's term as President ended in 1967: he did not seek renewal, and no successor matched his assertiveness for two decades. QMV would still apply in principle (a French concession), but in practice, where 'very important interests of one or more partners are at stake', the Council was expected to continue discussions, with a view to reaching unanimity 'within a reasonable time' – or, for the French, for as long as it took.[99] On paper, this was an agreement to disagree; in practice, unanimity was preserved even as the EEC moved into its third stage. France therefore returned to its Brussels chair in February. And a series of meetings from May to July agreed on a financial settlement to run to late 1969, the full activation of the CAP in 1967, and the completion of the customs union by July 1968.

It was a bruising crisis, and left traces. 'Brussels', observed Ralf Lahr, a key German negotiator, 'operates now only on cash and not on credit'. Trust might be slowly rebuilt over subsequent months – but only until a further crisis shook relations between France and the Five late in 1967.[100] This concerned, not the 'deepening' of the EEC's supranational institutions, but the 'widening' of the Community to new members – chiefly the United Kingdom.

The United Kingdom: two vetoes and Soames

In the Churchillian 'three circles' view of Britain's place in the world – as a transatlantic partner, at the centre of the Commonwealth, and as a European power – Europe in the post-war years came third. The UK joined none of the European Communities at their foundation. With the United States, by contrast, informality, frankness and trust prevailed: American power was viewed as benign and Britain's junior role in the partnership acceptable. Reinforcing Atlantic co-operation was central to Prime Minister Macmillan's 'grand design', which appeared to yield fruit in the renewal of nuclear sharing with the United States from 1958, after a 12-year gap.[101] This nicely mirrored de Gaulle's view of Britain, which he saw as summed up forever by Churchill's statement of 4 June 1944, that the British would always choose the open sea against Europe.[102]

Macmillan had been de Gaulle's leading Allied advocate in Algiers in 1943. But he could never cash in on past services:

gratitude, supposing he felt it, never shaped de Gaulle's policy. So Adenauer was invited to Colombey, whereas Macmillan was not; and by October 1963, when both men left office, de Gaulle had had twice as many conversations with the Chancellor as with the Prime Minister.[103]

Nor did early meetings with Macmillan go well. Visiting Paris on 30 June 1958, Macmillan tried to warn de Gaulle off implementing the EEC.[104] De Gaulle replied blandly that closer economic cooperation with the UK, though welcome, must not upset existing agreements between the Six.[105] Then Macmillan tried to bring de Gaulle round to the alternative FTA plan, offering nuclear assistance (which required American consent) if he agreed and threatening the withdrawal of British troops from Europe if he did not. De Gaulle rightly took this as bluff and rejected the FTA outright on 14 November 1958.[106] Britain went on to establish the European Free Trade Association (EFTA) with six non-EEC countries (Denmark, Norway, Sweden, Austria, Portugal, and Switzerland) in 1960.

Khrushchev's opening of the Berlin crisis, also in November 1958, brought a new source of divergence: de Gaulle viewed Macmillan's reaction – flying to Moscow for talks – as culpably soft. At Rambouillet in March 1960, talks about nuclear co-operation remained dependent on American consent; de Gaulle was equally non-committal on any possible association agreement between the UK and the EEC, and treated Macmillan to bitter reminiscences of British wartime behaviour.[107] De Gaulle's state visit to Britain that April was successful but, at barely three days, brief. He made only two further English visits – to Macmillan's country residence at Birch Grove in November 1961, and to London for Churchill's funeral in February 1965.[108]

Macmillan's half-application, 1961–1963

The de Gaulle–Macmillan relationship did not, therefore, offer a promising springboard for the application to join the EEC which Macmillan launched on 31 July 1961. He had, it is true, given de Gaulle advance notice. But the timing, with the CAP far from secure and the Fouchet Plan in mid-negotiation, was poor. Above all, Macmillan's initiative was oblique: he told Parliament he proposed an 'application under Article 237 of the Treaty of Rome in order to initiate negotiations to see if satisfactory arrangements can be made to meet the special interests of the United Kingdom, of the Commonwealth and of the European Free Trade Association'.[109] On 10 October the chief UK negotiator, Edward Heath, confirmed that EEC entry must not damage British trade relations with the Commonwealth. The UK therefore sought exemption from the common external tariff for 27 Commonwealth products, plus assurances of 'equivalent outlets' in the EEC to compensate the Commonwealth for the drop in their exports towards the UK; association or EEC membership for the other seven EFTA states; and a transition period of 12–15 years before the CAP applied to the UK.[110]

The Five, and Hallstein, and de Gaulle all (rightly) found these claims to special treatment exorbitant.[111] It is, indeed, less surprising that de Gaulle vetoed British entry after 18 months than that it took so long. But a British candidacy was of interest to the Five because the UK was both a big export market and a major power capable of balancing France. And de Gaulle was reluctant to take sole responsibility for a veto while still trying to secure agreement to the Fouchet Plan. So the British candidacy was allowed to spin out – though according to Couve, no serious negotiating happened before May 1962.[112]

De Gaulle discussed the application with Macmillan three times. The Birch Grove meeting, on 24–5 November 1961, achieved no result. De Gaulle was unimpressed by Macmillan's alarmist vision of the consequences of failure, including (again) possible withdrawal of British troops from Germany. Macmillan privately put de Gaulle's unreceptiveness down to his 'pride, his inherited hatred of England (since Joan of Arc)', adding that 'he goes back to his distrust and dislike, like a dog to his vomit'.[113]

By the second meeting, at the Château de Champs on 2–3 June 1962, Macmillan had scaled down his conditions, accepting that the UK would need to enter the CAP sooner and transform its relations with the Commonwealth. De Gaulle conceded that Macmillan's new-found European determination had impressed him.[114] But he remained worried by the effects on the EEC's structure and functioning of the entry of Britain, and possibly other countries, and sceptical about Macmillan's willingness to co-operate with Europe on defence: 'you are coming to Europe but you haven't reached it yet', he told Macmillan.[115] Nor did the two leaders progress on the detail of the British application.[116] The French Foreign Ministry still, therefore, expected negotiations to stall.[117]

The Château de Champs talks were thus a false dawn. The contrast was striking between their guarded tones and the enthusiasm of the Franco-German exchange of visits that followed. By September de Gaulle was telling Hervé Alphand that the British would try to sabotage the EEC from within.[118] Macmillan, delighted at securing acceptance of his plans the same month from the conferences both of the Commonwealth and of his Conservative Party, failed to see that his efforts to reassure them weakened his European credentials.[119] When detailed negotiations finally got underway in autumn 1962, the Commonwealth and agriculture remained sticking-points, with France taking a tougher position than the Five.[120] De Gaulle could afford to be tough: he was free of the Algerian millstone and had just won a referendum and parliamentary elections.[121]

This was the unpromising context of the last Macmillan–de Gaulle meeting, at Rambouillet on 15–16 December 1962. Macmillan travelled to France worried by the cancellation of the US Skybolt missile, which left Britain without any future nuclear deterrent to succeed its ageing V-bomber fleet.[122] He might, possibly, have proved his European commitment by proposing to develop a substitute missile system jointly with France. Instead, according to the British account of the talks (though not the French), he told de Gaulle that he planned to ask Kennedy for the American Polaris system.[123] On 16 December de Gaulle told Macmillan of his fundamental objection to British entry: 'France's weight within the Common Market is considerable. If Great Britain joined, along with the Norwegians, the Danes, and the Irish, no one could say what would become of the Common Market, or of Europe itself.'[124] Macmillan replied, with tears in his eyes, that 'It was not fair to have a year's negotiation and then bring forward an objection of principle.' De Gaulle, Macmillan continued, 'seemed rather shaken'.[125] If he was, he soon recovered. Three days later he told the Council of Ministers that 'I wanted to put my hand on his shoulder and say, like Edith Piaf in her song, "Ne pleurez pas, milord".' The episode soon appeared in the newspapers: as Jackson remarks, 'it is hard to imagine a more calculatedly contemptuous leak'.[126]

The first veto, January 1963

De Gaulle vetoed the British application four weeks later, on 14 January 1963, in a passage of his press conference that was no less categorical for being gift-wrapped in warm words about Churchill, Britain's wartime role, and Macmillan's leadership.[127] He was confident that Adenauer, with whom he would sign the Élysée Treaty eight days later, would not object. When the more pro-British Schröder tried to revive talks, the French formally imposed their adjournment *sine die* at the Council of Ministers of 28 January. The decision was de Gaulle's alone: he had not, for example, told Pisani, who recalled bitterly that he was still negotiating farm prices with the Heath team when news of the veto came through.[128] Couve had urged patience for another few months, by which time 'everyone would agree that agreement was impossible', but 'he wanted to break the negotiations himself rather than allow them to bog down'.[129]

Anyone seeking reasons for de Gaulle's first veto is spoilt for choice. One is simple Anglophobia, and rancour at his treatment during the war. Both certainly existed. Letting himself go in private, he could indulge in an Anglophobe litany scarcely distinguishable from Vichy propaganda, including the Hundred Years' War, Fashoda, Dunkirk, and Mers-el-Kébir.[130] But de Gaulle's emotional impulses coincided with, rather than determining, his statecraft, which he founded on a reasoned appreciation of France's national interest.

Two aspects of the EEC held particular importance for France, and British entry threatened both. The first, which he evoked in detail during the press conference, was agriculture: Britain was having difficulty breaking its reliance on cheap food from across the world, a practice incompatible with the CAP.[131] That the CAP, the most important EEC policy for France, was not yet anchored within the EEC's institutions was further cause for disquiet. While de Gaulle's later claim that 'Having failed from without to prevent the birth of the Community, [the British] now planned to paralyze it from within'[132] insulted the good faith of Macmillan and Heath, it was foreseeable that the British, once in the EEC, would seek to modify the CAP.

De Gaulle's second concern arose from his hopes of making Europe into a military power independent of the United States. British entry, in de Gaulle's view, gravely threatened this. Especially if other states joined, it would beget 'a colossal Atlantic community under American dependence and leadership which would soon swallow up the European Community'.[133] Privately, de Gaulle called Britain the Americans' 'Trojan Horse' in Europe.[134] The Macmillan–Kennedy meeting at Nassau merely crystallised his long-term views. According to Roussel, until Nassau de Gaulle had not despaired of a military alliance with the British that would balance the United States.[135] But the British purchase of Polaris, de Gaulle argued later, 'demonstrated an allegiance outside of that to a real Europe'.[136] Nassau prompted him to veto the British application outright rather than let negotiations fizzle out. For Pisani this, not the CAP, was crucial: 'He was a strategist, not a merchant'.[137]

In Couve's view, had the British taken a strong European position on either of these issues, their application might have succeeded. A clear acceptance of the CAP would have made the UK candidacy hard to refuse; joining France in a nuclear missile force 'would have proven [Britain] was genuinely European'.[138] The British had good reasons for their position on both issues: disquiet at higher food prices, and Commonwealth loyalties, for agriculture, and the greater attractiveness of a viable off-the-shelf product, Polaris, over the uncertainties of a missile project with France, for defence. But both together wrecked their European candidacy.

In principle, de Gaulle's veto was not permanent. The British might, he told the January 1963 press conference, 'moor themselves to the continent' one day.[139] Two days later, he presciently told Peyrefitte that UK entry would come in four to eight years under a rejuvenated Tory government after a Labour one (he was two years short).[140] At the end of 1965 he told the television interviewer Michel Droit that the EEC would include 'one day, probably, England', adding in his end-of-year broadcast that the imminent restart of the EEC would, hopefully, lead 'other neighbours' to join.[141] These were slim, oblique indications. But they were enough to encourage Harold Wilson, Britain's Labour Prime Minister from 16 October 1964, to present a second application.

The velvet veto, 1967

De Gaulle expected, and mistrusted, the second British candidacy, which Wilson announced on 10 May 1967. At his press conference of 16 May he outlined a position previously rehearsed with Peyrefitte and the Council of Ministers: the British had made progress, but significant difficulties remained. The Common Market was not yet complete; the British still needed to adjust their food imports; Britain was not a continental country, and risked transforming the EEC into a mere free trade area; the special relationship with the United States was a problem. To this was added a new objection: the pound sterling had recently shown weakness, and currency instability would disrupt the EEC.[142] Patience might be needed until 'this great people' had accomplished 'the necessary transformation' sufficiently to be welcomed in. But this was not, he insisted, a veto.[143]

This second application was harder to refuse than the first because Wilson, unlike Macmillan, was not asking for special treatment. And although Britain was still buying Polaris, Wilson was showing independence from the United States in his refusal to support the Vietnam War. Meeting on 10 July, the Six acknowledged that the British were not asking for major adjustments or exceptions to core EEC policies, and were ready to explore co-operation in foreign policy and defence.[144] The Five, and the Commission, were thus far more favourable to British entry than in 1963.

The devaluation of sterling, on 18 November 1967, gave de Gaulle his opportunity. At his press conference of 27 November he highlighted the economic and monetary problems of British entry, then questioned British consistency and motives more brutally than in any previous assessment. The British, he said, had first refused to sign the Rome Treaty, then tried to wreck it by creating an FTA, then sought to bend the EEC to their own will with Macmillan's application; lack of interest in the early Wilson premiership had preceded, finally, a second candidacy which still threatened transforming the EEC into an American-dominated FTA. A 'vast and profound mutation' was therefore required before the UK could join.[145] Couve confirmed the veto, against the 'Friendly Five' and the Commission, in December.

At the heart of the veto, observes Ludlow, was that 'Paris perceived enlargement to be a threat to its power'. Britain, with nuclear weapons, a permanent seat on the UN Security Council, and a global network of influence, was a rival for European leadership as the Five were not – and could block the independent political Europe that de Gaulle had again started to hope for after Erhard's departure. The CAP, meanwhile, only had secure finances to 1969; Germany and Italy, worried about its cost, would find Britain an ally ready to derail it. And the French genuinely (and exaggeratedly) feared that the UK would aim to transform the EEC into an FTA in which American capital would buy up European firms.[146]

Coming on top of the Empty Chair episode, the second veto created lasting resentments among the Five's leaders, who no longer believed France's claim that UK entry would damage the Community. De Gaulle, they concluded, would always block both 'deepening' and 'widening' of the EEC. There was nothing for it but to sit out the rest of his presidency.[147]

The Soames affair

Yet within 15 months de Gaulle made a direct approach to the British. The context, by late 1968, had changed dramatically. West Germany's refusal to revalue the deutschmark and thereby reduce pressure on the franc, and the development of Brandt's *Ostpolitik*, both provoked French worries about German power and independence. The UK now appeared as a possible balance more than a threat – and, perhaps too, as negotiations of a definitive financial system for the CAP approached, not as an adversary bent on wrecking the CAP, but as a useful financial contributor and export market. Might not an agreement with the British ease rather than endanger a financial settlement? Michel Debré, loyal Gaullist and Foreign Minister since July 1968, became the advocate of this pro-British viewpoint.[148]

At Debré's prompting, de Gaulle sounded out the British ambassador, Sir Christopher Soames, over lunch on 4 February 1969. As Churchill's son-in-law, Soames inspired de Gaulle's trust – in principle.[149] Might the British, de Gaulle wondered, be prepared to discuss a different European Community, a political concert of great powers with no interference from the Commission?[150] Soames wrote a report for the Foreign Office and got the Élysée chief of staff Bernard Tricot to sign it as accurate. What happened next showed how deeply the Foreign Office had come to mistrust de Gaulle. The British, and especially Foreign Minister Michael Stewart, suspected the French of planning to leak Soames's report, compromising Britain's position with the 'friendly Five'. Wilson and

Stewart accordingly leaked first, showing the report to Kiesinger in Bonn on 10 February, and in writing to the leaders of the other four countries. When *Le Figaro* published an article on the talks on 21 February, the Foreign Office published the full Soames record, commenting that de Gaulle sought to dissolve the EEC. The French rightly viewed publication as a betrayal of diplomatic confidentiality, and de Gaulle was furious. By seeking a form of revenge for the humiliations of 1963 and 1967, the Foreign Office had wrecked what might have been a promising opening in Anglo-French relations.[151] 'Perhaps it is better', wrote de Gaulle acidly on 26 February, 'that any uncertainty one might have had about real British intentions has thus been, most decidedly, dissipated.'[152]

Conclusion

Was de Gaulle the 'good European' who brought the Treaty of Rome to life as a functioning reality, or the unreconstructed nationalist who sabotaged a smooth path towards European federalism? The answer, inevitably, is a bit of both.

Not the least of his accomplishments was achieved outside the EEC framework. Franco-German reconciliation had begun a decade before his presidency, but de Gaulle was uniquely placed, as leader of Free France, to give it exceptional legitimacy, an emotional dimension, and finally a treaty to build on. The Colombey meeting, the Mass at Reims, the speeches at Bonn or Ludwigsburg, and the embrace at the Élysée are founding symbols of a unique partnership. Because no one since 1945 had told the Germans they were a great people, de Gaulle 'exercised a decisive influence for the renewal of German identity after World War 2'.[153] The downturn in relations after 1963 was unimportant in the long term; the de Gaulle–Adenauer partnership set an example which others would follow. The treaty helped ensure reconciliation in depth, and represented a model and foundation when President Macron and Chancellor Merkel sought to breathe new life into the partnership in 2019, signing their own treaty at Aachen, on another 22 January.

De Gaulle can also be credited with ensuring the realisation of the Rome Treaty's most tangible intended outcomes, the customs union and the CAP. Achieving the customs union required de Gaulle not only to make the (quite easy) choice between EEC and

FTA but also to ensure, through the Rueff–Pinay plan late in 1958, that France could face European competition. De Gaulle could take these temporarily unpopular economic measures where his Fourth Republic predecessors could not. The stability he provided was also vital to the relentless negotiations needed to implement the CAP: the Five knew that they would have de Gaulle, and Couve, to deal with for the indefinite future. With the customs union and the CAP underway, moreover, the EEC, with its market of 200 million consumers, could become a formidable player in successive rounds of GATT negotiations.

De Gaulle's successful pursuit of the CAP was perhaps his most double-edged achievement because it promoted a degree of supranationality, around the Commission, that the French appeared to think a price worth paying.[154] He thus created a monster at the polar opposite to his preferences: a close-knit policy community, centred on the Commission's agriculture directorate, drawing in agriculture ministers and farmers' unions, which gobbled up most of the EEC budget, and was impervious for decades to all but the most determined interventions by outsiders, including national governments.[155]

The CAP aside, de Gaulle prevented the 'deepening' as well as the 'widening' of the EEC. The Empty Chair crisis he provoked led to QMV being effectively introduced only in the mid-1980s. This two-decade extension of unanimity promoted a culture of consensus which has continued within the Council of Ministers. The Commission, though left stronger than de Gaulle had hoped, lost much of its role as a political leader and agenda-setter within the EEC to the member states, and with it its credibility as the future government of a federal Europe. For federalists, these blocking actions appear profoundly negative; for nationalists, simple realism. The record of the ensuing half-century suggests that national identities were stronger, and appetites for a federal Europe weaker, than de Gaulle's critics had hoped. Similarly, de Gaulle's double veto on British (and Danish, and Irish) entry may appear either as the selfish exclusion of a rival, or as a necessary refusal of a disruptive element during the EEC's formative years. The half-hearted nature of Macmillan's application lends credence to the latter view for 1963. It is harder to sustain for 1967 given Wilson's more straightforward candidacy. De Gaulle's departure would greatly improve the UK's chances of entry – as part of a package that also guaranteed the future of the CAP and its finances.

Alongside his positive and negative achievements lies de Gaulle's clear failure to achieve a political Europe via the Fouchet Plan. The plan failed because France's partners, especially Belgium and Holland, feared a French bid for political hegemony and a reorientation of European policy away from the United States. All of his private statements suggest that their mistrust was justified. Regular summits of heads of state and government did begin from December 1974, and were later institutionalised, within the European Union, as the European Council. But they only started once de Gaulle and his successor Pompidou had left the scene.

A final element of de Gaulle's record was his style. The unilateral decisions, the threats, the obstruction, the Empty Chair, changed the EEC's culture: as one senior Eurocrat put it in 1964, it sanded away the trust and good faith Europeans had brought to the early negotiations, in favour of a naked assertion of national interest.[156] This might have happened anyway as policy adjustments required to implement the Rome Treaty started to bite. But de Gaulle's – and Couve's – brutality as negotiators marked a brusque change, and inspired emulation by other leaders, notably Britain's Margaret Thatcher.

Writing in 1971, Couve de Murville observed that despite considerable 'technical' successes, including the CAP, the atmosphere in the EEC by 1969 was one of disenchantment and even pessimism. This reflected, in part, doubts about the EEC's purpose and development: what was an acceptable measure of supranationality, which new states might be admitted, and should the EEC be a political as well as an economic organisation?[157] These questions found answers, at least partially, at the summit at Den Haag on 1–2 December 1969. That such a resolution could take place barely seven months after de Gaulle's departure is an eloquent testimony to the blockages that he personally had created.

Notes

1 *DM*i, pp. 380–90: pp. 387–8.
2 Olivier Guichard, *Mon Général* (Paris: Grasset, 1980), p. 279; Pierre Maillard, *De Gaulle et l'Europe, entre la nation et Maastricht* (Paris: Tallandier, 1995), pp. 116–17.

3 Press conference, 21 December 1951, *DM*II, pp. 480–93: p. 481; cf. also Compiègne speech, 7 March 1948, *DM*II, pp. 169–75: p. 173.
4 Press conference, 12 November 1953, *DM*II, pp. 586–600: pp. 587–8.
5 Bordeaux speech, 25 September 1949: *DM*II, pp. 304–10: pp. 309–10; Press conference, 16 March 1950: *DM*II, pp. 344–58: pp. 348–50.
6 Press conference, 12 November 1953, *DM*II, pp. 586–600: p. 588; Declaration, 17 August 1950, *DM*II, pp. 379–90: p. 381.
7 Nîmes speech, 7 January 1951, *DM*II, pp. 401–8.
8 Compiègne speech, 7 March 1948: *DM*II, pp. 169–75: p. 173.
9 Press conference, 25 February 1953, *DM*II, pp. 564–75: pp. 569–70.
10 *DM*II, pp. 586–600: p. 587.
11 Press conference, 28 February 1953, *DM*II, pp. 564–75: p. 565.
12 Jean Lacouture, *De Gaulle*, vol. II: *Le Politique, 1944–1959* (Paris: Le Seuil, 1985), p. 645; Jean Touchard, *Le Gaullisme, 1940–1969* (Paris: Le Seuil, 1978), p. 213.
13 Maillard, *De Gaulle et l'Europe*, pp. 132–3.
14 Michael Sutton, *France and the Construction of Europe, 1944–2007: The Geopolitical Imperative* (New York and Oxford: Berghahn, 2007), p. 126.
15 Maurice Vaïsse, *La Grandeur. Politique étrangère du général de Gaulle, 1958–1969* (Paris: Fayard, 1998), p. 168.
16 For the Rueff-Pinay plan, see below, p. 371.
17 N. Piers Ludlow, *The European Community and the Crises of the 1960s: Negotiating the Gaullist Challenge* (London: Routledge, 2006), pp. 53–5.
18 Broadcast interview with Michel Droit, 14 December 1965, *DM*IV, pp. 422–33: p. 423.
19 Maurice Couve de Murville, *Une Politique étrangère, 1958–1969* (Paris: Plon, 1971), pp. 348–50.
20 Alain Peyrefitte, *C'était de Gaulle*, vol. I (Paris: Éditions de Fallois/Fayard, 1994), pp. 158–9 (27 June 1962).
21 *DM*III, pp. 216–21: pp. 220–1.
22 *DM*III, pp. 234–51: p. 245.
23 Broadcast, 31 December 1960, *DM*III, pp. 266–9: p. 268.
24 Georges-Henri Soutou, 'Le Général de Gaulle et le plan Fouchet', in Institut Charles de Gaulle, *De Gaulle en son siècle*, vol. V: *L'Europe* (Paris: Plon, 1992), pp. 126–43: p. 137.
25 *DM*III, pp. 401–17: pp. 404–9.
26 Note au sujet de l'organisation de l'Europe, Rambouillet, 30 juillet 1960, *LNC*III, pp. 255–6.
27 Alain Peyrefitte, *C'était de Gaulle*, vol. I (Paris: Éditions de Fallois/Fayard, 1994), p. 378 (13 February 1963); vol. II (Paris: Éditions de Fallois/Fayard, 1997), p. 20 (30 January 1963).
28 Maurice Couve de Murville, Intervention, *De Gaulle en son siècle* V, p. 183; Michel Debré, *Gouverner. Mémoires, 1958–1962* (Paris: Albin Michel, 1988), p. 428.
29 Soutou, 'Le plan Fouchet', p. 141.

30 *MH*, pp. 183, 189.
31 Soutou, 'Le plan Fouchet', p. 141.
32 Vaïsse, *La Grandeur*, pp. 188–90.
33 *Ibid.*, p. 178.
34 Edward A. Kolodziej, *French International Policy under de Gaulle and Pompidou: The Politics of Grandeur* (Ithaca, NY: Cornell University Press, 1974), pp. 253–4.
35 Jean Lacouture, *De Gaulle*, vol. III: *Le Souverain* (Paris: Le Seuil, 1986) p. 326.
36 Peter Schunck, 'De Gaulle et ses voisins allemands jusqu'à la rencontre avec Adenauer. Le Problème politique et militaire d'une vie', *De Gaulle en son siècle* V, pp. 325–42: p. 325.
37 Pierre Maillard, *De Gaulle et l'Allemagne. Le Rêve inachevé* (Paris: Plon, 1990), p. 145.
38 Vaïsse, *La Grandeur*, pp. 229, 234.
39 Peter Mangold, *The Almost Impossible Ally: Harold Macmillan and Charles de Gaulle* (London: I.B.Tauris, 2006), p. 109.
40 Vaïsse, *La Grandeur*, pp. 228–30.
41 Berndt von Staden, 'Charles de Gaulle et la politique extérieure de la République fédérale d'Allemagne', *De Gaulle en son siècle* V, pp. 342–52: p. 351.
42 Couve de Murville, *Politique étrangère*, p. 262.
43 Wilfrid H. Kohl, *French Nuclear Diplomacy* (Princeton, NJ: Princeton University Press, 1971), pp. 283–5, 294–5.
44 Alain Peyrefitte, *C'était de Gaulle* II, pp. 112–13 (25 June 1963), 117 (22 January 1964); Beatrice Heuser, 'The European dream of Franz Josef Strauss', *Journal of European Integration History*, 4(1), 1998, pp. 75–103: p. 93; Pierre Maillard, Intervention, *De Gaulle en son siècle* V, pp. 416–17.
45 Timothy Garton Ash, *In Europe's Name: Germany and the Divided Continent* (London: Vintage Books, 1994 [1993]), p. 24.
46 *DM*III, pp. 82–94: pp. 84–5.
47 von Staden, 'Charles de Gaulle et la politique extérieure', p. 344.
48 Couve de Murville, *Politique étrangère*, p. 243.
49 Maillard, *De Gaulle et l'Allemagne*, p. 174.
50 Peyrefitte, *C'était de Gaulle* I, pp. 153–4 (27 June 1962); Maillard, *De Gaulle et l'Allemagne*, pp. 175–6.
51 *LNC*III, p. 489.
52 For the Bonn speech of 5 September (*DM*IV, pp. 6–7), cf. https://www.youtube.com/watch?v=dqQdyKbyRXY, accessed 30 July 2020.
53 Maillard, *De Gaulle et l'Allemagne*, pp. 207–8.
54 Jacques Bariéty, 'De Gaulle, Adenauer et la genèse du traité de l'Élysée du 22 janvier 1963', *De Gaulle en son siècle* V, pp. 361–2.
55 Vaïsse, *La Grandeur*, pp. 248–9; French-German Treaty of 22 January 1963, www.fransamaltingvongeusau.com/documents/dl2/h6/2.6.3.pdf, accessed 1 October 2019.

56 Garret Joseph Martin, *General de Gaulle's Cold War: Challenging American Hegemony, 1963–1968* (New York and Oxford: Berghahn, 2013), pp. 22–3.
57 Maillard, *De Gaulle et l'Allemagne*, p. 215.
58 Alfred Grosser, *Affaires extérieures: La politique de la France, 1944/ 1984* (Paris: Flammarion, 1984), p. 185.
59 Peyrefitte, *C'était de Gaulle* II, p. 228 (24 April 1963).
60 Vaïsse, *La Grandeur*, pp. 260–2.
61 Jacques Morizet, Intervention, *De Gaulle en son siècle* V, pp. 419–20.
62 Peyrefitte, *C'était de Gaulle* II, p. 231 (3 July 1963).
63 C.L. Sulzberger, *The Last of the Giants* (London: Weidenfeld & Nicolson, 1970), p. 46.
64 Peyrefitte, *C'était de Gaulle* II, p. 247 (21 November 1963).
65 Peyrefitte, *C'était de Gaulle* II, pp. 257–8 (23 June/3 July 1964).
66 Heuser, 'The European dream', pp. 75–103: pp. 95–7.
67 *DM*IV, pp. 222–37: p. 230.
68 von Staden, 'Charles de Gaulle et la politique extérieure', p. 349.
69 Peyrefitte, *C'était de Gaulle* II, pp. 257, 303 (10 November 1965).
70 'Exposé au Conseil des Affaires étrangères sur l'Allemagne', 4 February 1966, *LNC*III, pp. 777–80; Éric Roussel, *Charles de Gaulle* (Paris: Gallimard, 2002), pp. 793–5.
71 *DM*V, pp. 96–117: pp. 101–2.
72 Couve de Murville, *Politique étrangère*, p. 273.
73 Pierre Messmer, *Après tant de batailles... mémoires* (Paris: Albin Michel, 1992), p. 292.
74 Bernard Ledwidge, *De Gaulle* (London: Weidenfeld & Nicolson, 1982), p. 323.
75 Grosser, *Affaires extérieures*, p. 185; Jacqueline Plum, 'La Jeunesse et la réconciliation des peuples. L'OFAJ, une volonté du Général et du Chancelier', in Fondation Charles de Gaulle, *Charles de Gaulle et la jeunesse* (Paris: Plon, 2005), pp. 241–7.
76 Pierre Maillard, 'La Réconciliation franco-allemande: problèmes et limites', *De Gaulle en son siècle* V, pp. 403–7; Maillard, *De Gaulle et l'Allemagne*, pp. 235–6.
77 Maillard, *De Gaulle et l'Allemagne*, p. 230.
78 Roussel, *Charles de Gaulle*, pp. 893–4; Couve de Murville, *Politique étrangère*, p. 282.
79 Henry Kissinger, *The White House Years* (London: Weidenfeld & Nicolson, 1977), p. 110.
80 John T.S. Keeler, 'De Gaulle et la politique agricole commune de l'Europe: logique et héritages de l'intégration nationaliste', *De Gaulle en son siècle* V, pp. 155–67: p. 166.
81 Nevers speech, 13 June 1948, *DM*II, pp. 193–7: p. 195.
82 Keeler, 'De Gaulle et la politique agricole commune', p. 156.
83 Peyrefitte, *C'était de Gaulle* II, pp. 298.

84 Peyrefitte, *C'était de Gaulle* II, pp. 356 (27 March 1963), 366 (25 March 1964), 571–3 (17 June 1965).
85 *MH*, p. 159.
86 Maillard, *De Gaulle et l'Allemagne*, p. 184.
87 *LNC*III, p. 433.
88 Maillard, *De Gaulle et l'Allemagne*, p. 229; Peyrefitte, *C'était de Gaulle* II, pp. 251–4; Keeler, 'De Gaulle et la politique agricole commune', pp. 155–67; p. 159.
89 Ludlow, *The European Community*, pp. 54–5.
90 *Le Monde*, 22 October 1964; Keeler, 'De Gaulle et la politique agricole commune', p. 160.
91 Ludlow, *The European Community*, pp. 66–7; Couve de Murville, *Politique étrangère*, p. 330.
92 Peyrefitte, *C'était de Gaulle* II, p. 286 (12 June 1965); *MH*, p. 184.
93 Edgard Pisani, *Le Général indivis* (Paris: Albin Michel, 1974), pp. 63–4.
94 Peyrefitte, *C'était de Gaulle* II, pp. 293–5 (28 July 1965).
95 *DM*IV, pp. 372–92: pp. 377–81; Ludlow, *The European Community*, pp. 76–7.
96 Ludlow, *The European Community*, pp. 82, 119–20.
97 Martin, *Cold War*, pp. 48–50; Ludlow, *The European Community*, pp. 201–2.
98 Ludlow, *The European Community*, pp. 92, 112.
99 Extraordinary session of the Council, Luxembourg, 17 to 18 and 28 to 29 January 1966, www.internationaldemocracywatch.org/attachments/297_Luxembourg%20Compromise.pdf, accessed 12 October 2019.
100 Ludlow, *The European Community*, pp. 105–7.
101 Mangold, *Almost Impossible*, pp. 95–6, 144.
102 *WM*II, p. 227; Peyrefitte, *C'était de Gaulle* I, p. 370 (24 January 1963). See also above, p. 129.
103 Mangold, *Almost Impossible*, p. 90.
104 *MH*, p. 188; Vaïsse, *La Grandeur*, p. 166.
105 *LNC*III, p. 21.
106 Alistair Horne, *Macmillan 1957–1986* (London: Macmillan, 1989), pp. 109, 112–13; Mangold, *Almost Impossible*, pp. 101–3, 117.
107 Mangold, *Almost Impossible*, pp. 147–9.
108 Mangold, *Almost Impossible*, pp. 93–4.
109 Hansard, 2 August 1961.
110 Couve de Murville, *Politique étrangère*, p. 400; Vaïsse, *La Grandeur*, pp. 197–8; Mangold, *Almost Impossible*, pp. 160–2.
111 Vaïsse, *La Grandeur*, p. 199.
112 Couve de Murville, *Politique étrangère*, p. 402.
113 Macmillan's diary, 29 November 1961, quoted in Horne, *Macmillan 1957–1986*, pp. 318–19.
114 Vaïsse, *La Grandeur*, p. 201.

115 Françoise de La Serre, 'De Gaulle et la candidature britannique aux Communautés européennes', *De Gaulle en son siècle* v, pp. 192–202: pp. 193–4; Peyrefitte, *C'était de Gaulle* I, pp. 299–303 (6 June 1962); Vaïsse, *La grandeur*, p. 218.
116 Couve de Murville, *Politique étrangère*, pp. 403–4; Maillard, *De Gaulle et l'Allemagne*, p. 206.
117 Julian Jackson, *A Certain Idea of France: The Life of Charles de Gaulle* (London: Allen Lane, 2018), pp. 589–90.
118 Hervé Alphand, *L'Étonnement d'être* (Paris: Fayard 1977), p. 386.
119 Horne, *Macmillan 1957–1986*, pp. 357–9.
120 Vaïsse, *La Grandeur*, pp. 202–3.
121 See above, pp. 262–3.
122 See above, p. 301.
123 Vaïsse, *La Grandeur*, pp. 205, 215.
124 *Ibid.*, pp. 206–7.
125 Horne, *Macmillan 1957–1986*, p. 432.
126 Jackson, *A Certain Idea*, p. 591; *Le Monde*, 30 January 1963.
127 *DM*IV, pp. 61–79: pp. 66–70.
128 Pisani, *Le Général indivis*, pp. 106–8.
129 Maurice Couve de Murville, Serge Maffert, and Maurice Vaïsse, 'Entretien avec Maurice Couve de Murville', in Institut Charles de Gaulle, *De Gaulle en son siècle*, vol. IV: *La Sécurité et l'indépendance de la France* (Paris: Plon, 1992), pp. 221–6.
130 Peyrefitte, *C'était de Gaulle* I, p. 153 (27 June 1962); Sulzberger, *Giants*, p. 55.
131 *DM*IV, pp. 67–8.
132 *MH*, p. 188.
133 *DM*IV, p. 69.
134 Peyrefitte, *C'était de Gaulle* I, p. 282 (24 January 1963).
135 Roussel, *Charles de Gaulle*, p. 739.
136 Press conference, 28 October 1966, *DM*V, pp. 96–107: p. 102.
137 Pisani, *Le Général indivis*, p. 105.
138 Couve de Murville, *Politique étrangère*, p. 409; Sulzberger, *Giants*, p. 963.
139 *DM*IV, pp. 69, 71.
140 Peyrefitte, *C'était de Gaulle* I, pp. 354–6 (16 January 1963).
141 Broadcast interview with Michel Droit, 14 December 1965, *DM*IV, pp. 422–33: p. 422.
142 Alain Peyrefitte, *C'était de Gaulle*, vol. III (Paris: Éditions de Fallois/Fayard, 2000), pp. 266–72 (February-July 1967).
143 *DM*V, pp. 155–74: pp. 168–74.
144 Vaïsse, *La Grandeur*, p. 601.
145 *DM*V, pp. 227–47: pp. 241–5.
146 Ludlow, *The European Community*, pp. 166–9.
147 Ludlow, *The European Community*, p. 159.
148 Ledwidge, *De Gaulle*, p. 360; Ludlow, *The European Community*, pp. 170–1; Maillard, *De Gaulle et l'Europe*, p. 269.

149 Bernard Tricot, 'Witness', in Robert O. Paxton and Nicholas Wahl (eds), *De Gaulle and the United States: A Centennial Reappraisal* (Oxford: Berg, 1994), pp. 233–5.
150 Vaïsse, *La Grandeur*, pp. 608–9.
151 Vaïsse, *La Grandeur*, pp. 610–11; Ledwidge, *De Gaulle*, pp. 363–7.
152 *LNC*III, p. 1035.
153 Gerhard Kiersch, 'De Gaulle et l'identité allemande', *De Gaulle en son siècle* v, pp. 304–13: p. 310; von Staden, 'Charles de Gaulle et la politique extérieure', p. 352.
154 Ludlow, *The European Community*, pp. 201–4.
155 Cf. Wyn Grant, *The Common Agricultural Policy* (Basingstoke: Macmillan, 1997).
156 Ludlow, *The European Community*, p. 52.
157 Couve de Murville, *Politique étrangère*, p. 345.

Further reading

The following material is in addition to the general works on de Gaulle's foreign policy listed for Chapter 11.

General works on France and Europe include Alain Guyomarch, Howard Machin, and Ella Ritchie, *France in the European Union* (Basingstoke: Macmillan, 1998); Michel R. Gueldry, *France and European Integration: Towards a Transnational Polity?* (Westport, CN: Praeger, 2001); and Michael Sutton, *France and the Construction of Europe, 1944–2007: The Geopolitical Imperative* (New York and Oxford: Berghahn, 2007).

De Gaulle's European policy and the complex reactions of the other member states are well covered in N. Piers Ludlow, *The European Community and the Crises of the 1960s: Negotiating the Gaullist Challenge* (London: Routledge, 2006).

For Franco-British relations, see Neville Waites (ed.), *Troubled Neighbours: Franco-British Relations in the Twentieth Century* (London: Weidenfeld & Nicolson, 1971); and Peter Mangold, *The Almost Impossible Ally: Harold Macmillan and Charles de Gaulle* (London: I.B.Tauris, 2006). A contemporary account of de Gaulle's veto is Nora Beloff, *The General Says No: Britain's Exclusion from Europe* (Harmondsworth: Penguin Books, 1963). Harold Macmillan writes of the veto in *At the End of the Day, 1961–1963* (London: Macmillan, 1973).

On Franco-German relations, see Alistair Cole, *Franco-German Relations* (Harlow: Pearson, 2001); Gisela Hendriks and Annette Morgan, *The Franco-German Axis in European Integration* (Cheltenham: Edward Elgar, 2001); and Douglas Webber (ed.), *The Franco-German Relationship in the European Union* (London: Routledge, 1999).

Pierre Maillard, de Gaulle's former diplomatic adviser, covered Franco-German relations in *De Gaulle et l'Allemagne. Le rêve inachevé* (Paris: Plon, 1990) and his European policy in *De Gaulle et l'Europe entre la nation et Maastricht* (Paris: Tallandier, 1995). Europe is also covered very fully in Institut Charles de Gaulle, *De Gaulle en son siècle*, vol. V: *L'Europe* (Paris: Plon, 1992).

13 May 1968: economy, society, and the limits of presidential power

France under de Gaulle achieved economic results that its twenty-first-century leaders could only dream of. Gross Domestic Product (GDP) grew by 5% or more annually, exceeding, per head, that of the UK by 1967; unemployment stayed under 3%; household living standards rose steadily, and with them access to an unprecedented range of consumer goods; educational opportunities expanded; white-collar jobs opened up to the children of workers or peasants.[1] De Gaulle did not achieve this single-handedly; France, like other Western countries, had enjoyed strong economic growth through the 1950s. But the stability he brought certainly reinforced the trend.

Yet in May 1968 France suffered its gravest social and political crisis since the war. Rioting, chiefly by students, and the police reaction, left hundreds injured (though mercifully few dead). Over two weeks, some 10 million workers joined a near-general strike. Students occupied their universities and workers their factories. Public services, transport, and petrol distribution were paralysed. And de Gaulle suddenly appeared as 'a querulous old man, caught in a situation beyond his grasp, and tugging desperately at unresponsive controls'.[2] De Gaulle's own recollections confirm this. 'Everything was slipping through my hands', he said to Malraux; he had found the situation 'impossible to grasp' and had nearly resigned, he told Michel Droit in a televised interview.[3] Despite a Gaullist landslide at snap parliamentary elections called in June, his presidency never fully recovered.

De Gaulle's personal record deepens the paradox of an apparently successful President engulfed in a tidal wave of protest. No Western leader had expanded university education faster. None had thought as much about transforming the condition of workers. None had called so vigorously for the United States to leave Vietnam – a central demand of the worldwide student movement. De Gaulle even advanced the condition of women, albeit from an antediluvian starting-point: the vote in 1944, the right (from 1965) for a married woman to open a bank account and exercise a profession without her husband's permission, and the legalisation of contraception in 1967 (though not its reimbursement by the Social Security system) were all passed on his watch. None of this counted for the protesters.

Resolving these paradoxes is a central purpose of this chapter, and the importance of the 'Events' of May 1968 for the de Gaulle presidency justifies giving them a central place in it. They are to be explained, in part, by the economic, social, and educational record of the preceding decade. Equally, however, that record should not only be examined through the lens of May 1968: its legacy also stretches into the ensuing decades.

Economic growth and social inequality

De Gaulle inherited a dynamic economy from the Fourth Republic.[4] And although he gave less attention to economic and social questions than to foreign and defence policy (or, till 1962, Algeria), he still had his own ideas about them. But they did not form a coherent whole.

First, as he said in 1961, 'We must achieve the rank of a great industrial state, or resign ourselves to decline.'[5] France needed internationally competitive industries capable of underpinning her political independence economically. Thus, as he wrote in his memoirs, 'the aim of the struggle for prosperity was not so much to make life more comfortable ... as to build up the wealth, the power and the greatness of France as a whole'.[6] Hence, second, he accepted the end of tariff barriers within the Six under the Treaty of Rome. International competition was the necessary spur for modernisation.

Third, de Gaulle also accepted, in the name of modernisation, the need to 'leave the door wide open to the spirit of enterprise, individual and collective, with its chances of gain and risks of loss'.[7] He never liked moneyed interests, nor they him, but he knew he had to rely on them.[8]

Fourth, a vigorous belief in state intervention balanced his guarded acceptance of free enterprise. 'The state is the inevitable leader of this immense movement [of modernisation]', he said in 1963. 'It guides it, plans it, often implements it and pays the largest share of it.'[9] By contrast, 'laissez-faire capitalism' was no better than 'totalitarian communism'.[10] The Planning Commissariat de Gaulle had established before leaving power in 1946 was central to his ambitions; in 1961 he called the Plan an 'ardent obligation' – and was only with difficulty dissuaded from giving it an imperative, Soviet-style character.[11] It was for the state, too, to encourage 'national champions' – internationally competitive large firms, nationalised or private; and to develop *grands projets* of investments to ensure France's independence in strategic sectors like oil or aerospace.

Fifth, de Gaulle remained committed to the *association capital-travail* of RPF days, now renamed 'participation', which in May 1958 he called a form of 'internal decolonisation', destined to 'dealienate' wage-earners from their work.[12] 'I have always sought, rather hesitantly' he wrote to Marcel Loichot, author of a work entitled *La Réforme pancapitaliste* (1966), 'a practical way to achieve a change in the very condition of workers, not just their standard of living.'[13] Even if 'his experience might say "not now, not like this ..."', he never lost sight of the goal.[14]

Sixth, de Gaulle was a fiscal conservative, determined to preserve the value of the franc (after one big devaluation in December 1958) through balanced budgets, low inflation, and a favourable balance of foreign trade. Almost his last piece of writing was in praise of monetary stability, not just for its economic benefits, but for the moral underpinning it gave the state.[15]

Each of these positions reflects successive accretions of de Gaulle's experience. 'Participation' draws on the social Catholicism of his youth; the mistrust of private business arises from the bourgeoisie's support for Vichy; the predilection for planning and state ownership from the provisional government of 1944–1946; the acceptance of open markets from the commitment, from 1958, to implement the Treaty of Rome. If there are common threads, they are a view of the economy as an instrument to serve France, and a strong dose of pragmatism: 'In economy as in politics or strategy', he wrote, 'I do not believe that there can be absolute truth, but only circumstances.'[16] Yet the presidency revealed tensions within de Gaulle's economic positions.

Planning would become increasingly incompatible with an open economy.[17] And de Gaulle's search for a 'third way' between Communism and capitalism sat ill with the classical liberal positions associated with his fiscal and monetary conservatism.[18]

Georges Pompidou, de Gaulle's longest-serving Prime Minister (14 April 1962 – 10 July 1968), had rather different economic instincts. This was important because de Gaulle intervened periodically rather than constantly in economic policy; indeed, he chose Pompidou above all as a safe economic manager. But Pompidou, who had run Rothschild's Bank in the 1950s, was far closer than the President to private business, and believed the state should 'leave as much space as possible for private initiative'.[19] Growth mattered more than low inflation and balanced budgets to Pompidou, who viewed rising household prosperity as the best antidote to social tensions.[20] He was accordingly sceptical about 'participation', which he cheerfully professed to his ministers not to understand.[21] These were mostly differences of degree, but they surfaced regularly during Pompidou's long premiership; 'participation' in particular proved an increasingly bitter source of discord.

Economic policy: between conservatism and reform

De Gaulle's preferences found expression above all in a conservative fiscal and monetary policy, a statist industrial policy, and, in social policy, a rather timid attempt to introduce 'participation'.

Fiscal and monetary conservatism produced a series of unpopular economic measures, even as France's overall prosperity grew. The founding economic act of de Gaulle's rule, the December 1958 Rueff–Pinay plan undertaken to ready France for the EEC, combined a purely cosmetic currency reform (the 'New Franc', issued from 1960, was worth 100 'Old Francs'), a 'once-and-for-all' devaluation of 17.5%, aimed at improving competitiveness, and public spending cuts such as an end to war veterans' pensions.[22] Then came a clampdown on public sector wages. This provoked industrial unrest culminating, in March 1963, in a major coalminers' strike.[23] By early April the government had conceded most of the miners' demands – but not before trying and failing to stop the strike by placing the miners under military discipline. This was the low point of de Gaulle's presidential popularity.[24]

The miners' successes unleashed public sector wages and then inflation, which de Gaulle attempted to stop with a 'Stabilisation Plan' in September 1963. This included spending cuts, new taxes, a credit squeeze and wide-ranging controls on prices.[25] It reduced inflation to 3% in months, but slowed economic growth and failed to tackle the poor competitiveness of many French firms.[26] Pompidou was sceptical about the plan, but de Gaulle and Finance Minister Giscard d'Estaing extended it, against his wishes, into 1965, then 1967.[27]

Living standards were also held back, from 1967, by Social Security reforms, which brought farmers into the system for the first time but forced higher contributions and lower pay-outs onto existing contributors, and cut trade union representation on Social Security boards.[28] Adopted during the holiday month of August 1967, by *ordonnances* under Article 38 of the Constitution, with no parliamentary debate, the measures proved deeply unpopular. Between Rueff–Pinay, the Stabilisation Plan, and the 1967 reforms, there was thus hardly a moment in the presidency when government policy did not offer the French reasons to grumble.

De Gaulle's relentless pursuit of economic and financial stability was paralleled by his, and Pompidou's, promotion of large industrial concerns – national champions. Measures used included accelerated depreciation allowances, tax breaks for research and development, credits and technical assistance to exporters, regional aids, and selective credit from nationalised banks. Mergers increased twentyfold in a decade, in sectors ranging from banking and consumer electronics to shipyards and textiles. Public money, meanwhile, was funnelled into *grands projets* whose chief aim was France's technological independence for political, military, or prestige reasons. These gave France the bases of a nuclear power industry, of a civilian missile launching site (Kourou), and of Europe's major civil aviation constructor (Airbus).[29] They also included expensive failures. The *Plan Calcul* of 1966 did not create a French computer industry. The Anglo-French supersonic airliner Concorde, meanwhile, was a technological triumph but an economic black hole.

'Participation', probably the policy closest to de Gaulle's heart, was the most imperfectly achieved. An *ordonnance* of 7 January 1959 made a very limited start, offering a voluntary profit-sharing scheme: by 1965 only 1.5% of workers had benefited from it.[30] Then, in 1966, an amendment to the budget tabled (with de Gaulle's approval) by Louis Vallon, a left-wing Gaullist, required the government to prepare a further bill. Pompidou set up a committee, which reported in July that neither side of industry was favourable: employers feared for their right to manage, trade unions for workers' basic pay.[31] Pompidou prepared suitably cautious legislation; de Gaulle demanded something more ambitious.[32] The outcome, published as *ordonnances* on 18 August 1967, *required* profitable firms of 100 or more employees to create a profit-sharing fund. Bonuses, capped at 10% of annual pay, would be distributed to workers as shares or long-term bonds. Business was reassured: workers would not co-manage their companies, or even the profit-sharing funds. Even then, many firms dragged their feet.[33] De Gaulle claimed that 'behind these dispositions lies the creation of a new social order'.[34] But he was soon demanding a further big reform – to which Pompidou expressed hostility in the Council of Ministers. That was in April 1968.[35]

Economic policy: outcomes and critiques

From most angles, the de Gaulle presidency's economic record was impressive. France's industry 'underwent greater transformation in ten years than during the preceding half century', achieving a trade surplus in manufactured goods. Rising business confidence pushed fixed investments up from 17.9% of GNP in 1953–1958 to 22.3% a decade later. Gold and foreign exchange reserves grew tenfold from 1957 to 1967.[36] Automobile production would triple, against 1959 levels, by 1973.[37] All sectors of the population saw their living standards rise, and the chance of upward social mobility through education appeared to beckon for millions.[38]

De Gaulle had contributed by giving France stable institutions, reinforcing business confidence, and by ensuring, through the Rueff–Pinay measures, that France successfully met the challenge of the EEC's open frontiers. But the record is open to criticism from two angles. For neo-liberals, his policies stored up economic problems that proved damaging a decade later. For analysts of French society, his record added to divisions and inequalities that contributed to the crisis of May 1968.

Neo-liberals criticise de Gaulle's statism. France's planning system, they argue, was a distraction in an increasingly open and complex economy, its ambitions easily blown off course by international developments or by policy shifts like the Stabilisation Plan.[39] Selective state intervention, instead of concentrating, on the Japanese model, on expanding international markets, had focused excessively on high-tech prestige projects.[40] Business disliked public money being poured into Concorde, or the *Plan Calcul*, or even the *force de frappe*, when some of the basics of modernisation were neglected:[41] France's telephone system, with 11 phones per 100 inhabitants in 1964, was the worst in Western Europe, while motorway building lagged painfully behind France's European partners.[42] Too many 'national champions', meanwhile, became sprawling conglomerates, insufficiently specialised and too complex to manage well. This made them uncompetitive, and price controls, by failing to deal with the underlying causes of inflation, could not help.[43] And the French economic model would prove ill-fitted to face the West's post-1973 economic crisis.

For social critics, Gaullist modernisation left significant groups behind, notably farmers and small businesses. Real farm prices fell by 16% between 1959 and 1969; peasants' income was 30% lower on average than that of industrial workers.[44] Some 3 million French people left the land between 1945 and 1970, more or less completing France's long-drawn-out industrialisation. Attached to the centuries-old round of rural life, de Gaulle was anxious not to make the process too brutal.[45] His Agriculture Minister from 1961 to 1966, Edgard Pisani, formed a successful partnership with Michel Debatisse and the young farmers' movement to improve farmers' education, investment, and productivity, all the while fighting in Brussels to get Europe to pay for France's farm subsidies. Despite this relative success, however, agriculture as a whole remained an endemic source of protest – including in May 1968.

No partnership was found with small and medium enterprises (SMEs), the second 'left-behind' sector. Some prospered as subcontractors in the modernised France; many more did not. For Gaullist planners, they were the economic equivalents of the *piedsnoirs*, destined for extinction – and certainly not to receive the selective credit reserved for national champions. The neglect of SMEs by Gaullist governments was a political error (like *pieds-*

noirs, small business people gravitated towards the extreme anti-Gaullist Right) but also an economic one: elsewhere in Europe, SMEs delivered some of the biggest productivity improvements.[46]

The third and largest group to feel left behind was the working class. Between 1956 and 1966, executives and managers saw their real pre-tax income rise by 48.7%; for workers as a whole the figure was 31.6%; for workers on the minimum wage, 6% – mostly in a one-off rise in 1958. The low-paid, many of them young, thus fell steadily further behind all other employees.[47] In those pre-Thatcher, pre-Reagan years, France had one of the Western world's most inequitable distributions of income, uncorrected by a similarly unfair tax system.[48] Access to decent housing, in chronically short supply, was particularly unequal. In 1968, 47% of farm workers and 44% of manual workers lived in overcrowded dwellings, but only 14% of professionals and managers. In 1958–1972, private-sector housing construction rose some five times as fast as that of public sector, low-cost, housing units – from which the poorest families were frequently excluded anyway.[49] For the poorest of the poor, immigrants who did France's least attractive jobs, all that remained was the shanty towns on the edges of France's major cities.

The pressure groups and the public

Workers facing inequality wanted different things: higher wages, certainly, but also more control over their work. Younger workers, especially if freshly arrived from the countryside, wanted to be treated as economic citizens rather than as mere factors of production. Both types of demand fed into May 1968.[50]

De Gaulle was sensitive to the qualitative demands. Talking to the left-wing Gaullist David Rousset on 25 April 1968, de Gaulle said 'We need to condemn capitalism and capitalist society. We need to condemn it explicitly. We need to condemn totalitarian communism. We need to find a new path, participation'. He complained, however, that he felt 'alone'; the 'men of goodwill' who might back him were absent both from the Gaullist ranks and from those of the Left.[51] But de Gaulle had a vision (which neither side of industry shared), not a working project. A less ambitious approach – to raise taxes on the best-off (admittedly difficult given his parliamentary majority), to cover more social spending by progressive taxation rather than contributions – might have achieved at least some of what he wanted.[52]

His complaint about a lack of partners, however, was well founded. France's trade union movement was weak, with membership at some 20% of the total workforce, and divided. The Communist-led Confédération Générale du Travail (CGT) dominated the scene, and opposed (at least openly) 'class collaboration' with government and business. It competed with a breakaway union, Force Ouvrière (FO), officially moderate but infiltrated by Trotskyists; a Catholic union, the Confédération Française des Travailleurs Chrétiens (CFTC), and the left-wing reformist Confédération Française Démocratique du Travail (CFDT). Teachers had their own Fédération de l'Éducation Nationale (FEN), university teachers the Syndicat National de l'Enseignement Supérieur (SNESup), and students the Union Nationale des Étudiants Français (UNEF). The CFDT was the most attuned to workers' qualitative demands, which it tried to negotiate with the chief employers' organisation, the Confédération Nationale du Patronat Français (CNPF) – to no effect.[53] Union weakness, employers' hostility, and an unfavourable legal framework meant that collective bargaining, the simplest outlet for working-class discontent, was marginal in France compared with other European countries. This in turn reinforced the unions' weakness.[54] Meanwhile France's old anarcho-syndicalist working-class traditions, marked by long periods of passivity plus short outbursts of rebellion, were still alive.[55]

The state, however, was also to blame for the lack of dialogue. Publicly, de Gaulle urged unions to join in preparing the Plan.[56] In practice, however, even moderate interest groups felt tolerated rather than welcomed by a regime that always feared they would obstruct rational policy-making.[57] For Williams and Harrison, the big farmers' protests of 1961 and 1963, the 1963 miners' strike, and May 1968 'could have been avoided by ministers with an ear to the ground'. Instead, having failed to build constructive relationships with interest groups – except, to a degree, the CNPF and young farmers – ministers had contributed to a yawning gulf between the regime and civil society.[58]

This was reflected in the public's negative view of Gaullist economic and social policy. Between 1964 and 1968, positive minus negative opinions in IFOP polls averaged −17 for economic performance and −23 on social issues (though the somewhat better April 1968 figures were −8 and −18).[59] And by 1967, as Charlot notes, 'the great majority of the French thought their standard of living was marking time'.[60] Pessimism about the economic outlook also gained ground from 1966: 50% in April 1968 thought things would get worse in future.[61] These worries, moreover, increasingly displaced Algerian or foreign policy, on which de Gaulle was judged most favourably, as the public's main concerns.[62]

The French had some reason to be worried. The year 1967 saw faltering growth, the slowest increase in real incomes for a decade, rising inflation, sagging competitiveness, and a deteriorating trade balance.[63] Unemployment rose by some 3,000 per month by late 1967, including a high proportion of young people and even some graduates.[64] Trivial by comparison with later economic shocks (the unemployment rate was 2.6% at the start of 1968, 2.9% by May), the slowdown of 1967 was worrying at the time, especially as the Stabilisation Plan remained in force and the *ordonnances* on Social Security contributions ate into take-home pay.[65]

These developments fuelled working-class resentments of employers and of the regime.[66] In spring 1967, strikes broke out at Rhodiaceta near Lyon, then at the Saint-Nazaire shipyards, then at the Usinor steelworks in Lorraine and Dunkirk. A series of more or less violent industrial conflicts followed, some with factory occupations, some including farmers, in Saint-Nazaire, Besançon, Le Mans, Lyon, Caen, and Redon. The prefect of Sarthe (Le Mans) described them as a 'dress rehearsal' in December 1967. So, months later, would Peyrefitte.[67] In January 1968, meanwhile, François Ceyrac, head of the CNPF, alerted Finance Minister Debré to political dangers arising from rising youth unemployment.[68]

Yet France on 1 May 1968 did not *appear* to be on the brink of a social explosion. That day's trade union parade through Paris – the first permitted in 15 years – passed off peacefully.[69] De Gaulle's personal popularity remained buoyant, at 57% positive to 32% negative opinions from January to April 1968, against an average over the presidency of 59% to 29%.[70] In April, trade union leaders had told Ceyrac, who was planning time off for an operation, that they expected May to be quiet.[71] They would be as surprised as anybody by what followed. And it was France's campuses that supplied the spark.

Education: expansion and its discontents

An expansion in public services marked the Gaullist era, just as much as industrial growth or the construction of a nuclear arsenal. France's health sector added more jobs in the 1960s than the whole of industry. So did education. And student numbers also multiplied faster than industrial jobs.[72] Driven partly by the baby boom (in 1966, 34% of France's population was under 20), partly by public policy, growth in education brought challenges that were not always well met, or even understood.

As leader of Free France, de Gaulle had been an inspiration to young people. As President, he made a point of speaking to the young on overseas visits, and especially to students – in Mexico City, Moscow, Montreal, Krakow, or Bucharest. He gave France a full ministry of Youth and Sport, and a Ministry of Culture, which tripled the number of local 'houses of youth and culture' (first launched under his provisional government in 1944).[73] His father had taught him to aspire to intellectual excellence. He read some three books a week as President; his correspondence is peppered with letters to novelists and historians.[74] De Gaulle was anything but an uncultured soldier.

But he was rarely at ease with France's intellectuals, and they, with few exceptions (the most illustrious being Malraux, his Culture Minister for a decade), leaned Left and viewed him as little better than a dictator. A defining moment took place in February 1959 when de Gaulle appeared at the annual ball of the École Normale Supérieure, seedbed of France's intellectual elite: not one student would shake his hand.[75] He never set foot in a French institute of higher education again, and never gave a speech directly to French youth.[76] And no social category was more anti-Gaullist than young people with higher education.[77]

De Gaulle still favoured widening educational opportunities. Characteristically, however, he viewed such expansion as necessary to meet the nation's needs more than individual aspirations, and wanted to mould the system in consequence.[78] Most contentiously, prompted by his adviser Jacques Narbonne, he favoured streaming in secondary schools and selection at entry to university.[79] Both ran against the egalitarian ethos of France's teaching profession. Selection, in particular, broke the tradition that passing the *baccalauréat*, the wide-ranging high school (*lycée*) leaving examination, should allow entry to the university of an individual's choice. Pompidou, a former *lycée* teacher, shared many of his old profession's preferences, and was sceptical about de Gaulle's 'democratic elitism'.[80] And de Gaulle's relative lack of attention to domestic affairs meant that Pompidou would shape policy as much as the President.

Education: the policy record

On paper, the Gaullists' record of education reform is impressive. They generalised subsidies to Catholic schools, raised the school leaving age, created middle schools, and oversaw an across-the-board expansion, especially of secondary and higher education. But they made relatively little headway against a culture of 'legalism, mistrust, and resistance to change' in a system penetrated by divided and divisive sectional interests, not least the teaching unions.[81]

The Catholic schools question had divided French politics since the separation of Church and state in 1905. Catholics wanted the state to contribute to institutions (like that of de Gaulle's father) where religious teaching was available; for their opponents, a secular state had no business doing so. But after 1945, half of secondary school pupils, and a quarter of primary, were in Catholic establishments, financed by a private donation system broken by inflation. The 'Debré law' of 1959 was a practical solution to this funding crisis: Church schools, in return for a state subsidy, would contract to provide the same core education as state schools, in addition to religious instruction. Neither Catholics nor secular activists liked the compromise and Debré had to use Article 49–3 to get it through Parliament. But despite periodic challenges, notably from François Mitterrand's left-wing government in 1984, the settlement has survived.[82]

A decree of 1959 raised the school leaving age from 14 to 16. By 1967, when it came into force, two-thirds of 14–16-year-olds were already in full-time education. To accommodate them, Christian Fouchet, Education Minister from December 1962, created a system of middle schools, *Collèges d'Enseignement Secondaire*. But the technical secondary education that de Gaulle had wanted did not flourish, and the culture did not change with the new intake. The secondary system remained 'a bastion of the older bourgeois values, with its emphasis on examinations, encyclopaedic syllabuses and abstract exposition, and with its impersonality, its neglect of discussion and out-of-school activities, and its lack of interest in fostering responsibility among its pupils'.[83]

Pupil numbers, meanwhile, soared. The primary sector grew first, from 5.1 million in 1950 to 6.9 million in 1957. Numbers in secondary schools rose from 1.5 million in 1956 to 3.5 million in 1967.[84] And in 1968, 19.6% of 18-year-olds passed the *baccalauréat*, against 5.1% in 1950.[85] Many of these entered the university system, where student numbers rose from 97,000 in 1945 to 180,600 in 1958, and 460,000 in 1967, 30% of them in Paris.[86]

Education spending also rose – by an annual 10.4% in real terms from 1958 to 1969, and as a share of gross domestic product from 1.85% in 1957 to 3.33% in 1968 (military spending's share fell from 6.34% to 4.17% in the same period). Higher education absorbed a growing proportion of the education budget: 7.8% in 1957, but 17.8% in 1969. Spending per student more than doubled in the de Gaulle presidency; so did student scholarships. University teachers were recruited massively (there were 2.5 lecturers for 100 students in 1957, but 4.6 ten years later), and paid better.[87]

Yet French higher education suffered from a growing malaise, for three reasons. First, the unprecedented resources devoted to it still did not keep pace with expansion.[88] The result was overcrowded lectures, understocked and understaffed libraries, and a high dropout rate among students defeated by the logistical rather than the intellectual challenge of study.

Secondly, the sector remained a bastion of inequality. Certainly, higher education was now accessible (with near-zero tuition fees) to the offspring of the middle classes, not only those of the solid bourgeoisie. But among children of farm workers, for example, only one in a thousand was likely to reach university.[89] Moreover, degrees no longer guaranteed 'graduate-level' positions; indeed, the economic downturn of 1967 left some graduates jobless. Children of the elite, meanwhile, increasingly gravitated, not to the universities, but to the *grandes écoles*, the highly selective (and often fee-paying) top end of the higher education pyramid. Equality of opportunity, guaranteed in principle by free access to university to anyone with the *baccalauréat*, thus proved fictional.[90] For de Gaulle, the remedy lay in orientation and selection, to guide students according to their talents and thin out oversubscribed arts courses with mediocre job prospects. In private, he even commended the Soviet example.[91] Resisted over four years by Fouchet, Pompidou, and the teachers' unions, de Gaulle replaced Fouchet with Peyrefitte in 1967, hoping for a more compliant minister. He chaired a meeting in April 1968 at which Peyrefitte was formally asked to draft a bill introducing selection.[92] But to students and many teachers, selection could only mean more inequality.

A third source of malaise was cultural. Barely reformed since Napoleon, France's universities were as conservative as the secondary sector. Students living in halls of residence were allowed neither pictures nor visitors in their rooms.[93] May 1968 began, in many universities, in November 1967, with agitation over visiting rights.[94] The issue was discussed in the Council of Ministers (itself a reflection of the system's hyper-centralisation) on 14 February 1968: Peyrefitte proposed that 'girls' of over 21 might visit 'boys' over 21 in halls, if they left by midnight – a minimal concession with no chance of meeting students' aspirations.[95]

Students of the late 1950s had channelled their political energies into the left-wing Catholic youth movement, or into the PCF's student section, which together fought over the leadership of UNEF. But the PCF's timid stance on the Algerian war discredited it among students; the Catholics' support also shrank; and the government punished UNEF for opposing the war by excluding it from consultations on higher education policy. De Gaulle, indeed, had stated in 1963 that he would not visit a university 'until the UNEF has been put in its place'.[96] UNEF declined from 100,000 members in 1961 to 50,000 in 1968. By April 1968, after a particularly ferocious power struggle at the top, it was leaderless, the left-wing vice-president Jacques Sauvageot acting as a stand-in.[97] The government had effectively deprived itself of responsible partners in the student body.

Into this arena of leaderless discontent stepped the *gauchistes*, a galaxy of far-Left activists including Trotskyists, Maoists, and – the most surreal group – Situationists. All held the government, and the PCF, in contempt. Some 350 *gauchistes* attended an international far-Left rally in Berlin in February 1968, where Peyrefitte claims they learnt anti-police street tactics.[98] They used two issues, shared by the whole international youth movement, to mobilise: sexual freedom (and thus campus visiting rights), and Vietnam. The point of Vietnam was not to call for peace or negotiations, but to show that 'if the most powerful nation in the world could be beaten by a small but determined people, revolution elsewhere, anywhere, was possible'.[99] Grounded in tangible grievances, the *gauchistes*' May 1968 was never troubled with moderate or achievable demands. They went straight for Utopia.

The case of Nanterre

It was no accident that May 1968 began at Nanterre, 12 kilometres west of Paris. Nanterre accommodated the overspill from the Sorbonne, the central Paris university. By 1968, the campus, surrounded by a shanty town, had 15,000 students, no library, and no café; buses into Paris were slow and infrequent. Here was a crucible of university discontents, where 'the only private distraction was sex, and the only communal activity, politics'. The authorities discouraged both.[100]

In March 1967, police intervened to end a sit-in at Nanterre's women's hall of residence.[101] A vocal 'peace in Vietnam' group appeared in October. In November the sociology students went on strike against their curriculum – more about selling soap than about understanding the world, said one of them, a French-born German citizen, Daniel Cohn-Bendit. It was Cohn-Bendit who, on 8 January 1968, interrupted a speech by the Youth and Sport Minister, François Missoffe, who was opening the campus swimming pool. The pool, Cohn-Bendit claimed, was a 'Hitlerian' attempt to distract attention from sexual issues facing young people. Though ruffled, Missoffe, whose daughter studied at Nanterre, was disinclined to pursue the matter. Peyrefitte, however, wanted Cohn-Bendit excluded from the university. Attempts by police to remove him were blocked by a crowd of as many as 1,000 angry students.[102]

There matters rested for two months. Then, on 19 March, a Nanterre student was arrested in connection with violent protests in Paris against the Vietnam War. That and another police visit on campus, this time seeking drugs, prompted the creation of a new student group, which briefly occupied the university's administration building on 22 March. The '22 March Movement', with neither structure nor official leadership, was certainly inspired by Cohn-

Bendit – whom Peyrefitte now wanted deported from France.[103] But neither Christian Fouchet, now Interior Minister, nor Jean Grappin, Dean of Nanterre, would act without the other. So Cohn-Bendit stayed.[104] Grappin, caught between militant students and a hardline minister, briefly closed down Nanterre altogether, then reopened it at the beginning of April. Regular disruption ensued. De Gaulle himself was less than helpful to his Education Minister. When Peyrefitte requested police measures (including searches and bugging) against Cohn-Bendit and other *gauchiste* leaders, the General responded that they were 'just kids'.[105]

By April, Peyrefitte had resolved simply to hold out through the examinations season, and then 'clean out' the Nanterre campus.[106] The *gauchistes*, and the university authorities, decided otherwise. On 26 April, Cohn-Bendit and his friends shouted down a speech at Nanterre by the PCF's education spokesman Pierre Juquin. Then, on 2 May, students commandeered a lecture theatre to hold a political meeting. Grappin closed the campus again. And, crucially, eight students involved in the occupation of the administration block on 22 March were summoned to a disciplinary hearing – in Paris.[107] With Nanterre closed, protest would now move to the capital.

Peyrefitte later claimed that May 1968 could have been avoided by taking tough action against a handful of *gauchiste* leaders like Cohn-Bendit. The opposite may also be suggested: that Peyrefitte's heavy-handedness, especially in January, escalated the unrest. But even Peyrefitte probably failed to grasp the scale of what was about to happen.

The 'Events' of May 1968

The May 'Events' proper began on Friday 3 May, as Nanterre students used the main courtyard of the Sorbonne to protest against the disciplinary hearings. From the government viewpoint, what followed divides into four roughly week-long periods. From 3–11 May, in Pompidou's absence, an indecisive government faced a crescendo of riots. From 11–18 May, Pompidou took charge, and made concessions to the students – only to see striking workers join the nationwide unrest. De Gaulle was reticent about Pompidou's strategy, but was himself abroad from 14 May. Returning on 18

May, he attempted, in the third week, to apply a tougher line, which his own ministers refused; and his broadcast of 24 May, announcing a referendum, failed to halt what had become a near-general strike. The fourth week, 24–31 May, saw the near-breakdown of government and de Gaulle's sudden departure for Baden-Baden, before a dramatic rallying of the Gaullist forces and the announcement of a snap parliamentary election. There followed a long postscript through June marked by periodic violence between police and protesters, a drift back to work, and a Gaullist triumph at the elections. On 10 July, an exhausted Pompidou resigned.

Indecisive government, 3–11 May

Paris saw four nights of rioting on 3, 6, 7, and 10 May. After the first, Rector Jean Roche of Paris announced the closure of the Sorbonne. The police made 596 arrests and detained 27 people; two of them received immediate two-month sentences. The SNESup union, dominated by young lecturers, backed the student movement. Its secretary-general, Alain Geismar, became, with Sauvageot for UNEF and Cohn-Bendit, one of the movement's three spokesmen. They had three immediate demands: to reopen Nanterre and the Sorbonne, to free their imprisoned comrades, and to withdraw police from the Latin Quarter around the Sorbonne. Meanwhile students occupied several provincial universities, and the UNEF, the CGT, and the CFDT announced a big demonstration for 14 May.

In principle the troubles were a public order matter: the government's problem, not the President's. But Pompidou had been away, in Iran then Afghanistan, since 2 May. Louis Joxe, his interim replacement, lacked his authority. The result was 'a classic example of how not to manage a crisis, of dithering, crossed lines of authority, flights from responsibility and of too little and too late'.[108] And de Gaulle, according to his chief of staff Bernard Tricot, had aged by 1967: his attention wandered late in the day and he tired more easily.[109] Having failed to take the students seriously in March, he now felt overtaken by events. His instinct was to harden.

At meetings on both 5 and 8 May, on Peyrefitte's account, de Gaulle called for live ammunition to be used against protesters. That, he said, was how riots were ended in France: the students were fighting with metal bolts and cobble stones, clubs and pick-axe handles; and 'the State has a prerogative, to bring down those who would bring it down'.[110] De Gaulle's ministers refused; Joxe even doubted that he really meant it.[111] Then, on the crucial night of 10 May, de Gaulle went to bed at 10pm just as barricades began to go up in the Latin Quarter. Until 2am, no one would give the order to Maurice Grimaud, the prefect of police, to have them dismantled. By then, the barricades were well installed. The ensuing fighting left 1,000 students and 400 police injured and was broadcast on France's 'peripheral' radio stations, RTL and Europe-1.[112]

Next morning at 6.30, de Gaulle met with Joxe, Fouchet, and Defence Minister Pierre Messmer and proposed calling in the army. Messmer was opposed: professional units would follow their training and shoot to kill; conscripts risked fraternising with the students; both, he said, would aggravate the situation. De Gaulle did not insist. But he did approve his adviser Jacques Foccart, who began recruiting a counter-demonstration force, the Comités de Défense de la République (CDRs), around the Service d'Action Civique (SAC), the strong-arm organisation that supplied marshals for Gaullist party meetings.[113]

Meanwhile the government dithered over the Sorbonne. On May 5 de Gaulle appeared resolved to keep it closed indefinitely. In the National Assembly three days later, Peyrefitte suggested reopening it if the protests ended. *France-Soir* simply announced that it would reopen the next day, which it did not. On 11 May, de Gaulle agreed with Peyrefitte: the Sorbonne should be reopened, if the demonstrations ended, and with identity controls at entry points and a low-level police presence in the Latin Quarter. If that failed, the government would use Article 16 of the Constitution to take emergency powers.[114]

Given the protesters' declared determination to occupy the Sorbonne at the earliest opportunity, this was a recipe for further confrontation or worse. It was never applied. Pompidou returned on 11 May resolved to take control. At 8pm he gathered ministers, including Joxe, Fouchet, Messmer, Guichard, and Peyrefitte, at Matignon (the Prime Minister's office) and told them he intended to reopen the Sorbonne unconditionally. 'The General no longer exists', he added, according to Joxe. 'De Gaulle is dead. There's nothing left.' At 9pm, at the Élysée, he secured de Gaulle's agreement – possibly by threatening to resign, possibly by impressing de Gaulle with his decisiveness. He then recorded a speech that was broadcast at 11.15pm. The riots, he claimed, were the work of 'agitators'. But the Sorbonne would reopen that Monday morning, 13 May, and the Court of Appeal would give a speedy (and, he implied, lenient) verdict on the imprisoned students.[115]

Prime ministerial government, 11–18 May

Pompidou was now in charge, and confident enough to tell de Gaulle that his planned presidential visit to Romania should go ahead. Probably, he wanted the General out of the way; he told Peyrefitte that de Gaulle had aged and no longer measured the consequences of his actions, a view several ministers shared.[116] De Gaulle delegated his powers to Pompidou and left for Bucharest on 14 May. Each morning, a serene, confident, and resolute Pompidou held a crisis meeting with his own staffers plus Fouchet, Messmer, Grimaud, and sometimes Foccart. They shared a determination not to fire on demonstrators as previous regimes had done in (notably) 1830, 1848, 1871, and 1934.[117]

On 13 May the Sorbonne reopened, and the Appeal Court freed the prisoners detained or convicted a week earlier. Pompidou gave a widely respected speech to the National Assembly on 14 May, analysing the student unrest as a 'crisis of civilisation'; two days later, in a second television broadcast, he announced an amnesty for illegal acts connected with the unrest committed since February. Not one of these conciliatory gestures worked.

If Sunday 12 May was quiet enough, the Monday saw a one-day general strike and a giant demonstration in which Cohn-Bendit's and UNEF's forces combined uneasily (and without mixing) with the CGT. The PCF's Waldeck Rochet and Jacques Duclos joined the march, along with centre-Left leaders like Guy Mollet, François Mitterrand, or Pierre Mendès-France (a member of de Gaulle's Provisional Government in 1944–1945, Prime Minister in 1954–1955, now a determined opponent of the Fifth Republic) – and about 230,000 others, according to (conservative) police estimates.[118] That evening the *gauchistes* occupied the Sorbonne.[119]

There was no rioting over the ensuing week – because the students had got what they wanted. They occupied the Sorbonne, Nanterre, a clutch of provincial faculties, the Beaux-Arts school, and the national theatre at the Odéon, declaring each independent of state authority. To the Sorbonne, infused with a surreal, revolutionary-romantic atmosphere, gravitated 'students, revolutionaries, camp followers, run-away children, idealists, derelicts, delinquents'. They had the choice between teach-ins in the lecture theatres, power struggles between *gauchiste* groups in the committee rooms, and sex in the stairwells.[120] Cohn-Bendit, Geismar and Sauvageot appeared, and debated convincingly, on television. France's riot police, meanwhile, were now stretched between the capital and big farmers' protests in Brittany. But half were in Paris.[121]

The week's most disturbing developments, however, occurred far from the campuses. On 14 May workers at Sud-Aviation's Bougenais plant near Nantes went on strike, occupied their factory, and locked up their managers. By the morning of 18 May, 2 million workers across France were out – or rather, in, as factory occupations became the norm. Strikes hit railways and the Paris Metro, taxis, post, and telephones, and, in part, the state broadcasting system; the trade unions could hardly keep up with an entirely spontaneous movement.[122]

Had Pompidou got it wrong? For de Gaulle, speaking on 2 June to Peyrefitte, 'the evening Pompidou opened the Sorbonne was when the authority of the state collapsed'.[123] Pompidou, however, later argued that he had avoided disaster by retreating to a defendable position: that 'I preferred to give them the Sorbonne than have them seize it.'[124] Neither university teachers nor the Parisian public, moreover, backed tough action. Three hundred professors from the Letters Faculty, and five Nobel prize-winners, had publicly deplored police violence against students and demanded the reopening of the Sorbonne and an amnesty.[125] Polls on 8 and 17 May indicated support for students running at 60% across Paris.[126] Far better, Pompidou reasoned, to let the movement play itself out.[127] But he had underestimated the workers' willingness to join in.

On 18 May de Gaulle, for the last time in his life, gave a speech in a university. But that was in Bucharest. Then, like Pompidou a week earlier, he cut his visit by half a day and flew home, determined to act.

Divided government, 18–24 May

De Gaulle had a barbed word for every one of the ministers, including Pompidou, who greeted him at Orly airport that evening.[128] His anger had not abated at the special meeting with security chiefs held the next day, Sunday 19 May. The Odéon, de Gaulle demanded, must be evacuated that very day, the Sorbonne the next. If the police were 'traumatised' by recent events, they should be given rough alcohol. Maurice Grimaud, successor to Maurice Papon as Prefect of the Paris Police, demurred. Re-taking these sites, he said, would immobilise police forces indefinitely when they were needed to protect public services. Pompidou, Fouchet, and Messmer backed him, and won.[129] Though both its heads were now safely in Paris, France's executive was still divided and dysfunctional.[130] And the slogan released in that day's official communiqué, 'Yes to reform, No to chaos!', was soon mocked on the streets.[131]

De Gaulle himself was bitterly aware of the limits to his authority. He complained to Foccart on 21 May that neither Fouchet nor Peyrefitte had applied the reforms – selection – he had demanded and that his ministers were 'non-existent'.[132] Two days later, at the next Council of Ministers, he was still hurling reproaches at Pompidou.[133] Meanwhile the strikes spread, involving up to 10 million workers by 24 May. The radio turned firmly against the government.[134] The student movement, too, returned to violence after Cohn-Bendit had finally been banned from French territory; there were riots on the nights of 22 and 23 May.[135] That the government survived a vote of censure in the National Assembly was meagre consolation: Parliament had become almost an irrelevance. Nor did the vote of Pompidou's promised amnesty law gain any purchase on the situation.

During this third week of the crisis, France's divided government did not have *a* strategy. Rather, as Jackson observes, it developed *three* strategies, in parallel and not necessarily co-ordinated.[136] One was to build up Foccart's CDRs as a Gaullist force capable of taking to the streets. They were now attracting not just confirmed Gaullists but former OAS and far-Right activists motivated by anti-Communism. On the night of 22 May, their headquarters survived a full-scale attack by a thousand or so students throwing Molotov cocktails.[137] The second strategy was Pompidou's: to negotiate an end to the strikes with the trade unions. The third was de Gaulle's: a referendum on the theme of 'participation'.[138] This he announced in a televised broadcast on 24 May.

The broadcast, as Lacouture remarks, was a serviceable social-democratic reading of the situation, concluding with the offer of a referendum on wide-ranging reforms to higher education and industrial relations. But it did not measure up to the crisis.[139] Its main message, 'participation', was buried in too many others and insufficiently developed.[140] De Gaulle looked 'old, tired and out of touch'. Worse, his threat to resign if the country voted No turned the Events into a crisis of his presidency and of the regime. As soon as he had watched it, de Gaulle admitted that 'I got it wrong'.[141]

That night saw the month's worst rioting, and the first two deaths: a student hit in the chest by a grenade splinter and a police superintendent in Lyon run down by a driverless lorry pushed out from among the protesters. Demonstrators attacked firemen, and 130 trees in the Latin Quarter were cut down with chain-saws (according to some observers, by *agents provocateurs* in a bid to alarm public opinion). In a rare student incursion to the right bank of the Seine, the Paris Bourse was set alight. Pompidou called the Lyon demonstration an attempt to start a civil war.[142] De Gaulle's return had done nothing to prevent France from slipping further towards a breakdown of government.

Crisis and reflux, 25–31 May

As Paris woke to the wreckage on Saturday 25 May, de Gaulle's referendum was already in difficulty. The Left decried it as a bid to prolong his personal rule. And, crucially, France's trade unions – plus, out of solidarity, their Belgian comrades – refused to print ballot papers, threatening the referendum's material feasibility.[143] Meanwhile the state broadcasting service was now offering just one minimal news bulletin daily from non-strikers. The focus now shifted to the second strategy, Pompidou's negotiations.

The CGT had wanted a big national negotiation since the start of the strikes. If it could take the credit for a generous settlement, its own credibility would be reinforced and the *gauchistes*' challenge seen off.[144] Pompidou claimed de Gaulle had told him to 'settle at any price'. He certainly agreed that the inflexible Debré, who as Finance Minister should have been at the table, would be kept firmly away.[145]

The talks at the Labour Ministry, in the rue de Grenelle, lasted from Saturday 25 May till early on Monday 27 May. Pompidou and his social affairs team, including the young Jacques Chirac, met representatives from all the main unions plus the CNPF and the small business confederation. The headline element of what became known as the 'Grenelle accords', a 35% rise in the minimum wage, was agreed very fast: the employers were keen to settle, and only 250,000 workers were currently on the minimum wage. A 10% average rise in other wages was also readily agreed, and a half-hour cut in the working week by 1970. Pay lost through strike action was to be made up by 31 December, and unions obtained a legal right to organise within firms. But Pompidou successfully resisted demands for the repeal of the 1967 Social Security *ordonnances* and for the indexation of all wages on inflation.[146]

The Grenelle accords were an outline agreement, requiring plant-level approval from rank-and-file workers. And the workers wanted more, and more qualitative measures giving them more job control.[147] Renault's Billancourt factory, the emblematic heart of industrial France where CGT leader Georges Séguy presented the accords in person on the morning of 27 May, set the national tone by rejecting them in a show of hands. At the Council of Ministers that afternoon, de Gaulle told Pompidou he had done his best and still had the backing of the President and government. But Pompidou's strategy, like de Gaulle's, had failed, at least for the moment.[148] There remained the CDRs, but they were more a resource than a strategy: Foccart planned a demonstration for 31 May, but without any guarantee of results. He also worried that the former OAS types he had recruited, however useful in a scrap, might slip the leash.[149]

With the rejection of Grenelle, de Gaulle again tried to call in the army. 'Public order', he told his ministers on 27 May, 'has always been one of the army's essential missions.'[150] Messmer's view was the precise opposite: 'the use of the army in matters of this kind is an old legacy of the eighteenth and nineteenth centuries, and it is a detestable one'. For the army to be brought in, he required written authorisation for it to shoot.[151] None was forthcoming. Grimaud and Michel Fourquet, chief of the general staff, backed Messmer for practical reasons.[152] So de Gaulle's call to use lethal force was again rejected – as was his proposal to ban a big left-wing meeting at the Charléty sports stadium.

From 27 May the government showed signs of falling apart. In each ministry, pre-prepared plans for a general strike were put into action – and found not to work.[153] Peyrefitte's resignation, first offered two weeks earlier, was finally accepted by Pompidou on 28 May. Other ministers, Tricot told de Gaulle, were increasingly passive in the face of events.[154] Meanwhile the initiative was with the Left. The PCF and the CGT, hitherto considered by Pompidou as more prudent than revolutionary, began to shed their role as stabilising forces. Mendès-France was acclaimed at the *gauchiste* meeting at Charléty, and soon touted, even by leading Gaullists in letters to the General, as a potential prime minister who could end the unrest.[155] Mitterrand announced his own candidacy for a presidential election (which had not been called), and his support for a provisional government under Mendès; a wide range of anti-Gaullists from the Left to the extreme Right suddenly supported him. Waldeck Rochet, too, started talking about a provisional government, with strong PCF representation, and called a big Communist demonstration for Wednesday 29 May. The Communists might not want to make the revolution alone – but they were determined that if the Gaullist state did collapse, they, and no other left-wing force, should take power.[156]

Later, the PCF's new assertiveness appeared as a gift to the Gaullists in rallying to them a population increasingly disenchanted with the May upheavals.[157] At the time, however, the Gaullists, the CNPF, and the intelligence services had real fears that the Communists had access to weapons and would attempt to seize public buildings after their march.[158] Gaullists opposed to firing on demonstrators had no such scruples towards armed Communists attempting a coup. Fouchet ordered the police to use live rounds if key public buildings were attacked; Messmer moved two regiments of paratroopers close to Paris from their bases in the south-west; Pompidou ordered tanks from the Satory camp to positions in Issy-les-Moulineaux, just south of the capital; Foccart put a helicopter on standby to evacuate de Gaulle from the Élysée if necessary.[159]

By this time de Gaulle had slipped into one of his moods of deep gloom. He could not sleep; his wife Yvonne's account of being insulted in the street – and by the driver of a DS, Citroën's high-end model – distressed him; he despaired at his government's failure to act. 'What can I do?', he asked Foccart. 'Can anything be done?'[160]

The next day he left Paris.

The trip was carefully prepared. That morning, Wednesday 29 May at 10.30am, his son-in-law, General Alain de Boissieu, was waiting for him at the Élysée. De Gaulle ordered Tricot to postpone that afternoon's Council of Ministers by 24 hours, and told Xavier de la Chevalerie, his *directeur de cabinet*, that he was taking a day's rest in Colombey. Telephoning Pompidou, he said he needed a break, concluding 'I'm old, you're young, you're the future ... *Au revoir, je vous embrasse*' – a wholly unaccustomed, and dramatic, form of farewell. He had also ordered his aide-de-camp François Flohic to prepare a uniform and 'maps going further east than Colombey, without anyone seeing you'. Three helicopters flew east from Issy-les-Moulineaux carrying the General, de Boissieu, Flohic, and Yvonne, as well as the usual gendarmes and bodyguards.[161]

The official destination, reported by that afternoon's *Le Monde*, was Colombey. Pompidou, and de Gaulle's staff, wondered if he planned to return. Their worries were compounded at lunchtime, when it became clear that de Gaulle was not at Colombey at all. De Boissieu called Foccart from Colombey at 2.15pm to say that 'it was for Pompidou to play' and that an 'emissary' would be sent to him with instructions, which was hardly reassuring. Only in the early evening did they learn that de Gaulle was finally back at home.[162]

In fact, he had gone to Baden-Baden, reaching the residence of General Jacques Massu, commander of French forces in Germany, at 2.50pm. His family joined him shortly after in two light aircraft.[163] De Gaulle left Baden-Baden shortly after 4pm, reaching Colombey at 6.10 with Yvonne and Flohic. From there he telephoned Tricot and Pompidou. After a night's rest he returned to the Élysée at 12.30 on Thursday 30 May.

Why Baden-Baden? And what was his state of mind? Witnesses differ. Massu depicts an emotionally drained General, ready to resign, whom he single-handedly bucked up and returned to the fray.[164] Peyrefitte, and to a degree de Boissieu, present a journey deliberately undertaken for dramatic political effect.[165] Each version has some truth. Foccart, Pompidou, and de Boissieu also recall a demoralised, exhausted de Gaulle. De Gaulle himself said he had contemplated resignation. But the care of his preparations, and the very brief time he actually spent at Baden-Baden, suggest the opposite of a man about to throw in the towel.

Five complementary explanations can be offered. The first was for de Gaulle to clear his head and get away from the oppressive atmosphere of the Élysée, a residence he always disliked. Second, on a day his intelligence services signalled as particularly dangerous, he aimed to ensure his own safety and that of his family: there would be no siege of the Élysée, and no hostage-taking, and the family had enough luggage for a long stay.[166] Third, he wanted to check the army's willingness to back him against any eventuality. Massu was the ideal officer to consult: before giving him other missions and making him a five-star general, de Gaulle had sacked him from his command in Algiers. Massu was categorical: Algeria was history; the army could be counted on. Fourth, de Gaulle wished to consider his options. They included resigning, invoking Article 16 of the Constitution, moving the government to eastern France, or even, he told Foccart and Chaban-Delmas the next day, 're-doing Free France' and 'reconquering France starting from Strasbourg'.[167] Finally, as de Gaulle had told de Boissieu before they left for Issy, 'I want to plunge the French, including the government, into a state of doubt and anxiety so that I can get a grip on the situation.'[168] A void at the top, he reasoned, would create a demand for his return. His disappearance certainly generated consternation among his closest associates, Pompidou and Foccart among them. Pompidou would never quite forgive him.

The de Gaulle who returned to the Élysée on 30 May was a transformed, vigorous, 77-year-old. He wrote a cheque to cover costs of Foccart's demonstration, now brought forward to that afternoon, lunched, spoke to Pompidou, chaired the Council of Ministers, and recorded a short but crucial radio broadcast that went out at 4.30pm. He had accepted Pompidou's amendments to the 436-word speech. In particular, where de Gaulle had written that he would simply postpone the referendum, he now added – at Pompidou's insistence, again backed by a threat of resignation – that he would dissolve the Assembly.[169] The Left, Pompidou reasoned, could hardly tell the trade unions to sabotage elections, the most democratic route to the 'people's government' they were demanding. So parliamentary elections would follow, said de Gaulle – unless someone attempted to 'gag the whole French people', just as they had tried to stop 'students from studying, teachers from teaching, and workers from working'. In such an eventuality, he said, he would take all necessary steps (meaning Article 16 and emergency powers) and encourage 'citizens' action' (meaning the CDRs) to maintain the Republic – because France was threatened with dictatorship and 'totalitarian communism'.[170]

The speech of 24 May had been true but sounded false, wrote Peyrefitte; his words six days later were 'perhaps false' but rang true.[171] De Gaulle was unfair on the PCF, which had spent the month trying to contain revolution, not promote it. This, however, was not a detached analysis but a fighting speech, comparable to the broadcasts that had ended Barricades Week in 1960 or the Generals' Putsch in 1961. De Gaulle's voice was firmer than six days earlier; the radio offered no visual reminder of his age; and the timing was perfect. Public opinion had begun to turn after the violence of the night of 24 May: if there had been *agents provocateurs*, they had worked well.[172] The comfortably off suddenly felt the breath of real revolution on their necks. And although the government had lost the state broadcasting system, newspapers like *Le Monde* and *Combat* moderated their earlier sympathy with the students. When young workers, or the unemployed, began requisitioning food from peasants, when students claimed that street demonstrations were a superior form of democracy, when goods disappeared from shops and petrol from the pumps, and the television went dead, that only reinforced the effect.[173] On 27 May, for the first time, a majority of Parisian respondents expressed their hostility to the demonstrations.[174] Public support now flowed to the Gaullists.

Foccart and his CDRs gave it ample opportunity for expression. Their march up the Champs Élysées began just 90 minutes after de Gaulle's broadcast that 30 May. The intelligence services had predicted 30,000 people.[175] In the event they were some 400,000, more than for any single left-wing demonstration of May.[176] Robert Poujade, the Gaullist party's secretary-general, who headed the march along with Debré, Malraux, Foccart, and Maurice Schumann, recalls the crowd yelling 'de Gaulle is not alone!'[177] There were more sinister chants too, including 'Cohn-Bendit to Dachau!'[178] But the sheer numbers signalled a turn of the tide. Meanwhile Industry Minister Olivier Guichard released the government's emergency petrol reserves, allowing Parisians to take a Whitsun holiday break (the resulting road deaths far exceeded those from civil unrest).[179]

De Gaulle's broadcast and his supporters' march galvanised public opinion. On 31 May a poll indicated that 84% of Parisians now supported a speedy return to work, and only 28% the continuation of street demonstrations.[180] Opinions of Mitterrand had sharply deteriorated; for Pompidou and (especially) de Gaulle, they had improved.[181] The same day saw a big government reshuffle. In the provinces, meanwhile, further pro-Gaullist demonstrations highlighted the turn of the tide. De Gaulle, it appeared, had won.

The triumph of the Right, 1 June – 10 July 1968

Slowly, throughout June, students drifted off on holiday and workers returned to their machines, on the Grenelle terms they had recently refused. The police steadily evacuated occupied buildings and plants: Renault's Flins factory on 6 June, the Odéon on 14 and the Sorbonne on 16 June, four weeks after de Gaulle had first ordered them cleared; the Beaux-Arts on 27 June, the medicine and science faculties on 5 July. Renault-Billancourt was back at work on 16 June, and Citroën eight days later, leaving just Dunkirk steel and Lyon engineering holding out. Some evacuations, especially if in the suburbs away from the media, were violent: Raymond Marcellin, the new Interior Minister, had fewer scruples than Fouchet, and most of the victims were workers not students. A young worker had been shot in the Calvados on 30 May; on 10 June a young *lycée* student supporting the Flins workers drowned after being chased by police into a canal; next day two Peugeot-Sochaux workers were killed in a pitched battle with police. Anger at these deaths triggered a final 'barricades night' in Paris on 11 June. On 18 June a PCF bill poster was shot in Arras, with a gun supplied by the Marseille SAC.[182] The June death toll was thus four, against three in May.[183]

The continuing violence, even when caused by the 'forces of order',[184] played into a Gaullist campaign focused on the Communist threat and on the necessary return to normality. The final barricades night, especially, got copious television coverage, sending a clear message about 'student' violence. Fear, of disorder and of Communism, had been one mainspring of the Gaullist vote since the RPF; in 1968 it was as effective as ever.[185] Anti-Communism drew in a wave of new Gaullist party members, whose total doubled.[186] And for the only time in its existence, Gaullism was reconciled with the far Right: de Gaulle chose 18 June to issue pardons for Raoul Salan and ten other OAS convicts still in prison, and

Jacques Soustelle and Georges Bidault were allowed to return to France; measures that contrasted with the dissolution of several Trotskyist and Maoist groups decreed six days earlier.[187]

To a degree, de Gaulle himself played to the hard-Right theme. In his interview with Michel Droit on 7 June, he blamed the PCF's 'totalitarian enterprise', not for starting May 1968, but for taking it over and paralysing the country. But he also portrayed the crisis as having deep roots in French society, and himself as the real 'revolutionary', citing achievements such as the Liberation, votes for women, nationalisations, decolonisation, modernising France's defences, starting 'the liberation of the French of Canada', beginning the rapprochement of Eastern and Western Europe, and promoting the emergence of less developed countries. Next on the agenda was 'participation' – again – and 'a complete reform of the University'.[188] The task of reform, he added on the day before the second ballot – no longer reluctant, as ten years earlier, to intervene in a parliamentary election – would be 'tough' and needed 'a Parliament capable of supporting, with a strong, coherent majority, the necessary policy'.[189] The tensions of de Gaulle's last ten months in office were already there: on a majority that sprang from a conservative desire for order, he intended to impose a programme of radical reform.

The election results reflected this. At the first round, the Gaullist-led coalition, newly baptised Union pour la Défense de la République (UDR), achieved an unprecedented 46.4% of the vote, of which 37.3% went to the Gaullist party proper, and 8.4% to Giscard d'Estaing's Républicains Indépendants. Against a quarrelsome, divided Left, the coalition then swept the board at the run-off on 30 June. With 293 out of 487 seats, the Gaullists achieved the first single-party parliamentary majority in French republican history.[190] But their voters appeared more as a classic conservative electorate than a cross-class Gaullist one: strongly supported among farmers and other rural inhabitants, managers, and small business, the UDR lost ground among workers, whose support, at 31%, was 11 points down on de Gaulle's in 1965.[191] Such an electorate was not likely to greet de Gaulle's planned reforms with enthusiasm.

Pompidou was at least as much the architect of the triumph as de Gaulle, but now said he needed a rest. Tired out after over six years in the premiership, culminating in the stress of May, he had offered to resign on 30 May. De Gaulle was far from displeased; he had been planning to replace him with Couve de Murville since at least 1967.[192] Pompidou was de Gaulle's likely successor; both men knew it; both thought that Pompidou would improve his chances by shedding the burdens of office.[193] Pompidou's departure should therefore have been simple to agree. Instead, mishandled by both men, it poisoned their relations.

De Gaulle and Pompidou had differences going back to 1965 at least. Pompidou had been irked that de Gaulle had not told him earlier that he would seek a second presidential term; he knew that de Gaulle had wanted to replace him in 1967;[194] and he believed that the long-drawn-out Stabilisation Plan had contributed to the recent unrest.[195] De Gaulle, meanwhile, judged Pompidou negatively for his record in the Ben Barka affair, for apparently seeking to take over the Gaullist party from 1966, and above all for his lukewarm attitude towards 'participation'.[196]

May 1968 had yielded more bones of contention. Pompidou believed that he deserved most of the credit for avoiding disaster, that de Gaulle had been 'absent' even when in the Élysée, and above all, that his conduct in leaving French territory for several hours without even informing his own Prime Minister was 'singularly cavalier'.[197] De Gaulle, meanwhile, considered that Pompidou had let things go in May, especially by reopening the Sorbonne and conceding too much at Grenelle.[198] He was also displeased with his own record in the crisis, and held that against witnesses, Pompidou above all.[199]

Curiously, however, de Gaulle showed reluctance to let Pompidou go, perhaps thinking that if he could only bring him round to backing 'participation' whole-heartedly, Pompidou would be a much more credible advocate of it than Couve.[200] Pompidou, meanwhile, showed hesitancy about resigning, perhaps because he feared (with reason) that his rivals in government would seek to undermine him once he left.[201] At all events, Pompidou twice told Tricot that he wished to leave, and Tricot was twice instructed to tell him that the General wanted him to stay. Only on the third occasion, on 4 July, did de Gaulle not ask Tricot to insist.[202] Then, on the morning of Saturday 6 July, after a sleepless night, Pompidou telephoned Tricot to announce, after all, that he would stay – only to be told that de Gaulle had already offered the job to Couve.

Pompidou was shocked and hurt that de Gaulle should have accepted his resignation without receiving a formal letter or even having a face-to-face meeting, and concluded that de Gaulle had never wanted to keep him, that their relationship had never been more than merely functional: 'all that', he wrote afterwards, 'left an ashen taste in my mouth'.[203] But then, as de Gaulle had told Foccart on Friday 5 July, 'I didn't ask Pompidou to go, I asked him to stay. But he doesn't want to. He is tired, wrung-out, and has had enough.'[204]

Officially, cordial relations were maintained. The Pompidous lunched at the Élysée on Tuesday 9 July; 'your husband held out' in May, de Gaulle told Madame Claude Pompidou.[205] Next day de Gaulle replied to Pompidou's formal letter of resignation, promising 'particularly close' relations in the future, and hoping that Pompidou would be ready 'to assume any mandate that the nation may give you'.[206] Far from remaining 'particularly close', however, their relations unravelled further, until and beyond de Gaulle's own departure.

Conclusion

With or without de Gaulle, France would have experienced unrest in 1968. An international protest movement, linked to the Vietnam War, generational change, the renewal of Marxist thought, and the failure of the post-war boom to benefit all social groups equally, was sweeping the Western world. France, with its long-standing revolutionary tradition, could hardly escape it. Observers since Tocqueville (and more recently, Michel Crozier) had analysed how the weakness of organised interest groups within French civil society limited peaceful, non-dramatic channels to express discontent, while a highly centralised state funnelled social conflicts to the top. All that suggested a particularly effervescent time for France.

De Gaulle still bears responsibility for events turning out as they did. Certainly, claims that he starved France of social and educational spending in order to build his Bomb are overdone. And his foreign policy was popular. But there was a problem of emphasis: as Hoffmann remarks, 'De Gaulle wanted prosperity for *grandeur*, the French wanted *grandeur* as a by-product of prosperity.'[207] Over a decade when his own strong political position, plus high growth and rising tax revenues, offered unique opportunities, his record of domestic reform is fairly thin: the financing of Church schools, the raising of the school leaving age, the reform of aid to agriculture, and the first bases of regional government in France were the main achievements. He failed to secure either selection to enter university, or 'participation'. Though he cared about both, he gave neither the *sustained* attention he gave to Algeria, or to the Bomb; nor did he maintain pressure on a reticent Prime Minister and government. The result suggests that even backed by a parliamentary majority, the president in Fifth Republic France is far from omnipotent: as in other democracies, successful policy-making requires the patient mustering of support, within and beyond government.

De Gaulle might talk about condemning capitalism, or dream of transforming the condition of the working class, but he never undertook the concrete redistributive measures that might have limited France's extreme (for the time) inequality. Again, Pompidou, who was more interested in making the cake bigger than in changing its distribution, had little appetite for such policies. But de Gaulle's own conservative fiscal and monetary beliefs, and thus his acceptance of a continuous downward pressure on wages in the name of low inflation and a strong franc, were also responsible. Expressed in the Rueff–Pinay reforms and the Stabilisation Plan, they were the heart of his economic policy as it was implemented.

In short, de Gaulle allowed the economic and social policy outcomes of his presidency to be more conservative than his rhetoric, contributing to the discontents of May 1968. But May 1968 was also a revolt against a style of authority. It was hardly surprising that de Gaulle, returning to power to re-establish the authority of the French state, should have carried to a new level its besetting defects of top-heaviness and distance from civil society; he distrusted (most) interest groups and their leaders, as prone to maximise their particular advantages at the expense of the general good. Curiously, too, the emergence of a stable parliamentary majority rendered the crisis harder to handle. A change of government, the regular solution of earlier regimes to crises, became vastly more dramatic after 1958. As Grimaud remarked, de Gaulle's Fifth Republic lacked shock-absorbers.[208] Political authority thus remained more authoritarian and uncompromising than society had become, lending a particular edge to May 1968.[209] Ambroise Roux, one of France's leading industrialists, compared the atmosphere of de Gaulle's France to that of a strict convent school – where discipline, in May 1968, suddenly collapsed.[210]

With the young, de Gaulle's disconnect was total. He literally never talked to them (as he talked to young audiences abroad), still less listened. He might encounter them in his periodic 'crowd baths', but there was no dialogue. Without dialogue, the common ground between de Gaulle and young people on a range of subjects including the Third World and non-alignment, Vietnam, or alienation in the workplace, could not emerge.[211]

As for the crisis itself, May 1968 was not de Gaulle's finest hour – and his own comments show that he knew it. At the start, in Pompidou's absence, he failed to constitute a crisis team that might have contained the violence. As the government lost control, his repeated recommendation was to use lethal force against protesters, some of whom were violent but none of whom was seriously armed. In this, fortunately, his government, his prefect of police, and his army chief blocked him (with Maurice Papon as prefect of police – he had only left the post in December 1966 – the outcome might have been far bloodier, given Papon's previous record). After 11 May, he agreed to Pompidou's policy of conciliation, but criticised his Prime Minister behind his back, among other things for being afraid to kill students ('you can't govern with scruples like that', he told Flohic).[212] His first broadcast, made fully three weeks after the start of the unrest, was only effective in ensuring that France now faced a regime crisis. The second, in the wake of his dramatic departure to Baden-Baden, certainly had a rousing effect – but played to a febrile anti-Communism rather than offering a unifying, Gaullist vision of the future.

The short-term impact of May 1968 on France's economy was slighter than expected; growth suffered a brief dip, the budget deficit grew but was under control in 1969, and the trade balance was back in surplus by 1970. Within France, there was a significant, if limited, reduction in inequalities as the share of wages in total added value rose by 2.2 points and the ratio of a senior manager's salary to a worker's wage fell from 4.5 to 4.[213] And modest rises in social spending were paid for by delays to defence programmes.[214]

Politically, the most obvious outcomes were the defeat of the revolutionaries, electoral setbacks for the left-wing parties, and the triumph of the Gaullist-led Right. In the longer term, the new ferment on the left gave rise to new movements hardly represented in May 1968 itself – feminism, ecology, and anti-racism. Some of these were harnessed in the new Socialist Party, re-founded by François Mitterrand in 1971 and victorious a decade later.

The Gaullists' electoral success, however, could not mask the damage done to the larger Gaullist project – and to de Gaulle himself. As Pompidou cruelly remarked, 'General de Gaulle's France was brought back to its true dimensions'. After May, and even more after the Soviet invasion of Czechoslovakia on 21 August, there was to be no war on the dollar, no lessons to the world on détente or on Europe from the Atlantic to the Urals.[215] De Gaulle's own record in May damaged him among Gaullists and the wider electorate.[216] On 31 May – the day after his successful broadcast – only 35% of Parisians – admittedly not the most supportive group – wanted him to serve his term till 1972, against 54% who wanted him to step down earlier.[217] The net result of May and the elections was thus to diminish de Gaulle and to reinforce a newly muscular, and newly reactionary, Gaullist party. Much of his record over his last ten months in power can be viewed as a bid to escape the resulting state of near-dependence on a type of organisation he still despised.

Notes

1 R.W. Johnson, *The Long March of the French Left* (London: Macmillan, 1981), p. 127; Philip M. Williams and Martin Harrison, *Politics and Society in de Gaulle's Republic* (New York: Doubleday, 1972), p. 7n.
2 Williams and Harrison, *Politics and Society*, p. 329.
3 André Malraux, *Les Chênes qu'on abat ...* (Paris: Gallimard, 1971), p. 28; Broadcast conversation with Michel Droit, 7 June 1968, *DM*v, pp. 294–310: p. 295.
4 Stephen S. Cohen, 'Twenty Years of the Gaullist Economy', in William G. Andrews and Stanley Hoffmann (eds), *The Fifth Republic at Twenty* (Albany: State University of New York Press, 1981), pp. 240–50: p. 240.
5 Broadcast, 14 June 1961, *DM*III, pp. 224–9: p. 225.
6 *MH*, p. 160.
7 Press conference, 4 February 1965, *DM*IV, pp. 325–42: p. 327.
8 Henri Lerner, 'De Gaulle et le patronat', in Institut Charles de Gaulle, *De Gaulle en son siècle*, vol. III: *Moderniser la France* (Paris: Plon, 1992), pp. 181–94: p. 194.

9. Press conference, 29 July 1963, *DM*IV, pp. 112–30: pp. 113–14.
10. Press conference, 4 February 1965, *DM*IV, pp. 325–42: p. 327.
11. Michel Debré, *Gouverner. Mémoires, 1958–1962* (Paris: Albin Michel, 1988), p. 69; Broadcast, 8 May 1961, *DM*III, pp. 310–14: p. 314.
12. Philippe Dechartre, 'La Participation', in *De Gaulle en son siècle* III, pp. 300–2.
13. *LNC*III, p. 809.
14. Olivier Guichard, *Mon Général* (Paris: Grasset, 1980), pp. 275–7.
15. *MH*, p. 374.
16. *WM*III, p. 120.
17. Bela Balassa, 'The French Economy under the Fifth Republic, 1958–1978', in Andrews and Hoffmann, *The Fifth Republic at Twenty*, pp. 204–26: p. 209.
18. Élie Cohen, 'Les Rapports entre le président de la République et le premier ministre sur les questions économiques', in Institut Charles de Gaulle, Association Française de Science Politique, *De Gaulle et ses Premiers Ministres, 1959–1969* (Paris: Plon, 1990), pp. 225–37: p. 229.
19. Lerner, 'De Gaulle et le patronat', p. 186.
20. Michel Jobert, *L'Autre Regard* (Paris: Grasset, 1976), p. 63.
21. Volkar Lauber, 'The Gaullist Model of Economic Modernization', in Andrews and Hoffmann, *The Fifth Republic at Twenty*, pp. 227–39: p. 230; Alain Peyrefitte, *Le Mal français* (Paris: Plon, 1976), p. 399.
22. Cohen, 'Les Rapports', p. 230; Christian Morrisson, 'Le Partage des bénéfices de la croissance sous le général de Gaulle de 1958 à 1969', in *De Gaulle en son siècle* III, pp. 245–54: p. 251.
23. George Ross, 'Gaullism and Organised Labor: Two Decades of Failure?', in Andrews and Hoffmann, *The Fifth Republic at Twenty*, pp. 330–47: pp. 334–5; Morrisson, 'Le Partage des bénéfices', pp. 246–7.
24. Philippe Alexandre, *Le Duel de Gaulle–Pompidou* (Paris: Grasset, 1970), p. 141; Éric Roussel, *Georges Pompidou, 1911–1974*, 2nd edn (Paris: Jean-Claude Lattès, 1994), p. 156; Jean Charlot, *Les Français et de Gaulle* (Paris: Plon, 1971), pp. 205, 293.
25. *MH*, p. 374; Roussel, *Pompidou*, p. 159; Lyon speech, 28 September 1963, *DM*IV, pp. 134–8.
26. Cohen, 'Les Rapports', p. 231; Morrisson, 'Le Partage des bénéfices', pp. 246–7.
27. Alain Peyrefitte, *C'était de Gaulle*, vol. III (Paris: Éditions de Fallois/Fayard, 2000), p. 391; Alexandre, *Le Duel*, pp. 152–4, 183; Georges Pompidou, *Pour rétablir une vérité* (Paris: Flammarion, 1982), p. 180.
28. Williams and Harrison, *Politics and Society*, p. 226.
29. Cohen, 'Les Rapports', pp. 232–3.
30. Williams and Harrison, *Politics and Society*, p. 296.
31. Roussel, *Pompidou*, p. 193.
32. De Gaulle to Pompidou, 13 May 1967, *LNC*III, p. 893.
33. Williams and Harrison, *Politics and Society*, p. 300.

34 Peyrefitte, *C'était de Gaulle* III, pp. 239–41 (31 July 1967).
35 Alexandre, *Le Duel*, p. 217.
36 Balassa, 'The French Economy', pp. 204–26.
37 Cohen, 'Twenty Years', p. 242.
38 Johnson, *Long March*, p. 127.
39 Balassa, 'The French Economy', pp. 209, 225.
40 Cohen, 'Les Rapports', pp. 234–5.
41 Lerner, 'De Gaulle et le patronat', pp. 184–6.
42 Peyrefitte, *C'était de Gaulle* III, pp. 63–6 (8 April 1964); Peyrefitte, *Le Mal français*, p. 62.
43 Cohen, 'Les Rapports', p. 236; Suzanne Berger, 'Lame Ducks and National Champions: Industrial Policy in the Fifth Republic', in Andrews and Hoffmann, *The Fifth Republic at Twenty*, pp. 292–310, p. 299; Balassa, 'The French Economy', pp. 211–12.
44 Williams and Harrison, *Politics and Society*, pp. 12–13.
45 *MH*, pp. 156–7.
46 Stanley Hoffmann, *Decline or Renewal? France since the 1930s* (New York: Viking Press, 1974), p. 106; Lauber, 'The Gaullist Model', pp. 231–2; Cohen, 'Twenty Years', p. 241.
47 Williams and Harrison, *Politics and Society*, p. 11n; Henri Weber, *Le Parti des patrons. Le CNPF, 1946–1990*, 2nd edn (Paris: Le Seuil, 1991), p. 215.
48 Morrisson, 'Le Partage des bénéfices', pp. 245–54; Johnson, *Long March*, pp. 118–21; Lauber, 'The Gaullist Model', p. 232; Jane Marceau, *Class and Status in France: Economic Change and Social Immobility, 1945–1975* (Oxford: Clarendon Press, 1977), pp. 59, 62, 185.
49 Marceau, *Class and Status*, pp. 70–3.
50 Johnson, *Long March*, p. 132; Jackson, *A Certain Idea*, p. 721.
51 Alexandre, *Le Duel*, p. 216.
52 Morrisson, 'Le Partage des bénéfices', p. 254.
53 Weber, *Le Parti des patrons*, p. 195.
54 Janice McCormick, 'Gaullism and Collective Bargaining: The Effect of the Fifth Republic on French Industrial Relations', in Andrews and Hoffmann, *The Fifth Republic at Twenty*, pp. 348–66.
55 Johnson, *Long March*, p. 130.
56 Broadcast, 19 April 1963, *DM*IV, pp. 92–6; pp. 92–4.
57 Williams and Harrison, *Politics and Society*, p. 165; Ross, 'Gaullism and Organised Labor', pp. 336–7.
58 Williams and Harrison, *Politics and Society*, pp. 165–6.
59 Jean Charlot, *Les Français et de Gaulle*, pp. 292–4.
60 Jean Charlot, *The Gaullist Phenomenon* (London: George Allen & Unwin, 1971), p. 60.
61 Charlot, *Les Français et de Gaulle*, pp. 296.
62 Charlot, *Les Français et de Gaulle*, pp. 254–8.
63 Jean Touchard, *Le Gaullisme, 1940–1969* (Paris: Le Seuil, 1978), p. 279; Anthony Rowley, 'La Modernisation économique de la

France', in *De Gaulle en son siècle* III, pp. 174–80: p. 178; Peyrefitte, *C'était de Gaulle* III, pp. 448–59.
64 Peyrefitte, *C'était de Gaulle* III, p. 241; Roussel, *Pompidou*, p. 214.
65 Ross, 'Gaullism and Organised Labor', p. 339.
66 David Goldey, 'A Precarious Regime: The Events of May 1968', in Philip M. Williams, *French Politicians and Elections, 1951–1969* (Cambridge: Cambridge University Press, 1970), pp. 226–60: p. 246.
67 Michelle Zancarini-Fournel, *Les Luttes et les rêves: une histoire populaire de la France de 1685 à nos jours* (Paris: La Découverte, 2016), pp. 792–3; Peyrefitte, *C'était de Gaulle* III, pp. 237–8.
68 Weber, *Le Parti des patrons*, p. 206.
69 Goldey, 'Events', p. 236.
70 Charlot, *Les Français et de Gaulle*, pp. 204–8.
71 Weber, *Le Parti des patrons*, p. 205.
72 Cohen, 'Twenty Years', pp. 242–3.
73 Laurent Besse, 'Des Maisons pour les jeunes: le soutien gouvernemental pour les MJC, 1959–1965', in Fondation Charles de Gaulle, *Charles de Gaulle et la jeunesse* (Paris: Plon, 2005), pp. 199–220.
74 Julian Jackson, *A Certain Idea of France: The Life of Charles de Gaulle* (London: Allen Lane, 2018), p. 711.
75 Peyrefitte, *C'était de Gaulle* III, pp. 23–8.
76 Ludovine Bantigny, 'Un Enjeu politique: la jeunesse. Étude de deux décennies (1950 et 1960)', in *Charles de Gaulle et la jeunesse*, pp. 315, 323.
77 Charlot, *Les Français et de Gaulle*, p. 120.
78 Françoise Mayeur, 'De Gaulle et l'Éducation nationale (1958–1969)', in *De Gaulle en son siècle* III, pp. 585–97: p. 586; *MH*, pp. 357–65.
79 Bruno Poucet, 'Un enseignement pour une seule jeunesse', in *Charles de Gaulle et la jeunesse*, pp. 257–76; Notes to Pompidou, 11 March 1964, and to Jacques Narbonne, 5 June 1964, *LNC*III, pp. 631, 649.
80 Poucet, 'Un enseignement', pp. 257–76.
81 Williams and Harrison, *Politics and Society*, p. 234.
82 Bruno Poucet, 'De Gaulle et les enjeux scolaires', in Fondation Charles de Gaulle, *Charles de Gaulle, chrétien, homme d'état* (Paris: Plon, 2005), pp. 233–52.
83 Williams and Harrison, *Politics and Society*, p. 19.
84 Jean-Claude Eicher, 'Note sur l'évolution de l'effort financier public en faveur de l'éducation sous la présidence du général de Gaulle', in *De Gaulle en son siècle* III, pp. 598–609: pp. 600–1.
85 Williams and Harrison, *Politics and Society*, p. 19.
86 Paul Gagnon, 'The Fifth Republic and Education: Modernity, Democracy, Culture', in Andrews and Hoffmann (eds), *The Fifth Republic at Twenty*, pp. 367–81: pp. 368–70.
87 Eicher, 'Note sur l'évolution', pp. 598–609; Claude Lelièvre, 'Les Idées du Général de Gaulle en matière d'éducation et de jeunesse', in *Charles de Gaulle et la jeunesse*, pp. 277–80.

88 Edward L. Morse, *Foreign Policy and Interdependence in Gaullist France* (Princeton, NJ: Princeton University Press, 1973), p. 166.
89 Williams and Harrison, *Politics and Society*, p. 14.
90 Gagnon, 'The Fifth Republic and Education', p. 371; Goldey, 'Events', p. 236; Marceau, *Class and Status*, p. 109.
91 Peyrefitte, *C'était de Gaulle* III, p. 397 (14 November 1967).
92 Françoise Mayeur, 'De Gaulle et l'Éducation nationale', p. 594.
93 John Gretton, *Students and Workers: An Analytical Account of Dissent in France, May–June 1968* (London: Macdonald, 1969), p. 73.
94 Patrick Guiol, Intervention, in *De Gaulle en son siècle* III, pp. 384–7.
95 Peyrefitte, *C'était de Gaulle* III, p. 426 (14 February 1968).
96 Alain Larcan, Intervention, in *Charles de Gaulle et la jeunesse*, pp. 350–1.
97 Williams and Harrison, *Politics and Society*, pp. 317–19.
98 Peyrefitte, *C'était de Gaulle* III, p. 430.
99 Goldey, 'Events', p. 234.
100 Goldey, 'Events', pp. 237–8.
101 *Le Monde*, 23 March 1967.
102 Peyrefitte, *C'était de Gaulle* III, p. 424 (26 January 1968).
103 Peyrefitte, *C'était de Gaulle* III, p. 432 (19 March 1968); Marie-Geneviève Dezes, Intervention, in *De Gaulle en son siècle* III, pp. 390–1; Zancarini-Fournel, *Les Luttes*, p. 797.
104 Peyrefitte, *C'était de Gaulle* III, p. 433 (23 March 1968).
105 Peyrefitte, *C'était de Gaulle* III, pp. 435–6 (25 March 1968).
106 Peyrefitte, *C'était de Gaulle* III, p. 467 (4 April 1968).
107 Gretton, *Students and Workers*, p. 80.
108 Goldey, 'Events', p. 228.
109 Jackson, *A Certain Idea*, p. 706.
110 Peyrefitte, *C'était de Gaulle* III, pp. 467–9 (5 May 1968), 481 (8 May 1968).
111 Peyrefitte, *C'était de Gaulle* III, p. 481.
112 Goldey, 'Events', p. 243; Roussel, *Pompidou*, p. 225.
113 Pierre Lefranc, *Avec de Gaulle* (Paris: Plon, 1989 [1979]), p. 337; Roussel, *Pompidou*, p. 225.
114 Peyrefitte, *C'était de Gaulle* III, p. 502 (11 May 1968); Robert Poujade, *Avec de Gaulle et Pompidou. Mémoires* (Paris: L'Archipel, 2011), p. 123.
115 Roussel, *Pompidou*, pp. 226–8; Peyrefitte, *C'était de Gaulle* III, pp. 508–9 (11 May 1968); Alexandre, *Le Duel*, p. 221; Pompidou, *Pour rétablir*, pp. 217–18.
116 Peyrefitte, *C'était de Gaulle* III, pp. 512–14 (13 May 1968); Roussel, *Pompidou*, p. 237n.
117 Peyrefitte, *C'était de Gaulle* III, p. 517; Jacques Foccart, *Le Général en mai. Journal de l'Élysée – II, 1968–1969* (Paris: Fayard/Jeune Afrique, 1998), p. 107.
118 Roussel, *Pompidou*, p. 231; Zancarini-Fournel, *Les Luttes*, pp. 806–7; Goldey, 'Events', p. 248; Poujade, *Avec de Gaulle*, p. 129.

119　Poujade, *Avec de Gaulle*, p. 105.
120　Goldey, 'Events', pp. 248–9; Poujade, *Avec de Gaulle*, p. 105.
121　Émilie Charrier et Grégory Zeigin, '9 janvier 1969. Des forces de police en ordre', in Philippe Artières and Emmanuelle Giry (eds), *68, les archives du pouvoir. Chroniques inédites d'un État face à la crise* (Paris: Archives Nationales/L'Iconoclaste, 2018), pp. 268–72.
122　Weber, *Le Parti des patrons*, pp. 206–7.
123　Peyrefitte, *C'était de Gaulle* III, p. 573.
124　Pompidou, *Pour rétablir*, pp. 184–5.
125　Peyrefitte, *C'était de Gaulle* III, pp. 481 (8 May 1968), 500 (11 May 1968).
126　IFOP, 'La Crise de mai 68', https://www.ifop.com/publication/ifop-col lectors-n4-la-crise-de-mai-1968/, pp. 5, 9, accessed 4 November 2019.
127　Roussel, *Pompidou*, p. 229.
128　Alexandre, *Le Duel*, p. 225; Peyrefitte, *C'était de Gaulle* III, pp. 524–5 (18 May 1968).
129　Roussel, *Pompidou*, p. 236; Maurice Grimaud, *En mai fais ce qu'il te plaît* (Paris: Stock, 1977), pp. 209–11; Jean Lacouture, *De Gaulle*, vol. III: *Le Souverain* (Paris: Le Seuil, 1986), p. 681; Lefranc, *Avec de Gaulle*, p. 342.
130　Hoffmann, *Decline or Renewal?*, p. 167.
131　The obscure medieval word he had found for chaos was *chienlit*, which was not scatological in origin but sounded as if it was (Lacouture, *De Gaulle* III, p. 682).
132　Foccart, *Le Général en mai*, pp. 117–19.
133　Alexandre, *Le Duel*, p. 229.
134　Weber, *Le Parti des patrons*, pp. 206–7; Foccart, *Le Général en mai*, p. 112.
135　Mark Kurlansky, *1968: The Year that Rocked the World* (London: Jonathan Cape, 2004), p. 236.
136　Jackson, *A Certain Idea*, p. 724.
137　Foccart, *Le Général en mai*, pp. 116–25.
138　Peyrefitte, *C'était de Gaulle* III, pp. 533–5.
139　*DMv*, pp. 288–91; Lacouture, *De Gaulle* III, p. 686.
140　Guichard, *Mon Général*, p. 427.
141　Goldey, 'Events', p. 254; Alexandre, *Le Duel*, p. 231.
142　Grimaud, *En mai*, p. 243; Zancarini-Fournel, *Les Luttes*, pp. 821–2.
143　C.L. Sulzberger, *An Age of Mediocrity: Memoirs and Diaries, 1963–1972* (New York: Macmillan, 1973), p. 434.
144　Jean-Jacques Becker, 'Communisme et gaullisme dans la crise de Mai 68', in Stéphane Courtois and Marc Lazar (eds), *Cinquante ans d'une passion française. De Gaulle et les communistes* (Paris: Balland, 1991), pp. 109–25: pp. 113–14.
145　Pompidou, *Pour rétablir*, p. 191; Guichard, *Mon Général*, p. 429.
146　Emmanuelle Giry, '25–7 mai 1968. Négociations rue de Grenelle', in Artières and Giry, *68, les archives du pouvoir*, pp. 116–21.

147 Becker, 'Communisme et gaullisme', p. 116.
148 Becker, 'Communisme et gaullisme', pp. 116–17; Peyrefitte, *C'était de Gaulle* III, p. 546 (27 May 1968).
149 Foccart, *Le Général en mai*, pp. 128, 135.
150 Peyrefitte, *C'était de Gaulle* III, p. 547 (27 May 1968).
151 Pierre Messmer, 'Témoignage', in *De Gaulle et ses Premiers Ministres, 1959–1969*, pp. 203–4.
152 Grimaud, *En mai*, pp. 251–3.
153 *Ibid.*, p. 206.
154 Foccart, *Le Général en mai*, pp. 131, 140.
155 Roussel, *Pompidou*, pp. 242–3.
156 Goldey, Events, p. 251; Becker, 'Communisme et gaullisme', pp. 118–20.
157 Guichard, *Mon Général*, pp. 429–30.
158 Weber, *Le Parti des patrons*, p. 208.
159 Foccart, *Le Général en mai*, p. 136; Laurent Jeanpierre, '9 juillet 1968. Les leçons de Christian Fouchet', in Artières and Giry, *68, les archives du pouvoir*, pp. 246–51; Pompidou, *Pour rétablir*, pp. 189–90; Pierre Messmer, 'Témoignage', *De Gaulle et ses Premiers Ministres*, pp. 203–4.
160 Foccart, *Le Général en mai*, pp. 141–2.
161 Alain de Boissieu, *Pour servir le Général* (Paris: Plon, 1982), pp. 184–8; Jackson, *A Certain Idea*, pp. 728–9; François Flohic, *Souvenirs d'Outre-Gaulle* (Paris: Plon, 1979), p. 176; Pompidou, *Pour rétablir*, p. 191.
162 Foccart, *Le Général en mai*, p. 148.
163 Flohic, *Souvenirs*, pp. 179–80.
164 Jacques Massu, *Baden 68. Souvenirs d'une fidélité gaulliste* (Paris: Plon, 1983).
165 Peyrefitte, *C'était de Gaulle* III, p. 554 (29 May 1968); de Boissieu, *Pour servir*, p. 193.
166 Eric Roussel, *Charles de Gaulle* (Paris: Gallimard, 2002), pp. 874–6; de Boissieu, *Pour servir*, pp. 185–8.
167 Broadcast interview with Michel Droit, 7 June 1968 *DMv*, pp. 294–310: p. 295; Foccart, *Le Général en mai*, pp. 150–3; Jacques Chaban-Delmas, *Mémoires pour demain* (Paris: Flammarion, 1997), p. 409.
168 de Boissieu, *Pour servir*, pp. 185–8.
169 Emmanuelle Giry, '30 mai 1968. Le Général de Gaulle s'adresse à la nation', in Artières and Giry, *68, les archives du pouvoir*, pp. 130–9; Alexandre, *Le Duel*, pp. 243–5.
170 Broadcast, 30 May 1968, pp. 292–3.
171 Peyrefitte, *C'était de Gaulle* III, p. 569 (30 May 1968).
172 Grimaud, *En mai*, p. 253.
173 Goldey, 'Events', pp. 250–5.
174 IFOP 'La Crise de mai 68', p. 14.
175 Frédéric Turpin, *Jacques Foccart. Dans l'ombre du pouvoir* (Paris: CNRS editions, 2015), p. 246.

176 Jackson, *A Certain Idea*, p. 735.
177 Poujade, *Avec de Gaulle*, p. 142.
178 *Le Monde*, 1 June 1968.
179 Peyrefitte, *C'était de Gaulle* III, p. 571.
180 IFOP, 'La Crise de mai 68', p. 16.
181 *Ibid.*, p. 18.
182 *Le Monde*, 24 April 2018.
183 Michelle Zancarini-Fournel, '10–11 juin 1968. Des luttes mortelles', in Artières and Giry, *68, les archives du pouvoir*, pp. 152–61; Zancarini-Fournel, *Les luttes*, pp. 822–3.
184 *Le Monde*, 24 April 2018.
185 David Goldey, 'The Party of Fear: The Election of June 1968', in Williams, *French Politicians and Elections, 1951–1969*, pp. 261–81: pp. 262–3; Zancarini-Fournel, 'Des luttes mortelles', p. 153.
186 Robert Poujade, interview with the author, 17 September 1991; Charlot, *The Gaullist Phenomenon*, p. 131.
187 Roussel, *Pompidou*, p. 252.
188 *DM*v, pp. 294–310: pp. 304–7; Touchard, *Le Gaullisme, 1940–1969*, pp. 282–3.
189 *DM*v, pp. 313–15.
190 Alain Lancelot, *Les Élections sous la Ve République* (Paris: Presses Universitaires de France, 1983), pp. 49–52.
191 Charlot, *The Gaullist Phenomenon*, p. 83; Johnson, *Long March*, pp. 82–3.
192 Alexandre, *Le Duel*, p. 226; Foccart, *Le Général en mai*, p. 278.
193 Foccart, *Le Général en mai*, pp. 228, 253, 256.
194 See above, p. 275.
195 Pompidou, *Pour rétablir*, p. 180.
196 Alexandre, *Le Duel*, pp. 185–7, Jacques Foccart, *Foccart parle. Entretiens avec Philippe Gaillard*, vol. I (Paris: Fayard/Jeune Afrique, 1995), p. 393.
197 Pompidou, *Pour rétablir*, pp. 198, 202.
198 Peyrefitte, *C'était de Gaulle* III, p. 578; Flohic, *Souvenirs*, pp. 162–3.
199 Guichard, *Mon Général*, p. 450.
200 Pompidou, *Pour rétablir*, p. 200.
201 Alexandre, *Le Duel*, p. 253.
202 Bernard Tricot, 'Les Rapports entre le président de la République et le premier ministre, juillet 1967–avril 1969', in *De Gaulle et ses Premiers Ministres, 1959–1969*, pp. 127–49: p. 139.
203 Pompidou, *Pour rétablir*, pp. 202–4.
204 Foccart, *Le Général en mai*, p. 261.
205 Pompidou, *Pour rétablir*, p. 203.
206 *LNC*III, pp. 982–3.
207 Hoffmann, *Decline or Renewal?*, p. 323.
208 Maurice Grimaud, Intervention in *De Gaulle en son siècle* III, pp. 379–82.

209 Hoffmann, *Decline or Renewal?*, p. 103.
210 Weber, *Le Parti des patrons*, pp. 214–15.
211 Patrick Guiol, Intervention, in *De Gaulle en son siècle* III, pp. 384–7.
212 Peyrefitte, *C'était de Gaulle* III, p. 578; Flohic, *Souvenirs*, pp. 163–4.
213 Morrisson, 'Le Partage des bénéfices', pp. 248–9.
214 Wilfrid H. Kohl, *French Nuclear Diplomacy* (Princeton, NJ: Princeton University Press, 1971), p. 199.
215 Pompidou, *Pour rétablir*, p. 196.
216 Guichard, *Mon Général*, p. 432.
217 IFOP 'La Crise de mai 68', p. 18.

Further reading

Julian Jackson, *A Certain Idea of France* (London: Allen Lane, 2018), chapters 24, 27, and 28, covers the social and economic record and May 1968.

De Gaulle's *Memoirs of Hope* (London: Weidenfeld & Nicolson, 1971), chapters 4 and 9, cover the economic record – with Chapter 9 breaking off in 1963. His *Discours et Messages*, vol. v (Paris: Plon, 1970) cover the May 1968 period.

The social and economic record of the 1960s is covered in William G. Andrews and Stanley Hoffmann (eds), *The Fifth Republic at Twenty* (Albany: State University of New York Press, 1981); Jane Marceau, *Class and Status in France: Economic Change and Social Immobility, 1945–1975* (Oxford: Clarendon Press, 1977); Philip M. Williams and Martin Harrison, *Politics and Society in de Gaulle's Republic* (New York: Doubleday, 1972); and Institut Charles de Gaulle, *De Gaulle en son siècle*, vol. III: *Moderniser la France* (Paris: Plon, 1992).

David Goldey's two chapters in Philip M. Williams, *French Politicians and Elections, 1951–1969* (Cambridge: Cambridge University Press, 1970), offer an excellent summary of the May 'events' and the June elections. Fuller studies include John Gretton, *Students and Workers: An Analytical Account of Dissent in France, May-June 1968* (London: Macdonald, 1969); David Hanley and A.P. Kerr (eds), *May 68: Coming of Age* (Basingstoke: Macmillan, 1989); and Julian Jackson, Anna-Louise Milne and James S. Williams (eds), *May 68: Rethinking France's Last Revolution* (Basingstoke: Palgrave, 2011). The year 1968 in the wider world is covered in Tony Judt, *Postwar: A History of Europe since 1945* (London: Heinemann, 2009), chapters 12–13; David Caute, *Sixty-Eight: The Year of the Barricades* (London: Hamish Hamilton, 1988); and Mark Kurlansky, *1968: The Year that Rocked the World* (London: Jonathan Cape, 2004).

Numerous memoirs and diaries in French cover the inside story of May 1968 from the government perspective. Most illuminating are Alain

Peyrefitte, *C'était de Gaulle*, vol. III (Paris: Éditions de Fallois/Fayard, 2000), and Jacques Foccart, *Le Général en mai. Journal de l'Élysée – II: 1968–1969* (Paris: Fayard/Jeune Afrique, 1998). Philippe Artières and Emmanuelle Giry (eds), *68, les archives du pouvoir. Chroniques inédites d'un état face à la crise* (Paris: Archives Nationales/L'Iconoclaste, 2018) is equally revealing on the written record.

Philippe Alexandre's *Le Duel de Gaulle–Pompidou* (Paris: Grasset, 1970) is an excellent analysis of relations between President and Prime Minister.

The polling institute IFOP offers a good record of public opinion through the crisis in IFOP, 'La Crise de mai 68', www.ifop.com/publication/ifop-collectors-n4-la-crise-de-mai-1968/

14 Departure, death, afterlives, 1968–2020

On 31 March 1969, visiting Washington for Eisenhower's state funeral, de Gaulle told ambassador Hervé Alphand that he would be gone in a month: he felt certain of losing the coming referendum on reforms to France's Senate and regions, set for 27 April. He had called the vote 'because I cannot govern without being sure of having the mass of the French behind me. But the present Parliament is the result of the Great Fear of May 1968. It doesn't represent the current state of people's minds.'[1] De Gaulle's own independence within France's political system was as important to him as France's independence within the world system; without it, the game was not worth the candle.

In 1968, independence for de Gaulle meant the freedom to undertake major reforms, if necessary against the very conservative Parliament elected in June. He announced the agenda at his press conference of 9 September 1968. The new Education Minister, Edgar Faure, would present a university reform that autumn. A reform to give workers a voice in the management of firms would follow. And France's embryonic regional structures would be reinforced, and the Senate merged with the Economic and Social Council. Because the Senate could not be expected to reform itself, moreover, the necessary constitutional amendment would be put to referendum. All three reforms were part of an overall project – to extend and reinforce 'participation' in French society.[2]

The press conference was de Gaulle's last. He devoted barely a quarter of it to international issues. In the past, the average had been two-thirds, but the legacy of May 1968, and the Soviet invasion of Czechoslovakia, had left his foreign policy in disarray.

There were to be no more international fireworks, only a visit to Turkey in October 1968, and the brief farewell to Eisenhower. The 'pivot to the West' signalled by Nixon's visit in February 1969 was significant, but hardly triumphant. De Gaulle's last ten months in power unfolded on a domestic, not a world stage.

At the background of domestic politics lay one question: would the President, who turned 78 in November, serve his full seven-year term, till December 1972? Foccart, his loyal adviser, wrote in his diary that the General's memory was still 'fantastic' – but also that he was ageing and fatigued. De Gaulle's son-in-law Alain de Boissieu had heard him say he planned to leave as soon as his reforms were completed; he had even heard Philippe de Gaulle urge his father to quit.[3]

Speculation about de Gaulle's future was fuelled by the presence of an obvious successor: Georges Pompidou. Pompidou, de Gaulle had told his press conference, was 'in the reserve of the Republic'.[4] That sounded, probably intentionally, like the deep freeze. But Pompidou had other ideas.

Reform and reaction, 1968–1969

Faure's 'framework law', the first of the three reforms, aimed to recast France's universities on a more human scale. Huge faculties were divided into smaller departments, each with a governing council including representatives elected from academics, students, and other staff; lectures were to be complemented by more seminars, examinations by assessed coursework; interdisciplinarity was encouraged, and political expression allowed; the idea of selection at entry was abandoned.[5] Such liberalism appalled the Gaullist parliamentarians. Faure's bill still passed by 441 votes to 0 in the National Assembly, but only after being much watered down. And the apparent unanimity did not prevent later grumbling, from conservative politicians, from advisers like Foccart, and from professors annoyed at the dilution of their own power.[6]

Then, in mid-November 1968, France faced a currency crisis. Worried by the impact of the Grenelle settlement on France's competitiveness and the budget deficit, investors began offloading their francs. The Germans refused to take the pressure off by revaluing the deutschmark. The Bank of France spent hard-earned gold reserves to defend the currency but many experts, and ministers promoted by Pompidou, including Marcellin (Interior), Chalandon (Industry) and Chirac (Budget), judged devaluation inevitable. Instead, de Gaulle resorted to an austerity package (exchange controls, limitations on imports, raised taxes and interest rates, and tougher price controls) that required the budget to be re-cast hours after the Assembly had voted it.[7] On 24 November he ruled out devaluation, blamed the crisis (justly) on the May events – and acknowledged that 'countries better off than ourselves' had assisted by buying francs.[8] He meant the Americans. Saving the franc had cost France a portion of independence. There could be no more attacks on the dollar. Currency crises were associated with the instability of the Third and Fourth Republics. This one, France's first in a decade, left de Gaulle demoralised.[9]

It was an unpromising moment to consider de Gaulle's long-cherished plan to reform industrial relations. In the midst of the franc crisis, the head of the CNPF, Paul Huvelin, expressed his worries about the effects of 'participation' on business in *Le Monde*.[10] The CNPF's hostility, and that of many Gaullists, was matched by that of the unions, for whom 'participation' smacked of class collaboration. By the year's end, in any case, the planned reform was nowhere near ready. Even when it was, it would not correspond to the proper object of a referendum under Article 11 of the Constitution: the 'organisation of the public authorities'. So the 'change in the very condition of workers' that de Gaulle had wanted since RPF days went to the bottom of the reform pile – and its place as the object of a possible popular vote was taken by the Senate and regional reform.[11]

France's 21 regions, each grouping 2 or more of the 95 *départements*, had been created in 1964. Chaired by a regional prefect, the regional economic development councils (CODERs) brought together interest-group representatives, government nominees, and delegates of local councils. Their rationale was partly technical: the region was considered a more rational framework than the *département* for planning large-scale industrial or infrastructure projects. But it was also political. Local government remained dominated by Fourth Republic politicians. New regional structures might loosen the stranglehold of these *notables* on France's territories; create a space where '*forces vives*', dynamic groups like young farmers, young managers, or even moderate trade unionists, could contribute to a progressive, Gaullist-led, consensus for development; and, in time, reinforce Gaullist positions in local councils.[12] De Gaulle had offered a further justification for regional reform in his Lyon speech of 24 March 1968. France's 'centuries-old effort of centralisation', necessary in the past to build the nation, had done its job; now, powers should be passed back from centre to regions.[13] Under the 1969 reform, new regional councils, replacing the CODERs, would include local elected officials but also Deputies (mostly Gaullist), and, for 40% of their representation, economic and social representatives – and thus, it was to be hoped, the *forces vives*. The reformed regions would gain new powers over town and country planning and public investments.[14] This was still, however, a modest, incremental change. Too limited for the modernists, the reform was still considered a threat by the *notables* – and by traditionalist Gaullists who feared it would undermine national unity.[15]

The stronghold in Paris of conservative, rural France was the upper house of Parliament, comprising 283 Senators elected by mayors and (mostly rural) local councillors. In 1958 de Gaulle, expecting an obstructive National Assembly, had viewed the Senate as his ally. In fact, the Gaullists conquered the Assembly, while the Senate, though unable to block laws outright, proved an irritant over policy areas including agriculture, Algeria, or the Bomb. Worse, its president, Gaston Monnerville, had accused de Gaulle of an 'abuse of authority' over the 1962 constitutional reform.[16] Now de Gaulle wanted to merge the Senate with the Economic and Social Council, a consultative body representing economic and social groups. The merged Assembly would also be purely consultative: it might issue opinions about legislation, but without being able to amend or block it, even temporarily.[17]

The idea was hardly new: it appeared in de Gaulle's Bayeux speech of 16 June 1946, and again in a speech given at Lille on 23 April 1966.[18] Alain Poher, who had succeeded Monnerville as president of the Senate in October 1968, had sought conciliation with de Gaulle, for example through better representation of towns in the Senate, or closer co-operation with the Economic and Social Council. But this fell far short of de Gaulle's plan.[19]

His reform sprang, in part, from the same considerations as the regional project: a revived upper house incorporating the *forces vives* via group representation would be a more dynamic assembly than the Senate, channelling demands from a wide section of civil society, not just established rural interests.[20] The project also reflected his long-standing mistrust of the *notables*, whom he considered to have been pro-Vichy.[21] There was, finally, a purely political motive, which he confided to Foccart: 'The Senate will always be against us. The main thing now is to make sure they don't bother us any more: they won't be legislators any longer.'[22] Here was a challenge that the Senators, and the mayors and councillors who supported them, were determined to resist.

None of de Gaulle's reforms – to the universities, to industrial relations, to the regions and Senate – mobilised the Gaullist majority elected in June 1968; rather the reverse. An added difficulty was that Couve de Murville, an excellent executant of de Gaulle's policies over a decade as Foreign Minister, was a mediocre Prime Minister who failed to weld his government into a team.[23] Foccart reported the gloomy atmosphere among Gaullist parliamentarians, extending even to Jacques Chaban-Delmas, President of the National Assembly, throughout the autumn.[24] Doubting de Gaulle's ability to continue till 1972, they increasingly looked to the successor in the wings.

Pompidou and the succession

Pompidou was now simply a Deputy for the rural *département* of Cantal. But as honorary president of the Gaullist parliamentary group, he was well placed to rally his fellow-parliamentarians to his future candidacy.[25] Meanwhile his friends in government kept him informed of de Gaulle's criticisms of him in the Council of Ministers, while he himself did not spare the General and his reforms in private conversations.[26]

What irreparably damaged relations between the two men, however, was the Marković affair. Stevan Marković, a bodyguard of the film star Alain Delon, was found dead on a rubbish dump on 1 October 1968. The police investigation revealed that he had organised, and photographed for purposes of blackmail, orgies for show-business clients at houses near Paris. By mid-October, rumours were circulating that a Marković contact had named Pompidou's wife Claude in a statement. De Gaulle had wanted

Pompidou informed, but Couve dragged his feet, and Justice Minister René Capitant, a long-term enemy of Pompidou, appears to have welcomed the news; neither, wrote Pompidou later, had shown 'the slightest reaction of a man of honour'.[27] The police investigation appeared more focused on involving the Pompidous than on identifying the murderer. Pompidou spoke to de Gaulle in person about the affair twice in November, and was fobbed off with vague statements of sympathy – and even a suggestion that Claude ought to have chosen her friends more carefully.[28] On 15 January, Foccart recorded Pompidou's fury at the continuing investigation, which mentioned Claude at every turn.[29] It suggested to Pompidou that de Gaulle wanted him damaged; the near-filial relationship he had built with the General over 24 years, shaken in May 1968, was now over.[30]

The political fall-out soon followed. On 17 January, speaking to the press during a visit to Rome, Pompidou casually remarked that 'it was no secret' that he would be a candidate at the next presidential election.[31] De Gaulle replied by official communiqué five days later: he had the 'duty and the intention' of 'fulfilling [his] mandate to its close'. Pompidou confirmed his candidacy from Geneva on 13 February, stating that 'I will have, God willing, a national destiny'.[32] Two weeks later, his speech to France's Chambers of Commerce, a hymn of praise (bolder then than it would have been 50 years later) for healthy business profits, was interpreted by *Le Monde* as the start of a presidential campaign.[33] Was Pompidou betting on de Gaulle losing his referendum and resigning? Probably not – but his repeated statements of availability still weighed on the campaign. De Gaulle certainly found them premature and hurtful.[34] Mindful of the referendum, however, on 12 March he entertained the Pompidous to dinner at the Élysée. Four months earlier this might have looked like a gesture of support, especially to Claude. Now, the dinner was too late and its effect diluted by the Debrés being invited too. The atmosphere was chilly, and de Gaulle never saw Pompidou again.[35]

Towards the referendum, February–April 1969

Despite a much-trumpeted consultation in autumn 1968, the text of the Senate and regional reform was mostly drafted by a small inner circle.[36] As expected, the revamped Senate would have the right to issue 'opinions', not to vote legislation. Changes were also planned to rules governing the eventuality of a president resigning or dying in office (the prime minister, not the president of the Senate as in the 1958 Constitution, would become caretaker president pending an election) and procedures for constitutional revision. At de Gaulle's insistence, voters were given the whole text to help decide: nearly 10,000 words, 14 pages of close print, which would repeal or amend 21 of the Constitution's 92 articles.[37] De Gaulle also insisted on a single vote on this unwieldy package: voters would not, in particular, be allowed to back the (relatively popular) regional reform while refusing (rather unpopular) Senate proposal. Thus 'the General ensured that the struggle would be a hard one – and that if he won, the victory would have real significance'.[38]

As 1969 opened, the reform lacked enthusiastic supporters even in government. But de Gaulle took the plunge anyway, announcing the referendum for 'this springtime' during a speech at Quimper (Brittany) on 2 February. On 19 February, the Council of Ministers fixed the vote for 27 April.[39]

Publicly optimistic, de Gaulle was privately the opposite; apparently favourable, the opinion polls also showed the fragility of his support. At first, indeed, de Gaulle tried to wriggle out of his own referendum; the date of 27 April, he claimed disingenuously, only committed the government, not himself.[40] The Gaullist 'barons' demurred: whatever its merits, they said, the referendum could not now be abandoned.[41] So de Gaulle sought to breathe life into his inert text with a broadcast on 11 March 1969. What he was offering, he claimed with much exaggeration, was 'the great French reform of our century' which would allow each person to 'participate actively' in his, or her, own destiny.[42]

The opinion polls in mid-March appeared to offer him solid backing; among voters who had made up their minds, 54% planned to vote Yes, and 46% No.[43] But the detailed figures were less upbeat. While 54% of respondents supported the regional reform, only 26% favoured the Senate changes. Even (Gaullist) UDR supporters were luke-warm: only 47% backed the Senate changes.[44] De Gaulle's core supporters, therefore, were looking quite soft.

Everyone else attacked the project throughout March. Communists, Socialists, Radicals, and the centrist Centre Démocrate all declared for a No vote. The Conseil d'État issued a negative opinion of the referendum project, as it had for that of October 1962: constitutional amendments, it said, had to be adopted with Parliament's agreement under Article 89 of the Constitution, not simply submitted to referendum under Article 11.[45] All these adversaries might be counted as the usual suspects. Less readily dismissed was René Cassin, the first jurist of Free France, who now called for a No vote.[46] Worse, the campaign was supposed to be run from the Prime Minister's office, but Couve proved incapable of galvanising his own troops, and especially an unenthusiastic UDR.[47] Meanwhile the hitherto unknown Alain Poher came across as 'reasonable, reassuring, moderate' as he fought to save his Senate.[48]

De Gaulle's doubts now took another form. Late in March he told Alphand, and Foccart, and de Boissieu, that he expected to lose the referendum and to resign immediately, and that such a departure would suit him; to de Boissieu he added that his resignation, and Pompidou's likely election, would settle France's institutions definitively.[49] That he planned to resign if he lost was hardly a revelation; he had said the same in 1958, 1961 and (twice) in 1962. Nevertheless, at the start of the campaign only a quarter of poll respondents believed de Gaulle would go. When, therefore, he confirmed his intention publicly, on 10 April in his last televised interview with Michel Droit, adding that a No would set France on a road to 'adventure', he ensured that the vote would be as much about him as about the reforms.[50]

Polls on 11–12 April showed the Yes vote holding at 55%.[51] Jacques Duhamel, the most pro-Gaullist of Centrists, and former Finance Minister Valéry Giscard d'Estaing, still notionally a Gaullist ally at the head of his Républicains Indépendants, were the last politicians, in mid-April, to declare their preferences: both backed a No vote.[52] De Gaulle dismissed Giscard as 'nothing', and told his son that the referendum would pass.[53] To others, however – even to leading Gaullists heading for campaign meetings – he gave the impression almost of looking forward to defeat and departure. Meanwhile the rumour gained ground that a No vote would be a vote for Pompidou.[54] On 21–2 April, for the first time, a poll showed 53% of respondents for No – the same level as the final result.[55]

On Wednesday 23 April, de Gaulle told his last Council of Ministers that 'We hope to meet next week. If this were not to happen, then a chapter of France's history would be closed'.[56] Two days later, he recorded a final broadcast. It was not his best. Over half was devoted to the chaos that would engulf France if he left – and to a promise not to run for a third term in 1972.[57] After lunch de Gaulle left the Élysée with Yvonne, pausing on the way out to shake hands – for the first time – with the military commander of the palace. On reaching Colombey he told Charlotte, the servant, that they were home for good.[58]

Defeat and departure, April 1969

'To vote Yes on 27 April', de Gaulle told François Goguel six months later, 'you really needed to be a Gaullist.'[59] Every non-Gaullist political force opposed him. But then, so (nearly) had they in October 1962, when de Gaulle had won comfortably. The one strictly political difference, Giscard's switch from Yes in 1962 to No in 1969, was significant, but he was followed by just half his troops: hardly enough to bring the Yes down nearly 15 points, from 62.3% to 47.6%. Rather, Giscard represented a wider phenomenon. In 1962, aside from the issue of de Gaulle's continuation in power, the referendum had been about one important, straightforward question: the direct election of the president. The turgid text of 1969 offered no such simplicity. The referendum was therefore even more about the person of de Gaulle, and on much less favourable terms. For the old recipe, 'me or chaos', could hardly work: in May 1968, France had had de Gaulle *and* chaos. Now, moreover, Pompidou, the real victor of the June elections, was available.[60] Worse, people brought their grievances to the polling-booth. 'Professors upset by the effects of Edgar Faure's university reform, local *notables* threatened by the plan for new regions, businessmen worried about participation in industries, shopkeepers upset by new taxes and higher payments for social security – all these turned away from de Gaulle'.[61]

The aggrieved were overwhelmingly male, according to the poll of 21–22 April. Fully 56% of women voters supported de Gaulle – but only 40% of men. Housewives and the retired remained loyal, by 63%–37%. But 53% of farmers, 56% of blue-collar workers, 61% of middle managers, small business people, and white-collar workers, and 70% of senior managers, voted No.[62] Among *all* working groups, support dropped by 9–15 points between March and April.[63] There were even 21 No voters in Colombey, an unprecedented phenomenon.[64]

Whatever de Gaulle's conceptions of democracy, he was no dictator. At 10.30pm on polling day, he telephoned a terse communiqué to Tricot: 'I am ceasing to exercise my functions as President of the Republic. This decision takes effect today at noon.' It reached Agence France Presse at 12.10am on Monday 28 April. His staff had emptied their offices, and his, by 12 noon. De Gaulle accepted neither his ex-president's pension nor his *ex officio* seat on the Constitutional Council. But he kept a small Paris office and secretariat.[65] He planned a clean break from the politics of his country.[66] The first test was the election of his successor.

The Gaullist 'barons' chose Pompidou, quietly over lunch, on 28 April.[67] De Gaulle was realistic enough to wish him success, in a private letter dated 30 April – adding that it would have been preferable for Pompidou not to have started his campaign several weeks early.[68] But he refused any public gesture of support, leaving France for a holiday in Ireland early on 10 May, and staying till after polling day.[69]

The last 'public' photos of de Gaulle show him striding the windblown hills of Cork or Tipperary, alone or with Yvonne and occasionally Flohic. The apparent isolation of the images was overdone. Prime Minister Jack Lynch had greeted the de Gaulles at Cork airport. France's ambassador in Dublin joined them for some of the early days. Lynch hosted a lunch in Dublin for them at the end of their stay, where de Gaulle proposed a toast to 'the whole of Ireland' (the 'troubles' in the North were just gathering pace).[70] On 17 June, they dined with President Eamonn De Valera: according to Roussel, the two presidents voiced their shared Anglophobia in English, a language de Gaulle never used with the British or Americans.[71]

Meanwhile Pompidou successfully converted de Gaulle's referendum defeat into his own presidential victory, winning back the support of Giscard and Duhamel and seeing off unexpectedly strong challenges from Poher and from Jacques Duclos, the Communist candidate. His 44.5% first-round score, based around a still-cohesive Gaullist base, was only a whisker short of de Gaulle's 44.7% in 1965, though on a lower turnout and with a more obviously conservative composition (fewer workers, more managers and small business people); at the run-off on 15 June, he won easily with 58.2% against Poher. In Ireland, de Gaulle ordered champagne, and sent Pompidou a brief letter of congratulation.[72] But he gloomily told Flohic that 'France's slide into mediocrity will continue',[73] before returning home on 19 June. Perhaps Pompidou's early measures justified his predecessor's pessimism. He unceremoniously ditched workplace 'participation'. He devalued the franc in August 1969. And at a European summit at Den Haag in December, he opened the door to serious negotiations with Britain about joining the EEC.

A brief retirement, 1969–1970

Philippe de Gaulle later claimed that sadness at his departure had broken his father's heart.[74] This seems hard to square both with his own earlier equanimity at the prospect of losing the referendum, and with his earlier confidences to Philippe that he planned to leave office on turning 80.[75] Indeed, one interpretation of the referendum is that it was an elaborate form of political suicide.[76] This is exaggerated: de Gaulle did not set out to lose. Rather, he followed the only course consistent with his own conception of how to wield power, knowing the risks and preparing for the worst.[77] But in the end no amount of preparation could ready him for the severance.[78]

Many French people also found the referendum result traumatic. De Gaulle received some 50,000 letters after April 1969, in which guilt ('It took your leaving to make me realise how great your place was') was mingled with love, sorrow, surprise, anger, and shame at the ingratitude of the French.[79] A poll in summer 1969 found that de Gaulle's departure was most regretted, not by a bourgeoisie mostly delighted with Pompidou, but by workers and the retired.[80] The manner of his departure shocked even his opponents because it showed that – contrary to their prejudices – he was a democrat after all.[81]

De Gaulle lived less than 17 months after returning from Ireland. His retirement, at Colombey, was conventional. He enjoyed the visits of grandchildren, walked in the woods next to La Boisserie, and wrote his memoirs. His one foreign trip, in June 1970, was to Spain, where he visited General Franco – a meeting that would have caused a furore had he been in office. The *caudillo* appears to have disappointed him. A planned visit to China (and Mao) never took place.[82]

De Gaulle had authorised the publication of five volumes of his major speeches – those he had written out and kept – and they appeared in September 1970. Then came *Renewal*, the first volume of his *Memoirs of Hope*, on 23 October 1970; de Gaulle had injured his hand signing 300 copies two weeks earlier. He planned for two further volumes, to appear in 1971 and 1972, closing his unfinished presidential term.[83] The *Memoirs of Hope* maintain the superlative writing style, and the tendentiousness, of the *War Memoirs*, but the subject-matter (despite Algeria) lent itself less to a dramatic treatment, and there are no revelations comparable to those of his epic quarrels with his allies.

Philippe saw his father on 27 September 1970 and found him in good humour and excellent physical form: they went mushrooming and he jumped across a ditch to pick some chanterelles. Saying farewell, however, he looked at Philippe as if for the last time, which it was.[84] A month later de Gaulle's former staffer Pierre-Louis Blanc found him musing on September's Middle Eastern terror attacks, inequalities between nations, and – astonishingly for a man of his convictions – the need for a world government.[85]

Just after 7pm on 9 November 1970, as he settled to a game of patience, de Gaulle suffered a rupture of the aorta, the largest artery, provoking extreme pain, massive internal bleeding, and loss of consciousness. He died in barely half an hour, 13 days short of his eightieth birthday.[86] His will, written in 1952, specified a simple funeral in the little church at Colombey, for family, Companions of the Liberation, and the village council – and no speeches or fanfares.[87] These arrangements were hardly adequate to accommodate the outpouring of emotion at his death, summed up with economy and poignancy by Jacques Faizant's cartoon of Marianne, symbol of France, weeping beside a fallen oak. Some 30,000–40,000 mourners converged on Colombey on 12 November hoping to accompany him to his simple grave. On the same day, at President Pompidou's instigation, a requiem Mass was held in Notre-Dame cathedral in Paris. Some 80 heads of state attended.[88]

Afterlives

De Gaulle had never ceased to make enemies: senior officers, Vichyites, Communists, supporters of *Algérie française*, parliamentarians who identified democracy with the rule of the National Assembly, Atlanticists, and Euro-federalists, all had reason to detest him.[89] A coalition of the discontented had overthrown him. In death he triumphed over all of them. In the short term, as Jean Daniel of the left-wing *Nouvel Observateur* wrote, 'Damaged in 1965, broken in May '68, killed off in April 1969, the Gaullian magic has returned to life, and in dazzling fashion.'[90] In the half-century since his death, a powerful de Gaulle myth has submerged oppositions and critiques.

Colombey was an early focus of the mythologising. From 9 November 1971, the Order of the Liberation began organising annual 'pilgrimages' with a visit to the grave and Mass in the church. The same year – on 18 June – a subscription opened to commemorate the General with a great monument, on a hill visible from La Boisserie. Although de Gaulle's will had specified no monuments or statues, a 44-metre-high Cross of Lorraine was opened by Pompidou on 18 June 1972. After Yvonne's death in 1979, the ground floor of La Boisserie opened to the public, adding a further 'pilgrim' site. Meanwhile the politicians began using the village for their own purposes. Giscard visited, as President, in November 1975, but was greeted with shouts of 'Traitor!'. Chirac, leading the (neo-)Gaullist opposition to Giscard, organised a 40,000-person march to Colombey for 18 June 1980.[91] The general public came in their hundreds of thousands every year of the 1970s, and took home any number of more or less kitsch souvenirs made in Germany, Spain, Greece, China, Japan as well as France. Even in the late 1990s the annual number still exceeded 100,000.[92]

But de Gaulle is physically commemorated far beyond Colombey: indeed, as Jackson observes, 'De Gaulle is everywhere' – on the names of streets and squares in 3,600 French localities as well as towns in Europe, Africa, and Latin America, in Colorado, Texas, Iowa, Louisiana, and Ohio.[93] France's Communists began commemorating him on street names less than ten years after his departure – in Vénissieux, where he shared the privilege with Thorez, Lenin, and Mandela.[94] From 1990, statues appeared – in Quebec, Warsaw, Bucharest, Moscow, and next to Carlton Gardens in London.[95]

The year 1990 was crucial because it marked a triple anniversary – 100 years since his birth, 50 since the *Appel du 18 juin*, 20 since his death. Commemorated materially across the world, de

Gaulle became an immaterial 'site of memory', an essential reference point of France's identity. The leaders who sent tributes at that year's gigantic international conference ranged from Nixon to Yasser Arafat (who always wore the Cross of Lorraine pendant de Gaulle had sent him in 1970).[96] The Left rallied almost unanimously. Régis Debray, former companion-in-arms of Che Guevara, hailed de Gaulle as 'the first man of the twenty-first century'.[97]

For the French public there was no doubt. In a 1990 poll, 45% of respondents named de Gaulle the most important *world* figure of the twentieth century: Roosevelt, Mao Tse-Tung, and Stalin each scored just 1%.[98] In both 2005 and 2010, he easily topped polls for the greatest Frenchman of all time, coming well ahead of Napoleon, Charlemagne, Jean Jaurès, or Louis XIV. He was viewed as good as well as great: in 1990, 27% of respondents considered his role had been 'very positive' and 57% 'fairly positive', against a mere 4% of respondents who took a negative view. Polls in 2010, though the questions were posed rather differently, showed very little change, as if the views of the French had been fixed by 1990.[99]

This hyperbolic approval of de Gaulle was given at a time when Gaullism, the creed of a political party for a generation and more after his death, was viewed – by 67% of respondents in 2010 – as an irrelevance, with little contemporary meaning.[100] It is the historic figure whom the French revere.

This reverence springs in part from his ability to represent to the French what was best about themselves. Within his inner circle, he inspired fierce devotion, even love. Partisan Gaullism survived until 2002, when Chirac merged the Gaullist party with the non-Gaullist moderate Right. But it was the non-Gaullists, often the most eloquent in their tributes, who turned majority support into near-unanimity. For the historian Michel Winock, who describes himself as a 'posthumous Gaullist', 'We had the impression, as long as he lived, that we French were not so mediocre'.[101] His appeal to left-wingers arose partly from his ability to transcend the milieu from which he emerged: a soldier of bourgeois, Catholic, and traditionalist origins, he constantly clashed with the army, the ruling class, the Church, and the conservatives.[102]

His appeal also arises from private qualities, and from nostalgia for a lost age of political and personal integrity: 'Can one imagine today', writes Hazareesingh, 'a French statesman insisting, as de

Gaulle did, on paying out of his own pocket for the meals of members of his family when he invited them to the Élysée?'[103] He was capable, too, of a touching personal attentiveness: for example, getting up early in his dressing-gown to make coffee for Joxe, who was spending a night at Colombey before departing on a dangerous mission to Algeria.[104] As Sulzberger noted wryly, 'The old General works a limited number of hours each day and spends at least part of them in personally answering letters from unimportant people – like a note I got from him.'[105] His correspondence is littered with personal letters, often of condolence on the loss of a spouse, addressed to people such as Spears with whom he was politically on execrable terms.[106] His love for his daughter Anne is perhaps the most eloquent testimony of the human warmth of this man who so frequently appeared as cold, distant, and formidable.

Yet for all of his intimate, personal qualities, assessing de Gaulle means, essentially, assessing his public achievements. And it is hard, as Jackson observes, to escape the heroic frame of reference de Gaulle himself set out for them. Thus when Johnson calls de Gaulle in the late 1960s 'an aging, erratic, and entirely mortal conservative politician', he seems hardly to have taken the measure of the man.[107] Yet Johnson's detachment from the de Gaulle myth is a necessity for any critical appreciation.

The achievement

The *Appel du 18 juin* remains both the founding moment of Gaullism and the single act for which de Gaulle is best remembered; 43% of poll respondents in 1990 cited de Gaulle as primarily 'the man of 18 June', and 84% approved of the speech. He supplied the Resistance with an indispensable focus and symbol; and 'with cunning, tactical skill and strategic vision, he leveraged his minuscule resources into securing for France a place among the victorious powers'.[108] His resistance leadership was approved by 75% in 1990.[109]

De Gaulle was, secondly, the 'man of the liberation' (27% of respondents in 1990): as Hazareesingh observes, 'His march down the Champs-Élysées in Paris in August 1944 remains one of the iconic moments in modern French collective memory.'[110] But his role then was substance as much as symbol. He ensured, as no-one else could have, a safe transition from Vichy's rule to that of an uncontested, and republican, state. And his provisional government's social and economic settlement lasted four decades.

The achievement of Free France and the Liberation era was matched by that of the presidency, beginning with the resolution of the Algerian conflict. De Gaulle was instrumental in halting three insurrections by white settlers, the army, or both, in 1958, 1960, and 1961. He extricated France from a hideous war that had caused the downfall of successive governments and then of the Fourth Republic. Algerian independence was approved by 64% to 18% of the 1990 sample.[111] For sub-Saharan Africa, meanwhile, he ensured a peaceful transition to independence.

De Gaulle's new Constitution not only brought France much-needed political stability; it brought consensus on the nature of the regime, arguably for the first time since 1789. De Gaulle was 'the man of the Fifth Republic' for 15% of the 1990 sample, and 88% approved the direct election of the president.[112] Political stability was matched by economic: the franc kept its value for a decade after 1958, France's trade and budget deficits were diminished or even reversed, and strong growth sustained without interruption. Remarkably, 62% of the 1990 sample took de Gaulle at his own self-evaluation as a 'man above parties', and 63%, rising to 75% in 2010, considered that his economic policies benefited all French people and not only the privileged.[113] Public services grew as fast as the economy; the thorny issue of subsidies to Catholic schools was finally resolved; France was given a full-blown Culture Ministry. And when, after a decade, de Gaulle felt he had lost the confidence of the French, he departed within hours – a gesture approved by 62% of the 1990 sample.[114]

Beyond the Hexagon, de Gaulle might infuriate his allies, but he restored France's self-respect, a degree of independence, and the capacity to be taken seriously. And not only the self-respect of France: as he set his seal on the process of Franco-German reconciliation in 1962, he lavished praise on the German people like no other statesman. He could, because he was de Gaulle. His brief words thrown out in their own languages to crowds across the world redounded to the credit of their listeners but also, inevitably, to that of France. Meanwhile France's new-found economic stability allowed de Gaulle to implement the Rome Treaty faster and more fully than any Fourth Republic politician could have. He equipped France with nuclear weapons (a success at least in his own terms), and modernised her armed forces. His withdrawal from NATO posed the question of Europe's defence relations with the United States as no speech could have done. His attempt to re-cast the international system was undertaken in the name of peace, not national aggrandisement, and his diplomacy had an exemplary power. His triptych of 'Détente, entente, cooperation' in East–West relations was on everybody's lips by early 1968; Nixon acknowledged de Gaulle's 'crucial role' in his own decision to recognise Communist China.[115] Within months of ending the Algerian War, de Gaulle had made France a source of inspiration to the Third World, notably through his firm independence of the United States and criticism of the Vietnam War. And he ensured that in per capita terms, France was second to none in aid to less developed countries. Looking back, poll respondents in both 1990 and 2010 identified grandeur and independence as essential, and respectable, foreign policy aims of the de Gaulle presidency.[116]

There are more intangible achievements, too. No-one else has managed to unite so many of the French – nearly all on 26 August 1944, an overwhelming majority in September 1958, and again nearly all since his death.[117] Even the Communists became positive from 1974.[118] De Gaulle's rhetoric, too, favoured unity more than division, inviting the French to aim high for their country rather than to despise or envy their neighbours or political opponents. His pedagogy, said Kissinger, aimed to show the French what it meant to be truly independent; for Winock, he offered a 'substitute for the great people that we had ceased to be'.[119]

The final intangible was the intuitions, some inconsequential (that Jacqueline Kennedy would marry a Greek shipowner), others of crucial importance. He understood in 1940 – as the essential premise of the *Appel du 18 juin* – that Europe's war was a world war. He realised that the Soviets did not seek war, at least from 1958, that the Sino-Soviet conflict would dislocate the world Communist movement, that East European peoples retained strong national aspirations, and that Europe would not be forever divided. He understood and acted upon the aspiration of colonised peoples to independence. He foresaw the collapse of the Bretton Woods monetary system, and the challenge that the – essentially technocratic – 'Monnet method' of European integration would pose to Europe's democratic systems. He warned two American presidents of the dangers of being sucked into Vietnam, and was ignored; he perfectly anticipated the corrosive effects on Israeli society of a prolonged occupation of Palestinian territories; he expected the breakup of Yugoslavia after Tito's death.[120] His often-repeated view that the United States could not indefinitely be counted on to defend Europe looked insulting in the 1960s; in the Trump era it appears as common sense. Few statesmen of any generation have got so much right.

And few can point to a comparable record of achievement: all at once liberator, founding father, educator in civic virtues, protector of the nation, and, after April 1969, a bit of a martyr, suitable for a Catholic country.[121]

But to stop there would be to ignore the failures, and worse, of his record.

A critical appraisal

No aspect of de Gaulle's achievement is beyond criticism. This applies even to de Gaulle's record as France's leader in war and liberation, which, though the least open to reproach, invites several qualifications. First, his extreme mistrust of his allies (who often, it is true, invited it) was at times counter-productive and a source of unnecessary conflict. Second, his account of the war and liberation overemphasises the role of the Free French at the expense both of the Allies and of the internal Resistance. Third, the claim that de Gaulle saved France from civil war at the Liberation is also overdone: France's Communists, though tempted by revolution in 1944, had no backing from Moscow, faced hundreds of thousands of Allied troops on French territory, and were therefore unlikely insurrectionists. Fourth, whatever the achievements of the Liberation government, de Gaulle still left France in a parlous economic state when he resigned in January 1946. Fifth and finally, his record in the colonies Free France ruled was one of intensified economic exploitation (also practised by the British), fierce repression in the Levant in 1943, and excessively cautious openings, at Brazzaville and in the granting of citizenship to a handful of Algerians, to colonial aspirations.

Turning to Algeria, the picture becomes altogether more sombre. De Gaulle's direct responsibility for the bloody repression in Guelma and Sétif in May 1945 is not established; but it happened on his watch and his memoirs show no awareness of its devastating human and political effect. After his return to power, his Algerian policy was marked by deception, lack of realism, and brutality. To French Algerians, he vowed in 1960 not to hand over power to the FLN,[122] before doing just that in 1962. Over the long-drawn-out contacts and negotiations with the FLN, he took up untenable positions – a permanent cease-fire as precondition for negotiations, no exclusive role for the FLN as representing the Algerian people, a possible partition of Algeria, shared sovereignty over the Sahara – which he would later have to shed, prolonging the conflict unnecessarily. But the worst stains on his treatment of Algeria, and indeed on his whole career, were the Challe Plan and the treatment of the *harkis*. The Challe Plan, with its free-fire zones and mass displacement of populations, inflicted colossal suffering on some 2 million rural Algerians, and would meet the definition of a war crime under present-day international law. The military victory it achieved was worthless, managing at most to buttress a tawdry claim that Algerian independence had been freely granted. As the war ended, de Gaulle's reluctance to welcome onto French soil Algerians who had fought for France cost thousands of *harkis* their lives. Even the peaceful decolonisation of sub-Saharan Africa was a flawed process, the French Community evaporating within months of its creation.

At home, de Gaulle's most lasting legacy after 1958 was his Constitution – which he violated by calling the referendums of October 1962 and April 1969. The 'president above parties', its central figure imagined by de Gaulle since 1946, was an illusion, even in de Gaulle's time and certainly after. The lack of synchronisation between presidential and parliamentary terms, and the lack of clarity about who was really to govern France, produced, after 1986, three periods, totalling nine years, of confused 'cohabitation' between a president and a government of opposed political camps; resolution only came with the shortening of the presidential term to five years from 2002. The weakening of Parliament, combined with the government's offhand attitude towards interest groups, deprived France's political system of safety valves, contributing to the upheavals of May 1968. De Gaulle's most cherished domestic project, *participation*, might have become reality had he devoted the time to building a coalition around it; instead, it came to almost nothing and he blamed Pompidou's obstruction for its failure. As for his behaviour in May 1968, his consistent advocacy of using lethal force against protesters, his attempt to rush up the blind alley of a referendum, and his deliberate severance, however brief, of all communication with his own government and staff, add up to a mishandling of the crisis barely compensated by the success of his broadcast on returning from Baden-Baden. Consistently with his own (negative) self-evaluation, this was the most unfavourably judged aspect of his record for the 1990 poll sample, with 30% applauding his record to 32% disapproving.[123]

The grand design of de Gaulle's foreign policy, meanwhile, was left unrealised. De Gaulle did not end the Cold War, or create a political Europe, or reshape the world order, or settle European defence. He underestimated the essential role of Communist ideology in perpetuating Soviet rule, and overestimated the capacity of national sentiment in Eastern Europe to break it. His hope of turning Western Europe into a power bloc capable of acting independently of both superpowers was frustrated both by his partners' reluctance to accept the French leadership proposed in the Fouchet Plan, and by his own refusal to accept the degree of supranationality which alone might have permitted such a power bloc to be formed. His ambition to turn France into a broker between Germany and the Soviet Union, essential to his initiatives of 1966, proved illusory: West Germany launched its *Ostpolitik*, Russians and Americans engaged directly in their version of détente, and France was by-passed.

Indeed, de Gaulle's whole vision of French *grandeur* and a multipolar world was flawed from the start. It entailed, not so much equality between nation states, as a redrawing of the line separating great powers from the rest just sufficiently to include France in the great-power category, with the direction of the world's affairs entrusted to the resulting oligarchy. France playing the role of equal partner with the United States did not, for de Gaulle, mean the Netherlands could claim equality with France.[124] But there was no logical justification for denying any nation its chance of *grandeur*, or indeed its possession of the Bomb. A similar argument could be made in relation to the withdrawal from NATO's integrated command: de Gaulle was claiming a special position for France which he did not wish other powers to seek. For West Germany, for example, to have followed France and ordered all American troops and weapons off its soil would have destroyed NATO, wrecking the cornerstone of post-war West European security and turning de Gaulle's pessimism about the viability of the American commitment into a self-fulfilling prophecy.

Within Western Europe, meanwhile, de Gaulle's 'realistic' approach and refusal of supranationality transformed the workings of the EEC for the worse. By practising diplomacy, in an inversion of Clausewitz, as the continuation of war by other means,[125] de Gaulle made the EEC into an arena for the confrontation of selfish national interests, emptying the organisation of much of the idealism with which it had started. Clashes became more confrontational and compromises more elusive. And the only supranational initiative he allowed (indeed, fought for), on agriculture, locked France and Western Europe into a Common Agricultural Policy which benefited a few large farmers, promoted an unsustainable, intensive form of agriculture, and, defended by a cohesive policy community, proved recalcitrant to reform. Even the reconciliation with West Germany did not measure up to the promise of the 1962 honeymoon. The Élysée Treaty and the affair of the preamble opened a falling-out between the two neighbours which lasted until the 1970s.[126]

De Gaulle's relationship with the Third World, finally, was more a marriage of reason than the expression of France's special humanitarian vocation. Third World leaders liked de Gaulle's advocacy of Vietnam (often simply identified with the Viet Cong) against the United States, and of the Arab states against Israel. De Gaulle saw in the Third World an opportunity to benefit from American errors.[127] But his commitment in no way excluded the creation of French protectorates in the former colonies of sub-Saharan Africa, the devotion of much of France's aid budget to military assistance to favoured (and repressive) regimes, and the brutal treatment of Third World countries which, like Tunisia in 1961, crossed France. As Williams and Harrison ironically remarked, left-wing admiration for de Gaulle's anti-Americanism overlooked 'his bomb, his paratroops in his African satrapies, his support of Portugal and Katanga at the UN, and his sales of arms to South Africa'.[128]

Legacies and myths

No aspect of de Gaulle's achievement, therefore, appears as an unqualified success, though some, and notably his leadership of Free France, come close. How much of the achievement remains, half a century on? Institutionally, a great deal: from 1944–1946, women's suffrage and the Social Security system; from 1958–1969, the Constitution – flawed, certainly, but the least bad France has had; the Culture Ministry; the École Nationale d'Administration; France's regions, now enlarged and transformed. To these may be added France's status as a nuclear power, and, still, as one of the few powers capable of projecting military force across the globe; Europe's Common Agricultural Policy, for better and for worse; and the Élysée Treaty, a framework – once fences had been mended in the 1970s – for Franco-German co-operation at all levels. In foreign policy beyond Europe, France's special economic and military relations with former colonies remain, though on a less exclusive basis. By contrast, almost nothing remains of the grand design, and France has even rejoined the NATO command.

At least as important are the intangible aspects of the de Gaulle legacy – the de Gaulle myths, in which aspects of France's past are transformed, simplified, even distorted, and given a heroic dimension in the name of a greater good, the pride of French people in themselves and their country and the papering-over of their historic divisions. Not surprisingly, the myths cover the most painful periods of France's recent history – the war and the Occupation, decolonisation, and France's loss of status as a first-rank power. The French people, according to the canon of de Gaulle's wartime speeches, were united in resisting the Occupation; Vichy was not France but a handful of criminals; the Free French and the Resistance liberated Paris, or even France. The trauma of Algeria is treated by a benign narrative of decolonisation, starting with the January 1944 Brazzaville speech, which glosses over Sétif, Indochina, and the Challe Plan, and culminates in the granting of independence to Algeria and sub-Saharan Africa and the opening of a new chapter of mutually beneficial co-operation. The passage from world war to

Cold War, finally, and France's demotion to the status of second-rank power, were associated with 'Yalta', a supposed cynical deal by the United States, Britain, and the Soviet Union, to divide Europe into spheres of influence. Breaking 'Yalta' became synonymous with France's mission to re-cast the international system.

Not one of the myths withstood prolonged contact with reality. The Gaullist narrative of war and resistance, hegemonic during his presidency, was increasingly challenged from the 1970s; and Jacques Chirac's 1995 speech accepting the responsibility of France in the deportation of Jews to Nazi death camps firmly contradicted the Gaullist view that 'France', from 18 June 1940, was in London or Algiers, never in Vichy. No consensual account of the Algerian conflict (which was only officially acknowledged as a war in 1999) has emerged, either between France and Algeria or among the French population. As for the 'Yalta' myth, it could not readily survive a speedy process of European reunification, beginning with the breach of the Berlin wall, which left France sidelined.

The purpose of the Gaullist myths was to bind the wounds of a people divided and humiliated by the experiences of military defeat, political incoherence, international demotion, and colonial conflict; France could not hope to be the great and victorious power that de Gaulle wanted her to be if the French people did not believe in it. But the myths' temporary functionality carried the risk that the adjustment to reality would be all the harder.[129] For France to be a medium power, a major player in Europe but with no special claim to lead the continent, with a less than glorious imperial history and an ambiguous wartime role, was scarcely consistent with the Gaullist 'certain idea of France' (the British, of course, suffered from comparable difficulties, compounded by the illusion of having 'won the war'). For both countries, the adjustment is still underway, and the wartime legacy has become a hindrance more than a help.

Judged against his own vaulting ambitions for France and for the world, de Gaulle's record inevitably falls very short. Against almost any other criteria his achievement remains colossal. To have led France from comprehensive defeat to the status of a victorious power; to have crafted a comprehensive post-liberation settlement; to have extricated France, despite everything, from the Algerian imbroglio; to have given his country a new Constitution – any one of these would have ensured de Gaulle a place as one of France's leading statesmen. To have managed all four, and considerably more, is altogether exceptional. Three characteristics stand out. The first was that at his best, and like his Anglo-Saxon allies and adversaries Roosevelt and Churchill, he offered hope over the airwaves and appealed to the best sentiments of his people. The second is that de Gaulle succeeded both as a wartime and as a peacetime leader – like Roosevelt but unlike Churchill, whose peacetime record was mediocre. The third was that de Gaulle had started from almost nothing – a dingy office, a table, and a few chairs on the Victoria Embankment – and in this he differed from both Roosevelt and Churchill. Hence the verdict of Stanley Hoffmann, the Viennese Jew who first heard de Gaulle's broadcasts as a boy hiding in occupied France: 'His is the greatness of having left France greater than he found her, and of all his life having produced extraordinary results from mediocre resources.'[130]

Notes

1. Hervé Alphand, *L'Étonnement d'être* (Paris: Fayard 1977), p. 519.
2. Press conference of 9 September 1968, *DM*v, pp. 318–35: pp. 321–30.
3. Jacques Foccart, *Le Général en mai. Journal de l'Élysée – II, 1968–1969* (Paris: Fayard/Jeune Afrique, 1998), pp. 360, 364, 399–400, 539, 687.
4. Press conference of 9 September 1968, *DM*v, pp. 318–35: pp. 323–4.
5. Paul Gagnon, 'The Fifth Republic and Education: Modernity, Democracy, Culture', in William G. Andrews and Stanley Hoffmann (eds), *The Fifth Republic at Twenty* (Albany: State University of New York Press, 1981), pp. 367–81: pp. 371–3.
6. Philip M. Williams and Martin Harrison, *Politics and Society in de Gaulle's Republic* (New York: Doubleday, 1972), pp. 321–4; Foccart, *Le Général en mai*, p. 623.
7. Williams and Harrison, *Politics and Society*, p. 335.
8. Broadcast speech, 24 November 1968, *DM*v, pp. 354–7.
9. Foccart, *Le Général en mai*, pp. 443, 458–60.
10. *Le Monde*, 22 November 1968.
11. Jean Lacouture, *De Gaulle*, vol. III: *Le Souverain* (Paris: Le Seuil, 1986), p. 730.
12. Williams and Harrison, *Politics and Society*, p. 245; Alain Chatriot, 'À la recherche des "forces vives"', in Serge Berstein, Pierre Birnbaum, and Jean-Pierre Rioux (eds), *De Gaulle et les élites* (Paris: La Découverte, 2008), pp. 219–37.
13. Lyon speech, 24 March 1968, *DM*v, pp. 270–3.
14. Williams and Harrison, *Politics and Society*, p. 247.

15 Stanley Hoffmann, *Decline or Renewal? France since the 1930s* (New York: Viking Press, 1974), pp. 179–80; Foccart, *Le Général en mai*, p. 439.
16 See above, p. 263.
17 Serge Berstein, '1968–1969: une nouvelle trahison des élites?', in Berstein, Birnbaum, and Rioux, *De Gaulle et les élites*, pp. 300–15: p. 311.
18 *DM*II, pp. 5–11: p. 9; *DM*V, pp. 27–30: p. 30.
19 Jean Mastias, 'De Gaulle et la seconde Chambre du Parlement français', in Institut Charles de Gaulle, *De Gaulle en son siècle*, vol. II: *La République* (Paris: Plon, 1992), pp. 472–84: p. 481.
20 Mastias, 'De Gaulle et la seconde Chambre', p. 480.
21 Hoffmann, *Decline or Renewal?*, p. 195.
22 Foccart, *Le Général en mai*, p. 353.
23 Williams and Harrison, *Politics and Society*, p. 334; Foccart, *Le Général en mai*, p. 505.
24 Foccart, *Le Général en mai*, pp. 356, 405, 485.
25 Philippe Alexandre, *Le Duel de Gaulle–Pompidou* (Paris: Grasset, 1970), pp. 316–19.
26 Alexandre, *Le Duel*, pp. 273–5, 284–5; Lacouture, *De Gaulle* III, p. 743.
27 Georges Pompidou, *Pour rétablir une vérité* (Paris: Flammarion, 1982), pp. 255–65.
28 Foccart, *Le Général en mai*, pp. 411–19, 449; Éric Roussel, *Georges Pompidou, 1911–1974* (Paris: Jean-Claude Lattès, 1994 [1984]), pp. 260–4; Julian Jackson, *A Certain Idea of France: The Life of Charles de Gaulle* (London: Allen Lane, 2018), p. 746.
29 Foccart, *Le Général en mai*, p. 535.
30 Éric Roussel, *Charles de Gaulle* (Paris: Gallimard, 2002), p. 899; Roussel, *Pompidou*, pp. 271–3.
31 Alexandre, *Le Duel*, p. 315.
32 Roussel, *Charles de Gaulle*, p. 901.
33 *Le Monde*, 1 March 1969.
34 Pierre Lefranc, *Avec de Gaulle* (Paris: Plon, 1989 [1979]), p. 372; Pierre-Louis Blanc, *De Gaulle au soir de sa vie* (Paris: Fayard, 1990), p. 365.
35 Roussel, *Pompidou*, p. 279.
36 Williams and Harrison, *Politics and Society*, p. 338.
37 Williams and Harrison, *Politics and Society*, pp. 338 and n, 364.
38 Philip Williams, *French Politicians and Elections, 1951–1969* (Cambridge: Cambridge University Press, 1970), p. 283.
39 *DM*V, pp. 375–9: pp. 378–9; Jacques Foccart, *Foccart parle. Entretiens avec Philippe Gaillard*, vol. I (Paris: Fayard/Jeune Afrique, 1995), p. 439.
40 Bernard Tricot, 'Les Rapports entre le président de la République et le premier ministre, juillet 1967–avril 1969', in Institut Charles de Gaulle, Association Française de Science Politique, *De Gaulle et ses*

Premiers Ministres, 1959–1969 (Paris: Plon, 1990), pp. 127–49: p. 144; Foccart, *Le Général en mai*, p. 619.
41 Foccart, *Le Général en mai*, p. 621.
42 *DM*v, pp. 385–8: p. 386.
43 Alain Lancelot and Pierre Weill, 'L'Évolution politique des électeurs français de février à juin 1969', *Revue française de science politique*, 20, 1970, pp. 248–81: p. 250.
44 Lancelot and Weill, 'L'Évolution politique', pp. 252–4.
45 Alexandre, *Le Duel*, pp. 353–4; televised interview with Michel Droit, *DM*v, pp. 389–403: pp. 391–3.
46 Roussel, *Charles de Gaulle*, p. 905.
47 Lefranc, *Avec de Gaulle*, p. 375.
48 Williams, *French Politicians*, p. 284.
49 Foccart, *Le Général en mai*, p. 659; Alphand, *L'Étonnement*, p. 519; Alain de Boissieu, *Pour servir le Général* (Paris: Plon, 1982), p. 210.
50 *DM*v, pp. 389–403: p. 402; Lancelot and Weill, 'L'Évolution politique', pp. 255–6.
51 Lancelot and Weill, 'L'Évolution politique', p. 256.
52 Roussel, *Charles de Gaulle*, p. 906.
53 Foccart, *Le Général en mai*, p. 692; Philippe de Gaulle, *De Gaulle mon père. Entretiens avec Michel Tauriac*, vol. II (Paris: Plon, 2003), pp. 414–15.
54 Foccart, *Le Général en mai*, pp. 690, 696, 713.
55 Lancelot and Weill, 'L'Évolution politique', p. 257.
56 Roussel, *Charles de Gaulle*, pp. 906–7.
57 *DM*v, pp. 405–6.
58 Roussel, *Charles de Gaulle*, p. 907.
59 Lacouture, *De Gaulle* III, p. 772.
60 Williams, *French Politicians*, p. 283.
61 Foccart, *Le Général en mai*, pp. 745–6; Hoffmann, *Decline or Renewal?*, p. 107.
62 Serge Berstein, '1968–1969: une nouvelle trahison?', p. 301.
63 Lancelot and Weill, 'L'Évolution politique', pp. 258–60.
64 Foccart, *Le Général en mai*, p. 743.
65 Foccart, *Foccart parle*, p. 445; Roussel, *Charles de Gaulle*, p. 909.
66 Foccart, *Le Général en mai*, pp. 728–9.
67 Jacques Chaban-Delmas, *Mémoires pour demain* (Paris: Flammarion, 1997), p. 423.
68 *LNC*III, pp. 1050–1051.
69 François Flohic, *Souvenirs d'Outre-Gaulle* (Paris: Plon, 1979), p. 201.
70 Flohic, *Souvenirs d'Outre-Gaulle*, p. 224.
71 Roussel, *Charles de Gaulle*, pp. 916–17.
72 Olivier Guichard, *Mon Général* (Paris: Grasset, 1980), p. 454.
73 Flohic, *Souvenirs d'Outre-Gaulle*, p. 221.
74 Roussel, *Charles de Gaulle*, p. 910.
75 Philippe de Gaulle, *De Gaulle mon père* II, pp. 380, 467.

76 J.E.S. Hayward, 'Presidential suicide by plebiscite: de Gaulle's exit, April 1969', *Parliamentary Affairs*, 22, June 1969, pp. 289–319.
77 Guichard, *Mon Général*, p. 9.
78 Blanc, *De Gaulle au soir*, p. 70.
79 Sudhir Hazareesingh, *In the Shadow of the General: Modern France and the Myth of de Gaulle* (New York: Oxford University Press, 2012), pp. 109–10.
80 Williams and Harrison, *Politics and Society*, p. 357n.
81 Guy Sorman, in Institut Charles de Gaulle, *De Gaulle en son siècle*, vol. I: *Dans la mémoire des hommes et des peuples* (Paris: Plon, 1991), p. 520.
82 Blanc, *De Gaulle au soir*, p. 97.
83 Blanc, *De Gaulle au soir*, p. 70.
84 Philippe de Gaulle, *De Gaulle mon père* II, pp. 461–3.
85 Blanc, *De Gaulle au soir*, p. 26.
86 Philippe de Gaulle, *De Gaulle mon père* II, p. 479.
87 Philippe de Gaulle, *De Gaulle mon père* II, p. 468.
88 Philippe de Gaulle, *De Gaulle mon père* II, pp. 468, 493; Hazareesingh, *In the Shadow*, p. 111.
89 Hazareesingh, *In the Shadow*, pp. 10–12.
90 Hazareesingh, *In the Shadow*, p. 111.
91 Hazareesingh, *In the Shadow*, pp. 124–31.
92 Hazareesingh, *In the Shadow*, pp. 131–41.
93 Hazareesingh, *In the Shadow*, pp. xii–xiv, 146; Jackson, *A Certain Idea*, p. xxix.
94 Hazareesingh, *In the Shadow*, p. 150.
95 Hazareesingh, *In the Shadow*, pp. 145, 150.
96 Hazareesingh, *In the Shadow*, p. 154; Institut Charles de Gaulle, *De Gaulle en son siècle* I, p. 5.
97 Régis Debray, *Charles de Gaulle, Futurist of the Nation* (London: Verso, 1994).
98 Raymond Barre, 'De Gaulle et les Français. La Nostalgie de la grandeur', in SOFRES, *L'État de l'opinion 1991* (Paris: Le Seuil, 1991), pp. 19–38: p. 27.
99 SOFRES, 'De Gaulle, quarante ans après sa mort', October 2010, https://www.tns-sofres.com/sites/default/files/2010.11.08-de-gaulle.pdf, accessed 12 November 2019.
100 SOFRES, 'De Gaulle, quarante ans après'; Roussel, *Charles de Gaulle*, pp. i–ii.
101 Michel Winock, 'De Gaulle: exercice de mémoire', in Institut Charles de Gaulle, *De Gaulle en son siècle* I, pp. 520–3.
102 Pierre Lefranc, *Avec de Gaulle* (Paris: Plon, 1989 [1979]), p. 379.
103 Hazareesingh, *In the Shadow*, p. 179.
104 Blanc, *De Gaulle au soir*, p. 369.
105 C.L. Sulzberger, *The Last of the Giants* (London: Weidenfeld & Nicolson, 1970), p. 642.

106 *LNC*III, p. 1008.
107 Jackson, *A Certain Idea*, p. xxxii; R.W. Johnson, *The Long March of the French Left* (London: Macmillan, 1981), p. 98.
108 Jackson, *A Certain Idea*, p. 775.
109 Barre, 'De Gaulle et les Français', pp. 27, 30.
110 Hazareesingh, *In the Shadow*, p. xiii.
111 Barre, 'De Gaulle et les Français', pp. 27, 30.
112 Barre, 'De Gaulle et les Français', pp. 27, 30.
113 Barre, 'De Gaulle et les Français', p. 32; SOFRES, 'De Gaulle, quarante ans après'.
114 Barre, 'De Gaulle et les Français', p. 30.
115 Hoffmann, *Decline or Renewal?*, p. 306; Richard Nixon, in Institut Charles de Gaulle, *De Gaulle en son siècle* I, p. 79.
116 Barre, 'De Gaulle et les Français', p. 31; SOFRES, 'De Gaulle, quarante ans après'.
117 Jean Charlot, 'Le Gaullisme', in Jean-François Sirinelli (ed.), *Histoire des droites en France*, vol. I (Paris: Gallimard, 1992), pp. 653–89: p. 676.
118 Marie-Claire Lavabre, 'Les communistes et de Gaulle', p. 570.
119 Winock, 'De Gaulle: exercice de mémoire', p. 523.
120 Jackson, *A Certain Idea*, p. 771.
121 Hazareesingh, *In the Shadow*, p. 4.
122 Broadcast, 29 January 1960, *DM*III, pp. 163–4.
123 Barre, 'De Gaulle et les Français', p. 30.
124 Alfred Grosser, 'Pour l'admiration critique, contre l'adulation mystique', in Institut Charles de Gaulle, *De Gaulle en son siècle* I, pp. 503–5.
125 Blanc, *De Gaulle au soir*, p. 152.
126 Paul Noack, 'Il est venu et reparti comme un étranger: Charles de Gaulle vu par les Allemands de l'Ouest entre 1958 et 1970', in Institut Charles de Gaulle, *De Gaulle en son siècle* I, p. 397.
127 Nicholas Wahl, 'De Gaulle et le Tiers monde: une alliance de raison?', in Institut du Droit de la Paix et du Développement de l'Université de Nice and Institut Charles de Gaulle (eds), *De Gaulle et le Tiers Monde*, actes du colloque de Nice, 25–6 février 1983 (Paris: Pedone, 1984), pp. 382–3.
128 Williams and Harrison, *Politics and Society*, p. 360.
129 Hoffmann, *Decline or Renewal?*, p. 242.
130 Hoffmann, *Decline or Renewal?*, p. 279.

Further reading

The following material is in addition to the works listed for Chapter 13.

Julian Jackson, *A Certain Idea of France* (London: Allen Lane, 2018), chapters 29–30, covers the last months and the legacy.

J.E.S. Hayward, 'Presidential suicide by plebiscite: de Gaulle's exit, April 1969', *Parliamentary Affairs*, 22, June1969, pp. 289–319 is a good study of the final referendum.

Pierre-Louis Blanc, *De Gaulle au soir de sa vie* (Paris: Fayard, 1990) is the only account specifically devoted to the last months.

Sudhir Hazareesingh, *In the Shadow of the General: Modern France and the Myth of de Gaulle* (New York: Oxford University Press, 2012) is the standard work on the legacy, along with the essays in Institut Charles de Gaulle, *De Gaulle en son siècle*, vol. I: *Dans la mémoire des hommes et des peuples* (Paris: Plon, 1991).

Opinion polls for two anniversary years are given in Raymond Barre, 'De Gaulle et les Français. La nostalgie de la grandeur', in SOFRES, *L'État de l'opinion 1991* (Paris: Le Seuil, 1991), pp. 19–38, and SOFRES, 'De Gaulle, quarante ans après sa mort', October2010, www.tns-sofres.com/sites/default/files/2010.11.08-de-gaulle.pdf

Index

Abbas, Ferhat 113, 162–3, 200, 201, 222, 229, 230, 232
Aboulker, José, 88, 98
Acheson, Dean 298, 343
Acre 73–4
Action Française 5, 10, 19, 77
Adenauer, Konrad 291, 296, 302–3, 311, 331, 334, 336–7, 339–44, 347, 351, 354, 358
Africa 43, 44, 45, 188, 220, 235, 240–4, 245, 246, 251, 262, 265, 287, 314, 340, 423, 426, 429, 431; coups d'état 244; French aid 242; and Free French 48–51, 55, 69–71, 76–7, 82, 110, 112, 114; French military presence, post-independence 243; *see also* Brazzaville; *Françafrique*
Africa, North 34, 36, 45, 46, 51, 54, 65, 69, 71, 74, 77, 81, 87–90, 96–109, 113, 121, 176, 189, 205, 245, 294
Africa, South 238, 245, 432
Afrique Équatoriale Française (AEF) 48, 50, 51, 69, 70, 75–7, 83, 89, 114
Afrique Occidentale Française (AOF) 48, 69, 71, 89, 106
Agriculture, French 3, 334, 346, 347, 374
Ailleret, General Charles 308

Algeria 2, 43, 49, 65, 69, 88, 89, 104–6, 110, 112, 113, 114, 119, 143, 160, 162–3, 165, 169, 188, 189, 193, 197–203, 204, 206, 210, 212, 215, 220, 221–41, 245, 246, 248, 250, 251, 262, 264, 272, 275, 305, 307, 309, 340, 393, 399, 414, 422, 425, 429, 432, 433; agriculture 199; Assembly (1947–56) 198; *colons* 198; French aid 233, 234, 242, 247; independence (1962) 114, 160, 221, 224–8, 233, 235, 247, 281, 292, 426, 429, 432; population 198; self-determination 226; voters and elections 113, 198, 222, 225, 226
Algerian War (1954–62) 18, 189, 191, 216, 245, 252, 279, 287, 291, 292, 299, 381, 426, 427, 433; aftermath 235, 236; and mainland France 224, 234; cease-fire (1962) 224, 228, 232, 235; chronology 222; concentration camps 238; Évian–Lugrin talks (1961) 223, 231, 232; free-fire zones 238; French troop numbers 200, 201, 221, 233; Les Rousses–Évian talks (1962) 224, 232, 339; Melun talks (1960) 223, 230; napalm 238; rapes 237; summary executions 238, 239; torture 202–3, 237–9

Algiers 38, 39, 43, 48, 51, 55, 88, 89, 96, 97, 98, 99, 100, 104, 105, 106, 108, 109, 110, 111, 113, 116, 119, 128, 130–4, 139, 159, 162, 188, 198, 200, 201, 204–211, 214–6, 225–7, 230, 231, 233, 272, 275, 350, 393, 433; Battle of (1957) 201, 202, 237; insurrection (May 1958) 197, 206, 208, 215
Allied Military Government in Occupied Territory (AMGOT) 118–9
Alphand, Hervé 39, 131, 160, 297, 353, 411, 418
ancien régime (pre-1789) 3, 21
Anfa 99, 100, 101, 103, 108
Anglo-Free French agreement (7 August 1940) 66
anti-Semitism 5, 8, 11, 43, 83, 104, 250
apparentements (1951 elections) 183, 185
Arab nationalism 46, 71, 75, 164, 165
Arab-Israeli war (1967) 249, 312, 315
Arafat, Yasser 250, 320, 424
Aragon, Louis 190
Armée de Libération Nationale (ALN – Algeria) 200, 201, 204, 224, 230, 232, 236–9
Armée Secrète 102, 103, 115, 116, 117
armistice (22 June 1940) 1, 7, 12, 25, 26, 33–6, 45, 100, 104
Aron, Raymond 179, 190, 250
association capital-travail 179, 184, 192, 370
Atlantic Charter (1941) 83
Auriol, Vincent 183, 186, 197, 209–12, 214
Auschwitz 250

Baden-Baden 384, 392, 400, 430
'barons' of Gaullism 189, 192, 417, 420

Barrès, Maurice 11
Barricades Week (Algiers, 1960) 226, 229, 264, 277, 394
Bayeux 130, 179; de G.'s speech on constitution (1946) 176, 177, 186, 192, 213, 259, 261, 414
BBC 2, 25, 35, 37, 67, 74, 83, 97, 102, 133
Bedell Smith, Walter 55
Beirut 15, 75, 76, 97, 164, 165
Belgium 8, 290, 302, 331, 337, 360
Ben Barka affair 245, 271, 397
Ben Bella, Ahmed 200, 203, 229
Ben Gurion, David 248, 250
Ben Khedda, Ben Youssef 232
Benelux countries 183, 334
Bergson, Henri 11, 17, 18
Berlin 97, 182, 288, 298, 319, 341–3, 351, 381; crisis (1958–61) 292, 296–7, 302, 340; wall 297, 433
Béthouart, General Antoine 88, 89
Beynet, General Paul 164
Biafra 244
Bidault, Georges 115, 136, 139, 164, 176, 177, 183, 209, 396
Bingen, Jacques 40, 115, 117
Bir-Hakeim 69, 77, 117, 143
Bizerte 205, 245, 251
Blanc, Pierre-Louis 422
Blum, Léon 6, 10, 11, 22, 23, 43, 85, 177
Boisson, Pierre 48, 69–71, 100, 104, 106
Bollaert, Émile 40, 115, 117
bombing, of France by Allies 120
Bordeaux 33, 34, 84, 141, 184
Boris, Georges 43, 83
Bouchinet-Serrueles, Claude 112
Boumediene, Houari 232, 235, 238, 239
Bourdieu, Pierre 238
Bourguiba, Habib 166, 204, 205, 245
Brandt, Willy 312, 320, 343, 345, 346, 357
Brasillach, Robert 154

Brazil 247
Brazzaville 50, 69, 72, 73, 74, 82, 97, 161, 220, 241; conference (1944) 51, 114, 160, 161, 180, 205, 220, 428, 432
Brest 35, 67
Bretton Woods monetary system 304, 305, 319, 427
Brezhnev, Leonid 311
Brigue 157
Britain *see* United Kingdom
Brooke, General Sir Alan 45, 47, 87
Brossolette, Pierre 40, 80, 100, 102, 103, 115
Bruneval 67, 178
Bucharest 310, 378, 386, 387, 423
Bundestag (West Germany) 303, 343
Bundy, McGeorge 293, 301, 309
Bureau Central de Renseignements et d'Action (BCRA) 52, 117

Cairo 43, 50, 69, 72–5, 201
Cameroon 38, 50, 69, 70, 240, 242, 244
Camus, Albert 190
Canada 85, 86, 119, 291, 307, 312–4, 318, 396
Capitant, René, 98, 139, 179, 416
Carlton Gardens (London) 41, 44, 47, 65, 80, 131, 423
Casablanca 36, 55, 88, 89, 99, 106
Casey, Richard 75
Cassin, René, 40, 43, 66, 72, 82, 83, 85, 178, 250, 418
Catroux, General Georges 42, 44, 48, 72, 73, 104, 112, 113, 114, 178
Ceausescu, Nicolai 312
Central Intelligence Agency (CIA) 302
Cerny, Philip 309
Ceux de la Résistance (Resistance group) 102
Ceyrac, François 377
Chaban-Delmas, Jacques 39, 118, 133–5, 178, 184, 185, 189, 204, 240, 275, 276, 393, 415

Chad 50, 69, 240, 244
Chalandon, Albin 268, 275, 276, 413
Challe, General Maurice 222, 224, 226, 227, 231
Challe Plan (1959–61) 222, 224, 229, 236–40, 246, 251, 429, 432
Charlot, Jean 182, 215, 264, 266, 268, 377
Charonne (metro station) 227
Châtel, Yves-Charles 88, 89
China (People's Republic) 131, 247, 248, 250, 290, 292, 302, 318, 319, 344, 421, 423, 427
Chirac, Jacques 390, 413, 423, 424, 433
Choltitz, General Dietrich von 135–6
Christian Democrats 9, 103, 150, 267, 268, 336, 349
Churchill, Winston S. 38, 39, 41, 48, 57, 65–76, 83, 86, 89, 90, 97, 99, 100, 101, 117, 121, 130, 132, 134, 142, 157, 158, 169, 190, 350, 351, 354, 357, 434; and de G. (1940) 25, 34–6, 47, 65–7, 69–70; at Anfa (1943) 99–101; assessment of de G. 38, 41; attempts to break with de G. 46, 48, 105, 106, 130; Europe and the open sea' quotation 129, 350; funeral 351; hostility to de G. 97; and Levant 71–2, 74–6, 164–5; and Roosevelt 54, 83, 97, 99, 100, 101, 119, 120, 121, 128, 129, 142; rows with de G. 47, 55, 71, 74, 100, 129–30
Church–State relations (France) 3, 4, 5, 131, 180
Citroën (car manufacturer) 192, 262, 391, 395
Clark, General Mark 87–9
Clausewitz Carl von 431
Cogan Charles 320
Cohn-Bendit, Daniel 382–4, 386–8, 394

Cold War 178, 192, 220, 250, 287, 288–90, 298, 303, 307, 309, 315, 320, 335, 340, 430, 433
Colombey-les-Deux-Églises *see* de Gaulle, Charles
Combat (Resistance group) 14, 77, 79, 80, 81, 84, 102, 205, 394
Comité d'Action Militaire (COMAC) 116, 118, 133, 134, 138
Comité Français de la Libération Nationale (CFLN) 82, 83, 96, 106–121, 128–30, 140, 231, 275, 331; recognition 118, 121, 132
Comité National Français (CNF) 68, 76, 78, 79, 80, 82, 83, 84, 97, 99, 102, 104
Comité Parisien de Libération (CPL) 116, 134, 136, 141
Comités de Défense de la République (CDRs) 385, 388, 390, 394
Common Agricultural Policy (CAP) 333, 341, 344, 346–8, 350–5, 357, 358–60, 431, 432
Communist Party, French (PCF) 4, 6, 7, 26, 52, 53, 57, 77–80, 84, 85, 101–3, 108–9, 111, 119, 132, 137, 139–41, 143, 150–1, 154, 157, 167–9, 175–84, 187, 205, 208, 212, 227, 261, 310, 311, 332, 376, 381, 383, 386, 391, 394–6, 417, 428; in Resistance 53, 78–80, 97, 101–3, 111, 116–8, 133–5, 139
Concorde (Anglo–French airliner) 5, 372, 374
Conféderation Française Démocratique du Travail (CFDT) 376, 384
Confédération Générale du Travail (CGT) 80, 81, 180, 181, 376, 384, 386, 389–91
Confédération Nationale du Patronat Français (CNPF) 376, 377, 390, 391, 413
Confrérie Notre-Dame (Resistance network) 78

Conseil de la Défense de l'Empire (CDE) 82, 83
Conseil National de la Résistance (CNR) 53, 96, 103, 105, 108, 111, 115–8, 121, 134–41, 152–3
conservative parties (non-Gaullist) 103, 150, 176, 181, 183, 185, 186
Constantine (Algeria) 110, 113, 162, 198, 200, 228, 233
Constituent Assembly (1945–6) 149, 150, 151, 154, 167
Constitutional Council 213, 261, 263, 420
Consultative Assembly (1943–5) 104, 108, 110–2, 116, 117, 119, 121, 139, 149, 163, 331
Corbin, Charles 34, 36
Corsica 57, 107, 111, 132, 209, 215
Côte d'Ivoire 212, 240, 241, 243–4
Coty, René, 197, 203, 205, 206, 210, 211, 212, 215
Coulet, François 43, 130
Council of Ministers 272, 273, 349, 353, 354, 356, 373, 381, 388, 390, 392, 393, 415, 417, 418
Couve de Murville, Maurice 106, 244, 248, 268, 270, 275, 291, 292, 294, 300, 302, 310, 312, 314, 336, 341, 345, 348–9, 352, 354–6, 359, 360, 397, 415, 416, 418
Crémieux-Brilhac, Jean-Louis 43
Crozier, Michel 398
Cuban missile crisis (1962) 263, 290, 292, 298, 299
Czechoslovakia 6, 7, 316, 317, 346, 401, 411

d'Astier de la Vigerie, Emmanuel 79, 80, 81, 87, 98, 103
d'Astier de la Vigerie, François 98
d'Astier de la Vigerie, Henri 88
Dakar 45, 48, 69, 70, 71, 74, 82, 88, 188, 241
Daladier, Édouard 6, 7, 23, 85, 211
Damascus 73, 164–5

Darlan, Admiral François 72, 88, 89, 97, 98, 99
Darnand, Joseph 154
de Beauvoir, Simone 190
de Boissieu, General Alain (son-in-law) 391, 392, 393, 412, 418
de Gaulle, Anne (daughter) 9, 24, 25, 26, 175, 191, 274, 425
de Gaulle, Charles: and Africa 48, 69, 71, 76, 77, 112, 160, 166, 169, 180, 187, 188, 193, 220, 240, 242, 243, 244, 251, 265, 287, 431; and Algeria 110, 113–4, 162–3, 189, 193, 203, 205, 212, 216, 220–240, 272–5, 278, 279–80, 281, 287, 292, 295, 308, 339, 399, 426, 429, 432; *Appel du 18 juin* (1940) 1, 33, 35, 36, 37, 68, 85, 142, 292, 423, 425, 427; assassination attempts 227, 262, 343; assessment 25, 26, 89, 90, 143, 144, 169, 191, 193, 214, 216, 251, 252, 281, 319, 321, 360, 398, 401, 424, 434; authoritarianism, as president 279, 280, 399, 429; and Barricades Week (1960) 226, 229, 264, 277; Bayeux speech (1946) 176, 177, 186, 192, 213, 259, 261, 414; and bipolar international system 158, 251, 287–9, 291, 313, 317, 319, 320, 427, 430, 433; and Britain 20, 39, 44–8, 58, 65, 68, 71, 73, 76, 85, 90, 120, 143, 157, 165, 191, 278, 286, 301, 303, 314, 319, 331–2, 335, 350, 358, 359; and business 151–5, 179, 369–370, 374, 413, 419; Catholicism 8, 25, 26; childhood and adolescence 8, 10, 16; and China 247, 421; and Churchill 25, 34–6, 38, 41, 46–8, 55, 65–7, 69–72, 74–7, 97, 99–101, 105, 106, 128–30, 132, 164–5, 351; and 'civil affairs' agreement with Allies 118, 128–130; claims status as revolutionary 84, 141, 396; at Colombey-les-Deux-Églises 25, 168, 178, 186, 187, 203, 204, 205, 208, 209, 210, 211, 212, 214, 221, 277, 279, 291, 334, 339, 340, 351, 358, 392, 419, 420, 421, 422, 423, 425; communication, as president 276, 278, 280; and Communists 53, 79, 80, 84–5, 102, 108, 111–2, 132, 137, 141, 150, 157, 167, 179, 180, 310, 394, 396, 427; Constantine Plan (1958) 222, 228; constitutional ideas 10, 83, 136, 150, 151, 176–7, 192, 259–262; 'crossing of the desert' (1946–58) 169, 175–193, 203; 'crowd baths', 38, 140, 151, 192, 278, 400; death (1970) 422; and decolonisation 220, 231, 242, 246, 426, 429, 432; and détente 288, 298, 307, 310, 312, 340, 345, 401, 427; *dirigisme* 152, 180, 370, 374; *La Discorde chez l'ennemi* 18, 21; *Le Fil de l'épée* 11, 18, 21, 156; and Eastern bloc 311, 312, 317, 319, 346, 430; economic policy 155, 369, 375, 413; education policy 180, 192, 368, 378, 380, 399, 411; and *épuration* (1944–5) 153, 154; and Europe 156, 159, 192, 290, 302, 311, 319, 331–60, 427, 430, 431; and 'Europe from the Atlantic to the Urals', 192, 290, 297, 335, 401; suspected of fascism 21, 24, 53, 82, 184; and France 11, 16, 110, 120, 137, 149, 177, 191, 220, 246, 250, 259, 286, 287, 289, 320, 321, 335, 337, 432, 433; *La France et son armée* 21; and Free France 41–4, 66–8, 85, 89, 139, 177–9, 393, 426, 428, 432; and French aid to former colonies 242, 246, 427; and French army 16, 20, 24, 25, 36, 210, 222–7, 230, 233, 239, 385, 390, 393, 427; and French Community 240–2, 429; and French empire 48, 69,

71, 76, 77, 112, 160, 166, 169, 180, 187, 188, 193, 220, 428; and French public opinion 90, 141, 168, 178, 186, 205, 265, 267, 288, 314, 316, 321, 371, 377, 395, 398, 401, 417, 421, 424–7, 430; and Generals' Putsch (1961) 227, 277; and Germany 19, 159, 192, 302–3, 306, 308, 310–2, 319, 331–2, 335, 339–46, 358, 426, 430, 431; and *harkis* 236, 429; health 68, 166, 175, 203, 384, 412, 422; and 'independence-association' for Algeria 229, 233, 234, 240; and Indochina 161, 248; and internal Resistance 51–3, 58, 77, 82, 85, 101, 103, 105, 115–8, 128, 131–3, 136–9, 140, 143, 425; and international monetary system 304, 305, 316, 413, 427; intransigence 38, 39, 44, 90, 101, 156; and Israel 249–50; and Jews 11, 26, 83, 104, 110, 249–50, 315; and leadership 18, 37–8, 259; and legitimacy 259, 262, 264; and Levant 71–6, 112–3, 163–5, 428; and Macmillan 39, 48, 100, 104–7, 111, 113, 115, 119, 291, 292–3, 296, 301, 350–5; and May 1968, 277, 383–95, 398, 400, 411, 419, 430; *Memoirs of Hope* 175, 293, 422; military career 1, 8, 12–17, 22; as military intellectual 1, 15–18, 20, 21; and Morocco 165, 245; mythologised, post-1970 423; and national independence 286–7, 291, 298, 301, 307; and NATO 179, 192, 278, 287, 288, 291–4, 299–302, 305–6, 308, 318, 319, 427, 430; and non-aligned movement 251, 289; and nuclear deterrent 294–300, 303, 307–9, 319, 320, 427; and *paix des braves* (1958) 228; and 'participation' 76, 275, 370, 371, 388, 389, 396, 397, 411, 413, 421, 430;

and partitioning Algeria 232, 234–5, 429; personal coldness 17, 40, 425; personal warmth 17, 25, 39, 425; and Pétain 12, 14–6, 22, 24, 25, 104, 154; Phnom Penh speech (1966) 248, 251; and *pieds-noirs* 221, 226, 230–3, 235; and political parties 79, 151, 166, 167, 178, 179, 185, 190, 266; political skills 85, 168, 182, 185, 192; and Pompidou 190, 209, 229, 231–2, 262, 269, 270, 272–5, 314, 371–3, 379, 381–93, 396–8, 400–1, 412, 415–6, 419–21, 430; and presidential power 264, 269, 271, 273, 276, 429; press conferences (1959–68) 277–8; and prime ministers 273–6; prisoner of war (1916–18) 14, 17–19, 22; provincial tours 140, 265, 278; Quebec speech (1967) 313–5; racism 243, 290; 'realism' in international relations 286, 431; reforms (1944–6) 151–3; and regional reform plan (1969) 414, 417; resignation (1946) 149, 152, 166, 175, 428; resignation (1969) 259, 420, 426; return to power (1958) 169, 175, 197–8, 204–16; and Roosevelt 54–6, 71, 85–7, 90, 97–101, 119–21, 131–2, 142, 159; and RPF 175, 178–88; and Sahara 223, 232, 235, 278, 429; and self-determination for Algeria 222, 229–30, 241, 278; self-doubt 68, 71, 97, 175, 418; and Senate 263, 272, 296, 411, 413–8; and Soviet Union 56–7, 111, 143, 157, 192, 287, 290, 296–8, 310–3, 317, 340, 427, 430; and Third World 220, 225, 246, 250–1, 427, 431; and torture in Algeria 237; and Tunisia 166, 245, 431; undersecretary of state for war (1940) 7, 23, 25, 33–4; and United States 20, 53–5, 85, 90, 108, 114, 120,

131, 142–3, 159, 191, 286, 288, 291–307, 317–9, 331, 335, 341, 354, 428, 430; and universities 378, 381, 383, 387, 411; and UNR/UDR 266–9, 401, 418; *Vers l'Armée de métier* 19–21, 340; and Vietnam 248, 316, 369, 427–8, 431; *War Memoirs* 10, 11, 69, 111, 135–8, 157, 162–3, 176, 186, 190–1, 287, 422, 428; wartime broadcasts 37, 90, 99, 102, 132–3, 137, 143; wartime speeches 37, 84, 104, 114, 117, 136, 143, 190, 432; and workers 179, 369, 370, 372, 375, 396, 399, 411, 413, 421; working habits, as president 279; wounded (1914, 1915, 1916) 14
de Gaulle, Élisabeth (daughter) 24, 186, 190
de Gaulle, Henri (father) 8, 9, 10, 379
de Gaulle, Jeanne (mother) 8, 9, 10
de Gaulle, Philippe (son) 10, 24, 186, 234, 250, 412, 421–2
de Gaulle, Pierre (brother) 8, 181
de Gaulle, Yvonne (wife) 9, 24, 35, 262, 391, 392, 419, 420, 423
De Valera, Eamonn 420
Debatisse, Michel 374
Debré, Michel 112, 178, 189, 204, 206, 208, 212, 214–5, 227, 230, 232–4, 237, 260–2, 270, 274, 296, 333, 338, 357, 377, 379, 389, 394, 416
Défense de la France (Resistance group) 77
Defferre, Gaston 220, 240–1
Delbecque, Léon 189, 204–7, 214–5
Delestraint, General Charles 40, 81, 102, 103, 115
Delon Alain 415
Delouvrier, Paul 222, 229, 238
Dentz, General Henri 72–5, 154
Deuxième Division Blindée (Second Armoured Division, or 2DB) 134–5, 143, 156

Dewavrin, André, *alias* Colonel Passy 40, 42–5, 52, 67–8, 77–8, 100, 102, 117, 178
Dien Bien Phu 187, 201, 206, 220
Diethelm, André, 83, 138, 179
Dreyfus Affair 5, 8, 9, 10, 15, 21
Droit, Michel 267, 277, 355, 396, 418
Dubček, Alexander 317
Dublin 420
Duclos, Jacques 386, 420
Duff Cooper, Alfred 48, 119, 120, 130, 132, 165, 167, 169
Duhamel ,Jacques 418, 420
Dulac, General André, 210
Dulles, Allen 55
Dulles, John Foster 291, 292
Dunkirk 33, 41, 229, 354, 377, 395
Duras, Marguerite 190
Duverger, Maurice 205, 263

Éboué, Félix 50, 114
Economic and Social Council 411, 414
Eden, Sir Anthony (Lord Avon) 39, 45, 47–8, 72, 105, 118–20, 130–1, 142, 144, 165
Education, French 378–9; Church schools 180, 379, 399, 426; spending 309, 380; student numbers 378, 380
Egypt 46, 50, 69, 71, 73, 75, 165, 201, 249, 289
Eisenhower, Dwight D. 55–6, 87–8, 96, 104–6, 117, 119–21, 129–30, 134–5, 138, 156–7, 205, 229, 248, 290–6, 304, 319, 411, 412
elections, cantonal: (1949) 181–2; (1955) 188
elections, municipal: (1945) 150; (1947) 181–2; (1953) 182; (1965) 269
elections, parliamentary 261; (1945) 149–50, 166–7; (1946, June) 176; (1951) 175, 181, 185; (1958) 213, 266; (1962) 263, 267, 272, 299;

(1967) 267, 268; (1968) 267, 268, 272, 396, 401, 419
elections, presidential: (1958) 214, 261; (1965) 264, 265, 267, 275, 277, 305, 349; (1969) 420
Ély, General Paul 207, 292
Élysée Palace (presidential residence) 211, 212, 265, 298, 385, 391, 392, 393, 398, 416, 419
Élysée Treaty (France–West Germany, 1963) 287, 302–3, 306, 310, 314, 339, 343–4, 354, 358, 431–2; and long-term Franco-German co-operation 345; preamble 303, 343–5
Empty Chair crisis (1965–6) 348–350, 357, 359
épuration (1944–5) 153–5
Erhard, Ludwig 303, 334, 341–5, 356
Euratom 333, 334
European Agricultural Guidance and Guarantee Fund (EAGGF) 347–8
European Coal and Steel Community (ECSC) 183, 332, 339, 340
European Commission 333–4, 337, 347–9, 359
European Council of Ministers 333, 348–50, 359
European Defence Community (EDC) 187, 332
European Economic Community (EEC) 301–5, 319, 321, 331–4, 337, 340–3, 346, 349–51, 354, 356, 360, 371, 373, 431
European Free Trade Association (EFTA) 351–2
Évian accords (1962) 224, 228, 232–6, 248, 251, 262, 266, 272, 287

Fall of France (1940) 1, 7, 11, 23, 54
Fanfani, Amintore 336
Farès, Abderrahmane 222, 228
Faure, Edgar 80, 411, 412, 419

Fifth Republic 214, 260; constitution 177, 213, 221, 234, 240, 241, 259–71, 281, 372, 413, 417, 418, 426, 429, 432; constitution, Article 16 227, 261, 272, 279, 280, 385, 393; constitutional amendment (1962) 260, 262–3, 414; presidency 213, 261–3, 269, 271, 281, 399
'flexible response' (nuclear doctrine) 299–300, 317, 341–2
Flohic, François 264, 392, 420
Foccart, Jacques: and Africa 188–9, 243, 246, 265; and Algeria 225–7, 242–4, 246, 251; and 'barons' 189, 417, 420; conversations with de G. 275, 313–4, 388, 398, 412, 415–6, 418; in May 1958 203–6, 209, 211, 214–5; in May 1968 315, 385–6, 388, 390–4 ; and RPF 177–8, 187–9, 203; and UNR/UDR 265–6, 269
Fondation Anne de Gaulle 191
Foot M.R.D. 133, 140
Force Ouvrière (FO) 376
Forces Françaises de l'Intérieur (FFI) 117–8, 130, 132–6, 138, 140, 153
Fouchet, Christian 42, 158, 179, 236, 302, 335–6, 339, 342–3, 379, 381, 383–8, 391, 395
Fouchet Plan (1961–2) 302, 335–6, 339, 342–3, 351–2, 360, 430
Fourquet, General Michel 390
Fourth Republic 176–7, 179, 185, 187, 191, 197–8, 203, 205, 213, 214, 248, 260, 264, 265, 273, 279, 281, 295, 340, 369
Françafrique 240, 242, 243, 245, 251
France, economy 155, 167, 183, 368
Franco, General Francisco 421
Franco–Soviet treaty (1944) 158, 160
Francs-Tireurs et Partisans (FTP) 80, 102, 111, 117

Franc-Tireur (Resistance group) 77, 79, 81, 84, 102
Free French 8, 11, 26, 33, 36–57, 65–80, 82–90, 97–9, 102, 105, 109, 121, 131, 139, 161, 179, 184, 247, 266, 274, 279, 336, 428, 432; armies 51, 69, 105, 109, 156; constitutional doctrine 82–3; manifesto (June 1942), 81, 85; quarrelsomeness 43
Frenay, Henri 79, 80, 81, 103, 139
French Community 213, 234, 240–2, 246, 275, 429
French empire 35, 48, 49, 55, 89, 112, 160, 169, 187, 188, 220; as asset for Free France 50; forced labour 51, 114
Frey, Roger 189
Front de Libération Nationale (FLN – Algeria) 199– 206, 215–6, 221–32, 234–9, 242, 251, 274, 279, 429; diplomacy 200–1; Soummam conference 1956, 201; violence 199–201
Front National (Communist-led Resistance group) 102, 103, 111

Gabon 50, 70, 240, 243–4
Gaillard, Félix 202, 204–5, 207, 215, 295
Gamelin, General Maurice 23
Garton Ash, Timothy 341
gauchistes 381, 383, 386–7, 389, 391
Geismar, Alain 384, 387
General Agreement on Tariffs and Trade (GATT) 304, 341, 347, 349, 359
Generals' Putsch (Algiers, 1961) 215, 223, 226–7, 231, 240, 272, 277, 279, 394
Geneva Convention (1949) 237
Georges, General Alphonse 100, 106, 108
Germany 2, 5–8, 12, 34–5, 53, 65, 74, 78, 83, 97, 98, 101, 107, 116, 120, 135, 136, 151, 153, 169, 183, 294, 300, 305, 308–9, 313, 314, 334, 352, 357, 392, 423; de G. and 8, 15–16, 19, 22–3, 26, 37, 40, 45, 136, 139, 142, 156–9, 160, 167, 176, 180, 182, 248, 287, 290, 292, 297, 299, 302–3, 310, 319, 331–2, 335, 339–47, 430–1; East 296, 311; *see also* Berlin; Élysée Treaty; Oder-Neisse line
Gibraltar 42, 70, 88, 89, 331
Giono, Jean 190
Giraud, General Henri 22, 88–9, 96–112
Giscard d'Estaing, Valéry 263, 267, 310, 372, 396, 418–20, 423
Goguel, François 265, 419
Gomulka, Wladislav 312
Gorse, Georges 43, 178
Gouin Félix 110, 176
Gouvernement Provisoire de la République Algérienne (GPRA) 222, 225, 228, 232–3
Gouvernement Provisoire de la République Française (GPRF) 1, 8, 33, 82, 121, 128–43, 149, 160–1, 166, 220, 225, 386, 426, 428; recognition 54, 58, 96, 142–3
Grappin, Jean 383
Grenelle accords (May 1968) 390, 395
Grenier, Fernand 102, 111
Grimaud, Maurice 385–6, 388, 390, 399
Gromyko, Andrei 291, 310
Guderian, Heinz 1, 20
Guelma 163, 169, 198, 200, 429
Guichard, Olivier 16, 38, 189, 192, 203, 206, 214–5, 266, 269, 314, 385, 394
Guillaumat, Pierre 237, 292, 295
Guinea 240, 241, 244
Guy, Claude 42, 175, 177

Hadj, Messali 162, 200, 224, 231
Hallstein, Walter 348, 349, 350, 352
harkis 236–7, 240, 429

Harrison, Martin 271, 280, 376, 431
Hazareesingh, Sudhir 190, 424–5
Heath, Edward 352, 354
Helleu, Jean 112–3
Helsinki Accords (1975) 313
Hettier de Boislambert, Claude 42, 50, 70
Hiroshima 294
Hitler, Adolf 6, 7, 19, 20, 23, 40, 55, 72, 135, 156, 298, 349
Ho Chi Minh 161, 162, 248
Hoffmann, Stanley 37, 168, 277, 398, 434
Hopkins, Harry 87
Houphouët-Boigny, Félix 114, 212, 241–3
housing and inequality 375
Howorth, Jolyon 309
Hudson (Lockheed aircraft) 79
Hull, Cordell 55, 86, 119, 131, 142

India 48, 250, 289
Indochina 42, 48, 54, 114, 161–2, 167, 169, 183, 187–9, 198, 202, 220–1, 237, 248, 432
Iraq 46, 71–2, 75, 165, 249, 321
Israel 71, 248, 249, 312, 318, 431
Italy 2, 53, 87, 107, 109, 119, 131, 142, 157, 183, 248, 290, 300, 302, 331, 334, 337, 357

Jackson, Julian 277, 353, 388, 423, 425
Japan 161, 423
Jaurès, Jean 11, 424
Jennings, Eric 51
Johnson, Daniel 313, 314
Johnson, Lyndon 248–9, 291, 301, 306, 309, 312, 316–8
Johnson, R.W., 281, 425
Jordan 249, 292
Jouhaud, General Edmond 227
Joxe, Louis 223–4, 231–3, 236, 384–5, 425
Juin, General Alphonse 89, 90, 109, 113

KC-135 (tanker aircraft) 295, 308–9
Kennedy, Jacqueline 427
Kennedy, John F., 201, 248, 290–303, 340, 342–4, 353, 355
Khrushchev, Nikita 289, 291–2, 296–8, 311, 340, 351
Kiesinger, Kurt-Georg 345, 358
Kissinger, Henry 318, 320, 346, 427
Koenig, General Marie-Pierre 42, 69, 117–8, 130, 133–5, 159, 160
Kolodziej, Edward 317, 318
Kosygin, Alexei 249, 311
Koufra 69
Krakow 378
Krim, Belkacem 200, 232

Lacouture, Jean 214, 389
Lagaillarde, Pierre 206
Larminat, Edgard de 42, 83, 90, 105
Latin America 85, 247, 318, 423
Laval, Pierre 88, 97, 135, 154
Le Monde 158, 205, 238, 392, 394, 413, 416
Le Troquer, André 85, 211
League of Nations 71, 75
Leahy, Admiral William 54, 131
Lebanon 14, 46, 71–2, 74–5, 112, 114, 165, 220, 292
Lebrun, Albert 11
Lecanuet, Jean 349
Leclerc, General (*alias* of Philippe de Hautecloque) 42, 48, 50, 69, 83, 90, 99, 105, 113, 134–6, 156, 161
Lefranc, Pierre 39, 177, 178, 187, 189, 204, 210, 227, 269
Legentilhomme, General Paul 42, 77
Lemnitzer, General Lyman 318
Lesage, Jean 313
Levant 14, 21, 42, 46, 48, 69–77, 89, 99, 112–3, 157, 159, 164–5, 428
Liberation (1944–5) 129, 133–4, 137, 140, 143, 281, 425, 428; of Paris (August 1944) 128, 132–4, 136–7, 142, 149, 432
Libération (Resistance group) 77, 79

Liberation Committees 112, 116, 134, 140
Libération-Nord (Resistance group) 77, 80, 102
Libération-Sud (Resistance group) 80, 81, 102
Libya 46, 69, 72, 99
Lille 9, 84, 155, 269, 414
Loichot, Marcel 370
Louis XIV 287, 424
Lübke, Heinrich 342
Lublin Committee 157–8
Ludlow, N. Piers 356
Luizet, Charles 107, 135–6
Luns, Joseph 337–8
Luxembourg 290, 302, 331, 348, 349; Compromise (1966) 349
Lynch, Jack 420
Lysander (Westland aircraft) 44, 79, 81
Lyttleton, Sir Oliver 73, 75

Macmillan, Harold 189; British Minister Resident in Algiers 39, 48, 100, 104–7, 111, 113, 115, 119, 121, 350; Prime minister 290–3, 296–8, 300–1, 342; and UK application to join EEC 301, 350–6, 359
McNamara, Robert 300, 301
Macron, Emmanuel 358
Madagascar 46, 74, 76–7, 87–9, 99, 114, 183, 188, 240–3
Mainz 14–15
Malraux, André, 179, 180, 189, 190, 268, 368, 378, 394
Mansholt, Sicco 347
Mao Tse-Tung 421, 424
maquis (rural Resistance) 116, 118, 133, 139, 153
Marcellin, Raymond 395, 413
Marseille 80, 133, 140, 180, 182, 198, 395
Marshall, General George 87, 183, 333
Masmoudi, Mohammed 188, 204–5

Massigli, René, 44, 109, 113, 120, 132
Massu, General Jacques 207, 226, 392–3
Matignon, Hôtel (prime minister's office) 265–6, 274, 385
Mauriac, Claude 141–2, 149, 155, 175
Maurras, Charles 5, 11, 26
May 1968 'Events' 2, 248, 267, 268, 272, 275, 277, 280–1, 316–7, 368–9, 373–7, 381–97, 399, 401, 411, 416, 419, 430; 'dress rehearsals' (1967–8) 377; aftermath 395, 400; and public opinion 387, 394; chronology 383; deaths 389, 395; strikes 316, 387–90, 395
mechanised warfare 1, 22, 106
Médéa 223, 230
Menace (Operation) 70
Mendès-France, Pierre 155, 178, 187–9, 202, 209, 212, 386, 391
Merkel, Angela 358
Mers-el-Kébir 45, 65–6, 71, 89, 233, 354
Messmer, Pierre 42, 160–1, 178, 243–4, 268, 312, 317, 341, 345, 385–6, 388, 390–1
Metz 14, 16–17, 98
Mexico 43, 247
Mexico City 247, 378
Meyer, Émile 11, 22
Michelet, Edmond 189
Middle East 21, 43, 45, 47, 71–5, 85, 164, 248–50, 319
Milice (Vichy paramilitaries) 116, 154
Mirage (Dassault aircraft) 245, 249, 295–6, 307, 309
Missoffe, François 382
Mitterrand, François 197, 211, 267, 379, 386, 391, 395, 401
Moch, Jules 184, 208
Mohammed V (Sultan of Morocco) 101, 113, 166, 245
Mollet, Guy 202, 203, 207–9, 212, 214, 234, 333, 386

Molotov, Vyacheslav 56, 340
Monnerville Gaston 211, 263, 414
Monnet Jean 34, 36, 41, 43, 104–7, 131, 152, 160, 332, 334, 339, 343, 428
Montcornet 1, 15, 17
Montgomery, General Sir Bernard 48, 99, 130
Montreal 313–4, 378
Morocco 36, 69, 88–9, 99–101, 106, 113–4, 165, 169, 189, 201, 220, 238, 240, 242, 245; French aid 245
Morton, Desmond 47, 67, 68, 76, 77, 130
Moscow 4, 7, 57, 76, 97, 111, 140–2, 157, 179, 190, 201, 297, 302, 306, 310–2, 344–5, 351, 378, 423, 428
Mostaganem 226
Moulin, Jean 78–81, 96, 100–3, 105, 111, 115
Mouvement National Algérien (MNA) 223–4, 231
Mouvement Républicain Populaire (MRP) 150, 167, 176–8, 181–3, 185, 202, 209, 212
Mouvements Unis de la Résistance (MUR) 102–3
Multilateral Force (MLF) 299–303, 319, 341, 344
Munich conference (1938) 6, 7, 19, 343
Murphy, Robert 88, 98, 100, 101, 104–7, 119, 205
Mururoa 307, 315
Muselier, Admiral Émile 42, 67–8, 76, 86

Nanterre 382–4, 386
Napoleon I, Emperor 3, 10, 21, 259, 349, 381, 424
Napoleon III, Emperor 3
Narbonne, Jacques 378
Nassau 301, 355

National Assembly 3, 81, 181–2, 187, 197–8, 205, 207, 210–3, 222, 225–6, 261–3, 267, 270, 271, 275, 332, 341, 385–6, 388, 412–5, 423; powers limited (1958) 260, 270
nationalisations (1944–6) 151
Netherlands 290, 302, 331, 337, 347, 360, 430
New Caledonia 48, 50, 55, 87, 89
New York 54, 86, 87, 225, 288; de G. visits 132
Nixon, Richard 17, 250, 318–21, 412, 424, 427
Noguès, Charles 36, 48, 88–9, 100–1, 104, 106
Normandy 25, 46, 120, 129–30, 133, 135, 140; landings (June 1944) 52, 56, 96, 121, 128–9, 176
Norstad, General Lauris 293–4
notables 140, 184–6, 192, 413, 415, 419
nuclear non-proliferation treaty (1968) 308, 318
nuclear weapons, French 294–6, 299–300, 307–8; costs 295, 307–9; effectiveness 309, 319; *tous azimuts* doctrine 308, 317

Odéon (theatre) 386, 388, 395
Oder-Neisse line (German–Polish frontier) 157–8, 297, 310–2, 342
Oran 89, 162, 198, 200, 229, 233, 239
Organisation Civile et Militaire (OCM) (Resistance group) 77, 102
Organisation de l'Armée Secrète (OAS) 223, 227–8, 232, 234–5, 262, 279, 388, 390, 395

Palestine 46, 71, 73, 165
Palewski, Gaston 43, 44, 177, 178, 189
Papon, Maurice 141, 155, 224, 388, 400

Paris 6, 9, 25, 33, 34, 39, 77, 84, 97, 102, 103, 112, 115, 116, 120, 128, 133, 138, 139, 141, 157, 162, 166, 168, 198, 203, 204, 207, 209, 211–2, 214, 231, 245, 262, 265, 266, 275, 349, 356, 401, 420, 422, 425; Commune (1871) 3, 5, 135; in de G.'s childhood and youth 8, 10; de G.'s weekly visits (1950s) 187, 205; Gaullist strength in (1947, 1953) 181–2; Liberation (August 1944) 132–7, 142, 143, 149; in May 1968 'Events' 377, 380–392, 394–5; NATO headquarters 288; police 6, 135, 155, 208, 224, 227, 279, 368, 382–8, 391, 395, 400, 415–6; summit (May 1960) 296–7; treaty, ceding Quebec to Britain (1763) 313; treaty, creating ECSC (1950) 183; venue for Vietnam peace talks (1968) 248, 316; visits from heads of state and government (1958–60) 291, 351

Parodi, Alexandre 117, 134–6, 139, 178

Partial Nuclear Test Ban Treaty (PTBT, 1963) 302, 318

Patriotic Militias 140–1, 150

Patton, General George 133

Peake, Charles 97, 130

Pearl Harbor 46, 86, 176

Péguy, Charles 11

Pétain, Marshal Philippe 16, 17, 33, 35, 54, 55, 65, 97, 120, 135, 177, 185; and 1940 armistice 1, 7, 34; relations with de G. 12–15, 21–2, 24, 25, 26, 154; and Giraud 98, 100; and Torch landings 89; Vichy head of state 34, 72, 82, 104, 108

Petit-Clamart 262

Peyrefitte, Alain: and Algeria 234; as Education Minister 314, 377, 381–3, 385–6, 388, 391; de G.'s confidant 221, 246, 259, 270, 273, 286, 287, 293, 295, 296, 298, 307, 313, 314, 320, 335, 337, 345, 347, 349, 355, 384, 386–7, 392, 394; as Information Minister 276–7, 310, 344; and presidency 'above parties' 267, 269

Peyrouton, Marcel 104, 106

Pflimlin, Pierre 202, 206–12, 215, 334

Philip, André, 40, 80, 97, 99, 211

Phnom Penh 248, 250–1

Piaf, Édith 353

pieds-noirs (Algeria) 198, 201, 208, 221, 226, 229–36, 374–5; migration to France (from 1962) 235

Pinay, Antoine 186, 209, 212, 334, 359, 371, 372, 373, 399

Pineau Christian 80–1, 84, 178

Pisani Edgard 348, 354, 355, 374

Planning, economic 152, 370, 371, 374, 376

Pleven René, 41, 43–4, 50, 83, 85–6, 155–6, 178, 205

Poher Alain 414, 418, 421

Poland 7, 11, 14, 19–20, 24, 157, 310–11, 320

Polaris missiles 300, 301, 303, 353, 355, 356

Pompidou, Claude 398, 415, 416

Pompidou, Georges 189–90, 209, 300, 303, 341, 401, 413, 423; and Algeria 222–3, 229, 231–2, 274; as successor to de G. 275, 360, 397, 412–3, 415–22; disagrees with de G. 232, 263, 269, 275, 314, 371–3, 379, 381, 388, 397, 399–400; in May 1968, 383–93, 395–6, 400; Marković affair 415–6; Prime Minister 262, 263, 270, 272–5, 312, 336, 371–3; resignation (July 1968) 396–8

Popular Front 6, 41, 71

Porch, Douglas 115, 117

Potsdam (summit 1945) 159

Poujade Robert 394

Provisional Government (1944–6) see Gouvernement Provisoire de la République Française (GPRF)
Psichari, Ernest 11

Qualified Majority Voting (QMV) on EEC Council of Ministers 333, 348, 349–50, 359
Quebec 85, 142, 159, 307, 313–9, 423
Queuille, Henri 183

Rachid Ali al-Gaylani 72–3
Radical Party 4, 5, 6, 150, 167, 176, 178, 181, 182, 183, 417
Ramadier, Paul 178, 181
Rassemblement du Peuple Français (RPF) 175, 178–93, 203, 204, 208, 214, 220, 248, 266, 268, 274, 331, 370, 395, 413; and violence 184; debts 184, 187; decline (from 1948) 181–6; disowned by de G. (1953) 175, 186; electorate 181; last years 187; membership 180, 184; surge (1947) 180–1
referenda 261; (1945) 150; (1946, May) 176; (1946, October) 177; (1958) 213, 215, 216, 225, 241, 259; (1961) 225, 226, 230, 231, 234, 272; (1962, April) 224, 226, 228, 232, 234, 272; (1962, October) 262, 263, 266, 272, 299, 419, 429; (1969) 250, 416, 420, 421, 429
regions, French 413; proposed reform of (1969) 414
Renault (car manufacturer) 151, 179, 390, 395
Renault, Gilbert *alias* Colonel Rémy 77–80, 178, 180, 185
Resistance, within France 33, 36, 38, 41, 87, 107, 115, 116, 119–20, 133–4, 153, 154, 167, 178, 185, 189, 190, 240, 425, 428, 432; and Free French 43, 45, 51–3, 56–8, 65, 77–82, 84–5, 87, 90, 96–7, 101–6, 108, 110–2, 117–8, 121, 128, 131, 133–4, 143, 425, 428, 432; decommissioned (1944) 137–42; and Paris 77, 134–6 ; *see also* Conseil National de la Résistance (CNR); Communist Party, French (PCF)
Resurrection (planned military operation, May 1958) 208–11, 215
Reynaud, Paul 7, 15, 22–3, 26, 33–5, 43, 262
Rhineland 23
Rocard, Michel 238
Roche, Jean 384
Rochet, Waldeck 310, 386, 391
Rol-Tanguy, Henri 135, 136
Romania 310, 312, 386
Rome 131, 333, 334, 335, 341, 346, 347, 349, 356, 358, 360, 416
Roosevelt, Franklin Delano 47, 71, 83, 103, 106, 128, 129, 158, 159, 166, 205, 424, 434; and de G. 53–6, 85–8, 90, 97–101, 105, 118–121, 131–2, 142, 159; see also Allied Military Government in Occupied Territory (AMGOT)
Rostow, Walt 309
Roussel, Éric 355, 420
Rousset, David 375
Roux, Ambroise 399
Royal Air Force (RAF) 66, 72, 79
Rudelle, Odile 264
Rueff, Jacques (and Rueff-Pinay plan) 334, 359, 371–3, 399
Ruhr 159
Russia 2, 3, 6, 14, 56, 57, 111, 287, 290, 297, 311, 317, 340; see also Union of Soviet Socialist Republics (USSR)

Saad Dahlab 232
Sahara 188, 198, 223, 232–5, 239, 245, 278, 295, 429
Saint-Cyr (officer training school) 1, 8, 12, 15, 16, 17, 35, 42, 109

Saint-Pierre-et-Miquelon 68, 86, 89
Sakhiet-Sidi-Youssef 204–5, 225, 238, 245
Salan, General Raoul 201, 206, 207, 210, 215, 221, 222, 224, 226, 227, 228, 235, 279, 395
Sartre, Jean-Paul 190
Sauvageot, Jacques 381, 384, 387
Schröder, Gerhard 342, 354
Schuman, Robert 183, 339
Schumann, Maurice 43, 67, 83, 177, 178, 394
Séguy, Georges 390
Sékou Touré, 241, 244
Senate 5, 6, 71, 261, 263, 272, 296, 411, 413–8
Senegal 69, 240–4
Senghor, Léopold 114, 242–3
Sétif 162–3, 169, 198, 429, 432
Sino-Soviet split 247, 289, 427
Soames, Sir Christopher 357–8
social security system 116, 152, 419, 432
Socialist Party, French 4, 6, 80, 103, 150, 167, 176–8, 181–3, 185, 202, 207–12, 401, 417
Sorbonne (Paris university) 205, 382–8, 395, 397
Soustelle, Jacques 43, 44, 177–8, 189, 204, 206, 208, 214–5, 221, 226, 396
South Africa 245
Soviet Union *see* Union of Soviet Socialist Republics (USSR)
Spaak, Paul-Henri 338
Spain 421
Spears, Major-General Sir Edward 35, 39, 42, 47, 51, 73–5, 112–3, 163, 425
Special Operations Executive (SOE) 44
Stabilisation Plan (1963) 372, 374, 377, 397, 399
Stalin, Joseph 38, 57, 111, 141–3, 150, 157–8, 160, 169, 182, 189, 349, 424

Stalingrad 65
Stark, Admiral Harold 55, 87, 103
State Department (United States) 54, 55, 86, 87, 119, 142, 293, 305
Stavisky riots (1934) 6, 10
Stewart, Michael 357
Stimson, Henry 55
Strasbourg 84, 156, 178, 393
Stuttgart 157, 159
Suez expedition (1956) 248, 249
Sulzberger, Cyrus 179, 186, 188, 190, 233, 288, 290, 425
Supreme Headquarters Allied Expeditionary Force (SHAEF) 96, 117, 130
Syndicat National de l'Enseignement Supérieur (SNESup) 376, 384
Syria 14, 46, 68, 71–7, 87–8, 112, 114, 119, 143, 154, 163–7, 169, 220, 249

Takoradi air route 50, 69
tanks 1, 15, 17, 23, 113
Tende 157
Terrenoire, Louis 189
Thatcher, Margaret 360, 375
Thierry d'Argenlieu, Admiral Georges 70, 87, 161
Third Force 182, 183, 185
Third Republic 2–8, 26, 34, 53, 79, 81–3, 84, 90, 103, 149, 150, 176, 259, 260
Thorez, Maurice 139–41, 150, 423
Tixier, Adrien 86, 87, 163
Tixier-Vignancour, Jean-Louis 267
Tocqueville, Alexis de 398
Torch (operation) 85, 88, 89, 96, 98, 102, 121
Toulon 45, 70
trade unions, French 4, 81, 103, 372–3, 376, 384, 388–9, 393, 413; *see also* Confédération Française Démocratique du Travail (CFDT), Confédération Générale du Travail (CGT)

Treaty of Rome (1957) 331–5, 341, 346–7, 349, 351, 356, 358, 360, 369, 370, 426
Tricot, Bernard 357, 384, 391, 392, 397, 420
tripartisme 150, 151, 178
Tripoli (Libya) 99
Truman, Harry S. 159, 178, 188
Trump, Donald 428
Tunis 38, 57, 105, 109, 111, 188, 201, 203
Tunisia 48, 69, 88, 113, 114, 165, 169, 189, 201, 204, 220, 238, 240, 242, 245, 431; French aid to 245

Union Démocratique et Sociale de la Résistance (UDSR) 178, 183, 185, 202
Union Nationale des Étudiants Français (UNEF) 376, 381, 384, 386
Union of Soviet Socialist Republics (USSR) 6, 7, 13, 14, 19, 45, 46, 53, 77, 116, 131, 140, 176, 180, 189, 192, 231, 287, 289, 296–8, 302, 306, 308, 340, 345–6, 401, 411, 430, 433; and Free French 53, 56–8, 90, 97, 99, 111, 118, 142, 143; de G. believes has 'softened' 189, 192, 289, 296, 307, 317, 427; de G. condemns, over Czechoslovakia 317; de G. expects war with 176, 192; de G. visits (1966) 291, 310–2; German invasion of (June 1941) 53, 78; Treaty with France (1944) 157–8, 160, 169
Union pour la Défense de la République (UDR) 268, 396, 417, 418
Union pour la Nouvelle République (UNR) 213, 266, 267, 268, 269, 271, 275; electoral support 268
United Kingdom (UK) 2, 3, 46, 242, 247, 291–4, 296, 300, 302, 306, 308–9, 331, 333–5, 337–8, 342, 344, 346, 368, 428, 433; applications to join EEC 278, 301, 303, 337, 342, 350–7, 359, 421; and Free French 35, 38, 44–8, 51, 54, 57, 65–77, 99, 104, 105, 110, 112–3, 117, 118, 120, 129–30, 132, 142, 191, 286; and Polaris 301, 353; post-war alliance with 157; Soames affair 357–8; supports France at Yalta 158; *see also* Churchill; Levant; War Cabinet
United Nations 87, 104, 142, 158, 165, 241, 249, 356, 432; and Algeria 200, 201, 205, 222–5, 232, 235, 251; Couve criticises Vietnam war in 248; de G.'s hostility to 225, 244, 247, 286
United States 2, 17, 20, 88–9, 152, 163, 169, 176, 183, 201, 231, 243, 245, 291, 295–8, 310, 311, 312, 315, 319, 320, 321, 331, 334, 335, 338, 344, 350, 354, 356, 369, 427, 428, 430, 431, 433; and Algeria 201, 205, 225, 229; and Free French 33, 46–7, 50, 51, 53–6, 80, 81, 85, 86, 87, 90, 97, 99–101, 103–5, 108, 109, 111, 112, 114, 118, 119, 120, 128–9, 131–2, 135, 138, 142, 143, 156, 191; de G. challenges (1958–68) 247–8, 250, 288–90, 292–4, 299–306, 308, 313, 318, 337, 340–1, 369, 431; loans to France 152, 155, 159, 160, 205; Marshall Aid 183, 333; post-war conflicts with de G. 156–9; rapprochement (1968–9) 318–9, 412–3

Vaïsse, Maurice 338
Val d'Aosta 157, 159
Vallon, Louis 373
Vendroux Jacques (brother-in-law) 9, 177, 178, 190
Verdun 14, 15
Vian, Boris 190

Vichy regime 34, 42, 43, 49, 55, 78, 114, 130, 131, 139, 141, 143, 149, 167, 179, 181, 201, 237, 250, 275, 321, 354, 370, 415, 426; and Americans 54–5, 88–90, 96–100, 119; and British 45–7, 71, 72; and *épuration* (1944–46) 138, 153–5; and Free French 36, 37, 51, 81–6, 100, 109, 110, 112, 119, 432–3; and French empire 50–1, 68–70, 72–6, 86, 114, 161; and North Africa (1942–3) 88–90, 96–100, 104, 106, 110; and Resistance 116
Viénot, Pierre 130, 131
Viet Minh 161, 187, 248
Vietnam 161, 162, 248, 250, 304, 306, 310, 316, 318, 344, 356, 369, 382, 398, 400, 428, 431
Villon, Pierre 116, 138
Vinogradov, Sergei 188, 190
Volapük 332, 336

War Cabinet (United Kingdom) 34, 35, 105, 106
Warsaw Pact 288, 299, 312, 316, 317, 320

Washington DC 54–6, 76, 86, 87, 105, 142, 247, 265, 277, 295, 297, 298, 299, 306; de G. visits 131, 159, 288, 319, 411
Wavell, General Sir Archibald 72
Weber, Max 108, 110, 137, 264
Weygand, General Maxime 33, 36
Williams, Philip 270, 271, 280, 376, 431
Wilson, Edwin 55, 73, 119, 356, 357
Wilson, General Sir Henry Maitland 72–3, 134
Wilson, Harold 355, 356, 359
Winant John 55, 87, 129
Winock Michel 424, 427
working class, French 4, 6, 375, 399
Wright, Vincent 264

Yalta (summit, 1945) 158–9, 289, 298, 317, 319, 433
Yourcenar, Marguerite 190

Zeller, General André, 227
Zorin, Valerian 310